**Fourth Edition**

# Interracial Communication

## Theory into Practice

**Mark P. Orbe**
*Western Michigan University*

**Tina M. Harris**
*Louisiana State University*

WAVELAND

PRESS, INC.

Long Grove, Illinois

For information about this book, contact:
    Waveland Press, Inc.
    4180 IL Route 83, Suite 101
    Long Grove, IL  60047-9580
    (847) 634-0081
    info@waveland.com
    www.waveland.com

**Photo credits**
p. 22, Eyecandy Images/Alamy Stock Photo; p. 49, World History Archive/ Alamy Stock Photo; p. 51, Paul Prescott/Shutterstock; p. 130, Anamaria Mejia/ Alamy Stock Photo; p. 149, Design Pics/Alamy Stock Photo; p. 336, Jelani Photography/Shutterstock

# Contents

## PART I
### FOUNDATIONS FOR
### INTERRACIAL COMMUNICATION THEORY AND PRACTICE

# PART II
## INTERRACIAL COMMUNICATION IN SPECIFIC CONTEXTS

# Preface

The 1970s witnessed a surge of books on the topic of communication and race: *Transracial Communication* (1973) by Arthur Smith, *Interracial Communication* (1974) by Andrea Rich, and *Crossing Difference . . . Interracial Communication* (1976) by Jon Blubaugh and Dorthy Pennington. We draw our inspiration from these authors who worked to set a valuable foundation for current work in interracial communication. The earlier editions of *Interracial Communication: Theory Into Practice* used this scholarship, as well as that of countless other scholars and practitioners, to provide you with a textbook that focuses on communication and the dynamics of race.

With the fourth edition of this textbook, we are more committed than ever to our primary objective—to provide a current, extensive textbook on interracial communication that promotes moving from the theoretical to the practical. The sociopolitical climate of the United States in the wake of the Donald Trump presidency has underscored the urgency of the many topics and issues addressed in this new edition. It is an even richer resource for professors teaching an undergraduate or graduate course on interracial communication and scholars with specific interest in the intersection of race and communication. More importantly, we have directed our efforts towards illuminating the ways that existing literature can be applied to everyday interactions. We distinguish ourselves from other textbooks in that we dedicate all of our attention to the interactions between people from diverse racial/ethnic groups, which can be of particular interest to those teaching a related course (i.e., intercultural communication, race relations, communication and racism, etc.). It is of equal importance that we make this book accessible to persons outside of academia who will find the book an invaluable, instrumental, and socially relevant resource in facilitating positive interracial dialogue in their respective communities and spaces. Because current and projected demographic trends demonstrate that the racial landscape of the world is constantly changing and evolving, the ability to communicate across racial and ethnic groups is and will continue to be crucial to personal, social, and professional success in the 21st century.

## CHANGES TO THE FOURTH EDITION

The first edition of our text was written in 1999–2000 and published in 2001. Since that time, we each have had the opportunity to use the book, for both undergraduate and graduate courses, many times. Our teaching experiences, interactions with students, conversations with colleagues across the United States, and research agendas involving race and communication have helped us to recognize the many different ways in which the effectiveness and utility of this text could be improved. This is increasingly important in light of overwhelming evidence that a post-racial United States is certifiably a myth. After the murder of George Floyd by police in 2020 and the ensuing racial unrest, racial tensions reached an all-time high. We entered the revision process well aware of the vast ground we need to cover to demonstrate how systemic oppression has impacted relationships, media, organizations, and identities. In this fourth edition, we further emphasize how racism is not an issue solely impacting BIPOC; *it is impacting us all*. Thus, we keep the spirit of the book by stressing that race continues to be a salient issue, and communication is a vital key to addressing one of the most significant barriers to effective race relations.

As in previous editions, each chapter includes Author Reflections, Case Studies, Opportunities for Extended Learning, Research Spotlights, and Recommended Contemporary Readings. The Case Studies and Research Spotlights highlight the pervasiveness of interracial communication in real world contexts and social science research.

The chapters in Part I are significantly revised. Chapter 1 begins with a box dedicated to the controversy surrounding critical race theory. Discussion was added on the predicted impact of the changing racial demographics on interracial communication. A section on culturally competent interracial communication emphasizes the significance of cultural competency and mindfulness in achieving optimal interracial communication. The authors share their experiences teaching interracial communication in an international context. The chapter also covers recent efforts of community-level programs and collective action to engage in dialogue about race and the shift to virtual learning in the interracial communication classroom during the COVID-19 pandemic and racial unrest of 2020. Chapter 2 begins with a new case study on Indigenous land grants to introduce the history of racial classifications. In-depth content was added on the 1619 Project to stress the importance of a counternarrative to previous public narratives on race. A box addressing the issue of reparations highlights the discussion of the role of history in race. We added considerable discussion about the Trump era backlash after the two terms of the Obama presidency and addressed domestic terrorism beyond 9/11. The #BlackLivesMatter social movement is also discussed as the tipping point of racial tensions after the murder of George Floyd. An important section was added about contemporary social justice activism in response to police brutality, the racial turmoil of 2020 and the Trump presidency, which stoked racism, xenophobia, and an unprecedented rise in hate crimes against AAPI people and police brutality against African Americans. In Chapter 3, we updated the power of verbal codes and added discussion of the preferred term Arab Americans versus Middle Easterners. A new box was created to feature Stewart's (2017) article, "Language of Appeasement," on efforts towards diversity and inclusion. A Research Highlight focuses on expectancy violation theory (EVT) and race. The chapter now includes speech community theory to address communication styles across racial and ethnic groups. Chapter 4 begins with a case study of an incident involving racism, ancestry.com, and a race-related lawsuit. New discussions include Wilmot's views of self, other, and relationship; image management, and ethnic-racial socialization. Horizontal socialization was included to acknowledge the influence of friends on identity development. Chapter 5 opens with a case study on colorism and the movie *In the Heights*. Black feminist thought is included in the discussion of intersectionality. The discussion of socioeconomic status is enriched with the addition of middle/upper-class privileges, classism., and a Research Highlight on gender, race and class privilege. The concept of nationality/regionality is introduced as a salient aspect of identity. The intersection of race and abilities was updated with a box containing recent Census Bureau data. Chapter 6 opens with a case study on the moniker "Karen" and its prevalence in public discourse. Three new theories were added: [counter]public sphere theory, conflict face-negotiation theory, and the theory of hyper(in)visibility. A case study addresses efforts to ban race-centered educational materials.

The chapters in Part II also underwent meaningful and substantive revisions. Chapter 7 addresses international perspectives on interracial communication, with specific attention given to colorism. The chapter includes a more nuanced introduction to the definition of colorism (i.e., skin tone socialization) and how it, as an ideology, has spread globally through colonialism. A box discusses the movie *Passing* (2021) and the characters' struggle with colorism. Aspects of the global business of skin whitening products are discussed. The chapter concludes with DoSomething.Org's guidelines for confronting racism. Chapter 8 includes Millen et al.'s (2019) four factors impacting friendships. The chapter also addresses the sociopolitical climate's impact on interracial friendships and relationships. The new box "Mix It Up" highlights the Southern Poverty Law Center's international campaign designed to encourage people to develop interracial friendships. The section on internet dating was substantively revised to include new social media data and Lee's (2017) broader category of digital sexual racism. The chapter looks at the Netflix hit series *Bridgerton*'s (2020–present) depiction of interracial romance. The Research Highlight "Not All Diversity Interactions Are Created Equal" is a longitudinal study of cross-racial interactions. The barriers to interracial relationships section is tied directly to the racial unrest of 2020. Hudson's (2020) "interpersonalizing cultural difference" work and related four subprocesses compliment the chapter's encouragement of interracial friendships. Chapter 9 has a new case study about the world's largest racial discrimination settlement of $137 million paid by Tesla to an African American employee. A new box includes the Center for Creative Leadership's (CLL) 4-Step Framework for

Action toward legitimate workplace inclusivity. The chapter has a case study dedicated to interracial communication trailblazer Dr. Dorthy Pennington and her interview about Black Lives/All Lives Matter. The concept of the concrete ceiling was added to address barriers to workplace success unique to Black women. In Chapter 10, the opening case study revisits the Un-Fair Campaign in Minnesota, followed by extensive coverage of Colin Kaepernick, his social activism, the NFL, and the Black Lives Matter movement. We added more findings on the relationship between racism and virtual reality, hate crimes, and intimate/interpersonal partner violence. There are new boxes on racial healing and residential segregation. The section on critical thinking about existing research now includes the Harris and Abbott (2011) racial microaggression identification and confrontation model. Chapter 11 opens with a case study about the differential treatment of Meghan Markle and Kate Middleton by British media. New boxes address the historic seasons of TV's *Big Brother* and *The Bachelor/Bachelorette* franchise and the ensuing racism each has faced. The newer stereotypes of the Black best friend, the angry Black person, thug, fresh off the boat, and Kung Fu warriors are included. Also discussed is how the resurgence of white nationalism and reactions to it have influenced media use. Finally, in Chapter 12, we discuss the continued importance of applying theories and concepts to real world experiences. The chapter starts with a case study of country singer Morgan Wallen and his use of the n-word. A new Research Highlight focuses on Castle Bell's 2019 study of interracial communication barriers. We revisit the Harris and Abbott (2011) model and discuss the concept of advocate-mentor by Harris and Lee (2019) as an addition/alternative to allyship, stressing the use of one's societal privilege to seek social justice. The Research Highlight distinguishing debate and dialogue demonstrates the qualities necessary for competent interracial conflict resolution. The chapter concludes with a charge to our readers to recognize the value and importance of communication in deconstructing racist ideologies that remain a pervasive part of Western culture.

## NOTE TO OUR READERS

It has been 21 years since the first edition, and we can honestly say that this book truly remains a labor of love for us. We have attempted to author a book that simultaneously reflects our professional and personal interests in interracial communication. As you read the book, we hope that you will sense our passion for this subject area. Both of us have spent considerable time thinking about race/ethnicity issues and "doing race" during our daily interactions. Our academic careers have been tremendously satisfying, and what we find most inspiring is our individual and collective efforts to engage in scholarship that promotes greater understanding of the inextricable relationships between race, culture, and communication. We have taught more than a dozen different interracial communication classes and made presentations to various groups across the United States and beyond. Yet, we hesitate when others identify us as "experts" in this area. While our individual and collective numerous achievements reflect a significant level of competency, we remain keenly aware that there is so much more to learn. So, as we progress through the 21st century, we invite you to join us in a life journey that will continue to be full of challenges *and* rewards.

Authoring a book on a topic such as interracial communication is not an easy task. Trying to reach a consensus among all concerned parties (colleagues, editors, authors, reviewers, students, practitioners) remains a fruitless endeavor. Some agreed on *which* topics should be covered, but disagreements arose in terms of *how* they should be treated and *where* they should appear. Terms and theories changed between editions due to the changing times and political climate. We fully anticipate that as you read through the text, you may find yourself agreeing and/or disagreeing with different approaches that we have taken. In fact, we don't believe that there will be any person who will agree with everything that is included in this book. Nevertheless, we do believe wholeheartedly that this book provides a comprehensive foundation from which dialogue on interracial communication can emerge. We remain even more convinced that we do not have "the" answers to competent interracial communication. Instead, we have built on a resource that provides a framework for multiple answers. As the reader, then, you are very much an active participant in this process!

Through every edition, it has always been our intention to create a book that is "user friendly" to educators who bring a diverse set of experiences to teaching interracial communication and to students. Student feedback from past interracial and intercultural communication classes indicated a greater need for opportunities for extended learning. Students wished to become more actively engaged in the topics of discussion. In light of this recommendation, and others collected from professors, students, and diversity consultants, we have written a book that remains both theoretical and practical. Before you begin reading, there are a couple of things to which we would like to draw your attention.

- Existing research and discussions of interracial communication have given a hypervisibility to European American/African American relations (see Frankenberg, 1993). Throughout the new edition, we have attempted to extend our discussion beyond this particular type of interracial interaction to include insights into Latinx, Asian Americans, Native Americans, and Arab Americans. However, complicating the effort was the problem that existing research has largely ignored these groups. Social issues such as immigration, terrorism, racialized police brutality, hate crimes, and virtual racism have heightened awareness of the salience of race for certain racial/ethnic groups, which has been troubling for many reasons. We felt it was imperative to include and strengthen our discussions of experiences in a race conscious society. Scholars have broadened their research agendas to be more inclusive, and we tried to provide a more balanced coverage of all racial/ethnic groups with each edition.

- Different racial/ethnic group members will come to discussions about race and communication with different levels of awareness. They will also come with different levels of power and privilege (see Chapters 3 and 10). Regardless of these differences, however, we believe that ALL individuals must be included in discussions on race (see Chapter 1 for guidelines). Throughout the book, we have attempted to strike a tone that is direct and candid, but not "preachy." Our goal is to provide a resource that prepares individuals for an open and honest dialogue about race (see Chapter 12). This is not an easy task, but we hope that we were able to negotiate these tensions effectively.

- We have worked very hard to address issues that were raised by scholars who have reviewed the manuscript in various stages of development and those who adopted past editions in their classrooms. In this regard, we attempted to include some discussion on a wide array of topics and focused our attention on those that seemed to be most important. However, like the first, second, and third editions, we see this fourth edition of *Interracial Communication: Theory into Practice* as an ongoing process of discovery. We invite you to contact us with your suggestions, criticisms, and insights.

Mark P. Orbe
mark.orbe@wmich.edu
Tina M. Harris
tharris4@lsu.edu

# ACKNOWLEDGMENTS

Together we have several people to acknowledge for providing crucial support for the completion of the fourth edition of this text. We are especially indebted to Neil Rowe, founder and publisher of Waveland Press, for believing in us and the textbook and presenting this wonderful opportunity to continue our much-needed work. Neil's interest in a fourth edition is a testament to his commitment to this work and its relevance to both the communication field and society as a whole. A heartfelt thank you is also extended to Carol Rowe for her impeccable feedback and insight in making our book even more cohesive, thorough, and relevant. We have learned that race continues to matter in more complicated yet necessary ways; we learned that lesson all too well from 2020 and the presidency of Donald Trump. The authors dove into this newest edition with a desire to cast a wide yet thorough net. We extend a special thanks to colleagues across the globe who have been consistently supportive of our work and who provided reviews and feedback along the way: Brenda Allen, Harry Amana, Cecil Blake, Sakile K. Camara, Guo-Ming Chen, Joyce Chen, Melbourne Cummings, Navita Cummings James, Patricia S. E. Darlington, Elizabeth F. Desnoyers-Colas, Eleanor Dombrowski, Doris Fields, Gail A. Hankins, Michael Hecht, Patricia S. Hill, Daniel White Hodge, Felecia Jordan-Jackson, Venita Kelley, Robert L. Krizek, Marilyn J. Matelski, Mark Lawrence McPhail, Betty Morris, Chuka Onwumechili, Dorthy Pennington, Frank G. Pérez, Laura Perkins, Pravin Rodrigues, Raymond I. Schuck, Jim Schnell, the late Anntarie Lanita Sims, William J. Starosta, Nancy Street, Angharad Valdivia, Jennifer L. Willis-Rivera, and Julia T. Wood. At each stage of the process we were able to benefit significantly from their insights. This fourth edition is much stronger due to the efforts of many scholars and practitioners across the United States.

We would also like to include individual acknowledgments.

**Mark P. Orbe**: Writing four editions of this book reflects 20+ years of a personal, cultural, and professional journey for me. In revising it, I could not believe how much I have learned about interracial communication since teaching my first course in 2000. In this regard, I am indebted to all my students who made sure that I learned something new each and every semester. To my past, current, and future students, Dumela!

**Tina M. Harris**: Amazingly, we have entered into our fourth edition of a textbook that is needed now more than ever. The ongoing journey of this textbook has been a level of growth for me as a teacher-scholar, advocate-mentor, and person concerned with issues of race, for which I am incredibly grateful. Mom, thank you for your continued support and love. Dad, I wish you were here to share in the work God is doing through your Baby Girl! I am thankful for my siblings, Greg, Sonya, and Ken. Each of you encouraged me in your own special way, and for that I am grateful. To Lauren, Andrea, and Jennifer (Wood)—my perpetual cheerleaders—I praise God for placing each of you by my side as I did the work I was commissioned to do. Thanks to all other family members and friends who have supported me on this journey. You are a Godsend!

# PART I

# Foundations for Interracial Communication Theory and Practice

# 1

# Studying
# Interracial Communication

Critical race theory (CRT) began in the 1980s as a legal scholarly framework. It challenged traditional thinking that believed racial discrimination could be solved by expanding constitutional rights and then allowing individuals who were discriminated against to seek legal remedies. CRT scholars believed that such solutions weren't effective because racism is so pervasive and embedded into the foundation of the U.S. legal system and society as a whole. Race, according to CRT, is a socially constructed category that is used to oppress and exploit people of color. According to a 2021 survey, nearly 80% of people in the United States have not heard of CRT, and a larger percentage do not have a working knowledge of what the theory entails. Yet, that hasn't stopped a core group of critics from rejecting the framework as helpful in navigating the repercussions of slavery and racism. CRT critics believe that teaching the theory pits different races against one another, wrongly blames current European Americans for long-standing racially oppressive systems, and further divides an already divided country. As you learn about CRT (see Chapter 6) and other ideas related to interracial communication, think about whether you agree with the critics.

Source: Camera, L. (2021, June 1). What is critical race theory and why are people so upset about it? *U.S. News & World Report.* https://www.usnews.com/news/national-news/articles/what-is-critical-race-theory-and-why-are-people-so-upset-about-it

African American historian W. E. B. Du Bois (1903/2012) predicted that the primary issue of the 20th century in the United States would be related to the "problem of the color line" (p. 3). From where we stand today, his words—written more than 120 years ago—appear hauntingly accurate. Without question, race relations in the United States remain an important issue that we continue to grapple with today. But do you think that Du Bois could have anticipated all the changes that have occurred since he offered his prediction? Take a minute to reflect on some of the following events and how they have changed the nature of the United States: land expansion and population shifts westward, the Great Depression, world wars, the Cold War, civil rights movements, race riots, multiple waves of immigration, drastic migration patterns, technological advances, population explosions, a competitive global economy, the pervasive impact of social media platforms, global warming and climate change, the influence of current-day social movements like #BlackLivesMatter. This list is hardly definitive, but it does highlight some of the major events and developments that the United States has experienced. Clearly, the world that existed in 1902 when Du Bois wrote his now famous prediction was drastically different. Yet, how does his forecast ring so hauntingly true regarding race relations?

Could DuBois and other civil rights leaders at the turn of the 20th century have predicted that the 21st century would see the United States elect its first president of African descent? Most think that this would be doubtful, especially given that over 70% of people in the United States in 2008 believed that they would not see an African American U.S. president in their lifetime (cited in Orbe, 2016). For many, the election of an African American to the White House symbolized the American Dream achieved. But what did the accomplishment mean in terms of race and race relations? For some, the election of President Barack Obama in 2008 meant that race was no longer a serious issue—that the United States had moved into a "post-racial" state.

The unprecedented resistance to the Obama administration, the rise of political conservatism, the increase in white supremacist group membership, and heightened racial tensions quickly put the idea of a "post-racial" society to rest. In fact, the election of President Donald Trump, according to some scholars like Cooper (2018), can be understood—at least in part—as a backlash to the election of President Barack Obama. The argument is that President Trump used fear of others (e.g., African Americans, Muslims, Latino/a/s immigrants, etc.) to prime European Americans' racial resentment of the overreported advancement of people of color and discrimination against them. Fanning the racial anxieties of voters, it appears, was a key element in the success of Trump's political rhetoric to galvanize conservative, traditional U.S. voters (Sugino, 2020). A similar rhetorical approach can be seen in his attitude to international affairs. Consider, for example, his statement that the United States should increase immigration from "desirable" nations like Norway and Japan while curbing immigration from "shithole countries" like El Salvador, Haiti, and African countries (Bahrainwala, 2021).

It would be an understatement to say that race continues to be a pressing issue in the United States (Kendi, 2019). The magnitude and intensity of protests against racist practices—related to police brutality, voting suppression, immigration, hate crimes, and Indigenous rights to traditional lands—symbolize the status of race relations. For centuries, racism has been embedded in the fabric of U.S. society. Yet, many remain ignorant about how systems related to health care, housing, economics, education, the criminal justice system, etc. have been constructed and protected over generations in ways that disenfranchise people of color. Many U.S. Americans, especially white people, believe that racism is wrong and also believe that a "color-blind approach" to race is the way to eliminate the problem (Orbe, 2016). These individuals, for instance, are quick to respond to any statements that #BlackLivesMatter with a forceful #AllLivesMatter; their belief is that drawing special attention to one racial group while ignoring others is a problem (Edgar & Johnson, 2018). This approach, according to Orbe (2015), reflects a "post-racial" ideology that ignores the problematic consequences that race and racism have on people of color in the United States. These differences in perception, stemming from drastically different experiences, present challenges for productive interracial communication. However, we believe that every challenge also can be regarded as an opportunity—and this book represents our intention to cultivate stronger race relations through communication.

---

**Box 1.1**                    *Public Perceptions of U.S. Race Relations*

### The Impact of Presidential Elections

The election of Barack Obama as the 44th U.S. president, and the first self-identified African American U.S. president, had an immediate effect on perceptions of race relations. One day after his historic election in 2008, 70% of U.S. Americans surveyed said that race relations would improve (Washington, 2012). Yet, in April 2012, survey results indicated that only 33% described race relations as getting better. When President Trump took office in 2016, one survey reported that a majority of U.S. Americans (52%) believed that race relations would worsen, something that seemed to reach a low in 2020 (Villarreal, 2021). Yet, more than a third of U.S. American adults expected race relations to improve following the election of President Joe Biden in 2020. How do your own perceptions compare to these survey results? How influential is the sitting president on race relations in the United States? As national leaders, do they represent the most important person in setting the tone for an entire country?

---

The basic premise of this book is that the field of communication, as well as other related disciplines, has much to offer us in working through the racial and ethnic differences that hinder meaningful communication. U.S. Americans from all racial and ethnic groups must learn how to communicate competently with one another. During the early to mid-1970s, several books emerged that dealt specifically with the subject of interracial communication (Blubaugh & Pennington, 1976; Rich, 1974; A. Smith, 1973). These resources were valuable in setting a foundation for the scholarly study of interracial communication. Given the significant societal changes and scholarly advances in the communication discipline, however, their usefulness for addressing race relations in the 21st century is somewhat limited. Our intention is to honor these scholars, as well as countless others, by creating an up-to-date interracial communication resource guide that provides theoretical understanding and clear direction for application.

Toward this objective, the book is divided into two parts. Part I focuses on providing a foundation for studying interracial communication and includes chapters on the history of race and racial categories, the importance of language, the development of racial and cultural identities, and various theoretical approaches. In Part II, we use this foundation to understand how interracial communication plays out in a number of contexts (international, friendship and romantic relationships, workplace, conflict, and the mass media). The final chapter in Part II (Chapter 12) makes the connection between theory and practice explicit, especially as it relates to the future of race relations in the United States.

In this opening chapter, we provide a general introduction to the topic of interracial communication. First, we offer a specific definition of interracial communication, followed by a clear rationale of why studying this area is important. Next, we explain the concept of racial locations and encourage you to acknowledge how social positioning affects perceptions of self and others. Finally, we provide some practical insight into how instructors and students can create a positive, productive climate for discussions on issues related to race. Specifically, we advocate for cultivating a sense of community among discussion participants and suggest several possible guidelines toward engaging in meaningful interracial dialogue.

Two important points should be made before you read any further. First, we initially authored this book to be used in interracial and intercultural communication classes at the undergraduate level. As our vision for the book developed, we realized it could be a valuable resource in any number of courses, including those in sociology, psychology, ethnic studies, and education (both undergraduate and graduate). In addition, we hope *Interracial Communication: Theory into Practice* will be useful for individuals and groups outside the university setting who are interested in promoting more productive race relations in the United States. Much of our focus in highlighting how communication theory and research is applicable to everyday life interactions occurs within the context of a classroom setting. However, in our minds, *a classroom is any place where continued learning/teaching can occur.* In this regard, the principles shared in this book can apply to community-based groups and formal study circles, as well as long-distance learning and other types of learning that occur through the cyberspace community. In a very real sense, the world is a classroom, and we hope this book is a valuable resource for those committed to using competent communication practices to improve the relationships between and within different racial/ethnic groups.

Second, we acknowledge the power of language, and therefore we have been mindful about using specific terms and labels. Chapter 3 focuses on the importance of language in interracial communication and discusses why we use certain racial and ethnic labels over other alternatives. We think it is vital that you understand why labels are important beyond issues of so-called political correctness. Both scholarly and personal evidence clearly shows that, in most cases, one universally accepted label for any specific racial or ethnic group does not exist. We have chosen labels that are parallel across racial and ethnic groups (e.g., Asian American, African American, European American, Latino/a/x American or Latin@s, and Native American). In addition, we have decided to use both racial and ethnic markers (instead of focusing on race alone). This decision may initially seem odd, given that this is a book on interracial, not interethnic, communication. But according to most scientific information on race—including how the U.S. government currently defines it—Latino/a/x Americans (Hispanics, Chicano/a/x) represent an ethnic group with members that cut across different racial groups. Thus, in order to include "interracial" communication that involves Latino/a/x Americans and other "racialized" groups, we consciously use descriptors such as "race/ethnicity" or "race and ethnicity." This is an important distinction since race and ethnicity can mean different things in different contexts (Bilge et al., 2021).

## DEFINING INTERRACIAL COMMUNICATION

Early writing on **interracial communication** defined it specifically as communication between whites and nonwhites (Rich, 1974) or more generally as communication between people of different racial groups within the same nation-state (Blubaugh & Pennington, 1976). Interracial communication was distinguished from other types of communication. **Interpersonal communication** traditionally refers to interactions between two people regardless of similarities or differences in race; the term is often synonymous with **intraracial communication**. **International communication** refers to communication between nations, frequently through representatives of those nations (Rich, 1974). **Intercultural communication** was used specifically to refer to situations in which people of different cultures (nations) communicated. **Interethnic communication**, sometimes used interchangeably with interracial communication, referred to communication between two people from different ethnic groups. Some scholars (e.g., Graves, 2004) use this term to expose the myths of racial categories (see Chapter 2). Others use interethnic communication to illustrate the differences between race and ethnicity and to highlight how interethnic communication could also be intraracial communication (e.g., interactions between a Japanese American and Filipino American or between a German American and French American).

Over time, the study of intercultural communication has gained a prominent place within the communication discipline. It also has emerged as an umbrella term to include all aspects of communication that involve cultural differences. Currently, this includes researching interactions affected by age, race/ethnicity, abilities, gender, national origin, and/or spirituality. Interracial communication, then, is typically seen as one subset of many forms of intercultural communication. We believe this framework has been a mixed blessing for interracial communication study. On one hand, scholars interested in studying how communication is experienced across racial lines are able to draw from a significant body of existing intercultural research and theory. Because of this, we have a "home" in the discipline complete with various frameworks to use in our research. On the other hand, such a positioning appears to have had a marginalizing effect on interracial communication study. Because intercultural theoretical frameworks are designed to apply generally to a variety of contexts, they do little to reveal the unique dynamics of any one type of intercultural communication. In addition, intercultural communication study has become so broad that minimal attention is devoted to any one particular aspect. Teaching a class on intercultural communication is challenging, because most instructors attempt to include materials from various areas of intergroup relations. Thus, issues of race are oftentimes covered in insubstantial ways. One of the major points of this book is that interracial communication is such a complex process—similar to, yet different from, intercultural communication—that existing treatments of it as a form of intercultural communication are not adequate.

For our purposes here, we are operating from the following definition of interracial communication: *the transactional process of message exchange between individuals in a situational context where racial difference is perceived as a salient factor by at least one person.* This working definition acknowledges that interracial communication can be seen as situated along an interpersonal/intergroup continuum. For instance, can you think of examples of communication that have occurred between two individuals who may be

---

| *Box 1.2* | *Racism Breeds Stupidity* |
|---|---|

### The Effect of Racial Bias on Cognitive Ability

The headline in the local newspaper read "Study Finds That Racism Can Breed Stupidity" (Cook, 2003). While three words—"racism," "breed," and "stupidity"—seemed to sensationalize the scientific study that was the basis of the article, the findings were interesting. Researchers at Dartmouth College (Richeson et al., 2003) studied how racial bias, and interaction with African Americans, affected European Americans' ability to perform basic tests. According to the findings of the study, "the more biased people are, the more their brain power is taxed by contact with someone of another race" (Cook, 2003, p. A4). Interracial contact caused racially biased European Americans to struggle not to say or do anything offensive. Researchers found that the effect was so strong that even a 5-minute conversation with an African American person left some European Americans unable to perform well on a basic cognitive test. Based on the findings, the researchers concluded that when racially biased European Americans were involved in interracial interactions—even briefly—it taxed the part of their brain in charge of executive control. The result is a temporary inability to perform well on other tasks.

- What do you make of these research findings?
- Do you agree that this happens? If so, to what effect? Do you think that generational differences exist?
- Do you think that a similar effect exists for European Americans who are conscious of their white privilege during interracial interactions?

from different racial groups but whose relationship seems to transcend differences? If racial differences are not central to the interaction, communication between these individuals may be more interpersonal than interracial. As you will see in Chapter 6, the idea of **transracial communication** (interactions in which members are able to transcend their racial differences) was first generated by Molefi Kete Asante (A. Smith, 1973). However, the more central role that perceived racial differences play within an interaction—from the perspective of at least one participant—the more intergroup the interaction becomes.

## WHY STUDY INTERRACIAL COMMUNICATION?

Over the past couple of decades, several basic arguments have emerged to justify attention to cultural diversity when studying various aspects of human communication. Most of these have related more directly to intercultural communication than to interracial communication (e.g., J. Martin & Nakayama, 2018). Although some of these arguments appear equally applicable to interracial communication, others do not seem to fit the unique dynamics of race relations. Therefore, within the context of these general arguments and more specific ones related to the cultural diversity in the United States (e.g., Verkuyten & Yogeeswaran, 2020), we offer four reasons why the study of interracial communication is important.

First, race continues to be one of the most important issues in the United States. From its inception, U.S. culture has reflected its multiracial population (even though political, legal, and social practices have valued certain racial groups over others). Because of the contradiction of the realities of racism and democracy (e.g., equal opportunity), the United States has often downplayed the issue of race and racism. We believe that in order to fulfill the democratic principles on which it is based, the United States must work through the issues related to racial differences. Racial and ethnic diversity is a primary strength of the United States. However, it can also be the country's biggest weakness if we are unwilling to talk honestly and openly. Although calls for advocating a "color-blind society"—one in which racial and ethnic differences are downplayed or ignored—are admirable, they are largely premature for a society that still has unresolved issues with race (Ono, 2010). The African proverb, the way out is back through, instructs us that we need to work through our history with race and racism before we can move forward.

Second, shifts in the racial and ethnic composition of the United States will increase the need for competent interracial communication. As you can see in Table 1.1, the U.S. population continues to grow and become more and more diverse. This reflects huge increases in people of color. For example, there were 23 million Asian Americans in 2021, the fastest growing racial group. In 2010, 4.8% of census respondents (14.7 million) identified as Asian; in 2020 that population grew by 35.5% (19.9 million). In combination with another race, the percentage increase was 55.5 (N. Jones et al., 2021). The number of nonwhite racial and ethnic groups increased in recent years, while the white population

**Table 1.1     U.S. Racial Diversity and Population Milestones**

| Race | 1915 100 Million | 1967 200 million | 2010 300 million |
|---|---|---|---|
| European descent | 88.0% | 76.6% | 63.7% |
| African descent | 10.7% | 13.8% | 12.6% |
| Latino/a/x descent | n/a | 6.5% | 16.4% |
| Others | 0.3% | 3.2% | 7.3% |

decreased. According to the 2020 U.S. Census, European Americans currently remain the majority (57.8%); however, that majority is shrinking each year (8.6% from 2010 to 2020). In fact, every state except one (Hawaii) experienced an increase in their populations of color—something that will continue given the population shifts related to age, race, and ethnicity (Frey, 2021). People who are biracial or multiracial increased from 9 million in 2010 to 33.8 million in 2020—a 276% increase. Given these projections, the need to communicate competently with different racial and ethnic groups is paramount.

Third, the past, present, and future of all racial and ethnic groups are interconnected. In tangible and not so tangible ways, our successes (and failures) are inextricably linked. Long gone is the general belief that the United States is a big melting pot where citizens shed their racial, ethnic, and cultural pasts and become (simply) "Americans." Instead, metaphors of a big salad or bowl of gumbo are offered. Within this vision of the United States, cultural groups maintain their racial and ethnic identities and, in doing so, contribute unique aspects of their culture to the larger society. Learning about different racial and ethnic groups is simultaneously exciting, intimidating, interesting, anxiety provoking, and transformative. It can also trigger a healthy self-examination of the values, norms, and practices associated with our own racial/ethnic groups. Remember, without this process we cannot take advantage of all the benefits that come with being a racially diverse society. To paraphrase Rev. Dr. Martin Luther King, Jr., we can either learn to work together collaboratively or perish individually.

Demographers predict that the United States will become a majority-minority country by the middle of the 21st century, a reality that is already being experienced in many elementary schools.

Fourth, and finally, productive race relations are only feasible through communication practices that reflect certain levels of cultural competency (Presbitero & Attar, 2018). Culturally competent interracial communication requires that individuals function in ways that are perceived as both effective

---

### Box 1.3

## Defining Important Concepts

Because of your interest in the topic, we assume you are familiar with many of the basic ideas central to understanding interracial communication processes. But we acknowledge the importance of not assuming that everyone is operating from the same definition for certain terms. Therefore, we have defined some basic concepts related to interracial communication to provide a common foundation. Throughout the text, we have included definitions whenever we introduce concepts that you may not be familiar with (e.g., discussions of privilege in Chapter 4). These definitions draw from a great body of interdisciplinary work with which we've engaged over time.

**Culture:** Learned and shared values, beliefs, and behaviors common to a particular group of people. Culture forges a group's identity and assists in its survival. Race is culture, and a person's culture is more than their race.

**Race:** A largely social—yet powerful—construction of human difference that has been used to classify human beings into separate value-based categories. Chapter 2 describes the four groups that make up a dominant racial hierarchy in the United States.

**Ethnicity:** A cultural marker that indicates shared traditions, heritage, and ancestral origins. Ethnicity is defined psychologically and historically. In most contexts, ethnicity is different from race and nationality. For instance, your race may be Asian, your nationality Asian American, and your ethnic makeup might be Hmong.

**Ethnocentrism:** Belief in the normalcy or rightness of one's culture and consciously or unconsciously evaluating aspects of other cultures by using your own as a standard. All of us operate from within certain levels of ethnocentrism.

**Microculture:** Term used to describe groups (in our case racial/ethnic groups) that are culturally different from those of the majority group (macroculture). We generally use this term to refer to African, Asian, Latino/a/x, and Native American cultures instead of **minorities**.

**Stereotypes:** Overgeneralizations of group characteristics or behaviors that are applied universally to individuals of those groups. **Metastereotypes** are the perceptions that individuals have concerning how others perceive them.

**Racial prejudice:** Inaccurate and/or negative beliefs that espouse or support the superiority of one racial group.

**Racial discrimination:** Acting upon your racial prejudice when communicating with others. All people can have racial prejudice and practice racial discrimination.

**Racism:** Racial prejudice + societal power = racism. In other words, racism is the systematic subordination of certain racial groups by the groups in power. Even if there were no racist individuals, racism would still exist through systems that were created and maintained to marginalize people of color.

(achieving one's objective) *and* appropriate (taking into account others' perspectives, norms and expectations) (Orbe, 2019). This book highlights the central role that culturally competent communication plays in the future of race relations. We recognize that race relations are an important aspect of study for all nations, not simply the United States. Although some similarities obviously exist, each country has a relatively unique history in terms of race. We have chosen to focus on the importance of interracial communication within the United States because that is what we know and where we believe we can have the greatest impact. However, we specifically address racial and ethnic groups in different countries in Chapter 7 and include examples throughout the book.

In short, this book represents a scholarly, social, and personal mission to contribute to interracial understanding. We are not simply reporting on abstract ideas related to communication. We are, in essence, talking about our lived experiences and those of our family, friends, colleagues, students, and neighbors. Communication theory and research has much to offer in terms of the everyday interactions of racially/ethnically diverse people. Our explicit goal is to advocate for using this body of knowledge to improve race relations in the United States. In other words, we want to practice what we preach and to give others a resource so they can do the same.

One last comment about the importance of bringing the issue of race to the forefront of human communication: Given the history of race relations in the United States (see Chapter 2), many people appear more willing to discuss "culture" generally than "race" more specifically. Simply put, race continues to be a taboo topic for many (Orbe, 2018). And it is this very point that makes centralizing the issue of race so important for all of us. Race cannot be separated from interpersonal or intercultural communication processes. Scholars who study race as part of research in these areas have provided some valuable insights. Nevertheless, we argue that research that does not centralize issues of race cannot get at the unique ways that race affects (to some extent) all communication in the United States. Starting here, and continuing throughout the entire book, we hope to increase your awareness as to the various ways that race influences how individuals communicate.

## ACKNOWLEDGING RACIAL LOCATIONS

An important starting point for competent interracial communication is to acknowledge that individuals have similar and different vantage points from which they see the world. These vantage points, or standpoints, are the result of a person's field of experience as defined by social group membership (Collins, 2022). Standpoint theories are based on one simple idea: The world looks different depending on your social standing (B. Allen, 1998). Standpoint theories have largely been used by scholars to understand how women and men come to see the world differently (Harding, 2004). Given the assumption that societal groups with varying access to institutional power bases have different standpoints, standpoint theories appear to offer a productive framework to link existing interracial communication theory and research to everyday life applications. In fact, the value of using standpoint theories as a framework for studying race relations has not gone unnoticed by scholars (J. Hall, 2020; Wood, 2005).

A key idea of standpoint theories is that social locations—including those based on gender, race, class, and so forth—shape people's lives (Wood, 2005).

---

**Box 1.4**                                                          *Author Reflections*

## My Racial Location

One of the important keys to promoting competent interracial communication is the recognition that each of us experiences life from a particular racial location. Because we have asked you to identify your racial location, it is only fair that we also publicly acknowledge our own. This is important because it helps identify us, the authors of this book, as human beings with a particular set of life experiences. Clearly, our racial locations inform our understanding of interracial communication. Therefore, throughout the book, we share our personal experiences through a series of personal reflections. This first reflection serves as an introduction to how I give consciousness to my racial standpoint.

A central component of my racial standpoint revolves around the fact that I don't fit neatly into any one racial or ethnic category. My grandfather came to the United States from the Philippines in the early 1900s; the Spanish lineage is clear given our family names (Orbe, Ortega). Some of my mother's relatives reportedly came over on the *Mayflower*. Like many European Americans, her lineage is a mixture of many different European cultures (Swiss, English, French). So, my racial standpoint is informed by the fact that I am biracial and multiethnic. However, it is not that simple. Other factors complicate the particular perspective I bring to discussions of interracial communication.

I am a fifty-something man who was raised in a diverse low-income housing project (predominantly African American with a significant number of Puerto Ricans) in the upper Northeast. In this regard, other cultural factors—age, region, socioeconomic status—also inform my racial standpoint. Except what I've seen reproduced through the media, I don't have any specific memory of the civil rights movement. I've always attended predominantly African American churches (both Baptist and nondenominational ones) and have always felt a part of different African American communities. For instance, in college, I pledged a predominantly Black Greek affiliate organization; these brothers remain my closest friends. My wife also comes from a multiracial lineage (African, European, and Native American); she has always identified most closely with her Blackness. We have three adult children who were raised to embrace strongly all aspects of their racial and ethnic heritage. Over time, they developed their own unique racial locations.

Through these descriptions it should be apparent that my racial location (like yours) is closely tied to age, gender, spirituality, class, sexual orientation, and region. So, what's your story? How are our racial perspectives similar yet different? As we explained earlier, acknowledging and coming to understand self and other racial locations are important steps toward competent interracial communication.

—MPO

This idea is grounded in the analyses of the master–slave relationship that realized that each occupied a distinct location in terms of their lives (Harding, 2004). Within this text, we focus on the social location primarily defined through racial and ethnic group membership. In simple terms, this concept helps people to understand that a person's racial/ethnic identity influences how that person experiences, perceives, and comes to understand the world around him or her. Everyone has a **racial location**, defined primarily in terms of the racial and ethnic groups to which that person belongs. However, according to standpoint theory, there is an important distinction between occupying a racial location and having a racial standpoint (O'Brien Hallstein, 2000). A racial standpoint is achieved—earned through critical reflections on power relations and through the creation of a political stance that exists in opposition to dominant cultural systems (Wood, 2005, p. 61). Being a person of color does not necessarily mean that you have a racial standpoint. In other words, racial standpoint can, but does not necessarily, develop from being a person of color. Racial standpoints are not achieved individually; they can only be accomplished through working with other people of color (O'Brien Hallstein, 2000). **Racial standpoint**, then, refers to more than social location or experience; it encompasses a critical, oppositional understanding of how one's life is shaped by larger social and political forces. By definition, European Americans cannot achieve a racial standpoint; however, they can develop multiple standpoints shaped by membership in traditionally marginalized groups defined by sex, sexual orientation, and socioeconomic status (Wood, 2005).

Standpoint theory is based on the premise that our perceptions of the world around us are largely influenced by social group membership. In other words, our set of life experiences shape—and are shaped by—our memberships with different cultural groups like those based on sex, race/ethnicity, sexual orientation, and so on. According to standpoint theorists (Harding, 2004), life is not experienced the same for all members of any given culture. In explicit and implicit ways, our racial locations affect how we communicate as well as how we perceive the communication of others. Acknowledging the locations of different social groups, then, is an important step in competent communication. Part of this involves recognizing that different U.S. racial and ethnic group members perceive the world differently based on their experiences living in a largely segregated society. The largest difference in racial standpoints, it is reasoned, is between those racial and ethnic groups that have the most and least societal power (Collins, 2022). Based on the arguments of standpoint theorists, European Americans and U.S. Americans of color have different—even possibly oppositional—understandings of the world. In other words, they see life drastically differently based on the social standing of their racial/ethnic group membership. This can be seen when different racial and ethnic groups perceive the police, policing, and police brutality through what Rengifo and Slocum (2020) regard as "identity prisms;" the result are significantly different perceptions. Understanding how racial locations create different worldviews, in this regard, assists in beginning the process toward greater interracial understanding.

In the past, some scholars have criticized standpoint theories because they focused on the common standpoint of a particular social group while minimizing the diversity within that particular group. For instance, traditionally, standpoint theorists have written extensively about the social positioning of women with little attention to how race/ethnicity further complicates group membership (Bell et al., 2000; Collins, 1998). The challenge for us is to use standpoint theories in ways that encourage identifying the commonalities among a particular racial, ethnic group while simultaneously acknowledging internal differences (Wood,

---

*BOX 1.5*                                                      *Author Reflections*

### Searching for My Racial/Ethnic Identity

In the first section of this textbook, we discussed the importance of history and multiple identities in understanding interracial/interethnic communication. As my coauthor has indicated in his personal reflection, it is important for you, the reader, to understand our racial/cultural standpoints. Here, I will share with you my journey for self-understanding.

By all appearances, I am African American; however, my family history will tell you otherwise. I am in my fifties and for many years have wondered about the details of my heritage. My father (who passed away in 1996) was in the Navy. When I was 2½ years old, we were stationed in Rota, Spain for 4½ years and were immersed in Spanish culture. Both my father and mother worked, and my older brother and sister were in school. Our maid, Milagros (no, we were not rich), took care of me during the day, and she taught me how to speak Spanish fluently and all about the rituals of the Spanish people. I felt as if I were a part of her culture.

After living in Spain, we moved to Pensacola, Florida, and then to Atlanta, Georgia, to be closer to my parents' families. As we moved across the world, it was my age, family status, and interpersonal interactions that shaped who I was. It was not until I was around family and peers with southern dialects, different life experiences, and few interracial/interethnic interactions that I became aware of my racial standpoint. I was accused of "not being Black enough" because I spoke "proper" English. One vivid memory involves being left out of the "best friend game" by my Jewish friend and a Pentecostal European American friend. They both decided that they were each other's friend because they knew each other longer than they knew me. I was the odd person out: Everyone had a best friend except me. I knew immediately that the reason I was not chosen was possibly because of my race/ethnicity.

My quest for learning about my family's history and realization of how we are socialized to view racial/ethnic groups has challenged me to explore the significance of racial/ethnic identity in a society that values a racial hierarchy. Although we do not have a family tree that shows us where we came from, I do find some peace in knowing a few pieces of the puzzle have been completed. I am aware that both of my grandmothers are of Native American and European descent. However, there is a big puzzle piece that does not complete the picture of who my family and I are. For this very reason, I am committed to becoming continually aware of the importance of our multiple identities in an increasingly diverse society. I want to have knowledge of my rich ethnic heritage to pass on to my future children.

—TMH

2005). Balancing these goals—seeing a person as both an individual and as a member of a particular racial/ethnic group—is difficult but necessary to achieve competent interracial communication (see intercultural dialectics in Chapter 12). This point is extremely important because it helps us avoid mass generalizations that stereotype all racial and ethnic group members as the same. As such, standpoint theories remind us to see the great diversity within racial and ethnic groups based on individual and other cultural elements like age, education, gender, sexual orientation, and socioeconomic status (Wood, 2005).

Through this brief overview of standpoint theories, you can see why identifying your racial location is an important ingredient for competent, meaningful interracial communication. Location identification is invaluable because it helps you acknowledge a specific life perspective and recognize its influence on how you perceive the world. In addition, it promotes an understanding that different racial locations potentially generate contrasting perceptions of reality. Nevertheless, remember that standpoint theories also require a conscious effort to pay attention to the various locations within any one particular racial or ethnic group. In other words, this approach to interracial communication hinges on your abilities to understand the possible commonalties of people who share a common racial group while simultaneously recognizing intragroup differences. Focusing on how racial identity is just one aspect of our multicultural selves, Chapter 5 discusses the cultural diversity *within* different racial and ethnic groups.

## CULTURALLY COMPETENT INTERRACIAL COMMUNICATION

In many interracial contexts—social, professional, and educational—the issue of race and racism continues to be a taboo topic. Lack of opportunity and high levels of anxiety and uncertainty decrease the likelihood that honest, meaningful dialogue regarding racial issues will take place. Ironically, these are exactly the type of interactions whereby anxiety and uncertainty are reduced and advances are made. Thus, a vicious cycle is created. People generally do not have sufficient opportunities to discuss issues related to race outside their largely intraracial network. As you might expect, we believe that the classroom holds the greatest potential for producing high-quality, substantial, and meaningful exchanges regarding race and racism.

Unfortunately, in the past, "the issue of race on college campuses has been one of the most profound and controversial topics in higher education" (Muthuswamy et al., 2006, p. 105). While the racial and ethnic diversity on college campuses has increased, inequalities continue to exist for students, faculty, and staff (Zamudio-Suarez, 2021). Racial and ethnic diversity alone, according to McAllister and Irvine (2000), is not enough—formal and informal opportunities for interaction are necessary. The reality is that many campuses may have numerical diversity but lack any sort of interactional diversity through which different racial and ethnic group members experience sustained meaningful interracial interactions (Sanders & Orbe, 2016). On most campuses, these opportunities must be cultivated by university faculty and staff; however, some question whether or not these individuals are prepared to facilitate interracial dialogues (Kezar et al., 2020). Just because they may be experts in their respective fields does not mean that they possess the necessary cultural communication competencies to address current racial tensions.

As described earlier in this chapter, **cultural competency** refers to the ability to communicate in ways regarded as both effective and appropriate. As conceptualized by Orbe (2019), cultural competence involves honest self-assessment, an enhanced knowledge and understanding of self and others, a specific set of adaptive communication skills, as well as a desire for and commitment to successful interactions with others. Culturally competent communicators engage in a variety of behaviors. First, they practice **mindfulness** in their communication with others, which involves maintaining a constant awareness of one's actions and thoughts and what motivates them. Second, they work to become aware of how their own **unconscious bias**—socio-cultural stereotypes about certain groups of people that individuals form outside their conscious awareness— inform their perceptions of self and others. Lastly, they approach their interactions with others with **cultural humility,** remaining humble and respectful as they embrace a lifelong commitment to self-reflection, self-critique, and searching for what they do not know. Cultural competency is not something that people are born with; instead, it is something that takes significant time, energy, and effort. According to health communication scholar John Oetzel, cultural humility is part attitude and part ability; "it focuses on self-reflection, growth and desire to learn and critique oneself" (quoted in Alexander et al., 2014, p. 15).

Cultural communication competency is necessary to maximize interracial communication encounters. Most individuals believe that their communication is "fine," and oftentimes place the blame of any miscommunication on others. This belief is not consistent with the ideals of cultural competency and the result most often is a less meaningful and successful exchange of ideas. Professional development opportunities aimed at strengthening the cultural competencies of faculty members have emerged recently (S. Williams et al., 2020). With an explicit focus on issues related to diversity, inclusion, access, and equity, these ongoing efforts have been crucial to working collaborating with faculty to promote learning that is inclusive, collaborative, and respectful (Weiss, 2015). Without this type of professional development, interracial interactions typically fall short of their potential.

Based on the work of different scholars (e.g., Freire, 1970/2000; Orbe, 2018), it is important to distinguish between different types of interactions. We can define **talk**, for instance, as unidirectional messages sent with little attention to or opportunity for feedback. Talk is one-way communication that oftentimes takes the form of a lecture. **Discussion**, in comparison, involves multi-directional messages exchanged between two or more people. If talk involves talking *at* someone, discussion typically involves people talking *with* others. The goal for this type of interaction is often to persuade the other person to see things in particular way; therefore discussions typically take the form of debates. Discussion becomes **communication** when the series of messages that are exchanged ultimately result in creating shared meaning and mutual understanding. Too often, we assume that we have shared meaning when we communicate with others, but we fail to recognize that individuals bring different sets of assumptions, perceptions, and understandings that lead to miscommunication. Because of this, some scholars (e.g., Shakirova et al., 2018) believe that communication failures are the norm, especially interactions that involve people from diverse backgrounds. In this book, we focus on the great potential of the last form of interracial interaction—**dialogue**. Multiple conceptualizations of dialogue exist, and most reflect a common focus on its transformative nature (e.g., Freire, 1970/2000; Orbe, 2018). By and large, dialogue is defined as an exchange in which people who have different beliefs and perspectives develop mutual understanding that transforms how they see themselves and others.

As you can probably imagine, cultivating an environment where dialogue can emerge is quite difficult. Throughout society, people often use dialogue to describe different events; however, true dialogue never occurs (Roper, 2019). We see this on our college campuses all the time. Different events promise "difficult dialogues on race," yet the interactions at these programs never go beyond talk, debate, and/or discussion. Our intention here is to advocate for striving for interracial communication (i.e., successful cocreated shared meaning and mutual understanding) with the potential for interracial dialogue to emerge. Just because you are talking with someone from a different racial/ethnic group, that doesn't mean that you are successfully communicating with them. The next section describes the crucial components of interracial interactions that go beyond mere "talk" or "discussion."

## FOSTERING INTERRACIAL DIALOGUE

We believe, as does Johannesen (1971), that dialogue is best viewed as an attitude, orientation, or philosophy. Compare this approach to dialogue with popular myths that describe dialogue as simple, relatively effortless, and easy to maintain (Roper, 2019). Within this more common perspective, dialogue is seen as a strategy or technique—consciously achieved with little or no preparation. But our use of the concept of dialogue is different from "honest expression," "frank conversation, "or "good communication." To foster an environment where dialogue can emerge, community members must work hard to promote a supportive (caring) climate in which genuineness, empathic understanding, unconditional positive regard, and mutual equality are maintained (Johannesen, 1971). Setting the stage for dialogue also includes addressing existing power differentials from which speech is enacted and utilizing tactics to empower those persons who enter a specific situational context with less social, organizational, and/or personal power than others (Peters & Besley, 2021).

According to Tanno (1998), six elements are crucial to the promotion of dialogue. The first element is *connection*, a recognition that our past, present, and future are inextricably tied together. As a way to prepare for dialogue, community members must come to understand how their shared history (sometimes at odds, sometimes together) informs, to a certain extent, current interactions. Connection also involves simultaneously recognizing both similarities and differences.

The second element is a *commitment* over time. Dialogue cannot be scheduled. It does not have a clear, explicit start and end. One of the defining characteristics of dialogue is that it represents a process, one in which all parties are actively involved and committed. In other words, dialogue can only emerge through commitment and time.

The third key element to dialogue is a developed *realness/closeness* both in terms of physical and psychological distance. Genuineness, honesty, and candor—even that which initially may be potentially offensive—all are central to the emergence of dialogue (Johannesen, 1971). A central element of dialogue is the desire, ability, and commitment to "keep it real" even when such an endeavor may result in some tension or hostility.

As it relates to freedom of expression, a fourth element of dialogue is the *creation/maintenance* of space where everyone's *voice* is valued. This includes the recognition and an appreciation that each person may speak for a variety of voices (professional, personal, cultural). For instance, within dialogue, the perspective of a layperson describing their own lived experiences is valued and appreciated with the same regard as a researcher's or scholar's perspective.

The fifth element of dialogue includes an *engagement of mind, heart, and soul*. The mind may be where logic and reasoning are located; however, the heart and soul are where emotion, commitment, accountability, and responsibility reside. Attempts to isolate some aspects (fact, logic, reason) with no or little consideration of others (emotions, experiences, intuitions) does not contribute to a healthy communication environment. Instead, it creates a traditional, hostile climate where certain voices are privileged over others.

The final element that is crucial in setting the stage for dialogue is *self-reflection*. According to Tanno (1998), all of the other elements previously described depend on each person's resolution to engage in self-reflection that is critical, constructive, and continuous. Such a process of self-examination can be initially difficult, and ultimately painful, especially when dealing with such issues as cultural oppression, societal power, and privilege. However, the process by which persons situate themselves—professionally, culturally, and personally—within the context of a healthy communication environment is crucial to establishing a readiness for dialogue. Through self-reflection, an understanding can emerge where individuals begin to recognize the relevance of their lived experience in perceptions of self and others. In this regard, "objective" positions stemming from a "neutral standpoint" are acknowledged as problematic. So, as we work to discuss the saliency of interracial communication, we must continue to engage in self-reflexivity. Through this process, we are encouraged to recognize that neutralization (apathy) only perpetuates the problem of racism.

As you probably noticed, cultural communication competency and facilitating dialogue go hand and hand. Interracial exchanges between individuals without substantial cultural competencies are likely to result in less-than-desirable outcomes. Part of being culturally competent is recognizing the importance of creating an environment conductive to dialogue; this includes

---

**Box 1.6**                                                    *Research Highlight*

## The Challenges and Opportunities
## with Teaching Interracial Communication

Both authors of this text have close to 50 years of combined experience teaching interracial communication courses. The second author has taught interracial communication as a study abroad course in Costa Rica for years. During the summer of 2019, the first author joined her and students from two different universities worked together for an amazing month-long experience. Over the years, both of us have had many "success" stories regarding our interracial classes; we also have shared the significant challenges we have encountered at different times. Teaching interracial communication has always been important— yet never easy. This is especially true as race relations intensify in the United States (Kezar et al., 2020). In a 2020 article, Michael Arrington discussed his experiences teaching the interracial communication course in the U.S. South. His autoethnographic account vividly described his experiences attempting to facilitate student growth and implementing the necessary elements to foster classroom dialogue (Arrington, 2020). As you read through the section on dialogue, what were your initial thoughts? Is dialogue too idealistic, something that is unlikely in college classrooms? What needs to be done to set the stage for dialogue? Are classes that don't experience dialogue a failure?

---

understanding power dynamics and local politics. All of these efforts are crucial to move beyond superficial discussions and toward interracial dialogue.

Accordingly, we turn next to the importance of classroom climate in promoting interracial dialogue. Race can be an emotional, personal, and/or challenging topic for both students and instructors (Arrington, 2020). This is especially true for European American (white) students who "feel that they cannot honestly discuss racially charged issues without fear of the ultimate social shame—being labeled as racist" (A. Miller & Harris, 2005, p. 238). A positive, productive classroom climate is, therefore, essential to maximizing discussions related to race, racism, and interracial communication. The ideal learning community is one that supports diverse student capabilities, offers multiple opportunities to participate, and promotes brave spaces where individuals can ask questions and make mistakes (S. Williams et al., 2020). Remember that we adopt a broad conceptualization of a classroom, defining it as any place where sustained teaching and learning can occur. So while a standard definition of classroom suggests university and college classes, our conceptualization is also relevant to interracial communication teaching and learning in various contexts.

## Building a Positive Learning Community in the Classroom

We tend to use the label **community** to describe any number of settings (e.g., neighborhoods, colleges, churches). Peck's (1987) writings on what he calls "true community" appear to offer the most productive approach, especially in terms of the interracial communication classroom. He restricts the use of community to a "group of individuals who have learned how to communicate honestly with each other" (p. 50). Those who are part of a true community have relationships that go deeper than typical interactions that only involve "masks of composure." They also involve a significant level of commitment to "rejoice together" and "to delight in each other, make others' conditions our own" (p. 50).

Building a sense of community in any classroom is ideal in that it is central to student engagement and satisfaction (Berry, 2019). It appears essential for courses that involve topics related to issues of culture, race, and oppression. Sometimes it can seem like an impossible task, especially given the time and commitment it takes. Because race continues to be a volatile issue in the United States, studying interracial communication typically involves some tension. The most productive instances of interracial communication, at least initially, work to sustain rather than resolve this tension (Orbe, 2018). This involves probing the awkwardness that sometimes comes with learning new perspectives, especially those that appear to conflict with a person's existing views. It also includes dealing with a range of emotions—anger, fear, pride, guilt, joy, shame—associated with understanding your own racial location. Negotiating the tensions that accompany such strong emotions can encourage classroom participants (including both instructors and students) to recognize racial/ethnic differences while also seeing the commonalities among different cultural groups.

Cultivating a sense of community in the classroom is facilitated by the instructor, who as the initial leader has responsibility to maximize learning (McKinney et al., 2006). Community can be established through culturally responsive classroom management (Weiss, 2015), which values collaboration, inclusivity, and respect. Yet, creating inclusive communities is not simply the responsibility of the teacher, it also requires a conscious effort for each member of the class (S. Williams et al., 2020). A major aspect of building classroom community involves establishing relationships. According to Palmer (1993), "real learning does not happen until students are brought into relationship with the teacher, with each other, and with the subject" (p. 5). So, how do we go about cultivating a sense of community in interracial communication classes? Peck (1987) identifies six characteristics of "true community": (1) inclusiveness, (2) commitment, (3) consensus, (4) contemplation, (5) vulnerability, and (6) graceful fighting. As you will see, each of these elements of community contributes to maximizing the potential for interracial communication interactions.

**Inclusiveness** refers to a general acceptance and appreciation of differences, not as necessarily positive or negative but just as different. First and foremost, community must embrace different perspectives and regard them as valuable (Peck, 1987). Maintaining ingroup/outgroup status within the interracial communication classroom and excluding some individuals because of their differences is counterproductive to cultivating a sense of community. Community members must establish and maintain a sense of inclusiveness.

**Commitment** involves a strong willingness to coexist and work through any barriers that hinder community development (Peck, 1987). Part of your commitment to community is a faithfulness to work through both the positive

Creating an inclusive classroom committed to respect, dignity, and a genuine desire to learn from others is a crucial part of setting the stage for dialogic moments.

and negative experiences associated with the tensions of racial interactions. In other words, being committed to community involves "hang[ing] in there when the going gets rough" (p. 62). Typically, it is exactly this sense of commitment that allows people to absorb any differences in racialized locations as a healthy means of community development and preservation.

**Consensus** is another important aspect of community. Interracial communities, in the true sense of the word, work through differences in opinions and seek a general agreement or accord among their members. Racial and ethnic differences are not "ignored, denied, hidden, or changed; instead they are celebrated as gifts" (Peck, 1987, p. 62). In every situation, developing a consensus requires acknowledging and processing cultural differences. In the interracial communication classroom, reaching a consensus does not imply forced adherence to majority beliefs. Instead, it involves collaborative efforts to obtain a win–win situation or possibly "agreeing to disagree."

**Contemplation** is crucial to this process. Individuals are consciously aware of their particular racial location as well as their collective standing as a community. This awareness involves an increased realization of self, others, and how these two interact with the larger external surroundings. Becoming more aware of your multicultural selves is an important component of this process, and Chapters 4 and 5 are designed to facilitate greater self-discovery in this area. Constant reflection on the process toward community is necessary.

**Vulnerability**, the fifth characteristic of community, involves individuals discarding any masks of inauthencity and exposing their inner selves to others (Peck, 1987). In other words, a certain degree of susceptibility must be assumed. For interracial communication instructors, this means creating a relatively safe place where students are accepted for who they are and who they are becoming. It also involves assuming the risks associated with sharing personal stories related to culture, race/ethnicity, and social oppressions. Vulnerability is contagious. Students are more willing to take risks and make themselves vulnerable when they perceive the instructor as personally engaged in the process of building community.

**Graceful fighting** is the final characteristic of community (Peck, 1987). As described earlier, tension in the interracial communication classroom is to be expected. Conflict is a natural process inherent to any intergroup setting and should not be avoided, minimized, or disregarded. The notion that "if we can resolve our conflicts then someday we will be able to live together in community" (p. 72) is an illusion. A community is built *through* the negotiation (not avoidance) of conflict. But how do we participate in graceful fighting? The next section explores this important question through guidelines to facilitating dialogue in the interracial communication classroom.

## Practical Guidelines for Facilitating Dialogue

We do not particularly like the term graceful fighting to describe the type of communication that we want to promote during interracial interactions. The word *fighting* has a negative connotation; it triggers images of nasty disagreements, physical confrontations, or screaming matches. Nevertheless, we do believe that our ideas of creating a positive learning community in the interracial communication classroom are consistent with Peck's writings on graceful fighting. In short, we see it as referring to an expectation that agreements and disagreements are to be articulated, negotiated, and possibly resolved, productively. One point needs to be raised before outlining the process of creating ground rules for discussion: some general differences in how different racial/ethnic groups engage in conflict.

A number of general ground rules exist that commonly are adopted to guide effective group discussions. Chances are, based on your experiences with working with different types of groups, you could generate a list of conversational guidelines, such as the following. Be open minded. Be a respectful, active listener; do not interrupt or plan what you want to say until you understand the speaker's views. Increase participation by giving everyone the opportunity to speak. Recognize that everyone has blind spots and opportunities for growth. Focus on understanding, not necessarily agreement. Use "I" statements when articulating thoughts, emotions, and ideas. Avoid making compound statements that include the word "but," because it negates your first statement; instead strive to use "and" as a conjunction. Act responsibly and explain why certain things people say are offensive to you. Assume that people are inherently good and always do the best they can with what information they have. As you read each of these guidelines, we hope that you understand how they contribute to a positive learning environment generally, and more specifically to classes focused on engaging issues of race and racism. We also hope that you see them as an important foundation for cultivating a space where dialogue can emerge.

A number of programs embrace the conceptualization of dialogue as described in previous sections. For instance, the W. K. Kellogg Foundation sponsors an annual National Day of Racial Healing, an effort that offers individuals, organizations, and communities a chance to come together and take collective action for a more just and equitable world (see Box 10.2). This program is grounded in the premise that racial healing is supported through respectful dialogue, recognition and affirmation of all people and their respective experiences, and an expressed connection to cultural histories and practices.

Committing to engagement with an explicit dialogue orientation is an important foundation through which everyone can embrace opportunities for increased awareness and consciousness, something that ultimately can lead to deeper understanding, empathy, and agency in terms of specific problematic thoughts and behaviors. The Caring Across Generations (2020) program offers several specific guidelines to holding dialogues on racism.

- Be clear and open about the purpose of the conversation before inviting people and during the conversation.
- Set ground rules for respectful conversation.
- Active listening is a must.
- Remain open, with curiosity modeled by responding with questions before responding with your own interpretation or explanation of impact in regards to someone else's comments.
- Recognize and acknowledge people's experiences. The person/people you are in conversation with are bringing their own perspective, shaped by their own experiences (culture, history, practices, upbringing).
- Be mindful to take breaks to recenter when conversations feel uncomfortable or too wrought with conflict to be productive. Build in moments for deep breathing, pauses to reflect and recenter, and moments to be aware of mind, body, and emotional alignment.
- Everyone has agency, and, regardless of agreement and alignment, everyone is worthy of being valued in the dignity of their humanity.
- DON'T assume intent. DO center impact over intent.
- Dismantling racism is not a checklist, a meeting, or a one-time commitment. Make small, realistic, challenging commitments to grow, learn, and evolve.

Do you agree with each of these guidelines? Why or why not? Consistent with the characteristics of cultivating a sense of community and elements to promote dialogue, it is important to recognize that a consensus of all participants must be gained in terms of classroom discussion guidelines. If just one person does not agree with a ground rule, it should not be adopted unless altered to everyone's satisfaction. Of course, some members may provide convincing arguments that persuade others to adopt certain guidelines. This, however, should not translate into peer pressure or intimidation. Again, after some extended discussion on each guideline, a consensus needs to be reached or it is not adopted by the classroom community. Because the dynamics of each community are different, specific ground rules are likely to be different from group to another. We must also take into consideration the specific situational context (dyadic, small group, open discussion) and communication channel used by the group.

The COVID global pandemic fostered a universal shift to online learning within the United States. For many professors and students—even those who had significant experience with virtual asynchronous formats—this affected their teaching and learning in significant ways. Given our dialogic approach to engaging in interracial communication content, we found that whatever challenges (e.g., opportunities) existed within in-person classrooms also were present with online offerings. This is consistent with the findings of Eschmann (2020a) who studied the existence of racial microaggressions in virtual learning environments. While virtual learning does not allow for the type of immediacy possible through in-person classrooms, it can provide a safe means to engage issues of race and racism if managed well. Virtual classrooms are not limited to boring PowerPoint slide presentations with uninspiring professor voice-overs. Lecturettes and experiential-learning activities combined with stimulating discussions via small break-out groups can be engaging and meaningful. With this type of critical public pedagogy, transformative interracial dialogues can emerge despite difficulties (Stokke, 2021). The essential point is that the mode of delivery for the interracial communication classroom (in-person, virtually, or a hybrid format) should have an impact on the type of guidelines that are used. One of the Opportunities for Extended Learning at the end of this chapter facilitates further exploration of this idea.

Another factor that should be recognized when creating guidelines for class discussions is the readiness levels of the participants of the group—this includes both the instructor/facilitator and students/participants (Arrington, 2020). It is important to note that the various ground rules that we have generated do not apply universally. Each community must create a set of communication norms that meet the expectations and competencies for their particular members.

In some instances, different groups will be willing and able to incorporate additional guidelines that reflect their deeper understanding of race, racism, and race relations in the United States. For instance, some interracial communication classes—depending on participants' levels of cultural competency and readiness to engage in difficult dialogues regarding race and racism—may decide to adopt one or more of the following guidelines (Arrington, 2020).

1. Communicate with the assumption that racism, and other forms of oppression, exist in the United States.

2. Agree not to blame ourselves or others for misinformation that we have learned in the past; instead, assume a responsibility for not repeating misinformation once we have learned otherwise.

3. Avoid making sweeping generalizations of individuals based solely on their racial/ethnic group membership (e.g., I can't understand why Asian Americans always . . .).

4. Acknowledge the powerful role of the media on the socialization of each community member.

5. Resist placing the extra burden of "racial spokesperson" or "expert" on anyone.

Each of these five examples represents another guideline that your class-room community may want to adopt as they engage in meaningful interracial communication. What other guidelines, relatively unique to your situation, might you also adopt? Once a consensus has been reached on a workable set of guidelines, repeatedly share them with the class so members have access to them. Over the course of the life of the community, review, reemphasize, chal-lenge, and/or revise your guidelines. As the relational immediacy of the stu-dents and instructors increases, so might the need for additional guidelines for classroom discussions. Other rules may no longer seem relevant. The key is to create and maintain a set of communication ground rules that serve to guide your discussions on race and racism.

## Conclusion

Chapter 1 was designed to introduce you to the study of interracial com-munication in the United States and to outline the importance of cultivating a sense of community to maximize the potential for productive dialogue on top-ics related to race. Interwoven throughout this chapter are several important assumptions that are central to effective interracial understanding. We sum-marize them here to facilitate your navigation of future chapters.

The first assumption deals with the history of race. Although race is largely a socially constructed concept, it must be studied because it is such an impor-tant external cue in communication interactions. Race matters in the United States and other countries around the world. Ethnic differences may be a more credible marker (scientifically), yet people see and react to perceived racial dif-ferences. Second, relying on racial and ethnic stereotypes when communicating with individual group members is counterproductive. Seeing others as individu-als, while maintaining an awareness of general cultural norms, promotes com-petent, meaningful interracial communication. The third assumption has to do with honest self-reflection in terms of the social positioning that your particular racial/ethnic group occupies. Acknowledging, and coming to understand, self and other racial locations is crucial to maximizing interracial communication interactions. Fourth, research and theory within the field of communication has significant contributions to make in terms of advocating for productive commu-nication within and across different racial and ethnic groups. And while we do not assume that communication is a cure-all, it does appear to be the primary means to advance race relations at a time when the world most needs it.

## Key Terms

| | |
|---|---|
| interpersonal communication | transracial communication |
| intraracial communication | culture |
| international communication | race |
| intercultural communication | ethnicity |
| interethnic communication | ethnocentrism |

microculture
racial prejudice
racial discrimination
racism
stereotypes
metastereotypes
racial location
racial standpoint
cultural competency
mindfulness
unconscious bias
cultural humility

talk
discussion
communication
dialogue
community
inclusiveness
commitment
consensus
contemplation
vulnerability
graceful fighting

## *OPPORTUNITIES FOR EXTENDED LEARNING*

1. Some communication scholars do not necessarily agree with our definition of interracial communication. For instance, Marsha Houston (2002) contends that the history of race (and racism) is integral to U.S. history. As such, she states that race is always a salient issue—either explicitly or implicitly—when people from different racial and ethnic groups interact. Break into small groups and discuss her contention; what are your thoughts about the saliency of race in everyday interactions?

2. In his award-winning book *How To Be an Antiracist*, Ibram X. Kendi (2019) provides operational definitions for different concepts related to race, racism, and power. For instance, he defines race as "a power construct of collected or merged difference that lives socially" (p. 35) and racist as "one who is supporting a racist policy through their actions or inaction or expressing a racist idea" (p. 13). Compare his definitions to the ones in this chapter. Which do you find most helpful, current, and productive? Kendi has multiple other definitions (at the beginning of each chapter); if you have access to his book, check his definitions and decide if you would amend the definitions in this chapter.

3. In an attempt to understand your particular racial location, create a list of statements in response to the question: What does it mean to be _____ [insert racial/ethnic group] in the United States? Once you have compiled your list, share it with others within and outside your racial/ethnic group. What similarities and differences exist? Learning about others' racial locations is an excellent way to generate an increased level of understanding of your own racial location.

4. Find out more about the racial and ethnic composition of your local community by visiting https://data.census.gov/cedsci/. At this U.S. Census Bureau website, you can get current demographic information about particular communities (by zip code or city) and states, as well as the entire United States. Compare and contrast your local community with others across the country.

5. As indicated in the chapter, guidelines for classroom discussions should reflect the specific dynamics of a particular group. Think about what guidelines might be necessary for computer chat rooms or classes conducted via

the internet. How might these be similar to, yet different from, more traditional classrooms?

6. One strategy for facilitating discussions related to race, racism, and communication is to generate a list of propositions (Sanders & Orbe, 2016). First, break the class into groups. Then give each group one of the following statements (and/or create your own); instruct group members to reach a consensus if at all possible.

   a. In the contemporary United States, people of color cannot be racist.

   b. Racism can be unconscious and unintentional.

   c. Many European American men in the United States are currently the victims of reverse discrimination.

   d. All European Americans, because of the privilege in the United States, are inherently racist.

   e. Asian Americans can be racist against other people of color, like African and Latino/a Americans.

## RECOMMENDED CONTEMPORARY READINGS

Adebayo, C. T., Walker, K., Hawkins, M., Olukotun, O., Shaw, L., Sahlstein Parcell, E., Dressel, A., Luft, H., & Mkandawire-Valhmu, L. (2020). Race and Blackness: A thematic review of communication challenges confronting the Black community within the U.S. health care system. *Journal of Transcultural Nursing, 31*(4), 397–405. doi.org/10.1177/1043659619889111

Alsaidi, S., Velez, B. L., Smith, L., Jacob, A., & Salem, N. (2021). "Arab, brown, and other": Voices of Muslim Arab American women on identity, discrimination, and well-being. *Cultural Diversity and Ethnic Minority Psychology.* Advance online publication. https://doi.org/10.1037/cdp0000440

Chuang, E., Fiter, R. J., Sanon, O. C., Wang, A., Hope, A. A., Schechter, C. B., & Gong, M. N. (2020). Race and ethnicity and satisfaction with communication in the intensive care unit. *American Journal of Hospice and Palliative Medicine, 37*(10), 823–829. doi.org/10.1177/1049909120916126

Dickerson, D. L., Brown, R. A., Klein, D. J., Agniel, D., Johnson, C., & D'Amico, E. J. (2019). Overt perceived discrimination and racial microaggressions and their association with health risk behaviors among a sample of urban American Indian/Alaska Native adolescents. *Journal of Racial and Ethnic Health Disparities, 6*(4), 733–742. https://doi.org/10.1007/s40615-019-00572-1

Nameni, A., & Dowlatabadi, H. (2019). A study of the level of intercultural communicative competence and intercultural sensitivity of Iranian medical students based on ethnicity. *Journal of Intercultural Communication Research, 48*(1), 21–34. doi.org/10.1080/17475759.2018.1549586

Nuru, A. K., & Arendt, C. E. (2018). Not so safe a space: Women activists of color's responses to racial microaggressions by white women allies. *Southern Communication Journal, 84*(2), 85–98. https://doi.org/10.1080/1041794X.2018.1505940

Woodhead, C., Onwumere, J., Rhead, R., Bora-White, M., Chui, Z., Clifford, N., Connor, L., Gunasinghe, C., Harwood, H., Meriez, P., Mir, G., Jones Nielsen, J., Rafferty, A. M., Stanley, N., Peprah, D., & Hatch, S. L. (2021). Race, ethnicity and COVID-19 vaccination: A qualitative study of UK healthcare staff. *Ethnicity & Health*, 1–20. doi.org/10.1080/13557858.2021.1936464

# 2

# The History of Race

**CASE STUDY**     **Indigenous Land Acknowledgements**

Indigenous Peoples' Day was first adopted by the Berkeley (CA) City Council in 1991, and observed the following year in lieu of the Columbus Quincentennial, marking the 500th anniversary of his arrival in the Americas. This holiday featured public acknowledgment that Indigenous groups lived on the land prior to European arrival and demonstrated support for Native American history and ongoing suffering from the legacy of conquest. In recent years, Indigenous Land Acknowledgements across the United States have been created to further such recognition. At their core, these statements are used to recognize and affirm "Indigenous Peoples as traditional stewards of this land and the enduring relationship that exists between Indigenous Peoples and their traditional territories" (Small, 2010).

Advocates and supporters applaud different organizations—including a number of U.S. colleges and universities—who have created and included Indigenous Land Acknowledgements in different public events. Such recognition is important given how history has worked to erase Indigenous culture from the U.S. landscape. Critics, on the other hand, describe such efforts as little more than symbolic with little effect on Native American community's material, political, or economic conditions. They recognize acknowledgement as an admittance of wrongdoing but also challenge organizations to commit to making restitution (Wilkie, 2021).

Have you heard of Indigenous Land Acknowledgements? Does your school have one that is used for different campus events? What are your thoughts and experiences with this attempt at racial reconciliation? Do land acknowledgements represent an important advancement in race relations in the United States, or do they reflect nothing more than an empty symbol? What types of restitution might be appropriate in order to extend these efforts to include more tangible actions?

The presence of race in the United States is like the presence of the air we breathe—something always around us that we use constantly, sometimes without much thought. How often have you thought about the racial categories in which you and others are placed? This chapter is designed to give you a brief historical overview of the concept of race in the United States (Chapter 7 will provide some information about race more globally). Tracing the history of the evolution of race and racial classifications is important in identifying the various ways that current designations affect our everyday communication.

The concept of race is a highly complex one, reflected in the great body of literature that deals with issues associated with this social construct. In fact, some might suggest the issue of race is central to nearly every aspect of the national agenda of the United States. Thus, we acknowledge that this text is simply an introduction to the various perspectives on race. We have included a variety of references that will give you a more in-depth treatment of the issues discussed here. Our hope is that you will take the initiative to do further reading (see Opportunities for Extended Learning and Recommended Contemporary Readings at the end of each chapter for some direction).

As evidenced throughout this book, the United States is a country where, in the words of Cornell West (1993), *race matters*. Attempts to promote a deeper understanding of the complexities inherent in interracial communication must begin with an exploration of the development of the idea of race and racial designations.

## HISTORY OF RACIAL CLASSIFICATION

Humans are an amazingly diverse species, but this diversity is not due to a finite number of subtypes or **races**. Rather, the vast majority of human genetic diversity reflects local adaptations and, most of all, our individual uniqueness. The concept of race as we know it did not exist in the ancient world (Snowden, 1970). Over the years, many scholars have examined the emergence of the idea of race and attempted to document the developmental history of racial classifications. Some (e.g., Gosset, 1963) suggest that a French physician, Francois Bernier, was the first to write about the idea of race in 1684. Bernier created a racial categorization scheme that separated groups of people based on two elements: skin color and facial features. The result was the formulation of four racial groups: Europeans, Africans, Orientals, and Lapps (people from northern Scandinavia). Other scholars (e.g., West, 1982) point to the work of Arthur de Gobineau (1816–1882), whose work divided the human race into three types (White, Black, and Yellow), with the white race described as the most superior of the three. But the most influential of all racial classifications, especially as they relate to the ideas of race in contemporary times, was established by Johann Friedrich Blumenbach in the late 1700s. When tracing the history of race, nearly all scholars point to Blumenbach's typology (first created in 1775, revised in 1781, and a third revision in 1795) as a central force in the creation of racial divisions (Lasker & Tyzzer, 1982; Montagu, 1964, 1997; Spickard, 1992). Because his ideas served as a foundation for much of the subsequent work on race, our coverage of the history of race begins with a focus on his work.

Blumenbach (1752–1840) was a German anatomist and naturalist who had studied under Carolus Linnaeus. In 1758, Linnaeus constructed a system of classification of all living things (Bahk & Jandt, 2004). According to the Linnaean system, all human beings are members of a certain kingdom (Animalia), phylum (Chordata), class (Mammalia), order (Primates), family (*Hominidae*), genus (*Homo*), and species (*sapiens*) (Spickard, 1992). Each level of this pyramid-like typology contains a number of specific subdivisions of the level above. Blumenbach's work was based on the premise, supplied by Linnaeus, that all human beings belonged to a species known as *Homo sapiens*. His work focused on extending this system down one more level to human *races*, primarily based on geography and observed physical differences.

It is important to note that Blumenbach's original text (1775/1969) recorded only four races based primarily on the "perceived superior beauty" of people from the region of the Caucasus Mountains. Interestingly, these four groups were defined primarily by geography and not presented in the rank order favored by most Europeans (Gould, 1994). Instead, the Americanus, describing the native populations of the New World, were listed first. Second were the Europaeus (**Caucasians**), who included the light-skinned people of Europe and adjacent parts of Asia and Africa. The Asiaticus, or Mongolian variety, were listed third. This grouping included most of the other inhabitants of Asia not covered in the Europaeus category. Finally listed were the Afer (Ethiopian) group, who represented the dark-skinned people of Africa. This initial taxonomy, like the earlier work of Linnaeus, did not imply any inherent form of social hierarchy. Of note, Blumenbach is cited as the founder of racial classification because, unlike his predecessors, he purportedly advanced the earlier work by rearranging races along a hierarchical order with Caucasians occupying the most superior position.

In the simplest terms, Blumenbach's 1795 work (1865/1963) incorporated an additional ordering mechanism into his classification of race. This one addition would set in motion a series of developments that led to our current state of racial relations. In essence, "he radically changed the geometry of human order from a geographically based model without explicit ranking to a hierarchy of worth . . . [based on] a Caucasian ideal" (Gould, 1994, p. 69). He accomplished this by recognizing one particular group as closest to the created ideal and then characterizing the remaining groups as progressive derivations from this standard. In order to create a symmetrical pyramid, Blumenbach added the Malay classification in 1795. This grouping included the Polynesians and Melanesians of the Pacific, as well as the aborigines of Australia. The result was an implied racist ranking of Europeans first, Africans and Asians last, and Malays and Americans between them (see Figure 2.1). Over the years, the implied worth of human races—as indicated by the conventional hierarchy created by Blumenbach—has permeated the various attempts at racial classification. Most systems of classification divide humankind into at least four groups based primarily on skin color and physical features: Red, Yellow, Black, and White (Native Americans/Alaskan Natives, Asians, Africans, and Europeans, respectively). Subsequent sections in this chapter explore the biological and social nature of racial classifications, as well as how these perspectives inform our current perceptions of race, ethnic-

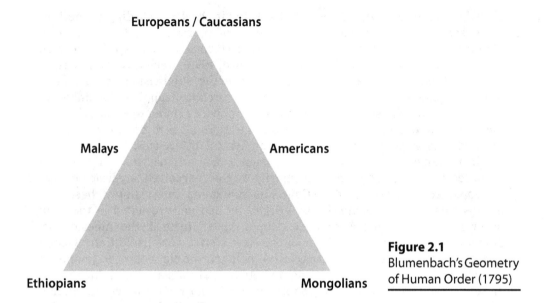

**Figure 2.1**
Blumenbach's Geometry
of Human Order (1795)

ity, and interracial communication. However, before doing so, we need to explore the ways that earlier racial classifications were used in terms of world, national, and local events.

## ECONOMIC AND POLITICAL EXPANSION AND RACE

The history of race is intertwined with one of the major themes of the past five centuries of world history: economic and political expansion of European countries (Tolbert, 1989). As a way to justify their domination of Native populations of land they deemed desirable, Europeans developed and maintained ideologies and belief systems that supported their policies. A greater understanding of how race has been used by some as a means of economic and political expansion is an important aspect of the history of race. According to Tolbert, three specific ideologies warrant attention: (1) the idea of a "chosen people," (2) racism, and (3) colonialism.

### A Chosen People

The first ideology that helps us understand the role of race in international affairs is a version of the Judeo-Christian concept of a **chosen people**. This idea appears both in the Hebrew Scriptures and the New Testament. Within this interpretation (C. E. Jackson & Tolbert, 1989), Europeans were the race chosen by God. It was their responsibility, therefore, to reclaim the world in his name. One movement related to this idea become known as Manifest Destiny.

Throughout the history of European expansion into the "new world," the idea that their efforts were consistent with spiritual teachings was prevalent.

The term **Manifest Destiny** began to appear in print regularly within the United States around the mid-1800s. At that time, it referred to the idea that the United States had the right—granted by God—to spread across the entire North American continent (Brewer, 2006; Rathbun, 2001). The religious sentiment of U.S. Americans at this time in history was extremely high; in fact, many believed that the land across North America was sacred land that had been given to them by God.

It was in the name of Manifest Destiny that Europeans proceeded with their expansion in North America. Although initially embracing Europeans as potential traders, Native peoples faced grave adjustments in the face of a relentless encroachment by these strangers. The principles inherent in a Manifest Destiny clearly clashed with the nearly universal Native American belief that the land was a living entity the Creator had entrusted to them for preservation and protection (C. E. Jackson & Tolbert, 1989). Years of wars, disease, and negotiations, including the 1830s national "removal policy" that called for the resettlement to Oklahoma of all Native Americans living east of the Mississippi, had a devastating impact on Native populations. By 1850, for instance, the estimated 12 million Native people in North America at the time of Columbus's arrival had been reduced to 250,000 (Tolbert, 1989). By 1914, the 138 million acres that Native peoples "oversaw" had been reduced to 56 million acres. Today there are approximately 326 land areas administered as federal reservations.

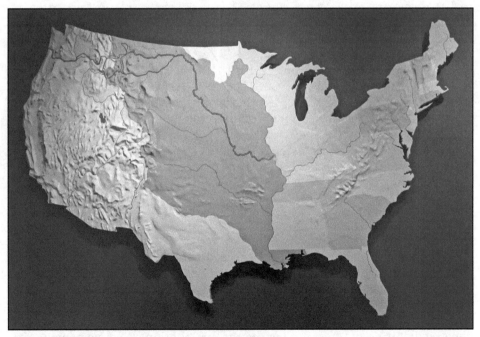

Manifest Destiny played an important role in the U.S. expansion across the Americas, including the Louisiana Purchase in 1803. This massive amount of land covers 15 current U.S. states and 2 Canadian provinces.

Native Americans were not the only people who were engulfed by the Europeans' expansion in the Americas (Brewer, 2006). The U.S. annexation of Texas from Mexico, the U.S. war with Mexico, and the subsequent acquisition of the New Mexico and California territories all were completed under a general charge of Manifest Destiny (Parrillo, 1996; Rathbun, 2001). Although Mexicanos were guaranteed, as new U.S. citizens, the protection of basic rights, discrimination and racism were commonplace. During prosperous times, with an urgent need for workers in agriculture, railways, and industry, Mexicans were welcomed by employers. In times of scarcity, however, they have been dismissed as "disposable field hands"—oftentimes without hearings or confirmation of their U.S. citizenship (West, 1982), an issue that continues today (C. Stewart et al., 2011). Much of the land in the southern and western regions of the United States was gained through efforts related to Manifest Destiny. Additional expansions—in Puerto Rico, the Philippine Islands, Alaska, and Hawaii—were also related (Brewer, 2006).

---

*Box 2.1*                                                          *Student Reflections*

### Embracing German Heritage in America

Although I am 100% German, I carry very little of the German culture in my blood. After all, my family moved to America when I was only 3 years old, and I have assimilated to the culture and its values quite well since then. However, I always felt a sense of shame and embarrassment whenever grade school kids found out that I was German. Maybe it is because the only time the teacher discussed anything German was when World War I and World War II came up on the lesson plan. My mother also felt a little embarrassed at times when in public, because whenever my siblings or I misbehaved, she would speak in German to us.... While I was taught to respect all people, no matter what color their skin, I was never taught of the injustices happening in the world around me. Sure, I went to high school and learned all about the civil rights movement and slavery, but I was never enlightened to how bad things still were in today's world. As much as I hate to say this, I feel that my high school has left me behind when it comes to social issues and the injustices surrounding them.

---

## Racism

According to Hodge (1989), racism is "the belief in, and practice of, the domination of one social group, identified as a 'race,' over another social group, identified as of another 'race'" (p. 28). To justify their economic and political expansion in the New World, European Americans relied on the perpetuation of racist thinking. Because Europeans believed that races were genetically different, most did not see the exploitation of Native people, Africans, and others as any different from the use of farm animals (Graves, 2004). Manifest Destiny, in this regard, had a significant impact on how people, and by extension institutions, regarded Native Americans, Africans, and others living in the Americas. Three important components of early racist thinking are especially relevant to understand the foundational years of the United States.

First, Europeans maintained that humankind consists of well-defined races. This basic belief was evident in the ways that diverse ethnic and cultural groups, like those included in the larger groupings known as Native Americans and African Americans, were regarded as similar when contrasted to European American norms. This ignored that great diversity existed within the various ethnic groups contained in one racial category; in fact, the diversity within groups was larger than between groups (Bahk & Jandt, 2004).

Second was a belief that some races are inherently superior to others. In order to support the idea of a chosen people—one that has superiority over other groups—European Americans attempted to prove the inferiority of other racial groups by ignoring the achieved levels of learning, wealth, community, and established spirituality of Native American and African civilizations. The history of European–Native relations, for example, was situated within a superiority–inferiority dynamic (Corbett, 2003). Labels for indigenous people reflected negative stereotypes (e.g., savages, barbarians, wild men) and rationalized the enactment of policies designed to transform them into "proper citizens" (Stromberg, 2006).

Third, the belief that the superior race should rule over inferior races was viewed as good for both European Americans (who were fulfilling their responsibilities as the so-called chosen people) and other racial groups (who would benefit from the European influences). For example, European Americans believed that Africans had a natural defect that made it nearly impossible for them to function as free women and men. Using this reasoning, slavery was deemed productive in partially civilizing these "savages" and introducing them to a faith by which they could achieve salvation (Tolbert, 1989).

| Box 2.2 | Student Reflections |
|---|---|

### Tracing Generational Roots

For the past few years, some of my relatives have been tracing our generational roots. Not to our surprise, we have traced our ancestry back to the McFadden Plantation of Sumter, South Carolina. It was not surprising because as an African American, I figured that my ancestors were slaves. It just amazed me to get a true and visible example of where my ancestors lived and experienced such harsh treatment. Bitterness did not overwhelm me, but I was negatively affected in the beginning. I felt a little angry about how many people's ancestors were robbed of their pride, dignity, tradition, and most importantly their sense of family and togetherness—things that seem to plague our community today.

## Colonialism

**Colonialism** is a formal system of domination that removes the power of self-determination from one group and gives it to another. Given the examples provided in earlier sections, it should be relatively clear how colonialism was central to European economic and political expansion. Comments from Spickard (1992), an expert on issues of race and ethnicity, summarize how this works.

> From the point of view of the dominant group, racial distinctions are a necessary tool of dominance. They serve to separate the subordinate people as Other. Putting simple, neat racial labels on dominated peoples—and creating negative myths about the moral qualities of those peoples—makes it easier for the dominators to ignore the individual humanity of their victims. It eases the guilt of oppression. (p. 19)

Spickard goes on to explain how categorizing various African peoples all in one racial group, "and associating that group with evil, sin, laziness, bestiality, sexuality, and irresponsibility," (p. 19) made it easier for European slave owners to rationalize treating people in inhumane ways. Perceptions couched in colonialist thinking continue in contemporary transnational and intercultural contexts. For instance, Shome (2011) writes about how white femininity remains privileged across the world, something that is steeped in colonialism.

The concepts of a "chosen people," Manifest Destiny, racism, and colonialism are closely woven together. Understanding the history of race is important. As you will see throughout this text, contemporary issues are oftentimes rooted within a long-standing history of racist thinking. With this foundation in place, the remainder of this chapter discusses race as a biological and/or social construct and the role of racial classifications in the contemporary Americas.

## THE BIOLOGICAL FOUNDATIONS OF RACE

By definition, a race is a "subdivision of a species; it consists of a population that has a different combination of gene frequencies from other populations of the species" (Lasker & Tyzzer, 1982, p. 458). In the 19th century, the popularity of Darwinian theory served as a catalyst for scientists who were attempting to prove the existence of racial differences. Throughout history, the so-called commonsense view of race was based on the idea that at one time a handful of supposedly pure races existed. These subgroups had physical features, blood, gene pools, and character qualities that diverged entirely from one another (Zuberi, 2000). For instance, popular thought is that most observers can still distinguish a "Caucasian type" by his or her light skin, blue eyes, fine sandy or light brown hair, high-bridged nose, and thin lips. In contrast, a "Negroid type" is identified by dark brown skin, brown or black eyes, tightly coiled dark hair, broad flat nose, and thick lips (Diamond, 1994). Similar prototypical classifications could be generated for the Mongoloid and other races. These racial categories are based on **phenotypes**: sets of observable characteristics of an individual (height, eye color, hair color, blood type and certain types of disease) resulting from the interaction of genotypes with localized environments. In more recent times, U.S. racial categorization has moved beyond such definitive divisions and acknowledged how intermarriage, immigration, and other determinants have made such phenotypes unreliable (Feliciano, 2015).

Over time, the increased number of interracial unions has contributed to a blurring of the distinct boundaries between "pure" races. However, additional problems arise within this commonsense approach when we look at specific examples within each racial category. For instance, Europeans who reside near the Mediterranean have dark, curly hair. The Khoisan peoples of southern Africa have facial features that closely resemble the people in northern Europe (Diamond, 1994). The !Kung San (Bushmen) have epicanthic eye folds, similar to Japanese and Chinese people (Begley, 1995).

Various scientists have engaged in countless studies searching for proof of the biological differences that reportedly exist in different racial groups. Some researchers, for example, conducted extensive analyses of geographical differences, only to come away with inconclusive findings. Once blood was ruled out as a possible distinguishing trait, some researchers began to study genetic composition (Bahk & Jandt, 2004). Others measured body parts—brains, calf muscles, jaws, lips, and noses—in attempts to link the more "inferior" races with apes (Valentine, 1995). In 1965, researchers studied gene clusters and proposed the formulation of hundreds, even thousands, of racial groups (Wright, 1994). Alternative bases for designating racial groups (e.g., by resistance to disease or by fingerprints) have also generated a wide variety of equally trivial divisions (Diamond, 1994). Regardless of what was being measured and how, scientists were not able to come up with consistent evidence or proof of biological differences between racial groups (Begley, 1995).

In fact, extensive research indicates that pure races never existed (Lasker & Tyzzer, 1982; Montagu, 1997; Spickard, 1992); all humankind belongs to the same species, *Homo sapiens*. National, religious, geographic, linguistic, and cultural groups do not necessarily coincide with racial groups. The cultural traits of such groups have no demonstrated genetic connection with racial traits. Because of this, the genetic variability within populations is greater than the variability between them (Bahk & Jandt, 2004). In other words, the biggest differences are *within* racial groups, not *between* them. This is not to say that physical features have no connection to geographical and genetic factors (the two primary factors in Blumenbach's work). But it is now understood that the few physical characteristics used to define races account for only a very tiny fraction of a person's total physical being (Graves, 2004).

Montagu (1964, 1997) was one of the first, and clearly the most successful, researchers to make use of scientifically established facts in debunking what he referred to as "man's most dangerous myth." His work has revealed how existing "racial mythologies" have supported countless attempts of "superior races" to prevail over more "inferior" ones. For example, think about the basic premises for slavery—Manifest Destiny and cheap labor—discussed earlier. A review of current events or even a quick search on the internet indicates that such beliefs still exist in some places across the United States. All of these ideologies have one characteristic in common: They reflect attempts to foster the advancement of a superior race. **Eugenics refers to the study of, or belief in, improving the quality of the human species by encouraging the reproduction of persons believed to have desirable traits and discouraging reproduction by those thought to have undesirable traits.** Throughout history, eugenics has fueled racist policies (e.g., bans on interracial unions, forced sterilization, ethnic genocide) aimed at fostering a superior white race.

As much as existing research has revealed the illogical notion of racial classifications as a means of self- and other identity, most people in the United States continue to use race as a way to distinguish human qualities, potential, and behaviors. Despite a lack of scientific evidence, race continues to be a largely accepted means of categorization. This is true for many people—not just those with racist ideas—who wrongly believe that racial differences are real (Graves, 2004). Now that we have debunked the myth of racial difference, we explain race as a sociopolitical construct. One point of caution first: Accepting that racial differences are not real does not make the effects of racism any less damaging. Future chapters reinforce this point.

## THE SOCIOPOLITICAL CONSTRUCTION OF RACE

According to Foss-Snowden (2011), race is commonly understood as a social construct intellectually. Yet, in everyday life, many people treat it as biologically accurate—with no critical interrogation. In the most basic sense, race cannot be considered a scientific construct if its categories are constantly being changed depending on laws, history, emotions, and politics (Nakashima, 1992). Instead, race is best understood as a product of social, political, and economic dynamics (rather than as a phenomenon based on biology). For instance, Pimentel and Balzhiser (2012) argue that U.S. Census categories are embedded in politics. They argue that the term *Hispanic* (defined as an ethnic not a racial group) was created to monitor population growth while not inflating the number of racial minorities. Identifying the various ways that different social, political, national, and regional groups define racial classifications reveals how political these decisions are.

| *Box 2.3* | *Author Reflections* |
|---|---|

### "Race, an Idea Whose Time Has Passed"

For most of us, challenging existing ideologies about race is not easy. Such a process involves letting go of some basic ideas that have been commonly accepted as fact by the larger society. I vividly remember the first time that someone confronted me with the idea that there was only one human race—that what we recognized as different racial groups were not, in fact, different races at all.

The assertion occurred in the early 1990s during a graduate seminar that I participated in as part of my doctoral program in interpersonal/intercultural communication. I remember publicly nodding in agreement with my fellow classmate's comments but privately thinking that she was playing around with the semantics of the word *race* or trying to intellectualize our conversation by using abstract academic jargon that had no relevance to everyday living.

But, somehow, that brief encounter planted a seed that would be nurtured as I continued to explore the complex dynamics of culture, race, and communication. In various places, I found other scholars and practitioners who embraced the idea of one human race. "Race, an idea whose time has passed," was a phrase I saw on T-shirts, bumper stickers, and posters. Upon greater exploration of this issue, I found more and more evidence that indicated the concept of race was a social construction, with little or no biological foundation. Trying to communicate this idea to others was not easy, nor always well received. During discussions with family, friends, and colleagues, I got a chance to see a wide variety of reactions, including those that mirrored my own initial response.

Undeterred from embracing this newfound idea, I consciously avoided using the term *race* and instead used *ethnicity*. I subsequently found out that this substitution was first suggested in 1950 (Montagu, 1978)—was I behind the times! Nevertheless, I began to use *interethnic* to describe the communication between African Americans and European Americans, *biethnic* to describe my cultural identity, and *multiethnic* to describe my family. Recently, I have shifted back to using racial terminology, especially in my teaching and research (or adopting a combination of the two: *race/ethnicity*). Attempts to describe the country as "post-racial" is premature (at best) and blatantly reinforcing the problematic state of race relations (at worst). Race is a powerful concept in the United States, and whether a scientific or social phenomenon, it is one that must be acknowledged when exploring the relationships between culture and communication. That is the only way to reduce its effect. As noted in Chapter 1, an African proverb captures the importance of working through our history with race and racism before moving forward: *The way out is back through.* Not to use the term *race* would be ineffective and unrepresentative in describing the type of research that I do.

What has your personal journey been like, in terms of understanding your own and others' racial/ethnic identity? What role has this book played in the process?

—MPO

## The Fluid Nature of Racial Categories

Roughly speaking, race has become a way to describe human variation created by the interplay of geography, migration, and inheritance (Lasker & Tyzzer, 1982). However, the ways in which we have categorized people by race has changed over time (Bahk & Jandt, 2004). For example, in the late 19th and early 20th centuries, some newly arrived European Americans, including Italians and the Irish, were defined as distinct racial groups (National Research Council, 2004). Eventually, these groups were accepted, along with other Europeans, as "white." In short, the fluid nature of racial categories speaks volumes about its existence as a social-historical construction (A. James & Tucker, 2003). As seen in Figure 2.2, the U.S. Census Bureau has

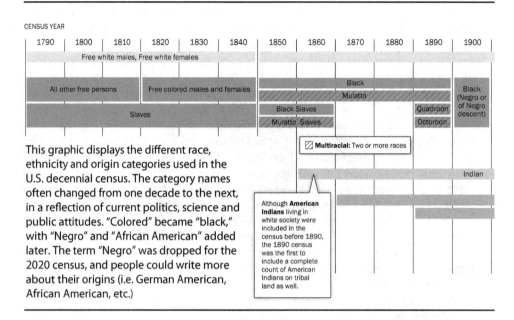

CENSUS YEAR

This graphic displays the different race, ethnicity and origin categories used in the U.S. decennial census. The category names often changed from one decade to the next, in a reflection of current politics, science and public attitudes. "Colored" became "black," with "Negro" and "African American" added later. The term "Negro" was dropped for the 2020 census, and people could write more about their origins (i.e. German American, African American, etc.)

Although **American Indians** living in white society were included in the census before 1890, the 1890 census was the first to include a complete count of American Indians on tribal land as well.

**Figure 2.2**    What Census Calls Us (1790–2020) (Pew Research Center, 2020)

used a wide variety of racial categories to classify its citizens. Changes have ranged from ones largely expected to others that appear novel, questionable, and/or illogical. For instance, did you realize the following?

- Early categories separated people of African descent based on the percentage of "Black blood" (e.g., Black, Mulatto, Quadroon, Octoroon).
- From 1920 to 1940 some Asian Indians were counted as members of a "Hindu" race.
- In the 1960 U.S. Census, Latin Americans were counted as white.
- The U.S. Census has stopped asking about race in their count of the residents of Puerto Rico because of the contrasting definitions of racial designations.
- Prior to 1977, Asian Indians were considered white but are now designated as Asian/Pacific Islanders.
- Current categories consider persons with origins traced to North Africa and the Middle East to be white.
- Latino/a/x or Hispanic people (from Mexican, Puerto Rican, Cuban, Central or South American, or other Spanish culture or origins) can be of any race.

Racial categories vary in different social networks. Historically, they have been defined based on geographical, cultural, economic, and political factors.

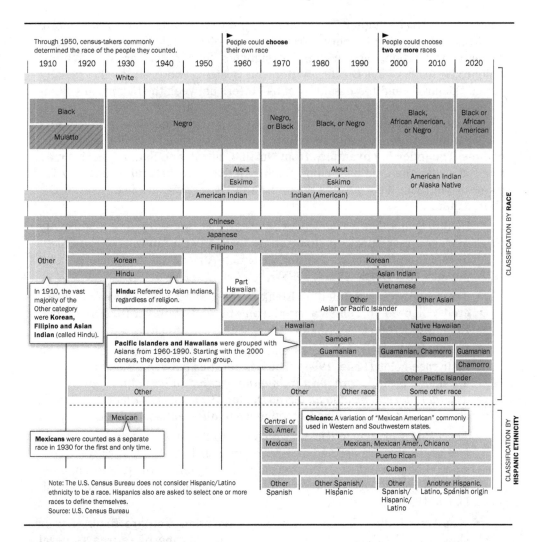

**Figure 2.2**    *(continued)*

In many cases, social distinctions based on race develop when two or more groups of people face economic, political, or status competition (Spickard, 1992). Competition for perceived limited resources creates and maintains a sense of us-versus-them. Depending on the introduction of additional players into the competition, these distinctions may change. People indigenous to what is now known as the Americas, for instance, did not experience themselves as Native Americans prior to the arrival of Europeans. Instead, they were Mayan, Pequot, Osage, Mohegan, Ottawa, Sioux, or Oneida, for example.

An important foundation for understanding racial/ethnic identities is how various counties and states officially define and designate their population in terms of race (see Chapter 7). Because of the world's attention to its historic fight against apartheid, South Africa has one of the best known systems of racial classification. The country designates four racial groups: Whites, Coloureds, Asians, and Blacks. Within this system, two groups—the racially mixed Coloureds and the Asians—act as buffers between the historically dominant whites and native Blacks (F. J. Davis, 1991). Although this type of racial classification may seem remote to most people living in the United States, several examples closer to home also illustrate the inconsistencies of racial designations. The following examples from North, Central, and South America may seem strange, alien, or confusing. Such reactions are natural, especially for those of you who have always accepted the rigid racial designations of the United States.

- In the United States any degree of African ancestry has historically made a person Black. Such is not the case in Latin America or the Caribbean. In some societies, any degree of non-African ancestry means that a person is not Black (Winn, 1995).

- The same person defined as Black in the United States may be considered Coloured in Jamaica or Martinique and white in the Dominican Republic (Urban et al., 2010).

- In Brazil, a survey of Blacks generated 40 different words to describe their race/color (Page, 1994). The possibilities between Black and white are many: *preto, cabra, escuro, mulato escuro, mulato claro, pardo, sarara, moreno*, and *branco de terra* (Degler, 1971). Some "Blacks" in Brazil change their designations as they move to different social classes.

- Three-fifths of Puerto Ricans who come to the mainland and are identified as Black were defined differently in their homeland. Most were considered *blanco* (white), *mulato* (mulatto), *trigueño* (wheat colored, olive skinned), or any of a number of color designations other than Black (F. J. Davis, 1991).

- To a West Indian, Black is a literal description: You are Black if your skin is black. If you are lighter—like the coloring of retired General Colin Powell—you would describe yourself as "middle-class brown" or "a light chocolate" (Gladwell, 1996).

These examples clearly illustrate the ambiguous ways that race has been defined in various American societies. How race is designated in each culture is best understood within its national, political, and economic history (for a comprehensive treatment, see Chapter 7).

## Race Designations in the United States

Another means of critically examining the sociopolitical construction of race in the United States is to trace the ways that different racial group members, including multiracial persons, have been designated. The first census, supervised by Thomas Jefferson in 1790, had three categories: "free [w]hites," "slaves," and "other free persons." This last category included free Blacks and "taxable Indians," referring to those Native Americans living in, or in close proximity to, European settlements (Wright, 1994). For most of the 19th century, distinctions were made between gradations of enslaved Blacks, including **mulattos** (one-half Black), **quadroons** (one-quarter Black), and **octoroons** (one-eighth Black) (F. J. Davis, 1991). After 1920, such distinctions were eliminated with the estimation that nearly three-quarters of all Blacks in the United States were racially mixed and that "pure" Blacks would soon disappear. This assumption, coupled with the socially accepted principles of hypodescent and the "one-drop rule," resulted in more exclusively rigid categories of white and Black persons.

Unlike many other countries, the United States has historically embraced a **one-drop rule**, whereby a single drop of Black blood makes a person Black (Rockquemore & Laszloffy, 2005). This idea was grounded in the concept of a pure "white race," one that would be forever tainted by even the most minuscule addition of Black blood. The rules of **hypodescent** were based on a similar assumption. According to Root (1992), this principle occurs in a "social system that maintains the fiction of monoracial identification of individuals by assigning a racially mixed person to the racial group in their heritage that has the least social status" (p. x). Both of these commonly accepted practices led to the continued social separation between Black and white worlds, despite the blurring of these distinctions (F. J. Davis, 1991; Root, 1992). For instance, some scholars (C. E. Jackson & Tolbert, 1989; Spickard, 1992) believe that attempts to cling to these sociopolitical distinctions, in addition to clear economic reasons, led many white slave owners to regard some of their children (born to enslaved African females) as slaves. Recent DNA evidence suggests this was the case with the children of President Thomas Jefferson and Sally Hemmings (who was one of Jefferson's slaves). Ironically, it was Thomas Jefferson who wrote extensively on how the government should categorize mixed-race persons (see Box 2.4).

Different states had varying legal specifications as to the degree of Black ancestry that qualified residents as "officially Black" (see Spickard, 1989). Many states, especially those in the Northeast, did not have such legal definitions. Others were quite specific in their statutes. For instance, a person with one "Negro or Mulatto" great-great-grandparent was defined as "Negro" in North Carolina or Louisiana. However, this same person could be "white" in several states where racial lineage was only traced to great-grandparents (e.g., Indiana, Tennessee, Maryland, and Florida) or grandparents (e.g., Oregon). Many of us would like to believe that such statutes are relics of an embarrassing distant past. However, many of these state laws remained on the books—if not in practice—until the late 20th century. Consider the following case: In 1986, the U.S. Supreme Court refused to review a ruling from a lower court in Louisiana. In this case, a woman, whose great-great-great-great-grandmother was an enslaved Black woman, sued over the right to change her race legally from Black to white (Wright, 1994). Although she could trace her lineage to the point where she could conclude that no more than 3/32 of her genetic heritage

---

**BOX 2.4**

### Early Writings on Mixed Race People

Racial designations have always been salient in the United States. As the founding fathers began to write key documents, complex definitions for what constitutes racially mixed people were created. The formulas provided below were written by Thomas Jefferson.

- Let the first crossing be of "*a*," pure Negro, with "*A*," pure white. The unit of blood of the issue being composed of the half of that of each parent, will be $a/2 + A/2$. Call it, for abbreviation, *h* (half blood)

- Let the second crossing be of *h* and B, the blood of the issue will be $b/2 + B/2$, or substituting for $h/2$ its equivalent, it will be $a/4 + A/4 + B2$ call it *q* (quateroon) being ¼ Negro blood.

- Let the third crossing be of *q* and C, their offspring will be $q/2 + C/2 = a/8 + A/8 + B/4 + C/2$, call this *e* (eighth), who having less than ¼ of *a*, or of pure Negro blood, to wit? only, is no longer a mulatto, so that a third cross clears the blood. ("What Constitutes a Mulatto?" 1995)

---

was Black, the state court's decision that she was legally Black in Louisiana was upheld.

The social construction of race is evident from the fact that there were no such definitions for other racial groups. Racial designation was inconsistent even in states with laws regarding African Americans. Most designations historically were completed by what was commonly known as the **eyeball test** ("No Place for Mankind," 1989). This nonscientific, random measure involved various untrained laypersons (e.g., census takers, hospital staff, educational administrators) making decisions about others' racial makeup based on personal perceptions of race-based physical characteristics (see Orbe, 2012). Such practices resulted in ambiguous, illogical, and inconsistent classifications.

This point is best illustrated through the example of three brothers who lived in Dulac (LA) in 1969. Part of the Houma nation, the brothers shared the same father and mother. Each man was given a racial designation by the personnel assisting with his birth. The oldest brother was born at home with the help of a midwife. Because the state of Louisiana did not recognize the Houma as an official Native American nation prior to 1950, he was classified as a Negro. Born in a local hospital after 1950, the second brother was designated as an Indian. The third brother was born in a New Orleans hospital 80 miles away; he was designated as white based primarily on his French family name (Stanton, 1971).

As we saw earlier, an analysis of the ways that individual states treated racial classification provides some insight into the unscientific nature of these designations. The examples described thus far have focused on the experiences of African American, Native American, and biracial people. Some states needed ways to name and define groups of people who were relatively unique to their geographical location (for example, the Creole of Louisiana and the Mestizo of Texas and New Mexico).

The state of Hawaii (added to U.S. territories at the end of the 19th century with statehood in 1959) provides an interesting insight into the social construction of race (Tolbert, 1989). Unlike other states that traditionally embraced the one-drop rule with little question, Hawaii has a long tradition of treating race designations more fluidly and inclusively because of the multiracial background of its native population. The first inhabitants came initially from the Marquesas Islands and then from Tahiti some 1,500 years ago (Howard, 1980). Hawaii's earliest residents were Polynesians, whose racial/ethnic composition represented a blend of Southeast Asia, Indonesia, and possibly the Middle East (F. J. Davis, 1991). After the arrival of several Spanish ships in the late 18th century, the Hawaiian Islands became the adopted home for a number of other racial groups, including those from China, Japan, the Philippines, Puerto Rico, and Portugal (Day, 1960). Unlike other parts of the United States, Hawaii has a history of greater acceptance of ethnic and racial intermarriages, which has resulted in an affirmed melting pot of cultures. Steeped in a strong tradition opposing rigid racial categories, residents have long used a variety of ways to describe themselves, including the creation of multiple ethnic and racial configurations.

In his book on language, race, and communication, Ray (2009) summarizes the state of race relations in the United States across different historical time periods (see Table 2.1). Focusing on Black-White relations, he describes how tens of millions of Africans were brought to the United States through the

**Table 2.1  U.S. Race Relations: Historical Perspective of Black-White Relations**

| | | |
|---|---|---|
| Colonial Era | 17th–18th Centuries | African Slave Trade <br> Three-fifths Compromise |
| Antebellum Era | Early 19th Century | North-South Tensions <br> Slavery Debates <br> Black Inferiority |
| Civil War/Reconstruction | 1880s–1890s | Emancipation Proclamation <br> African American Troops <br> Abolition of Slavery <br> *Plessy v. Ferguson* |
| Jim Crow Era | 1890s–1950s | Black Codes <br> Ku Klux Klan <br> NAACP Legal Initiatives <br> World Wars <br> *Brown v. Board of Education* |
| Modern Civil Rights Era | 1960s–21st century | Civil Rights Victories <br> Personal Accountability <br> Growing Middle Class <br> Enlightened Racism |

African Slave Trade and regarded as property throughout the 17th, 18th, and part of the 19th centuries. Attempts by African Americans, like Frederick Douglass, to argue for the abolition of slavery and equal rights for all were widely controversial (Mcclish, 2012). In fact, enslaved Africans were also treated as political pawns. The Three-fifths Clause, for example, was a political compromise whereby five enslaved Africans would be counted as three people (Willis, 2003). This allowed Southern states to gain some—but not too much—power in a political system where representation was, in part, related to population. The tensions between the northern states and southern states, including but not limited to the issue of slavery, led to the Civil War.

When Robert E. Lee surrendered to Ulysses S. Grant at Appomattox, the Civil War might have ended, but the issue of race relations was not solved—in fact, in many ways, it intensified. African Americans were legally and politically equal to European Americans, but they remained a socially and culturally oppressed group across the United States. In the southern states, **Jim Crow**—state and local laws that mandated racial segregation—was the norm for more than a half of century. This reality was negotiated by African Americans throughout their daily lives and challenged through various legal battles by national civil rights groups like the National Association for the Advancement of Colored People (NAACP). One of the most significant legal accomplishments occurred when separate but equal educational facilities for European Americans and African Americans was declared unconstitutional by the U.S. Supreme Court in 1954. *Brown v. Board of Education* paved the way for racial integration and was a major civil rights victory. The next couple of decades witnessed additional legal decisions that gradually removed existing barriers for authentic, productive race relations.

The advances in basic civil rights for African Americans led to many improvements. Greater racial equality increased opportunities to achieve the "American Dream." The belief in a color-blind society where hard work and determination bring success has facilitated a form of **enlightened racism** (Jhally & Lewis, 2003). High-profile, rags-to-riches stories conjure images of a Black upper class. The lack of collective success among African Americans is blamed on individual weaknesses (e.g., laziness, lack of initiative, etc.). Inequalities in terms of educational achievement, employment, family income/ poverty, health measures, etc. are attributed to personal failures. Given the proportionately high number of African Americans in prison, Alexander (2010) argues that a "new Jim Crow" has been created where a caste-like system creates communities that are denied the very rights supposedly gained through the civil rights movement. Throughout everyday life, racial discrimination against African Americans, and other racial and ethnic minoritized groups, continues in a wide variety of contexts (Nazione & Silk, 2011). The growing number of people of color in the United States and advances in civil rights legislation have resulted in some European Americans perceiving various forms of "reverse discrimination" in their educational, professional, and social lives (Camara & Orbe, 2011).

## THE SIGNIFICANCE OF RACE TODAY

According to a West African proverb, the story of the lion hunt will never be complete until the lions tell their side of the story. The insight generated through this statement is applicable to any discussion of history. Most U.S. history taught in schools, for example, is presented from the perspective of European American men (Serwer, 2019). The result is a master narrative that produces a collective memory for the general public (Huang & Chen, 2019). This has been the case for the history of race in the United States for centuries with significant aspects of history "white-washed" or ignored all together (Louis, 2021). Over the past few decades, however, critics have worked to remedy this problem and provide a more well-rounded perspective.

The 1619 Project released by *The New York Times* in 2019 is an excellent example of a counternarrative of race (Silverstein, 2021). Developed by Nikole Hannah-Jones and others, this comprehensive journalism project traces the history of the United States to 1619 when the first enslaved Africans arrived in the English colony of Virginia. This series of essays and supplemental materials asks the public to consider what U.S. history looks like when the consequences of slavery and contributions of African Americans are placed at the center of understanding (Serwer, 2019). This counternarrative—in direct opposition to master narratives that promote the ideals of freedom, democracy, equal opportunity, and justice for all (Sue, 2016)—is grounded in the idea that the legacy of slavery and racism have shaped, and continue to shape, U.S. life in all aspects. From this perspective, white supremacy is inherently tied to U.S. history, a core idea that is absent from the master narrative.

The 1619 Project garnered a significant amount of praise and, accordingly, was integrated into thousands and thousands of classrooms across the United States (Ellison, 2020). Not surprisingly, the curricula were also criticized by many, including President Trump who condemned the work as an attempt to destroy the country. In response, he established a 1776 Commission to promote "patriotic education" that praised the country as an exemplar for democracy (Trump, 2020). The debate over how U.S. history should be taught continues to be a controversial topic with the majority of state legislations attempting to restrict the inclusion of counternarratives in curricula (Stout & LeMee, 2021).

The importance of counternarratives cannot be understated—without them, one dominant version of history remains unchallenged and upheld as fact. Counternarratives, such as the 1619 Project, are not designed to replace the current U.S. history content. Instead, they represent an enhancement of traditional U.S. history curricula (Serwer, 2019). Without different historical perspectives, the master narrative of the United States as an ideal democracy steeped in equality, freedom, justice, and equal opportunity (e.g., "The American Dream") continues to exist with no acknowledgement as to the role that race and racism have played since its inception. According to Sue (2016), this leads European Americans to be reassured in the belief that the United States is a "post-racial" society where good, moral, and fair people can live harmoniously together with no collective action needed to address issues of racism. Creating and disseminating counter stories, or counternarratives (R. Miller et al., 2020), to historical texts is a much-needed critical move to create oppositional knowledge (Collins, 2016), something that ultimately works to promote more balanced, comprehensive understandings of history.

Race continues to be a significant sociopolitical marker in the United States because, in most people's minds, race is a fundamental way to understand human diversity. Regardless of the unscientific and illogical foundation, thinking along long-established racial categories dominates national discussions. And although racial categories have served as a means of discrimination throughout U.S. history, they have also facilitated a sense of identity and common experiences for many racial groups (Touré, 2011). In the face of historical uses of racial classification systems, many African Americans, for instance, have embraced their Blackness as a source of pride, unity, sense of belonging, and strength. In this regard, race and ethnicity function as a double-edged sword. Before concluding this chapter, we highlight several issues in the contemporary United States that illustrate this point—immigration and migration, tensions related to terrorism, presidential politics and race, and social justice activism.

## Box 2.5

### The Case for Reparations

According to Coates (2014), reparations for African Americans are not only connected to the effects of slavery but also are warranted because of the effects of Jim Crow, discriminatory practices, and legalized racism/discrimination by federal, state, and local policies in the United States. For example, the theft of black-owned land stretching back to the antebellum period—through terrorism, threats, and legal means—is well documented. In addition, the Federal Housing Administration created in 1934 to provide federal backing for loans refused to insure mortgages in African American neighborhoods (redlining) and subsidized subdivisions provided none of the homes were sold to African Americans—essentially state-sponsored segregation that continued for more than three decades (Rothstein, 2017). Before you make a conclusion regarding reparations, take some time to learn more about the following two cases. The first involves the Bruce family in Manhattan Beach, California. Wilma and Charles Bruce, an African American couple, built a resort in 1912 to provide beach access for African Americans; the city condemned and seized the property in 1924. In 2021, legislation returned the property to Bruce descendants, restoring the wealth they were denied for generations (Hajek et al., 2021; Xia, 2020). The second case involves the city of Evanston, Illinois, which has created a historic plan to distribute $10 million in reparations to Black residents (Adams, 2021). Both of these specific cases make a strong argument as to *why* reparations make sense and *how* they might be implemented on a local, state, and/or national level (Heyward, 2021).

## Immigration and Migration Tensions

In many ways, the United States is a country of immigrants. In fact, U.S. history has been shaped by four distinct waves of immigration (Pedraza, 2006). The first wave—covering the 18th to the middle of the 19th century—saw a large influx of immigrants from Northern and Western Europe. At the same time, there was forced immigration of persons from Africa and the forced migration of Native Americans. The second wave of immigrants came from Eastern and Southern Europe at the end of the 19th and beginning of the 20th century. Between 1924 and 1965, the third wave consisted of internal migration involving African Americans, Native Americans, Mexicans, and Puerto Ricans relocating from the south to the north. The final wave of immigration, covering the past 40 years, has witnessed a large influx of immigrants from Asia and South and Central America.

Contemporary immigration patterns are significantly different from those of the past (see Table 2.2). For example, the top five countries of origin for the foreign-born population in the United States in 1960 were: Italy, Germany, Canada, the United Kingdom, and Poland. In 2000, the top five countries were Mexico, China, the Philippines, India, and Cuba. This reflected a dramatic shift in terms of nationality, with the largest number of immigrants coming

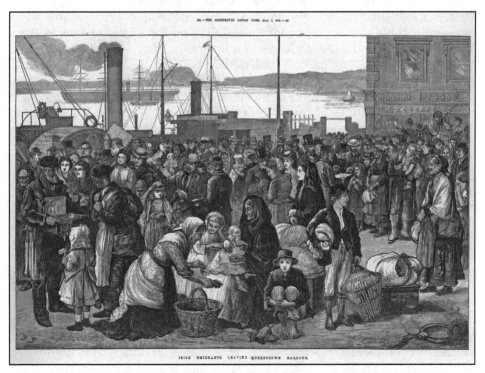

The first wave of immigration to the United States involved people from Western Europe, including large groups of individuals from Ireland; this photo shows emigrants leaving Queenstown, County Cork, Ireland in the mid-1800s.

**Table 2.2    Countries of Origin for U.S. Immigrants (1990–2019)**

| Top ten countries | 2020 | 2010 | 2000 | 1990 |
|---|---|---|---|---|
| Mexico | 10,924,662 | 11,711,103 | 9,177,487 | 4,298,014 |
| China | 2,795,333 | 2,166,526 | 1,518,652 | 921,070 |
| India | 2,618,558 | 1,780,322 | 1,022,552 | 450,406 |
| Philippines | 1,967,140 | 1,777,588 | 1,369,070 | 912,674 |
| El Salvador | 1,370,579 | 1,214,049 | 817,336 | 465,433 |
| Vietnam | 1,354,391 | 1,240,542 | 988,174 | 543,262 |
| Cuba | 1,314,570 | 1,104,679 | 872,716 | 736,971 |
| Dominican Republic | 1,125,208 | 879,187 | 687,677 | 347,858 |
| South Korea | 1,048,588 | 1,100,422 | 864,125 | 568,397 |
| Guatemala | 964,528 | 830,824 | 480,665 | 225,739 |
| All of Latin America | 22,073,519 | 21,224,087 | 16,086,974 | 8,407,837 |
| All Immigrants | 44,125,120 | 39,955,854 | 31,107,889 | 19,767,316 |

Source: Decennial Census, 1990, 2000; American Community Survey, 2010, 2020b.

from Central America and Asia (Huntington, 2005). In 2019, the top five coun-
tries were: Mexico, China, India, the Philippines, and El Salvador (Migration
Policy Institute, 2022). Latinx people are now the largest ethnic group in the
United States (Budiman, 2020). Puerto Ricans make up over 9% of this num-
ber—and double that if you count those living on the island of Puerto Rico.
Currently, they are the second largest Latinx group, after Mexican Americans.

The number of foreign-born individuals residing in the United States is
about 45 million people, which represents 13.7% of the country's population
(Batalova et al., 2021). While nearly 90% of all immigrants living in the United
States until the middle of the 20th century were of European or Canadian
descent (Suarez-Orozco, 2000), today, the majority of immigrants come from
the Asian (31.3%) and Latin American (50%) countries (ACS, 2020). While
early waves of immigrants experienced a process of natural, continuous, and
irreversible assimilation, such is not the case for more recent immigrants.
Many immigrants continue to function, in varying degrees, in both "new" and
"old" cultures (Mahalingam, 2006).

Scholars have critically examined immigration over time and concluded
that resistance to immigration is grounded in the politics of race (Merrill, 2006).
For instance, racist legislation (Page Act of 1875, Angell Treaty of 1880, and the
Chinese Exclusion Act of 1882) targeted different Asian American groups, denying them citizenship and limiting or prohibiting future immigration. Growing
anti-immigration sentiment has been understood by some as covertly reflective
of racial and ethnic tension (Domke et al., 2003). Others regard it as a tension
between an "outgroup" and the "ingroup" (Waisanen, 2012). Interestingly,
research reports that the percentage of adults with an unfavorable impression
of immigrants from Mexico has tripled in the last decade, with no similar negative trend for immigrants from other countries (e.g., C. Stewart et al., 2011).
Immigrants from certain geographical regions—mostly those in Africa and Cen-

tral and South America—are perceived in more negative terms than those who are from Europe or Asia. In response to this sentiment, social movements have been created to assist Latinx migrants with their attempts to become U.S. citizens while navigating immigrant and national identities (Lechuga, 2020).

## Post–September 11 Tensions Related to Terrorism

The war against terrorism was prompted by the attacks on the United States that occurred on September 11, 2001. Immediately following 9/11, Arab Americans—and any individuals perceived to be Arabic or Muslim—experienced a backlash of discrimination, harassment, and violence (Dias, 2021). A significant number of targets of this backlash were not Arab Muslims; instead, they included Sikhs, Arab Christians, South Asians, and Moroccans; the mistaken categorization occurred in the United States as well as across Europe (Hopkins et al., 2017). Merskin (2004) reported similar misperceptions in several speeches by then President Bush, whose rhetoric was based on stereotypical images of Arabs. Consistent with existing media and popular culture images, he portrayed Arabs as evil, bloodthirsty, animalistic terrorists. Such representations negate the diversity and multiplicity of diverse groups of people united by a cultural identification (Witteborn, 2004).

The political discourse surrounding historical events, like 9/11, helps create meaning for individuals, which in turn affects their opinions on different issues (Leudar & Nekvail, 2011). Not surprisingly, national polls documented a decrease in support for immigration immediately following 9/11. An analysis of poll data over the decade after the attacks documented persistent worries about another catastrophic terrorist attack and concerns about the impact on people's lives (Bloch-Eikon, 2011). This sentiment prompted support for the 2001 USA Patriot Act, which expanded legalized government surveillance of U.S. residents, primarily targeting Muslims and those of Arabic descent.

Since the September 11 attacks, Muslim Americans—and any one perceived to be Muslim—have reported increased racial profiling in airports and other public places.

According to Mujahid (2003), the act's racial focus on brown-skinned men and Muslims—both immigrants and citizens—resulted in ongoing interrogations, home invasions, detentions and arrests, special registration, and deportation that negatively impacted select communities. Like the issue of immigration discussed earlier, anti-terrorism efforts also reflected racialized patterns.

## Contemporary U.S. Presidential Politics and Race

The historic nature of Barack Obama's election as the 44th president of the United States has been documented by numerous national and international media outlets (Orbe, 2011). Much of the discussion about President Obama's election has focused on what it means in terms of race, racism, and racial relations. Immediately prior to the 2008 presidential election, 56% of U.S. Americans reported believing that race relations would improve if Obama were elected, a number that jumped to 70% the day after his election (Washington, 2012). While some research indicated a drop in perceptions of racial discrimination (Valentino & Brader, 2011), national public polls on race relations have demonstrated that the perceptions grew increasingly pessimistic after President Obama's election. For instance, polls in April 2013 reported that only 33% believed that race relations were getting better; 42% thought that they were staying about the same; and 23% described them as getting worse. Some U.S. Americans supposed, and continue to argue, that President Obama's election would mark the beginning of a "post-racial" society and would symbolize the end of racism (Orbe, 2011). Yet, the reality is that his political accomplishments have brought existing racialized attitudes to the surface of public discourse. Interestingly, President Obama largely downplayed, or remained silent, on racial issues during his presidency (Coates, 2012).

After Obama's election, people pointed to the diverse coalition that elected him—something that they believed would serve as a game changer for future elections. Politicians who attempted to be elected through division, fear, and exclusion would never be successful again (Blake, 2021). Yet, President Obama's election also resulted in an increase in both the numbers and visibility of white supremacists that fueled, to some extent, right-wing conservativism and the election of President Donald Trump. His election in 2016 was understood by many as a political reaction to the election of President Barack Obama (Cooper, 2018). While President Obama's election prompted optimism for harmony and inclusion, those hopes proved premature as President Trump's campaign seemed to focus on racial and cultural division, fear, and racialized nationalism. His message spoke to millions and millions of voters who felt as if their voice, interests, and values were ignored under the Obama administration. While much of Trump's campaign rhetoric used language that avoided overt racist tones (e.g., Make America Great Again), his slogans could be categorized as examples of "racist dog whistles"—public utterances that evoke racist connotations for followers but whose denotative meanings allow plausible denials to accusations of racism (Shapiro, 2020). Other times, the rhetoric was more overt (Sugino, 2020). This was evident as Trump kicked off his presidential bid with harsh words for Mexican immigrants, stating "They are not our friend, believe me. . . . They're bringing drugs. They're bringing crime. They're rapists" (as quoted in Reilly, 2016). His focus on promoting the danger of Mexico immigrants was central to his presidential bid as he promised to build a wall along the Mexican border and get Mexico to pay for it.

President Trump's disdain for immigrants of color was not limited to Mexico, however. As widely reported by major news outlets (e.g., Blake, 2018), his belief that immigrants from "shithole countries" (i.e., El Salvador, Haiti, and African countries) should be heavily restricted while immigrants from more "beneficial" countries (i.e., Norway, and certain Asian countries) were welcome reflected the centuries-old racial hierarchy described earlier in this chapter. Again, President Trump's rhetoric seemed to provide support for U.S. citizens who were frustrated with the racial politics under the Obama administration. This frustration appeared to fuel the "Unite the Right" rally in Charlottesville, Virginia in 2017. Large groups of white nationalists and others gathered there to protest the removal of a statue of General Robert E. Lee, who led the Confederate army during the Civil War (Keneally, 2018). Holding lit tiki torches, hundreds of white men marched through the campus of the University of Virginia, some chanting the Nazi-associated phrase "blood and soil." Others kept repeating "You will not replace us. Jews won't replace us" (as quoted in Jimenez, 2017).

The message of this protest was clear: A portion of the U.S. public was angry with the direction that racial politics was taking in the country. This anger and frustration were especially evident as the world watched the events of January 6, 2021, unfold at the U.S. Capitol Building. Generated by a belief that President Trump's loss was the result of a rigged election, a group of U.S. citizens stormed the center of national government and forcibly disrupted election-related hearings from taking place. Among the protestors were members of white supremacist, anti-government, and extremist groups like those from the militia movement. Fernando and Nasir (2021) described January 6 as the culmination of years of promised aggression toward the U.S. government. Among a sea of U.S. flags were also Trump campaign flags and Confederate flags, the latter of which are emblems long associated with white supremacy (J. Anderson, 2021).

## Contemporary Social Justice Activism

As reported by Nakamura (2021), hate crimes in the United States rose to the highest level in 12 years amid increasing attacks on African Americans and Asian Americans, something that generated a renewed sense of activism. This was evident in a variety of social justice initiatives, many of which were fueled by the power of social media. For instance, #StopAsianHate drew national attention in response to increased violence and discrimination against Asian and Asian American communities. The Native American protests against the Dakota Access Pipeline (#NoDAPL) became an international rallying cry for indigenous rights and climate change activism, ultimately attracting thousands to rural North Dakota. Fair Fight, a national voting rights organization led by Georgian Stacy Abrams, worked to fight voter suppression, particularly that which unjustly targets voters of color and young voters. Protests in support of the Deferred Action for Childhood Arrivals program (DACA) and/or the DREAM Act, which provide legal pathways for select immigrants to stay in the United States and in some cases become U.S. citizens, were also a part of a new age of activism. Each of these examples relates to a social justice movement fueled by unfair treatment of people of color in the United States and were inspired by the magnitude and intensity of the Black Lives Matter movement and its significant progress.

The origins of the Black Lives Matter movement can be traced back to 2012, when Trayvon Martin was killed by George Zimmerman (Lambert & Orbe, 2019). At the time, several protest hashtags, including #Justice4Trayvon and #HoodiesUp, appeared across social media. When Zimmerman was acquitted of murder in 2013, #BlackLivesMatter became the rallying cry across social media platforms. The hashtag emerged as a social media call to action for people interested in protesting a number of issues facing African Americans, including racial profiling, police brutality, mass incarceration, and the militarization of policing in Black communities (Edgar & Johnson, 2018). From its inception, #BlackLivesMatter was designed to improve the lives of all African Americans while simultaneously focusing on those individuals whose lives had been traditionally marginalized by traditional Black liberation movements (e.g., those who are LGBTQ+, undocumented, etc.). That goal differentiated Black Lives Matter from other civil rights movements closely aligned with the traditional Black church (House, 2018). The popularity and power of #BlackLivesMatter prompted different chapters to form across the United States and the world. As described by Lambert and Orbe (2019), these different grass-roots organizations have organized over a thousand demonstrations—rallies, assemblies, vigils, die-ins, and marches—worldwide. While these demonstrations effectively brought attention to the deaths of dozens of African Americans at the hands of police, it was the death of George Floyd in 2020 that raised the Black Lives Matter movement to a level of monumental significance.

## CONCLUSION

One central task of the study of interracial communication is to describe what we mean when we discuss race and racial categories. This chapter was designed to give you a historical perspective on these concepts. Specifically, we provided insight into the complex ways that designations based on race and ethnicity have been tied to social, political, and economic events. In addition, we focused on how the progression of race categories is tied to interracial communication in the 21st century.

Distinctions attributed to racial differences were initially used by Europeans in the 18th century to justify political and economic expansion. This continued well into the 20th century as the political and economic systems in the New World continued to take shape. Despite a lack of scientific evidence, race continues to be a largely accepted means of categorization in the United States.

Various attempts to prove the existence of racial differences have only resulted in revealing the myth of "pure" races. In fact, it is commonly accepted that the greatest variability of human differences occurs within traditional racial categories—not between them. The most compelling evidence indicates that race is a sociopolitical construction, one that is actively maintained by our communication in various contexts, including interpersonal, small group, organizational, and mass media (to be highlighted in Part II of this book). The reality remains, however, that most people continue to utilize this framework as a marker to distinguish human qualities, potential, and behaviors.

A historical foundation is important in setting the stage for our understanding of the complexities inherent in interracial communication today. First, it allows us to debunk the myths of superior and inferior racial groups. Second, it helps us affirm the existence of some differences when comparing various racial/ethnic groups while at the same time recognizing the similarities of all people belonging to one human race. Third, and finally, it provides an important context for understanding contemporary issues related to race and racism.

## KEY TERMS

| | | |
|---|---|---|
| chosen people | mulattos | hypodescent |
| Manifest Destiny | quadroons | eyeball test |
| colonialism | octoroons | Jim Crow |
| phenotype | one-drop rule | enlightened racism |

## OPPORTUNITIES FOR EXTENDED LEARNING

1. Take some time to watch an episode or two of *Skipped History*, a comedy web series that explores different historical events, people, and ideas that have been largely overlooked. Through presentations that are both accessible and funny, host Ben Tumin helps to create a counternarrative to U.S. history. For instance, you might start with an episode that explores the racially-motivated reasons why the United States entered its first major war abroad in the Philippines and ultimately created a new category ("noncitizen nationals") whereby Filipinos in the new U.S. territory were denied the right to vote (https://www.youtube.com/watch?v=1pY6XHJAcFQ). Other episodes focus on the origins of Black crime statistics, the U.S.-led coup in Guatemala, and how Confederate historians shaped the teaching of U.S. history.

2. The United States has long been regarded as "a nation of immigrants." Within this context, recently some have questioned how and why the label of "immigrant" has become stigmatized—especially for immigrants of color. Given this, take some time to reconsider some popular ideas about immigration by visiting https://www.carnegie.org/our-work/article/15-myths-about-immigration-debunked/. This resource can provide some insight in terms of dispelling popular myths that stigmatize immigrants and their families in the United States.

3. Learn more about land acknowledgements and other programs recognizing indigenous rights in Canada, Australia, and New Zealand. Spend some time comparing and contrasting how each country (including the United States)

has negotiated their past with native people. What similarities and differences do you see? What, in your eyes, would be an ideal situation?

4. Table 2.1 highlights the history of race relations between African Americans and European Americans according to Ray (2009). Spend some time conducting your own research online and see if you can replicate a parallel box that outlines the history of different racial/ethnic groups in the United States. For instance, you might focus on Native American/European American race relations or the history of Jewish Americans and African Americans.

5. Visit the BlackLivesMatter.com website and review the content. Pay particular attention to how the movement and its history are described. What news stories are included? What actions are suggested? What resources are listed? Do the descriptions differ from your understanding of #BLM prior to visiting the website? Does what you've learned from the media, family, and friends match what you found on the website?

6. Leung (2021) describes different potential proposals for changing certain categories for the 2030 U.S. Census. Given the progression of racial and ethnic categories over time (https://www.census.gov/data-tools/demo/race/MREAD_1790_2010.html provides an excellent interactive resource), what are your reactions to these proposed changes? How might they increase the accuracy of data collection for Latinx people and those with ancestral roots in the Middle East and North Africa? What, if any, other changes do you think would make this data gathering more accurate and meaningful?

## RECOMMENDED CONTEMPORARY READINGS

Cornejo, M., Kam, J. A., & Afifi, T. D. (2021). Discovering one's undocumented immigration status through family disclosures: The perspectives of U.S. college students with Deferred Action for Childhood Arrivals (DACA). *Journal of Applied Communication, 49*(3), 267–285. doi.org/10.1080/00909882.2021.1896022

Day, A. M., O'Shay-Wallace, S., Seeger, M. W., & McElmurry, S. P. (2019). Informational sources, social media use, and race in the Flint, Michigan, water crisis. *Communication Studies, 70*(3), 352–376. doi.org/10.1080/10510974.2019.1567566

Fridin, K., Wintersieck, A., Courey, J., & Thompson, J. (2017). Race and police brutality: The importance of media framing. *International Journal of Communication, 11*, 3394–3414.

Italiano, R., Ramirez, F., & Chattopadhyay, S. (2021). Perceptions of police use of force among U.S. adults and the role of communication accommodation in improving police-civilian interactions. *Journal of Applied Communication Research*, 1–18. doi.org/10.1080/00909882.2021.1930103

Mallya, D., & Susanti, R. (2021). Theorizing race, marginalization, and language in the digital media. *Communication & Society, 34*(2), doi.org/10.15581/003.34.2.403-415

Mixon-Mitchell, D., & Hanna, M. D. (2017). Race matters: Child protection and the communication process. *Journal of Ethnic & Cultural Diversity in Social Work, 26*(4), 366–381. doi.org/10.1080/15313204.2017.1344944

Oshiro, K. F., Weems, A. J., & Singer, J. N. (2020). Cyber racism about Black athletes: A critical race analysis of. http://TexAgs.com online brand community. *Communication & Sport*, doi.org/10.1177/2167479520911888

Wilson, D. A., & Atouba, Y. C. (2021). Making sense of attitudes toward the US national anthem protests: Examining the role of emphatic concern, and perspective-taking. *Howard Journal of Communications, 32*(1), 43–54. doi.org/10.1080/10646175.2020.1850373

# 3

# The Power of Verbal and Nonverbal Codes

**CASE STUDY**　　　**Keeping Native Languages Alive**

Of the 400 to 600 North American tribal languages believed to have existed, 150 still exist but many of them no longer have any first-language or native speakers—people who learned the tribal language before they started speaking English. For many, the loss of a language is the loss of a nation's culture; language is part of one's identity and reinforces an Indigenous way of thinking. Menominee is an Algonquian language; Algonquin tribes were among the first encountered by Europeans. Many place names in the East and Midwest (including Wisconsin, Milwaukee, and Michigan) are derived from Algonquian words.

　　The Menominee tribal language had an estimated 5 first-language speakers in 2019, all of them older than 80. The tribe trained Menominee language instructors to teach classes in the schools and at the College of Menominee Nation. The language is taught in day care and in kindergarten through middle school. It is an elective at the high school, and language instruction is offered at adult recreation centers. Historically, the Menominee language was not embraced; generations were discouraged from using it and even punished by schoolteachers for speaking anything but English.

　　Nineteenth century efforts by the U.S. government forced Native American assimilation through educational and socialization efforts. How important do you think language is to one's culture, identity, and sense of belonging?

Source: Tolan, T. (2019). Wisconsin's native tribes are taking action to keep their languages from dying out. *Milwaukee Magazine*.

While reading Chapters 1 and 2, how conscious were you of the terms used to describe different racial/ethnic groups? Did some labels offend you? Confuse you? Enlighten you? Deciding about the language to use—including labels, and naming—is one of the challenges in writing a book on interracial communication. Such decisions are difficult because racial/ethnic groups are not static entities (Rodriguez, 2002). Instead, the ways in which ingroup (as well as outgroup) members identify and label themselves change and evolve over time (Corona et al., 2017). Throughout the book, we have attempted to determine and utilize those terms and labels favored by the particular racial/ethnic group we are discussing.

As you will undoubtedly come to realize, if you have not done so already, verbal codes are a powerful element in communication processes. Contrary to the popular old adage, we believe "Sticks and stones may break your bones *and* that names can and will hurt you." Historically, the process by which racial/ethnic groups—as well as those cultural elements central to their locations—were labeled has in fact had a tremendous effect on self- and other perceptions. For example, did you notice in Chapters 1 and 2 that we avoided using the terms *America* or *American* to describe the land or people of the United States? Instead, we used phrases like North, Central, and/or South America to help specify the particular people/land to which we were referring. Using the term America to describe the United States—or using American to describe U.S. citizens—is egocentric and reduces the visibility, attention, and importance given to other diverse countries in the Americas (Canada, Mexico, Argentina, Brazil, etc.). In a historical sense, it is also important to recognize that "America" was the home to civilizations of people years prior to the

---

**Box 3.1**                                                        **Author Reflections**

### Language Choices Matter: A Process of Lifelong Learning

As explained in the next section, The Power of Verbal Codes, language choices matter. They help to co-create meaning, influence our understanding, and communicate our inner thoughts to others. Throughout the book, you will be introduced to a variety of words and phrases (e.g., Latinx, BIPOC, minoritized people, etc.) that I've learned to embrace over the years. Please note that each word and phrase reflect a conscious choice.

Recently, I learned about the power of the truncated passive voice—a sentence structure that is often used without little consciousness. Consider, for example, the following statement: *Black Americans were enslaved in the United States.* The statement is written in the truncated passive voice, with no identification about who enslaved Black Americans. Indeed, *European [white] Americans enslaved Black people.* In the previous sentence, the group committing the atrocity of slavery was left unnamed, invisible, and not held accountable. In the second sentence, the responsible parties are named.

Teaching others how to be "politically correct" has never been my goal. Instead, I hope to increase awareness and mindfulness of the power of verbal and nonverbal codes when communicating with others. Sensitivity to the potency of codes can help us make the best choices possible. My mantra is: A more conscious, informed communicator is a more competent communicator. The fantastic thing about being a lifelong learner is that as I work to increase my students' awareness, they are doing the same for me. #Teaching ↔ Learning

—MPO

arrival of Europeans. What became known as the New World to European settlers was, in the experiences of the indigenous people of the land, not "new" at all. Many knew it as Turtle Island (Gonzalez, 2002).

Our objective here is not to provide a laundry list of "politically correct" language for you to use when interacting with individuals who are racially/ethnically different. Given the complexity of interracial communication processes, such a list would be limited, ungeneralizable, and ultimately counterproductive. Instead, we want you to recognize the inherent power of language choices in determining levels of communication effectiveness. Specifically, this chapter discusses the importance of verbal codes in interracial communication and how societal power is directly related to issues of labeling and naming specific cultural groups. In addition, we highlight the power that nonverbal codes possess in the creation of meaning.

## THE POWER OF VERBAL CODES

Verbal codes, as part of a larger language system, are central to human communication processes. Although certainly it is incorrect to equate verbal codes with communication itself, the important role of verbal codes in communicative competency cannot be denied. For most individuals, however, their native language is a ubiquitous entity, one that is constantly in use but seldom critiqued or questioned consciously. Language—words, phrases, and styles—is natural and effortless when used with others who share a common speech community, a concept that we cover later in this chapter. In this regard, verbal codes are an abundant public resource that many utilize with little attention to their powerful nature. In terms of interracial communication, the power of verbal codes can be seen in the ways they have been used to label, and subsequently define, some *groups* of people while leaving others—the dominant or "standard" group—unlabeled. Prior to our discussion of the power of labels and naming, we provide some background information. Specifically, we want you to observe the important role that verbal codes play in human communication processes. This is best achieved by describing them as (1) a tool, (2) a prism, and (3) a display.

### Verbal Codes as a Tool

In their most basic form, verbal codes are a tool that humans have utilized—sometimes competently, sometimes not so competently—to communicate their ideas, thoughts, and feelings to others. Language systems include semantic, syntactic, pragmatic, and phonetic patterns and are accessed through either written or spoken channels. Verbal cues are the means by which our internal cognitions (beliefs, values, attitudes, emotions, etc.) can be shared with others. Communication comes from the Latin **communicare**, which means "to make common." Without establishing and locating common experience (some use the term **homophily** to describe the common experiences you share with others), communication would be impossible. Central to the human experience is the ability to share our internal cognitions with others.

The analogy of a toolbox is useful in understanding language systems. Think of a set of tools (verbal codes) used to communicate in different settings. No limitations are put on the number of tools that a person is capable of acquiring, nor is a person restricted from learning how to use multiple sets of tools. In fact, we would guess that many U.S. Americans find themselves using different language systems (toolboxes) for achieving different objectives in various communities of which they are a member. For instance, a student may draw from one set of tools when interacting with family members and another when discussing his or her chemistry test with a professor. In order to communicate competently, the same or different tools might be necessary when in the company of friends, professional colleagues, or those with a common interest or hobby. In essence, a well-stocked toolbox (language system) is essential to getting the job done through appropriate means (communicating competently).

---

*Box 3.2*                                                    *Research Highlight*

## Communication Barriers with International Teaching Assistants

Conventional wisdom tells us the best way to become proficient in another language is to travel to a country where you must speak the native language. For many international students, increased language proficiency—as well as opportunities for quality educational and cultural opportunities—make studying abroad an attractive option. When international graduate students also serve as teaching assistants, problems can arise. Students not being able to understand teaching assistants from other countries has become so prevalent that one state considered requiring refunds for students who complained in writing about their instructor's lack of English proficiency (Gravois, 2005). Hao (2011) analyzed a Midwestern university newspaper article, and subsequent letters to the editor, about an International Teaching Assistant (ITA) training program. While the article generally applauded the university's attempt to provide training to ITAs who needed additional assistance, Hao took issue with how the article placed all of the blame for communication problems between ITAs and students squarely on the ITAs. In a letter to the editor, he asked, "Don't you think that our students should also learn how to listen more carefully so that they can understand their ITAs?" and went on to reason, "We now live in a multicultural U.S. society, and unfortunately many of us are too lazy to learn another language and/or try to learn ways to communicate more effectively with people who are from different cultural backgrounds" (p. 310). Other letters disagreed with Hao's reasoning and insisted that outsiders must learn the dominant language and "that the responsibility lies with those who come to OUR country to better themselves in the English language" (p. 312). What are your thoughts on this issue? What, if any, experiences have you had with international faculty/TAs or traveling abroad that have solidified your perceptions? In short, do you think that the responsibility for communication competency lies primarily with the instructor, student, or both parties?

One aspect of verbal codes that sometimes hinders competent interracial communication is the **arbitrary nature of words**. Words do not have any inherent meaning. Instead, they are abstractions of the things they represent and are always incomplete representations. Meaning is created not by the codes themselves but by how the codes are interpreted by *both parties*. Some responsibility for specific verbal codes, therefore, must be assumed by both the senders and the receivers. This means assuming a **message orientation approach** to communication, one whereby both senders and receivers have some responsibility to create shared meaning (Burgoon et al., 2021).

## Verbal Codes as a Prism

Verbal codes are more than simply passive, neutral tools that we use to communicate our internal cognitions to others (Hymes, 1974). In addition to serving as an "instrument for voicing ideas," they also provide a guide for an individual's mental activity (Hoijer, 1994, p. 194). In other words, language serves a central role in providing linguistic, semantic, and verbal categories that have a direct relationship with how we understand abstract ideas. Language can be regarded as a prism that colors how we perceive reality. One of the central ideas associated with linguistic relativity is the Sapir-Whorf hypothesis (sometimes referred to as simply the Whorfian hypothesis).

The **Sapir-Whorf hypothesis** suggests that language structure is necessary in order to produce thought (Fong, 2000). Within this perspective, language is a guide to social reality. Although it helps articulate our experiences, it also plays a central role in defining them. In its most extreme form, this understanding of verbal codes suggests that the particular elements of a language system predispose us to think in particular ways and not in others (see Box 3.1). Edward Sapir explained that "human beings do not live in the objective world alone, nor alone in the world of social activity as ordinarily understood, but are very much at the mercy of the particular language which has become the medium for their society" (quoted in Mandelbaum, 1949, p. 162).

You may need a set of examples to help you understand this abstract concept. A significant amount of research has been completed on color terms and perceptions (e.g., Kay & Kempton, 1984) and provides support for the Sapir-Whorf hypothesis. For instance, you may hear the same item called blue, green, bluish green, teal, turquoise, seafoam green, or malachite. Depending on the particular person's set of life experiences (e.g., working as a salesperson for J. Crew clothing), perceptions of the item probably differed greatly. According to the Sapir-Whorf hypothesis, varying perceptions of reality are due to the differences in verbal abilities (color terms) of specific people. In other words, the ways in which a person thinks about a particular thought, object, or emotion is confined by the terms to which she or he has access. If one of your friends does not have the term *seafoam green* in her repertoire of color terms, she will not be able see something as seafoam green (even if others do). In this regard, her reality is shaped by her language structures.

| BOX 3.3 | Author Reflections |
|---|---|

### "Jungle Fever": Overlooking Negativity in Popular Vernacular

As we have discussed in this chapter, language is a prism or tool we use daily to communicate. Depending on a number of variables and factors, that language can be very powerful in shaping our identities and affecting how racially different people interact with and perceive each other. We must be sensitive to the fact or reality that, as racialized individuals, we will certainly have different interpretations of our shared experiences. We also need to be aware of how our language can manifest that power and cause even greater division between the races.

The phrase "jungle fever" entered popular culture vernacular as a result of Spike Lee's 1991 film of the same name. The movie was incredibly popular and played a very critical role in articulating for its audience, and society at large, the historical framing of Black/white love. According to Paulin (1997), the title

> reiterates dominant representations of interracial relationships . . . [as evidenced by] the underlying discourse of contamination implied by the clichéd title. Thus, *Jungle Fever* effectively reinscribes the notion that interracial love is the result of irrational, racialized, heated passion. The film serves to reproduce the notion that interracial desire is transgressive and that it contaminates pure blood lines. (p. 168)

When the movie was released, very few people took the time to deconstruct the meaning and power of the phrase "jungle fever"; it permeated everyday language and had very negative connotations. A closer listen to the lyrics of the title song takes us into the pressures of interracial romantic relationships. The upbeat tempo of the song distracts the listener from the savagery of the origins of interracial relations (i.e., slavery) where Blacks were objectified. Contemporary interracial relationships do not share the oppressive master/slave origins, but negative perceptions of Black/white romantic relationships are still very common (see Chapter 8). There remains a belief that romantic connections to a nonwhite person, specifically a Black person, will "infect" the European American partner with a disease that will ultimately kill him or her. The term remains a part of Black culture, but I have personally chosen to *not* use it in reference to interracial romantic relationships. It gives too much power to a phrase that demonizes relationships between the races.

Let's all be proactive in being careful about the words we use and the power we give insensitive and offensive language—one word at a time.

—TMH

## Verbal Cues as a Display

The importance of verbal codes in the communication process can be seen through the many roles they play. In addition to its use as a tool and a prism, verbal codes also serve as a display for our internal thoughts. The verbal choices we make as a means to communicate certain ideas do more than simply articulate those ideas. Although oftentimes unintentional, they provide additional information—beyond the presentation of our ideas—about internal cognitions regarding a particular subject. It has often been said that language is an index to, or reflection of, our internal thought patterns (Hymes, 1974). Consider the following example to help you understand how individuals' language choices sometimes communicate more about them than they always recognize.

In the English language, several verbal codes (synonyms) can be used to communicate any one idea. The unconscious or conscious choice of words can provide a great deal of insight in terms of how one feels about the idea—in some cases, even more than is directly communicated. Olsen (2006) describes the power of verbal codes in his article critiquing the treatment of Japanese Americans during World War II. In particular, he criticizes the ways in which the government, media, and historians used words and phrases that misrepresented what was done to people of Japanese ancestry living in the United States. He urges educators to use appropriate terms to teach students about how Japanese American citizens (not "non-aliens") were forcibly removed (not "evacuated") to concentration camps (not "relocation centers"). These shifts in language are important to avoid neutralizing the racist activities of the U.S. government (Mizuno, 2003). Do you see any parallels between this example and the verbal codes that are used to describe recent Mexican immigrants ("illegals" versus "undocumented") to the United States (C. Stewart et al., 2011), or citizens ("refugees" or "evacuees") who lost their homes during Hurricane Katrina (Edgerly, 2011)?

In February 1942, the U.S. government forcibly removed more than 110,000 people of Japanese ancestry from their homes and businesses; they were imprisoned in remote, military style camps. The Manzanar War Relocation Center pictured here was one of the ten camps. Photograph by Ansel Adams, Library of Congress.

The phrase **semantics of prejudice** can be used to describe how specific verbal codes can unintentionally reveal information about individuals' internal thoughts (regardless of attempts to shield them from display). For people whose involvement in varying forms of interracial communication is considerable, language choices often serve as a way to understand the perspectives of others. When you hear a new acquaintance refer to a third party as "Oriental" (as opposed to Asian, Korean, or Laotian), do you draw any conclusions about how that person regards people of Asian descent? How about if a person commented on the "savage-like behaviors of some Blacks" or someone who thinks that "Dominican girls are so exotic"? Would these language choices impact your perceptions of these peoples' views on race, ethnicity, and interracial communication? For those experienced in interracial communication—including both authors of this text—such language choices would certainly send up red flags!

# THE POWER OF LABELS

Part of human nature is to use labels to refer to other people and ourselves. Systems of classifications are a productive means by which we make sense out of a complex world. But we must critically examine the genesis and development of labels for particular categories. Labels communicate on many levels of meaning. They also implicitly work to establish, maintain, or challenge specific kinds of relationships between individuals and/or groups of individuals. Labels, as verbal codes, can be used strategically to communicate closeness or distance among individuals depending on the intentions and effects of the speech act. As noted in chapter 2, racial categories have served as a means of both discrimination and as a source of identity and common experiences for many groups. The labels designated for specific racial/ethnic groups in the United States are significant examples of the power of verbal codes.

Chapter 2 also highlighted the contextualization of language as a political act; how social, regional, and national groups define racial classifications indicates the political nature of these decisions. Asante (1998b) explains that whenever categories and labels are created to make certain concepts functional, the choices made are drawn from many different possibilities. Typically, the categories chosen create mechanisms that benefit some groups to the disadvantage of others. Some suggest that persons with political, social, and economic power occupy positions that allow them to label less powerful groups of people. In many instances, this is completed in ways that maintain or increase the power bases of those already in the most powerful societal positions.

## Privilege

Over the course of U.S. history, middle- and upper-class European American men have held most of the social, economic, and political power. From this position of privilege, they have consistently created and used labels to define other ethnic groups in ways that have benefited their own existence. Chapter 2 described how Africans, Asians, and those indigenous to North America never defined themselves as such until coming in contact with Europeans. Prior to European influences, the labels that were used reflected the diversity of particular groups of people based on ethnicity, culture, and other factors. Think about how one label based on race (e.g., Asian) has come to represent a multitude of diverse ethnic and cultural groups (e.g., Chinese, Filipino, Hmong, and Indonesians). Each label created a category that served the purpose of defining these groups from a European perspective.

---

**Box 3.4**                                                    *Student Reflections*

## Life as an "Oreo"

I cannot count how many times I have been told I talk or act white or have been called an "Oreo" (Black on the outside, white in the inside). I had no Black people around me besides my family since I moved to the suburbs. I did a 180 when I moved from the city to the burbs. I found myself trying to act "less Black" because I was young, and I wanted friends even though there wasn't another Black girl in my entire elementary school. In second grade, all of the girls in my class told me they wouldn't play with me because I was Black, and I was called a nigger more in elementary school than in the rest of my life. Since then, I embrace my race and love me for me. I know I speak properly; unfortunately the way I speak is being mistaken for talking white. However, I see it as representing Black people in the most positive way I know how. I know many people who dumb themselves down because they think that excelling in school or speaking correctly is a white thing, and that is a disgrace. We, as Black people, should be ashamed of ourselves when we equate success to acting white. We need to lift our fellow Black people up and be proud of our educated brothers and sisters.

---

The idea of **societal privilege** is an important concept in terms of the ways that certain groups have the power to label others while remaining unlabeled. Peggy McIntosh (2009) advanced understanding of how societal privilege operates within specific contexts and its effect on perceptions of "reality." Initially, she wrote about male privilege but then recognized that white privilege is especially relevant to discussions on interracial communication. Societal privilege, in this vein, refers to a generally favored state, one that has been earned or conferred by birth or luck. Unlike that which is earned, power from unearned privilege can look like strength, but what it typically represents is an *unearned entitlement*. According to McIntosh (1992), part of white privilege is seeing racism in terms of individual acts and not as largely invisible systems that confer dominance on European Americans. In terms of the power of labeling, a position of privilege is a position that remains largely unnamed and racially "neutral" (Rowe & Malhotra, 2006). White privilege can be seen in the ways that most people of European descent think of themselves as Americans with no race (A. Miller & Harris, 2005).

The remainder of this section presents an overview of the labels that have been used to describe the major racial/ethnic groups in the United States. Recognize that such groups are not merely static entities. As you will see, racial/ethnic groups—as we have come to understand them—are products of a lengthy, ongoing process of labeling and identification.

## African Americans

Research on the evolution of labels to describe persons of African descent is well documented (R. A. Davis, 1997). Variations have included African, Colored, Negro, Black, Afro-American, and African American. According to Holloway (1990), the different labels reflect changes in how persons of African descent negotiated their identity in the United States. This ranges from strong African identification, nationalism, integration, and attempts at assimilation to a renewed sense of cultural identification. Eligon (2020) sees recent shifts of African American self-identification as connected to issues of self-determination, strength, progress, and control. One major issue in labeling, for all racial/ethnic groups generally and people of African descent specifically, is the general preference for labels that have been generated from within the community (as opposed to those imposed by others).

Given the variety of choices, which term—Black or African American—is correct? Because of the diversity of thought within this heterogeneous group, one term is not necessarily more correct than the other. Celeste Watkins-Hayes, professor of African American studies at Northwestern University, describes the adoption of the term African American as a deliberate choice by Black communities to denote both African heritage and status as people born in the United States (Adams, 2020). Layers of racial identity are complex and personal; asking someone's preference is an opportunity for conversation. Research over the past few decades found that people of African descent were equally divided in the preference for the label "Black" or "African American." Interestingly, this was consistent across gender and level of education. However, those individuals who were younger, attended integrated schools, and were from larger non-Southern cities were more likely to prefer "African American" rather than "Black" (Sigelman et al., 2005).

R. A. Davis (1997) believes that an all-inclusive term like African American is not appropriate given the increasing diversity of people of African descent living in the United States (see also, Orbe & Drummond, 2009). According to Reimers (2005), more Black immigrants entered the United States since the end of World War II than during the slave era—the forced migration of 450,000 Blacks (p. 232). Recently, the largest numbers have come from the Caribbean (most notably the Dominican Republic, Cuba, Jamaica, and Haiti) and secondly from Africa (most notably Nigeria, Ethiopia, Morocco, Ghana, and Kenya) (Waters, 1999). Because of this, we need terms that embrace the diversity of Black Americans while also recognizing the differences in terms of culture, language, and national origin (El Nasser, 2003). In the end, Bilge et al. (2021) argue that African American is best used as an eth-

> ## Box 3.5
>
> ### Linguistic Profiling
>
> When communicating on the phone with someone whom you do not know, it is natural to make judgments about that person's race, gender, age, and other demographic elements (Groscurth, 2003). Recent research has indicated that this is especially true in terms of race. According to Rickford and Rickford (2000), an average U.S. American can correctly identify the race of speakers 80–90% of the time. While the process of making judgments is natural, it is illegal when individuals discriminate against others based on those judgments. In fact, this discriminatory act has been given a name, linguistic profiling.
>
> **Linguistic profiling** occurs when individuals listen to a person's voice on the phone, make conclusions about a person's race/ethnicity, and then discriminate against the person based on assumed race/ethnicity (Baugh, 2000b). In past years, several African Americans across the United States have sued apartment managers who, they claim, correctly assumed their race by their vocal patterns and then violated fair housing practices. Oftentimes these plaintiffs were not identified because of their use of Ebonics—something that for some signals ignorance (Baugh, 2000a) and triggers negative reactions (Groscurth, 2003). Instead, they used "standard" English but in ways in which their intonations and vocalics reflected the African American culture.
>
> - Do you think that linguistic profiling is prevalent?
> - In what contexts?
> - Do you think that there is such a thing as "sounding Black" or "sounding white?"
> - How does society perceive individuals whose language use does not "match" their racial and/or ethnic identity?
> - Is this becoming more, or less, common? Why?

nic identifier (specific to certain groups in the United States) whereas Black is a racial identifier that transcends national origins.

## Arab Americans

In this fourth edition of our book, we have opted to use Arab Americans instead of Middle Eastern Americans. This is because the identifier, Middle East, is imprecise, culturally and geographically biased, and Anglocentric with origins in the height of the British imperial century. The label, Arab Americans, describes a diverse ethnic group (Bilge et al., 2021) that shares a common linguistic, cultural, historical, and geographical bond (Alharbi, 2018). While this label encompasses people with a shared ancestry from a particular region in the world, it also reflects many different national identities, including: Armenia, Lebanon, Syria, United Arab Emirates, Turkey, Iraq, Iran, Israel, Palestine, Morocco, Oman, Yemen, Egypt, and Algeria.

Arab Americans have lived in the United States since the mid-1800s; most of the earliest immigrants were Chaldeans—Roman Catholics from present-day Iraq (Reimers, 2005). In the following years, other groups immigrated to the United States in substantial numbers from the late 1800s to the early to mid-1900s from countries including Armenia, Lebanon, and Syria. Presently, nearly 3.7 million U.S. Americans trace their roots to an Arab country (Arab American Institute, 2021). Arab Americans live in every state; however, one-third of the population of this ethnic group reside in three metropolitan areas (Los Angeles, Detroit, and New York). The majority of Arab Americans are native born, and nearly 82% of Arabs in the United States are citizens.

Prior to September 11, 2001, the label *Arab* was used to emphasize the commonality of all individuals of Arab descent regardless of national origin. However, after the terrorist attacks, the use of national labels such as Palestinian, Egyptian, or Lebanese were more frequently used (Witteborn, 2004). This was done to highlight the distinctions in terms of religion, nationality, and ethnic origins—an important consideration given the general ignorance about this diverse group. Many U.S. Americans automatically, but incorrectly, assumed that all Arab Americans were fundamentalist Muslim or "Islamists" (Swahn et al., 2003). In particular, the terrorist attacks on the United States on 9/11 prompted this perception because the terrorists were identified as Muslims. In fact, only 24% of Arabs living in the United States are Muslims (Pew Research Center, 2017). Many Arab Americans are Jewish (from both Israel and Arab nations), Christian (including large numbers of Lebanese Christians and Egyptian Copts), and members of the Baha'i faith from Iran (Reimers, 2005). Misunderstandings and lack of knowledge about the spiritual and cultural diversity of this ethnic group result in increased prejudice, discrimination, and attacks on all Arab Americans. Stereotyped reactions have also increased ethnic pride and a sense of nonwhite minoritization (Awad et al., 2021).

## Asian Americans

Most scholars trace the first wave of Asian immigrants in the United States back to Chinese laborers who arrived in California between 1850 and 1882 (Min, 2006). However, the first recorded Asians arrived in the United States prior to the signing of the Declaration of Independence; this small group of "Manila men" arrived in New Orleans in the 1760s. We make this point to draw attention to the fact that particular immigration patterns of different Asian American groups is varied and covers 250 years (Chan, 2003) and three different eras (Min, 2006).

In recent years, the label Asian has replaced the use of other terms, including "Mongolian," "Asiatic," and "Oriental." Asian American, a phrase coined by historian and civil rights activist Yuji Ichioka in the late 1960s, helps to unite different Asian ethnic groups (Shih et al., 2019). Currently, it is used as an umbrella term to describe both U.S. citizens and immigrants who trace their ancestral roots to Asia. Yet, the label is imprecise since it includes over 30 different groups from various Asian countries. These include large groups in the United States (those of Chinese, Filipino, Indian, Vietnamese, Korean, and Japanese descent) as well as smaller groups (those with Malaysian, Nepalese, Indonesian,

## Box 3.6

### Thinking Critically About the Model Minority Myth

Sociologist William Petersen used the term *model minority* in 1966 to describe how Japanese Americans overcame discrimination and achieved educational and economic success in U.S. society through a cultural emphasis on hard work (F. Wang, 2016).

There are 22 million Asian Americans from more than 20 countries; they comprise approximately 7% of the U.S. population (Budiman & Ruiz, 2021). Within this larger context, consider the following statistics:

- Asian Americans have the highest percentage of any racial group with a bachelor's degree or higher (54%).
- Asian Americans make up 17% of all U.S. physicians and surgeons.
- Nearly 12% of all engineers in the United States are Asian American.
- 23% of all computer and mathematical occupations in the United States are held by Asian Americans.
- The median household income for Asian Americans is $85,800—the highest among all racial groups (overall median household average is $61,800).

While these statistics provide evidence for the model minority label, a closer examination reveals inaccuracies with this racial stereotype. For instance, it is important to recognize that Asian Americans are a diverse group of people whose ancestors came from many different cultures (Shih et al., 2019). When analyses consider different Asian ethnic groups separately, the model minority stereotype becomes faulty. For instance, while Asian American groups from particular countries (e.g., China, India, Japan, and Korea) have benefited from high educational achievements, others (e.g., those from Southeast Asia) were refugees from predominantly agricultural countries where education was less emphasized. As such, some Asian Americans—like the Hmong, Vietnamese, Cambodians, and Laotians—have high percentages of people with educational levels far below the national average and the highest high school dropout rates in the country (Le, 2022). In California, almost 40% of Vietnamese refugees receive public assistance, as do an equal number of Cambodians, Hmong, and Laotians in Minnesota and Wisconsin. Asian Americans have the greatest income inequality of any ethnic group (Hassan & Carlsen, 2018). The top tenth in income earns 10.7 times as much as the bottom tenth; in comparison the top 10% of Blacks earn 9.8 times as much as the bottom 10% while the top 10% of both Hispanics and whites earn 7.8 times the bottom tenth.

While the model minority stereotype continues to dominate public thinking (Mudambi, 2019), it is most descriptive of members of some Asian American groups, but definitely not all. A more critical approach to understanding this phenomenon would be to recognize that other factors like national origin, age, and socioeconomic status impact educational and professional success. The myth of universal success makes the economic struggles of some Asian Americans invisible.

and Burmese ancestry). Because of the great diversity represented within this commonly used label, it is often helpful to use more specific identifiers when possible. This practice recognizes and distinguishes Asian Americans from Asian nationals, and it also helps differentiate among Asian nationalities. Such distinctions are important given those of Asian descent vary greatly in terms of their immigration history, cultural values and beliefs, socioeconomic status, primary languages, spiritual beliefs and practices, and overall identities.

While Asian American is a convenient label, Shrikant (2018) reports that few U.S. Americans of Asian descent actually identify themselves as such. Instead, they identify with their particular countries of origin. Still, many U.S. Americans treat Asian Americans as a panethnic group—seeing all Asian Americans as similar and with little, or no, recognition of differences within particular ethnic groups. Cultural differences, like those related to age, generation status and spirituality (Min, 2006), are given little consideration as to how they affect identity and communication. A key factor in how Asian Americans communicate has to do with their experiences within the United States—for instance, are they immigrants, first generation, or born in the United States? These important issues impact things like language ability, cultural values, and cultural identification.

## European Americans

As we discussed earlier, European Americans have historically remained unnamed because of their positions of privilege in the United States. In fact, this privileged social positioning results in little conscious awareness of their racial/ethnic identity for most persons of European descent (A. Miller & Harris, 2005). Unlike other racial/ethnic groups, the identity of this dominant group is not seen as central to everyday interactions. Hence, when faced with the question of self-identification (e.g., "What are you?" or "What race do you consider yourself?"), a common response from many European Americans is simply to label themselves as "Americans" with no particular racial or ethnic identity. This is part of white privilege.

It is important to recognize that labels for European Americans, like the other labels discussed in this section, have evolved over time. For instance, many groups that were not initially considered white (e.g., Catholic Irish immigrants or persons from Eastern Europe) eventually "achieved" status as white/European Americans (Roediger, 1994). Researchers (e.g., J. Martin et al., 1996) have examined which terms are most commonly used in self-identification by European Americans. They found that when forced to use a racial/ethnic marker, people of European descent most often chose "white," followed by "Caucasian." Labels that were least reported were "WASP" (White Anglo-Saxon Protestant) and "Anglo." Interestingly, Morrison and Chung (2011) found that people who use the label white, compared to those who use European American, are less supportive of multiculturalism, more racially prejudiced, and have less identification with people of color. Lastly, it is important to understand that Caucasian is problematically ethnocentric since it is based on the idea that a specific group of Europeans (natives of Caucasus) had the ideal physical appearance (Khan, 2011).

You've probably noticed that we have opted primarily to use *European American* throughout this book. When we do use the racial label, white, we follow contemporary writing style guides and leave it uncapitalized. This is done in attempts to use parallel terms that are geographically based, as reflected in the headings of this section. Although this rationale is strong, it—along with other language choices in terms of interracial communication—is not invoked without some concerns. For instance, some scholars, such as Frankenberg (1993), warn that using parallel terms "falsely equalizes communities, who are, in terms of current reality, unequally positioned in the racial order" (p. 231). This concern, like many explained throughout this chapter, demonstrates the imperfect nature of verbal codes.

## Jewish Americans

The history of Jewish people in the United States can be traced back to the early 17th century. However, large scale Jewish immigration was not seen until the 19th and 20th centuries when immigration was the result of persecution and economic difficulties in Eastern Europe. The most recent U.S. Census estimates put the Jewish population at 7.5 million; some estimates count the Jewish population in Israel as 6.8 million, making the U.S. Jewish community the largest in the world (PEW Research Center, 2021). Approximately 40% of Jewish Americans live along the east coast in six states (New York, New Jersey, Florida, Massachusetts, Maryland, and Connecticut) and Washington, D. C.

Jewish identity can be described as having different parts: ethnic identity (stemming from ancestral inheritance), religion (observance of spiritual rituals), and culture (celebration of traditions, both secular and religious) (Pew Research Center, 2021). In this regard, Jewish community exists in diverse forms in terms of worship cultural traditions, language, observance of various Jewish religious holidays, and identification with Israel (Bowen, 2016). Over the past two decades, more Jewish Americans (27%) have started to identify as Jewish in terms of ethnicity, rather than religion (Pew Research Center, 2021). One consequence is an acculturation toward dominant U.S. culture—fewer Jewish spouses, friends, neighbors, coworkers and feelings of lack of attachment to Jewish communities (Don-Yehiya, 2012). The label, Jewish American, then has become to represent an identification with Jewish heritage, something that fosters a sense of belonging across the United States (Weber, 2016).

Some distinctions are important here between race and ethnicity. The vast majority (92%) of Jewish Americans identify as European American and, because of their general appearance, are seen as white by others (Rubin, 2021). This fact, in addition to the complexities of defining one's Jewishness and a history of anti-Semitism, makes Jewish identity ambiguous and difficult to define in straightforward terms (Zauzmer, 2019). Some individuals demonstrate their Jewish identities through relational (e.g., marrying another Jewish person, raising children with Jewish traditions), social (e.g., sending children to Jewish day school, joining Jewish organizations), or personal choices (e.g., wearing a Star of David). In a recent survey, 8% of Jewish respondents identified as Black, Hispanic, or another race or ethnicity (PEW Research Center, 2021). Some of these individuals are part of Jewish families through intermarriage or adoption; a smaller number are Jewish through conversion. Like their European counterparts, Jews of color—those who are of African, Asian, Latinx, and Native descent—embrace and demonstrate their Jewish identities in a variety of ways. However, they also navigate their Jewishness without the cover of white privilege (Rubin, 2021).

## Latinx Americans

As we illustrated and discussed earlier, naming is not a neutral act. In many cases, we have seen how racial/ethnic labels have been used to downplay microlevel differences in order to maximize the distance between certain groups and European Americans. Such is the case for the term **Hispanic**, a label first sanctioned for official and generalized use in the United States in 1968 (Melville, 1988). *Hispanic American* is a term that traditionally has represented persons with a similar use of the Spanish language and other aspects of a Spanish culture, regardless of the distinct differences of the many groups that it includes. For instance, the label refers to those U.S. citizens from Mexico, Cuba, Spain, Chile, the Dominican Republic, and many other countries.

Research by Rinderle (2006) illustrates the complexity of names over time. Specifically, she traces the names for people of Mexican descent back to times before Spanish explorers arrived in the Americas. At that time, between 9 and 25 million people were living in what is now Mexico: Mayas in the south, Tarascos in the west, and Mixtecos and Mexicas/Aztecas in central Mexico. With the arrival of Columbus, a new term was invented: *Indio* (Indian). Over time, additional terms—some derived from within and some from outside the group—have been used. Mexican was introduced following the independence movement in 1810, Mestizo became prominent in the early 1900s, and Mexican American was popular following World War II. Since that time, other terms have emerged to describe this large cultural group: Hispanic (created by U.S. government officials), Chicano (which emerged from the Chicano movement), and Latino. Throughout the book, we use Latino/a/x or simply Latinx, a term that has gained in popularity in recent years, as a more efficient and gender-inclusive alternative (de Onis, 2017).

Researchers have found that different labels coincide with different orientations. According to Soto-Vasquez (2018), Hispanic is more acceptable for those people seeking to become a part of U.S. culture (assimilationist); in contrast, Chicanx is more aligned with activism, and Latinx is typically embraced by those with a multinational, pan-ethnic identity. Specific labels are informed by factors such as age, immigrant status, and region (Corona et al., 2017). For instance, Martinez and Gonzalez (2020) found that college graduates, non-Mexicans, first- and second-generation immigrants, and those in the western United States are more likely to prefer Latino/a/x over Hispanic. It is also important to recognize that even when individuals use the same term to describe themselves, different meanings can be attached (Delgado, 1998). This is certainly the case with Latinx (Dame-Griff, 2021). Finally, some Latinx Americans use La Raza to signify political unity among diverse cultural groups (Delgado, 1998). For many, La Raza encourages different Latinx communities to recognize the power of "one race," something advocated by the Chicano movement.

---

### Box 3.7

## Language of Appeasement

In a largely circulated and cited article entitled "Language of Appeasement," Dafina-Lazarus Stewart (2017) critiques current efforts in the name of diversity and inclusion. Ze (Stewart's nonbinary gender pronoun) reminds us that the student activism of the 1960s–1980s was not done with the goal of more acknowledgement and celebration of diversity; instead it was grounded in demands for ethnic studies departments, affinity spaces, and a greater commitment to recruit and retain minoritized faculty, staff, and students.

Stewart regards mainstream efforts at promoting diversity and inclusion as largely things that quiet criticism and protests of students and appease other stakeholders like trustees and donors. Such efforts, ze describes, do little to create systemic or transformative change on campus. True institutional change, according to Stewart, must shift the rhetoric from diversity and inclusion to commitments for equity and social justice. In other words, universities should not measure institutional success through incremental growth of the percentage of minoritized people and their involvement on campus. Alternatively, they must focus on issues of equity and social justice—and not equality among diverse people—that work to expose how university systems inherently disadvantage some people over others.

Spend some time researching your university or organization's efforts regarding these issues. Do you notice a trend to focus on equality, diversity, and inclusion, or are there efforts to move toward commitments regarding equity and social justice? What, if any, differences do these language shifts make toward long-term, systemic institutional change?

---

## Multiracial Americans

**Multiracial Americans**, a diverse group of individuals whose parents are from different racial and ethnic groups, have always existed within the United States. While some of these individuals identify in terms of one group of their ancestors, an increasing number of persons advocate for labels that affirm all aspects of their racial and ethnic heritage. Responding to the pressure of this growing population, the government responded by making the 2000 U.S. Census the first in which people could describe themselves as being of two or more races. In 2010, the U.S. Census recorded over 9 million persons who described themselves as more than one race—a 32% increase since 2000. In 2020, the census form included lines under the boxes for Black and for white; respondents could describe their racial backgrounds in more detail (Tavernise et al., 2021). Coding/processing capacity also improved to capture the additional detail. The multiracial population numbered 33.8 million people, a 276%

increase over the 2010 count making it the fastest growing racial group (N. Jones et al., 2021).

The increase in multiracial Americans reflects the growing diversity of the U.S. population. The change in the 2000 census may have reflected growing numbers of multiracial Americans who refused to be "boxed in" to a single racial category. Instead of seeing themselves as "half black" and "half white," many described themselves as fully black *and* fully white (Kellogg & Liddell, 2012). Others used newer terms like Eurasian (a person with one Asian and one European parent) or original labels like Cablinasian (the term used by Tiger Woods to describe his Caucasian, Black, American Indian, and Asian ancestry) (Nishime, 2012). The identity of multiracial Americans is dynamic and experiences changes over time, place, and context. This is especially true when multiracial individuals identify differently in different social contexts (D. Harris & Sim, 2001) and refuse to respond to attempts by others that they practice "racial allegiance" to one group over another.

As Joseph (2011) reminds us, multiracial identities continue to exist within a sociopolitical context where whiteness is situated as the preferred racial identity. Many factors are important to consider when understanding how multiracial Americans define themselves, including: levels of family identification, physical appearance, friends, relations with extended family members, and composition of neighborhood (Rockquemore & Brunsma, 2002). Logically, those families emphasizing multiracial and multiethnic diversity are much more likely to raise children who appreciate their diverse heritage and embrace their multicultural identities. But we would also note that it would be "logical" for families to adopt other descriptors, including the refusal to be labeled as anything other than a member of the "human race."

## Native Americans

Prior to the arrival of European explorers/settlers, diverse nations of native people—Oneida, Sage, Pequot, Mohegans, Blackfeet, Sioux, Cherokee, Potawatomi, and so on—lived off the land. Early writings of European settlers utilized various condescending labels to describe groups indigenous to what was named "America" (Stromberg, 2006). In the end, it was Christopher Columbus, thinking he had reached India via a quicker route, who incorrectly labeled these Native persons as Indians.

Currently, there are 574 federally recognized tribes of Native Americans and Alaska Natives in the United States (Fonseca, 2021). The Navajo Nation is the largest tribe (almost 400,000 citizens) followed closely by the Cherokee Nation (392,000). Tribes are allocated federal money based on the number of citizens. Each tribe determines how to count its population. The Navajo require one-quarter blood for eligibility while the Cherokee previously used lineal descent. As a result, tribal numbers can differ from census numbers, which are derived from self-identification. Descendants of Blacks enslaved by tribes fought for the right to tribal citizenship (Chavez & Kauer, 2021). In 2021 the Cherokee tribe removed the phrase "by blood" from its constitution, which allowed descendants of people enslaved by the tribe to qualify as Cherokee.

Approximately 9.7 million people identified as Native American and Alaska Native alone and in combination with another race (5.9 million) in the 2020 census, accounting for 2.9% of the U.S. population. Of this number, the biggest percentages of Native Americans and Alaska Natives live in Alaska (14.8%), New Mexico (8.9%), South Dakota (8.4%), Montana (6%), and North Dakota (4.8%) (Indian Country Today, 2021).

Like other racial and ethnic groups, there is a lack of agreement among Native Americans on one preferred term (Shaver, 1998). While "Indian" has been reported as the most commonly used by indigenous people, others strongly advocate for "First Nation people" (Heilbron & Guttman, 2000). Other terms used across North America include American Indian, Native People, and Indigenous or Aboriginal People. While groups are lumped together for statistical purposes, they can be quite culturally diverse (as can particular nations). When describing Alaskan Natives, for example, little attention is given to the diversity of people comprising this group. Like many of the other racial/ethnic groups discussed in this section, preferences for labeling Native Americans call for naming their specific nation whenever possible.

The case study at the beginning of the chapter highlights the language revitalization efforts of the Menominee. While some Native American communities had separate linguistic systems, others were multilingual (Kroskrity, 2018). Today, tribal members speak English, Spanish, Navajo, Ojibwe, and more than 100 other languages (Pluralism Project, 2020b). They live in towns, cities, on farms, and on reservations. Native Americans have rich and complex traditions developed for various ceremonial and decision-making processes (Stromberg, 2006). While each tribe has distinct lifeways, there are some common characteristics (Pluralism Project, 2020a). An oral tradition is one—reliance on spoken transmission of story and enacting ritual knowledge. Religious traditions are generally oriented toward the land and the existence of a spirit world.

> Native ways of life are at once endangered and alive and well. They are endangered by the legacy of U.S. Indian policies that have reduced many Native people's experience of American history to little more than the dispossession of land, resources, and culture. The vast majority of Native American languages are endangered; many have become extinct. And yet this is also a moment of profound rebirth of Native languages, cultures, traditions, and lifeways, as Native peoples maintain both the privacy and secrecy of important ancient rites and simultaneously adapt to changing times by creating new forms of community life and ritual. (Pluralism Project, 2020c)

## THE POWER OF NONVERBAL CODES

In his book *The Silent Language*, Edward T. Hall (1959) discussed the great importance of recognizing verbal and nonverbal behaviors in intercultural communication contexts. We can easily talk about verbal and nonverbal language in similar terms, although some key differences exist (e.g., the sequenc-

Recognizing the ways that nonverbal communication behaviors, like touch and the use of intimate space, used by different racial and ethnic groups is an important part of communication competency.

ing of verbal exchanges as compared to the continuity of nonverbal cues). In this section, we provide some specific attention to the crucial role that nonverbal cues play alongside specific forms of language. Although the exact percentage is questioned, communication scholars agree that the majority of meaning when communicating is derived from nonverbal cues (Burgoon et al., 2021). Attempting to identify precise formulas by which meaning is created is an inexact science. However, the point of these studies is clear: The role that nonverbal cues play in interracial communication processes is crucial.

Nonverbal codes are all types of communicative cues that do not rely on words or other linguistic systems (like American Sign Language). Studying the power of nonverbal codes is crucial for a number of different reasons (Burgoon et al., 2021). First, unlike verbal codes, nonverbal communication is omnipresent—no form of human communication exists without some nonverbal codes. Second, nonverbal codes are multifunctional in that they can complement, contradict, enhance, emphasize, or replace verbal codes. Third, while some nonverbal codes are culturally specific, others serve as a universal language system that transcends cultural differences. Fourth, when verbal and nonverbal codes contradict one another, people tend to believe the messages that are communicated nonverbally. Fifth, and finally, it is important to recognize the importance of nonverbal codes because they get significantly less attention compared to verbal codes. Formal classes or training in nonverbal communication is not the norm, but we typically get comprehensive instruction about verbal communication across educational experiences. Some might suggest that being nonverbally illiterate is even more problematic than being verbally illiterate.

## Types of Nonverbal Codes

Nonverbal codes are best understood in terms of the different forms that they take. When people think about nonverbal communication, most immediately focus on body movements or gestures (what communications scholars refer to as **kinesics**). Kinesics encompass all of the ways in which we use our hands, fingers arms, legs, and posture when communicating. They also include the various ways in which we use facial expressions and head movements. Think about how important kinesics are to communicate emotions that you and others are feeling. Generally speaking, the face is a good source for interpreting how someone is feeling, and the body gives us an indication as to how intense those feelings are. **Vocalics**, or paralanguage, are a second type of nonverbal code and include any vocal-auditory behavior except for spoken words (e.g., pitch, volume, tone, pauses, laughter, and sarcasm). This type of nonverbal code is also important in communicating emotions.

**Proxemics** (use of space) and **haptics** (use of touch) are two other types of nonverbal codes. The way that individuals use space and touch communicate a great deal. In terms of space, we typically examine the amount and use of space to get information about personal, social, and professional status and power. We also use proxemics and haptics to discern the relationship status of individuals. Classic studies have demonstrated the importance of touch in human survival (Montagu, 1978). Touch can be affectionate, comforting, congratulatory, instrumental, playful, controlling, or abusive. Different racial, ethnic, and cultural groups may have different norms for how individuals use space and touch (see Box 3.8).

---

### Box 3.8                                                    *Research Highlight*

## Nonverbal Communication Expectations and Race

Expectancy Violations Theory (EVT), the culmination of work by Judee Burgoon and others, offers a productive framework to understand the important role that individual, racial, and cultural expectations play within different interactions (Burgoon et al., 2021). The core idea of EVT is that our communication is informed by the expectations that we have coming into an interaction. These expectations are based on one's field of experience and can vary significantly from person to person and cultural group to cultural group. Regarding interracial communication, EVT helps competent communicators increase their understanding of expectations and how people respond when their expectations are violated.

Consider, for example, the research of L. Houston et al. (2018), who studied how one's expectations regarding customer service communication impacts overall satisfaction. The research team concluded that African Americans, in light of a history of mistreatment, had different expectations than did their European American counterparts—something that significantly impacted their assessment of authentic "service with a smile."

Can you generate a list of different communication expectations (e.g., greetings, eye contact, dress, touch, space) that might exist for people of different racial and ethnic backgrounds?

---

Three additional types of nonverbal cues can be grouped into place and time codes (Burgoon et al., 2021). **Environmental nonverbal codes** are those natural and human-made features of different settings. They can include temperature, lighting, furniture, colors, and materials used in construction/decoration. These things can have a significant impact on the type of interaction that occurs in different spaces. **Artifacts** refer to physical and personal objects that are used personally (e.g., clothes, jewelry) or spatially (e.g., objects in one's personal or professional space). While some artifacts are primarily functional or aesthetic, the choice of particular objects can communicate a lot about a person. Think, for example, about how some people choose artifacts that highlight different aspects of their racial and/or ethnic cultures. The final type of nonverbal code involves how we use time to communicate nonverbally; this is known as **chronemics**. On a personal level, people's use of time can be used to communicate their power, status, or level of interest in a person or activity. On a cultural level, scholars have studied how different groups generally adopt monochronic (e.g., European Americans) or polychronic (e.g., African Ameri-

**Table 3.1    Guide to Perceptions of Interracial Verbal and Nonverbal Codes**

| Specific behavior | Likely ingroup perception | Possible outgroup perception |
|---|---|---|
| Avoidance of direct eye contact by Latinx people | Used to communicate attentiveness or respect | A sign of inattentiveness; direct eye contact is preferred |
| An African American who aggressively challenges a point of disagreement | Acceptable means of dialogue; not regarded as verbal abuse or a precursor to violence | Arguments are viewed as inappropriate and a sign of potential immediate violence |
| Asian American use of finger gestures to beckon others | Appropriate if used by adults for children, but highly offensive if used to call adults | Appropriate gesture to use with both children and adults |
| Interruptions used by African Americans | Tolerated in individual/group discussions; attention is given to most assertive voice | Perceived as rude or aggressive; clear rules for turn taking must be maintained |
| Silence used by Native Americans | A sign of respect, thoughtfulness, and/or uncertainty/ambiguity | Silence indicates boredom, disagreement, or a refusal to participate/respond |
| The use of touch by Latinx people | Perceived as normal and appropriate for interpersonal interactions | Deemed as appropriate for some intimate or friendly interactions; otherwise perceived as a violation of personal space |
| Public displays of intense emotions by African Americans | Personal expressiveness is valued and regarded as appropriate in most settings | Violates U.S. societal expectations for self-controlled public behaviors; inappropriate for most public settings |
| Same-sex Asian American friends touching or holding hands | Seen as acceptable behavior that signifies closeness of platonic relationships | Perceived as inappropriate, especially for male friends |
| Latinx use of lengthy greetings or the exchange of pleasantries prior to business meetings | Regarded as an important element of establishing rapport with colleagues. | Seen as a waste of time; getting to the business at hand is valued. |

cans) time orientations (E. T. Hall, 1983). Time is compartmentalized and linear in monochronic cultures; one event follows another. Schedules, punctuality, and precision are valued. In polychronic cultures, events happen simultaneously; relationships are valued over scheduling, and time is more flexible. While these generalizations do not apply to all individuals in a particular racial group, they do help explain some racial misunderstandings when one person believes that being on time for pre-planned activities is more important than having flexibility so that personal relationships are prioritized over existing time constraints.

In the next section, we highlight a specific theory that provides a useful framework for understanding how distinct communication systems, including verbal and nonverbal codes and rules and values that dictate their usage, may exist for different racial and ethnic groups.

## Speech Community Theory

Speech community theory, also known as the ethnography of communication and speech codes theory, is useful in explaining the communication systems that exist within different racial and ethnic groups (Philipsen, 1997). According to Labov (1972), a **speech community** exists when a group of people understands goals and styles of communication in ways not shared by people outside of the group. In terms of interracial communication, speech community theory is useful for interactions with people with different language systems (e.g., a Spanish-speaking Cuban American and a Chinese-speaking Chinese American). It is also useful for those who use the same language (e.g., Spanish) but whose racial/ethnic groups have a different set of speech codes (e.g., a Spanish American and Mexican American). Simply put, speech community theory focuses on how different cultural groups (including those defined by racial/ ethnic differences) instill within their members distinct styles of communicating and interpreting the communication of others. Some instances of problematic interracial communication can be traced to a misunderstanding of the other person's speech code. Carbaugh (1999), for instance, presents an interesting analysis of how European Americans oftentimes misunderstand Native American speech codes, like those of the Blackfeet (see also Covarrubias, 2008).

Speech community theory is grounded in four assumptions (Philipsen, 1997). First, members of cultural communities create shared meaning among themselves. These communities are oftentimes defined by differences in language and geography, as well as other less visible boundaries. Second, communicators in any cultural group must coordinate their actions. Even though it may not be apparent to nonmembers, each speech code is guided by some order or system. Third, meanings and actions are particular to individual groups. During interracial interactions, attempts to understand another person's communication by using your own cultural norms may be ineffective. Fourth, each cultural community has a set of distinct resources for assigning meaning to its actions. Not only are patterns of communication different among some racial/ethnic groups but each group may also have its own set of meanings with which to understand its own codes.

Within the field of communication, this theoretical framework has proven instrumental in understanding how people from different cultural groups follow different sets of communication rules. For instance, Edgerly (2011) analyzed language choices in the wake of Hurricane Katrina. She studied hundreds of mass media texts to reveal how certain cultural codes—"refugee" vs. "citizen"—were used to reflect a discourse of difference when describing different persons. Homsey and Sandel (2012) examined the speech code of food and tradition within a Lebanese American community in the central United States. Based on ethnographic observations and in-depth interviews, these researchers identified Lebanese community speech codes that are gendered, generational, and steeped in tradition.

In short, speech community theory offers a valuable perspective on the communication styles of different racial/ethnic groups, helping us recognize the variations that exist in speech codes within and across groups.

## Understanding in the Context of Verbal and Nonverbal Codes

Oftentimes, people with little experience in intergroup relations desire a quick, easy, and foolproof list of the "dos and don'ts" for communicating with others who are racially or ethnically different. We have made a conscious attempt to avoid such a simplistic treatment of the complex issues related to interracial communication. We are often approached by colleagues, students, and others who are seeking insight into an interracial communication problem. Typically, they offer a brief summary of a problematic interracial case scenario and then ask the supposedly simple question, "What should I do?" We have found that, in almost all cases, there is never a simple answer to these types of inquiries. Most of the time, the best response we can come up with is, "It depends. . . ." Past experiences reveal that the most productive way to help people deal with interracial conflict is to provide some applied research guidelines to help them gain a more complete understanding of what they perceive as a relatively simple problem.

One of the most important considerations in choosing appropriate/effective language centers around the specific relationship between the parties involved, as well as the particular situational context. Where did the interaction take place? Who was present during the interaction? How well do you know the individuals? What past experiences do you share with one another? What do you (they) know about their (your) lived experiences? Within what relationship is the interaction enacted (classmates, coworkers, friends, acquaintances, strangers)? One basic axiom states that communication has both a content and relationship dimension. Within our discussion here, this axiom can be used to understand that certain verbal cues (content) will have varying meanings and effects depending on the status (relationship) of the parties involved. For instance, research has indicated that African American women often take offense when European American women assume a position of familiarity with their verbal codes (i.e., "Hey, girl, how are you?") in their interactions, which they perceive as premature (Orbe et al., 2002; Scott, 2016).

| Box 3.9 | Student Reflections |
|---|---|

### An Unusual Mix

I come from a family that is half Middle Eastern and half Irish. There seem to be very few people who have this mix; in fact, I have yet to meet any. My mother is the Irish person, and my father is Middle Eastern, Chaldean to be exact. In short, Chaldeans are Catholic Iraqis, and many left Iraq in search of a more culturally accepting environment being that they were often mistreated for practicing Christianity rather than Muslim traditions. My mother and father were engaged, but my father's family didn't want to accept my mother because she was a "white girl"—they wanted him to marry a Chaldean woman. My parents ended up getting married in Las Vegas, alone, because no one would come to their wedding.

This line of reasoning is also useful in offering insight into the importance of recognizing cultural ownership of certain verbal cues and the nonverbal codes that help shape meaning. Because of shared cultural experiences and an acknowledged relationship status, two members of a particular racial/ethnic group may use language that is appropriate between them but highly inappropriate when others (ingroup and especially outgroup) use it. One example is when Filipino American men use "pinoy" (pee-noy) to describe one another but regard the term as derogatory when used by non-Filipinos (Sing, 1989). The use of different variations of the "n-word" also helps illustrate the idea of cultural ownership and how meaning is cocreated between individuals (Watts, 2016). This is an important consideration given that, among some African Americans, the term reflects positivity and unity of ingroup relations. They argue that current use of the term is a form of **reappropriating language** whereby Black people embrace a once-negative label and redefine it as a means of empowerment (H. Smith, 2019). Other African Americans argue that any form of the word, given its negative history, should not be used. Regardless of where individuals fall within the debate of ingroup use, clearly it represents a word extremely offensive when used by non-African Americans (Cemone et al., 2020).

Remember the important point that, despite particular language choices, scholars believe a majority of the meaning of a message is communicated nonverbally. This crucial element of interracial communication does not cancel the importance of making good language choices. However, it does assist us in recognizing the key role that nonverbal cues play within the negotiation of meaning between racially/ethnically diverse persons. An increased consciousness of the meanings that others attach to your nonverbal behaviors—especially given that nonverbal cues are used more unconsciously than verbal ones—is crucial to competent interracial communication.

The most competent communicators, particularly those who are committed to maintaining and strengthening intergroup relations, acknowledge **intentionality** as a key issue in their response to certain verbal and nonverbal codes they regard as inappropriate or offensive. The most competent responses for the same communication code may be drastically different for those individuals who are identified as "unconscious incompetents" (naive offenders) as opposed to those whose choices are more consciously offensive (Howell, 1982). For instance, would your response to a child's use of a racially offensive term be the same as your response if one of your professors used it? This is not to say that intentionality is necessarily more important than the effects that certain verbal and nonverbal codes have on interactions. However, it does evaluate the motive (or lack thereof) behind using certain terms.

## CONCLUSION

After reading this chapter, you should have an increased awareness of the importance of verbal and nonverbal messages in interracial communication. Throughout this chapter, as well as in the remainder of the text, we have made a conscious attempt to avoid what might result in a definitive laundry list regarding the most appropriate verbal and nonverbal codes to use with different groups. Instead, our discussion highlights the need to recognize the crucial role that language systems play in our everyday lives.

Several general guidelines summarize the central points of this chapter. Although these bits of advice offer quick points of reference for everyday interactions, they are best understood within the context of the additional information provided within this chapter. In brief, competent interracial communicators do the following:

- Recognize the role that power plays within language, labels, and issues of naming (including ingroup cultural ownership of certain terms and phrases).

- Make informed choices about the verbal and nonverbal codes they use in particular situational contexts *and* assume responsibility for their effects. Practice mindfulness!

- Develop a deep understanding of the similarities and differences of verbal and nonverbal coding systems within and between different groups.

- Seek out additional information when needed! If an appropriate relationship has been established, this may mean asking specific people of color their perceptions of particular verbal cues. It may also include using other means, such as books, videos, and/or other educational resources.

## KEY TERMS

| | |
|---|---|
| communicare | semantics of prejudice |
| homophily | societal privilege |
| arbitrary nature of words | linguistic profiling |
| message orientation approach | multiracial Americans |
| Sapir-Whorf hypothesis | kinesics |

vocalics                                    artifacts
proxemics                                   chronemics
haptics                                     reappropriating language
environmental nonverbal codes

## OPPORTUNITIES FOR EXTENDED LEARNING

1. In order to gain a more personal understanding of the associative power of labels and names, visit the website for Project Implicit. (http://implicit.harvard.edu/implicit/). Click on one of the options for social attitudes. When you reach the list of Implicit Association Tests, choose "Race IAT." After taking the test, discuss your impressions of it with your friends, family, and classmates.

2. Take some time to learn more about how race impacts language. Similar to spoken languages, sign languages also have different dialects. Black American Sign Language (ASL) is the unique dialect that developed historically within segregated African American Deaf communities. Largely unknown to outsiders, Black ASL has become a symbol of solidarity and a vital part of identity within the Black deaf community. Learn more about this topic by watching a video from a recent documentary project, https://www.youtube.com/watch?v=oiLltM1tJ9M

3. Throughout the text, we've highlighted both author and student reflections to "personalize" the topics of each chapter. Peruse the different concepts in this chapter and write your own personal reflection about a particular experience, thoughts on a concept or issue, or a critique of a specific research finding.

4. Professor David Weber (2016) writes that an important component of his identity is being Jewish. He laces his comments to his primarily Protestant students with Yiddish expressions: "Put some *schmaltz* (i.e., personal warmth) into your oral reports!"; "Get started early on your essay, or you'll end up with *chozzeri* (junk) on the page" (p. 156). Some Yiddish words (e.g., "shmuck" meaning jerk or prick, and "schlep" meaning to drag or haul) have made their way into the general vocabulary of the larger population. Can you think of other terms, once specific to a particular racial or ethnic group, that have become a part of the general U.S. American vocabulary? Generate at least a couple of terms from each group highlighted in this chapter, using internet resources if necessary. Were you aware of the origins of all of these terms?

5. Generate a list of responses to the following sentence: "I find it offensive when I hear (*name of specific group*) using terms and phrases like (*name specific utterances*), because . . ." Share your responses with others. Is there a general agreement among people who are racially like and unlike you? Why or why not? How do your findings compare with the research shared throughout this chapter?

6. In small groups, brainstorm a list of labels, names, and terms used to describe the different racial and ethnic groups highlighted in this chapter

(African Americans, Asian Americans, Jewish Americans, Latinx Americans, Arab Americans, multiracial Americans, and Native Americans). Once a substantial list has been created, work as a group to place the terms on a "positive . . . neutral . . . negative" continuum. Following the activity, discuss patterns that emerged across the names for different racial and ethnic groups. For instance, did you notice many more negative labels than positive ones for most, if not all, groups? What does this tell us about how our language has shaped our sense of race and ethnicity in the United States?

7. Review the different perceptions of nonverbal behavior listed in Table 3.1. Then conduct some research—through one-on-one interviews, focus group discussions, on-line resources, etc.—and generate additional entries for different racial and ethnic groups. For instance, you might include some nonverbal behaviors for Arab Americans (e.g., primarily using their right hand and sitting in ways that the soles of their shoes/feet cannot be seen) that can have distinctly different ingroup and outgroup perceptions.

## RECOMMENDED CONTEMPORARY READINGS

Bishop, S. C. (2021). "What does a torture survivor look like?" Nonverbal communication in US asylum interviews and hearings. *Journal of International and Intercultural Communication.* doi.org/10.1080/17513057.2021.1881146

Buerkle, C. W. (2019). Adam mansplains everything: White-hipster masculinity as covert hegemony. *Southern Communication Journal, 84*(3), 170–182. doi.org/10.1080/1041794X.2019.1575898

Eschmann, R. (2020). Digital resistance: How online communication facilitates responses to racial microaggressions. *Sociology of Race and Ethnicity, 7*(2), 264–277. doi.org/10.1177/2332649220933307

Hamel, L. M., Moulder, R., Harper, F., Penner, L. A., Albrecht, T. L., & Eggly, S. (2020). Examining the dynamic nature of nonverbal communication between Black patients with cancer and their oncologists. *Cancer: Journal of the American Cancer Society, 127*(7), 1080–1090.

Marino, M. I., Bilge, N., Gutsche, R. E., & Holt, L. (2020). Who is credible (and where?): Using virtual reality to examine credibility and bias of perceived race/ethnicity in urban/suburban environments. *Howard Journal of Communications, 31*(3), 297–315. doi.org/10.1080/10646175.2020.1714514

Wong, T. S.-T. (2021). Crazy, rich, when Asian: Yellowface ambivalence and mockery in *Crazy Rich Asians. Journal of International and Intercultural Communication.* doi.org/10.1080/17513057.2020.1857426

# 4

# Racial and Ethnic Identity Negotiation

CASE STUDY        A New Age of Racial Discrimination
                          in the United States

In April 2017, a 19-year veteran police officer sued the city of Hastings (Michigan) for racial harassment and discrimination. In the lawsuit, Cleon Brown reported that other police officers, the police chief, and the town's mayor treated him differently because of his race. Allegedly, they called him "Kunta Kinte" (a character from the miniseries, *Roots*), mocked him by chanting "Black Lives Matter," greeted him with the Black Power fist salute, and continually made racially insensitive jokes. After initially complaining, he was bullied, shunned, excluded from mandatory training, and denied important information regarding police matters. After filing a $500,000 lawsuit through the Michigan Department of Civil Rights, the case was settled in 2018 without an admission of guilt from the city. In the end, Brown received a $65,000 settlement and resigned after his paid suspension ran out.

The case of Cleon Brown gained national attention—not because of the uniqueness of the alleged incidents but because Cleon Brown is a white man whose ancestry.com results reported that he was 18% African. The mistreatment, according to Brown, started after he shared the news with coworkers. The reactions appear consistent with other responses by European Americans to similar results from popular genetic tests (see Putman & Kvam, 2021). What are your thoughts about the merit of Brown's case? Do you think that the outcome was fair given that it involved white officers harassing and discriminating against another white officer in an all-white, small-town police department? Do you think that the outcome would have been different if Brown was a Black officer in the department? What role, if any, do you think that white privilege played in this case? Box 4.5 provides additional insight about the issue of genetic ancestral testing.

*Source*: Rojas, N. (2018, August 1). White police officer receives $65,000 settlement from city in racial discrimination suit. *Newsweek*. https://www.newsweek.com/cleon-brown-hastings-police-michigan-racial-discrimination-settlement-1052977

S ince the early 20th century, the topic of identity has been of great interest to scholars, especially those in social psychology and communication (Y. Kim, 2007). Within the field of intercultural communication generally, and interracial communication more specifically, identity research has experienced significant growth since the late 1980s. According to Cupach and Imahori (1993), identity is "self-conception—one's theory of oneself" (p. 113) and is studied from two contrasting views. The first focuses on discovering one's true self, typically through gradual stages of identity development. The second approach understands identity as a process, more of a verb than a noun. As articulated by Bardhan and Orbe (2012), this view sees identity negotiation as a matter of *becoming* and *being*. In this chapter, we provide explanations of both approaches as a means to increase your understanding of how identity development and negotiation impact communication in both explicit and implicit ways.

Some have described the United States as having a general preoccupation with identity issues (Field & Travisano, 1984; Tanno & Gonzalez, 1998). According to other scholars, cultural identities are bound to get more, rather than less, complex in the 21st century (Bardhan & Orbe, 2012). A good place to begin any discussion on racial/ethnic/cultural identity (the topic of both Chapters 4 and 5) is with some honest, straightforward self-assessment. How would you describe your cultural identity? What aspects of "who you are" come to mind quickly? (The exercise in Box 4.1 will help with your assessment.) How do these characteristics and/or roles reflect how you define "culture"? Is your response to this line of inquiry relatively easy, extremely difficult, or somewhere between the two? Have there been events in your life that triggered a search for a deeper understanding of your cultural identity? How comfortable do you feel identifying one specific aspect of your cultural identity as most central to who you are?

This chapter provides some detailed descriptions of theoretical frameworks that explain how racial/ethnic identities, as well as perceptions of racially/ethnically diverse others, are negotiated over time (R. Jackson et al., 2020).

---

**Box 4.1**                                                    *Who Am I?*

### An Exercise to Discover Your Identity

A common exercise used to help people self-assess their identity is known as the "Who Am I?" exercise (e.g., Kuhn & McPartland, 1954). Before reading any further, take a few minutes to reflect on how you define yourself. On the left side of a piece of paper, jot down "I am" 20 times. Then take a few minutes and complete each statement. Do this with the assumption that no one will see your list. The key is not to take a lot of time on this exercise. Just write down what pops into your mind in the order it occurs to you. Do not continue reading until you have completed this exercise.

Take a minute to read through your list and reflect on the descriptors that you provided to the question, "Who am I?" Pay attention to the types of responses you used to complete the sentences.

- How many of your items represent specific roles that you play in life (e.g., student, friend, mother/father, daughter/son)?

- Do other items refer to aspects of cultural groups to which you belong (e.g., women, Asian American, Generation X, LGBTQ+) and/or personal characteristics (e.g., handsome, intelligent, caring, aggressive)?

- Scholars suggest that the ordering of statements may also be significant in identifying a hierarchy of the most important aspects of your personal/cultural identity (Kuhn & McPartland, 1954). For instance, are the responses at the top of your list the most central to who you are?

- How might your list have changed given a different time, location, and set of consequences?

- If prompted, could you articulate why you listed the particular characteristics in the order they appear?

Although the information will not directly answer any of the questions just listed for any particular person, it will help you understand your own particular cultural standpoint. The first portion of this chapter details the stages that specific racial/ethnic group members experience as they form their particular racial/ethnic identities. Much of this information comes from the fields of social psychology. The remainder of the chapter presents sociological and communication frameworks that highlight the relational aspects of identity negotiation.

## APPROACHES TO STUDYING IDENTITY

The concept of identity is universal. Nevertheless, the way in which personal/cultural identities are played out in different cultures varies (Geertz, 1976). Research on how individuals come to understand who they are has generated a significant amount of information regarding what has been established as a complex, intricate, lifelong process (Moss & Faux, 2006). Much of the work on identity development has focused on how young children and adolescents engage in the process of formulating personal/cultural identities.

Most notable in the existing literature is the influence of Erik Erikson, whose work provides a framework for human development across the entire lifespan (Maree, 2021). According to Erikson (1963), the major task of adolescence is establishing an independent identity. Central to his ideas about identity formation is the recognition that individuals move through a series of interrelated stages in their psychosocial development. Each stage involves a particular aspect of identity crisis. Individuals are able to move to another stage by resolving issues related to current stages. This foundational work highlighted how culture, race, and ethnicity shape identity. In fact, Erikson's research explored both between-group and within-group comparisons of different racial and ethnic groups (Syed & Fish, 2018). Social science theorists have applied these fundamental ideas to a number of contexts, including the construction of ethnic minority identity in contemporary Chile (Merino & Tileaga, 2011), young Arab males (Khakimova et al., 2012), and African American adolescents (Floyd, 2010). In doing so, they extend Erikson's strong structural perspective—one which examines how historical, social, and political contexts interact with individual identity development (Syed & Fish, 2018).

## CULTURAL IDENTITY DEVELOPMENT MODELS

Scholars from multiple disciplines (communication, education, psychology, and sociology) have created a variety of models that help us understand how cultural identity is developed over time. These models are grounded in the work of Erikson (1963) and others and provide insight into the development and negotiation of personal identity in the context of societal categories. According to Phinney (1993), the formation of cultural identity generally involves three phases: (1) unexamined cultural identity, (2) cultural identity search, and (3) cultural identity achievement. Following a description of each of these identity formation components, we turn to the specific ways that scholars have described how macrocultural and microcultural group members (including those persons identifying as biracial) form their racial identities. As you will see, all of the existing racial identity development models (e.g., J. Banks, 1976; Hardiman, 1994; Helms, 1994; B. Jackson & Hardiman, 1983; Ponterotto & Pedersen, 1993) reflect Phinney's three general phases.

During the first stage of cultural identity formation, we function in society with an *unexamined cultural identity*. We take our cultural values, norms, beliefs, customs, and other characteristics for granted. Our culture is experienced as "natural" and generates little interest. Minoritized group members tend to become aware of racial differences and identities earlier than persons of European descent (M. Bell, 2021; Nance & Foeman, 2002). Even so, many children

Racial and ethnic identity development begins fairly early in life, typically as children enter their school-age years. An unexamined cultural identity may last longer, however, depending on a number of factors.

experience their early years from an unexamined cultural identity standpoint. At some point, however, something triggers a move into the next stage (*cultural identity search*). Typically, this shift can be caused by conflicting messages from family, friends, social organizations, or the media about race and ethnicity issues. Searching for our cultural identity involves an ongoing process of exploration, reflection, and evaluation. For some of us, this is completed in our young adult years. For others, it takes longer. Within the final stage of *cultural identity achievement*, we develop a clear, confident understanding and acceptance of ourselves. Subsequently, we internalize a strong cultural identity. Although this element is apparent in each of the racial identity development models we describe later in this chapter, one crucial element must be acknowledged: Our cultural identities are not static, fixed, or enduring. Instead, our identities are dynamic and subject to change over the course of our lives (Maree, 2021).

Identity formation, along these lines, is best seen as "becoming" rather than "being" (Sarup, 1996). The racial identity development models discussed here take on a linear, unidimensional form (R. Miller & Rotheram-Borus, 1994). Still, we must not oversimplify the complex ways that cultural identity is developed. Seldom does it occur in a neat, orderly fashion. Although some of us experience a straightforward progression of identity formation—moving from an unexamined state to an identity search and concluding with a clear sense of identity achievement—most eventually experience a "recycling" of stages based on new experiences (Helms, 1994). Because of this, the process of identity formation is more like a spiraling loop than a straight line.

Phinney's (1993) three general stages of cultural identity formation apply generically to all persons. Given the history of race in the United States (see Chapter 2), it should come as no surprise that the process racial/ethnic micro-cultural and macrocultural group members use to form their identities is similar yet different (Hughes et al., 2006). U.S. Americans of European descent create their identities within a dominant society that affirms the value of their culture (M. Bell, 2021). Persons of color within the United States, in contrast, must deal with social norms that define their life experiences as "sub-cultural." Because of this reality, microcultural and macrocultural group identity formation processes differ. People of color must form their racial identities within a larger society that does not necessarily value the same things. For example, think about how our society defines standards of beauty. Traditionally, beauty has been defined through European American standards in terms of skin color, hair texture, body shape, and facial features (Fujioka et al., 2009; R. Hall, 2013). How do you think identities are formed for individuals who do not match these standards? Without question, all persons are affected by these standards. However, you can see how the effects are different for people of color whose cultural standards contradict those of the microculture.

## Understanding Whiteness

The color of a person's skin holds social significance in the United States (Wander et al., 1999). Historically, much of the research and self-reflection related to race and racism has focused on experiences of racial/ethnic micro-cultures. Because European Americans were in the majority, their culture was less visible than others (Whitehead & Lerner, 2009) who seemed deviant and in the minority. Being "white" was a sign of normalcy, importance, or privilege (in that it is viewed as the standard to which other racial categories are compared). This perception exists in interpersonal, organizational, and mass-mediated contexts (Drew, 2011). This idea is not limited to race and ethnicity, though. Other macrocultures have also benefited from their majority status. Their experiences (e.g., heterosexuality, able-bodied, masculinity) have also remained unnamed and uninvestigated compared to those of specific microcultures.

**Whiteness**, by definition, is a "social construction which produces race privilege for white people by appearing 'neutral,' unlinked to racial politics, universal, and unmarked" (Rowe & Malhotra, 2006, p. 168). Studies that explore whiteness have increased tremendously in the past 10 years (D. McIntosh et al., 2018) and promise to continue to grow in the future (Nakayama, 2017). The interest in talking about whiteness has been seen in academic fields such as sociology, English, education, women's studies, and communication. We think it is important to address whiteness here before our discussions on racial/ethnic identity development. Based on our experiences and those of our colleagues across the United States, we have come to realize that many European Americans do not see themselves as cultural, racialized beings (M. Bell, 2021). Because of their relative privilege, they are more likely to focus on the cultures of other racial/ethnic groups. Therefore, when asked about their cultural identity, most European Americans struggle with understanding their whiteness as a racial entity. Some students even felt silly or embarrassed identifying themselves as "white people." This is because whiteness is an invisible social force that facilitates people of European descent as seeing themselves as "unraced" (A. Miller & Harris, 2005).

By naming and exploring European American culture, whiteness studies play an important part in competent interracial communication research and practice (Rowe & Malhotra, 2006). First, studying whiteness fosters an increased awareness of how race and racism shape the lives of European Americans (Frankenberg, 1993); it also confronts the idea of white racelessness (M. Bell, 2021). It helps all of us to view communication as a racialized process—meaning that our communication is structured by larger societal racial dynamics. Second, understanding whiteness sharpens our awareness of how racial categorization is used to reinforce old hierarchies in which some races are more superior than others (see Chapter 2). It also helps us recognize how whiteness signals dominance, normalcy, and privilege (rather than subordination, deviancy, and disadvantage) in the United States (Frankenberg, 1993). Finally, whiteness studies also assign each person a role in race relations. No longer can European Americans sit by the sidelines in discussions of race and racism. Naming and understanding their whiteness means they, as much as people of color, have a stake in issues related to race. In this regard, a critical attention to whiteness, and working to productively negotiate the privileges that come with it, is part of a larger attempt to better inform race relations (J. Warren & Hytten, 2004).

In short, whiteness studies enable us to advance our understanding of European American culture beyond that of a normalized and raceless category. Understanding whiteness helps us recognize how race shapes European Americans' lives (M. Bell, 2021). As this growing body of research develops, other important insights are gained. For instance, D. McIntosh et al. (2018) advance studies on whiteness in innovative ways. In particular, they study the role that communication plays in forming this aspect of social identity. Their edited book also points to an important aspect of this line of research: Understanding whiteness requires us to see how it relates to other aspects of a person's cultural identity. In other words, whiteness is not the only—or necessarily the most important—cultural marker we need to recognize. In addition, it is not static but continues to change over time (Nakayama, 2017). As such, we must increase our understanding of whiteness and how it intersects with other cultural elements, like socioeconomic status (Engen, 2016; Lawless, 2016), to inform a person's lived experiences (Frankenberg, 1993) (see Chapter 5). Next, we focus our attention on how the social identity of whiteness is developed.

## Macrocultural Identity Development Model

Ever since the work of Erik Erikson (1963), scholars have been interested in the concept of identity development. Over time, the focus of identity development models has moved from more generic stages to those specific to particular macrocultural and microcultural group experiences (see Table 4.1). Several majority identity development models (e.g., Hardiman, 1994; Helms, 1994) contain conceptually similar stages. We offer a brief description of Janet Helms's (1990, 1994) model because it is one of the most comprehensive.

In order to increase our awareness of how European Americans formulate their racial/ethnic identities, Helms outlines six specific stages: contact, disintegration, reintegration, pseudo-independence, immersion/emersion, and autonomy. The first stage in Helms's model is **contact**. Within this stage, European Americans' self-perception does not include any element of being a member of the "white race." Instead, they assume that racial/ethnic differences are best understood as differences in individuals' personalities. European American perceptions are guided by minimal knowledge of other racial/ethnic groups, which may result in behaviors that are naive, timid, and/or potentially offensive (Helms, 1990).

Within the second stage of **disintegration**, European Americans acknowledge that prejudice, discrimination, and racism exist and are forced to view themselves as dominant group members. Typical reactions at this stage include experiencing overwhelming feelings of guilt and confusion, seeing oneself as less prejudiced than other European Americans, or proudly protecting microcultural group members from negative interactions with "white bigots." In the **reintegration** stage, European Americans tend to focus less on themselves in comparison to microcultural group members and more on themselves as a member of the "white race." They may deny any responsibility for the social problems experienced by people of color.

## Minority Sympathy

Basically, I feel for minorities. I go out of my way to help those who are racially different from myself and try to pay more attention to them than, say, my fellow white Americans. Because I think most minorities have a tough hill to climb just to get on the same playing field as most whites. It sucks to say, but I view minorities as being disadvantaged, and I am quick to give them my sympathy. I think this is where my problem lies. Although some might not mind some sympathy now and then, some I'm sure don't need my sympathy and, frankly, don't want it. Fact is, though, I have few minority friends, if any. . . . Why is that so?

The fourth stage of majority group identity development is **pseudo-independence**, in which European Americans unintentionally believe their culture is more advanced and civilized than others. Within this stage, individuals accept people of color as a whole and become interested in helping them become successful in society. Consciously or unconsciously, however, the underlying assumption is that "successful" means becoming more like European Americans (Helms, 1990). Distinguishing the fifth stage of Helms's model, **immersion/emersion**, from the fourth stage (pseudo-independence) can be quite subtle. The basic difference is that European Americans in the pseudo-independence stage blame problems experienced by racial/ethnic group members on the group. In comparison, those at the immersion/emersion stage recognize that European Americans contribute to the problems. Most individuals, according to Helms (1994), do not advance to this stage of majority identity development.

The final stage of European American Identity development is **autonomy**. According to Helms (1994), this is the "stage in which the person attempts to interact with the world and commune with himself or herself from a positive, [w]hite, non-racist perspective" (p. 87). European Americans at this sixth stage are committed to working toward what they see as a nonracist position. Continual involvement in life experiences move them to this ideal.

## Microcultural Identity Development Model

As indicated by Table 4.1, various models describe the process of how microcultures (e.g., African Americans, Native Americans, Asian Americans, Arab Americans, and Latinx Americans) form their racial/ethnic identities (see also Cross, 2017). Each of these models overlaps considerably with other existing frameworks. The table lists four models of microcultural identity development, and recent research in this area continues to highlight that processes differ for African Americans and other people of color (e.g., Davis et al., 2010; Endale et al., 2018).

The model of racial-ethnic identity development by Phinney (1993) has been foundational to present-day understanding (Cross, 2017). According to

**Table 4.1    A Sampling of Racial Identity Development Models**

| Members of Microcultural Groups | Members of Macrocultural Groups | Multiracial Persons |
| --- | --- | --- |
| *J. A. Banks, 1976* | *Hardiman, 1994* | *J. H. Jacobs, 1992* |
| Psychological captivity | Unexamined identity | Pre-color constancy |
| Encapsulation | Acceptance | Racial ambivalence |
| Identity clarification | Resistance | Biracial identity |
| Biethnicity | Redefinition | |
| Multiethnicity | Immersion/emersion | |
| | Autonomy | |
| *B. W. Jackson & Hardiman, 1983* | *Helms, 1990, 1994* | *Kich, 1992* |
| Acceptance | Contact | Awareness of differentness |
| Resistance | Disintegration | Struggle for acceptance |
| Redefinition | Reintegration | Self-acceptance and assertion |
| Internalization | Pseudo-independence | |
| | Immersion/emersion | |
| | Autonomy | |
| *Phinney, 1993* | | *Poston, 1990* |
| Unexamined identity | | Personal identity |
| Conformity | | Choice of group categorization |
| Resistance/separation | | Enmeshment/denial |
| Integration | | Appreciation |
| | | Integration |
| *Ponterotto & Pedersen, 1993* | | |
| Dissonance | | |
| Resistance/denial | | |
| Introspection | | |
| Synergetic articulation | | |

Phinney (1993), the identity development process for U.S. racial/ethnic micro-cultural group members involves four stages: unexamined identity, conformity, resistance/separation, and integration. Note that a person does not typically arrive at the final stage and remain at that level for the rest of their life. Instead, people experience a recycling of stages as they engage in the process of dealing with life changes within their current sense of identity (B. Jackson & Hardiman, 1983). Because of this, the experience of identity formation is best understood as a series of continuous loops rather than a straight line. Phinney (1993) describes the first stage in this process as **unexamined identity**, a period of a microcultural group member's life with little or no exploration of racial/ethnic background. During this stage, individuals may have an extremely low awareness of their cultural heritage, often because of a lack of interest in particular cultural values, norms, language, and other elements.

The second stage (**conformity**) involves accepting and internalizing dominant group perspectives. For some people of color, this stage may include accepting negative group stereotypes (B. Jackson & Hardiman, 1983), which results in an intense desire to try and adopt the values of European American culture (Phinney, 1993). Each racial/ethnic group has ingroup terms that describe those in the conformity stage (e.g., an African American who is labeled as an "oreo"). J. Banks (1976), in his research on minority identity development, uses a particular phrase to convey this concept: "psychological captivity" (p. 191). He attributes the process of internalizing negative beliefs about one's own racial/ethnic group to self-rejection and low self-esteem. Stage 3, **resistance and separation**, typically begins when individuals experience some tension when trying to understand themselves in the midst of ingroup and outgroup cultural perceptions. It is difficult to determine exactly when stage 2 dissolves and stage 3 begins. Much of this process depends on when (if) a person of color begins to think critically about macrocultural values versus a microcultural standpoint. Once this process has started, however, the sense of resistance to Eurocentric perspectives grows more intense. Oftentimes this leads a person to search for an increased understanding of racial/ethnic group histories. The result is the development of an extreme sense of pride based on the significant accomplishments of other racial/ethnic group members, more open challenges to racism, and a conscious attempt to separate oneself from European Americans.

While the image of a "model minority" seems like a positive portrayal of Asian Americans, it is limiting to a large, diverse group of people who may or may not adhere to the stereotype.

Another important aspect of stage 3 is the initial transition that occurs between old identities (informed by outgroup cultural perspectives) and new ones (encouraged by a greater awareness of racial/ethnic pride). This process of identity transformation is continued in the fourth stage of microcultural identity development, **integration** (Phinney, 1993). The basic issue involves achieving a public racial/ethnic identity that is consistent with one's inner sense of self (B. Jackson & Hardiman, 1983). The ultimate outcome of this final stage of microcultural identity development is internalizing a confident and secure racial/ethnic identity, a key component of well-being and psychological health (Nelson et al., 2018; Willis & Neblett, 2020).

The next section deals specifically with how persons with more than one racial/ethnic heritage formulate their identities. Based on the descriptions provided earlier, you will be able to understand how bi-/multiracial identity development models are similar to, yet different from, Phinney's (1993) microcultural identity development model.

## Multiracial Identity Development Model

As noted in the previous chapter, the number of individuals in the United States identifying with more than one racial group is on the rise—the fastest growing racial group in 2020. Historically being "biracial" typically meant that a person had one African American and one European American parent; however, contemporary use of the term (and its more contemporary counterpart, "multiracial") reflects a great array of racial combinations (Saulny, 2011).

Identity development for biracial and multiracial people is unique. First, unlike microcultural and macrocultural based models, multiracial identity has no clear-cut ultimate outcome (Nance & Foeman, 2002). Because their identities do not fit into simple categories, the last stage in identity formation may be ambiguous and tentative. Second, existing models do not allow for several racial/ethnic identities simultaneously. Multiracial individuals typically have been forced to "choose" one over the other (Moreman, 2011; Poston, 1990). In reality, these persons may identify with one group, both groups, an emergent group (multiracial community), or all three simultaneously (Orbe, 2012). For some multiracial persons, self-identities may even change depending on the specific situational context (T. Harris, 2016; Kellogg & Liddell, 2012). Third, research indicates that the multiracial identity development takes on an even greater spiraling process when compared to the creation of monoracial identities (S. Alexander, 1994; Herring, 1994). Evidence shows that many biracial individuals repeat earlier stages as they mature (Nance & Foeman, 2002) and develop different peer groups (Kellogg & Liddell, 2012). This ongoing process is typically experienced with great intensity, awareness, and a sense of purpose

### "I'm Not Just One Race, but Two"

I have been told by others that I look Indian, Native American, Black, and biracial. My dad is Black, and my mom is Irish and German, which makes me biracial. I see being both Black and white as having the best of both worlds; I'm not just one race but two. I think by being mixed I have different views and standpoints than others that are of just one race. I have had to grow up being both, trying to be my own person who is Black and who is white. I'm not trying to become someone who is Black or someone who is just white, but someone who is me. I get along with both races. I have more white friends, but that doesn't mean that I don't get along with or identify with the Black side of me. I see the world Black and white and not just one or the other.

(Herring, 1994). As such, multiracial identity continues to be studied by researchers in different fields through a number of methodological approaches (e.g., Young, 2015).

While a number of models of biracial and multiracial identity development exist, we have chosen one that focuses on the positive, unique aspects experienced by biracial individuals. Poston (1990) identified the first stage of identity development for multiracial people as **personal identity**. Individuals at this initial stage are relatively young. Membership in any particular racial/ethnic group is secondary to the sense of self that is somewhat independent of their racial/ethnic heritage. In other words, children do not see themselves in racially specific terms. Instead, their identity is informed more by personality elements than cultural ones (Cross, 2017). **Choice of group categorization** is the second stage in multiracial identity development. At this stage, individuals gain an increased awareness of their race/ethnic heritage and are pushed to choose one particular identity. Historically, research on the lived experiences of multiracial persons clearly indicates an external pressure for them to make a specific racial/ethnic choice (Funderburg, 1993). The choice made at this stage involves a number of interrelated factors, including demographics of home neighborhood, parental presence/style/influence, physical appearance, influence of peer groups, and support of social groups (Kellogg & Liddell, 2012; Rockquemore & Brunsma, 2002).

Poston's third stage is **enmeshment/denial**. Following the choices made in the previous phase, this stage is characterized by an emotional tension (e.g., confusion, guilt, or self-hatred) because claiming one identity may not fully express who they are. In many cases, a multiracial person feels that their identity choice makes it difficult to identify with both parents. This conflict can result in feelings of disloyalty, abandonment, and/or guilt (Sebring, 1985). A sense of **appreciation** for one's multiple racial/ethnic background occurs at the fourth stage of multiracial identity development. Poston (1990) describes individuals at this stage as attempting to learn more about all of the racial/ethnic cultures that make up who they are. Although an appreciation of diverse cultures exists, multiracial persons still primarily identify with one racial/ethnic identity (as determined by the earlier choice of group categorization). Within this stage, individuals recognize and value each aspect of their racial/ethnic identity. Through **integration**, individuals carve out an identity that reflects their complete selves. This was not the case in earlier stages where their identities were necessarily more fragmented and incomplete.

Researchers continue to rely on various identity developmental models (e.g., Cross, 2017; Floyd, 2010). Consistent with the dominant worldview of the United States and most other Western cultures, much of this work has tended to view identity as an individual entity (J. Yin, 2018). Consider, for example, "I think, therefore I am," the famous adage by Descartes. Compare that idea with the African (Ubuntu) philosophy of "I am because we are." The former focuses on an individualistic sense of self, whereas the latter highlights how one's identity cannot be separated from relationships with others. A significant portion of earlier research on identity focuses on the formation of a personal identity through autonomy and independence. More recent scholarship reflects the idea that identity is constantly negotiated in a variety of ways—and never really "achieved" (Bardhan & Orbe, 2012). In the next section, we highlight a variety of theories that reflect this principle, an approach that has great potential to provide insight into the ongoing process of racial and ethnic identity negotiation.

## THE CO-CREATION OF IDENTITY

For the purposes of this chapter, we identify ourselves as scholars who see the important role that both the individual and the relational serve in identity negotiation. We attest that identity development simultaneously involves personal (personality) characteristics and cultural identities associated with particular roles, reference groups, and sociocultural categories. The most productive lens through which to understand identity is as both an individual entity (representative of traditional psychological perspectives) *and* as a relational one (representative of social communication theory).

Wilmot (1995) provides three different paradigmatic views of the related concepts of self, other, and relationship. First is *individual selves loosely connected*, which emphasizes the self. This paradigm is common in individualistic cultures like in the United States. *Embedded self* is a second paradigm in which self is best understood within the context of relationships. The relationship itself is viewed as a separate identity. Finally, the third paradigm described by Wilmot is the *nonseparable self/other/relationship*. This paradigm explicitly challenges the very notion of a separate, identifiable self and other. Instead, it highlights how we come-into-being through our interactions with others so much so that discussing any one of the concepts (i.e., self, other, relationship) necessitates talking about all three collectively. Like Wilmot, we embrace the idea that a person's cultural identity develops through interaction with others—and that identity is continuously negotiated, not developed toward a particular outcome (Bardhan & Orbe, 2012). In this section, we highlight different theoretical frameworks that are based on the idea that identities are co-created through communication involving self, others, and society.

### Symbolic Interactionism

One of the most influential works in identity scholarship is *Mind, Self, and Society* (Mead, 1934). George Herbert Mead described the concept of self in terms of its direct relationship to various segments of social life. His work marks a shift from a focus on the self to one on the communication (symbolic interaction) between self and others. Although some communication scholars have identified problems associated with Mead's work (e.g., Tanno & Gonzalez, 1998), his attention to the important relationship between self-identity and social life highlights the central role that communication plays in identity formulation. In this regard, Mead's contributions inform the current perspectives of cultural identity development, especially those that appear in the literature associated with the field of communication. Mead's work is fundamental to the work of both the Chicago and Iowa schools on symbolic interactionism (Meltzer & Petras, 1970). The framework provided in this section draws from these schools of thought, in addition to more current scholarship on racial/ethnic identity development (e.g., R. Jackson et al., 2020) that sees identity formation as a co-created entity.

Simply put, cultural identities are co-created and re-created in everyday interactions (Yep, 2002). This general idea is grounded in Mead's work and subsequently strengthened by the advances of his students. For instance, Blumer (1969) championed the idea that the sense of self emerges from a process of definition/redefinition that occurs through social interaction. In other words, identity is negotiated—formed, maintained, and modified—through our interactions with others. Identity also simultaneously influences these very interactions through our expectations and perceptions of others' behaviors (Cornejo & Kam, 2020). In essence, a person's sense of self can be seen as an integral part of that person's social behavior (and vice versa). Part of a person's social behavior includes finding appropriate names and labels (remember the discussion on the importance of language in Chapter 3) that locate the self in socially recognizable categories (Burke & Reitzes, 1981). Most often, we gain our self-identities through a process of contrasting ingroup and outgroup characteristics (Turner, 1987). In other words, we come to understand who we are as we compare and contrast ourselves with others. Helms (1994) suggests, for instance, that most European Americans largely define their "whiteness" in terms of the opposite or lack of "Blackness" (see, for example, Al-Ramahi et al., 2021).

Think about how others—especially those that play an important role in your life—interact with you. What messages do they send you about their perceptions of you through both their verbal and nonverbal cues (both directly and indirectly)? Do you accept, reject, and/or ignore their perceptions of you? Symbolic interactionists would suggest that the images others communicate to you are a central aspect of identity formation. Another central element is your reaction to such communication. Gradually, some of the meanings generated through interactions are generalized over time and become established as core elements of your identity (R. Jackson et al., 2020).

## Theories of Identity Management

A number of different theories offer valuable insight into how individuals manage their identities with others. In this section, we describe two specific theories—self-presentation theory and impression management theory—that assist in understanding image management. The theory of image management is based on several assumptions (Burgoon et al., 2021). First, individuals manage multiple images across different contexts. Second, image management focuses on behaviors that are associated with maximized outcomes. Third, individuals use different image management techniques (e.g., assertive or defensive) directed to a generalized audience. Fourth, and finally, image management concentrates specifically on how a single person encodes certain verbal and nonverbal behaviors (as opposed to the process of impression formation—how others decode that information). Before we describe these theoretical frameworks, one final important point needs to be made. Our racial and ethnic identities compose just a portion of our self-concepts. So, while this section focuses on how individuals communicate their racial and ethnic identities to others, it is important to recognize that these parts of our identity are impossible to separate from other parts of who we are. This topic is the focus of our next chapter.

Goffman's (1959) self-presentation theory is a classic framework for describing how individuals use verbal and nonverbal communication to convey positive images of themselves in public spaces. This theory draws on a theatre analogy to describe how people present themselves in everyday life through the different roles that they embrace and perform in public. According to Goffman, various situations and audiences call for different performances, and individuals make verbal and nonverbal choices as they take various stages. Self-presentation theory describes how communication varies as individuals perform in largely public spaces (front region of the stage) and those that are more private (back region of the stage). Remember that public performances do not exist in a vacuum. Instead, they occur in larger social and cultural contexts which are filled with preconceived notions about racial and ethnic group members. Can you think of times when your public performances of race and ethnicity were consciously different than those enact privately? How might these differences—our use of specific words, displays of artifacts, and dress choices—be related to decisions to conform or resist images traditionally associated with our racial and ethnic groups?

Impression management theory is also useful in understanding how individuals attempt to maximize positive views of themselves, while avoiding negative evaluations of others. According to Tedeschi and Norman (1985), impression management efforts are best understood through two basic dimensions. First, individuals use techniques that are either assertive or defensive. Assertive techniques are used to establish positive characteristics in the eyes of others. Defensive techniques are enacted when individuals experience or anticipate negative perceptions and employ techniques to avoid negative judgments. Second, impression management techniques are strategic or tactical. Strategic communication addresses long-term goals and consequences, whereas tactical communication focuses more on short-term goals. Burgoon et al. (2021) report that nonverbal image management typically is assertive and strategic, something that would be consistent with the type of communication that occurs within racially charged environments. These scholars highlight how individuals use vocalics (volume, tone, rate, pitch, etc.) and other nonverbal cues to generate positive judgments in terms of attraction, likability, and credibility.

Theories focused on identity management have been useful in enhancing our understanding of how racial and ethnic identities are negotiated in different contexts (Boylorn & Orbe, 2021). For instance, recent research has utilized these theories to understand the central role that societal power plays in performances of identity in everyday life (C. Moore et al., 2017), how stigmatized identities are situated across different historical periods (Tyler, 2018), and the motivational factors that lead to cyber-bullying and cyber hate (Kilvington, 2020).

## Communication Theory of Identity

According to the communication theory of identity (CTI), identity is a naturally communicative and relational phenomenon (Shin & Hecht, 2017). Communication builds, sustains, and transforms identity. At the same time, identity is expressed through communication (Jung & Hecht, 2004). Identity is best understood as multidimensional and holistic in nature. As such, a major assumption of CTI is that identity consists of four interconnected layers: personal, enacted, relational, and communal (R. Jackson et al., 2020).

The theory originators assert that the **personal frame** of identity encompasses an individual's self-concept or self-definition. The personal level of identity is partially constructed from the messages received from relational others; however, the location is within the individual. The personal layer of identity provides clues as to how individuals view themselves in general as well as in specific contexts and situations.

The second frame of identity is the **enacted frame**. This frame is based on the idea that identities are communicatively manifested during social interactions. According to CTI, identities emerge through our interactions with others and are communicated either directly or indirectly through social roles, behaviors, and symbols (Hecht et al., 2003). This frame treats self as a performance and makes communication the location of identity (Hecht et al., 2005).

---

**Box 4.4**                                                    *Student Reflections*

### Not Being "Mexican Enough"

When I was growing up, I developed a passion for sharing my Mexican heritage with others but was quickly shut down by many of my white friends. Some would always accuse me of not being "Mexican enough" or say things like, "Oh, you're one of them that really looks like one of us." But as I entered high school, things began to change. I learned not to be ashamed of my heritage but to embrace it and share it with others who could then reciprocate by sharing their religions, traditions, and customs with me.

---

The **relational frame**, the third location of identity, captures how identities emerge in reference to others (Shin & Hecht, 2017). According to CTI, identities are mutually constructed and negotiated through relationships (R. Jackson et al., 2020). There are three aspects of this frame. First, individuals reflect upon themselves in terms of the people with whom they interact. Second, people gain their identities through relationships with others. Third, relationships themselves, such as couples, constitute units of identity (Hecht et al., 2005).

Finally, the **communal frame** as a locus of identity points to a group of people or a particular community bonded by a collective memory (Hecht et al., 2003). The community has its own identity and illustrates the joint identities of the individuals who associate with it (Hecht et al., 2002). Thus, identities arise from group associations and social networks (Hecht et al., 2005).

Although we have discussed each of these four frames separately, CTI explains that the frames are always interrelated and never separate (Marsiglia & Hecht, 1999). The ways in which the different frames influence, confirm, and contradict one another helps to capture the ongoing process of identity negotiation. Within the CTI framework, it is known as **interpenetration** (Jung & Hecht, 2004). One's personal identity, for example, cannot be considered without the context of the relational, enacted, and communal layers (Hecht et al., 2005). Although the frames coexist and cooperate in the composition of a person's identity, they do not always work in accord; instead, they may contradict or compete with one another, revealing inevitable **identity gaps** (Jung & Hecht, 2004). For instance, a communal frame of identity for an ethnic group (e.g., Latinx) may have certain things associated with it (e.g., being able to speak Spanish, eating certain foods, participating in certain celebrations). Latinx Americans who do not do these things may still identify as Latinx (per-

---

**Box 4.5**                                                      *Research Highlight*

### Identity Negotiation in a World of Genetic Ancestry Testing

Genetic ancestry testing is a billion-dollar industry with over 40 different companies providing services to millions of people interested in uncovering their ancestral background. Through various commercials, people witness how different individuals discover parts of their ancestry previously unknown to them and then embark on world-wide adventures to embrace new aspects of their cultural identity through travel, food, people, customs, music, and dress.

According to Roth (2018), genetic testing results (typically pie charts with percentages of geographically based ancestry) are grossly oversimplified and designed to reveal a probability, not a definitive answer, to one's ancestry. The results are based on science that was created to address questions at a macro-level population level, not for specific individuals at the micro-level. In addition, Roth argues, a person's racial identity is not simply what's found in their genes—it is a social construction shaped by self, others, and society. In other words, racial identity is not determined solely by one's genes. Instead, ideas about race, ethnicity, and identity are informed by how individuals are socialized on these topics within a specific time period and social context.

Roth (2018) reminds us that 99% of DNA is identical, consequently genetic tests focus on only 1% of our DNA to offer insight into our ancestral composition. In light of this, Roth characterizes genetic ancestry test results as similar to a Rorschach Inkblot Test. Individuals can interpret the same results quite differently. Roth's research found that white test consumers are much more likely to adopt new racial or ethnic identities, whereas people of color find their test results interesting yet nothing that affects their racial/ethnic identity.

sonal layer); however, a struggle may exist in terms of how they communicate (enacted layer) and relate to other Latinx people (relational layer) (Hecht et al., 2002).

CTI has been used to explore racial and ethnic identity among various groups, including African Americans (R. Jackson et al., 2020), U.S. immigrants (Jung & Hecht, 2008; Urban & Orbe, 2010), Arab women (Witteborn, 2004), Jewish Americans (Faulkner, 2006; Hecht et al., 2002; Marsiglia & Hecht, 1999), as well as diverse younger participants from the southeast United States (Drummond & Orbe, 2009). Hecht and his colleagues, for instance, illustrated how Jewish Americans constantly create and negotiate their identities by revealing and concealing their Jewishness depending on varying situational and contextual salience of personal, communal, relational, or enacted layers of identity. Similarly, Marsiglia and Hecht demonstrated how the interaction between the communal and personal gendered Jewish identity is expressed in core symbols, labels, and behaviors. Finally, adding another dimension to CTI studies, Drummond and Orbe (2009) provided a nuanced understanding of how different seemingly innocent questions (i.e., "Where are you from," "Who are you trying to be?") reflect racial microaggressions that can prompt identity struggles between personal, enacted, and relational frames.

## FOCUS ON RACIAL/ETHNIC IDENTITY NEGOTIATION

So far, we have summarized some existing research on identity and identity formation to help you understand how persons come to define themselves culturally. Toward this objective, we have combined research on personal identity and cultural identity issues. This section continues to use these cultural identity perspectives, but we focus our attention more narrowly on racial/ethnic identity development. Specifically, we discuss three fundamental contributors to the co-creation of racial/ethnic identity (family and friends, dominant societal institutions/organizations, and media) to illustrate the process by which perceptions of racialized self and others are formed.

Before we examine these social institutions, we first introduce an important concept—**ethnic-racial socialization** (ERS). By definition, ERS refers to how individuals, through explicit and implicit messages, learn what race and ethnicity mean to them (Hughes et al., 2006). According to Minniear and Soliz (2019), ERS occurs frequently and explicitly in the context of family communication. This is important given the realities of race and racism in the United States (Umaña-Taylor & Hill, 2020) because ERS has been related to positive racial/ethnic identity and improved mental health (M.-T. Wang, Henry et al., 2020; M.-T. Wang, Smith et al., 2020). While families are oftentimes assumed to be the most important site of socialization, other scholars (e.g., Nelson et al., 2018) have studied the crucial role that peers play in ethnic-racial socialization. Based on the significance of this research, we begin our discussion on how family and friends impact our understandings of our racial and ethnic identities.

## Family and Friends

One of the central aspects of Mead's (1934) symbolic interactionism framework is the idea of a **generalized other**, a concept that refers to the collective body from which the individual sees the self. In other words, it is an individual's perception of the general way that others see them. Throughout your life, you have learned these perceptions from years of socialization and interaction with others. Each person has a number of **significant others** who have been particularly influential in identity development. Shin and Hecht (2017) refer to these individuals as orientational others. For most individuals, orientational others are family members (not restricted only to blood relations).

How do family and friends help co-create our racial/ethnic identity? The answer to this question is complicated. Racial/ethnic identity is developed in a number of ways, including direct communication about race/ethnic issues, role modeling, and general socialization (see, for example, Juang et al., 2017). An extremely powerful component of the co-creation of race/ethnic identity is reflected in the labels that family and friends use. C. Taylor (1992) notes that, "people do not acquire the languages needed for self-definition on their own. Rather, we are introduced to them through interaction with others who matter to us" (p. 32). Think back—as far as your memory reaches—to the terms and labels that friends and family members have used to describe you as well as themselves. How does your self-identity reflect some level of conscious or unconscious acceptance of these labels? Can you think of instances when you felt uncomfortable with the racial/ethnic labels used by or about family and friends? Such experiences reflect one aspect of the powerful role that family and friends play in the co-creation of identity (Dodd & Baldwin, 1998). In their work on multiracial families, Rockquemore and Brunsma (2002) acknowledge the importance of nuclear and extended family in creating healthy identities. Docan-Morgan (2011) found similar influences in her research on single-race families who decide on transracial adoptions.

As described by a number of communication scholars (e.g., Carrillo Rowe, 2016; Gangotena, 2016) one of the primary ways that racial/ethnic identity is created for people is through family stories. Most often, but not always, family stories are passed down orally from generation to generation and represent some truth or life lesson. In terms of those particular family stories that focus on race/ethnicity, many provide pertinent information used to develop perceptions of the racial/ethnic identities of self and others.

Navita Cummings James (2016) describes how significant stories from her youth (e.g., stories of lynching, murder, slavery) represented a specific set of beliefs and stereotypes about European Americans and African Americans, including the following:

- Black people are "just as good" as white people—and in some ways (e.g., morally) better.
- Black people have to be twice as good as whites to be considered half as good.

- White people probably have some kind of inferiority complex which drives them to continually "put down" Blacks and anyone else who is not white.
- White men are usually arrogant; white women are usually lazy.
- There are some good white people, but they are the exceptions. (p. 139)

These perceptions were gained through the communication of both European and African American sides of James's family. In addition, she is quick to point out that these childhood beliefs and stereotypes did not immediately become part of her self-identity. Instead, her work on family stories, culture, and identity suggests that family stories represent one source of cultural information used in the co-creation of racial/ethnic identity.

Family stories do not exist in isolation but in context with other stories that we gain from others, including our friends. The impact of one's peers, which in some cultural contexts may be just as important as the influence of one's family, is described as horizontal socialization (Eleftheriadou, 2010). This is especially true as individuals become teenagers and young adults. U. Moffitt and Syed (2020) studied ethnic-racial identity exploration among emerging adults. Their qualitative analysis found wide variation in racial and ethnic conversations, both in terms of content and structure. In particular, they report that peer interactions related to race oftentimes can be highly charged, resulting in both self-affirming exchanges and negative experiences of denial, disinterest, and discrimination. Not surprisingly, these experiences, and the ways in which young people respond to them, are impacted by the earlier ethnic-racial socialization from family (Marcelo & Yates, 2019). Family socialization exists within larger contexts like your local neighborhood, organizations, and other institutions (Rockquemore & Brunsma, 2002).

## Dominant Societal Institutions/Organizations

As we saw in the descriptions in the previous section, our family and friends typically (but certainly not always) serve an important role in providing information concerning our racial/ethnic identity (Dodd & Baldwin, 1998). For many parents with children of color, cultivating a positive racial/ethnic self-identity in their children is important (Orbe, 2012), especially for those who believe children from racial/ethnic microcultures who lack a strong, positive identity are prone to fail in dominant societal institutions/organizations. What do we mean by "dominant societal institutions/organizations"? This is a phrase that best represents various predominantly European American bodies that reflect the dominant cultural values of the United States (e.g., hospitals, schools, government agencies, police, etc.). Oftentimes, the messages that individuals receive from the institutions concerning their racial/ethnic identity either explicitly or implicitly contradict those from friends and family. In other words, certain institutions serve as the "recognition, nonrecognition, or misrecognition" of racial/ethnic identities (C. Taylor, 1992, p. 32). Think about how certain persons in authority—teachers, police officers, doctors, social workers—have interacted with you over the course of your life. How has their communication, both verbally and nonverbally, contained messages concerning their own as well your

**Box 4.6**                                                    *Author Reflections*

## The Unrelenting Question: "What *Are* You?"

While I was lecturing at another university several years ago, an African American woman described me as a "cultural enigma." Her comment was part of a question she was asking about the presentation that I had just given about my research. Although I probably shouldn't be, I am surprised at the level of intensity that often accompanies people's need to know my racial/ethnic/cultural identity. Within the context of this woman's comments, she seemed to accept the difficulty that occurs when people try to classify my cultural identities in terms of "either/or" categories (see MPO's personal reflection in Chapter 1). However, this is not typically the case. More often than not, people exhibit an intense need to know "what I am." In the past few years, I've experienced acquaintances and colleagues who do the following:

- Use direct questions ("What *are* you?" "Are you Black?" "What's your cultural background?—You have *something* in you, but I can't figure it out!")

- Touch the back of my head in an attempt to measure how "nappy/kinky" my hair is (I had just met this African American woman at a conference; this was her way of trying to figure out my racial background)

- Tell me that "everyone is dying to figure out what you are" and that "some people don't feel comfortable interacting with you until they know"

- Assume they know my race/ethnicity and then try to argue with others (including some of my good friends) when they are corrected!

Part of me wants to respond to these types of inquiries by saying, "What difference does it make?" But, of course, I realize that race and ethnicity do make a difference in the United States (as well as other countries).

Writing several editions of this book has increased my consciousness of how these experiences work in the co-creation of my racial/ethnic identity, especially in terms of how others see me. It's interesting because more often than not, people of color typically recognize that I've got "something in me," whereas some European Americans are quicker to designate me as a "white male." A lot of it has to do with the particular set of circumstances that surround our interaction. When I correct them (which is often, but not always), reactions include shock, apologies, embarrassment, and aggression. "You can say what you want, but I see you as a white man and that's how I'm going to interact with you!" responded one person. Although each of these interactions is both symbolic and significant to me, I imagine that most of these individuals are relatively unaware of the power of their verbal and nonverbal cues, which could be considered racial microaggressions. Part of their uncertainty and anxiety is probably fueled by a recognition that their self-identities are tied to how they identify me. As James Baldwin (1990) put it, "If I'm not who you say I am, then you're not who you think you are." So how do these interactions affect my racial/ethnic identity? I'm not exactly sure, but I do recognize that they definitely do have some impact—if they didn't, why would I remember them so vividly?

—MPO

racial/ethnic identity? Consciously or unconsciously you have dealt with these messages as part of an ongoing process of identity development.

The lived experiences of biracial and multiracial persons in the United States offer a vivid example of how the co-creation of racial/ethnic identity involves ingroup and outgroup perceptions (Harwood et al., 2006). Autoethnographical research indicates that multiracial families talk about race and ethnicity issues among themselves differently depending on a variety of interrelated factors (Orbe, 1999). These include the influence/presence of parents, racial/ethnic makeup of neighborhoods, and personal philosophies of race/racism (Fine & Johnson, 2016; Rockquemore & Brunsma, 2002). A growing number of parents are raising their children to resist pressure to choose one racial/ethnic identity (Docan-Morgan, 2011). Instead, they embrace a multiracial identity that allows them to express all aspects of who they are wherever they go. Problems occur when orientational others (e.g., a teacher or a social worker) fail to recognize this identity and continue to see them in traditional racial categories that follow a one-drop rule.

What happens, then, when a child must deal with conflicting messages about racial/ethnic identity? Consider the case described by Orbe (1999) of a young girl whose racial lineage consisted of African, European, Asian, and Native descent (in that approximate order). At birth, her parents believed the hospital records should indicate her "race/ethnicity" as multiracial and list all of her racial heritage (as was done with their first child). The assisting records nurse, based on her perceptions of the baby's mother, listed her race/ethnicity as "Black." The family's pediatrician (a Central American woman), despite knowing the multiracial family for over a year, recorded "white" in the appropriate box on another hospital form. Her designation was based on the girl's physical features (blond hair, bluish green eyes, and peach complexion). Despite some initial conflicting perceptions, the little girl was raised to see herself as multiracial. Nevertheless, distinct differences in how outgroup members described and perceived her continued to contradict this racial/ethnic identity.

This brief case study helps us understand the complex ways that interactions with authority figures must be negotiated within the context of family and friends' communication about racial/ethnic identities (Kellogg & Liddell, 2012). Only time will tell how her co-created self- identity will ultimately be formed in the context of interactions with family, friends, and members of the larger macroculture, and how she will be able to embrace an identity that does not force her to keep the different races and ethnicities separate in her sense of self (Moreman, 2011). We would suggest that all people experience some conflicting messages about their identities (although at various levels of intensity). This process is aptly described by Hegde (1998) as **identity emergence**. It refers to the multiple, sometimes contradicting, interactions that characterize the experiences of human life. One societal institution that plays a significant role in this process of identity emergence is the mass media. Because of the growing interest in the power of mass-mediated images, we separate it from other dominant societal organizations/institutions.

## Mass Media

Defined broadly, media are communication tools used to create, deliver, exchange, and store information. According to McLuhan and Fiore (2005), media refer to a variety of communication technologies that work to extend the range, speed, channels and overall capabilities of human communication. The particular forms of specific mediums (e.g., print media, radio, television, film, social media) influence the message given their capabilities (e.g., text, pictures, graphics, images, interactive features). In addition, other factors— speed of delivery, ease of utility, complexity, usability, visibility, impact/reach, relative advantage, etc.—also influence communication-based decisions surrounding media. With all of this in mind, this section highlights the media as a powerful source of socialization.

Considerable research exists on the impact of mass media representations on an individual's perceptions of race, ethnicity, and culture, both in terms of self and others (e.g., R. Jackson, 2006). Chapter 11 discusses how mass-mediated communication represents—and ultimately affects—interracial communication in a variety of contexts. Several theoretical frameworks have been created to assess the impacts of the mass media on perceptions of self and others. These include, but are not limited to, cultivation theory, agenda setting theory, critical theory, uses and gratification approach to media, social learning

---

### BOX 4.7

#### The New Trend on Racial Ambiguity

Over time, the media have always paid close attention to racial appearance in terms of who was included on screen and in print. Some scholars (A. James & Tucker, 2003) have noted a growing trend in the entertainment industry over the past few decades—the promotion of individuals who are racially ambiguous. They argue that actors, models, and other entertainers—Vin Diesel, The Rock, Jessica Alba, Zoe Saldana, Bruno Mars, Vanessa Hudgens, and Maya Rudolph—whose heritage is difficult to discern are highly marketable. Part of their popularity with younger audiences seems to relate to the lack of certainty about their racial and ethnic composition. In this regard, Sengupta (2018) argues that multiracial people with racially ambiguous appearances represent diversity and equality yet do so because they are more comfortably accepted by European Americans seeking a harmonious post-racial society.

- Think about your favorite movies, television shows, music videos, and blogs, and social media sites. Do they feature racially ambiguous persons?

- What were your initial perceptions of these individuals? Do you think that your perceptions were the same as others in, and outside of, your family/friend circle?

- How are they portrayed in the media?

- How, if at all, is their racial and ethnic identities discussed openly?

- Have you paid more attention thinking about their racial/ethnic heritage after taking this class?

theory, public sphere theory, critical media effects theory, hyper/in/visibility theory, and the theory of a spiral of silence. Each of these theoretical frameworks suggests different levels of mass media influence. However, one consistent idea is common across this diverse set of media theories: Mass media representations do have some impact on societal perceptions of self, culture, and society. According to G. Kellner (1995), media culture "provides the materials out of which many people construct their sense of class, of ethnicity and race, of nationality, of sexuality, of "us" and "them." Media culture helps shape the prevalent view of the world and deepest values. . . . Media culture provides the materials to create identities" (p. 1).

Much of the research on mass media representations and effects has focused on television images and their impact on viewers who watch large amounts of television programming (Tukachinsky et al., 2017). However, of equal or possibly greater importance are the mass-mediated representations found in mainstream books, films, magazines, newspapers, music, social media, and virtual images—all of which reinforce the racial/ethnic images found on television (Banjo, 2011; Sanders & Ramasubramanian, 2012). For children of color, these forms of mass media serve as a relentless source of dominant cultural values, beliefs, and attitudes (Tukachinsky et al., 2017). Mainstream mass media forms have been largely criticized for perpetuating negative racial/ethnic stereotypes (T. Harris & Hill, 1998). According to bell hooks, exposure to negative images is unavoidable for African Americans, given the pervasive nature of the mass media. "Opening a magazine or book, turning on the television set, watching a film, or looking at photographs in public spaces, we are most likely to see images of black people that reinforce and reinscribe white supremacy" (hooks, 1992, p. 1). A similar conclusion was also drawn from the research of Antoine (2011) and Curtin (2011) who explored how larger societal narratives communicated through the mass media impacted the identities of Native Americans.

Clearly, the messages contained in the mass media serve as another source of information concerning racial and ethnic groups with which all persons, regardless of cultural background, must deal. Halualani (1998) describes this process as a "struggle of culture"—the clash between cultural identities produced for us and by us (p. 265). In terms of Mead's (1934) focus on symbolic interactionism, we can see how mass-mediated images might contribute to how individuals understand their identities in terms of the "generalized other" (Cornejo & Kam, 2020). Technological advances, like the internet and various forms of social media, have intensified the impact of media in our understanding of self and others (Harlow & Benbrook, 2019).

When opportunities for substantial interracial interaction are limited because of personal, social, or physical distance, mass media representations have a greater impact on outgroup perceptions. The following excerpt illustrates the power of mass-mediated forms of communication not only on how individuals perceive themselves but also on how others perceive and interact with those who are racially/ethnically different from themselves.

> A white woman acquaintance at my university pulled me aside and in a serious voice announced that she understood what I had been talking about all

of these months about my ethnicity and race. "I saw the movie THE JOY LUCK CLUB with my husband over the weekend. I feel so close to you now, like I understand you so much better! Chinese women are so lucky to have relationships with their mothers with such deep emotions!" I felt confused and speechless and didn't know where to begin. In addition to the fact that I am not Chinese American, I wondered what in the world this woman and her husband have fantasized about my life and family relations based on this Hollywood movie. (K. Wong, 2002, p. 98)

Other scholars (Rodrigues, 2016) have written about similar problematic interactions with others who rely on mass-mediated images to form their expectations about interracial interactions. For instance, you can read about how one African American communication professor at a predominately white university in the South responded to students who expected her to behave like the Black women they had watched on different reality television shows (Boylorn, 2008).

## CONCLUSION

This chapter described how individuals come to understand racial/ethnic perceptions of self and others. Much of the discussion focused on how people co-create their individual racial and/or ethnic identities. Specifically, we described in some detail the commonalities and differences of macrocultural, microcultural, and multiracial identity development models. We also introduced different sociological and communication theories that encourage us to understand how identity is best understood as an individual, relational, and societal process. Within all of these descriptions, we discussed how our own identities are inextricably linked with the ways that we perceive others. In short, strong racial and ethnic identification impacts how we communicate with others—both ingroup and outgroup members (Bresnahan et al., 2009).

We began this chapter by highlighting how cultural identities are becoming increasingly complex and salient in society. The information provided here is substantial in illustrating the importance of race/ethnicity in matters of identity negotiation. It is also largely incomplete, given that identity, and, subsequently, interracial communication, is informed by other elements of sociocultural categories. Chapter 5 will complete our coverage of the multifaceted, complex process of identity co-creation.

### KEY TERMS

| | |
|---|---|
| whiteness | conformity |
| disintegration | resistance and separation |
| reintegration | integration |
| pseudo-independence | personal identity |
| immersion/emersion | choice of group categorization |
| autonomy | enmeshment/denial |
| unexamined identity | appreciation |

| personal frame | identity gaps |
| enacted frame | ethnic-racial socialization |
| relational frame | generalized other |
| communal frame | significant others |
| interpenetration | identity emergence |

## OPPORTUNITIES FOR EXTENDED LEARNING

1. Create a chapter outline for a book that describes your racial/ethnic identity development over the course of your life. Create a title for each chapter that captures a significant event or time in your life that symbolizes an increased degree of awareness in terms of race/ethnicity. Chapter 1 should contain details of your first memories, and your last chapter should describe your current perceptions (the chapters in between will describe the process by which you got from there to here). Share and explain your outlines with the class. The goal is to focus on understanding others' narratives and to search for commonalities and differences between individual's stories.

2. The media contain a number of excellent examples of individuals at different stages of racial/ethnic identity development. When growing up, what was your favorite television show, movie, cartoon strip, or book. Who were the main characters? Think about what you have learned about them. Based on their communication about self and others, can you make an educated guess at which stage of racial identity development they are? Do you have any evidence that this has changed over time? Are there characters at different stages? How is their communication similar and/or different? If time permits, compare your judgments with others.

3. Maria Primitiva Paz Root (1996) created a "Bill of Rights for Racially Mixed People" that includes the following: "I have the right not to keep the races separate within me," "I have the right to identify myself differently than strangers expect me to identify," and "I have the right to change my identity over my lifetime—and more than once." (See https://www.mixedpeopleshistory.com/bill-of-rights for a complete list.) Break up into small groups and discuss your reactions to these "rights." Do you agree or disagree? Is there anything that you might add to Root's list? How many of these statements apply to people in general? Do others seem most relevant to individuals with particular identities?

4. Spend some time exploring websites that promote the strengthening and prideful embrace of white identity. Pay particular attention to how the website's content uses technology to create and reinforce a specific form of identity for white people. Then apply the different stages of macrocultural racial identity to understand the foundation of the information and how it represents a particular form of whiteness.

5. Put in some effort investigating how whiteness is experienced in different areas of the United States. For instance, do some research on how some European American groups in the Northeast (e.g., New York, Philadelphia, and Boston) or Midwest (e.g., Chicago, Grand Rapids, Minneapolis) emphasize their ethnic identities through celebrations (St. Patrick's Day parade)

or other means ("Little Italy"). Do similar displays of ethnic pride occur for European Americans in other regions?

6. Review Wendy Roth's YouTube video *Genetic Ancestry Testing and the Meaning of Race* (https://www.youtube.com/watch?v=MQlmX7gvYRA). Explore her views on whether race is determined by our genes and/or through our socialization. Talk with individuals who have completed genetic ancestry testing and discuss their reasons for taking the test and how the results have shaped, if at all, their current identities.

7. Learn more about how facial analysis software, increasingly used by police departments and other organizations to monitor the public, uses codes that include algorithmic bias against people of color and women. Watch the TED talk by MIT graduate student Joy Buolamwini, who is on a mission for greater accountability of what has become known as the "coded gaze" of white-male-created algorithmic programs. (See https://www.ted.com/talks/joy_buolamwini_how_i_m_fighting_bias_in_algorithms?referrer=playlist-the_inherent_bias_in_our_techn for her brief yet compelling presentation.) For a more extensive treatment of this topic, watch Shalini Kantayya's award-winning documentary, *Coded Bias*.

## RECOMMENDED CONTEMPORARY READINGS

Cramer, L. M. (2020). Whiteness and the postracial imaginary in Disney's *Zootopia*. *Howard Journal of Communications, 31*(3), 264–281. doi.org/10.1080/10646175.2019.1666070

Labador, A., & Zhang, D. (2021). The "American dream" for whom?: Contouring Filipinos' and Filipino/a/x Americans' discursive negotiation of postcolonial identities. *Journal of International and Intercultural Communication.* doi.org/10.1080/17513057.2021.1945129

Lie, S. (2020). Asian-American Buddhist identity talk: National criticism of Buddhism in the U.S. *Journal of Communication & Religion, 43*(2), 5–21.

Maragh-Lloyd, R., & Corsbie-Massay, C. L. (2021). Embodying resistance: Understanding identity in a globalized digital future through the lens of mixed and multiracial Caribbeans. *Journal of International and Intercultural Communication.* doi.org/10.1080/17513057.2021.1940243

McCullough, K. M., Wong, Y. J., & Deng, K. (2021). Exploring the connections between watching Asian American YouTubers, racial identity, and self-esteem. *Asian American Journal of Psychology, 12*(1), 41–51. https://doi.org/10.1037/aap0000218

Rudick, C. K., & Golsan, K. B. (2018). Civility and white institutional presence: An exploration of white students' understanding of race-talk at a traditionally white institution. *Howard Journal of Communications, 29*(4), 335–352. doi.org/10.1080/10646175.2017.1392910

Sasser, J., Lecarie, E. K., Park, H., & Doane, L. D. (2021). Daily family connection and objective sleep in Latinx adolescents: The moderating role of familism values and family communication. *Journal of Youth and Adolescence, 50*, 506–520. doi.org/10.1007/s10964-020-01326-7

# 5

# Intersectionality of Identities

**CASE STUDY**         **Representation Matters:**
**Colorism and *In the Heights***

Lin-Manuel Miranda's Broadway musical, *In the Heights,* won a Tony award in 2008. Thirteen years later, the film adaptation was released. While the movie was praised for its artistic and cultural value, some critics were quick to point out problematic tensions over *Latinidad*—how "Latino-ness" was represented. Specifically, they criticized the lack of Afro-Latinx main characters in the show (e.g., Afro-Dominicans, Afro-Puerto Ricans, Afro-Cubans). In many ways, the film reflected a larger issue: Black Lives Matter in the Latinx community.

As we discuss in Chapter 7, colorism (ingroup bias based on skin color) exists across the world, including among Latinx people. In this chapter, you will learn how colorism is best understood through an intersectional lens: how race inherently relates to ethnicity, nationality, socioeconomic status, and other aspects of identity. Across the Americas, social caste systems exist where those with white, European features are at the top of the racial hierarchy and those with Black, African features are at the bottom (Chavez-Duenas & Adames, 2014). Colorism can be seen throughout all aspects of life—personal, social, cultural, and the media—where those with phenotypically white characteristics have greater privilege. In Caribbean countries with great national pride and multiracial ancestry (i.e., African, Indigenous, and Spanish ancestors), racial identification is not necessarily a fixed state (Alford, 2021). M*estizaje*—mixture—is an ideology in which everyone is considered to have mixed heritage and was one of the strategies used to de-emphasize privileges associated with phenotypically white characteristics. However, Afro-Latinos have experienced social caste systems in which Black Latinos are placed at the bottom and the whitest Latinos at the top. Popular phrases such as *mejorar la raza*—improve the race by marrying a white partner—reveal the hierarchical structure.

Reflect on your exposure and experiences with Latinx culture: How is colorism present? Can you think of examples in the media (e.g., television, film, advertisements, music, artistic expressions, etc.) that reinforce and/or counter colorism in the Latinx community? Within this larger context, how fair do you think the criticisms of *In the Heights* were?

To comprehend the dynamics of any particular cultural phenomenon, you must see how it relates to other aspects of culture (Connell, 2005). In other words, understanding race must involve going beyond race. Within this chapter, we explain how all individuals have multidimensional identities. Thus far, we have focused on racial and ethnic identity, but it is important to recognize how all of us belong to a variety of other cultural groups that share common attitudes, values, and norms of relating to one another.

Like the authors of this text, you are a member of many different cultural groups that influence who you are and what you think and feel—as well as how you communicate with others. Recognizing the multiple aspects of your cultural identity promotes a deeper understanding of the complexities of interracial communication beyond simple racial/ethnic designations. Chapter 5 provides a conceptual framework to enhance your understanding of how other elements of cultural identity (socioeconomic status, gender, nationality/regionality, age, sexual orientation, spirituality, and abilities) affect interracial communication. Throughout this chapter, continue the self-reflective process initiated in Chapter 4 and you will begin to discern how race and ethnicity—and other cultural elements—become more or less significant in different contexts.

## ACKNOWLEDGING MULTIPLE CULTURAL IDENTITIES

Cultural identities are central, dynamic, and multifaceted components of our understanding of self and others (Bardhan & Orbe, 2012; Rodriguez, 2002). Once formed (at least if we could freeze time for at a particular moment, before future points of negotiation), they provide an essential framework for organizing and interpreting our interactions with others. Mary Jane Collier (2000, 2002) and others have advanced a cultural identity theory (CIT) that provides a productive framework for acknowledging the existence and impact of complexities of cultural identity and interracial communication. The central premise of the theory is that each individual has multiple cultural identities that are formed through discourse with others. Individuals use communicative processes to construct and negotiate cultural group identities and relationships across contexts (Littlejohn et al., 2021). Consistent with the research referenced in Chapter 4, CIT is based on the idea that "cultural identities are negotiated, co-created, reinforced, and challenged through communication" (Collier, 2000, p. 31). CIT also helps shed light on the various ways our cultural identities are defined in relation to one another. This process assists in recognizing the diversity within cultural groups (Orbe et al., 2006). Group members

> have multiple cultural identities in addition to their shared group membership. Diversity, then, both within and between groups, is the starting point of CIT. Not only do individuals' identities consist of different and multiple cultural identities—race, ethnicity, gender, sexuality—but an individual's identification within a cultural group differs in salience and importance across various contexts. An African American identity may be less important than gender in a group of African Americans, but it might become extremely

important if someone is the only African American person in a class or organization. (Littlejohn et al., 2021, p. 427)

The theoretical framework of CIT serves as an excellent transition between the basic ideas presented in Chapter 4 and the focus here.

Two of the major ideas associated with CIT are avowal and ascription. **Avowal**, according to Collier (2002), refers to the perceived identity that a person or group enacts in a particular context. It consists of a more subjective identity, one that is typically viewed from the point of a specific individual. **Ascription**, in comparison, is how others perceive an individual or group. Although these two identity components can be described independently, they function together in inextricable ways (Moss & Faux, 2006). For instance, our self-identity is informed largely by our interactions with others, including our perceptions of how others perceive us. Others' perception of us (ascription)—or at least our perceptions of their perceptions—has a direct impact on how we come to see ourselves (avowal).

Another major aspect of CIT involves understanding the enduring/changing quality of cultural identity (Rodriguez, 2002). Typically passed down from one generation of group members to another, cultural identities are enduring in that historical group orientations inform present and future reality (Chen & Collier, 2012). Although our cultural identities possess an enduring quality, they simultaneously are also apt to change over time. Our cultural identities are dynamic and subject to constant examination, reexamination, and possibly alteration based on our interactions with others. This involves all aspects of our identity, including those more permanent (e.g., race/ethnicity and gender) as well as those more fluid (e.g., socioeconomic status and age). Most of us—especially students who have invested significant amounts of time, money, and energy in obtaining a college degree—foresee how this accomplishment might alter our self-identity in a number of ways (possibly regional/geographical location, and hopefully socioeconomic!). However, even with a stable cultural marker such as race, our identities may also change over time. Think about how an increased knowledge of self and others changes—if not your particular race/ethnicity—the ways you label, understand, and identify with a particular set of racial/ethnic lived experiences.

Furthermore, cultural identities comprise both context and relational levels of interpretation (Collier, 2002). This aspect of CIT recognizes that the meanings within interracial interactions are created not only by the content shared between interactants but also their relationship. Various aspects of *content* (e.g., language, jokes, self- and other labels) must be understood within the *context* of the participant's relationships (see Chapter 8). Take, for example, the use of *girl*. Among African American women, this term is used to refer to one another in a positive, affirming, and celebratory manner (Scott, 1996; 2016). In an interracial communication context, the use of *girl* by a European American woman to refer to an African American woman (e.g., "Hey, girl, how are you?") may generate a set of different meanings. The European American woman might perceive it as a way to establish rapport. The African American woman might perceive it as presumptuous, offensive, and insulting given the sociohistorical context of the United States and the absence of an established relationship (Orbe et al., 2002). In the context of an established, close relationship, *girl* may be used by both African American and European American women as a sign that racial differences may be transcended (B. Allen, 2016). Again, a competent interpretation of meaning involves both the content and relationship dimensions of the message.

A final aspect of CIT relates to the salience and intensity of particular cultural elements in any given interracial communication context (Moss & Faux, 2006). **Salience** "refers to the relative importance of one or two identities to others" (Collier, 2002, p. 305). This means acknowledging that in any given interaction, some aspects of cultural identity will be more salient than others. In this regard, interactions between people from two different racial and/or ethnic groups may be focused on a similar trait—thereby transcending racial/ethnic differences. For instance, in their collaborative research on their interracial friendship, Clark and Diggs (2002) describe how a common spiritual connection allowed them to negotiate any tensions they experienced related to racial differences. These two women (who describe themselves as friends, academic colleagues, and coauthors) explain how similarities in their spiritual selves became more important in their relationship than racial differences. This is not to say that racial differences were totally erased; in fact, they describe times when race had saliency in their friendship. Understanding how some cultural similarities, like those based within spirituality, can help individuals transcend racial differences is at the heart of this chapter.

In Chapter 1, we define interracial communication as interactions between two or more individuals in a situational context where racial difference is a salient issue. Given this definition, Clark and Diggs (2002) might have some interactions that are interracial (where racial differences impact their friendship) and some that are interpersonal (where their identities as spiritual beings allow them to minimize any racial differences). A productive way to visualize this distinction is to understand each interaction as falling somewhere on an interpersonal-interracial continuum (see Figure 5.1). Such a conceptualization reinforces the idea that any interaction isn't solely interpersonal or interracial but can shift depending on the interactions. An excellent example of this is described in Box 5.1.

| Interpersonal | Interracial |

**Figure 5.1**   Interpersonal-Interracial Continuum

Most communication involves multiple cultural identities, with the exceptions reflecting one single identity that overwhelms all others (R. Jackson et al., 2020). Think about this statement for a moment. Can you generate any examples of communication that are *solely* the result of one aspect of your cultural

| Box 5.1 | Author Reflections |
|---|---|

### A Shocking Racist Slip in the Workplace

I was talking with a staff member about a problem she was having and gave her some advice on what she could do. After venting for a moment, she finally made a decision and said, "Well, I guess I'll just sit here like a tar baby and keep my mouth shut." My mind automatically went blank. Immediately, I thought *"Surely,* I didn't just hear her say *tar baby."* In all my life, I have *never* heard anyone use this incredibly derogatory and racist phrase—until that day. As she continued to talk about the problem, I felt as if a knife were slowly being pulled from my stomach. Although she was not calling me a tar baby and there was no racial overtone in what was said, I couldn't help but feel the sting of her words. Stunned, I walked out of the office with nothing to say. What *could* I say? Tar baby was a term adapted from an African folktale to refer to a sticky mess or situation. The term eventually devolved to refer to Black people and was blatantly negative in nature and tone.

How could someone say something so racist and offensive in the workplace? Did this mean she might one day slip and call someone this incredibly racist term? Because this happened at work, I knew there would be consequences if I confronted her. I felt in my heart her intention was not to offend. This was a reflection of the era in which she grew up. She could become defensive or angry, or she might even cry. Worst case scenario, our department chair could get wind of it and file a complaint, maybe causing her to lose her job, and I didn't want that. I knew if I said something, our working relationship would be changed, to my detriment, and could make for a very tense environment. In the end, I decided this was not a battle I was emotionally, mentally, or spiritually ready to tackle. I've been fighting for so long that I opted to let this one go. Regardless of your racial standpoint or identity, maybe you can help me by joining the fight. It will make for a better world in the end; at least I hope and pray so.

—TMH

identity? More than likely, if you think critically, any example you can come up with reflects an intersection of various cultural elements. For example, you may have heard the statement, "It's a Black thang . . . ," a phrase illustrating how certain behaviors are directly related to a particular racial experience. (The second part of the phrase, "you wouldn't understand," highlights the difficulty of outgroup members' understanding ingroup cultural norms, values, and/or ideas.) However, how many times is something described as a "Black thang," when in essence it refers to something more than simply race? In many cases, "it's a Black thang" might be better described as "a Black *urban* thing," "a Black *Generation X* thing," and/or "a Black *working-class* thing." These phrases help acknowledge that some African Americans may not share certain cultural experiences (because of region, age, or socioeconomic status) and some non–African Americans may, because of similar cultural identities other than race/ethnicity.

# INTERSECTIONALITY

Take a minute to reflect on the idea that your interactions with others can represent different points on an interpersonal-interracial continuum. Interracial communication must be understood in the context of variables in addition to race/ethnicity. Later in this chapter, we discuss different aspects of culture (socioeconomic status, gender, nationality/regionality, age, sexual orientation, spirituality, and abilities) separately. In reality, these and other cultural markers are interlocking and inseparable. No person belongs solely to one single group. Instead, individuals simultaneously encompass multiple cultural identities. The best vantage point to come to understand human communication is through an acknowledgment that each person experiences life as a complex individual whose cultural group identities function in concert with other identities (M. Houston & Wood, 1996). **Intersectionality** refers to the combined impact of different cultural identities, especially those oppressed by systemic structures. Embracing this concept helps us generate deeper, more complex understanding of people's lives; it also assists in avoiding more superficial explanations of behavior based on one aspect of culture.

A key idea of intersectionality is recognizing how the experiences of people from one racial background may vary depending on other aspects of their cultural identity, such as gender, age, and (dis)ability.

Initially, the concept of intersectionality was used to describe the dynamics of race and gender related to violence against women of color through laws (Crenshaw, 1995, 2012). More specifically, it emerged from the work of Black feminist thought (Collins, 2022) that highlighted how Black women are oppressed in multiple ways: sexism within the Black community, racism within white feminist groups, and classism within both communities. This theoretical framework is instrumental in understanding how Black women share common experiences and simultaneously are different in other ways leading to diverse responses to intersectional oppressions. Expanding her work to other minoritized individuals, Crenshaw argues that intersectionality "is an analytic sensibility through which we analyze the relationship between our multiple identities and their connectedness to social power" (Crenshaw, 2015).

Over time, intersectionality has been used to understand how race, gender, class, ability, sexuality, nationality and other cultural elements simultaneously operate to produce a specific person (K. Chavez, 2012). Yep (2013) characterized two approaches to intersectionality: (1) a roster-like approach (a superficial listing of different cultural markers as characteristics of an individual) and (2) thick intersectionality (which focuses on the complexities of a person's identity—their lived experiences within a specific historical period and geographical location). In this chapter, we seek to use thick intersectionality as a means to promote competent interracial communication. This means that we do not focus solely on marginalized identities (Yep, 2016). Instead, one's communicative experiences must be understood as a complex, multidimensional phenomena (Carbado, 2013) marked by both advantages and disadvantages produced by societal systems (Purdie-Vaughns & Eibach, 2008). Yep's (2019) work on microaggressions is a good example of how productive a thick intersectional approach to understanding interracial communication can be.

Embracing intersectionality is central to cultural competency within interracial communication (Razzante et al., 2021). It helps to promote an understanding of how identity is multidimensional and a mixture of both privilege and disadvantage. It also helps to further our understanding of how societal power and privilege function at the interpersonal level (Collins, 2019). This is aptly described in the work of Cooper (2018), whose experiences as a Black southern female academic inform every aspect of her life including her teaching, research, and political activism. Her writing helps us to understand that intersectionality is not necessarily an account of personal identity but of power. In similar ways, Durham (2021) and A. Johnson (2021) embrace intersectionality as they move toward a more holistic, complete understanding of self.

| Box 5.2 | Student Reflections |
|---|---|

### Ethnic Gumbo

The actual makeup of my race, like most African Americans, is pretty diverse. I like to call it gumbo! My great-grandmother on my mother's side was Irish and Cherokee Indian. Her husband was Black (and who knows what else). My great-grandfather on my father's side was African American, Mexican, and Blackfoot Indian; however, even this is unreliable information because of family secrets about marriage, paternity of children, and because the name "Blackfoot" was used to describe a number of tribes besides that of actual Blackfeet Indians. I know little about my exact family history due to death and family members who refuse to talk about those who have passed away. I identify most with being Black, but to add even more confusion, my racial experience specifically relies on being a light-skinned Black because I have experienced both detrimental and beneficial racism within and outside of my own race.

Figure 5.2 provides a visual representation to understanding one's intersectional identity. One way to incorporate the idea of hierarchical organizations of identity as both fluid and enduring—a basic property of cultural identity theory—is to envision a pyramid of sorts. The more enduring aspects of an individual's self-identity exist at the top of the identity pyramid. Other more fluid cultural markers, whose salience and intensity vary depending on the particular situational context (T. Harris, 2016), are positioned at the bottom. This framework is productive in that it (1) embraces the interconnectedness of multiple cultural identities, (2) recognizes both the enduring and fluid nature of cultural markers, and (3) avoids the trap of building a rigid, definitive hierarchy of cultural identity for all people. Without assigning status to any one aspect of identity for all people, the pyramid highlights the concept that certain sets of lived experiences result in moving specific identity elements to the core of a particular person's self-concept. Some theorists see multiple identity hierarchies as largely fluid, changing from one situation to another; others believe

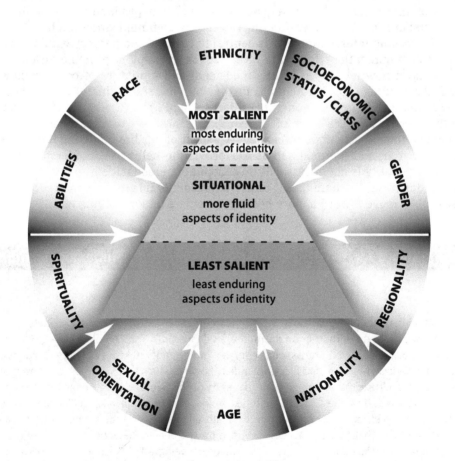

**Figure 5.2**   Cultural Identity Pyramid

the organization of key cultural identity markers is more enduring (R. Jackson et al., 2020). In reality, both perspectives are likely correct to some extent.

## POTENTIALLY SALIENT ASPECTS OF CULTURAL IDENTITY

Because our focus here is on interracial communication, it is not feasible to offer a detailed description of each aspect of culture that has the potential to impact interracial contact (see B. Allen, 2012). Such a task appears especially difficult given the broad ways in which culture has been defined by most communication scholars. Instead, we have identified several specific elements of cultural identity that seem especially relevant to interracial communication in the United States. Our selection, although not definitive, is the result of a thorough review of existing literature as well as our own research and lived experiences. Nevertheless, we acknowledge that additional elements of cultural identity may represent significant factors during interracial interactions. These are known as "differences that make a difference" (Goodnight, 1997, p. 270). To illustrate the process by which multiple cultural identities are enacted, we focus on seven specific elements: socioeconomic status, gender, nationality/regionality, age, sexual orientation, spirituality, and abilities.

In the sections to follow, each cultural aspect is described specifically in terms of its influence on communication processes. These descriptions (1) distinguish how each aspect represents a cultural identity marker, (2) generate an understanding of its relationship to perceptions of communication, (3) illustrate how it relates to privilege/disadvantage, and (4) highlight the ways it intersects with racial and ethnic identities in the context of intraracial and interracial communication. As you read, reflect on how multiple cultural identities are negotiated in different contexts. Specifically, ask yourself the following questions: What is the salience and intensity of this cultural marker within my self-concept? How is this directly related to particular situational contexts and relationships with others? Are there any cultural elements that are enacted with more salience and intensity than those marked by race/ethnicity? If so, within what contexts and/or relationships?

### Socioeconomic Status

**Socioeconomic status** (SES), or class, refers to the relative status according to income, wealth, power, and/or position. SES is a communicative entity, something that includes "a sense of community, status symbols, territories, rituals and gender and racial inflections" (MacLeod, 2009, p. 251). The field of communication has been slow to examine how SES impacts communication, although some significant work does exist (M. Houston & Wood, 1996; Moon & Rolison, 1998; Philipsen, 1975, 1976). One reason for this dearth of substantial research might be the lack of awareness and general silence about the role of SES in a country that values equal opportunity to achieve the "American dream" (Langston, 2020). Ehrenreich (1990) explains,

[U.S.] Americans are notorious for their lack of class consciousness or even class awareness. We have a much greater consciousness of race and gender issues than we do of class. Race and gender are immediate—and they are irreversible. Class is different: The American myth is that we can escape (transcend) our class. We can work our way up and out of it. (p. 103)

---

**Box 5.3**                                                              **Author Reflections**

## Impact of Socioeconomic Status on Self-Concept

I have quite a few memories about the role that socioeconomic status played in my self-concept and how I interacted with others. Growing up in a low-income housing project with subsidized rent meant that my family didn't have a lot, but neither did anyone else, so our lives seemed pretty "normal." This continued during elementary school when most of my classmates dressed like me, talked like me, and liked to do the same things as me (watching lots of TV, listening to music, and playing basketball, Kick-the-Can, Red Rover, and Cartoon Freeze Tag). Getting "free" or "reduced" lunch every day at school was the norm, not the exception.

One of my realizations of class differences occurred in the seventh grade when I attended a citywide junior high school. During one of my first days of school, I vividly remember one of the teachers taking attendance and asking each student what elementary school he or she had attended. I couldn't help but notice that she seemed to treat students differently based on that information. Such treatment seemed to strengthen the boundaries between "us" (the poor kids) and "them" (the rich kids). Although some friendships were able to cross class divisions, these were relatively few and seemed to only play out in certain circumstances (e.g., during college-prep courses where a few of *us* were able to interact with more of *them* on a more equal level). Differences in dress, speech, and interests clearly facilitated a social/class division in our school. Bringing your lunch—and looking down on those of us who ate school lunches—was the preferred norm. The few of *them who paid* for their lunch received tickets that were a different color from those tickets that were *given to us* free or at a reduced rate. Distinguishing markers based on class were everywhere.

Socioeconomic status is a way of life and does not necessarily change with your personal or family income. Thus, while my salary today is significantly higher than that of my parents, my life perspective in terms of class remains largely the same (see, for example, Orbe, 2021b). For example, I rarely buy anything not on clearance—even sale prices are too expensive for me! I initially struggled with our children who seemed to have very expensive taste and always wanted to buy things on the spot without checking prices or waiting to buy it off-season. I kept telling them that my shopping is smart, but they were convinced it's because I'm cheap. Our middle daughter started calling me "chmart" (a combination of the two!). Over time, my class consciousness has impacted how our children perceive money as adults. Because of my early experiences growing up—something I wouldn't trade for the world!—socioeconomic status remains an important issue in most of my interactions with others. What are some of your salient cultural issues? How are they tied to specific life memories?

—MPO

An important consideration when examining class differences is recognizing that SES is not equated with economic standing. Income (how much you make) is different from wealth (what assets you have access to); particular perspectives on life are associated with wealth, something that is more stable over time (Lui et al., 2006). Are you familiar with the terms "old money" and "new money"? Typically, the latter term refers to individuals whose economic standing has drastically improved, yet their values, interests, attitudes, and behaviors have remained fairly constant. The term has been used by the upper class to distinguish themselves from others who have more recently achieved economic success, emphasizing that how much money you have does not automatically translate into a particular "class of people." Beyond current levels of income, class also entails assumptions concerning levels of economic security, the importance of family and kinship ties, interests and leisure time activities, and specific communication styles (Orbe, 2021b). According to some scholars, class is all-encompassing and influences every aspect of our lives. "Class is your understanding of the world and where you fit in; it's composed of ideas, behaviors, attitudes, values, and languages; class is how you think, feel, act, look, dress, talk, move, walk" (Langston, 2020, p. 119). In short, "We experience class at every level of our lives" (p. 120).

**Classism** is most commonly understood as a top-down practice whereby middle- and upper-class persons perpetuate discriminatory behaviors toward those of lower-class standing. One aspect of classism is the maintenance of separation, including conscious efforts of "affluent" groups to do whatever they can to avoid contact with the "less fortunate" (Ehrenreich, 1990; Moss, 2003). Because of the lack of any substantial interaction between different classes, all socioeconomic groups maintain stereotypes about other classes. People from the middle- and upper-class segments of society often stereotype

---

### Box 5.4

## Middle/Upper-Class Privileges

Building on the work of Peggy McIntosh (1988), educators have identified different privileges that some groups have over others. Below are seven examples of middle/upper class privilege.

1. I can afford to live in neighborhoods where I feel "at home" and there are schools with great resources.
2. I can be pretty sure that my behaviors (e.g., swearing, sloppy dress, tardiness) will not be attributed to my social class.
3. I can talk with my mouth full and not have people blame it on my social class.
4. I can do well in a challenging situation without being called a credit to my class.
5. I can remain ignorant of the language and customs of other classes without any penalties.
6. I can worry about classism without being seen as self-serving.
7. I can invite my friends out for an evening and not worry about affording it.

the working class/underclass as ignorant, lazy, and hopelessly bigoted. It is important to recognize, though, that class prejudice (in the form of personal attitudes) functions at all levels of SES (Moon & Rolison, 1998). Wasteful, snobby, lazy, carefree, and prejudiced are some of the perceptions that members of a lower socioeconomic status have in regard to more affluent persons. Although the institutional power of individuals to enact policy based on these stereotypes varies, the influence of prejudice on interpersonal contact remains strong for all SES groups (Engen, 2016).

Socioeconomic status remains a largely invisible issue within the United States (Lawless, 2016; Lui et al., 2006). This is, in part, due to the reality that class standing is largely correlated with racial/ethnic identity and other cultural variables such as gender, family structure, and neighborhood composition (Langston, 2020). Therefore, many references to racial and ethnic groups typically reflect class distinctions more than racial/ethnic differences. Lui et al. (2006) provided an in-depth analysis of the roots of the racial wealth divide in the United States with insightful descriptions of how each racial group (Native Americans, African Americans, Latino/as, Asian Americans, and European Americans) has, or has not, accumulated wealth. Power differences have resulted in widely divergent differences in wealth. "For every dollar owned by the average white family in the United States, the average family of color has less than one dime" (p. 1). In 2019, the median Black household had about $23,000 of wealth compared to $184,00 for a median white household—12 cents per dollar (Kent & Ricketts, 2020). The median Hispanic family had $38,000 of wealth—21 cents per dollar of white median wealth.

Clearly, race intersects with socioeconomic status in meaningful ways (Hendrix, 2016; Swencionis et al., 2017). Looking at race and SES alone, however, does not give us a complete enough picture to predict the quality of interracial communication. Any productive analysis of the potential for interracial communication competency must not only account for race/ethnicity and SES but also all of the other aspects of cultural identity described in this chapter. For example, consider existing communication research that studied the experiences of those individuals who were the first in their families to attend college (Orbe, 2003; Putman & Thompson, 2006). While having college-educated parents has an established correlation with socioeconomic status, the researchers findings revealed that race, gender, age, and regionality were important aspects of the ability to succeed at college and maintain close ties at home. Studies on other issues, such as life expectancy, also demonstrate the importance of considering intersections of race, ethnicity, gender, and socioeconomic status (Neergaard, 2006).

## Gender

Of all of the aspects of cultural identity we have chosen to describe here, **gender** is the one most extensively researched by communication scholars. Julia Wood (1996, 1997, 2005) is one of the most influential gender communication researchers using a cross-cultural perspective (Wood & Dindia, 1998). Research has focused on both the similarities and the differences in gendered

Box 5.5                                                   *Research Highlight*

## Gender, Race, and Class Privilege—Missing White Woman Syndrome

Missing white woman syndrome (U.S. American news anchor, Gwen Ifill, is credited with creating the term) refers to the heightened media coverage of missing person cases involving young, white, middle- and upper-class women. The increased attention is markedly different than cases where a person of color from a lower-socioeconomic status is missing (Rosner, 2021). Reflecting a type of gendered and racialized hierarchy in U.S. cultural imagery, the phenomenon has also been highlighted in South Africa, Australia, New Zealand, and the United Kingdom. In addition to gender, race, and class, other factors (e.g., perceived attractiveness, body type, and youthfulness) also contribute to increased media coverage. Notably, media coverage of missing Black women is more likely to focus on the victims' problems (e.g., a troubled past). In comparison, news reports for missing white women tends to highlight their roles as daughter, mothers, or community members. The U.S. national sensation surrounding the case of 22-year-old Gabby Petito in 2021 is the most recent noteworthy example of missing white woman syndrome.

What can be done about how unconscious bias impacts media focus? Recent research by Parlsoe and Campbell (2021) offers one possibility. Their research focused on Canada's National Inquiry on Missing and Murdered Indigenous Women and Girls (MMIW), an effort inspired by activists concerned with the disproportionately high rate of disappearance and death of Indigenous women and trans persons. More specifically, the researchers highlight the ways in which social media platforms, like Twitter, can play a significant role in increased awareness. Their article reports on how the power of (cyber)activism can be leveraged to reframe Indigenous trauma, facilitate a greater collective identity, and mobilize a nation-building discourse around the issue.

communication (e.g., Canary & Dindia, 1998) and the intersections of gender and race/ethnicity (e.g., Carlo et al., 2012).

The interlocking nature of gender, race, and ethnicity are so powerful that they are simultaneously enacted with high degrees of salience and intensity (R. Jackson & Hopson, 2011; Tyree et al., 2012). Attempting to describe the impact of these identity markers on interracial communication is not feasible unless we also pay attention to other elements of identity in specific interactions. In some situational contexts, the commonality established through one identity aspect may serve as a strong foundation for competent interracial communication. Traditionally, sports represent a context where people from different racial and ethnic groups come together for a common purpose (winning) (Connell, 2005). After the advances made possible through programs that promote equal resources for women and men (e.g., Title IX programs), more women have experienced the synergy, collective energies, and close relationships that come with competitive sports at all levels. Some researchers criticize sports as simply another societal mechanism where the "politics of inequality" are played out (Kao et al., 2019), but other research indicates that positive, long-lasting interracial relationships are initiated through participation in various sports.

### "My Race Didn't Make a Difference"

I'm a typical Midwesterner. I grew up in a pretty good-sized town that had one major high school. We had some, but not a lot of, different races in our school. Like most schools, however, people pretty much stuck within their own cliques: jocks, band geeks, preppies, drama kids, brainiacs, druggies, etc. A few times someone might cross from one group to another, but not very often at all. The same went for race. . . . Sports were an exception, though. As an Asian, I was definitely a brainiac, but I also played soccer for 4 years—the only minority on the team. I really liked the fact that I could be friends with different groups of people at school. Playing soccer definitely allowed me to make friends that I normally wouldn't have, and I can be 100% sure in saying that my race didn't make a difference to my teammates. We practiced together, traveled together, and won and lost together.

Frustrated by issues of sexism within their communities, some women turn to women's coalitions to fight various oppressions (P. Allen, 1986). Interestingly, feminism is the only major human rights movement that is consistently not embraced by the individuals who have most benefitted (Vavrus, 2010). The goal of many of these organizations is to focus on the common experiences of all women, transcending barriers based on racial/ethnic, class, and sexual orientation differences. However, according to women of color, addressing commonalties based on sex while ignoring differences of race threatens the mobilization of women's collective power (Forbes, 2009). In many contexts, women of color are often read as threatening or aggressive when they assert themselves (Calafell, 2010). African American women report that their interpersonal interactions with European American women (even those perceived as well-intentioned) reflect a focus on common experiences while ignoring salient racial differences. Attempts at solidarity, according to Huling et al. (2016), come in phrases like "I never even notice that you're Black," "You're different than other Blacks," and "I understand your experiences as a Black oman because sexism is just as bad as racism" (p. 61).

Although rallying around issues central to women can create a unified front, it should not be done by ignoring differences based on race/ethnicity or class (K. Wong, 2016). Competent interracial female communicators recognize the negative impacts of downplaying the importance of race. Instead, they consider the crucial role that racialized lived experiences play in how all individuals perceive self and others (Frankenberg, 1993). Research on sexual harassment found that women must negotiate the double jeopardy of racism and sexism in organizations—something not always acknowledged by European Americans (J. Taylor & Richardson, 2006). African American women and Latinas were the targets of "racialized sexual harassment" (p. 84), including being treated as an "exotic erotic" figure in the workplace.

---

**BOX 5.7**                                              *Research Highlight*

## The Unconscious Bias

For the past 30 years, psychologists Mahzarin Banaji and Anthony Greenwald (2013) have studied the unconscious biases that exist in human brains, something that are known as *mindbugs*—"ingrained habits of thought that lead to errors in how we perceive, remember, reason, and make decisions" (p. 4). According to this line of research, mindbugs are learned mental habits that interrupt the brain's ability to perceive things as they really are. Over the course of our lives, culture and societal interactions contribute to our attitudes about things like race, gender, sexuality, age, and socioeconomic status. The bottom line is this: If you admit it or not, we all have mindbugs that unconsciously impact our views of others. Brenda Allen (2012) uses the idea of "thinking under the influence" (TUI) as a way to describe this human tendency. Psychology researchers have designed a series of tests as part of Project Implicit (see Chapter 3) that allow individuals to identify their implicit biases in terms of gender, age, disability, weight, sexuality, and race/ethnicity—including African Americans, European Americans, Native Americans, Asian Americans, and Arab Muslims.

---

## Nationality/Regionality

Traditionally, **nationality** has been used to refer to the nation in which one is born and holds citizenship. This simplistic definition, however, has grown increasingly complex given the large numbers of people who change their citizenship, have dual citizenships, or affiliate with multiple national cultures (Collier, 2002; Hao, 2021). For example, consider the lived experiences of Gust Yep (2002), who describes his "multicultural self" as follows.

> I am Asianlatinoamerican. Although I have never been to China, I am racially what my parents describe as "100% pure Chinese." During my formative years, we lived in Peru, South America, and later moved to the United States. . . . I am trilingual (English, Spanish, and Chinese) . . . I "look Asian American," yet at times my Latino culture is most prominent in some communication settings. I strongly identify with all three cultures, and they are more or less integrated into this complex entity that I label as "multicultural self." (p. 60)

While nationality is a salient cultural marker, regionality provides another layer of identity that is often just as important yet less acknowledged. **Regionality** refers to a specific area of a nation that has its own culture within the larger national culture. For instance, most U.S. Americans recognize that being born and raised in New England is significantly different than being born and raised in the Midwest, or in the rural South, or on the West Coast. While we commonly acknowledge regional differences within our own countries, we must do the same for other countries as well. Simply focusing on nationality can create nation-based stereotypes that do not account for important regional differences. In support of this idea, Mallinson and Brewster

(2005) highlight how different forms of "regiontalk" and other forms of non-verbal cues influence perceptions and communication behavior.

Some clarification may be necessary to distinguish nationality and region-ality from other cultural identity elements such as race and ethnicity. Paying attention to these differences should shed some light on how complex cultural identity perceptions can be. Literature on the cultural experiences of one racial group, that of Asian/Pacific Islanders, serves as an excellent point of analysis. Applying one label based on race to drastically diverse cultural groups is *problematic* because it ignores other cultural differences such as language and religion (Sodowsky et al., 1995). For many non–Asian Americans, *race* serves as a primary cultural marker and *ethnic* differences remain less visible. Consider that Asian Americans can be Chinese, Japanese, Filipino, Korean, Indian, Cambodian, Laotian, Hmong, etc. Looking at *nationality* brings additional complexities into the negotiation of multiple cultural identi-ties. Take, for instance, a Chinese person whose nationality may be most closely defined by the People's Republic of China, Taiwan, Hong Kong, or the United States. *Regional* differences (urban/rural, east/west/north/south) also come into play here. Imagine the differences of two Chinese Americans who were born and raised in different regions of the United States: one in Missis-sippi and the other in San Francisco's Chinatown (see Gong, 2016).

**Transnationalism** is another important concept to consider in this discus-sion. This idea captures the experience of today's immigrants, refugees, and sojourners who, instead of abandoning their old identities and assimilating, choose to simultaneously live in two (or more) cultures and construct bicul-tural identities (Bhattacharya, 2021; Carrillo Rowe, 2016; Mutua, 2016). This often means integrating multiple, often diametrically distinct, cultures into one social world (M. Hall, 2012; Pedraza, 2006). Although immigrants have almost always maintained connections with their country of origin (Vertovec, 2001), their embeddedness in two cultures has been facilitated (although not caused) by rapid, accessible transportation and communication technologies (Cheng, 2005). The maintenance of close ties with the country of origin was previously viewed as an early, temporary stage in immigrant assimilation, which—if it did not end—was perceived as an exception to the rule (Baia, 1999). Moreover, immigration to the host country was usually viewed as per-manent (Suárez-Orozco, 2000). However, recent research shows that individu-als continue to identify with multiple nations (Orbe & Drummond, 2011).

## Age

The United States has been described as an increasingly age-conscious society (McCann et al., 2004) "where children want to be adults, adults want to be children, and those in their twenties and thirties are considered to be in the 'prime of their life'" (p. 89). Age remains a salient issue in a culture where people celebrate significant transition ages (e.g., 16, 21, 30, 40, 50 years old), have their social and relational roles (e.g., married or single) judged on the basis of age, and oftentimes report a fear of aging. Think about different age groups (senior citizens, Generation X, baby boomers). What images do you typically associate with each group? Stereotypes related to age impact communication (K. Anderson et al., 2005).

Some communication research exists on the cultural aspects of different age groups (Hajek & Giles, 2002; Yen, 2009). Most of this work is based on the idea that the shared life histories of generations of U.S. Americans have resulted in a common culture of sorts, including common values, norms, languages, dress, and so on (McCann & Giles, 2002). Table 5.1 provides a snapshot of commonalities (Jayson, 2010). Consider millennials, the group whose numbers reached 72.1 million in 2019, surpassed the 71.6 million baby boomers as the largest adult generation (Fry, 2020). This cohort has been criticized for being entitled, self-absorbed, easily offended, and uniquely special—in essence, a bunch of "snowflakes" (Rangel, 2020). Members of this group reject this offensive characterization and highlight how current conditions (e.g., global financial crises, increased climate concerns, rising costs of living and education, and turbulent political landscape) have contributed to increases in poor mental health (Haslam-Ormerod, 2019).

Contrast the stereotypical characterizations of millennials with those associated with older generations, like the Silent Generation. Research indicated that most perceptions of older adults revolve around negative stereotypes: "greedy, lonely, afraid, incompetent, senile, sexless, inarticulate, forgetful,

**Table 5.1    Generational Cultural Identities**

| Generation and Birth Years | Key Events | Characteristics |
|---|---|---|
| Greatest (GI) Generation Born 1901–1924 | Great Depression, New Deal, Roaring 20s | Team-playing, optimistic, respect authority, strong sense of civic obligation, frugal |
| Silent Generation Born 1925–1945 | Great Depression, World War II, Korean War | Friendly, professional, conciliating, trustworthy, credentialed, expert |
| Baby Boomers Born 1946–1964 | JFK/MLK assassinations, Vietnam War, civil rights movement, women's movement | Values-oriented, idealistic, work-centric, seeking self-actualization, competitive, "Me generation" |
| Generation X Born 1965–1980 | Latchkey kids, rising divorce rates, HIV/AIDS, technology | Pragmatic, independent, self-reliant, individualistic, value work-life balance, protective of their children |
| Millennials (Generation Y) Born 1981–1995 | 9/11, Columbine, internet, social networking | Optimistic, civically engaged, self-confident, team-oriented, close to parents, technology-focused |
| Generation Z Born 1996–2010 | Racial/ethnic diversity, increased gun violence, intensified climate change, increased reliance on technology | Pragmatic, financially mindful, independent thinkers, politically progressive, shrewd customers, extensive social networkers |

depressed, stubborn" (McKay, 2000, p. 184). Such images are reinforced by the media (Barker & Giles, 2003). Dilip Jeste, a geriatric neuropsychiatrist, notes that the description of older adults as "elderly" is stigmatizing and offensive.

> There is a lot of ageism in the society—meaning that people over a certain age (e.g., 65) are considered as being uniformly frail and disabled. Thus, it is similar to sexism and racism in that it stereotypes people based on a characteristic over which they have no control—in this case, chronological age. (quoted in Vore, 2021)

As the U.S. population continues to age, competent communicators must be prepared to interact with people whose life experiences span generations of different racial events.

It is important to recognize that age is a cultural phenomenon. The concept of age, and the perceptions related to different age cohorts, is culturally linked (Uotinen, 1998). This even includes what is defined as "young" and "old." Among Native American cultures, for example, determination of who is "old" does not solely relate to chronological age; evidence of particular social roles (e.g., being a grandparent or being unable to work) is equally as important. As such, someone can be considered "young" at 80 if economically and financially functional or "old" at 45 if sick or frail (Barker & Giles, 2003).

In individualistic, Western countries, aging is perceived negatively (Hajek & Giles, 2002). In comparison, in more collectivistic cultures, (e.g., Laos and Thailand) older people are highly respected and valued because of their knowledge, wisdom, and sageness. Family-oriented Native Americans traditionally respect their elders for their knowledge and experience (Carson & Hand, 1999); as such, care of the elderly is the primary responsibility of relatives and a concern for the entire tribe (Barker & Giles, 2003). All of these things demonstrate the need to acknowledge racial, ethnic, and cultural influences on how individuals negotiate their lives. For instance, scholars have urged health care practitioners to consider race and ethnic identifications when creating health care policy, procedures, and public campaigns.

## Sexual Orientation

**Sexual orientation** refers to the direction of an individual's sexuality. Common terms used to reference sexual orientation are: heterosexual (straight), bisexual (bi), homosexual (lesbian and gay), and asexual (no sexual attraction to others or interest in sexual activity). Most definitions of sexual orientation include (1) a psychological component that refers to the target of an individual's erotic desire, and (2) a behavioral component that focuses on the sex of the individual's sexual partner(s) (Shively et al., 1984). The term sexual preference is sometimes used in place of sexual orientation; however, it implies an element of choice as opposed to the belief that sexual orientation is biologically predetermined and/or fixed early in life (Reiter, 1989).

Some scholars have reported that gays and lesbians are increasingly socially accepted in Western society (Seidman et al., 1999); however, the level of acceptance can vary significantly depending on region, local community, or particular context (Sanders, 2020). Other scholars contend that gays and lesbians continue to live as minorities in a heterosexist world that harbors negative attitudes toward anyone not "straight" (Hajek & Giles, 2002). Heterosexist attitudes maintain a double standard related to sexual orientation; heterosexuality is viewed as healthy when overtly shared, whereas homosexuality is not. Until the Supreme Court decision in June 2015 that the Fourteenth Amendment guarantees a right to same-sex marriage, same-sex relationships were not legally sanctioned or recognized in all states (at the time of the decision, 13 states banned same-sex marriage). Despite the mandated legal status, sexual orientation remains a contested social issue, especially within particular cultural communities (Nero, 2016; Stotlzfus-Brown, 2021). For instance, within

---

### Box 5.8

### LGBTQ and Jewish

Faulkner and colleagues (Faulkner, 2006; Faulkner & Hecht, 2011) examined how individuals negotiate different aspects of their identities in various ways. This research on LGBTQ (lesbian, gay, bisexual, transgendered, and queer-identifying) Jewish persons highlights the complex ways that the identity emergence process occurs.

> Some ... considered Jewish and gay as separate and non-competing categories where one identity was more salient to who they were. Some considered being Jewish as a secular, cultural designation that didn't influence being LGBTQ, often they did not think of being Jewish on a daily basis. Some saw a conflict between a religious Judaism and being LGBTQ as they worked to integrate them, whereas others absolutely integrated Jewish/LGBTQ as in a gay Havurot and couldn't separate the identities. (Faulkner, 2006, p. 113)

Can you see how, at times, difficulties can arise when people try to integrate different aspects of their identities? What examples can you think of where this would be an ongoing issue?

the context of friendships, research has shown that sex and sexual orientation shape the norms and expectations of others' behavior (Muraco, 2005). Heterosexual persons, especially heterosexual men, evaluate behaviors more favorably when the other person is straight (Herek, 2000). When communicating with gay and lesbian people, negative attitudes are communicated through heterosexist talk and discriminatory nonverbal behaviors, like increased physical distance (Alexander, 2021; Speer & Potter, 2000). While sometimes less visible than race, sexual orientation impacts our everyday communication (Silverman, 2021).

Living the life of a cultural outsider in the United States provides gays and lesbians with a perspective shared with many other cocultures. For many individuals, a basic assumption exists: A person who experiences oppression is more likely to identify with others who are also oppressed, regardless of the source of their oppression. Can the sting of confronting isms (racism, sexism, heterosexism) on a daily basis work toward creating a bond for two racially diverse people? According to Allen (2016), it can and did in her close interracial relationship with one of her colleagues, Anna. The two women have a great deal in common: baby boomers from the Midwest, raised with a similar socioeconomic status, and strong religious backgrounds. However, Allen attributes their strong friendship to sharing a similar marginalized position in society and concludes that, "despite our similarities in personal style and background, Anna and I would probably not have become such good friends if she were straight" (p. 220).

Race, ethnicity, and sexual orientation intersect in different ways for different individuals in different contexts (Galupo, 2007; Pattisapu & Calafell, 2012; Spieldenner & Castro, 2010). For example, Luna (1989) provides strong evidence that the discrimination gay communities face does not naturally lead to a greater vision of racial understanding and harmony. In fact, what appears prevalent in the gay male culture is a level of "gay racism" (p. 440) that parallels the prejudice in the larger society. For instance, M. Ng (2004) describes how the sexual identities of Asian males are strongly informed by European American males. He argues that, within gay youth culture, the only role that gay Asian American men are expected to play is that of the submissive, exotic, and passive stereotype. Similar forms of racial discrimination exist for women (Patel, 2019) and other people of color (Souleymanov et al., 2020). In summary, racial- and ethnic-based bias and discrimination continue to exist as a problematic issue in different areas of LGBTQ+ culture.

## Spirituality

**Spirituality** generally refers to an individual's identification with and belief in a higher power. In comparison, **religion** is the participation within a community of people who fellowship around common ways of worship (Pindar & Jones, 2012). Although religious and spiritual communities have not been studied extensively as cultural entities per se, group membership does represent an important aspect of cultural identity for many individuals (Silverman,

2021). This is especially true for certain racial and ethnic groups, like African Americans, who traditionally relied on religious organizations to meet both spiritual and tangible needs such as health care, education, and financial assistance (Hamlet, 2016; Youngblood & Winn, 2004). Examining various levels of spirituality in the context of interracial communication appears especially relevant, given that many people's perceptions of different racial/ethnic groups (as well as other cultural groups, such as women and gays and lesbians) are informed by such belief systems.

U.S. history demonstrates the central role of spiritual beliefs in the ways that different racial and ethnic groups have interacted. The call for a Manifest Destiny (see Chapter 2) was regarded as a "spiritual endeavor" and set the tone for how European Americans interacted with the people of color they found in North America (Brewer, 2006). Select biblical scriptures were often presented as evidence for the necessity and value of slavery and other oppressive measures against African Americans and other microcultures. The Ku Klux Klan, a self-defined religious organization, uses traditional Christian symbols like the cross as a means to illustrate their "spiritually inspired" actions (Ezekiel, 1997). Fighting back the advances and influences of groups that promised to kill the legacy of what it means to be a "real American" (by African Americans, Jews, Catholics, and so on), the KKK's ideology of white supremacy is grounded in "good old-fashioned Christian values." A similar

---

### Box 5.9

### Contemporary White Supremacist Groups

A special edition of ABC's *Nightline* featured a story on the "new Ku Klux Klan" that highlighted activities in Mississippi and Virginia (Bernstein, 2012). Although the KKK has traditionally been surrounded by secrecy, *Nightline* was welcomed by Steven Howard, the Grand Dragon of the Mississippi White Nights of the KKK who sought to increase awareness of the reinvigorated group. According to Mark Potok of the Southern Poverty Law Center (a group long on the front line in fighting hate groups), two of the largest hate group websites crashed because of unprecedented activity immediately following President Obama's 2008 election. While the first African American U.S. president was seen as the single most effective recruiting tool for the KKK, the election of President Donald Trump in 2016 prompted an additional rise in visibility to those individuals committed to resisting a new racial politics that threatened white supremacist values (J. Anderson, 2021). According to national reports, the number of U.S. hate crimes rose to new heights in 2021, with Asian Americans and African Americans as the most targeted groups (Nakamura, 2021). While the "new KKK" represents one reinvigorated white supremacist group, other contemporary groups also exist in various forms. What is your knowledge about these groups? How might you differentiate between groups that espouse white supremacist views through different rhetorical devices? What aspect of these organizations do you view as the biggest threat to productive racial relations? (See Jimenez, 2017 for one reporter's answer.)

sense of spirituality was intertwined with the messages of the Nation of Islam, guided by the Honorable Elijah Muhammad, Malcolm X, and minister Louis Farrakhan. For many Black Muslims, defining all European Americans as "white devils"—along with other teachings from the nation of Islam—were regarded as spiritual Truths (McPhail, 1998b). These religious beliefs, and the various ways in which they maintain tremendous barriers to productive inter-racial communication, are still apparent today.

Interestingly, many individuals indicate it is their spirituality that pro-motes interracial understanding that transcends racial and ethnic differences (see, for example, Clark & Diggs, 2002). Historical accounts provide various examples of how interracial coalitions based within an overarching spiritual purpose generated positive relations across racial and ethnic lines. According to Harris and DeTurk (2012) several specific themes are present in proactive multiracial diversity initiatives in religious organizations (e.g., agape/God-inspired love, racism as sin, peace and justice as core values). For many indi-viduals, the importance of their spirituality provides them with the common faith to interact, not as different racial or ethnic group members but as exten-sions of the same creator. Despite such beliefs, spiritual gatherings remain one of the most segregated aspects of society (Orbe & Elliott, 2012). Without ques-tion, spirituality seems to hold great potential for transcending racial/ethnic differences. Yet the "baggage" that comes with particular cultural systems oftentimes includes problematic perceptions, expectations, and behaviors that ultimately interrupt ideal relationships operating on purely spiritual levels (Gonzalez, 2002).

## Abilities

Another salient issue in negotiating identity **is ability**—the social effects of physical, emotional, or mental capabilities. Wilson (2021) reminds us that all identity categories "are not uniform, static, or unrelated but rather fluid, dynamic, and deeply interconnected" (p. 7). What one person experiences in terms of abilities is not necessarily the case for another. Box 5.10 summarizes various statistics regarding disabilities, but we must be aware of factors beyond numbers. The degree to which a disability affects one's everyday life may differ depending on factors such as the visibility of a disability and the stage of life at which it occurred (Comeforo, 2021; Cornett-DeVito & Worley, 2005). For instance, Deaf with a capital "D" refers to people who were born deaf; they learned to communicate in sign language as their first language. In contrast, deaf with a lowercase "d" refers to people with severe hearing prob-lems or those who became deaf later in life (Parrish-Sprowl, 2016).

> There is no singular disability experience, and no one person will experi-ence disability in exactly the same way as others similarly disabled. Nor will one's individual experience of disability remain static over time. How a per-son experiences disability is due to a huge number of factors, including not only the type of disability one has but also whether the disability is congeni-tal or acquired; how the disability is perceived by others; the level of stigma

attached to the disability; whether one's disability is visible to others; how one's disability experience intersects with one's experiences of gender, race, class, sexuality, age, geographic location, and religion (among other factors); and one's access to adequate health care, education, employment, family and community support, and social services. (Wilson, 2021, p. 19)

When we discuss abilities, most often we refer to able-bodied persons and people with disabilities, as if there were an objective process for the division. Yet who is counted as disabled is a cultural decision (Wilson, 2021). Society constructs its expectations for health, levels of performance, and what societies value. Individuals classified as disabled may not identify as such while others may feel impaired, but their difficulties are not recognized as a disability. One example of a constructed category is the millions of people who were classified as having a mental disorder until the American Psychiatric Association removed "homosexuality" from the second edition of the Diagnostic and Statistical Manual of Mental Disorders. Disability categories result from dominant assumptions about race, class, and gender.

---

### Box 5.10

### People With Disabilities (2020 Numbers)

- 44 million people with a disability (13.4% of total population); this includes those with a hearing difficulty (3.6%), vision difficulty (2.4%), cognitive difficulty (5.3%), ambulatory difficulty (6.6%), self-care difficulty (2.7%), and independent living difficulty (5%) (Paul et al., 2021)

- 11.8% of the disability population has a college degree

- 16.9% of the American Indian and Alaska Native population have a disability (highest of all racial/ethnic groups) (American Community Survey, 2020a)

- Approximately 8 million people with a disability (ages 18 to 64) were employed in 2020 (Paul et al., 2021)

- $40,858 was the median earnings for people with disabilities

---

Disability is a salient communicative issue (Harter et al., 2006). Research that conceptualizes persons with disabilities as a cultural group has resulted in a growing body of literature in and outside of the field of communication (D. Braithwaite & Thompson, 2000). Disability as culture views people with disabilities as forming distinct cultures or cocultures; this underscores the empowering potential of disability as a cultural identity (M. Cohen & Avanzino, 2010; Coopman, 2003). When discussing persons with disabilities as a cultural group, three points must be acknowledged. First, different frames serve to oppress persons with disabilities; these include labels such as "disabled," which are seen as "damaged" and "defective" (Harter et al., 2006) and a cultural stigma (Vidali, 2009). Historically, disability has been seen as a medical problem, an "impairment" that must be repaired (Coopman, 2003). Second, a person with a disability may identify with a community of other persons with disabilities generally or those with a particular disability (e.g., blind, deaf, or mobility-related disabilities). According to Waldrop and Stern (2003), almost half of the people with disabilities live with more than one type of disability. Third, like any other cultural group, differences in experiences (e.g., being born with a disability or having lived as a TAB—temporarily able-bodied person) affect the phases of identity development (Padden & Humphries, 1988), communication, and community life (Harter et al., 2006).

Persons with disabilities recognize that, more often than not, able-bodied persons primarily see them as disabled first and a person with other personality and cultural traits second (D. Braithwaite & Braithwaite, 2000). In most instances, a disability invokes a number of widely accepted stereotypes for people, including being "dependent, socially introverted, emotionally unstable, depressed, hypersensitive, and easily offended, especially with regard to their disability" (Coleman & DePaulo, 1991, p. 69). Based on these stereotypical images of persons with disabilities, many able-bodied persons' communication is characterized by one of two approaches (Chan, 1989). First, communicators try to ignore that any disability exists. This oftentimes results in ignoring people with disabilities completely. Second, able-bodied persons may become oversensitive to the disability and treat a person with a disability in an overly protective and/or patronizing manner. The best advice is to first look at a person's abilities before factoring in what might need to be accommodated in terms of disabilities.

The intersection of abilities and racial/ethnic identity (Cedillo, 2018) provides some interesting case scenarios of interracial communication. Take, for example, the experiences of Sucheng Chan (1989), a person with a disability who is of Asian descent. Her experiences are especially interesting because in many East Asian cultures, a strong folk belief exists that sees a person's physical state in this life as a reflection of how morally or sinfully she or he lived in previous lives. Reactions to her decision to marry an able-bodied man outside her racial/ethnic group provide an insightful illustration of how race was more of an important factor for some (her father-in-law), and her disability was for others (mother-in-law, parents' friends).

Within this section, we have highlighted the ways in which different aspects of cultural identity intersect with race/ethnicity to create particular sets of experiences. For organizational purposes, we have separated out each aspect of identity to highlight the ways in which it interacts with race/ethnicity. However, this isolation does not happen in real life situations. We all are multicultural—we are a combination of race/ethnicity, age, gender, spirituality, sexual orientation, nationality/regionality, socioeconomic status, and abilities—and these things all play some role in how we communicate with others. This fact is what makes interracial communication simultaneously so fascinating and challenging!

# CONCLUSION

Cultural identity, of which racial/ethnic identity is a part, is abstract, complex, multidimensional, and fluid. Developing a consciousness of the role that racial/ethnic differences play in the communication process is important. It should not be overemphasized, though, to the point of stereotyping people based on their race/ethnicity. In other words, treating people as if they are solely defined by one facet of their cultural identity is problematic and arguably the best formula for *ineffective* interracial communication. Consider the following quote from Audre Lorde (1984):

> As a Black lesbian feminist comfortable with the many different ingredients of my identity, and a woman committed to racial and sexual freedom from oppression, I find I am constantly being encouraged to pluck out one aspect of myself and present this as the meaningful whole, eclipsing or denying the other parts of self. But this is a destructive and fragmenting way to live. My fullest concentration of energy is available to me only when I integrate all the parts of who I am, opening, allowing power from particular sources of my living to flow back and forth freely through all of my different selves, without the restrictions of externally imposed definitions. Only then can I bring myself and my energies as a whole to the service of those struggles which I embrace as part of my living. (p. 120)

As Lorde points out, interacting with others based on a single aspect of our identity denies us the opportunity to participate as complete cultural beings. Race remains a salient issue in the United States. And we should recognize the role that race/ethnicity plays in the communication process alongside other elements of a person's multiple cultural identity. Ultimately, the ability to recognize the multiple identities of self and others—and identify key elements of cultural difference in any given interaction—appears to be a fundamental component of interracial communication competence (Collier, 2002). In addition, paying attention to the multiple cultural identities of others and the various ways they influence communicative behaviors generates opportunities for enhanced self-identity development.

## KEY TERMS

| | | |
|---|---|---|
| avowal | classism | transnationalism |
| ascription | gender | sexual orientation |
| salience | nationality | spirituality |
| intersectionality | regionality | religion |
| socioeconomic status | | |

## OPPORTUNITIES FOR EXTENDED LEARNING

1. Create a case study that details a particular scenario in which multiple cultural identities directly influence intraracial or interracial communication (for an example, see Box 5.6). Ideally, these should be based on real-life experiences. Share your case study with the rest of the class/group and discuss the importance of recognizing multiple cultural identities in communication competence.

2. Aimee Mullins is a well-known athlete, actress, fashion model, and accomplished public speaker. What typically gets her the most attention, however, is the fact that she has twelve pairs of legs (she was born with a medical condition that resulted in the amputation of both of her lower legs when she was 1). One of the powerful points that Mullins makes in her speeches is that her disability is not related to her legs or the ability to function but to the perceptions of others that make assumptions about her weakness, incompleteness, and inabilities. This important idea is at the heart of the photo exhibit titled "Impaired Perceptions," created by Brian Steel, a 33-year-old man who was diagnosed with congenital fiber-type disproportion when he was four months old. Battling ableism his entire life, his photos depict people with disabilities in ways that feature humanity. Steel's point is simple: "You cannot tell what a person is capable of or what their life is like simply by looking at them." Check out the eight photos featured at: http://edition.cnn.com/2013/01/25/health/brian-steel-impaired-perceptions/index.html. What are your impressions of the individuals in these photos? Are your impressions influenced by different abilities and disabilities, as well as by the gender, race, ethnicity, and age of the people in the photos?

3. Costumes that exaggerate, for example, the apparel or hairstyles of different racial and ethnic groups are fairly common. In fact, you can purchase a "Ghetto Fab wig" or "illegal alien jumpsuit" at mainstream stores like Kohl's and Target. Every fall, ethnic and racial stereotypes are popular costume themes at Ohio University, which has hosted one of the largest unofficial Halloween parties in the Midwest since the mid-1970s. A student organization at the university, Students Teaching About Racism in Society (STARS), created a poster campaign to make people reconsider how their costume choice reduces a culture to a caricature. Posters feature students of color from a variety of backgrounds holding pictures of costumes of their own groups. Some posters have the caption: "We're a culture, not a costume. This is not who I am and this is not okay." Others read: "You wear the costume for one night. I wear the stigma for life." You can check out five posters at: http://edition.cnn.com/2011/10/26/living/halloween-ethnic-costumes/index.html. What do you think about these posters? Do you see them as an overreaction to innocent fun or a productive way to educate others about the power of their actions?

4. Create an identity pyramid that reflects the various components of your self-identity in the context of reading this book (see Figure 5.2). First, complete the pyramid by listing your self-identity (which aspects of cultural identity are most salient to you). Then, use a different colored pen to com-

plete the list in terms of how others see you (e.g., which aspects of cultural identity to you think that they perceive are most salient to you). Once you've completed the task, break off into small groups and share why certain elements are more salient than others. What differences exist in terms of self (avowal) and others' (ascription) perceptions? What other cultural elements did you include that were not specifically described in this chapter (i.e., profession, education, etc.)?

5. According to Chen (2016), "names are not solely personal; they are cultural, social, and political" (p. 21). Within small groups of 3–5 people, have each person share their preferred name (first, middle, last, nickname, etc.) and explain how it symbolizes who they are. Make special note of the origins of your name (e.g., the historical, familial, cultural aspects), how different aspects also relate to your age, gender, spirituality, nationality/regionality, etc., and how your naming preferences may have changed over time.

6. Within this chapter, we explain how gender (identity) and sexual orientation (attraction) intersect with race and ethnicity in terms of interracial communication. These concepts, however, are oftentimes misunderstood. Spend some time engaging these issues further by reviewing Sam Killermann's *Genderbread person* v. 4.0 (https://www.genderbread.org/). This visual, easy to understand resource provides a valuable foundation for discussing key concepts (anatomical sex, gender identity, gender expression, and attraction) in ways that resist an overly simplistic, binary (either/or) understanding of these complex concepts. Remember the key to a more developed, nuanced understanding is through more developed, nuanced language!

7. View the TED-Ed video on *The Five Major World Religions* by John Bellaimey (https://www.youtube.com/watch?v=m6dCxo7t_aE). As you learn more about Hinduism, Judaism, Buddhism, Christianity, and Islam, pay close attention to the ways in which each belief system has similar and different core values. Time permitting, locate and review additional educational resources on other religions (Bahá'í, Confucianism, Dahomey mythology [African], Earth Lodge religion [Indigenous], New Age, etc.). What lessons about race, communication, and, more specifically, interracial communication can we take away from different religions?

## RECOMMENDED CONTEMPORARY READINGS

Capobianco, P. (2017). Transfiguring identity: Social relationships and intercultural communication between foreign "children" and Japanese "parents." *Journal of International and Intercultural Communication, 10*(4), 324–341. doi.org/10.1080/17513057.2017.1300311

Chen, Y.-W. (2019). When religion meets academia: Millennial Christians becoming cultural others on a minority-serving campus in the United States. *Journal of International and Intercultural Communication, 12*(4), 325–343. doi.org/10.1080/17513057.2018.1557732

Garcia-Louis, C., & Cortes, K. L. (2020). Rejecting Black and rejected back: AfroLatinx college students' experiences with anti-AfroLantinidad. *Journal of Latinos and Education*. doi: 10.1080/15348431.2020.1731692

Holladay, H. W. (2018). Reckoning with the "redneck:" *Duck Dynasty* and the boundaries of morally appropriate whiteness. *Southern Communication Journal, 83*(4), 256–266. doi.org/10.1080/1041794X.2018.1472797

Lee, J. (2021). Talking through race: Two raced women's Tinder stories. *Communication, Culture & Critique.* doi.org/10.1093/ccc/tcab030

Medhurst, J. M. (2020). Cooking up Southern Black identity in *Chef's Table's* "Mashama Bailey." *Southern Journal of Communication, 85*(4), 219–230. doi.org/10.1080/1041794X.2020.1801822

Whittington, E. Y., Castle Bell, G., & Otusanya, A. D. (2021). Exploring discursive challenges between African Americans and African-born U.S. immigrants from the standpoint of African Americans. *Southern Communication Journal, 86*(1), 71–83. doi.org/10.1080/1041794X.2020.1861479

# 6

# Theoretical Approaches to Studying Interracial Communication

**CASE STUDY**    "Karen": Derogatory Racial Insult and/or Important Cultural Critique?

In contemporary U.S. culture, "Karen" is a label that emerged to describe any white woman who exercises her white privilege to police, surveil, and regulate African Americans and other people of color in public spaces. This label was prompted by countless real-world incidents where Black people were harassed by white women who were offended by their everyday behaviors—actions that seemingly had little to no effect on them. Oftentimes, "Karens" leveraged their societal power by calling, or threatening to call, the police on African Americans for simply "living while Black." Social media generally, and Black meme creators more specifically, used humor, satire, and strategic critiques to offer social commentaries on the behavior of white women behaving badly (A. Williams, 2020). Social media critique of white women's problematic behaviors is important given the history of surveillance and regulation of Black bodies in public; in essence it plays a key role in challenging white racial dominance in everyday acts of racism. This form of social media activism also embraces a sense of agency whereby offenders are held accountable for their actions and face very real consequences (e.g., social critique, loss of social status, termination of employment, etc.).

As the use of "Karen" gained prominence, some white women spoke out criticizing the term as a racial slur—the equivalent of the "n-word" for white women (Shand-Baptiste, 2020). Additionally, critics decried the "cancel culture" that surrounded social media critiques of white women's behaviors. What is your opinion of this issue? Do you see value in social media critiques of "Karens," and/or do you believe that they unfairly stereotype and grossly overemphasize the behavior of a small number of white women? Furthermore, what are your thoughts about how media attention has prompted real consequences for everyday racist behaviors? Do you see it as "cancel culture" and/or "accountability culture"?

F or most college students, the word "theory" triggers visions of abstract, dull, unnecessarily complex ideas that "academic types" use to intellectualize the world around them. Many believe that theories hold little practical value in terms of their everyday life experiences. Although these perceptions are not universally shared by all students, they do seem to hold true for significant numbers. The goal of this chapter is to present different theoretical frameworks that allow us to understand communication phenomena in more complex ways. Without theories to guide our actions, studying different aspects of interracial communication would be haphazard, disjointed, and random. Good communication theories expand our knowledge beyond superficial understanding. They also have practical value in enhancing communication competency.

Theoretical frameworks as lenses that assist us in seeing the world clearly is a useful metaphor for making the connection between theory and practice. Think about eye examinations in which the doctor changed the lens and then asked you if the letters on the wall were clearer. Some lenses increased our vision slightly, whereas others made our vision blurrier. The key to the process was to try different lenses until 20/20 vision was achieved. Imagine the tremendous difference that corrective lenses make for those who have been experiencing life (sometimes unknowingly) without clear vision. According to Deetz (1992), "a theory is a way of seeing and thinking about the world. As such, it is better seen as the 'lens' one uses in observation rather than as the 'mirror' of nature" (p. 66). Theories are very much like lenses. They help us see communication phenomena with greater clarity.

This chapter introduces ten theoretical frameworks that hold great promise for increasing our understanding of interracial communication. A general description of each theory or model is presented, including its core building blocks—concepts (a thing conceived, idea, or notion) and propositions (statements that describe how concepts relate to one another). Consistent with the lens metaphor, we acknowledge that some theories may be a better personal fit for you than others. The key is to identify and concentrate on those theories and models that facilitate the greatest understanding in terms of your life experiences. Ultimately, we hope that you are able to use multiple theories/ lenses to view interracial communication. Before presenting these theories, however, let's look at the early work on interracial communication.

## INTERRACIAL COMMUNICATION MODELS

The earliest interracial communication models can be traced to the mid-1970s and linked to the increased attention to race relations in the United States at that time. During the 1960s and 1970s, people of color—most notably African Americans and Chicanx people—gained national attention as they confronted historical, political, and social practices that were discriminatory and oppressive. Although most civil rights struggles continue in the 21st century (Orbe, 2005), these historical acts of civil disobedience were instrumental in forcing a society to deal with social ills traditionally ignored by most European

Americans. Several communication scholars acknowledged the key role they could play in building productive relations among different racial/ethnic groups. For many scholars, interracial communication represented an area of both great academic and practical relevance beyond most traditional work that focused on culture from an international perspective.

The earliest interracial communication model stemmed from the work of Molefi Kete Asante (previously known as Arthur L. Smith). His transracial communication model focused on describing the process by which individuals could "cross racial lines" to communicate effectively (A. Smith, 1973). However, Asante avoided traditional approaches of racial differences (based on genetics) that were prevalent in most research. Instead, he focused on interactions that were impacted by perceived racial identity distinctions on the part of one or more individuals. Interracial communication, then, included interactions when perceived racial differences were a critical feature. According to this model, the goal of transracial communication is the **normalization** of communication. Normalization was used to describe the process of identifying and moving toward a central threshold where both parties can find common ground on which to base their communication. To this end, ethnic differences could be transcended.

Rich (1974) and colleagues (Rich & Ogawa, 1972) created an interracial communication model that approached interracial communication differently from the transracial model. The model focused on the process by which different nonwhite racial groups leave their own cultures and intersect with European American–dominated social structures. The researchers believed that people of color could live within their respective communities relatively uninfluenced by the dominant structures of European Americans by remaining closer to their native culture. Specific attention was paid to the various ways that other cultural factors (socioeconomic status, skin color, degree of cultural differences) influenced the communication between European Americans and people of color.

The work of Blubaugh and Pennington (1976) differs from the interracial communication model in two distinct ways. First, their analysis of interracial communication is not limited to white–nonwhite communication. It can be used to understand European American–African American interactions, as well as those involving different racial/ethnic minorities (e.g., Asian American–Latinx Americans, Native American-African Americans, etc.). Second, the cross difference model of communication recognizes that all racial/ethnic groups (including European Americans) share some aspects of a "common culture" affiliated with living in the United States. Furthermore, the model acknowledges the mutual influences of different racial/ethnic cultures on one another. The cross difference model focused on the importance of transcending racial differences while simultaneously understanding how such differences remain a part of one's culture. Blubaugh and Pennington believed that while cultural influences will still be apparent during interracial interactions, they must be diminished in order for communication to be effective. In short, the cross difference communication model advocates transcending (not erasing) racial differences so that persons can communicate on a "same-race (human race) basis" (p. 17).

## THEORIZING INTERRACIAL COMMUNICATION

The past 50 years have yielded significant changes in terms of the political, social, legal, and economic structures that inform race relations in the United States. Yet, many issues remain hauntingly similar. For this reason, early inter-racial communication models contain elements and approaches that are still pertinent to the 21st century. Still, they do not reflect some of the changing realities of the past five decades. The field of communication generally, and the area of intercultural/interracial communication specifically, offers a broad range of theoretical frameworks that provide insight into interactions and relationships among people of diverse racial and ethnic backgrounds.

The remainder of this chapter divides descriptions of 10 theories into three different sections. The first section covers theories that are more scien-

---

**Box 6.1**                                              *Research Highlight*

### Research as Activism: #CommunicationSoWhite

In recent years, the field of communication has been criticized for its lack of representation of scholars and scholarship from people of color. The most visible manifestation of this criticism was prompted by an analysis that found that scholars of color continue to be severely under-represented in publication rates, citation frequency, and editorial roles throughout the field of communication (Chakravartty et al., 2018). This study—highlighted through the hashtag #CommunicationSoWhite—sparked unprecedented conversations regarding issues of diversity, inclusion, equity, and access on multiple levels throughout the communication discipline (Murthy, 2020). More importantly, these conversations resulted in important changes in policy and practice within regional, national, and international organizations and the publication outlets that they sponsor. In no uncertain terms, this publication and the others that followed (e.g., Austin et al., 2023; E. Ng et al., 2020) reflect a strong tradition of engaged scholarship—applied research that explicitly works to make a difference.

While we've always featured scholars of color and their scholarship in every edition of this textbook, we've "stepped up our game" by highlighting even more theoretical frameworks that centralize the perspectives and experiences of people of the global majority. This is crucially important to provide a broader, more representative understanding of interracial communication—one that is not primarily informed by one dominant (e.g., European American) mindset. As Chakravartty et al. (2018) aptly asserted, "decades of scholarship show that publication and citation practices reproduce institutional racism" (p. 257). Historical knowledge production has reinforced whiteness as the norm and, consequently, limited our access to information that is desperately needed to fully comprehend the role that race plays in our communication with others. The theories in this section work explicitly to offer a lens into the world that is *not* dominated by one particular racial/ethnic location.

tific in nature (anxiety/uncertainty management theory, communication accommodation theory, and conflict face-negotiation theory). Next, we present three theories that assume a more interpretive approach to studying interracial communication (co-cultural theory, cultural contracts theory, and [counter]public sphere theory). The final section features four theories [critical race theory, afrocentricity, complicity theory, and theory of hyper(in)visibility] that feature a critical approach. As you read through this section, note how each theory provides insight into how racialized perspectives and locations (see Chapter 1) influence communication. Remember, your objective should be to use each theory as a lens to understand interracial communication with greater clarity.

## SOCIAL SCIENTIFIC THEORIES

Social scientific theories are the result of research that has used objective observations and study in the search for communication truths. Through an empirical process of testing different variables, these theories work to explain cause and effect relationships that assist with future predictions. Through testable hypotheses, social scientific theories seek to produce findings that are reliable and valid (Griffin et al., 2019). This section describes three such theories and their applicability to interracial communication contexts.

### Anxiety/Uncertainty Management (AUM) Theory

Anxiety/uncertainty management (AUM) theory has been used in a number of intercultural communication contexts (Gudykunst, 1988, 1993, 1995). It also serves as a valuable framework for interethnic and interracial interactions (Gudykunst & Hammer, 1988). AUM theory focuses on interactions between cultural ingroup members and "**strangers**"—unfamiliar others from outside the primary cultural community. AUM is designed to increase communication competence with strangers through (1) managing our anxiety about interacting with others who are from different racial/ethnic groups and (2) accurately predicting and explaining their behaviors (Gudykunst, 1995). Competent communication, then, refers to the process of minimizing misunderstandings and involves certain levels of self-consciousness and cultural competencies (Howell, 1982).

The main idea of AUM theory is that anxiety and uncertainty are the basic causes of communication failure

Cultural stereotypes, like those associated with young African American males, increase the uncertainty and anxiety present during interracial interactions and remain a large source of communication failure.

in intergroup interactions (Gudykunst, 2005). Although these two elements are closely related, they are different in a few crucial ways. **Anxiety** is an emotion triggered by anticipation of things yet to come. Gudykunst (1995) defines it as "the feeling of being uneasy, tense, worried, or apprehensive about what might happen" (p. 13). **Uncertainty** is best understood as a mental state of doubt about one's ability to predict an outcome. All communication encounters involve varying levels of anxiety and uncertainty. AUM theory suggests that minimal levels of these two elements can be productive in that they motivate us to keep focused on being competent communicators. However, levels of anxiety and uncertainty are closely tied to the degree of perceived cultural difference among individuals—the greater the perceived racial/ethnic differences, the more prevalent role that anxiety and uncertainty will play. Higher levels are the major cause of communication ineffectiveness.

According to AUM theory, three variables contribute to the prevalence of anxiety and uncertainty during interracial communication (Gudykunst, 2005). One of these variables involves motivational factors. How important is interracial communication success in any given context? How do these efforts work toward achieving certain needs, gaining valuable information, and other desired outcomes? Knowledge factors represent a second variable. Examples include expectations and awareness of other racial/ethnic groups, understanding different perspectives, and information gained through shared networks. Knowledge also involves a recognition of the similarities and differences of racial/ethnic groups. The third variable, skills, refers to factors that allow individuals to put knowledge bases into practice. They include the ability to practice empathy (not sympathy), tolerate ambiguity, and accommodate new behaviors.

Recent publications provide comprehensive explanations of the theory and its utility for contemporary research. Presbitero and Attar (2018) found that knowledge about other cultures mitigated the impact of anxiety and uncertainty. Salazar et al. (2021) demonstrated how AUM theory provides insight

---

**Box 6.2**                                               *Student Reflections*

### Experience Driven Racial Perceptions

I guess one could say that my first experience with being around all African Americans was when I worked at a concession stand. Now, I do not like to judge everyone of a race based on one group of people; however, it is hard not to with the situation I was in. These people in this city were rude, loud, and just plain disobedient. During pool hours, none of the people followed any of the pool rules. When they came to the concession stand, they were extremely rude and made my job difficult. From that time forward, I have had an image of African Americans all being like these people in this city. I guess that I do have stereotypes because of the experiences I have had growing up. That isn't to say that I am rude or outwardly mean to any of these people. I do not think that Asians can drive, but at the same time, a lot of white old people cannot drive either.

into the cultural factors involved in workplace cyberbullying, especially the communicative dynamics between cyberbullies, cybervictims, and cyberbystanders. Created decades ago, AUM theory remains an important lens through which we can enhance our understanding of interracial communication.

## Communication Accommodation Theory (CAT)

Communication Accommodation Theory (CAT) was first presented as a "speech" accommodation theory by Howard Giles and colleagues in the early to mid-1970s (Giles, 1973; Giles et al., 1973). It was initially a theoretical framework that focused on language and linguistic elements but has developed into an insightful lens through which all aspects of communication between different racial/ethnic groups can be understood. Specifically, CAT explains the ways that individuals adjust their communication during intergroup interactions (Shepard et al., 2001). Accommodation can be seen in almost all communication behaviors, including accent, rate, loudness, vocabulary, grammar, gestures, dress, and artifacts.

Following the foundations of social identity theory (Tajfel, 1978), CAT maintains that individuals derive a significant portion of their identity from groups to which they belong. As we discussed in Chapter 5, different aspects of a person's identity may be more important in different contexts (Gallois et al., 2005). During interactions where racial/ethnic differences are significant, CAT can be used to understand how a person's communication will be used to emphasize or downplay those aspects of group identity. In other words, CAT focuses on how verbal and nonverbal communication is used to achieve the desired level of social distance (immediate or distant) between ingroup and outgroup members.

Two major aspects of CAT are convergence and divergence (Y. Zhang & Giles, 2018). **Convergence** is adjusting and adapting communication to become more like the other person; convergence can be partial or complete. People may converge for different reasons, including a desire to again acceptance, social integration, or as a means for effective communication (Giles, 1973). In all intergroup interactions, and especially in the context of interracial communication, it is important to note that convergence may be toward a person's actual communication *or* a preconceived stereotype of how the racial/ethnic group members communicate (this is called **overaccommodation**). According to Y. Zhang and Giles (2018), persons react to others, not necessarily as individuals, but as representatives of different racial/ethnic groups. Clearly, convergence is not the best strategy in all situations. The success of convergence in intergroup interactions depends on a number of factors, including a person's ability to converge effectively and how their efforts are perceived by the other person.

**Divergence** is an active process in which communicators emphasize verbal and nonverbal differences between themselves and others; like convergence, it can be partial or complete. **Maintenance** is doing nothing (as opposed to convergence or divergence) about different communication styles. Convergence is typically the result of internal scripts and occurs on a largely unconscious level. In comparison, persons are often more aware of divergence in interracial interactions. In many cases, divergence is used by racial/ethnic microcultural group members as a means to maintain their identity, cultural pride, and distinctiveness (Gallois et al., 2005). It is important to understand that divergence (as well as convergence) can be mutual or nonmutual. In other words, one person or both persons can use divergence to emphasize the social distance between racial/ethnic groups.

CAT research continues to make important contributions to our understanding of interracial communication practice (Woods & Ruscher, 2021). For example, T. Dixon, Schell, Giles, and Grogos (2008) drew from the theory in their study of traffic stops in Cincinnati, Ohio. Focusing on the race of the driver and the officer, researchers reviewed 313 randomly sampled video recordings from police cars. Their analysis found that race made a difference in three areas: (a) African American drivers were more likely to experience extensive policing during the traffic stop, (b) the communication quality of European American drivers was generally more positive than that of African American drivers, and (c) police officer communication behavior was more positive during same-race interactions. Similar disparities in treatment were found in a parallel study of Latinx drivers (Giles et al., 2012). These studies reveal how accommodation occurs in racialized contexts. The most satisfying interracial interactions typically involve a delicate balance of convergence (as an indication of a willingness to communicate competently) and divergence (as a means to acknowledge the importance of racial/ethnic group identification) *for both persons.*

## Conflict Face-Negotiation Theory

Face-negotiation theory (FNT), largely based on the work of Stella Ting-Toomey (1988, 2017), is best understood as a cross-cultural conflict theory that explains how individuals from different cultures manage different interpersonal conflicts. Within the context of interracial communication, FNT provides a valuable framework to understand how larger cultural dimensions can impact a person's individual communication choices during everyday conflict situations.

The basic idea of FNT is that people of every culture are in constant negotiation of their public self-image, or **face**. Face is best understood relationally: it is "how we want others to see us and treat us and how we actually treat others in association with their social self-conception expectations" (Ting-Toomey, 2023, p. 54). Ting-Toomey uses the term, **facework**, to describe the verbal and nonverbal messages that we use to address four concerns: (1) self-face (concerns related to restoring one's own public image); (2) other-face (concerns related to defending and supporting others' needs); (3) mutual-face (concerns for both parties' public images); and (4) communal-face (concerns related to upholding ingroup public image).

Related to the fundamental idea of face is the recognition that different cultures may prioritize different cultural values that influence one's facework. Specifically, FNT highlights the differences between individualistic and collectivistic cultures. **Individualism** is a cultural value that prioritizes the individual and their needs, rights, and desires. The United States, Europe, and Australia are examples of individualistic cultures. In comparison, **collectivism** is a cultural value that prioritizes the larger group's identity, harmony, and loyalty. In collectivistic cultures like most countries in Asia, Latin America, and Africa "we-identity" is regarded as more important than "I-identity." A good example of how this cultural dimension plays out in everyday life can be seen in how different countries responded to the COVID pandemic. Collectivistic cultures, with a focus on other-concern, were more likely to adhere to safety restrictions willingly. Individualistic cultures, on the other hand, focused on self-concern by asserting their individual rights to accept or reject different governmental directives (e.g., vaccinations, masks, social distancing, etc.).

Different racial and ethnic groups typically have particular systems of communication, which reflect larger cultural values like individualism or collectivism.

Through the foundations of face, facework, face concern, and larger cultural dimensions, FNT offers a framework that highlights predicted styles of conflict management. Members of collectivistic cultures, with a high other-concern, are likely to utilize conflict styles that feature practices such as obliging (accommodating or giving into the wishes of others), compromising (seeking to find a middle ground through negotiation or bargaining), and avoiding (withdrawing from open discussion). In comparison, FNT predicts that persons from individualistic cultures with a focus on self-concern are likely to value conflict styles like dominating (viewing conflict as a contest to win) and integrating (problem solving through collaboration where both parties win). While FNT predicts that culture impacts one's conflict style, the theory also recognizes that different individuals may have varying degrees to which they see themselves as connected to larger cultures and their values. This concept, known as **self-construals**, demonstrates that ingroup differences regarding conflict practices are to be expected.

Through the work of Ting-Toomey and other scholars, FNT has provided great insight into how culture generally impacts our conflict communication (see Chapter 10) and, more specifically, the role of racial and ethnic differences. Married couples in southern Ghana utilized conflict styles informed by other-face and mutual face concerns (Affram et al., 2020). Research focused on various ethnic groups in Indonesia (Marta et al., 2021) also found that harmonious conflict styles informed by collectivistic cultural values could lead to enhanced social solidarity in diverse nations. Of particular interest to scholars focusing on interracial communication within U.S. conflicts, research informed by FNT generated insight into how Black feminists working in predominately white male work spaces could utilize a compromising conflict style to advocate for self-definition amid blatant discrimination based on race and sex.

As described by Ting-Toomey (2023), conflict face negotiation theory continues to develop in its scope, reach, and complexity. As a social scientific theory, it has proven to have great predictive value regarding the relationships between culture, communication, conflict, and related factors. It remains a valuable resource for interracial communication scholars and practitioners.

# INTERPRETIVE THEORIES

Interpretive, or humanistic, theories take a different approach than those that are more social scientific. They assume that multiple meanings (or truths) are possible and focus on understanding people's communicative experiences from within their particular perspectives (Griffin et al., 2019). The ultimate goal in terms of interracial communication, then, is to produce powerfully rich descriptions of communication that can be used as cultural guides in understanding individual and group behavior. In this section, we present three interpretative theories: co-cultural theory, cultural contracts theory, and [counter]public sphere theory.

## Co-Cultural Theory

Co-cultural communication refers to a particular form of intercultural communication research that centers on issues of societal power and dominance within the United States (e.g., Folb, 1997). Co-cultural communication theory, as described by Orbe (1998), helps us understand the ways that persons who are traditionally marginalized in society communicate in their everyday lives. Grounded in muted group (Kramarae, 1981) and standpoint theories (D. Smith, 1987), co-cultural theory focuses on the lived experiences of a variety of "nondominant" or **co-cultural groups**. It represents a relevant framework for studying the experiences of people of color, women, people with disabilities, and gays, lesbians, and bisexuals (Orbe & Roberts, 2012). In terms of interracial communication, it can be used to understand interracial communication from the perspectives of racial and ethnic microcultural group members. In its most basic form, co-cultural theory lends insight into how members of microcultures negotiate their underrepresented status with others (both as part of macrocultures and microcultures) in different situational contexts (Ramirez-Sanchez, 2008).

Co-cultural theory is based on the idea that, because of their marginalized societal positions, people of color have to develop certain communication orientations in order to survive and/or succeed in the United States (Orbe & Albrehi, 2023). However, it is important to recognize the vast diversity within and among different racial and ethnic groups. Therefore, the adoption and maintenance of certain practices—as well as the rationale behind such decisions—varies greatly. Six interrelated factors (field of experience, perceived costs and rewards, ability, preferred outcomes, communication approach, and situational context) influence strategies. **Field of experience** relates to the sum

---

**Box 6.3**                                                           *Author Reflections*

## Co-Cultural Communication Theory

In the spring of 1992, I was a graduate student in my last quarter of course work. During a graduate seminar on qualitative research methodologies, I worked with a colleague and friend, T. Ford-Ahmed, on a project about how African American graduate students negotiate racial prejudice at predominantly European American college campuses (Ford-Ahmed & Orbe, 1992). With the humblest of beginnings, that project launched a series of research projects that has contributed to the development of co-cultural communication theory (Orbe, 1998).

In this personal reflection, I want to highlight an idea inherent within co-cultural theory that may not be apparent from the discussion in this chapter. One of the assumptions of the theory is that co-cultural groups (e.g., people of color, women, people with disabilities, LGBTQ persons) respond to oppression (racism, sexism, ableism, heterosexism) in similar ways. In other words, traditionally marginalized group members draw from common communication tactics regardless of the type of oppression they face. Evidence from personal experience, as well as that gained from more scholarly endeavors, indicates that the types of strategies used vary significantly within and between different co-cultural groups depending on the particular standpoint of an individual.

This idea is tied to a personal philosophy that I've adopted over the years. I believe that people who come to understand the oppression(s) they face are more likely to understand their role in oppressing others. Differences in terms of how racism, sexism, ageism, heterosexism, and so on are played out clearly exist. However, I see them in strikingly similar terms in the way that they are tied to power, control, and dominance. Understanding the direct and indirect influences that power has on interracial communication is a crucial element of ultimate competency. We all possess varying levels of power, and no one is either just the oppressor *or* the oppressed. Simultaneously recognizing the similarities and differences across life experiences can facilitate the process of naming privilege and power in productive ways. I hope that co-cultural work, and extensions like dominant group theory (Razzante & Orbe, 2018), provide a theoretical/practical framework.

—MPO

of lived experiences for people of color. Through a lifelong series of experiences, individuals learn how to communicate with others. They also come to realize the consequences of certain forms of communication. Based on one's unique field of experience—which is simultaneously similar to yet different from the experience of others—an individual comes to recognize **perceived costs and rewards** are associated with different communication practices. In some instances, the advantages and disadvantages are clear; in others, they are less straightforward and more complex.

A third factor influencing interracial communication is the **ability** to enact certain strategies that establish and maintain a specific communication orientation. Consistent with communication accommodation theory, co-cultural theory understands that people of color have varying levels of success in using certain strategies (e.g., "passing" or networking with other people of color). Much depends on the specific dynamics inherent in any given **situational context**. This includes where the interaction takes place, other parties who are present, and the particular circumstances that facilitate the interaction. It should be apparent that situational context, like the other five factors, intersects in highly complex ways to influence interracial interactions (Orbe & Roberts, 2012).

The final two factors are **communication approach** and **preferred outcome**. Communication approach refers to the specific "voice" used by racial/ethnic microcultural group members in the United States. Is the communication approach aggressive, assertive, or nonassertive? Preferred outcome relates to the ultimate goal that the person of color has for the interaction: (1) Is he or she aiming to fit in and not bring any unnecessary attention to racial differences (assimilation)? (2) Is the goal to recognize racial and ethnic differences and work with others to ensure that these differences do not translate into unequal treatment (accommodation)? (3) Is the goal to limit interaction with European Americans and create affirming communities exclusively of people of color (separation)?

The explicit objective of co-cultural theory is not to predict the behaviors of people of color. Instead, it is to understand the complex factors that influence how they communicate in a society that traditionally has treated them as cultural outsiders (Orbe, 1998). This was evident in the work of Jun (2012) who found that Asian Americans who experience racially discriminatory messages (racial slurs, playground teasing, professional discrimination, etc.) are almost twice as likely to utilize nonassertive approaches compared to assertive or aggressive ones. Some of the nonassertive responses might reflect emotional shock and humiliation or a lack of experiences on which to draw. Other Asian Americans used this co-cultural approach strategically to avoid negative repercussions (see also Camara & Orbe, 2010). In comparison, Latinx and African American attorneys reportedly enacted assertive co-cultural practices when responding to racial microaggressions in the workplace (Orbe, 2021a).

| *Box 6.4* | *Research Highlight* |
|---|---|

### Co-Cultural Theory in Applied Contexts

To say that the COVID pandemic impacted every corner of the world is not an exaggeration. Initially reported in 2019, early reports traced the virus to China and some coverage framed this news in ways that prompted public suspicions of Chinese government officials. Public use of racist labels for COVID (e.g., "Chinese virus," "Kung flu," "Wuhan virus") exacerbated a racialized stigma on the pandemic. In times of extreme uncertainty, anxiety, and panic, such rhetoric impacted the lives of Asian Americans who reported a sharp increase in racial discrimination and hate crimes (Nakamura, 2021). #StopAsianHate emerged as a national response to such problematic treatment.

Jun et al. (2021) examined how Asian Americans responded to increased verbal and physical attacks during the pandemic. This research team utilized co-cultural theory to explore how individual characteristics and previous experiences with racial discrimination influenced particular responses. Asian Americans responded to racist interactions most frequently through nonassertive co-cultural practices, followed by more assertive and aggressive approaches. The researchers also found that individuals with salient ethnic identity and previous discrimination experiences were even more likely to respond nonassertively. Asian American males were more likely than their female counterparts to enact assertive approaches.

## Cultural Contracts Theory

Cultural contracts theory is a framework created by Ronald Jackson and colleagues. It is based on the idea that interracial relationships may or may not be coordinated, depending upon different dynamics, including power, boundaries, cultural loyalty, group identification, and maturity (R. Jackson, 2002a). As an extension of identity negotiation scholarship in general, and the work of Ting-Toomey (1993) in particular, cultural contracts theory defines the negotiation of cultural identity as "a process in which one considers the gain, loss, or exchange of his or her ability to interpret their own reality or worldview" (R. Jackson, 1999, p. 10). In short, the theory helps us to understand how individuals negotiate their racial and ethnic identities in different contexts (Drummond & Orbe, 2010; R. Jackson & Crawley, 2003).

Cultural contracts theory is based on three premises that describe the nature of identities (R. Jackson & Castle Bell, 2023). First, identities require affirmation to exist, something that is gained through a person's communication with others. Second, identities are constantly being exchanged and, therefore, represent a life-long process of activity. Third, and finally, identities are contractual. By definition, cultural contracts are used to reflect "an agreement between two or more interactants who have different interpretations of culture and have decided whether to coordinate their relationship with one other so that the relationship is deemed valuable to both" (R. Jackson, 2002b, p. 49). According to R. Jackson and Crawley (2003), many people are not aware of the cultural contracts that they have unknowingly agreed to ("signed"). In addition, they do not understand all of the implications of having signed them. Think, for instance, how most U.S. Americans learn about race and ethnicity identities (people who are like "us" and those who become "them"). We innocently learn racial and ethnic labels and rarely challenge all of the meaning that come with these labels (Drummond & Orbe, 2010).

According to the theory, three different types of cultural contracts exist. **Ready-to-sign cultural contracts** are pre-negotiated agreements designed to promote assimilation and maintain the status quo (R. Jackson & Castle Bell, 2023). From the perspective of the person in power, this type of contract typically means, "I am not going to change who I am, so if you want this relationship to work, you must act like me" (R. Jackson, 2002b, p. 48). Ready-to-sign contracts are often used by individuals who are entrenched in their own worldview and refuse to see the value in alternative perspectives, perceptions, and/or communication. People of color and white people who unknowingly agree to these contracts reaffirm traditional racial dynamics (Castle Bell, 2019).

The second type of cultural contracts are partly pre-negotiated and partly open for negotiation; **quasi-completed cultural contracts** attempt to balance maintaining the status quo and asserting one's identity within existing structures (R. Jackson, 2002b). Individuals who use this type of cultural contract demonstrate some willingness to negotiate but tempered by a desire to maintain one's own worldview—and maintain some measure of control (R. Jackson & Crawley, 2003). An example is the creative use of existing labels, such as multiracial individuals who object to having to choose one group to identity with and describe themselves as EuroAsian to include both European and Asian.

**Co-created cultural contracts**, the third category, are agreements that are "fully negotiable, with the only limits being personal preferences or requirements" (R. Jackson, 2002b, p. 49). This type of cultural contract differs from

Like all families, multiracial family identity is negotiated through different cultural contracts. Over time, ready-to-sign contracts are being replaced by quasi-completed and co-created agreements.

| Box 6.5 | Student Reflections |
| --- | --- |

### "I Just Love the Skin I Am in and Those Who Share It"

My name itself is reflection of my Blackness. My mom didn't make up my name, like most Black mothers are known for; she heard it on television and thought that it was unique. My last name is a slave name that I have inherited. My great-great-great grandmother was a slave who was impregnated by her slave master on a plantation in Alabama. That is all I know about my history. I never really thought about how much I didn't know my history until my coach asked people on the team where their family came from. People responded with "the Netherlands," "Germany," "Ireland," "Jamaica," etc. When he asked me, I had no response, but "Alabama." When I said that everyone laughed, but it is the sad truth. I am a living example of what slavery has done to Blacks in America; I don't know where I come from. I recently realized that I have had to learn so much about the white culture, but they haven't had to learn about mine. My high school U.S. history book was huge with small words, while my African American history book was very small with large letters. I love being Black and I wouldn't want to be anything else. I love how we talk loud and dramatic, I love how we show love through food, I love our deep connection to God, and I love how we sometimes are a connected community. I just love the skin I am in and those who share it. I am a Black American woman and I plan to continue to share, enjoy, and reflect on my Blackness. It is me and I am it.

the others in that individuals acknowledge and validate the cultural differences of all parties; as such, co-created cultural contracts are motivated by mutual satisfaction and respect—and not obligation. Co-created cultural contracts reflect a sentiment of "I am comfortable with you and value you for who you are, and I am not interested in changing you in any way" (p. 49). Enacting this type of agreement reflects an openness and desire to embrace alternative worldviews (R. Jackson & Castle Bell, 2023).

## [Counter]Public Sphere Theory

The intellectual tradition of public sphere theory can be traced back to European and U.S. thinkers such as Jürgen Habermas, John Dewey, Walter Lippmann, Stuart Mill, and Hannah Arendt. These scholars conceptualized a **public sphere** as an area of social life where different people come together and engage in sociopolitical issues and, ideally, utilize this engagement as a springboard to action. The work of Habermas (1989) was instrumental in advancing public sphere theorizing and sparking renewed attention to a theoretical framework useful to understanding the roles of citizens, deliberation, culture, and power in democratic societies. Specific to interracial communication, public sphere theory offers an intentional examination how modes of communication affect racial, political, and public life.

The work of Squires (2002) is especially important to understanding how race, power, and communication influence public spheres. Drawing from the critiques offered by Fraser (1992), she asserts that traditional public sphere theorizing failed to account for salient issues of culture and power in their conceptualizations of ideal spaces where political power was shifted from the state to the public majority. Through her work, she contends that two basic types of public spheres coexist: (1) a dominant public sphere, and (2) **subaltern counterpublics** created and maintained by historically marginalized group members. Counterpublics, by definition, "exist outside of state-sanctioned or mainstream spaces and reflect opposing perspectives from dominant public spheres" (Squires & Orbe, 2023, p. 241).

Black public spheres are a great example of counterpublics. Dawson's (1995) work, for instance, highlighted the success of churches, social and cultural organizations, and various media outlets that fostered important conversations within the African American community. Over time, such ingroup deliberations were critical to engage communal interests, rights, and strategies to resist white supremacist rule. According to Squires (2002), there are three specific types of Black public spheres. The first is an **enclave**, which is produced when societal norms deny access or meaningful participation in dominant public spheres. An enclave fosters an oppositional consciousness through debate, engagement, and strategizing in a manner largely independent from dominant group influence. Examples of Black enclaves include local artist collectives, community-based and faith-based organizations, and social media platforms like Black Twitter.

Unlike the independent nature of the enclave, a **counterpublic** is designed specifically to engage dominant public spheres through social protests and other acts of civil disobedience. The defining feature of this second type of Black public sphere is increased public communication between marginalized and dominant public spheres (Squires & Orbe, 2023). The focus is for marginalized groups to articulate communal interests on their own terms as they resist dominant group perspectives and seek solidarity with other marginalized groups. A variety of civil rights organizations, including the current #BlackLivesMatter movement, are examples of Black counterpublics.

The third and final type of Black public sphere is the **satellite**. The explicit goal of a satellite is to create and maintain a solid collective group identity within independent institutional spaces that allow for wider and more equitable public discourses than what is allowed in dominant public spheres. The preference for a separate public sphere typically is motivated by a desire to resist assimilation and remain true to group identity, goals, and ideals. Squires (2002) cites The Nation of Islam as a prime example of a Black satellite sphere.

Research in different communication contexts has drawn from Black public sphere theorizing to be informed by race, ethnicity, and culture. For instance, S. Jackson and Welles (2015) used the New York City Police Department's 2014 public relations campaign, #myNYPD, as a case study to demonstrate the power of citizen activists in creating a counterpublic. While the hashtag was designed to generate positive images of the police department, the campaign was "hijacked" by minoritized peoples who re-framed the social media campaign to highlight instances of racial profiling, racism, and police brutality. Gittens (2021) utilized the theoretical framework to study the power and diversity of Black counterpublic spheres that exist within aesthetic communities. The research focused on rapper 2 Chainz's Pink Trap House in Atlanta, Georgia and how its creation emerged as a symbol representing drug-infested neighborhoods and disruption of white suburban living spaces. According to Gittens, the Pink Trap House was a Black aesthetic counterpublic that materialized because of a lack of hidden space required for an enclave and the reduction of satellites that have been co-opted by state-sponsored institutions.

The recent surge of research on counterpublics (see also Larson & McHendry, 2019) demonstrates its utility in advancing our understanding of race, power, and communication. By recognizing how multiple public spheres exist in different forms—including those created by minoritized groups—we are at a better vantage point to understand more fully the diversity in how individuals and groups participate in democratic deliberations.

## CRITICAL THEORIES

The last grouping of interracial communication theories that we feature in this chapter are those that take a critical approach. Critical theories approach studying communication with an assumption that society is divided into different hierarchies, like those based on race, ethnicity, and other cultural markers. Consequently, these theories focus on issues of "power, context, socioeconomic relations, and historical/structural focuses" (Nakayama & Halualani, 2011, p. 1) to reveal how they shape everyday interactions in both explicit and implicit ways.

### Critical Race Theory

Compared to all of the theories presented in this chapter, critical race theory (CRT) represents a framework that was developed outside the field of communication (Calvert, 1997). Its origins can be traced back to the late 1970s and early 1980s (Crenshaw et al., 1995). Specifically, critical race theory was developed by civil rights activists who were seeing many of the gains achieved during the 1960s disappear (Matsuda et al., 1993). The earliest work in this area was done by scholars in critical legal studies. Their efforts generally challenged dominant values of equal opportunity and justice for all by highlighting the realities of race. As described by Griffin (2010), communication scholars have drawn on this theoretical approach to inform their research on race, ethnicity, and communication. Research has included the study of racialized language to describe multiracial persons (Nishime, 2012), President Barack Obama's use of different rhetorical strategies when communicating about race (Isaksen, 2011), and efforts to create a Latino/a critical theory that focuses on environmental justice advocacy (Anguiano et al., 2012).

Several core elements capture the essence of CRT (Matsuda et al., 1993). First, it recognizes that racism is an integral part of the United States. Instead of debating whether racism can ever be totally eliminated, critical race theorists work to challenge existing structures that reinforce racial oppression. Second, CRT rejects dominant legal and social claims of neutrality, objectivity, and colorblindness. It embraces the subjectivity that comes with a particular field of experience. As part of the rejection of neutrality, critical race theorists describe their work as explicitly political. The third core element rejects a historical approach to studying race. Instead, this theoretical approach insists on looking at interracial communication from within a contextual/historical context. The 1619 Project, described in Chapter 2, is a perfect example of this point.

Fourth, CRT recognizes the importance of experiential knowledge that comes from various microcultural standpoints. In other words, it (like Afrocentricity, discussed next) values insight grounded in the experiences of those racial and ethnic groups that have historically been marginalized. The fifth core element relates to the interdisciplinary and eclectic nature of critical race theory. The ideas of this theory are borrowed from several traditions, including Marxism, feminism, critical/cultural studies, and postmodernism. Finally, CRT actively works toward the elimination of racial oppression. Although the focus is on racial oppression, the theory also acknowledges other forms of oppression based on gender, class, and sexual orientation.

As described by Matsuda et al. (1993), the work of critical race theorists is both pragmatic and idealized. Specifically, their scholarship attempts to address the immediate needs of those who are oppressed—and in doing so, to work toward the ideals of equal opportunity and justice on which the United States was founded, especially within educational contexts (Dixson & Rousseau, 2005; T. Harris & Abbott, 2011). While CRT initially focused on dynamics specific to white supremacy, racism, and African Americans, it provides a fruitful foundation from which we can explore a variety of racialized experiences. For example, scholars of color have extended the core principles of CRT to examine different elements (e.g., assimilation, white settler colonialism, immigration, imperialism) used to racialize and marginalize different communities of color (Aguilar & Juarez, 2023). This includes Latina/o critical legal theory (Cabrera, 2019), Tribal critical race theory (Brayboy, 2005), and undocumented critical theory (Aguilar, 2019).

These new theoretical developments demonstrate the vitality of CRT and its importance in providing tools to investigate white supremacy and racism as well as ways to change existing power relations (Aguilar & Juarez, 2023). Today, CRT is used by academic scholars in various fields to describe how racism is embedded in all aspects of U.S. American life: education, health care, economics, housing, criminal justice system, and clean water. As such, CRT remains an important theoretical framework toward achieving a more complex understanding of how race affects our everyday communication.

| Box 6.6 | Case Study |
| --- | --- |

### Efforts to Ban Race-Centered Educational Materials

Passionate cries to ban U.S. educators from teaching critical race theory (CRT) have become commonplace. In many ways, this issue symbolizes a culture clash between those who insist that the United States grapple with its racist history and those who believe that it represents toxic propaganda that works to undercut patriotism and divide a country far removed from racism. Related to banning CRT from being taught are intensified efforts to ban books that highlight the reality of marginalized experiences. Good (2021) reports an unprecedented volume of efforts to ban books about people of color and LGBTQ+ people. Attempts to ban particular books because of controversial content is not new. The *Catcher in the Rye*, for instance, has the distinction of being the most banned book in the United States; it also is the second most taught book.

In 2020, the American Library Association identified hundreds of challenges to ban books because they were deemed to be divisive, immoral, dangerous, and/or potentially disturbing. For instance, *The Hate U Give* by Angie Thomas, was challenged for its profanity, diverse language, and anti-police message. *Stamped: Racism, Antiracism, and You* by Ibram X Kendi and Jason Reynolds was banned, in part, because it does not encompass racism against all people. *All American Boys*, a book by Jason Reynolds and Brendan Kiely about a Black teen assaulted by a white police officer, was banned for similar reasons and because it addressed "too much of a sensitive matter right now" (Good, 2021).

As students of interracial communication, what are your thoughts about banning certain educational resources at libraries, schools, and universities? What do you think is at the core of these challenges? What impact do you think such a practice has on existing perceptions of race (and other cultural elements) in the United States? How might we create age-appropriate resources to present the realities of that increased awareness and understanding? Is this an acceptable solution to the current debates? What other options exist?

## Afrocentricity

Asante (1988, 1998a) is the foremost scholar associated with Afrocentricity (also known as African-centered scholarship). His work has provided much of the framework for personal, social, educational, and theoretical/methodological development; other scholars from various disciplines have also contributed important ideas. In its most basic form, Afrocentricity places Africans and the interest of Africa at the center of research and practice. According to Austin (2006), the concept is used in two ways. First, it refers to a paradigm that makes Africa in general, and the ancient Nile Valley civilizations of Egypt and Nubia in particular, central to African Americans. Second, it describes an approach to African American experiences that reflects cultural pride and identification.

Do you see how this idea is consistent with standpoint and critical race theories? Afrocentricity is especially important given that for many years communication research on persons of African descent was completed within European frameworks (Asante, 1998a). The theory has provided a powerful critique of the problems with communication research solely situated in traditional Western thought (McPhail, 1998a). Afrocentricity is not meant to be placed above other perspectives. Instead, it should exist alongside other cultural/historical standpoints. In this regard, Afrocentric thought provides an alternative to traditional frameworks when exploring the perspectives of people of African descent. Other approaches, like an Asiacentric perspective (P. Wong et al., 1995), also offer valuable frameworks for studying interracial communication from non-European standpoints.

What exactly is an Afrocentric theoretical framework? First, it involves the development of a theoretical perspective that reflects African ways of knowing and interpreting the world (Ribeau, 2004). Afrocentricity assumes that people of African descent, despite some diverse lived experiences, share a common set of experiences, struggles, and origins. The African Diaspora provides a common cultural base that reflects a key set of values: harmony with nature, humaneness, rhythm, and communalism in terms of how wealth is produced, owned, and distributed. Second, Afrocentricity seeks agency and action through collective consciousness (Asante, 1988). In other words, Afrocentricity serves as a mechanism for embracing African ideals at the center of intellectual/personal life. It relies on the self-conscious actions of individuals with direct attention to the way they relate to one another.

One of the major components of Afrocentricity—as it relates to interracial communication—is that it represents an intellectual framework that sees people of African descent as participants (rather than subjects/objects) in their human existence. It also recognizes that features of the human condition (feeling, knowing, and acting) are interrelated and should not be viewed as separate (i.e., viewing emotion as irrational and less valuable than reason). According to Delgado (1998), Afrocentricity is important because it embraces an "alternative set of realities, experiences, and identities" (p. 423) for research attempting to view interracial communication from a non-Western perspective. From the beginning, U.S. history has been pluralistic, and interpretations of human existence (communication) from any one cultural standpoint are unproductive. Research on African American women's negotiation of hair within the workplace (Spellers, 2002) and the lyrics of popular rap songs that promote achieving balance, harmony, and transcendence in the community (Cummings & Roy, 2002) are excellent examples of applications of Afrocentricity.

In short, all analyses of race and communication are situated within a particular cultural location, complete with ideological assumptions. Afrocentricity proves a valuable lens in that it promotes a culturally centered analysis of interracial communication, in light of its explicit focus on Africa and the African diaspora. Through celebratory recognition of heritage, style, language, balance, diversity, and harmony, Afrocentricity makes valuable contributions to those that value diverse perspectives to a pluralistic world (F. Stewart, 2020). As such, Afrocentricity offers a theoretical framework that draws attention to existing problems with scholarship that solely reflects one group's cultural experiences.

## Complicity Theory

Complicity theory (McPhail 1994a, 2002) was created specifically to study issues of race, language, and communication (as opposed to theories that study culture more generally). It challenges our basic understanding of race, particularly as it relates to racial differences. Complicity theory is grounded in two key ideas. First, at the core of racism is a language system that divides and ranks human beings in black-and-white terms (McPhail, 1994b), creating a "language of negative difference" (McPhail, 1991, p. 2) that affects social reality. The results are social practices that perpetuate the principle of negative difference in human interaction. In other words, racism is not merely a problem of "Blacks" and "[w]hites"; it is a consequence of understanding the world through black-and-white terms (McPhail, 2002). Second, central to complicity theory is the assertion that dominance and marginality are not fixed states (McPhail, 1996b). According to complicity theory, racism reflects the Western predisposition toward **essentialism**—overgeneralizations based on a single cultural factor. Separate, distinct classifications fail to consider how racism exists within a social system that also marginalizes people based on gender, class, age, sexual orientation, and the like. Complicity theory advocates for efforts that avoid essentialist categories.

As a means to advance the ideas central to complicity theory, McPhail introduces three key concepts: complicity, coherence, and implicature. **Complicity** means "an agreement to disagree" (McPhail, 1991, p. 2). According to complicity theory, productive race relations can never occur when complicity is the norm. Instead, we must move from complicity to coherence. **Coherence** is a concept that emphasizes interconnectedness and commonality (McPhail, 2002) in attempts to facilitate "harmonic discourse" (Fine, 1991, p. 271). It avoids a focus on negative differences and critiques existing frameworks that depict human beings in terms of separate and distinct races (McPhail, 1998a). While complicity hinges on the idea of negative difference as oppositional forces, coherence sees difference as complementary (McPhail, 1996b). The final key concept, **implicature**, involves a basic acceptance of the belief that we are all implicated in each other's lives (McPhail, 2002). Implicature is more than having empathy for others; it includes the idea that "human beings are linguistically, materially, psychologically, and spiritually interrelated and interdependent" (Dace & McPhail, 2002, p. 99). In other words, implicature is grounded in the idea that we are all connected; what affects one of us affects all of us.

Complicity theory has been used by various communication scholars to critique existing representations of race. This has included analyses of feature films (McPhail, 1996a, 1996b; Orbe & Kinefuchi, 2008), interactions on U.S. college campuses (Patton, 2004), workplace dynamics (Evia & Patriarca, 2012), and rigid U.S. racial and ethnic categories (Orbe & Drummond, 2009)—all of which have been described as grounded in complicity. Other scholars have pointed to complicity theory as a helpful framework to transform the current state of race relations into more liberating dialogues (R.

Jackson, 2000) where true racial reconciliation can occur (Hatch, 2003). Complicity theory, through the work of McPhail (2009, 2023) and others continues to evolve.

McPhail's most recent writings question the role that rhetoric can play in erasing racism; he theorizes that racism may be a problem of psychiatry rather than simply rhetoric. In either case, the core ideas of this textbook reflect key principles associated with complicity theory and see its utility in understanding the power that language has within our psychological understanding of self, others, and society. Complicity theory, in this regard, represents one perspective committed to generating new paradigms designed to address racism and its related problems (McPhail, 2023).

## Theory of Hyper(in)visibility

The theory of hyper(in)visibility, our final framework, is based on the work of A. Johnson (2018) and Petermon (2014). The theory connects the personal to the political and systemic through examining how power is connected to ways of seeing. The core idea is that the images we see, and the ways we see them, impact how we interpret artifacts and understand the identities of people. The theory is useful in understanding the media, systemic power, and everyday interpersonal interactions.

**Visibility** refers to frequent and complex representations in media that contribute to greater understanding of the human experience beyond mere stereotypes (A. Johnson & Petermon, 2023). Invisibility is significantly different. For instance, racialized groups can experience **invisibility**, or a lack of mediated representation where certain groups are missing en masse. Further, a sense of **hypervisibility** can occur when racialized bodies are so heavily stereotyped in the media that they are believed wholeheartedly even when refuting information exists. **Hyper(in)visibility** exists when individuals cause others harm and feel justified because of their deeply held stereotypes of the person. In essence, this occurs when someone consumes a plethora of stereotypical mediated images of a group of people and the images inform how they interact with them. For instance, Johnson and Petermon describe how the hyper(in)visibility of Muslims (and others presumed to be Muslim) after 9/11 lead to increased instances of discrimination, dehumanization, and oppression by U.S. Americans who stereotyped them as terrorists (e.g., Yomtoob, 2013).

A. Johnson (2017) argues that the shooting of Michael Brown by police officer Darren Wilson in Ferguson, Missouri, is another prime example of hyper(in)visibility. Wilson felt justified in killing Brown because he saw him as a "monster" (p. 4). This perception, in the context of a hypervisible stereotype of Black men as dangerous, violent thugs, makes sense in that Wilson's understanding of Brown through dominant mediated stereotypes resulted in violent (deadly) behavior. Johnson argues that this is not an isolated event. Instead, hyper(in)visibility is a valuable framework to understand the deaths of Black men in the United States over time. Black bodies, and Black masculine bodies in particular, are hyper(in)visible prompting widespread stereotypes that continue to justify mistreatment.

As seen in the examples provided thus far, hyper(in)visibility occurs when individuals use pervasive stereotypes to justify the harm they cause others. This violence, according to A. Johnson and Petermon (2023), can take various forms. For instance, as with the case of Michael Brown and other Black men, it can result in physical violence (assault or murder). More common within interpersonal interactions, however, is the discursive violence that is prompted by hypervisible stereotypes. This includes name-calling, using derogatory terms, and microaggressions. Another form is legislative violence that exists through laws and ordinances like "stop and frisk," racial profiling, and immigration detainment. Additionally, violence can be political (e.g., voter suppression efforts, protests that disrupt democratic practice) and/or economic (e.g., redlining, unethical mortgage lending practices).

Despite being a relatively new development, the theory of hyper(in)visibility has proven to be insightful in understanding how visibility politics impact interracial interactions. For instance, Petermon (2014) explored how television in the late 1990s and 2000s witnessed an increase in characters of color, most notably African Americans. Yet, the goal to be more inclusive seldom went beyond restrictive stereotypical depictions, resulting in a sense of hypervisibility that lacked complex, diverse representations. A. Johnson (2018) found a similar dynamic within feature films, like *Straight Outta Compton*. Interestingly, even in shows created and produced by African Americans that embrace a multicultural, colorblind form of television, hyperinvisibility continues to exist (Petermon, 2018). This is the case because characters of color are often portrayed as racially neutral; as such, they fail to contribute to enhanced understandings of culturally diverse human experiences.

In short, the theory of hyper(in)visibility provides a valuable framework through which we can examine how media representations rooted in stereotypes promote different forms of interpersonal violence. In a world where traditional media forms have expanded to feature diverse social media platforms that seem to dominate the ways in which we communicate, the value of the theory is likely to increase over time.

## CONCLUSION

In 1979, Pennington reported that interracial communication research and theory was in its infancy. Her call for increased productivity focusing on the "deep structures" (p. 392) and different worldviews that inform interracial interactions did not go unnoticed. More recent research and theory faces additional challenges, especially in terms of its focus on difference and application to everyday practice. In addition, interracial communication research must continue to explore the value of alternative methods and theories (Austin et al., 2023). As illustrated by the broad range of frameworks described in this chapter, substantial options are available to theorists and practitioners interested in validating, critiquing, and/or extending research. However, challenges still exist.

First, theoretical frameworks must create a delicate balance between providing insights into the general cultural norms of each racial/ethnic group and acknowledging the great diversity within each group. Second, interracial communication theoretical frameworks must assume an action-sensitive approach to theory development and practical application. In a country (and larger world) where race relations continue to be highly adverse, communication scholars have a unique opportunity—and responsibility—to utilize theories in the discipline to improve the competence of everyday interracial interaction. Responding to this challenge, Part II extends theory into practice within a number of specific interracial communication contexts.

## KEY TERMS

| | |
|---|---|
| normalization | communication approach |
| strangers | preferred outcome |
| anxiety | ready-to-sign cultural contracts |
| uncertainty | quasi-completed cultural contracts |
| convergence | co-created cultural contracts |
| overaccommodation | public sphere |
| divergence | subaltern counterpublics |
| maintenance | enclave |
| face | counterpublic |
| facework | satellite |
| individualism | essentialism |
| collectivism | complicity |
| self-construals | coherence |
| co-cultural groups | implicature |
| field of experience | visibility |
| perceived costs and rewards | invisibility |
| ability | hypervisibility |
| situational context | hyper(in)visibility |

## OPPORTUNITIES FOR EXTENDED LEARNING

1. Brown and Chevrette (2021) provide a blueprint for engaging students with communication theories through popular culture. Using *The Greatest Showman* film, their work focuses specifically on using co-cultural theory to increase critical thinking regarding how dis/ability intersects with other marginalized identities. Select a popular culture text and analyze it using one of the theories in this chapter. Specifically, the analysis should focus on how the representation (e.g., characters, story lines, dialogue, music, visual cues, etc.) communicates about race, intersectionality, and communication. Use the exercise to explore the important role that popular culture serves in our thoughts, perceptions, and actions.

2. Select one theory and conduct a more thorough analysis of its usefulness in interracial communication. Start by locating and reading the references that we cite. Then reflect on the strengths and weaknesses of the theory. This will allow you to identify certain criticisms of each theory (something

that we did not do because of space limitations). During your analysis, ask yourself questions such as: What are the basic assumptions and main ideas of the theory? How does the theory help guide future research? How can it be applied to everyday interactions?

3. Gudykunst and his colleagues believe that anxiety and uncertainty are the primary sources of miscommunication for interracial interactions. Spend 10 to 15 minutes of class time brainstorming all of the different forms of interracial communication that are likely to cause unproductive anxiety and uncertainty. Pay particular attention to how you experience different levels of anxiety and uncertainty with the various racial and ethnic groups highlighted in Chapter 3. Conclude this reflective exercise by highlighting how you might utilize the three AUM factors (knowledge, ability, and motivation) to manage your anxiety and uncertainty with different groups.

4. The Fresh Prince of Bel-Air was a popular sitcom airing on NBC from 1990 to 1996. The program featured the adjustment of a street-smart teenager from West Philadelphia (Will Smith) after he was sent to live with wealthy extended family members in the exclusive community of Bel-Air. The entire series serves as a case study in communication accommodation theory. Use youtube.com, or other website resources, to review different episodes of the series (you may want to watch earlier seasons for the most explicit examples of the theory). Focus on the youngest characters—Will Smith and Hillary, Carleton, and Ashley Banks—and find different examples of how each person practices convergence, divergence, and maintenance in partial or complete ways. Can you find any examples of overaccommodation? Based on what you know about each character and the larger context of the show, can you suggest reasons for the accommodation exhibited by each of the characters? [Extra credit: Use communication accommodation theoretical concepts to compare and contrast the original *The Fresh Prince of Bel-Air* to its recent re-imagination, *Bel-Air*.]

5. Break the class into several groups and assign each group a particular theoretical framework. The objective of each group is to create a 3-hour cultural diversity training program that focuses on race relations. Group members must decide on the following details for the program: (1) Who is the target audience? (2) What structure will it follow? (3) What aspects of the theory will be used, and how will they be incorporated into the training? and (4) What types of experiential learning will be included? Time permitting, share your race relations training modules with the class.

6. Utilize credible virtual resources to further your engagement with interracial communication issues. For example, *Race/Related* is a weekly newsletter delivered to your inbox by *The New York Times*. The newsletter highlights articles that explore the countless ways race affects people's lives. The newspaper also features a monthly column, *Race Manners*, that helps readers resolve personal dilemmas involving race, culture, and identity. Peruse these materials with a keen eye toward how your understanding of the issues presented have been informed by the concepts, principles, and theories covered throughout this book. Visit nytimes.com/newsletters/race-related to sign up for the newsletter.

## RECOMMENDED CONTEMPORARY READINGS

Azocar, C. L., LaPoe, V., Carter Olson, C. S., LaPoe, B., & Hazarika, B. (2021). Indigenous communities and COVID 19: Reporting on resources and resilience. *Howard Journal of Communications*. doi.org/10.1080/10646175.2021.1892552

Blair, M., & Liu, M. (2019). Ethnically Chinese and culturally American: Exploring bicultural identity negotiation and co-cultural communication of Chinese-American female adoptees. *Journal of International and Intercultural Communication, 13*(4), 347–365. doi.org/10.1080/17513057.2019.1649710

Logan, N. (2021). A theory of corporate responsibility to race (CRR): Communication and racial justice in public relations. *Journal of Public Relations Research.* doi.org/10.1080/1062726X.2021.1881898

Onuzulike, U. (2021). Ethnicity and belonging among young Igbo in the United States: Explicating coculturation and ethnic communication theory. *Howard Journal of Communications, 32*(3), 156–170. doi.org/10.1080/10646175.2021.1878477

Teboul, J.-C. B. (2019). Other tongues at work: Foreign language accommodation in multilingual organizations in the U.S. *Howard Journal of Communications, 30*(5), 371–390. doi.org/10.1080/10646175.2018.1466745

Zenovich, J. A. (2018). Theorizing interracial communication in the former Yugoslavia. *Journal of Intercultural Communication Research, 47*(4), 343–360. doi.org/10.1080/17475759.2018.1473279

Zirulnik, M., & Orbe M. (2019). Black female pilot communicative experiences: Applications and extensions of co-cultural theory. *Howard Journal of Communications, 30*, 76–91. doi: 10.1080/10646175.2018.1439422

# PART II

# Interracial Communication in Specific Contexts

# 7

# Racial Hierarchies as International Communication Phenomena

| *CASE STUDY* | Colorism as a State of Mind |
| --- | --- |

For some communities of color, the term *colorstruck* (a fascination with lighter skin tones) sums up the idea of colorism—a preference for someone who is light skinned and has stereotypically European American or white features. The bias operating in this way of thinking is that those who do not conform to this ideal are viewed as being less desirable. Lighter skinned individuals are direct benefactors of this system, but they also have struggles with this value-based racial hierarchy. Trinidadian journalist Akiler Holder (2012) describes her struggles with being stereotyped because of her light-brown complexion and long hair. Colorism is an issue in Trinidad and Tobago, as it is in countries throughout the world.

*Washington Post* journalist DeNeen Brown (2009) describes the roots of colorism as beginning during slavery when darker skinned Black slaves were restricted to doing field work while lighter skinned Black slaves, who were typically children of slave masters, were assigned work indoors. This racial division was eventually internalized, perpetuating the belief that lighter is better (Holder, 2012). Lighter skinned women were either sold into prostitution or became mistresses to the master, which further perpetuated this misconception. All of these factors contributed to the stigma attached to darker skin color and to the damaged self-esteem of darker skinned Blacks, especially women, who were subjected to racial prejudice, or colorism, from both whites *and* Blacks.

Unfortunately, colorism did not end with the abolishment of slavery in 1865. In fact, this way of thinking was so ingrained in U.S. culture that the African American community in the 1960s popularized the following mantra: "If you are light, you are all right. If you are brown, you can stick around. If you are black, get back." This racial attitude rings true for many Trinidadians. Holder (2012) attributes the hostility from darker skinned women to feelings of inferiority and being insecure because of their skin color differences. Despite these tensions, she concludes that colorism is a state of mind that dark-skinned women must work to overcome.

Is colorism a new concept to you? How do you think it can be overcome? Is it an issue that affects both micro- and macrocultural groups? How will addressing it affect race relations? We hope these questions will prompt your thinking about the influence of race on interracial interactions.

# INTRODUCTION

Chapter Two provided a historic overview of race as a social construction and overwhelming evidence that racial hierarchies continue to inform our interpersonal interactions. With that foundation, we explore the international phenomenon of colorism in this chapter. Colorism is understood to be a term coined in 1982 by the Pulitzer Prize winning author Alice Walker (Norwood, 2015). **Colorism** is a form of ingroup bias involving the unequal treatment of individuals belonging to the same racial or ethnic minority group based primarily on differences in skin tone. Colorism can be a form of ingroup bias or across groups. "Because of its unique relationship to who and what is beautiful, it has a tendency, although not exclusively, to affect *and infect* women more than men (p. 586).

Wilder (2015) spent two decades deeply entrenched in Black women's color stories; her work highlights the history and current significance of colorism in the United States. "*Everyday colorism* is a system of language, beliefs, and practices that govern the everyday interactions and experiences of black women as it relates to skin tone" (p. 16). Everyday colorism occurs through the use of a language system (e.g., communication) comprised of internal scripts and external behaviors guiding daily interactions and experiences related to skin tone. Colorism is not unique to Black Americans; people of color around the world—from Africa, Latin America, Asia, and the Caribbean, etc.—are impacted by *global colorism*, or the widespread elevation of light skin tones over darker skin across all communities of color (p. 6). Negative messages of inferiority/superiority are learned through and perpetuated by relationships between ingroup members (e.g., racial/ethnic, cultural, and familial). For example, young Indian girls talking about beauty may find themselves saying things that value and affirm lighter skinned girls as the beauty standard, which might be largely due to messages from families and cultural communities. These messages are both implicit and explicit, thus heightening the girls' awareness of a racial hierarchy that directly affects perceptions of self and others.

Colorism is a system-wide issue that perpetuates self-loathing and has a far-reaching effect on many racial/ethnic communities (Landor & Smith, 2019). Other countries (such as Puerto Rico, Brazil, India, Mexico, and Africa) also use color stratification systems that place greater value on lighter skin over darker skin. Specifically, research has shown that "lighter skinned African Americans are more likely to have higher-status occupations, higher incomes, more years of schooling, live in better neighborhoods, and marry higher status individuals than their darker skinned counterparts" (Steele, 2016, p. 55). This also applies to other communities of color who value lighter skinned members and perceive them as attractive and possessing positive personality traits and qualities, thus contributing to the devaluation and denigration of darker skin. Rooted in European colonialism and slavery (Dixon & Telles, 2017), colorism and racism were dual psychological strategies designed to "divide and conquer" colonized territories, securing Europeans as the primary benefactors. Belief systems established centuries ago continue to cause spirals of oppression that inform and shape contemporary understandings and treatments of racial differences. This chapter explores how colorism is a racial ideology with consequences for historically marginalized groups as well as society at large. We will draw your attention to racial hierarchies that directly impact interracial communication.

Our focus is on communication's role in the perpetuation of this race-laden value system and its profoundly negative impact on a wide array of racial/ethnic microcultural groups throughout the world. These global negative messages originated from colonialism and slavery; however, they continue to exist and have become a significant part of ingroup discourse in many ways.

> Using the biological differences of skin color as a justification for the oppression and enslavement of Africans, European colonizers developed a social hierarchy that aligned whites at the top and blacks at the bottom. The inferiority associated with blackness translated into socially constructed ideas about skin tone and phenotype that continue to shape identity, status, and opportunity. (Wilder, 2015, p. 7)

The value placed on lighter, whiter skin continues to impact the psyche of marginalized groups through the messages communicated to them in interpersonal relationships (see Chapter 8), the media (see Chapter 11), and organizations (see Chapter 10).

Racism is different from colorism in that only those with societal power *and* racial prejudice can be guilty of practicing racism (see Chapter 1). Because marginalized groups do not have societal power, they cannot be racist. Colorism is a system of oppression in which (unfortunately) everyone can participate and is targeted at communities of color (read nonwhite). Skin tone determines the value and worth of individuals and privileges lighter skinned people while penalizing darker skinned people, thus perpetuating skin stratification. "Light-skinned people earn more money, complete more years of schooling, live in better neighborhoods, and marry higher status people than darker-skinned people of the same race or ethnicity" (Hunter, 2007, p. 237).

Throughout this chapter, we provide a comprehensive overview of how European conquest and colonization perpetuated and spread colorism globally. We begin with a discussion of the origins of colorism and its relationship to whiteness, followed by highlights of its impact on gender discrimination and self-esteem. We discuss skin tone socialization to offer insight into how ingroup members are socialized to adopt and believe the value-laden ideologies about skin color in racial communities. We will also discuss the impact of colorism on quality of life and self-perception. Colorism is a negative phenomenon and a serious impediment to competent interracial communication. We conclude with a challenge to all to (1) adopt culturally responsive practices to colorism and (2) examine our communication within and outside of our communities about skin color and the values we place on lighter skin tones. We hope our efforts contribute to dismantling yet another form of race-related systemic oppression impeding interracial communication.

## THE INTERSECTION OF COLORISM AND INTERRACIAL COMMUNICATION

Colorism has been explored and addressed in the social sciences yet remains an under-researched topic in the communication discipline. This is critical because communication—whether through the exchange of messages in interpersonal relationships or mass media messages to society—is at the core of how ideologies about race are maintained. Communication scholar Kimberly Moffitt (2020) centers communication in research on colorism and stresses the importance of intragroup dialogue within African American families and communities. Colorism exists in most, if not all, communities of color and is normalized.

The experience of Mexican American actress Eva Longoria illustrates the family's role in communication about colorism. She was called *"la prieta fea"* ("the ugly dark one"), while her blonde sister with green eyes defined the family's ideal of beauty (Satran, 2016). Such messages may be told with humor but that does not minimize the extent of the hurt caused by messages of rejection from family, and possibly the Mexican community—and their negative effect on self-perception. Colorism messages occur on an interpersonal level and reflect cultural and societal thinking that preserve an outdated and highly problematic valuation system. Just as racism is taught through relationships (e.g., family, friends, media), so is colorism. Racial attitudes and values are transferred between individuals through communication.

Colorism is an offshoot of colonialism and slavery; both the oppressor and the oppressed placed value on lighter skin color. Whiteness is understood to be the standard of beauty (Landor & Smith, 2019), and colorism perpetuates a skin paradigm where being lighter is ideal, as are Eurocentric features. This system of oppression has been internalized by many communities of color through internal scripts. As Parameswaran and Cardoza (2009) explain, the justification of this skin-based hierarchy, or epidermal signification, began in the late 17th century, which marked the beginnings of the modern science of race and the creation of scientific models of racial superiority. Colorism was solidified in the 19th century through colonialism's perpetuation of the biological argument of race. Physical attributes (e.g., skin color, hair, breasts, brain, buttocks) of natives, or indigenous people, were scrutinized by Europeans to prove their alleged innate inferiority, thus legitimizing institutions of slavery and territorial conquest.

Communication facilitates the maintenance of a racist ideology through the use of labels that magnify racial differences (e.g., "Darkies" for Africans, "Yellow Orientals" for East Asians, "Red Indians" for Native Americans, "Dark Natives" for South Asians) and create racial binaries between whites and nonwhites. Labels for light skin are positive, while the majority of terms for dark skin are negative and derogatory (Wilder, 2015). The language of skin color influences internalized scripts that "constitute the socially constructed ideas and expectations of various skin tones" (p. 159). Internalization of color scripts then influence behavior. Do you see evidence of this in your own life, or among your friends and family? We are all guilty of using racial labels as descriptors, and they become a problem when they are intentionally or unintentionally judgmental, negative, and value laden.

Colorism is more detrimental when it comes from interpersonally close others. A nationally representative sample of African Americans experiencing ingroup colorism reported having worse physical health outcomes than those experiencing outgroup colorism (Monk, 2021a). Participants reported having worse cardiovascular, cardiometabolic health, and pain disorders directly related to discrimination experienced from ingroup members. While outgroup colorism is certainly harmful, both forms have long-lasting effects for BIPOC experiencing such maltreatment. As discussed later, color standards are preserved through interpersonal and media messages that communicate racial inferiority. To counteract such messages, we must engage in dialogue with each other about these ideologies and promote healthy self-images and positive intraracial and interracial communication.

Significant mental and emotional energy is exerted in managing the social stressors that create a daunting reality that is difficult to negotiate. Societal level racism and colorism have negative consequences and devastating impacts on racialized groups, forcing members to deal with both systemic and internalized racism (Monk, 2021b).

> Even decades after the civil rights movement, skin-tone stratification and colorism have become normalized and remain embedded in contemporary America. Cultural messages continue to permeate throughout the United States, have been adopted across the world through media, and contribute to a profitable industry focused on obtaining the Eurocentric beauty ideal. . . . Like experiences of racism, colorist incidents can be overt or covert (ambiguous), systematic or sudden, intentional or unintentional, and experienced through language and/or symbols (e.g., the absence of people who look like you on television shows and in magazines). (Landor & Smith, 2019, p. 803)

Matters are worsened by the media (Mitchell Dove, 2021; Razack & Joseph, 2021), immigration (Hunter, 2002), socialization (T. Banks, 2000; Davis Tribble et al., 2019), and history (Barnett, 2004), all of which actively perpetuate racial hierarchies negatively impacting communication and relationships. For example, darkness and blackness are negative concepts that are used interchangeably and associated with evil, discouragement, despair, and bad luck. They are so ingrained in our minds that they have been transferred onto skin, resulting in skin color devaluation (Anderson & Cromwell, 1977).

*Box 7.1*                                                    *Author Reflections*

## Race: An International Issue

From 2008 to 2019, I served as a study abroad Program Director. I expected race to be a critical social issue, and several encounters validated that for me in disheartening yet enlightening ways. They taught me about international perspectives on race and how skin color is a universal concept central to a person's cultural identity.

While in Tanzania, many Tanzanians assumed I "belonged" because of my skin color until they heard my U.S. accent. They were confused and often asked, "My sister, why don't you speak Swahili?" I was labeled "white" because I couldn't speak the language and dressed in typical Western attire. Nevertheless, I respected the culture and language choices and accepted their perceptions of me. This did not, however, prepare me for my most salient racial encounter in Africa.

I was approached by a street vendor (*machin gua*) while souvenir shopping. Our polite exchanges gradually got intense and uncomfortable when I decided not to buy anything. I was browsing through his merchandise (a U.S. cultural shopping norm); in Tanzania, this was perceived as an informal contractual obligation to make a purchase—hence the machin gua's anger. I understood his frustration but did not anticipate his aggressive behavior. As I sprinted towards our tour bus, he followed me and continued to harass me. My white male colleague immediately rebuffed him, forcefully saying I was not interested in his goods. The machin gua immediately responded by pacing near the bus and then yelling at me, "Blackie! Blackie!" I was mortified that he resorted to a racial slur. He might as well have called me the n-word—it cut like a knife. The hurt and embarrassment were so deep that I eventually wept in silence. Many of our Tanzanian guides and staff later apologized and assured me this was atypical and inappropriate behavior. Despite their assurances, I kept wondering why my skin color was devalued in another country, a country where I assumed I would be celebrated.

I had to deal with a similar experience in Costa Rica with a small class of five women (four African American and one Caucasian American). Two of the African American women had a very emotional, tearful reaction to a guest lecture from an anthropologist on the history and evolution of three distinct racial groups: mestizos (whites), Afro-Caribbeans, and indigenous (Indians). He concluded that a long-standing racial hierarchy established at least a century ago through colonization and white privilege continues to exist and impact contemporary race relations. The students were more disheartened than surprised; one African American female felt completely devalued by this information.

As the Program Director, I was learning about race in Costa Rica as well and worked really hard to make connections between the United States and Costa Rica so that students would have a rewarding experience. Unfortunately, our tour bus driver's attempt at being an impromptu translator almost undid those efforts. He was uninformed about the country's history on race. When he paraphrased the professor's conclusion that Blacks are deemed less valuable than whites, he emphasized the conclusion by pointing his finger at the African American student and then the Caucasian American student. The students were devastated by the driver's insensitivity. His being white and privileged made the matter worse and very hurtful. He eventually apologized, but the larger issue remained: colorism is alive and well throughout the world. There were numerous discussions about the existing racial hierarchy throughout the remainder of the program. Colorism was recognized as a universal concept with typically negative outcomes for marginalized and systemically oppressed groups. Thankfully, student anger and hurt were replaced with an appreciation for their cultural experience despite the harsh reality with which they were becoming much too familiar.

A racial binary is pervasive (Black vs. white, bad vs. good) and shows no evidence of being eradicated. Study abroad programs and other educational initiatives can help society move away from racist ideologies such as this.

—TMH

## GLOBAL RACIAL HIERARCHIES

Colorism is a global phenomenon, and to understand its role in perpetuating negative racial dynamics, we will provide brief overviews of colorism in various countries. We highlight findings from research that capture the complex nuances of colorism and its implications for BIPOC. Skin color and colorism are related to status throughout the world (Dixon & Telles, 2017). The majority of research has investigated Western societies, where color and colorism have been closely related to race and racism. In Latin America, the two sets of concepts overlap. Although there are differences, Latin American countries share a history of European colonization, slavery, and racism with the United States. Spanish and Portuguese colonizers established a hierarchy based on race and color throughout colonial Latin America. They "explicitly (through *castas*) or implicitly adopted a racial/color hierarchy that put indigenous and Black populations at the bottom and European colonizers at the top" (p. 409). When Spain colonized Mexico and Latin America, it implemented *sistema de casta*, a racial caste system (Cantu, 2018). *Criolos* were at the top of the system—whites primarily of Spanish descent. Mestizos were mixed race, indigenous and Spanish. Lowest on the caste scale were *mulattos*, a Black and Spanish mix.

The 300-year Spanish colonial period in Mexico was highly stratified through the casta system. After independence in 1821, the new social hierarchy was based on wealth and education (Campos-Vázquez & Medina-Cortina, 2019). After the Mexican revolution, the government in 1917 promoted an ideology of *mestizaje* (mixture of races) as the national identity. Mexico no longer recognized ethnic/racial categories; the population was classified as indigenous or nonindigenous by self-reported ability to speak an indigenous language. While mestizaje promotes the idea that stratification is driven only by class and wealth and not by skin color, Villarreal's (2010) study of adults found that contemporary Mexicans socially stratify by skin color, resulting in darker skinned Mexicans having lower education levels, lower occupational status, and being more likely to be impoverished (e.g., less likely to be affluent).

Scientific ideas of white superiority gained prominence by the late 1800s, and many Latin American countries sought to "whiten" their populations through European immigration (Dixon & Telles, 2017). Brazil had more African slaves than any other country involved in the transatlantic slave trade (Monk, 2021b). It carried out a particularly large whitening campaign—**branqueamento/blanqueamiento** (Charles, 2021), which endorsed "the belief of the superiority of whiteness and the desire to aspire to whiteness" (p. 16). Brazil's branqueamento immigration project was highly successful. In less than a century of subsidized European immigration, more than 4.7 million free white laborers immigrated to Brazil compared to the 3.6 million slaves forcibly imported in three centuries of the slave trade (Telles & Garcia, 2013).

---

### Box 7.2                    One Drop: Shifting the Lens on Race

## Debunking Colorism

Yaba Blay (2021) is a creative producer, native ethnographer, scholar-activist, public speaker, and cultural consultant whose scholarship documents the global Black experience. She is a thought leader on Black racial identity, colorism, and beauty politics and the author of *One Drop: Shifting the Lens on Race.*

> In the United States, historically a Black person has come to be defined as any person with *any* known Black ancestry. Although this definition has been statutorily referred to as the "one Black ancestor rule," the "traceable amount rule," and the "hypodescent rule," it is more popularly known as the "one-drop rule," meaning that one single, solitary drop of Black blood is enough to render a person Black. Said differently, the one-drop rule holds that a person with *any* trace of Black ancestry, however small or (in)visible, cannot be considered white. (p. 4)

No other racial or ethnic group was defined this way in the United States, and no other nation used such a formula.

Colorism has pervaded the psyches of African American men and women. Blay asks that we reflect on the salience of colorism within marginalized communities and engage in conversations about racial politics reinscribed through dominant discourses.

Women and men with lighter skin and European features are prominently featured in print media, internet, and television media. The same is true for female love interests in movies and music videos. There is also visual coding in the context of politics in the Black community (e.g., who has historically been in the positions of leadership—including the U.S. presidency). Think about these observations, see who is in power, and make the connections of what phenotype is more powerful and valuable in this society. BIPOC did not create it, but many continue to operate from this worldview (Blackstone, 2021).

Blay has produced numerous viral media campaigns, including CNN's documentary "Who Is Black in America?" All her work encourages critical thinking by addressing the history of race and the evolution of colorism. She encourages *everyone* of all skin tones to value their skin color and ask questions prompting introspection on an individual and societal level about motivations driving racial hierarchies and willingness to preserve them through silence.

Elite Brazilians embraced miscegenation not because they believed in racial equality but because it promised to dilute the Black Brazilian population and produce lighter generations. Official surveys in most Latin American countries do not include skin color designations. The exception is Brazil—information on skin color is available in the official census (Campos-Vázquez & Medina-Cortina, 2019). Even after adjusting for self-identification into official race-color categories, skin tone is significantly associated with socioeconomic status in Brazil.

Skin-color discrimination in India predates both European colonialism and contemporary globalization (M. Jha, 2016). There are diverse scholarly views on the origin of skin-color stigma and its association with caste discrimination. One view finds the origin of color prejudice in the Hindu *varna* system of caste organization and color hierarchy. Another view was the now debunked Aryan race theory, which traced the lineage of Brahmins to Aryans. The third view is the orientalist and colonialist reinforcement of the caste hierarchy. Some scholars argue that the practice of skin-color discrimination in Indian society originated in a mythical Aryan race theory promoted by the elite upper castes. Inequality and darker-skin discrimination was always associated with lower-caste status and socioeconomic positions in India.

The caste system was a prescriptive guide for how labor was to be divided and how racial groups from different casts should or should not interact (Parameswaran & Cordoza, 2009). A widely accepted and recognized hierarchical ladder of caste in order of highest to lowest valued groups is: **Brahmins** (intellectuals and priests), **Kshatriyas** (rulers and warriors), **Vaishyas** (merchants and traders), **Shudras** (servants and manual workers), and **Untouchables** (workers who process animal and human waste). British colonialism reinforced the advantages of lighter skin castes. A "racist construction of the 'dark native' as barbaric, savage, primitive, exotic, passive, unruly and incapable of self-determination" resulted from British slavery, antimiscegenation laws, and "exclusion of Indian citizens from full participation in structures of power" (p. 223).

> Skin-color prejudice in postcolonial India is linked to the lasting impact of British imperialism and the historical legacy of institutionalized white supremacy and internalized racism that colonial rule normalized in Indian culture. Indian class hierarchy is shaped by colonial Western values that the upper classes were acculturated into, through the education system, socializing the upper and middle classes into disdain for the rest of Indians. Poor Indians are often described in newspapers and government reports as backward, uneducated, and uncivilized. (M. Jha, 2016, p. 66)

The system places a considerable burden on Indian women who continue to experience significant pressure to be light skinned—a patriarchal logic that exposes women to the dual oppressions of colorism and sexism and how those intersecting identities are treated. Women's status is further compromised by an erroneous belief in a "pure" caste system (Parameswaran & Cordoza, 2009). Lighter skin color is a symbol of a woman's potential to preserve and continue the upper caste system. As our later discussions will demonstrate, dark-skinned women from India and other ethnic groups are perceived as liabilities to family, self, and society, and they sometimes respond to unreasonable expectations with desperate measures (e.g., skin whitening).

Color preferences in Asia prior to any contact with the West were based on status and sun exposure (Dixon & Telles, 2017). People who worked outside in the sun were in low-status occupations whereas those who worked indoors enjoyed higher status. For women, lightness was associated with femininity, beauty, and purity. Over many centuries, whiteness in Japan symbolized class privilege, spiritual purity, and feminine beauty. In Japanese art, the Japanese were portrayed as whiter than Europeans. In the Philippines, East Asian ideas (defined by lighter skinned, economically powerful countries such as Japan and China) about success and beauty combined with the remnants of the color caste system imposed on the native Filipino population by the Spanish. Throughout Asia, lighter-skinned East Asians—especially mixed-race individuals possessing European features—are idealized and contrasted with darker skinned Filipinos, Cambodians, and Vietnamese.

In Chapter 2, we provided an overview and discussion of the history of colonialism in the United States, which is central to the existence of colorism. Here, we highlight how post-slavery responses to racial hierarchies inform contemporary intraracial and interracial communication. Negative attitudes towards blackness/darkness are evidenced throughout the world (Dixon & Telles, 2017). In the United States, the white standard of beauty was established as the standard and was eventually challenged, to some degree, by the Black is beautiful movement of the 1960s and 1970s. The Afro hairstyle became fashionable; full lips and dark skin were celebrated. James Brown's infamous chant "Say it loud! I'm Black and I'm proud" reverberated throughout the Black community and emerged as a form of empowerment and resistance to the dominant ideals.

In Jamaica, different racial/ethnic/cultural groups in the creole society cling tightly to their heritage (Charles, 2003). However, the racial hierarchy places African and European cultures at odds. People who have embraced their African heritage resist European norms and values. Others assimilate to avoid being associated with individuals at the bottom of the hierarchy. Assimilating to European culture perpetuates not only an unattainable ideal but also relegates African heritage to the bottom rung. Charles's research also revealed a pattern of colorism driven by the psychological scars of colonialism. Assimilating has created an ingroup discourse where negative messages are communicated to members, namely children, and blackness (e.g., skin color, physical features, hair texture) is believed to be bad. Brown is better than black, and white is better than brown. Portrayals of success in Jamaica involve individuals who are white, fair, and brown. In a society in which color distinctions are important, individuals incorporate varying degrees of whiteness/brownness/blackness as they construct their identities to give meaning and purpose to their lives.

*Box 7.3*                                                      *Student Reflections*

### Racial Experience of a British Transplant

As a [British] Black woman, I label myself depending on who is asking. For instance, if I have attended a cultural event where there are individuals from African countries, I will say that I am English, but my parents are from Ghana. However, since being in the U.S. these last few months, I simply say that I am English. Since beginning [this] communications class, I definitely feel as if I am more aware of race than I was before. For instance, my roommates' friends seem to label me as the "Black girl from England" and sometimes I just wonder why I cannot be known as "the girl from England," but since they are white, I would not want to make a big deal out of it and make it into a racial issue because I feel that it could make the situation awkward. Last semester, it was interesting because a range of comments were made towards me, which I did not really think about at the time. Things like, "I did not know there were Black people in England," "I didn't know Black people spoke like you in England," "Was this [television] programme specifically targeted at ethnic minorities?" Since race was not something I was completely conscious about, these comments to me were simply regarded as standard, but now I really do wish I asked more about what they had meant.

Another thing I have noticed since being here is I am treated differently by some of the African American females, and I have been told that it is "because I am from London" and apparently there is a stereotype attached to that as being "stuck up" and thinking that I am "superior," which I believe is ridiculous. I just believe I am a regular Black female trying to obtain an education, and it really is as simple as that.

## COLORISM AS A SOCIALIZING PROCESS

The only way colorism can survive is through socialization. Relationships on individual, institutional, and societal levels are the breeding ground for good and bad indoctrination about various issues. Children, for example, do not adopt racial caste systems until their family, teachers, and others teach them the behaviors and attitudes associated with the structure. That means skin tone valuation is a socialization process. How have you been taught to think about skin color differences? Have you heard family or friends say being lighter/whiter is better? While you may or may not relate to this, colorism is a reality for many, and this way of thinking has many consequences and outcomes. Both covert and overt messages communicated to micro- and macrocultural groups send a resounding message that, contrary to popular belief, race *still* does matter. This was evident in the 2021 movie *Passing* based on the 1929 book by Nella Arsen (see Box 7.4).

Family is a major contributing factor to our skin color attitudes and how we think about race. Communication with family members establishes socialization patterns and processes prevalent in shaping racial attitudes (Wilder,

---

**Box 7.4**

### The Price of *Passing*

The film *Passing* tells the story of Irene Redfield, a biracial woman, and her childhood friend Clare living in Jim Crow 1929. Both women are light-skinned African Americans, but the striking difference between them is that Clare has chosen to live her life as a white woman; she is "passing." Clare's decision to deny her race is partially due to rejection from her white relatives after her father dies. She later marries a wealthy white man, who tells Clare he hates Black people—not knowing he has married a Black woman. Irene has married a Black man and embraces her Blackness. An unexpected meeting rekindles the friendship between Clare and Irene, complicated by the women keeping Clare's secret. Clare has dyed blond hair and has created a believable narrative about her background that her husband believes to be true.

The movie uniquely addresses the issues of passing and colorism by drawing parallels between the characters and highlighting their markedly different approaches to their identities. While Clare is in complete denial of her Blackness, Irene is accepting of who she is and navigates her life to minimize the negative impact societal racism has on her and her family. The friendship sheds light on the anguish the women experience because of their skin tone and colorism. *Passing* provides audiences a peek into a cultural phenomenon that has been in existence for decades. It reveals the personal turmoil biracial/multiracial and light skinned people suffer when choosing to give up their identities because of societal pressure—a choice that comes with anguish and many risks.

The film is a personal project of filmmaker Rebecca Hall, who is also an actor. She wrote the screenplay and used the movie as an opportunity to process her own family history; her Black grandfather passed as a white man his whole life. *Passing* provides audiences with a nuanced understanding of a very complex and real phenomenon that is more common than we might think.

---

2015), which have a significant impact on one's life experiences and psychological well-being (Matthews & Johnson, 2015; Monk, 2021a). These experiences are often gendered (Mitchell Dove, 2021); skin-tone discrimination (along with other physical characteristics, such as hair texture and physical features) more negatively affects women than men (Adams et al., 2020). In-depth interviews with African American women revealed the effects of family socialization (Wilder & Cain, 2011). Women identified both implicit and explicit messages regarding skin color bias exchanged among and between family members, particularly between women. The mixed-race grandmother of one interviewee had the strongest feelings about colorism, which she explicitly communicated to her family members. The interviewee, who was very light skinned, shared that her grandmother delivered harsh warnings against light- and dark-skinned African Americans being romantically and sexually involved. These admonishments made it quite clear to female family members that the grandmother demonized dark-skinned individuals, whom she believed posed a threat to the alleged purity of her light-skinned family.

Socialization processes include establishing a hierarchy of skin tones and other physical characteristics such as hair texture.

This story, along with many others, is important to our understanding of colorism as a communication phenomenon. Wilder and Cain (2011) found that communication is largely responsible for maintaining the schisms between racial groups. Much like racist thinking, these socialization patterns support the belief that colorism is taught by and learned through the family. Families provide our first exposure to the concept of race, and by extension to skin-tone bias and colorism. For interview participants, colorism was a part of the normative framework, or normal way of conceptualizing race, and this extended to the dominant views toward skin tone within the Black community in general. Because Black womanhood is recognized as a cornerstone in Black families, mothers, grandmothers, and other female family members were consistently identified as the main sources of knowledge. These maternal figures were also identified as reaffirming and transformative agents who, subsequently and actively, worked to perpetuate what has become the norm regarding ideologies about skin-tone bias and discrimination. In the end, these messages were adopted and accepted as truth and rarely challenged. A multidimensional process of color socialization does exist (K. Moffitt, 2020). Thus, it is safe to conclude that colorism makes competent intraracial and interracial communication challenging.

Wilder's (2015) interviews with Black women who reported having direct experience with colorism and family socialization are enlightening. Participants identified their families, schools, relationships, and the media as maintaining these scripts and practices. These people and societal institutions were also recognized as directly shaping attitudes toward light and dark skin, which Wilder concludes is a signifier of "an inheritance of similar attitudes . . . [from] earlier generations of black Americans" (p. 159). It must also be noted that this process involves what Wilder calls ritualistic, compensatory, and discriminatory practices.

---

**Box 7.5**                                                    *Research Highlight*

### Addressing Colorism via Social Media

From a scholarly standpoint, colorism was popularized by Black scholars and broadened to extend understanding of this phenomenon to different cultural contexts. Indiana professor Radhika Parameswaran is a leading scholar in the area of colorism and media who tackles this very difficult topic from many angles. Parameswaran was interviewed by graphic designer Juyoti Gupta (2020) because of Parameswaran's interest in fair and just media. Gupta attempts to bring international attention to the worldwide issue of colorism via social media.

Parameswaran and Gupta have a pointed discussion about how colorism is plaguing Indian women. They discuss skin lightening and consumerism, standards of beauty, and marriageability, and charge everyone to think critically about colorism and the influence of advertisements and interpersonal networks in feeding this bias. Parameswaran's many points provide food for thought about how we can deconstruct racial hierarchies dividing our racial communities. One of her insights is on intersectionality in relation to skin tone. "[Skin whitening is] a problem that connects with ideas of class. We see poor people as darker skinned. We see South Indians as darker skinned and therefore less beautiful, etc. We see people of lower caste as more dark-skinned. It is important to keep in mind that colourism is widespread and that it connects with a host of social problems."

What are your thoughts about colorism? Do you think it is as much of a problem as the researchers report? Are all communities of color affected in a similar way? What role does the macrocultural group have in addressing this social issue?

---

## Racial/Ethnic Communities

This chapter might be prompting you to ask yourself, "What does this have to do with me?" Although not directly affected by colorism, you are most likely interacting and in relationships with people facing this very real issue. If these negative beliefs about dark-skinned people are internalized, then race becomes salient in a very unique way and impacts how you interact with each other. Just imagine how disheartening it is to be a member in any racial/ethnic group in the world where people with lighter skinned or European features are deemed more beautiful and more successful. That feeling is magnified when both micro- and macrocultures internalize those messages, further reinforcing the negative value associated with dark skin. Burge et al. (2020) explored colorism in politics. Study participants were from diverse ethnicities, and Black participants deviated from a colorist ideology and expressed preference for darker skinned candidates. Wilder and Cain's (2011) participants shared how family teachings are oftentimes Afrocentric and affirming yet challenged when they enter white spaces. The findings offer hope that colorism can be dismantled through positive intraracial and interracial communication. They also serve as a springboard for a discussion of the larger, international implications of colorism as it informs our relationships across the globe.

Racial and ethnic diversity within communities create tensions over what aspects of one's cultural identity are valued. There is increasing evidence that our relationships with ingroup members and society inform the value we place on others and ourselves. Similar to family, we value the role that our racial/ethnic community members play in our lives (Charles, 2021).

Darker skinned immigrant Latinas reported having lower self-esteem and lower feelings of attractiveness, and they wanted to be lighter skinned because of the negative value placed on dark skin (Telzer & Vazquez, 2009). The bias was communicated to the women by their families and society throughout their lives. A similar pattern exists among South-Asian Canadian and European-Canadian women. In general, all women were dissatisfied with their bodies (Sahay & Piran, 1997), suggesting a general pressure to ascribe to societal standards of beauty. In terms of race, South-Asian Canadian women desired lighter skin but not necessarily white skin. Sahay and Piran suggest that "shifting away from white skin and more toward light skin [may have been] precipitated perhaps by spillover effects from the *Black Is Beautiful* movement, the advent of civil rights movements, multiculturalism, racial integration, and equal opportunity programs" (p. 167). This is further substantiated by the fact that lighter skinned South Asian-Canadian women had "higher body satisfaction than all women," followed by medium-skinned and then dark-skinned South Asian-Canadian women.

Medium skinned women experience fewer negative reactions; however, they are not light enough to feel secure or to benefit from the advantages of having light skin. This middle position may produce a sense of inadequacy and account for the fact that this group exhibited the lowest body satisfaction (Sahay & Piran, 1997, p. 168). Skin tone has a negative effect on the self-esteem and self-efficacy of Black men and women (Thompson & Keith, 2001). It also increases the likelihood of being shot by police (Crutchfield et al., 2017). Darker skinned men reported lower self-efficacy or belief in oneself to achieve personal success. Dark-skinned women from a working class background expressed lower self-esteem, and dark-skinned women overall were perceived as unattractive.

Flores and Telles (2012) reanalyzed data from a research project using the PERLA (Project on Ethnicity and Race in Latin America) skin color variable to test skin color bias. They found that interviewers in the 2006 Mexico Panel Study practiced extreme color bias while rating the skin tone of study participants by using the highly subjective classification process of physically eyeing participants and rating them on a scale from 1 (very light) to 11 (very dark). (This is similar to the eyeball test in Chapter 2.) Regardless of actual physical skin color, high-income people were classified as white (or *güero*) and were nearly twice as likely to be classified as such than were low-income persons of the same race. Flores and Telles call this **money whitening**—assigning color categories based on class. So, even though a person is physically dark skinned, their economic standing places them in a higher status group, which confirms color bias and provides insight into this phenomenon on a social level. Unlike other research on victims of color bias, this study shows that conscious or subconscious bias has serious implications for other contexts. The interviewers were probably volunteers, which means they may have learned bias in the workplace, favored lighter skinned, upwardly mobile people, and discriminated against darker skinned individuals. This behavior perpetuates the systemic nature of color bias that is beyond the victim's control. As such, it becomes even more important for people to begin thinking critically about their attitudes toward skin color and the impact of those attitudes on intraracial and interracial interactions. Just as color bias in the original panel study reproduced social inequality in Mexican society, it does the same in all other countries throughout the world.

## Skin Color as Social Capital

Have you ever noticed any advantages or disadvantages you have because of your own skin color? If not, it is very likely that others have interacted with you in response to your perceived racial identity. If you are a Caucasian American person, then you have probably received benefits because of how you are perceived. Lighter skinned individuals are associated with positive (e.g., trustworthy, smart, hardworking, rich, attractive) characteristics while darker skinned individuals are associated with negative (e.g., criminal, lazy, unintelligent) ones. Whiteness, and lighter skin, has been set as a societal standard for beauty, thus creating significant pressure for individuals, communities, and society as a whole to conform. This mindset fosters an unattainable ideal and preserves a value-laden racial hierarchy that underprivileges some and over privileges others. **Social capital** refers to the potential of individuals to secure benefits through membership in social structures (Bhandari & Yasunobu, 2009). Lighter skinned individuals accrue social capital because of society's regard for lighter skin tones. They are held in higher esteem within and outside their community and enjoy societal privileges and benefits because of the racial hierarchies ingrained in our social psyche (Flores & Telles, 2012; J. Hall, 2020).

Schwartzman (2007) refers to this as **racial boundary-crossing**. Her nationwide household survey in Brazil revealed that money whitening is a significant pay off for light-skinned individuals. Although a person cannot change their skin color to their advantage, their education can be a vehicle toward that end. The survey showed that nonwhite parents with more education were more likely to marry whites than nonwhites, and interracial couples (one nonwhite and one white partner) with more education were also likely to categorize their children as white more often than less educated interracial couples. These patterns of behavior demonstrate how deeply ingrained societal attitudes are in the daily lives of many people—so much so that personal decisions about relationships and child-rearing are made based on value laden racial hierarchies. Thus, colorism is maintained as a global phenomenon in very implicit and explicit ways.

Social capital is linked to many factors (e.g., education, income, skin color). Regardless of whether a person possesses many of these "valuable qualities," their light skin provides accessibility to benefits denied to darker skinned individuals. For women, there is an expectation that they must be light skinned to be considered beautiful. For example, many people have heard, "She is pretty, for a dark-skinned woman." The statement implies that a woman's darkness disqualifies her from being beautiful. For lighter skinned women, this physical quality is a form of social capital in that they are reaping privileges at a higher rate than darker skinned women (Wilder & Cain, 2011). Findings from a national survey provided critical evidence about the impact of skin color on life outcomes for women of African and Mexican descent (Hunter, 2002). Light-skinned women who closely resembled whites reaped considerably more rewards than dark-skinned women, even in instances where they did not work or study as hard as darker skinned women. Lighter skinned African American women were also found to earn higher wages even though they had the same credentials as darker skinned African American women. The data also showed that light-skinned women had a clear advantage when it came to marriage, in that they were more likely to marry men of high status than were darker skinned women, thus perpetuating colorist ideology. Light skin is both social capital and a stratifying agent for women regarding life chances (Mathews & Johnson, 2015).

> Positive characteristics and traits are attributed to those with lighter skin, while those with darker complexions are frequently placed into stereotypical categories and judged severely by their physical appearance. Though discrepancies between light and dark complexions speak generally to categorizations of race, colorism is a specific phenomenon of stratification that has been formed within the African-American community.... Since light complexions have been socially construed to define beauty, African American women who possess this trait benefit from an elevated social capital. A woman's social relationships (i.e., social ties or social network) can additionally affect how many and how advantageous her resources are to other outlets (such as employment and/or education. As women are judged excessively by their physical appearance, those considered to possess more beauty will have better chances when encountering the social world. Bias preferences for skin color can lead equally qualifying women to dramatically different life outcomes. (pp. 250, 253)

Skin color as social capital originated in slavery, and as a result skin-tone bias has divided the Black community for almost as long as racism has divided the United States (Wilder, 2015). Colorism caused division in the Black community based on one's proximity to whiteness. Slave owners assigned lighter-skinned slaves to indoor work. Because of their partial white heritage, light-skinned Blacks were considered superior to dark-skinned Blacks. In some cases, light-skinned biracials accepted the privilege of light skin and the stigma of dark skin to form their own social class that enjoyed more opportunities in the white-dominated society. They became the Black Elite and their educational and religious institutions implemented separatist standards.

> Organizational colorism thrived through exclusionary social clubs and societies.... Throughout the years, these stereotypical beliefs made their way from one generation to the next, and some African Americans today con-

tinue to place a premium on lighter skin tone, seeing the different shades of brown as varying degrees of status, acceptance, and achievement. (p. 9)

Canotal (2009) notes that in the United States there were "social distinction[s] between blacks, mulattoes and whites, where freed fair skinned people of mixed race would often try and marry other people of fair complexion in order to dilute the darkness of their skin in their offspring" (p. 35). He supports his conclusion from a gender perspective, explaining that light-skinned Black men are more "palatable" in the workplace than are dark-skinned Black males, thus suggesting that "light-skinned black men are seen as more likely to assimilate into the work environment, not alienate their clients, and not appear threatening" (p. 31). This stratification based on skin tone exists in both professional and personal relationships. "The preponderance of the evidence strongly suggests that the significance of colorism in shaping the life chances, trajectories, and outcomes among African Americans continued mostly unabated from slavery to the early twenty-first century" (Monk, 2021b, p. 82).

## Skin Whitening and the Price of Beauty

Skin lightening industries have globalized bleaching and spread a worldwide message perpetuating racial bias privileging lighter skin over darker skin. Groups across nationalities, races, ethnicities, and cultures have embraced this ideology and actively place value on people according to their skin tone. For those born into a race-based caste, lighter skinned individuals are perceived as instant benefactors of privileges over darker skinned group members. Pressure to ascribe to cultural standards of beauty prompts some individuals to resort to **skin whitening** (Chauhan & Tiwari, 2019; Verma, 2010). Globalization and the mass media helped spread white/light supremacy throughout the world. Entertainment—from India's Bollywood to Latin America's telenovelas—and advertising industries throughout the globe portray images of a global beauty that is rooted in whiteness. Skin lightening and cosmetic surgeries exploded during the 20th century, becoming a multibillion-dollar global industry (Dixon & Telles, 2017). In China, Malaysia, the Philippines, and South Korea, approximately 40% of women use such products. The strength of the skin-bleaching industry is perceived as evidence of a global preference for lighter skin. Light-skin preference and white supremacy have become increasingly united, globalized, and commodified.

A. P. Harris (2008) explains that colorism in the Americas is inextricably connected with histories of slavery and indigenous conquest; light skin and European features became the standard. Several Latin American nations launched whitening campaigns in the late 19th and early 20th centuries. Whitening is currently tied to conformity to societal and communal standards of beauty and is a huge and very lucrative global industry. What is more disconcerting is that women, and men, from all racial/ethnic backgrounds are falling victim to colorism.

Most scholars contest the idea that preferences for lighter skin are neutral, aesthetic, individual preferences (often promoted in advertising) rather than the product of colonial domination and the rhetoric of white supremacy throughout the world (Dixon & Telles, 2017). Some see the desire for lighter skin as a rational response to perceived better life outcomes (a view promoted by multinational corporations and the mass media). Conceptualizing skin color as a form of capital forms the basis for considering skin-lightening practices as rational. Light skin tone can be "transformed into social capital (social networks), symbolic capital (esteem or status), or even economic capital (high-paying job or promotion)" (p. 412). It is also interpreted as beauty, which serves as a form of social capital providing access to education, romantic partners, social networks, and jobs. "If skin color is a form of capital, then individuals may rationally seek to acquire lightness/whiteness in the same way they seek to acquire other forms of capital, although in doing so they replicate the ideologies, and the material consequences, of light/white supremacy" (p. 412).

Research has investigated associations between skin color and life outcomes in terms of educational experiences, marital prospects, occupational status, and mental/physical health, including self-esteem. As noted earlier, colorism can have a negative impact on self-perception and identity (Mathews & Johnson, 2015). The findings regarding self-esteem, however, are complex. According to Charles (2003), "we cannot assume that bleaching is done as a result of low self-esteem" (p. 720). In interviews, Jamaican youth "cited a beauty-related reason for bleaching. One participant said she loved the 'brown thing' because it made her look better. Another used the bleaching cream to prevent acne and keep her skin smooth" (p. 720). The findings suggest that self-hate or low self-esteem is not a consequence of skin bleaching for these participants; rather "[s]kin bleaching is the contemporary evidence of the deep-rooted and lingering psychological scars of slavery in particular and colonization in general" (p. 712). Some individuals who engage in skin lightening assert that becoming white is not their goal; rather they are seeking an improved version of themselves (Dixon & Telles, 2017).

While lighter skin tone generally creates advantages and privileges, perceptions of skin tone are relative and based on one's subjective experiences with race and skin tone (Landor & Smith, 2019). Research has found that the consequences of skin-tone bias depend on racial identity and skin-tone satisfaction, The issue is complex and indicates the importance of examining social identity factors. Skin-tone trauma is a complex, multilayered topic affected by the intersection of gender, race, and socioeconomic position.

According to S. Jha and Adelman (2009), there is a global bias in the preference for light-skinned females, which undoubtedly has an impact on all relationships, including the selection of a romantic or marriage partner. This bias is present in social media, specifically internet dating (see discussion of racial bias in online dating in Chapter 8). Jha and Adelman analyzed the publicly available online profiles and preferences of brides and grooms in India and the "success story wedding photos" (200 of them) posted on four Indian matrimonial websites, finding a significant bias. Males preferred brides with lighter skin than their own and were more likely than females to make that preference

Colorism in India has a more significant impact on women than men. This means that men of all shades are at an advantage when choosing a lighter-skinned marriage partner.

blatantly clear. The photos showed the brides to be consistently lighter skinned than grooms, with dark-skinned women essentially nonexistent in these success stories. The study illustrates how technology both perpetuates and *intensifies* colorism, which is consistent with other findings that racist ideologies are gaining momentum in the age of social media (see Chapter 11). Visual images embedded within these internet sites continue to devalue and invalidate darker skinned Indian women, which is probably the case with women of color from other racial/ethnic communities.

Verma (2010) comments that skin whitening "pays a colossal premium to being fair which is equivalent to prestige, desirability, attractiveness and, in the case of women, impressive points on the marriage scoreboard" (p. 464). Verma attributes this obsession to the caste system, "which planted the seeds of eminence for fair skin as it was generally the domain of the upper classes and the lower classes were always portrayed as the dark ones" (p. 465). Lightening of India occurred through invasion from the Dutch, Mughal, Portuguese, and the British, who were all of lighter skin color than the Indians. The continued glorification of light skin due to British governance and societal obsession with skin whitening/lightening products is evidence that colorism is a mainstay for many within the Indian community.

There was a popular Indian soap opera, *Saat Phere* ("Seven Circles Around the Fire," a Hindu marriage ritual), that aired from 2005 to 2009 (Perry, 2005). The lead female character, Saloni, was played by a beautiful actress, Rajashree Thakur. As the actress explained, "It's not that Saloni isn't beautiful. . . . It's that she's dark. Because of her complexion, her family thinks no one will marry her." Cory Wallia, Bollywood's top makeup artist, explained that the desire for whiteness has little to do with beauty but is related to ethnicity: "Indians are more racist with other Indians than any American ever was with his slaves."

Professor Parameswaran notes that the idea that the powerful have always been light skinned is a global phenomenon; colorism "manifests in myriad ways in most cultures" (quoted in Gajanan, 2020). Saraswati (2021) studied mass media representations and the preference for light-skinned women in Indonesia. Her research found that the preference existed prior to European colonialism and that lighter was not always considered better if the woman's race was not the preferred race. After Dutch colonialism, the preference was Caucasian white; after the Japanese took over, the preference was for Japanese white. Saraswati proposed the idea of cosmopolitan whiteness to rethink whiteness beyond racial and ethnic categories and to think of it as constructed through feelings. Whiteness, thus, is not coded as specific biological features or originating from a specific place; it is about *appearing* white and experiencing the privileges and cosmopolitan lifestyles attached to it.

In India, the forces of colonialism, caste-based systems, and globalization contribute to colorism (Gajanan, 2020). In families, light-skinned children enjoy preferential treatment; in the workplace, people feel they must appear lighter to succeed. Unilever introduced a product called "Fair and Lovely" in 1975 when there were very few products for skin whitening. By 2020, Unilever's cream held 70% of the skin-lightening market. Public scrutiny and criticism of marketing campaigns that emphasized light skin as a positive quality resulted in Unilever changing the name to "Glow & Lovely" in 2020. Mirusha Yogaraja, a filmmaker and writer, said changing the name does nothing—the product is still being sold to people for whom colorism is extremely prevalent. Parameswaran agrees that the name change is superficial.

> For colorism to even head toward something like ending, there has to be multi-frontal campaign to end it. Start within families and school systems. Change the books we read and the illustrations we look at. Change marriage practices. Undo white supremacy in general. (quoted in Gajanan, 2020)

Skin whitening is also a very popular phenomenon in Africa (Rao, 2019). Skin lighteners are popular among young, urban, educated women from formerly colonized countries (Dixon & Telles, 2017). In Nigeria, South Africa, and Togo, 77%, 35%, and 59% of women, respectively, regularly use skin-lightening products. The World Health Organization (WHO) warns that skin bleaching can cause psychosis, cancer, and damage to the liver and kidneys. Another, even more dangerous, skin-bleaching treatment is the injection of glutathione or the consumption of tablets containing the substance. Skincare companies in Africa have increasingly used the treatment, which unfortunately is marketed to pregnant women to lighten the skins of their babies in utero. The skincare and cosmetics industries are taking advantage of African women's desire for lighter skin; 40% of African women bleach their skin. Social media platforms are replete with advertisements for skin products. Shingi Mtero teaches a course on the politics of skin bleaching at Rhodes University (South Africa) and notes the many nuances surrounding skin lightening. If men want lighter skin, then women may assimilate to that standard to increase the chances of getting married, which is a form of social capital; people also believe lighter skin will help them find better jobs.

> Whiteness has been elevated and presented as a universal standard of prog-
> ress. When people say it's about whiteness, it's not necessarily to physically
> be white, it's about wanting to access things white people have easy access
> to—privileges, economic and social status. (quoted in Rao, 2019)

Given these assumptions, the decision to use skin lightening products could be
characterized as a businesslike decision, which makes banning the products, as
Ghana, Rwanda, and the Côte d'Ivoire have attempted, less likely to succeed.

As you can see, colorism is a large-scale social issue. Will institutions be
willing to take on the problem or be successful in doing so? We must question
what is driving the market for skin whiteners, the industry producing them, and
the consumer. Digital activism through platforms such as Change.com can aid
communities and societies in combatting global messages that lighter is better
and that social capital can be achieved through purchasing these products.

## Transforming Attitudes Toward Racial Hierarchies

Colorism is a social disease that plagues communities on both a national
and international level. This is evidenced by the fact that skin color and colorism are related to status throughout the world (Dixon & Telles, 2017). The
social constructions of color and colorism are closely related to race and racism, which should not be a surprise.

> Although all these concepts deal, on some level, with categorizing human
> difference, their use and meaning are not consistent across societies. What
> is nearly always consistent is a color hierarchy in which white or light skin
> is considered more desirable and modern, whereas darker skin is consid-
> ered less valuable and primitive. (p. 418)

Colorism is a by-product of racism and colonialist ideology, but it exists as
its own substructure operating at both individual and institutional levels. Colorism is experienced apart from racism but, as a substructure, interacts with
the larger structures of race, gender, and class and must be understood within
that larger context. "Colorism is a form of internalized racism, and, as such,
colorism mirrors many of the same qualities of racism" (Wilder, 2015, p. 160).
It is a socially constructed ideology of who people are and what they should be
based on the color of their skin.

We cannot deny this reality; there is substantive evidence that the ves-
tiges of institutionalized racism via slavery and other forms of systemic
oppression continue to have negative impacts on intraracial and interracial
relationships. Colorism leads to stratification by skin color, which challenges
relationships. Skin tone socialization occurs through interpersonal networks.
It is a vicious cycle, but it can be stopped. We need to think critically about
our communication so that we improve our attitudes toward racial differences and work toward dismantling racial hierarchies. This includes recognizing that the meaning ascribed to words is learned through association
with other phenomena (Mathews & Johnson, 2015). Black women too frequently learn that dark is associated with stigmatized, negative qualities

such as ugly, immoral, and hated. Thus, to change such perceptions, we need to change our communication.

Race relations can only improve by reeducating ourselves and society about racial differences, which includes prejudice reduction and collective action towards social change (J. Dixon et al., 2010). This requires mobilization among disadvantaged groups that will destabilize institutions and challenge the status quo. This can only occur through communication within intraracial and interracial relationships. Figure 7.1 provides a visual illustration of how this process would work. Before beginning the process, we must first admit that colorism affects us all. We can them move forward with eradicating colorism, which involves (1) debunking and de-institutionalizing myths about light, brown, and dark skin; (2) having frank and open discussions about colorism at the moment it occurs; (3) educating through empowerment among groups; and (4) building community-level coalitions where differences are valued and appreciated.

**Figure 7.1**    Communication Is the Path to Social Change

After conducting her in-depth interviews with African American women, Wilder (2015) encouraged using a communication approach to combat colorism. This is a global issue that affects many historically oppressed groups, but we strongly encourage *everyone* to rethink the value placed on lighter skinned individuals and their social capital. Wilder's advice is crucial. Just as open and honest dialogue can change racial attitudes in general, the same is true for colorism. Wilder suggests the road we can take to dismantle the racial hierarchies negatively impacting our perceptions across and within racial communities.

> I think it all comes down to talking about it. I mean when you don't talk about something . . . and then it turns into a big boil, and it's a lot more dramatic. So I think if you as a community, or as a race, if you voice these issues and you say, "well you know this is what's going on," and you ask yourself why is this, rather than just accepting it for . . . the situation that it's always been. I think things can get a lot better. (pp. 168–169)

Having pointed conversations about race with family, friends, and coworkers is critical to removing color bias. Wilder (2015) says these discourses should take place in the moment. When we hear biased comments against a person or group because of their skin color (or make them ourselves), we should take the time to discuss with the offending party how hurtful that language is. More importantly, there should be discussion of the power this language has in shaping racial attitudes. Sure, these comments might be made in private or in a casual context, but what happens when our words offend or hurt someone? Or limit their opportunities for professional advancement? As we have seen, women and men of color have attested to the consequences colorism has on their self-perceptions and treatment by society. In order to have healthy intraracial and interracial communication, we must choose to communicate positive, affirming messages that celebrate our many shades and hues.

---

*Box 7.6*

## Confront Colorism Guide

The organization DoSomething.Org tackles colorism by offering people ways to best confront it. Below are select tips that encourage people to get involved in identifying and addressing colorism in their interpersonal interactions, in the media, and in society (Menjivar, 2021).

**Watch for problematic behavior in friends and acquaintances**

- Limited time spent in the sun to avoid skin getting darker
- Use of makeup or skin products that make skin appear lighter
- Approval of memes on social media that joke about differences between light- and dark-skinned people

**Watch for exclusion in media**

- Do all film or television characters have lighter skin, or are dark-skinned characters in less important or stereotypical roles?
- Do lists of the most beautiful celebrities only include people with lighter skin?
- Do Twitter threads of influential activists and figures to follow online include anyone with darker skin?

**How to address colorism**

- Education about and acknowledgement of colorism instances help dismantle skin-tone bias and promote healing
- Listen to and support those impacted.
- Verbally and calmly confront colorists
- Embrace hard conversations
- Increase moral courage and be actively involved

## CONCLUSION

Prior to reading this chapter, many of you were probably unaware of colorism or what it means for microcultures, let alone society at large. Others might have had direct experience with it and can relate to it. Because of or in spite of your racial/ethnic background, we hope you will become an active change agent in how we learn to value race and skin color. Standing by idly and doing nothing gives power to antiquated ways of thinking, doing more harm than good. So, it benefits us all to commit to changing our perceptions of skin color.

Our communication with family members, friends, and colleagues is critical to dismantling all forms of racial prejudice and discrimination. Those relationships are where we learn about racial differences and should be where we work to unlearn our negative thoughts about skin color and its perceived value. In theory, there is a fundamental belief that all humans are equal; the reality, however, is that many do not share this thinking. Therefore, we must make it our practice to begin addressing troubling ideologies through pointed discussions about skin color bias. These discourses, along with other discussions about race, can improve race relations and provide us with the communication skills necessary for competent communication and healthy relationships within and between our many racial/ethnic communities.

### KEY TERMS

| | |
|---|---|
| colorism | shudras |
| branqueamento/blanqueamiento | untouchables |
| mulatto | money whitening |
| caste system | social capital |
| brahmins | racial boundary-crossing |
| kshatriyas | skin whitening |
| vaishyas | |

### RECOMMENDED CONTEMPORARY READINGS

Cardwell, M. E. (2021). Examining interracial family narratives using critical multiracial theory. *Review of Communication, 21*(3), 206–222.

Chatterjee, S., & Rastogi, S. (2022). Television culture and the beauty bias problem: An analysis of India's postmillennial television serials. *Media Asia, 49*(3), 213–234.

Crutchfield, K., Sparks, D. M., Williams, M., & Findley, E. (2021). In my feelings: Exploring implicit skin tone bias among preservice teachers. *College teaching.* DOI:10.1080/87567555.2021.1979456

Cummings, K. (2019). Sisters in the shadows: An examination of Prince's "strange relationship" with Black women. *Howard Journal of Communications, 30*(2), 144–163.

Foy, S. L., & Ray, R. (2019). Skin in the game: Colorism and the subtle operation of stereotypes in men's college basketball. *American Journal of Sociology, 125*(3), 730–785. https://doi-org.libezp.lib.lsu.edu/10.1086/707243

Harris, K. L. (2018). Biracial American colorism: Passing for white. *American Behavioral Scientist, 62*(14), 2072–2086. https://doi-org.libezp.lib.lsu.edu/10.1177/0002764218810747

Keyes, L., Smaol, E., & Nikolova, S. (2020). The complex relationship between colorism and poor health outcomes with African Americans: A systematic review. *Analyses of Social Issues and Public Policy, 20*(1), 676–697.

Reece, R. L. (2019). Color crit: Critical race theory and the history and future of colorism in the United States. *Journal of Black Studies, 50*(1), 3–25. https://doi-org.libezp.lib.lsu.edu/10.1177/0021934718803735

Reece, R. L. (2021). The gender of colorism: Understanding the intersection of skin tone and gender inequality. *Journal of Economics, Race, and Policy, 4*, 47–55.

Stewart, Q., Cobb, R., & Keith, V. (2020). The color of death: Race, observed skin tone, and all-cause mortality in the United States. *Ethnicity & Health, 25*(7), 1018–1040.

## OPPORTUNITIES FOR EXTENDED LEARNING

1. After reading this chapter, you should have a strong sense of what colorism is and its impact on various communities throughout the world. How is colorism impacting peers your age throughout the world? What similarities are there? Differences? How are different genders being impacted by colorism? Do an internet search for hashtag movements designed to fight colorism. Make note of the countries, organizations, and people using social media to draw attention to this very important social issue. How effective are they in educating people about colorism? What racial groups and countries are the focus of these digital campaigns? How are victims of colorism empowered?

2. In small groups, create a street poll that asks passersby about their awareness of colorism as an international issue. For example, you might begin by asking people to define colorism and then offer examples of it. Aim to ask 5–6 questions. As a class, choose the 10 best questions and conduct interviews with strangers and willing friends. This activity will allow you to gauge the level of awareness about this social issue and to identify any patterns that affect perspectives on colorism.

3. White privilege is directly related to colorism. Use the internet or your own recall to create two separate lists of women and men in popular culture (e.g., singers, actors, athletes) who are considered beautiful in two different countries (for example, the United States and Japan). Summarize your observations about common physical characteristics shared by the two cultures that perpetuate a Eurocentric beauty standard. During a class discussion, share your findings, comparing and contrasting them with the findings of classmates. Relate the outcome to colorism.

4. Go to a bookstore or choose a few online international magazines targeted to men and women. Looking primarily at the product ads and photos accompanying feature articles, how is diversity being addressed? Are there any people of color in the magazine? Are they light skinned? Dark skinned? How would you describe their physical features? Do they "conform" to certain cultural standards? Compare and contrast the similarities and differences.

5. Nicki Minaj, Rihanna, Michael Jackson, Priyanka Chopra, Sammy Sosa, LaToya Jackson, Lil Kim, and Beyonce are among the celebrities featured

in the online pictorial titled "Celebrities Who Bleached Their Skin" (https://www.glossyfied.com/celebrities-who-bleached-their-skin/). "Before" and "after" photos show remarkable differences in their physical appearance as a result of bleaching their skin. While there are no definitive answers to explain how they have been able to significantly alter their appearance, the photos are evidence that colorism is embedded in the psyche of these entertainers who have great influence on their fans and others. As a class, or on your own, try to find celebrities from the countries discussed in the section on skin whitening. Is it really bleaching, or is it photoshopping? Are there clues that the people pictured are suffering from self-hate? How are they trying to conform to white standards of beauty?

6. As a class, watch the YouTube video titled "Immediate Skin Lightening" by Super Princess Jo (https://www.youtube.com/watch?v=gJ7iqR841840), which is a tutorial for lightening your skin in a relatively short period of time. Have a discussion about what you see, and then take about 10–15 minutes to read the comments below the video. What is the overall tone of the comments? What are specific words or phrases used in response to the message in the video that show colorism is present? What kind of social capital do commenters believe can be gained from skin lightening? Be sure to discuss how the video's message is probably impacting a global audience, as there are nearly 4 million views.

# 8

# Friendships and Romantic Relationships

**CASE STUDY** — **Interracial Love Denied**

LaKambria Welch, 24, of Booneville, Mississippi, had what she describes as her "first direct contact with pure racism" when she confronted a business employee on behalf of her recently engaged brother. Welch and her brother are Black, and the fiancée is white. The couple had reserved Boone's Camp Event Hall for their wedding. They were startled and confused when they received a message that their reservation was canceled, and they would not be allowed to rent the space due to "the venue's 'beliefs.'" The event hall learned that the couple was interracial after someone searched the soon-to-be-bride's social media and saw their pictures.

Welch drove to the event hall to ask why the couple's request to book the venue was denied. She decided to record the encounter with the employee who greeted her. When asked why the reservation was canceled, the woman echoed the message in the email and attempted to explain. "First of all, we don't do gay weddings or mixed race, because of our Christian race—I mean, our Christian beliefs." Welch explained that she, too, is Christian and asked the woman to tell her where in the Bible it states that interracial marriages are forbidden. The woman then stated, "Well, I don't want to argue my faith. Yeah, we just don't participate. We just choose not to." When Welch confirmed that this is the woman's "Christian belief," the woman agreed, saying, "Yes ma'am."

In her email to ABC News, Welch says that she was left "shaking" after the conversation, which is strikingly different from the calm she displays in the video. Welch was heartbroken that the woman expressed such hurtful things to her. In 2016, Mississippi passed House Bill 1523, the "religious freedom" law, designed to protect religious beliefs and moral convictions held by businesses. Businesses can refuse to offer products and services to individuals whose lifestyles are perceived as a violation of the business's beliefs and convictions. While the law provides protection for beliefs against same-sex marriages and transgender people, it does not apply to denying service due to race. The event hall violated the rights of the couple. After much public criticism from the video, it briefly deactivated its Facebook page.

When the page was reactivated, it contained a lengthy apology. Although the post no longer exists, a screenshot of the page revealed that the post's female author is a Mississippi native who was raised to believe in and maintain the unspoken racial boundaries separating African Americans and European Americans. She noted that she was forced to confront those beliefs after her husband asked her to identify scripture denouncing interracial relationships. After finding none, she conceded that she was wrong.

Were you surprised that a business would deny a request to serve as a venue for the wedding? Until a Supreme Court Ruling in 1967, interracial marriage was illegal in multiple states. Have attitudes changed to match legal requirements? What would you do if someone expressed opposition to an interracial marriage?

Jacobo, J. (2019). *Mississippi venue apparently denied interracial couple's wedding over 'Christian belief,' video shows.* ABC News. https://abcnews.go.com/US/mississippi-venue-apparently-denied-interracial-couples-wedding-christian/story?id=65356377

## THE STATE OF INTERRACIAL RELATIONSHIPS

Interpersonal relationships are a vital part of our lives as humans. Everyone wants to have a sense of belonging and connection, and we fulfill those needs through our relationships with our families, partners, friends, and *framilies* (i.e., friends who are considered family) or families of choice. Not having these connections can have an adverse effect on one's health. The saying that "No [hu]man is an island" is a testament to this reality. While it is good and healthy for us to sometimes have alone time, it is important for us to find our way back to those closest to us. Generally, people agree that relationships are fundamental to human existence, but what happens when racial differences are present? Depending on circumstances, the rules and expectations we have for our relationships change when it comes to race. Race has had a profound impact on institutions and societal interactions, so it's not unreasonable to assume that it affects our personal relationships.

This chapter uses friendships and romantic relationships as a context for understanding how biases, prejudices, and stereotypes consciously and subconsciously impact our interpersonal interactions. Categorizing people is sometimes helpful to our sense-making process, but it is problematic when these schemas cause us to generalize about people or groups and serve as a barrier to positive and healthy interracial relationships. This chapter is designed to address the impact that race has on decisions about the persons with whom we choose to establish interpersonal relationships. It will also help us better understand how systemic racism unnecessarily complicates interracial friendships (IRFs) and interracial romantic relationships (IRRs).

The numbers of interracial romantic relationships (and friendships) have increased as the U.S. population has become more diverse (Livingston & Brown, 2017). IRFs and IRRs occur naturally when there is increased ethnic diversity providing more opportunities for racially different people to encoun-

| Box 8.1 | Author Reflections |

## Accountability and Support in My Interracial Relationships

Much like the rest of the world, the racial unrest in response to the murders of George Floyd, Breonna Taylor, and so many other African Americans at the hands of police was very poignant for me for multiple reasons. One specific thing it prompted me to do was to take stock of my interracial relationships. I have several non-Black women with whom I am very close, and I also have relationships with several others as acquaintances, colleagues, and peers. Most of these relationships or connections are due to something that we share. In the relationships where there is emotional closeness and trust, my friends and I have felt comfortable talking about a variety of issues including race. Even though our lived experiences are different, it has been comforting to know that our racial differences are not a barrier.

Thankfully, I have several relationships with white women who have absolutely no issues with or concerns about discussing race with me. That is not at the core of our relationship, but it is one aspect that is very important to me. I am accepted for who I am. All of me. What impresses me is that these women have always been "woke" and feel it is just the right thing to do to speak out against racism and use their privilege to address it whenever possible. I don't always know when this happens, but they will sometimes briefly mention their anger or frustration about an incident or express empathy towards me and the racism that I continue to experience on a regular basis.

—TMH

ter one another. While racial proximity does not guarantee relational intimacy, it does increase significantly the potential for it to occur. During our formative years, we enter what could be called a relational boot camp. Within our familial units, we learn myriad social rules and how to communicate with people. Lessons are learned through observation and, in some cases, explicit instructions, that ultimately prepare us for relationships with people outside of the family, such as friends, coworkers, and romantic partners. Much like a family, friendship is "a mutual involvement between two people . . . characterized by affection, satisfaction, enjoyment, openness, respect, and a sense of feeling important to the other" (LeCroy, 1988).

Millen et al. (2019) explain that friendships are valuable interpersonal connections to have. These connections are impacted by internal and external factors, some of which are out of one's control. These factors include: "(a) **environmental factors**—opportunities to be together; (b) **situational factors**—frequency of interaction and desire to interact with the other person; (c) **individual factors**—social skills, responsiveness, and physical attraction; and (d) **dyadic factors**—similarities, reciprocity of liking, and self-disclosure" (p. 577). We spend most of our time in same-race environments (Tatum, 2017). As a result, our relational patterning and socializing fosters same-race relationships. Several mitigating factors might limit our opportunities to have interracial relationships, whether platonic or romantic. We hope that identifying and discussing those factors provides a better understanding of their impact on race relations.

As discussed in Chapter 1, the current sociopolitical climate in the United States has had a profound impact on interracial relationships as well as same-race relationships. There have been a number of social media posts (i.e., Tik-Tok, Facebook) where people claimed being disowned by conservative family members. A study by global news agency Reuters shortly after the 2016 presidential election found an increase in the number of arguments people had with family and friends over politics (Pinsker, 2021; Whitesides, 2017). Relationships were formally terminated or partners chose to cut off all communication because friends aligned with President's Trump's divisive rhetoric of racism, sexism, ethnocentrism, and white supremacy that "strengthen[ed] boundaries against Muslims, Mexicans, and other nonwhite groups" (Olivier et al., 2019, p. 7). Although the study did not explore interracial communication, the findings suggest that familial divisions over race on a societal level have undoubtedly impacted intrafamilial communication about racially diverse relationships. These ideological differences are hindering opportunities for racial reconciliation (e.g., healing racial tensions) and the development of healthy interracial relationships. We strongly encourage society to rethink its attitudes toward racial differences.

Significant attention has been directed to IRRs, as they have been viewed as tainting fictional "pure races." The number of interracial marriages in 1967 was 3%, rising to 7% in 1980, and reaching 17% in 2015 (Livingston & Brown, 2017). The number of people married to someone of a different ethnicity in-

---

### Box 8.2

## "Mix It Up!": Not Just for Kids!

After giving a 2009 lecture at the University of West Georgia, Lecia Brooks of the Southern Poverty Law Center (SPLC) spoke with staffers Deirdre Haywood-Rouse and Doris Kieh of the university's Center for Diversity and Inclusion about the SPLC's "Mix It Up at Lunch Day" program. The program is part of an international campaign that "strives to break down racial, cultural, and social barriers in schools" by encouraging students to "identify, question and cross social boundaries by sitting with new friends at lunch" (Ehrenhalt, 2018). The university has since joined 48 other colleges and universities and 3,200+ K–12 schools in encouraging purposive interracial interactions in a healthy and productive way. An impressive 580 people participated in October of 2018, which included students, faculty, staff, and administrators at four designated locations on campus.

UWG is a microcosm of the world, with its student body representing 70 different countries and 38 states. The lunch hour gives everyone the opportunity to talk about culture, ability, race, and campus inclusion and their diversity experiences at the school. The end goal is to help students become less anxious about interacting with an outgroup member and more comfortable with opening up to someone who can potentially be a friend.

creased from 3 million in 1980 to 11 million in 2015. Asian (29%) and Hispanic (27%) newlyweds are more likely than Black (18%) or white (11%) newlyweds to have married someone of a different ethnicity. Table 8.1 shows the most prevalent form of intermarriages. Intermarriage was highest for Hispanic/white couples and lowest for Hispanic/Multiracial.

**Table 8.1   Ethnicity of Intermarriage Couples**

| Racial Combination | % of Heterosexual Marriages |
|---|---|
| Hispanic/white | 42% |
| Asian/white | 15% |
| Multiracial/white | 12% |
| Black/white | 11% |
| Hispanic/Black | 5% |
| American Indian/white | 3% |
| Hispanic/Asian | 3% |
| Hispanic/Multiracial | 3% |

**Table 8.2   Intermarriages by Gender in 2015 and Ethnicity in 1980 and 2015**

| | Intermarriage by Gender 2015 | | Intermarriage | |
| | Female | Male | 1980 | 2015 |
|---|---|---|---|---|
| Asians | 36% | 21% | 33% | 29% |
| Blacks | 12% | 24% | 5% | 18% |
| Hispanics | 28% | 26% | 26% | 27% |
| Whites | 10% | 12% | 4% | 11% |

Views about the impact of interracial marriage on society vary depending on age, education, gender, and location (Livingston & Brown, 2017). In 2017, 39% of adults believed intermarriage was good for society, 52% believed it did not make much difference, and 9% believed society was worse off. Younger people, individuals with at least a bachelor's degree, men, and people living in urban areas were more likely to characterize intermarriage as a good thing. Attitudes about the idea of a close relative marrying someone of a different ethnicity have changed since 2000 when 31% were opposed. In 2017, 10% were opposed. While these trends are encouraging and possibly speak to attitudinal changes toward IRRs and race relations in general, we hope this will translate into interracial relationships being perceived as natural as same-race relationships.

# HISTORY OF RACE RELATIONS

As discussed in Chapter Two, state and local statutes in the United States that legalized racial segregation were known as Jim Crow laws. The landmark U.S. Supreme Court decision in *Brown v. Board of Education* (1954) ruled that racial segregation in public schools was unconstitutional—"separate but equal" education and other facilities were inherently unequal. In 1952, Oliver

Brown led the court case on behalf of his daughter Linda who was barred by the school board from enrolling in the nearby all-white Sumner School in their Topeka, Kansas, neighborhood. Angry with this racial injustice that forced his daughter and other Black children to shuttle to schools elsewhere, Brown partnered with the NAACP (National Association for the Advancement of Colored People) and other plaintiffs to file the lawsuit. Two years later, the Court overturned legalized separation by race in classrooms throughout the country, ruling the practice violated the Fourteenth Amendment, which guarantees equal protection under the law. This victory was an important one because fought it against the dominant ideology that African Americans were inferior and sent messages of affirmation and validation for Black youth (and adults alike) to the Black community. By directing the nation's attention to Black subjugation, the ruling spurred freedom rides, sit-ins, voter registration efforts, and other actions leading to civil rights legislation in the 1960s (Rothstein, 2014). The ruling set a legal precedent that could be used to overturn Jim Crow laws.

This legally and socially sanctioned racial segregation set the stage for whites and BIPOC to informally maintain their relational distance from each other, a by-product of which has been the fostering of prejudice and negative attitudes (Sigelman et al., 1996). Because people relied on information relayed to them by others and not their own interracial experiences, this worked to stigmatize interracial relationships and intimacy across groups. However, this was not universal in that many recognized the falsehoods driving racial segregation and saw the value in other racial groups and the importance of interracial relationships. As such, ending segregation increased the possibilities for interracial contact, which could be a critical path to positive interactions. Yet,

> having friends of the other race or living in environments where interracial contact is commonplace does not guarantee that [B]lacks and whites will perceive race relations as more amicable or that they will feel more committed to engaging in social intercourse. (p. 792)

African Americans are more likely than European Americans to perceive interracial relations as problematic; African Americans perceive hostility to be widespread. Even if the positive effects of interracial contact are modest, they have the potential to ease the climate of race relations.

Self-segregation is another factor that hinders race relations. Tatum (2017) explains that, for African American students in a context where they are in the numerical minority, choosing to be around same-race friends offers a sense of support, solidarity, and closeness absent from cross-race friends who have not shared the same experiences. There is a constant burden of

> having to strive to do your best and show that you can do just as much as everybody else. Your white friends can't understand that, and it's really hard to communicate to them. Only someone else of the same racial, same ethnic background would understand something like that. (p. 154)

The ability to see oneself as part of a larger group is an important coping strategy. M. Houston (1997) also partially attributes social distancing to mistrust, which is discussed in the next section.

As mentioned in the case study at the beginning of the chapter, **antimiscegenation laws** in a number of states prohibited marriages between whites and nonwhites. The general concern was that white/nonwhite unions would produce untold horrors (Pettigrew et al., 1982), but it was the racial pairings between whites and Blacks in particular that were seen as most disturbing because they represented what many believed were "opposites along the race continuum" (Foeman & Nance, 1999, p. 540). Extreme measures such as slavery and internment camps were used to maintain "pure" bloodlines. Until 1910, interethnic marriages among European Americans were the most prevalent type of intermarriage (Davidson & Schneider, 1992). When white partners chose to marry nonwhite persons, they were seen as "race traitors" and subjected to death and violence.

In 1967, the Supreme Court ruled in *Loving v. Virginia* that antimiscegenation laws were unconstitutional, finding that their impact on individuals in interracial relationships was cruel and dehumanizing (Roberts, 2015). Virginia residents Richard (European American) and Mildred (African American) Loving were legally married in Washington, DC. They returned to their home state, Virginia, and were arrested and prosecuted in 1959. The Lovings were accused of violating the Racial Integrity Act, which outlawed such unions because intermixing with "Black blood" would render "white blood" impure. The couple pleaded guilty and were given the choice of spending one year in prison or leaving Virginia for 25 years. They returned to Washington, DC but in 1964 filed an action in federal court. Their case overturned antimiscegenation

---

## Box 8.3

### Relationship Stigmas Surrounding Intimate Interracial Relationships

Interracial romantic relationships have long been stigmatized and framed as abnormal, unhealthy, and undesirable. Rosenthal and Starks (2015) call this *relationship stigma*, and their study found that friends of partners in an interracial romantic relationship were the ones who stigmatized the relationship. The partner(s) ultimately internalized those judgements and experienced "lower relationship commitment, trust, love, and sexual communication, as well as greater odds of intimate partner aggression victimization" (p. 384). In other words, the partners allowed the judgement of others to dictate their happiness. Instead of remaining committed to their partner, they placed greater value on the friends' perception of the relationship, which is racial bias.

Another relationship stigma is that interracial relationships are more violent than same-race relationships. Field et al. (2015) tested this stereotype by comparing both relationship types and the likelihood that physical violence will be committed against an intimate partner. Their 1,174 student-participants were from four U.S. universities and one Canadian university. According to self-reports, there were minor differences between racial groups and minor assaults. Not surprisingly, the findings did not reveal greater instances of partner violence in interracial romantic relationships.

laws in 17 states and had a significant impact on marital law. Despite this monumental accomplishment, the remnants of historic racism continue to frame IRRs as taboo.

To better understand interracial relationships, we continue our discussion with recent trends in online dating. We include internet dating in this chapter due to the increasing importance of social media in 21st-century communication. We then discuss the mental models or theories of and barriers to interracial relationships, followed by an explanation of the most noted interracial relationship development model. The chapter concludes with a challenge for all to rethink their attitudes toward interracial friendship and romantic relationships.

## DATING AND RACE IN VIRTUAL SPACES

Over the last decade or so, people have become increasingly dependent on social media for various reasons. Whether it is for news, research, entertainment, gaming, or interpersonal connections, most of us are engaging with technology on a very regular basis.

> The internet is where social issues, including race, are negotiated and renegotiated. In the digital world one can comment, post, and browse topics anonymously with little fear of repercussion. Similarly, online dating allows people to express sexual preferences for whites or Asians or Blacks without public judgment. (Curington et al., 2021, p. 44)

One of the earliest studies of internet dating was conducted by Tsunokai et al. (2009). The researchers tested the hypothesis that racial/ethnic differences and birth cohort (generation) would be strong predictors for dating preferences and online dating. The cohorts were determined by the generation in which they were born: the Silent Generation (1925–1945), baby boomers (1946–1964), Generation X (1965–1980), and millennials (1981–1996). The four major racial/ethnic groups included in the study were African Americans, Asian Americans, European Americans, and Hispanics. As predicted, the Silent Generation (oldest) expressed the least willingness to date anyone outside of their racial group. Tsunokai et al. attributed this resistance to critical events such as Jim Crow laws and the civil rights movement occurring during the group's formative years that likely shaped their worldview regarding race. Conversely, millennials were most open to interracial dating. Other important findings were that whites and Asians were most opposed to dating African Americans, and African Americans were most opposed to dating whites. Asian Americans demonstrated an overwhelmingly strong preference for dating whites over all racial groups. Multiracial people were willing to date any race except white.

Dating apps such as Tinder, Zooks, OkCupid, and eharmony have grown in popularity and are now a normal part of dating. People still meet partners in-person but dating apps have become a part of societal norms. They are convenient and provide opportunities for greater partner compatibility. The utopian view was that online dating had the potential to democratize courtship—to eliminate racial barriers, to disrupt residential and occupational barriers, and to connect people while ignoring differences. However, racial discrimination online, while deeply rooted in the past and seemingly covert, is also a new form of racism that interacts with technologies to produce experiences and consequences distinct from traditional racism (Curington et al., 2021). New technologies are perceived as more objective but reflect and reproduce existing inequities. Individual preferences "massively and systematically segregate cyberspace, reinforce categorical thinking, and police digital self-presentation, all without the need of in-person avoidance and confrontation" (p. 4).

Tsunokai continued his exploration of online dating as one of the authors of a study of 1,200 men and women on the U.S. version of Match.com (McGrath et al., 2016). The researchers looked at the profiles and racial preferences of participants to determine how biracial and monoracial daters feel about dating someone with a different background. As previously discussed, the number of interracial marriages in the United States has increased. One-in-six new marriages is interracial or interethnic. Biracial people, as offspring of interracial relationships, would ideally view racial categories as fluid and malleable, be less likely to stereotype people, and would be more willing to interact with people different from themselves. But are ethnic boundaries blurring as the United States becomes more ethnically diverse? The study found that race continues to play a significant role in who is asked for a date.

The percentage of biracial daters who indicated a willingness to date someone outside their ethnic group was about 87%; however, 92% sought a white partner, 81% were willing to date Hispanics, and 71% would date "others" (McGrath et al., 2016). About 87% of monoracial daters also said they would date someone outside their ethnicity. But again, 91% stated a preference for dating whites, followed by Hispanics (81%), "other" (71%), Asians (67%) and Blacks (62%). Certain ethnic combinations were less inclined to date someone outside of their own ethnicity. Biracial individuals who identified as white (e.g., Asian-white, Hispanic-white, and other-white) were less likely to indicate a preference to date outside of their racial/ethnic category compared to biracial daters as a whole. Tinder's published self-study found that its subscribers believe dating services "make them more open-minded about dating someone outside their own race or ethnicity" (Notopoulos, 2018). Tinder's data, however, only gauged willingness to interracially date—not actual dating behavior.

While societal attitudes toward interracial dating have improved, there are still many barriers that impact these relationships (Ranzini & Rosenbaum, 2020). App users both directly and indirectly express preferences for partners from certain racial groups, rejecting some while accepting others. Dating preferences may be perceived as racist because they reflect a rejection of others due to stereotypes and limited exposure to outgroup members. OkCupid chief marketing officer Melissa Hobley suggests that these behaviors reflect real life norms and that users behave the same way online and offline (Brown, 2018). Yet those attitudes are likely the products of systemic racism—the legacy of slavery and antimiscegenation laws that made interracial relationships socially taboo (Papamarko, 2017). "It is an oxymoron to describe racial preferences as individual because race is by definition a social construct, a manufactured distinction generated through the regulation of intimate life" (Curington et al., 2021, p. 13).

While dating sites present opportunities to connect with individuals one might not otherwise meet, there are strong indications that racial bias exists in online dating. Curington et al. (2021) refer to this as **digital sexual racism**. Racial bias in online dating is the "conflation of race with tired tropes about masculinity, femininity, class, and real people reduced to exotic caricatures" (S. Lee, 2017). Assigning specific qualities to all members of a social group exaggerates differences. Dehumanizing stereotypes have been ingrained in our culture for centuries and have surfaced in digital spaces. This results in users "avoiding, ignoring, and filtering out potential love interests simply because of their race" (Holt, 2021).

Popular dating sites employ a swipe-to-reject process that too often puts people of color at a disadvantage (S. Lee, 2017). This suggests that judgments based on photos, thus phenotypic features, are affected by stereotypes and implicit biases and amplified through technology. In theory, online dating should level the dating field, but it seems to have the reverse effect on how people are choosing a mate. People are possibly relying on misinformation to either reject someone or consider someone a viable romantic partner. This can be seen in three of the common stereotypes experienced by people of color in online dating, which are described below. Perceptions are not based on the qualities of an individual—rather, expectations are based on long-standing stereotypes about particular groups, frequently reinforced by media portrayals.

**Race fetishization** is a sexual obsession with or unnatural preference for individuals solely because of their racial group membership (S. Lee, 2017). Perpetrator behaviors range "from overtly sexual messages to microaggressions disguised as compliments," such as only dating Asian women because they are submissive, Black men because they are endowed, and Latinas because they are "spicy." These positive biases perpetuate racism and contribute to discrimination (Wynne, 2020).

> Amid rampant digital misogyny, minority women must also contend with being fetishized on the basis of their racial identities. As such, white women are objectified "only" for their gender identity, while minority women are doubly objectified for both their gender and their race. (Curington et al., p. 99)

**The race checklist** consists of subjectively favorable beliefs about individuals based on stereotypes—a mental categorization of qualities or characteristics a person is expected to have as a member of a particular group (S. Lee, 2017). For example, when one sees an Asian person, one might assume a stellar academic record (recall our discussion of model minorities). These checklists can damage relationships because they objectify, marginalize, and devalue the person. They can also cause individuals to feel pressured to comply with unrealistic expectations. A response for some people is to reject a positive stereotype or attempt to explain the dehumanizing nature of said stereotype, but they run the risk of being labelled overly sensitive because the attribution was a "compliment" and not negative.

**Racial devaluation**, in contrast, ascribes negative stereotypes. Susie Lee (2017) explains that photo-based dating apps combined with implicit bias "have the unfortunate consequence of really reinforcing toxic and pervasive stereotypes that undermine individual dignity." Perceiving negative qualities based on racial categories debases people. When this happens to a person of color, it increases the likelihood of rejection and not being chosen.

**Racial preferences** are illegal in education, employment, housing, and lending, but digital dating platforms build filters for race and ethnicity into their structures. Unfortunately, filtering out people based on race is a normal practice on dating apps. The rationale offered is that preferences indicate individual choice rather than discrimination. In other words, preferences are described as natural and simple matters of attraction. The presumption that preferences are personal and benign ignores that they are the product of exclusionary social constructs.

> Narratives about personal choice have long since obscured prejudice, fear, and desires for segregation. They elide the deep, pervasive impact of historical antimiscegenation sanctions and overstate the equality of contemporary society. They glide past the deep fissures of racial marginalization reflected in and encouraged by centuries of legislation and social practice. Despite what we may tell ourselves, mate preference is never completely personal, nor is racial taste in romantic partners inconsequential. (Curington et al., 2021, p. 3)

Many individuals have ingrained racist ideas, resulting in profiles listing, for example, "No Asians" or "No Blacks" (Stokel-Walker, 2018). Ranzini and Rosenbaum (2020) found that, regardless of race or ethnicity, all Tinder users preferred "a Caucasian-looking profile over the alternative under all name conditions" (p. 44). Ultimately, even progressive white singles "still swipe on and message people of their own race to a larger degree" (Holt, 2021). Race is the most important predictor of how white daters select whom to date, but the vast majority of African American and Asian Americans also select from within their ethnicity. Black men and Asian women outmarry more often than Black women and Asian men (Curington et al., 2021). Black women and Asian men are the least preferred both online and in person (Notopoulos, 2018). Excluded by the vast majority of clients, online dating matches for those individuals are far less likely (Papamarko, 2017). Same-sex white daters prefer to date only whites (homophily), while Asians, Latinos, and African Americans exhibit higher rates of heterophily (Rafalow et al., 2017). Rejection is very high for minority men who are least desired by white gay men (Lundquist & Lin, 2015). Rejection is both covert and overt, and oftentimes leads African Americans, Latinx people, and Asians to avoid dating apps altogether to protect their confidence and self-esteem (Brown, 2018; S. Lee, 2017). According to Ranzini and Rosenbaum (2020), race becomes a large determinant of a users' dating market value, which is higher for whites and lower for all other races and ethnicities.

## MENTAL MODELS OF INTERRACIAL RELATIONSHIPS

Mental models of interracial relationships were created and shaped by legislation, history, cultural events, and personal biases that ultimately inform individual choices. To challenge misrepresentations, we need new mental models of what these relationships should be. IRRs are subjected to more scrutiny and pressure from others (e.g., family, friends, coworkers, strangers, society) than are IRFs. Cross-sex interracial friendships, however, may be subjected to similar pressure because of the *perceived threat* to a pure race (e.g., shift from friendship to romance) (Kunst et al., 2021). Interracial relationships in general are at greater risk of dissolving than same-race relationships. This disheartening outcome suggests that racial differences and other factors are barriers to relationship development. Because IRFs are viewed as less taboo than IRRs, we will use that relational context as the basis for understanding the reality of these relationships and how they are managed. We will provide an overview of theories suggesting that increased intergroup contact will lead to change in racial attitudes. This contact involves communication and interaction, which most likely begins in the context of a friendship (T. Hudson, 2022; Kunst et al., 2021).

Interracial interactions (e.g., "interracial friendliness" and "interracial conflict") are occurring primarily in schools and colleges (T. Hudson, 2022) due to increased opportunities for intergroup relations (Stackman et al., 2016). These will only increase with the predicted shift in the racial majority in 2050, hence the need to be informed and knowledgeable about racial/ethnic diversity and positive interracial communication. Although a culturally diverse environment would theoretically lead to more interracial relationships, qualitatively meaningful interracial interactions are not guaranteed. Data from a survey of undergraduate sexual/romantic relationships at an elite university found racial homophily strongly evident; Black students were particularly isolated (McClintock & Murry, 2010). In a multiracial middle school, friendship groups were predominantly segregated, which suggests family and community discouraged establishing IRFs (M.-H. Wu, 2021).

Schools have responded by developing race-focused curriculum and creating more integrated educational environments to reduce negative racial stereotyping among all young children (Welner, 2006). These interpersonal encounters may also break the use of self-segregation as a coping strategy (Tatum, 2017). Self-segregation does buffer against feelings of isolation (Buggs, 2017b; Schieferdecker & Wessler, 2017), but interracial interactions can also be encouraged. If all parties are to benefit from these interactions, there must be comfort with interracial differences (Carlson et al., 2003). Successful interethnic friendships (IRFs) require relational commitment to establish compatibility, trust, and enjoyable companionship (T. Hudson, 2022). Friends are then more inclined to work through relationship difficulties through open and honest discussions, which may reduce frequent miscommunication or arguments.

IRRs are rooted in a history of enslavement, objectification, and racial hierarchies. This tension was evident in the first season of the Netflix series *Bridgerton*, which cast a Black man and a white woman as lovers. *Bridgerton* was released seven months after the Black Lives Matter movement of 2020. Despite objections to using colorblind casting of the characters, viewers were asked to not "apply contemporary American politics to characters from 19th century London" (Marine, 2021). For some, that season was a catalyst for pub-

---

**Box 8.4**                                                       ***Research Highlight***

## Michael Banton's Six Orders of Interracial Contact

Banton's (1967) six **orders of interracial contact** is a foundation body of work many researchers reference in their understanding of race relations. Although his work is 44 years old, it is still relevant and pertinent to current race relations. His primary argument is that racism and racial prejudice can be dismantled through more interactions between racial groups. This was a general observation on the heels of desegregation. Banton explained that the first four orders (peripheral contact, institutionalized contact, pluralism, and assimilation) discourage and two orders (acculturation and integration) encourage an appreciation of racial/ethnic difference in varying degrees. They reflect a progression from no contact to colonialism to minimum social interaction (e.g., coexistence) or an adoption of dominant group attitudes and beliefs.

As this order suggests, interracial contact can be strained by systemic oppression that discourages such interactions. As a consequence, virtually no effort is put forth to accommodate for the differences between individuals. In an ideal world, authentic interracial contact would occur through the two more positive orders. Acculturation involves racial/ethnic group members learning about a culture (dominant group) while maintaining their biological racial/ethnic identity. This allows all racial/ethnic groups to live in two worlds simultaneously.

A progression toward integration means minor consideration is given to racial distinctions while interracial interactions are maximized. Relational partners choose to nurture interracial friendships by moving across racial/ethnic lines. Ideally, interracial contact would greatly contribute to competent interracial communication. Unfortunately, various barriers prevent this utopian state of race relations from occurring. In order to achieve this complex, yet attainable, goal of positive interracial communication, we must first consider what barriers prevent this process from occurring.

The contact hypothesis fails to address the quality of interactions. Opportunities must be created for enriching and affirming relationships where differences and similarities are valued and appreciated. The contact hypothesis was not used to dismantle the Jim Crow laws of years gone by but to address the aftereffect of such a dramatic change in society. As N. Miller (2002) notes, the contact hypothesis functions under the assumption held by social interventionists that being in the presence of outgroup members (e.g., friendships) will lead to a transformation in thought processes regarding racial and ethnic differences, hence positive race relations. This theory does not, however, address the possibility of IRRs resulting from these intergroup interactions.

Increased contact between people from different racial/ethnic backgrounds leads to an increased likelihood that interracial friendships can develop, which can be mutually beneficial.

lic conversations about the still taboo nature of romantic relationships between African Americans and European Americans (see T. Harris & Sanders, in press). People who disapproved of the interracial pairing in the series used the slur "jungle fever." Some may view *Bridgerton* the way people did when Spike Lee's 1991 film *Jungle Fever* was released, which was that it "confirm[ed] the dominant belief that interracial sexual relations are wrong or immoral" (Paulin, 1997, p. 168). The slur jungle fever implies that IRRs are driven by sexual curiosity about the racially different other and reiterate "dominant representations of interracial relationships" through "the underlying discourse of contamination implied by the clichéd title" (p. 168). For some African American women, these relationships are a rejection of their racialized and gendered bodies (T. Hudson, 2022).

## Contact Hypothesis and Race Relations

Psychologist Gordon Allport (1958) predicted that race relations could improve through interpersonal relationships. His **contact hypothesis** suggested that increased interactions between racial groups will reduce prejudiced thoughts and beliefs if four conditions exist: equal status, common goals, intergroup cooperation, and support of authorities. In the years since Allport devised the hypothesis, there have been a number of developments. Pettigrew et al. (2011) found that Allport's conditions facilitate the effect but are not necessary. Positive outcomes of contact are greater trust and forgiveness, as people learn how others view the world. Contact reduces anxiety and increases empathy. Friendship is an important factor; it facilitates self-disclosure, leading to positive attitudes resistant to change. Others have found that emotion predicts discrimination twice as strongly as stereotypes or beliefs (Bergsieker et al., 2010). Contact may reduce prejudice because of decategorization (facilitating seeing someone as an individual rather than only as a member of a group) or recategorization (changing conceptual representations of groups

**Table 8.3    Contact Theories, Concepts, and Models**

| Theory | Author | Assumptions |
|---|---|---|
| Contact Hypothesis | Allport (1958) | Increased interracial interactions = reduced prejudiced thoughts and beliefs |
| Structural Theory | Kouri & Lasswell (1993) | Demographics = mutual attraction |
| | | Endogamy—marriage within group (e.g., race/ethnicity or religion) |
| | | Homogamy—similarity between partners including social status, education, etc. |
| Racial Motivation Theory | Spaights & Dixon (1984) | Interest in interactions *because* of racial difference and its appeal/attractiveness (exoticization) |

from us/them to "we") (Dovidio, Love, et al., 2017). IRFs provide an opportunity for individuals and society to think critically about racial stereotypes. Through contact and interactions, we become wiser, more attuned to our intimacy needs, and more discriminating in our friendship choices (Schieferdecker & Wessler, 2017).

The general assumption of the contact hypothesis has evolved, resulting in several theories, concepts and models that address societal influences on intergroup relations. In the following section, we offer an overview of these conceptualizations.

## Interaction Theories and Related Concepts

Two theories related to the contact hypothesis are **structural theory** and **racial motivation theory.** Recognizing that theories on romantic relationships have largely been racially exclusive, focusing solely on whites, scholars developed theories to explain why some IRRs do or do not exist. Although these occur naturally much like same-race romantic relationships, there were not many theories developed to explain how they begin.

Kouri and Lasswell (1993) developed the structural theory to better understand motivations for relational involvement. Structural theory suggests that mutual attraction between relationally different partners is due to demographics (e.g., socioeconomic status, education, occupation, residence) and may lead to interracial marriage. **Endogamy** occurs when people marry within their group (e.g., race/ethnicity or religion), and **homogamy** is a preference for a mate of the same social standing, social status, or educational background. Both partners seek similarities they deem integral to their identities and what they believe is important in a partner. Prioritizing these qualities can create closure and eliminate all others from their "selection pool" who might be a better match (Kalmijn, 1998). **Hypergamy** is an interest in or willingness to marry someone of a different status. It accounts for partner attributes and qualities not traditionally deemed pertinent to the relationship.

Spaights and Dixon (1984) created the **racial motivation theory** to explain when a person is involved in an IRR *because* of racial difference. They asserted that African Americans in IRRs are rebelling against an oppressive society for financial gain or to attain social status. This assertion was driven by their belief that all relationships between African Americans and European Americans are anomalies and doomed to fail—a problematic assumption given that there are successful IRRs. The theory also suggests that motivation can be driven by an attraction attributed to race, a curiosity about myths of sexual prowess and promiscuity, rebellion against family, demonstrating a liberal attitude, or an interest in a cultural experience. Racial motivation theory may explain some, but not all, individual motivations for being in an IRR. Education, interracial contact, group size, chance encounters, geographic location, and preference are also important to a hypergamous approach to dating (Qian, 1998).

We suggest that individuals must actively seek opportunities for interracial encounters and assess the racial composition of their own friendships through a relationship inventory. This involves evaluating your relationships and gauging how many are intraracial and how many are interracial. If there is not much diversity, to what do you attribute the homogeneity of your relationships? Are there issues of mistrust? Is there a sense of safety in those same-race friendships that may be absent from IRFs? Or have there just not been any opportunities to branch out and establish IRFs? These questions are not to condemn or judge but to prompt thinking about how racial differences and separation exist within our personal networks (i.e., family, friendships)—perhaps ingrained attitudes that affect our interpersonal relationships. Yes, there is a certain level of comfort and solidarity that comes from ingroup relationships, but it is our hope that taking inventory of our relationships will trigger openness to the possibility of IRFs that evolve organically. As we can see in Box 8.5, learning about racial identity development and racial dynamics in classrooms and communities provides new perspectives and fosters strategies for productive dialogue. The problem is that "we may be living in a color-*silent* society, where we have learned to avoid *talking about* racial difference" (Tatum, 2017, p. 24). Dialogue about race and racism helps instill the confidence we need to break the silence about race at home, with friends, and at work.

Ethnicity and race related conversations can consist of positive, self-affirming exchanges or they can be negative experiences of identity denial, disinterest, and discrimination (U. Moffitt & Syed, 2020). "This may be particularly true if friends hold differing beliefs or have had divergent ethnicity and race related experiences" (p. 69). For instance, if one person describes a discrimination experience and the other person does not ask supportive follow-up questions or changes the subject, the person who shared the experience may feel invalidated and less motivated to pursue such conversations in the future. If, instead, the listener shows active engagement with the story, both parties help one another gain meaning from the experience.

The role of such conversations in ethnic-racial identity development relates both to *what* is being said and *how* the conversation is structured (U. Moffitt & Syed, 2020). *Scaffolding* refers to how a listener responds to and encourages the

Box 8.5

## Not All Diversity Interactions Are Created Equal: Cross-Racial Interaction, Close Interracial Friendship, and College Student Outcomes

An important and oftentimes overlooked benefit of college is the opportunities students have to experience increased interracial contact and foster meaningful relationships with their peers. Currently, there is limited research available about whether and when these interracial friendships come into existence. Bowman and Park (2015) recognized this void and conducted a 4-year longitudinal study involving 2,932 undergraduates enrolled at 28 institutions throughout the United States

The findings from this study support other studies that also found that there are many benefits associated with cross-racial interaction. More specifically, students can and do develop real interracial relationships while enrolled in college. At the time of publication, the authors assert this was the first study of its kind to be conducted, which makes the findings even more important. They attribute these relational opportunities to "frequent exposure to novel situations and information" that might be directly related to student growth and desired outcomes.

T. Hudson (2022) extended the work of these researchers in her theory of interpersonalizing cultural difference. She identified four subprocesses that college students can utilize for developing and sustaining interracial relationships that ultimately prepare them for living and working in a diverse society. The four subprocesses require that partners (1) cultivate trust and establish a silent contract, (2) embrace similarity yet remember their differences, (3) explore other cultures, and (4) bridge differences to connect. Her research illustrates how colleges and universities can support interracial friendships and help students engage positively and meaningfully with culturally different peers.

conversation partner. Asking supportive questions for elaboration and building on interpretations of a story are positive scaffolding while changing the subject and asking questions that negate the storyteller's experience of interpretation of the event are negative scaffolding. Effective conversations with friends about experiences related to ethnicity and race are themselves constructions of ethnic and racial identity. The researchers found that the types of stories told in ethnicity and race related exchanges between friends were shaped by ethnic-racial inequality, discrimination, and the largely segregated experiences of white students.

As the theories, models, and concepts in this section suggest, the assumption that increased interactions will reduce bias or contribute to a change in racial attitudes is reasonable. It is important, however, to recognize the influence of the quality of the communication on these interactions. If a person genuinely enters these encounters with an open mind, then the prediction that increased contact reduces prejudice has validity. If the outgroup biases are strong, however, then the frequency of those encounters will have little impact on either party, which decreases the likelihood of developing a genuine interracial relationship.

## BARRIERS TO INTERRACIAL RELATIONSHIPS

The racial unrest of 2020 prompted people to have frank and difficult conversations with their family members, friends, colleagues, and, sometimes, strangers about race and social justice. Racialized experiences are undeniable, and they are different for all people and racial groups. Those different realities and the inability or refusal to acknowledge them forced many BIPOC and some white people to either terminate or set boundaries within those relationships. There was explicit discussion about the rules that should be followed if partners were going to discuss race and social justice.

There was also the caveat that there should be no expectation that BIPOC friends and colleagues will assume the role of educator in relationships (T. Hudson, 2022). U. Moffitt and Syed (2020) found that white members of a cross-racial dyad were more likely to experience some form of being educated with the friend of color engaging in the emotional labor of providing information.

> While such a conversation may prove novel, illuminating, or uncomfortable for the white friend, the friend of color may find such work taxing. The line between a positive exchange and a burdensome or disappointing endeavor may be thin, and it might be in a very different place for the two parties involved. (p. 89)

The onus for learning and finding credible resources about racism and fighting racial injustice lies with each person. While the interracial relationship may involve such discussions, the partners need to determine how these social issues impact them as friends and raced beings outside of the relationship. Racial literacy is a skill set that enables conversations about race (Mills, 2021). IRFs can provide a better understanding of the lived experiences of people of different ethnicities through witnessing one another's racial reality. Meaningful communication expressing accommodation and affirmation is a key element in racial literacy and empathy.

### Challenges to Friendships

Stow (2017) explains that friendship is "a practice; a set of hard-won, complicated habits that are used to bridge trouble, difficulty, and differences of personality, experience, and aspiration" (p. 297). These qualities are of particular importance in interracial friendships. Friends have different worldviews and realities that influence how they interact and communicate with each other. They may also deal with pressure or barriers from others outside of the relationship (i.e., family, friends, strangers) or from the partner (Roy et al., 2020) to end the relationship. When those factors are rooted in racism, we must remember that each partner in an IRF or IRR brings a racial perspective to the relationship that cannot and should not be ignored. "Race does not disappear in relationships that traverse racial lines" (Buggs, 2017b). If left unattended or unacknowledged, barriers can cause relationship termination (Schieferdecker & Wessler, 2017). Actively working to preserve and nurture a relationship includes being aware of potential barriers.

One barrier is stereotypes (M.-H. Wu, 2021). Partners very likely have preconceived notions about each other's racial group, and those perceptions guide interactions. For example, Asian men are perceived as being less masculine than white men while Black women are perceived as relatively masculine (Chuang et al., 2021) Disparaging distortions communicate which group members are ideal and play a role in which romantic partners are desirable (Mills, 2021). Individuals in stigmatized groups aware of these misperceptions may be anxious and stressed (Dovidio, Love, et al., 2017). The stereotypes restrict choices of interactional partners for those acting on preconceived notions and affect behavior in interactions for those unfairly characterized.

Another barrier is mistrust by one or both relational partners (Kunst et al., 2021). Communication scholar Marsha Houston (1997) attributes this long-standing mistrust and suspicion between racial/ethnic groups to the history of race relations. Shelton et al. (2010) confirmed this assumption through their study of intimacy in developing interracial friendships between African Americans and European Americans. When comparing same-race and interracial relationships, intimacy was greater in intraracial friendships for African Americans because partners had shared concerns. As students at predominately white institutions (PWIs), African Americans may work harder to establish and maintain intimacy vis-à-vis self-disclosure with other African Americans because of a smaller social network on campus (Kunst et al., 2021). This may also create reservations about sharing with European American friends (Shelton et al., 2010). In contrast, European Americans saw no difference in intimacy levels across relationships, which the researchers attributed to "social desirability concerns" (p. 84). The European American participants wanted to be viewed favorably by the researchers and chose to conceal negative interracial experiences. The behavior could also reflect white privilege, in that white individuals rarely have to think about race and are unaware of the lack of intimacy in some IRFs.

Colorblindness is another barrier. Examples of this attitude are "I never notice race" or "Race doesn't matter; I only look at who people are" (Mills, 2021). A variation of the barrier is colormuteness, a description of opting out of any discussion of race or maintaining silence when witnessing bias. Colorblindness is more prevalent with white individuals; other individuals are less likely to be oblivious to the impact of ethnic and racial categories on everyday lived experiences (U. Moffitt & Syed, 2020). The language of colorblindness "promotes silence on the topic of race and washes over the existence and impact of racism and discrimination" (p. 71). It avoids discomfort and creates a perception of open-mindedness that can disguise contradictory feelings (Buggs, 2017a).

Intentionality versus emotionality is a barrier for these relationships as well. Intentionality is the degree to which a certain behavior is perceived as purposefully causing hurt or harm. If an interracial relationship is to be "real," then both parties must be willing to discuss the offending behavior, if the offense was intentional, and what consequences there are for (un)intentional harms. Communicating about an offense and the underlying intent helps partners understand the emotionality of an interracial interaction gone bad. Emotionality involves negative emotions or feelings stemming from first- and secondhand observation(s) of offending behavior. For example, you are angered by your friend's use of a racial slur. Although you are not a part of the offending group, you are willing to have a frank discussion about the verbal infraction to address racism on the individual level.

Racial homophily, which is the tendency to be attracted to people of the same race (Gilkes Borr, 2019), is also a barrier. When homophily was first introduced by Lazarsfeld and Merton in 1954, it referred to general similarities that draw people together and has come to include race (i.e., racial homogeneity). Racial homophily is natural because we are drawn to the familiar. It becomes a barrier to interracial relationships when people actively avoid or dismiss connections to outgroup members. As the majority group, white individuals oftentimes practice racial homophily as a normalized approach to social networking and connection. For BIPOC, racial homophily can be a necessity for affirmation and survival in situations where there are few non-white people in an organization or geographic location (McClintock & Murry, 2010). In one example of racial homophily, Black college students "manipulated their campus placements and time commitments to access predominantly Black spaces at the expense of cross-racial relationships" (Gilkes Borr, 2019, p. 322). Racial homophily can deter interracial friendships by reducing the possibility of interpersonal interactions because it segregates racial groups.

## Social Forces

Most societies socialize members to adopt a homogamous approach to mate selection. Kalmijn (1998) identified three social forces impacting this process: (1) preferences for certain spousal characteristics in marriage candidates, (2) the interference of third parties in the selection process (i.e., social group influence—families, friends, and institutions), and (3) constraints in the marriage market. All three are important, but we will briefly explain and address the first and second because they are deemed most salient for interracial partners.

Those closest to us will surely influence decisions about IRRs (Buggs, 2017b; Ross & Woodley, 2020). For example, Hohmann-Marriott and Amato (2008) identified several challenges in IRRs that are largely absent from same-race relationships: "greater likelihood of having experienced a parental divorce," "fewer socioeconomic resources," additional partner differences (e.g., "religion, age, and country of birth"), "fewer sources of social support," and "fewer shared values" (p. 847). IRR and same-race couples share similar problems, but IRR couples experience unique difficulties from outside sources. Interracial marriages have historically experienced opposition from

---

**BOX 8.6**                                                      **CASE STUDY**

## "BMMW": An Interracial Dating Continuum

In a class discussion a few years ago, my students and I were discussing attitudes towards IRR, and I asked them to explain how people are taught certain relational norms about those kinds of relationships. One male Indian student eagerly raised his hand to describe a general attitude about interracial dating among Indians: "Date BMMW." The class and I became very interested in this semi-formal approach and asked for elaboration. A second Indian male chimed in and explained this as an approval continuum (from "B" to "W") created for the community to inform them about and guide them through the racial hierarchy they must use if they choose to date interracially. The closer they are to the "W" on the continuum, the more approval of the IRR there will be. Each letter represents a racial/ethnic group (B = Blacks, M = Mexicans, M = Muslims, and W = Whites). Based on the general premise of this continuum, romantic involvement with a Black person would face less approval and acceptance than all other racial groups.

Many of us had never heard of this continuum, but it is consistent with studies on IRR (B. Miller et al., 2021; Robnett & Feliciano, 2011). In general, darker-skinned groups are found to be less attractive or appealing than whiter or lighter-skinned groups. This value system practiced within the Indian community is an example of colorism, which is an international phenomenon (see Chapter 7). Other racial/ethnic groups most likely have similar philosophies about IRRs, which is a troubling commentary given the inevitability of racial diversity by 2050. For these and other reasons, it is imperative that we become more open-minded about IRRs, as they will become the rule and not the exception.

---

external forces, which is oftentimes driven by the fear of intermixing and an unfounded fear that group cohesion and homogeneity are being threatened (e.g., "watering down of the races").

The first social force, preference for marriage candidates, is affected by resources. One of the important partner qualities for both males and females is socioeconomic resources (Lewis, 2016). A partner is expected to bring monetary resources "to the table" to help meet basic needs and "produce economic well-being and status . . . [that] is shared by the family members" (Kalmijn, 1998, p. 399). Thus, there is a general expectation that the partner will contribute to the family's financial well-being and stability.

Cultural resources reference the importance of shared or similar cultural or racial/ethnic backgrounds between partners (Lewis, 2016), leading to similar values and opinions. Shared similarity increases one's attractiveness and the likelihood of shared conversations, activities, and mutual understanding central to and independent of their racial/ethnic differences. This will also include having a similar educational background, which may be a gateway for interracial marriage. For example, a microcultural group member with a doctorate may desire a same-race mate, but limited dating options may make other cultural resources (e.g., political beliefs, education) more salient than race/ethnicity.

Social group is the second social force influencing partner choice. Some third parties insert themselves in the lives of family members to prevent IRRs in new generations (B. Miller et al., 2021). This may be due in part to the unfounded fear of intermixing and the potential "threat" to group cohesion and homogeneity. This is what Gordon (1964) calls group identification and includes a desire to preserve the racial/ethnic group's social history. This was the case for Chinese, Japanese, and Korean college international students (Ritter, 2015). Forty-seven students were interviewed, and 35 expressed a preference for dating someone from their same culture, which was directly tied to parental

| Box 8.7 | Author Reflections |
|---|---|

### The Life of an "Equal Opportunity Dater"

I, somewhat jokingly, tell people that I was an "equal opportunity dater"—open to dating women from all different racial and ethnic groups. The truth is that I really didn't have lots of women interested in me in high school . . . so I wasn't exactly in a position to be overly picky. ☺ Growing up and attending schools with significant amounts of diversity, it probably wasn't surprising that I dated European American, African American, and Puerto Rican women. I met my spouse in 1983 when I was in the second year of my undergraduate studies at Ohio University; she was in her first year. It sounds like a cliché, but the truth is that I knew that I was going to marry her the first time we met (yes, she is that amazing!).

While both my spouse and I have multiracial backgrounds, and both have European ancestry, people see us as an interracial couple. This makes sense given that she has always identified as an African American woman, and I have negotiated my European and Spanish/Filipino background in different ways. Yet, when it comes to our marriage, race is seldom the issue that causes the most disagreement. We both are similar in terms of age, ability, nationality, and spirituality, and are different when it comes to gender, regionality, and socioeconomic status. When I think about the issues that we continue to negotiate even after 30+ years of marriage, it seems like socioeconomic status is the most salient. As you might recall from my personal reflection in Chapter 5, I was raised in low-income housing projects; my spouse, on the other hand, was raised in a solidly middle-class neighborhood. This background has cultivated different views on money, spending, and saving—things that sometimes cause disagreements. And while socioeconomic status is at the core of this issue, I can't help but see how our gender identities (she's more feminine and I am more masculine) and regional backgrounds (she was born and raised in the Midwest, and I in the Northeast) influence our ability to communicate competently with one another.

It is important to note that all relationships, to some extent, are multicultural—all couples have both similarities and differences that must be recognized. While interracial relationships may still get the most attention, other intercultural pairings can be just as challenging. What are your views of relationships that are interfaith? Intergenerational? International? Interability? Can you see how racial difference isn't always the most salient issue in relationships?

—MPO

approval. They also revealed a racial hierarchy should they consider dating other groups with European Americans and Asian Americans acceptable but no interest in African Americans, Latinx, and Southeast Asian students.

Group sanctions, another aspect of the second social force, involves institutions imposing sanctions against violators of group norms and expectations regarding IRRs (Lewis, 2016). State sanctions (e.g., antimiscegenation laws) no longer exist, but family sanctions do and are more informal and have relational consequences (Kalmijn, 1998). Sanctions include (1) meeting with potential partners to discourage interest; (2) becoming a matchmaker and selecting more appropriate mates; (3) offering unsolicited advice and opinions to discourage interest; and (4) punishing by withdrawing emotional and relational support. The church is also an institution that potentially imposes sanctions against IRRs (e.g., interfaith marriages) (Rose & Firmin, 2016; Royer, 2014). Some religions believe interfaith/interracial marriages decrease the lifeblood of the faith and are a form of intermixing. There is also an assumption that sacred texts such as the Bible speak against intermixing, thereby bolstering arguments against IRRs amongst its members and society at large.

## INTERRACIAL RELATIONSHIP DEVELOPMENT MODEL

Foeman and Nance's (1999) **interracial relational development model** (IRDM) describes the process of successfully managing IRRs (specifically African American/European American) in the face of external forces. The four stages are: (1) racial awareness, (2) coping with social definitions of race, (3) identity emergence, and (4) maintenance. Three films do an impressive job of demonstrating how couples progress through the four stages. T. Harris and Trego (2008) use the films *Something New* (Hamri, 2005), *Guess Who's Coming to Dinner* (1967), and its remake *Guess Who?* (2005) to illustrate this relationship progression.

Data suggest that African American women are least likely to date interracially than women from other racial/ethnic groups.

## Racial Awareness

Stage 1 involves awareness of a mutual attraction and possibility for intimate involvement. Attraction is both an interpersonal and cultural experience where partners must address social frames (e.g., complex racial past) and inform outsiders (e.g., family, friends) of the relationship. "Interracial couples work their way through the awareness stage by engaging in communication behaviors related to their mutual attraction and sensitivity" (Foeman & Nance, 1999, p. 550). Outsiders will likely view the partners in the interracial relationship in different ways. Partners face the stereotype that they are in an IRR because they "have low self-esteem and poor relationship quality (commitment, satisfaction, realistic expectations, the level to which expectations were met, and partner preferences)" (Gurung & Duong, 1999, pp. 652–653).

## Coping

The second stage is coping and involves partners pulling toward each other and away from others in their interpersonal networks (Brummett & Afifi, 2019; Ross & Woodley, 2020). The partners are in the early stages of dating and might be influenced by others' opinions. In this stage, the pressure from family members and friends propel the couple together. Rather than choosing to fight with others about their relationship, they fight *for* their relationship by creating proactive strategies. The couple may choose to spend more time with each other and less time with those who are unsupportive. They may develop new networks that support the relationship. "Communication will function at this stage to relay strategies and enact them as necessary" (Foeman & Nance, 1999, p. 552). In short, the couple protects itself by choosing to enact responses that preserve the relationship.

## Identity Emergence

If the couple is able to withstand the initial pressures placed on them, then they transition to stage three, identity emergence. During this stage, partners make their relationship official and present themselves to others as a romantic couple (Foeman & Nance, 2002). Interracial couples can reframe their experience for outsiders and emphasize that they are choosing a path on their own terms rather than one prescribed by others. "Communication functions to provide the voice and words to recast their world" (p. 553). The posture they take with others is very defensive and protective. They actively work toward defending the relationship with an awareness that they live in a racially charged culture with negative racial attitudes towards IRRs. As partners and as a couple, they are committed to simultaneously nurturing their relationship and protecting it from others who object to it (Brummett & Afifi, 2019). This may involve verbal confrontations with family members or friends, or even strangers, who express opposition to their relationship. Partners express a deep relationship commitment to themselves and to others in spite of the consequences. If their efforts to manage the relationship are successful, then they move forward to the next stage. If struggles create tension in the relationship, then they may very well regress or choose to end the relationship.

## Maintenance

The final stage, maintenance, requires long-term relational commitment and continued communication about "how they present themselves and how others speak about them" (Foeman & Nance, 2002, p. 248). Relational partners must work through their differences and defend themselves from the external forces attempting to dissolve the relationship (Castle Bell & Hastings, 2011). This likely includes marital (or relational) perspective taking, which involves an openness to having one's perception of their partner be challenged and "causes the partner to dig deeper into gaining an understanding of their partner's experiences" (Ross & Woodley, 2020, p. 47).

## MYTHS AND SMOKE SCREENS ABOUT IRRs

According to research, there are several myths and misconceptions about IRRs (Karanja, 2019). We have already discussed the social forces that oftentimes exert a significant amount of pressure on relational partners who are from different racial groups. We even read firsthand accounts of informal systems (e.g., Indian racial continuum) that discourage romantic involvement between racially different individuals. Below, we provide a list of common myths researchers have explored and offer evidence that challenges the arguments made against IRRs that are grounded in misinformation.

**Myth 1:** Individuals involved in IRRs have "nonnormative" (read "abnormal") sexual attitudes (Yancey, 2003).

**Fact:** There are no differences between same-race and interracial relationships in the way of sexual intimacy, thus debunking the myth that individuals involved in interracial sexuality have permissive sexual attitudes (Yancey, 2003).

**Myth 2:** People involved in IRRs have lower self-esteem and poorer relationship quality (commitment, satisfaction, realistic expectations, the level to which expectations were met, and partner preferences) than people in same-race/ethnicity relationships (Ellithorpe, 2016).

**Fact:** Findings suggest no differences between these groups. In fact, those involved in such relationships most likely have high self-esteem and confidence, which may be necessary to defy societal norms and date outside of their racial/ethnic group.

**Myth 3:** Partners in interracial relationships are less satisfied with their relationship than same-race partners (Troy et al., 2006).

**Fact:** Interracial romantic relationship partners have significantly higher levels of relationship satisfaction compared to those in intraracial relationships (Genç & Su, 2021).

**Myth 4:** IRRs experience more conflict and have less relationship quality than same-race relationships. (Troy et al., 2006)

**Fact:** No differences were found or reported between the two groups. (Yancey, 2003)

## PROBLEMS, PROGRESS, AND FUTURE DIRECTIONS

Whether an interracial relationship is a friendship or romance, there are relational dynamics that often times require partners to develop coping strategies to buffer against attacks on the relationship. Such factors as family and societal disapproval, language barriers, logistics, cultural barriers and traditions, and children exert so much pressure that partners are forced to decide whether to put forth the effort necessary to preserve and maintain the relationship. Our societal attitudes towards racial difference cause us to prejudge racially different others, which is problematic; therefore, it is incumbent upon us to create new models or ways of thinking about race and IRRs. This can be achieved, in part, through an increased understanding of how these relationships work. This will facilitate progress in understanding the establishment and maintenance of interracial interactions, which is critical to positive race relations.

After reading this chapter, we hope you have come to think more positively about interracial romantic relationships. Much like same-race partners, interracial partners enter relationships out of a basic human need for emotional intimacy with another person. They desire a relationship with someone who has life goals, attitudes, beliefs, and values similar to their own. So the next time you see an interracial couple and you think to yourself, "Why are *they* together?" ask yourself if you would ask the same question of a same-race couple. The answer goes beyond the physical differences that seem to separate the partners from each other. We must rethink our own and others' perceptions of the cross-race mate selection process. With the increasing racial diversity we are experiencing in the United States, we should avoid asking the "whys" and understand the "why nots" of interracial romantic relationships. This process involves actively pursuing diverse geographical spaces and locations and opportunities for increased contact and quality interactions with racially diverse outgroup members that will ideally lead to reduced prejudicial attitudes. Living and working in a diverse society is facilitated by cultivating trust, embracing similarity while remembering differences, exploring other cultures, and bridging differences to connect.

## CONCLUSION

The United States., like many other countries, has a sordid past when it comes to race relations. It is driven by a racial hierarchy that has dictated how our institutions are created and, by extension, the kinds of relationships we are expected (or not) to have. Slavery and the Jim Crow Laws laid the foundation for contemporary race relations in that there remains a high level of mistrust, prejudice, and bias between racial groups. As a society, we continue to be socialized to avoid interracial relationships because they are either a threat to a collective group or an individual; sometimes it is both. This is unfortunate because it perpetuates a false narrative that interracial communication is innately unnatural, difficult, and to be avoided at all costs.

It is a reality that IRFs and IRRs will increase significantly as the U.S. population becomes even more diverse. The ever-changing racial/ethnic landscape of the country guarantees there will be increased interracial interactions at work, school, and in other public spaces. Rather than fearing them, we should approach these interpersonal exchanges as opportunities for personal growth that can lead to a truly inclusive world. More importantly, these relationships will go a long way in achieving the broader goal of destigmatizing IRFs and IRRs and normalizing them as we do same-race relationships.

## KEY TERMS

| | |
|---|---|
| environmental factors | orders of interracial contact |
| situational factors | contact hypothesis |
| individual factors | structural theory |
| dyadic factors | endogamy |
| *Brown v. Board of Education* | homogamy |
| antimiscegenation laws | hypergamy |
| digital sexual racism | racial motivation theory |
| race fetishization | intentionality |
| race checklist | emotionality |
| race devaluation | racial homophily |
| racial preferences | interracial relational development model |

## RECOMMENDED CONTEMPORARY READINGS

Brummett, E. A., & Steuber, K. R. (2015). To reveal or conceal?: Privacy management processes among interracial romantic partners. *Western Journal of Communication, 79*(1), 22–44.

Cardwell, M. E. (2021). Examining interracial family narratives using critical multiracial theory. *Review of Communication, 21*(3), 206–222.

Caselli, A. J., & Machia, L. V. (2021). Discrimination is not just Black and White in romantic relationships: A consideration of perspective taking and self-expansion. *Journal of Personality and Social Psychology.* https://doi.org/10.1037/pspi0000380.supp (Supplemental)

Greenland, K., Augoustinos, M., Andreouli, E., & Taulke-Johnson, R. (2020). Cross-group friendships, the irony of harmony, and the social construction of "discrimination." *Ethnic and Racial Studies, 43*(7), 1169–1188. https://doi.org/10.1080/01419870.2019.1648845

Greif, G. L., Stubbs, V. D., & Woolley, M. E. (2022). Clinical suggestions for family therapists based on interviews with white women married to Black men. *Contemporary Family Therapy: An International Journal,* 1–16. https://doi.org/10.1007/s10591-021-09629-y

Punyanunt-Carter, N. M., & Rodriguez, N. B. (2020). An examination of equity and inter-dependence theory as predictors of maintenance behaviours: Interracial vs. intrara-cial dating relationships. *Journal of Intercultural Communication Research*, 49(6), 617–631.

Rastogi, R., & Juvonen, J. (2019). Interminority friendships and intergroup attitudes across middle school: Quantity and stability of Black-Latino ties. *Journal of Youth & Adolescence*, 48(8), 1619–1630. https://doi.org/10.1007/s10964-019-01044-9

Robinson, W. T., Muse, C., Hewett, R., Balogun, M. O., Elrahman, J., Nordling, A., Abdulkerim, N., & Matsumoto, A. (2021). Regular white people things: The pres-ence of white fragility in interracial families. *Family Relations*, 70(4), 973–992. https://doi.org/10.1111/fare.12549

## OPPORTUNITIES FOR EXTENDED LEARNING

1. Twitter is notoriously popular for bringing awareness to a wide variety of issues, topics, and interests through hashtag movements. Some example hashtags that have been popular and were used to affirm and support interra-cial romantic relationships are #diversity and #loveconquersall, #blackwom-enwhitemen, and #interracialcouple. What are some other hashtags that have been used recently in the same way? What incidents seem to have inspired them? What kind of support are people giving interracial couples? What is the overall tone of the comments responding to these movements? What racial pairings seem to be most common? Given what you have learned about dating preferences and patterns, does this seem to coincide with what you believe?

2. In pairs, use your device of choice (i.e., phone, laptop) and scroll public pro-files of strangers on social media that neither of you knows. Pull up their photo albums, and in complete silence, scroll the pictures and make note of any interesting patterns you see such as the kinds of activities, the average number of people in each photo, and the different racial groups. Be sure to write down any thoughts you might have about your observations. After 5–10 minutes of scrolling, share your observations with each other and discuss your impressions. Be sure to discuss the ratio of intraracial and interracial friends observed and the factors that contributed to or hindered these rela-tionships from occurring.

3. Take a moment and create two separate top 5 lists of the rules or lessons you were taught about interracial relationships—one for friendships and one for romantic relationships. Think about the specific things that you were told "to do" and "not to do" in relationships with people of a different race. Also, write down who was the source of that lesson (i.e., who told it to you). Once the lists are completed, review them and make note of which ones you fol-lowed and which ones you disregarded. What are the reasons why these rules were shared? Were they because of stereotypes about specific racial groups? Did family members communicate most of the negative messages? How many discouraged the relationships from forming. This semi-inven-tory might reveal how certain lessons and ways of thinking about race rela-tions are handed down from generation to generation and influenced by society. It will also encourage you to think about your own beliefs about interracial relationships and what factors contribute to shaping them.

4. If you have not already seen the 2018 romantic comedy *Crazy Rich Asians*, watch this example of a ground-breaking movie featuring an all-Asian cast. It received praise from audiences and movie critics alike regarding issues of racial representation. Lost in these critiques, however, are the struggles the couple is forced to deal with as they attempt to move through and beyond their differences. As you watch the movie, make note of the different scenes and intercharacter interactions that illustrate the difficulties. Specifically, pay attention to (a) the extent to which their racial differences are magnified or minimized; (b) whether the movie perpetuates stereotypes about IRR or a specific racial group; and (c) the stressors that attempt to prevent the relationship from progressing. Using Foeman and Nance's (1999) interracial romantic relationship model, identify what stage the couple is in and the events they experience that cause them to be in any of the stages.

5. Universities are unique spaces because they provide students with opportunities to meet students from different races, ethnicities, and cultures. Students can participate in programs, activities, and organizations designed to bring them together and foster close relationships. In class and in small groups of five, do a search of your university's home page for different things it has done and is doing to encourage these kinds of interactions. Review them for their potential effectiveness and ability to encourage positive race relations on campus. Also discuss which ones, if any, are familiar and how effective the university has been in promoting them.

6. Imagine that a friend has come to you to discuss how to handle a white friend who keeps asking for advice on fighting for racial justice. As a BIPOC, your friend feels a great deal of stress, although recognizing that the questioner is well-meaning. This is a common problem for many of your BIPOC friends. Make a list of 10 rules that the white friend can follow to become more educated about how to do their part in addressing racism and preserving interracial relationships. Make a list of a mix of strategies and rules your BIPOC friend should use and follow to deal with the stress of racism and its impact on their overall well-being and interracial relationships.

# 9

# Interracial Communication in the Workplace

**CASE STUDY**      **The Hefty Price of Workplace Racism**

Owen Diaz worked at the Tesla factory in Fremont, California, from 2015 to 2016. During his nine-month tenure there, he was exposed to a hostile working environment by his colleagues. In a federal lawsuit, Diaz asserted that he was called the N-word by other employees, told to "Go back to Africa," and was subjected to racist and derogatory pictures drawn and placed throughout the factory (Hernandez, 2021). These prejudicial, discriminatory, and racist behaviors were nothing like what Diaz was expecting prior to working for what he anticipated was a "modern workplace." Instead, he found a "scene straight from the Jim Crow era." Rather than suffering in silence, Diaz complained about the discrimination. His claims were never taken seriously, and no interventions were ever made to stop the hostile behaviors.

In October 2021, a San Francisco jury awarded $130 million in punitive damages and $6.9 million in emotional damages. Diaz's lawyer asserted the verdict sent a strong message to Tesla to "clean up its workplace" and noted the historical significance of the "largest award in a racial harassment case involving a single plaintiff in U.S. history."

The racially hostile work environment to which Diaz was subjected prompted him to seek a legal remedy to the workplace racism. His lawyer stressed that those in power need to "take proactive measures to protect employees against racist conduct." Tesla's vice president of people posted a statement on Tesla's website that witnesses corroborated the use of the N-word but that it was often used in a "friendly manner." The statement further said Tesla strongly believed the facts did not justify the verdict and, despite not being perfect in 2015 and 2016, the company had come a long way from five years earlier.

In November 2021, Tesla challenged the award asking for a new trial or for the damages to be reduced, claiming the amount was unprecedented. In April 2022, a federal judge reduced the award to $15 million ($13.5 million punitive damages; $1.5 million compensatory damages) based on other court rulings in discrimination cases (Torchinsky, 2022). The judge affirmed that the evidence pointed to a factory saturated with racism, which undoubtedly causes profound emotional harm for employees.

What effect do you think the court case had or will have on employee relationships at Tesla? What risks are there for employees who witness these acts and say or do nothing? Why would a company ignore complaints about racism as blatantly evident as graffiti, which apparently was not removed for months? Compensatory damages are meant to cover actual losses. Why is (or is not) $1.5 million an appropriate amount? What do you think would be the best approach to address the racial divide at the factory?

We wrote this textbook to provide an overview of the history of race relations and interracial communication and the identification of contexts where racial differences become salient and impact interactions. In Chapter 8, we discussed friendship and romantic relationships. In this chapter, we shift our attention to professional relationships, specifically those in the workplace. Organizational communication differs from other relational contexts because the workplace has different expectations and goals. In all contexts, we expect interpersonal and interracial interactions to be, at a minimum, considerate. Expectations are higher in the workplace because communication is key to the organization's goals and identity. Members must work to create a culture where differences are respected and appreciated so that the skills of all organization members can surface and contribute to positive outcomes.

To understand the impact of interracial communication on the workplace, we begin with a discussion of four approaches by organizations to racial, ethnic, and cultural diversity. We then discuss the racializing of organizational cultures, followed by a presentation of general organizational principles and insight into practicing diversity management. We recognize that these suggestions are by no means absolutes; rather, we share them as food for thought as you consider the impact of race on your daily life and the lives of others.

When you enter the workforce, you very likely will work with racially diverse people. That means each of you will need to accommodate your communication behaviors and styles to reach common ground and understanding. Working in groups for class projects and dealing with people who have different personalities, views, and perspectives is good preparation for life after graduation. Your colleagues at work may be even more diverse in their thinking and behaviors than you ever thought possible. Nevertheless, we challenge you to take advantage of the opportunities you have in college to become more knowledgeable about and skilled in working with racially, ethnically, and culturally diverse others.

## COMMUNICATING THROUGH DIFFERENCES IN ORGANIZATIONS

Organizations emerge from collaborations between people to achieve collective action or goals (Littlejohn et al., 2021). Organizations are constructed in different ways depending on the goals and attitudes of people in the organization. Organizational communication research covers three core areas: the role of communication in organizing, issues of control and resistance in organizations, and relationships that exist within organizations. It is through communication that our social realities are created, and organizing is accomplished through communication, which is "contextual, historically situated, and political" (p. 300). Structures (patterns of rules and norms) are created through the process of communicating with others—whether individual relationships or large institutions. In order to effectively address the influence of race on organizational cultures, we narrow our focus to relationships theory. Specifically, we address how interactions among and between organization members become more important as the demographic and racial landscape changes.

**Human relations theory** focuses on people and their needs, including attention and recognition. Relationships are important, and being part of a supportive team is a motivating factor for productivity in an organization. The

---

**Box 9.1**                                              *Research Highlight*

## The Racial Foundation of Organizational Communication

In 2003, organizational communication scholars Karen Lee Ashcraft and Brenda Allen noted that organizational communication scholarship "rarely and inadequately attends to racial issues" and "the ways in which we routinely frame race preserve the whiteness of the field, even as we claim to do otherwise" (p. 6). They analyzed six highly regarded organizational communication textbooks and paid specific attention to the visibility or invisibility of race in chapter discussions. In short, there was concern for the profound silence regarding the topic of race.

Their analysis identified five messages about race. First, they found that race is treated as a single concept deemed relevant only in certain circumstances. Second, race is only relevant when it involves cultural differences that can be controlled or managed to facilitate organizational performance. Third, cultural difference and international variations are synonymous; nation of origin is portrayed as the strongest influence on cultural disposition, neglecting cultural variation and race relations within national boundaries. Fourth, there are four sources of racial discrimination: (1) personal bias; (2) interpersonal misunderstanding; (3) organizational mismanagement of cultural differences; and (4) disproportionate demographics. Racial discrimination is characterized as the unfortunate practices of people within organizations—not as a systemic discrimination or an organizational product. Fifth, whiteness is the organizational normal.

Ashcraft and Allen conclude that organizational communication textbooks frame race in ways that bury or ignore the pervasive nature of whiteness as an overarching framework for understanding and describing organizational culture. In short, textbooks that continue to be held in high regard fail to give critical attention to racialized experiences (rendering them silent) and privilege dominant experiences (e.g., whiteness). This biased approach ultimately advances an unchallenged assumption that theory is race neutral and race is an atheoretical (or less theoretical) matter.

Women in the workplace are forced to deal with resistance to their intersecting (e.g., race and gendered) identities, which can result in workplace conflict.

theory examines interpersonal—including interracial—relationships among employees in the workplace. It acknowledges and recognizes the multiple identities of organizational members. As noted above, some needs of organizations vary, but competent approaches and strategies that contribute to positive interracial communication amongst organizational members is essential in all organizations. When people in positions of power are sensitized to employee identities that have been shaped by experiences and informed by race, gender, socioeconomic status, and professional history, the probabilities for cooperation and productivity increase. This recognition of and adaptation to human diversity within the workplace contributes to a truly inclusive organization.

Diversity and inclusivity in the workplace (and beyond) are necessary in an ever-changing world. Box 9.2 offers a constructive framework for addressing diversity in the workplace. The work to get there is hard and will assuredly involve resistance due in part to preconceived notions (e.g., stereotypes, racial prejudice) about racially different others that unnecessarily hamper workplace interracial relationships. To overcome that resistance, we offer positive and effective examples for facilitating constructive workplace communication.

Organizations are based on ideologies that can benefit some individuals and disadvantage others. Corporate colonization theory describes situations in which corporate interests dominate those of the individual, thus privileging managerial interests over the interests of identity, community, or democracy (Littlejohn et al., 2021). "Gender, race, and class, as well as other identity markers, are important ideological components that have been addressed in the theorizing of organizational communication, and a special concern is how communication enables individuals to resist control and hegemony" (p. 337).

While organizational communication research has become somewhat more inclusive, it continues to ignore historic and systemic forms of oppression as a source for the racialized experiences of outgroup members. We must commit to engaging in discussions of race with people that do not minimize their life experiences. This requires a recognition that there is a resistance to change among many people that becomes magnified when we discuss racial

## Box 9.2

## Taking REAL Action

The Center for Creative Leadership (CCL) is a premier leadership development organization founded in 1970 to develop leadership that directly benefits society worldwide. To help institutions understand the dynamics of diversity, equity and inclusion in the workplace, CCL developed their REAL™ framework. The ultimate goal is to establish a process of discovery to meet the unique challenges in organizations based on their particular contexts and histories.

The REAL framework is a 4-step process (Leading Effectively Staff, 2022). Step 1 is *revealing relevant opportunities*. This is a discovery stage to gain awareness of an institution's specific context before setting a direction—rather than setting an agenda or copying initiatives from other organizations. Current leadership should be aware of their power and privilege and the influence of both on their leadership. As such, they should work with members to determine relevant opportunities for change and strategic action. In Step 2, *elevating equity*, CCL highlights the importance of providing all individuals the opportunities

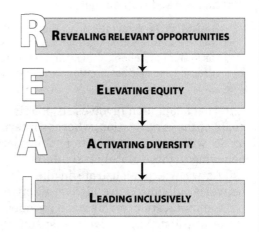

and resources required to gain their full potential. Senior leaders acknowledge societal inequities in their businesses and develop an action plan. *Activating diversity* is the third step, which includes recognizing differences—exploring the impact of diversity on perspectives, assumptions, and approaches in order to identify ways to engage the contributions of everyone. Step 4, *leading inclusively*, includes leaders actively and vigilantly promoting full participation of each employee, customer, and strategic partner, which will contribute to a sense of belonging for everyone. The last step not only involves policies and practices but also the ability to envision and enact new ways of leading.

This 4-step process challenges organizational leadership to take a hard look at itself in order to actualize inclusive leadership and foster allyship. CCL advises taking action to establish effective conversations at every organizational level. Without meaningful conversations, it is difficult to overcome the divisions among individuals whose backgrounds and perspectives are vastly different. This can be achieved through direct conversations about diversity, which will ultimately break down silos and communication barriers within the organization and between its members. Organizations desiring a better culture must begin with having better conversations about difficult topics. Through communication, individuals can learn about unconscious biases that shape experiences within and outside of the workplace. This involves collaboration between members facilitated by a culture of openness, respect for differences, and understanding.

demographics in our organizations (Wiggins-Romesburg & Githens, 2018). In the following section, we will offer examples of specific organizational cultures that reflect this hesitancy to deconstruct the racial hierarchy that perpetuates privilege and power and complicates race relations.

## THEORY OF RESPONSIVENESS TO WORKPLACE DIVERSITY

**Organizational culture** is the accumulated shared learning of a group from its experience solving problems of external adaptation and internal integration that has worked well enough that it is

> taught to new members as the correct way to perceive, think, feel and behave in relation to those problems. This accumulated learning is a pattern or system of beliefs, values, and behavioral norms that come to be taken for granted as basic assumptions and eventually drop out of awareness. (Schein, 2017, p. 6)

External adaptation involves responding to the environment's influence on the goals of the organization, whereas internal integration has to do with changes made within the organization. Members adapt their ways of thinking and behaving to those closely resembling those of the organization.

As we will demonstrate in the following sections, authentic interactions between individuals are highly effective in improving race relations. Authentic communication involves being open and sharing one's feelings honestly while also listening actively, respectfully, and empathetically to what others have to say. Authentic communication strengthens relationships, builds trust, and promotes inclusivity. It is imperative to recognize that a culture of belonging in which everyone's ideas and perspectives are valued helps people feel comfortable revealing their authentic selves, thus helping an organization foster true belonging.

Recall our discussion in Chapter 7 that intergroup contact can lead to changes in racial attitudes. Authentic communication and increased interactions can potentially decrease discrimination in the United States. Since 1997, more than 1.8 million complaints of workplace discrimination have been filed with the EEOC (Flynn, 2022). The number of complaints filed in 2020 was 67,448; yet only 17.4% of cases are resolved in favor of the person filing. In 2021, employers paid approximately $484 million in settlements. Of note is that racial discrimination claims have the lowest success rate (15%) and a majority (61%) of workers have experienced or witnessed workplace discrimination. These data show us that systemic racism is difficult to dismantle and remains a barrier for many in the workplace. Despite the evidence that racism and other forms of systemic oppression exist, corporations are either willing to do little or nothing to change the culture and/or employees are deterred from reporting racism because of the low success rate across industries. Table 9.1 shows states with the highest number of discrimination cases by type of workplace discrimination.

**Table 9.1    States with the Most Employment Discrimination Cases per 100K (2009–2018)**

| Age | Color and Race | Equal Pay |
|---|---|---|
| 1 Alabama 5.8 | 1 Alabama 8.3 | 1 Alabama 1.1 |
| 1 New Mexico 5.8 | 2 Mississippi 7.2 | 2 New Mexico 1.0 |
| 3 Illinois 5.3 | 3 Arkansas 5.8 | 3 Alaska 0.7 |
| **National Origin** | **Religion** | **Sex** |
| 1 New Mexico 5.0 | 1 Colorado 1.1 | 1 Alabama 9.7 |
| 2 Colorado 3.1 | 2 Alabama 0.9 | 2 Mississippi 8.8 |
| 2 Florida 3.1 | 2 Georgia 0.9 | 3 Arkansas 8.7 |

Source: Paychex®, 2019

## Dialogic Approach

Institutions of higher education are a type of organization where opportunities for education about racial, ethnic, and cultural diversity exist and are oftentimes addressed directly through curriculum and myriad initiatives. As a student, you can probably think of a few ways your university is trying to implement these changes. One example may be the multicultural general education requirement all students must fulfill for graduation. These courses will ideally expose students to diversity and new ways of thinking about difference. What is ignored, however, is *how* the students are expected to engage with this topic. Will reading a novel by an Arab American female author be sufficient in changing student views on this group? Are students sharing their personal experiences with race, ethnicity, and culture that complement what is being learned? Are they better served by a variety of teaching strategies that facilitate learning and move them out of their comfort zone? These are all questions that must be asked if dialogue or communication is to be recognized as a vital means for improving interracial communication in the workplace and other interpersonal contexts.

The research of two communication scholars supports our conclusion that communication is key to positive race relations. Deetz and Simpson (2004) introduced a theory that addresses the role of communication in this transformative process. They focused on communication concepts and practices that facilitate voice and developing an appreciation of otherness as part of dialogic interaction. The **politically responsive constructionist theory of communication (PRCT)** recognizes the importance of political realities in sociohistorical context. Deetz and Simpson explain that "communication in its dialogic form is productive rather than reproductive. It produces what self and other can experience, rather than reproducing what either has" (p. 143). In other words, communication produces something new rather than a product of self-interest. They further explain that "by attending to the centrality of difference in organizations, we can see more clearly that transformation requires not simply a rapprochement of perspective but a more careful examination of a wider range of voices" (p. 150).

While similarities are important, working *through* our differences might yield more significant and critical changes in race relations. Deetz and Simpson (2004) suggest that these interactions have the potential to call into question a person's beliefs, worldviews, and assumptions about the world and for them to reexamine assumptions that privilege the self at the expense of the other.

> Failure to attend carefully to the otherness around us limits our own perspective, produces incomplete and inadequate decision-relevant information, and does violence to those "others" who positions are often already institutionally and culturally marginalized. Encounters with the other must go beyond the notions of exchange [to] recognize the central importance of radical difference to our own capacity for growth in understanding.

As they explain, challenging unexamined assumptions is not for the purpose of inducing guilt but to provide an understanding of a world where systemic oppression is real. This may cause a shift in thinking about the legacy of institutional racism and its effect on contemporary experiences with race and racism.

**Table 9.2   Features of Dialogue from a Politically Responsive Constructionist Lens**

| Dialogue Is | Dialogue Is Not |
| --- | --- |
| Historically situated | Hypothetical or acontextual |
| Productive | Reproductive |
| Engaging | Passive |
| Empowering | Demeaning |
| Transformative | Satisfied with the status quo |
| About exploring different perspectives | About being "right" |
| Politically responsive | "Politically correct" |

(Deetz & Simpson, 2004)

A fundamental argument of PRCT is that adopting a colorblindness mentality should be avoided. Colorblindness, as discussed in Chapter 8, is where racial and ethnic differences are ignored or minimized. This way of thinking is replaced by a constructionist lens that facilitates meaningful dialogue. The practice of avoiding discussions or shutting down conversations about divisive issues ultimately functions to obscure power by maintaining one view of reality at the expense of another (Heath & Borda, 2021). As such, calls for civility in the context of organizational power can be a strategy to suppress conflict and maintain the status quo. Such strategies are more appropriately labeled cordial speech rather than civility.

Cordial speech involves people adapting their communication behaviors to the powerful, thus maintaining the current power hierarchy. Civility has been central to studies in dialogue and deliberation, but definitions vary substantially. Some scholars have suggested *discursive opening* as a guideline for what counts as civil interaction. "Discursive opening shifts our attention away from strict definitions describing what civility 'is,' and asks instead *what work civility does*—that is, it initiates and maintains the possibility for further conversation among those with deeply held differences" (Heath & Borda, 2021, p. 9). This approach opens discussion for dissenting views while maintaining respect for individuals and invites diverse perspectives. It is honest discourse about race and all issues experienced by those who are systemically oppressed.

Simpson (2008) conducted an in-depth qualitative study about diversity and college campuses. Her focus groups and individual interviews with students, faculty, and administrators from both the macroculture (i.e., European American) and microculture (i.e., African American, Asian American, Latinx American) revealed distinctly different approaches to navigating discussions about the issue of race. Simpson found that people of color are oftentimes taught as children by their parents to avoid "making waves" during interracial interactions. This approach might include, for example, avoiding discussions about race-related experiences or the topic of race at all. Because whites rarely, if ever, have to deal with or witness racism, becoming aware of and acknowledging the reality of racism and privilege can create hesitancy or apprehension. Simpson concludes that scholars and administrators who are dedicated and committed to "diversity, justice, equality, and fairness" should move away from colorblindness and create an environment where people from different racial/ethnic backgrounds feel comfortable revealing their experiences and opinions.

**Table 9.3    Student Responses to the Question "What can, or should, be done to make the campus climate more open and welcoming for students of color?"**

| White Student Responses | Student of Color Responses |
| --- | --- |
| "I don't know because from experience everyone seems to enjoy themselves and feels welcome." | "How can you be welcome if there aren't many people you can relate to?" |
| "CU puts so much emphasis on ethnicity these days that I'm beginning to feel like a minority." | "In 5 years I have not had one minority teacher. This is part of the problem." |
| "Nothing different—a special effort should not be made to make certain people feel welcome—they need to learn to do it for themselves." | "Have the president talk with me. Have the chancellor talk with me. Re-educate faculty, staff, and students about their own lack of awareness on racial issues. They all need to understand their lack of awareness helps to continually perpetuate racism." |
| "It seems that you have convocations for people and personally I think that should be enough. If you do any more it may be looked at as favoritism." | "I don't really care. I'm leaving." |

(Simpson, 2008)

There are key concepts or characteristics with which we should all become familiar to better understand what qualifies as "true dialogue" (Simpson, 2008). Open-mindedness, perspective taking, and empathy are critical elements. Ignoring or minimizing differences and perspectives is counterproductive to honest and open interracial communication in the workplace and in other contexts.

Exploring this notion of a dialogic approach to workplace communication, researchers conducted focus groups with students from different races/ethnicities at a university to identify responses (e.g., curriculum, lecture content,

---

**Box 9.3**                                                    *Author Reflections*

## Diversity Is More than Just Rhetoric

Throughout my career, I have consistently been either "the first" or one of a few Black women to achieve several accomplishments and accolades at two different predominately white institutions (PWIs) in the south. I was the first (if our collective history is correct) African American female to be awarded tenure and promotion to the highest faculty rank and am now the nation's first endowed chair of race, media, and cultural literacy at my current institution. Reflecting on this process, I am reminded that I could not have gotten here were it not for my family and sister-friends who have provided me with constant support through the ups and downs. What has cemented our relationships is the fact that our *social locations* (e.g., race, class, gender, professional status, education, physical ability) have bonded us and created unique experiences and realities others sometimes do not or cannot understand. BIPOC oftentimes have to create their own connections and social support as they strive to succeed professionally in spaces where they are in the minority. Those relationships are typically with other Black women since they have similar lived experiences. In the case of Black women, these relationships become essential when an organization's public rhetoric celebrating diversity on the institutional level fails to translate into action on the individual level. Lack of inclusion and other challenges ultimately cause additional work-related stressors and potentially impede professional success for Black women. Ultimately, organizations must create an inclusive environment that is authentic and maintain ongoing efforts to boldly recognize and challenge systemic oppression.

Organizational leaders must be more responsive to diversity beyond rhetoric. Yes, organizations and institutions must become diverse, but what happens when BIPOC members "get there"? They should not be tokenized; rather, organizations and their leaders must work aggressively towards creating an environment genuinely receptive to change. Diversity training as well as discussions and strategic plans that aim to eliminate ideologies and behaviors resistant to diversity by individuals and institutions are essential. These efforts should also involve, for example, abolishing grooming policies that unfairly target women of color (see, for example, Bennett-Alexander & Harrison, 2016). Sister-friends are an excellent antidote to being the only Black woman in a professional setting. Ideally, organizations would strive to be more diverse; until then, BIPOC must actively seek nurturing and affirming relationships to help them navigate these very alienating spaces.

—TMH

etc.) to race and diversity within the classroom (Simpson et al., 2007). Although the participants were not coworkers, they were members of a community where interactions that take place are similar to those in the workplace. The expectations become higher when addressing diversity, or the lack thereof, on college campus. The students explained that it is important for instructors to familiarize themselves with a broad range of racial realities. Doing so contributes to creating an open and welcoming environment in the classroom and elsewhere on campus. They also reported that professors should directly address how their discipline responds to race and diversity in its scholarship. Without such analysis, post-secondary education will remain an exclusive profession that marginalizes BIPOC realities and experiences. Faculty members, administrators, and students from all racial, ethnic, and cultural backgrounds need to engage in self-reflection and cultural sensitivity as institutions adapt to the changing racial landscape.

## Interaction-Based Approach

An interaction-based approach to workplace communication carries an expectation that community members will have constant interactions. Michigan State University tested this theory by creating a racially and ethnically diverse community environment on campus. The residential community increased the opportunities for interracial interactions in hopes of bridging racial divides. The **multiracial unity living experience (MRULE)** was established in 1996 by two faculty members committed to facilitating student discussion around social issues through what they call the three pillars: social justice, human agency, and action research. MRULE's website stresses that its primary goals are to help students create genuine relationships and promote social justice. It is anticipated that these interactions will involve open and honest dialogue that allows individuals to transcend their differences due to race, gender, class, sexuality, and nationality. Social justice involves community members promoting acceptance, fairness, and equality in all areas of public life, not just on campus.

Intergroup contact at a young age can lead to positive interracial and intercultural relationships.

The program founders envisioned creating a community where diverse groups of students would participate in peer-to-peer education coupled with weekly round table dialogues facilitated by trained peer leaders and monthly socials. Co-founder David Thomas explains that the program stresses "solidarity, cohesiveness and working across racial difference" while working towards justice through "a dedicated, engaged practice of building relationships dedicated to dismantling oppressive structures and constructively contributing to the world." Activities at the core of the program include year-round roundtable discussions (RTDs), and the communication-intensive focus is evident in the number of hours invested by MRULE community members. The program has Intercultural Aides (ICAs) (Resident Advisor equivalent) who facilitate 264 hours of RTDs annually, guide 330 students weekly in conversations, and participate in a weekly average of 760 interpersonal conversations with residents and 1,000+ conversations with students about academic success every semester. The seminars offered require that the leaders "[cover] a range of issues on race and culture, [conduct] research material to present to their groups, [facilitate] dialogues, [lead] group activities and outings, and [build] genuine relationships among themselves and their participants" (Muthuswamy et al., 2006). MRULE has since added community service, university-wide curriculum, and community building trips aimed to move knowledge from theory to practice within the organization itself and the world.

A study was designed to determine if two-year MRULE participants experienced cognitive and behavioral changes in their residence halls. When compared to nonparticipants, MRULE student attitudes were "significantly more positive towards issues related to race" (Muthuswamy et al., 2006, p. 118). The findings support the use of the MRULE model in other communities and organizational contexts through "creating interactional diversity" that emphasized "peer education, holistic communication, and a commitment to situating race-related dialogue within the purview of interpersonal relationships and communication contexts" (p. 118). The researchers acknowledge that there is a "self-selection effect" or "self-selection bias" among the students because they *chose* to participate in the program. An organizational culture was created that was not reflective of "typical" student interactions on campus. Replicating the results in real world contexts may not be possible if they lack the necessary diversity, opportunities for authentic, organic interactions, and an institutional commitment to diversity. Nevertheless, we remain hopeful that these efforts are a move toward improved race relations. MRULE's success supports the premises of the contact hypothesis.

## Applied Approach

Whitehead (2009) looked at language choice in a racial diversity training session, specifically the use of racial categories by speakers in their accounts of someone else's actions. Whitehead conducted same-race focus groups ("white group" and "People of Color group") with organizational members and then a general session among all participations. Conversation analysis revealed that people racialized their dialogue in three ways. **Generalizing race** involved no explanatory properties associated with a specific racial category. There was a failure to recognize "racial privilege as a situational characteristic of which-ever 'ingroup' constitutes the majority in any given neighborhood" and ignor-ing the significance of white privilege (p. 332). **Localizing race** refers to limiting the use of race as an explanation for action to particular situations. Speakers who qualify the use of race to a particular instance present them-selves as individuals who use race only when it is warranted. **Alluding to race** involves the use of language to imply a racial meaning. They do not explicitly connect race with a practice, but they indirectly make the association. These strategies may be employed by speakers to avoid being categorized as biased. However, racial prejudice was present in their communication behaviors and decreased the likelihood of an inclusive organizational environment.

Latinx Americans attempting to garner organizational success confront workplace discrimination. This group is the largest microculture in the United States, but they are disproportionately underrepresented in highly compen-sated positions in corporations (Blancero et al., 2018). More than 50% of His-panics experience discrimination and believe that their workplaces talk about

### Pulled Over for Being a Good Samaritan

At my old job, I worked as a server. We had bussers there. All but one of the bussers were African American. Many of the bussers lived in the Athens-Clark County public housing system [and] . . . would ride the city bus to work. Many times they would call a friend to pick them up or I would take them home. The first time I drove my friend(s) home, I pulled [over] . . . to stop and let my friend out. [He said] "This is no place for a white kid after dark." So the next day, I said, "Look, I know what you mean, and I'm not trying to be a hero, but I'm driving you home, man. C'mon."

Well, immediately following my leaving the neighborhood, I was pulled over by Athens' finest. The white cop insisted that I had just bought drugs. Now I give him a lot of leeway, because, well, I have been with people who have bought drugs here before, and because I know some of my friends sell drugs in here. I proceeded to tell him that I drove my friend home from work. He proceeded to tell me no white kid drives a Black guy home from work into the projects and that I should quit lying. I said roughly, "Look, dude, I'm really not in the mood for you right now. I don't have anything on me. I just had a really long night, and I have to use the restroom, so if you want to search my &*^$#* and get this over with so I can go home, then please do so. If not, I need to be on my way." Not to be outdone, he pro-ceeded to lecture me on how to speak respectfully to an officer (which under normal cir-cumstances I do), then let me go by saying I should not come around here anymore.

I was pissed. I was racially profiled (like Blacks are all the time) by a white cop. His motiva-tions were based on stereotypes, and he would not accept that he was wrong. Not only that but all of the public housing saw me get pulled over so now when I come back I am going to have to deal with the suspicion that I am in cahoots with the police.

inclusivity and diversity but do not change policies or culture to make that happen (Acosta, 2021). Data from LinkedIn reveals that 70% of Latinx professionals believe that, if their complexions were a lighter tone, then they would advance further in their careers. This speaks to the issue of colorism discussed in Chapter 7. More than three-quarters of Latinx repress parts of their personas at work, which they consider necessary in order to advance (Hewlett et al., 2016). They modify their appearance, nonverbals, and communication style to conform to traditionally white, male standards. A large majority (63%) do not feel included, do not feel invited to share ideas, and do not believe their ideas are heard and valued in the workplace. Similarly, Latinx women are scrutinized on many levels as well. Like all women, they face challenges to leadership and career success sometimes because of lower pay for equal work, prejudicial perceptions that women belong at home, or employers who will not hire or promote women because of the belief that personal obligations will affect their job performance (Bonilla-Rodriguez, 2016).

With diversity comes the potential for competition amongst racial groups for resources and positions (Gordils et al., 2021). This creates a unique situation for historically marginalized groups because not only must they deal with difficult communication with majority group members but they also face in-group competition. Perceived interracial competition is associated with higher levels of racial bias and stereotyping plus negative intergroup outcomes, such as avoidance, anxiety, and mistrust.

## Deconstructing Whiteness: White Leader Prototype

Another phenomenon perpetuating a racial divide is the white leader prototype, a public relations theory positing that professional roles are racially constructed through ideological discourses that perpetuate white privilege (Logan, 2011). This is one of many barriers to achieving diversity, equality, and inclusion (DEI). Logan (2021) places the responsibility for DEI on powerful corporations that have historically benefitted from the discrimination against people of color. Diversity and inclusion efforts have increased the employment of people of color, but they have been ineffective in achieving racial equity in the workplace. While Latinx people comprise 18.5% of the population, only 20 individuals were chief executive officers in 2021; Black people comprise 13.4% of the country, and only 6 were CEOs (Kurt, 2022). Logan (2021) argues that

> corporations were discursively constructed as sites of privilege and exclusion, inculcating and reproducing the durable perception that only certain people belong there. Or perhaps more precisely that different types of people belong there, but in different capacities—capacities that primarily were determined by one's race, gender and/or sexuality. For example, Black people "belonged" as the help—custodians, cooks, security, and so on. White women belonged as secretaries and in other support roles, and cisgender white men belonged as managers and future leaders. (p. 4)

Despite decades of alleged efforts to diversify the workplace, the distribution of power and privilege continues to benefit white males.

Another study explored the white leader prototype to determine whether the association of whites with leadership was a function of cultural exposure or of white dominance (Hu et al., 2016). Chinese participants associated leadership with being Chinese rather than white, which supports the cultural exposure explanation and indicates that exposing individuals to a diverse set of leaders can reduce racial bias in leader prototypes. Communicators who are aware of the racialized history of the corporation and the processes of exclusion that has perpetuated can work to create equitable change (Logan, 2021).

> Breaking down barriers to the authentic adoption of DEI is vital for twenty-first-century communicators who want to take up the challenging, but rewarding, work of engaging in the kind of insider activism necessary to lead corporations to embrace one of their most important social responsibilities. (p. 13)

---

### Box 9.5

## John Raible's (2009) Revised Checklist for Allies Against Racism

The following is a sampling of items from Raible's checklist of behaviors that identify individuals as allies in the struggle against racism.

Part I includes ally behaviors demonstrating that an individual "gets it." Part 2 identifies problem areas and behaviors one should avoid in fighting racism.

**Part 1**

Think about how often and how consistently you exhibit the ally behaviors below.

_____ I continually educate myself about racism and multicultural issues.

_____ I can identify racism as it is happening.

_____ I use my privilege to communicate information from the dominant group to marginalized groups.

_____ I reach out to initiate personal contact with people of different races.

_____ I can accept leadership from people of color as well as from white people.

_____ I can relax, socialize, and feel at ease with people of color and with whites.

**Part 2**

The following are some problem areas where individuals sometimes get stuck. These were developed specifically for white individuals. Do any of these apply to you?

_____ I speak for people of color and attempt to explain their positions.

_____ I intellectualize about the struggle rather than live it daily.

_____ I wait for people of color to raise white people's awareness.

_____ I know fewer than five individual peers of color intimately (i.e., adults, not younger students or children)

These findings are consistent with several reports from various sources. Despite white males accounting for only 30% of the U.S. population, they constitute 62% of political officeholders (Villarreal, 2021), 79% of the directors of S&P 500 companies (Kurt, 2022), and 71% of engineers and architects (Fry et al., 2021), for example. This continued pattern of homogeneity in leadership in U.S. corporations sends a very clear message of a lack of commitment to diversity, equity, and inclusion. Successful interracial mentoring would be a start in changing perceptions; it would involve leaders in all institutions and organizations working aggressively with groups, interest groups, and concerned citizens to identify qualified candidates to succeed in a certain profession or industry. This would also require an allotment of financial resources and the development of long-term, sustainable programs designed to retain these

---

**BOX 9.6**                                                                **CASE STUDY**

### Interracial Communication Trailblazer

Dorthy Pennington is an associate professor of communications studies at the University of Kansas. In 1976, Jon Blubaugh and she published a trailblazing book, *Crossing Difference: Interracial Communication*, that included the importance of understanding power dynamics. Pennington has dedicated her career to research and teaching about how to overcome barriers to interracial and intercultural communication. She was interviewed about her perspective on racial unrest in spring 2020 in response to the police killing of George Floyd and public arguments around the false binary of Black Lives/All Lives Matter (Hellman, 2020). Throughout the interview, she stressed that there are "hot moments" or "precipitous moments" where mass media and society are consumed by interracial communication.

"People who are out there on the battlefront, so to speak, want practical answers that they can use in their organization, rather than something theoretical that needs to be further explained to them." Pennington suggests there are six things that can facilitate better race relations.

1. Identification with the other, thus crossing racial barriers

2. Having a spirit of goodwill (a predisposition for good, genuine race relations)

3. Knowledge, education, awareness, and information that help you understand the other person better

4. Ethic of caring (concern about other people's welfare)

5. Having adequate skills (knowing and doing what is necessary for cordial race relations)

6. A willingness to positively engage (being action-oriented, reaching out, taking the initiative in establishing and maintaining good race relations)

Pennington states that these are her "ways of bringing the races together." When asked if the commitment to racial justice will last, she explains that institutions and organizations will do their part due to EEOC mandates. She also notes that these places are using DEI language "as a way of coming to grips with the fact that that's what the world will require in a global marketplace."

diverse employees. It is imperative that these efforts be authentic and genu-ine—not "going through the motions" to project a progressive or performative image. Rather, the efforts must be driven by a commitment to welcome and nurture racially, ethnically, culturally, and ideologically diverse perspectives, thus enriching the overarching goals of workplaces.

## RACIALIZING THE ORGANIZATIONAL CONTEXT

Our discussion thus far has demonstrated how race is fluid in its produc-tion of meaning within an individual. We can see more clearly that our racial/ethnic identities become more salient or less salient as we go from one social context to another. This fluidity means organizations (as well as other public and private contexts) oftentimes face difficulty in adjusting to the diversity amongst their members. Both ingroup and outgroup members have qualita-tively different experiences that must be considered.

Corporate America, community-based organizations, and schools are insti-tutions that have recognized the significance of the racial diversity of their members and considered the degree to which the organizational context influ-ences organizational communication. Organizational communication can be complex because of the different work habits of employees and management and their respective individual identities. Weick (1979) argues that there are three specific organizational contexts that directly influence how members communicate: (1) the **physical context** is where the communication takes place (e.g., boss's office, employee lounge); (2) the **social context**, which is the relationship of the communicators (e.g., peers, leader/manager, supervisor/employee), and (3) **chronological context**—the role of time in influencing the interaction (e.g., morning vs. afternoon meetings). Communication processes are negotiated by members as they consider the effects of the different con-texts on their interpersonal interactions.

As we have noted, the U.S. population is becoming increasingly racially diverse, which will affect our relationships in both private and public spheres (see Chapters 1 and 10). Consider this example. Milagros is from Spain and accepted a job with a U.S. firm. Adjusting to her new culture was difficult because Spanish culture is very relaxed and tight-knit. Her new job was uncomfortable because her coworkers were very competitive and culturally insensitive. Eventually, Milagros decided it was less stressful to adapt to the new company and host culture. Although the company did not seem to embrace diversity, she accepted it and chose to learn the organization's culture without losing her Spanish heritage.

In this scenario, Milagros's coworkers and manager did not consider the potential problems of her transition into a new culture. They expected her to fit in and work to achieve the American Dream as they do, rather than volunteer-ing to help her adapt to the U.S. and company cultures. The organization seems resistant to adapting to demographic changes occurring throughout the indus-try. Although the company recruits BIPOC employees from the United States and abroad, the leadership and members of the organization do not seem genuine about creating an inclusive workplace environment. They seem concerned primarily with status, power, and interpersonal differences. The organization's hiring of diverse individuals means cultural and ethnic differences are a reality that may increase uncertainty for many. However, the organization must experience these growing pains to become a truly diverse organization.

For there to be meaningful change, the organization, its leadership, and its members must be authentic in their appreciation of racial/ethnic differences while working towards their organizational and individual professional goals. This means expending the resources for supporting its members as the organization redefines itself as authentically diverse. Organizational members must avoid perceiving and treating each other as if they are one-dimensional with a single identity. Racial/ethnic diversity can bring new, rich ideas to an organization that has traditionally been unidimensional. The organization and its members should not become so consumed by race that their mission and purpose fall by the wayside. Organizations must be sure their goals and attempts to diversify its members will work in concert with each other to improve its overall mission. In the following section, we discuss the influence of race/ethnicity on profit and nonprofit organizations.

## General Organizational Principles

Corporations and communities alike are now being forced to examine what image they are going to project to society as a whole. We have shifted our thinking from the melting pot metaphor to the salad bowl to reflect a more inclusive approach to diversity that nullifies the previous assimilationist approach. Others have chosen the rainbow or mosaic metaphors to describe various ethnicities working/living next to one another. These metaphors are important to our discussion of interracial communication within organizations because, as we have previously discussed, all aspects of our identities impact how we communicate with each other in the workplace.

## Practicing Diversity Management

Managing diversity in a constantly changing organizational culture is an essential skill. Despite the apparent need for equipping organization members with the knowledge to navigate a diverse workplace, organizations remain unprepared. Kecia Thomas, a coauthor of the article in Box 9.7, is an expert in the psychology of workplace diversity and diversity training. She argues that diversity management must begin with leaders who have a commitment to and place value on an inclusive workplace. To become change agents, leaders must engage in communication behaviors that support individuals in a diverse working environment. They must also be aware of double standards, microaggressions, and/or stereotypes that are barriers to competent communication between racial groups.

As a visionary for an organization, the leader must practice goal setting, framing, accountability, and readiness. Each stage in this process leads to a behavioral outcome reflective of adaptation and cultural sensitivity (K. Thomas & Davis, 2006). **Goal setting** involves establishing diversity goals that can be measured by relationships with minority communities within and outside of the organization. This also includes increasing mentoring relationships for more

---

| Box 9.7 | Research Highlight |
|---|---|

## Workplace Diversity

"When I look at you, I don't see color." "Oh, they had to fill a quota, and that's why we have so many Hispanics." These comments are all too common and capture the wide-ranging reactions people have to workplace diversity, race relations, or racially/ethnically different friends.

Recognizing the problem with this kind of worldview, Plaut et al. (2018) examined the implications of a colorblindness approach versus a multiculturalism approach. They define colorblindness as the minimization of the use and significance of racial group membership, suggesting that race should not and does not matter. Multiculturalism, in contrast, advocates that group membership matters and should be acknowledged, respected, and valued. The researchers looked at the approaches to determine the implications of each for stereotyping and prejudice, sensitivity to discrimination, intergroup interaction, and people's experiences with discrimination in institutions.

Whites are more likely to endorse colorblindness, which facilitates maintaining an egalitarian self-image. While the approach can represent a vision of an equitable society, it can also justify current inequalities. This means that people high in colorblindness are less sensitive to racism, which can result in being less attuned to the realities experienced by people of color.

The multicultural approach has strong support across groups but is more likely to be endorsed by microethnic (i.e., microcultural) than macroethnic (i.e., macrocultural) groups. Perceived threat is sometimes a problem. Diversity is frequently associated with nonwhite groups, which can result in macroethnic groups feeling excluded. Research suggests the multicultural perspective relates to less implicit and explicit prejudice than colorblindness. Employees of color who work in departments in which white coworkers hold multicultural attitudes feel more engaged and perceive less risk of bias.

The findings are nuanced in terms of whether avoiding or attending to race fosters or reduces discrimination. As noted above, both colorblindness and multiculturalism have negative aspects. The former can maintain current racial hierarchies and diminish sensitivity to racism. The latter has the potential to provoke threat in interracial interactions. In addition, highlighting diversity initiatives sometimes creates a deceptive impression of organizational fairness that undermines detection of discrimination.

The authors conclude their exploration with this question "If avoiding race increases inequality but attending to it incites resistance, how do we balance those concerns?" (Plaut et al., 2018, p. 204).

As these findings suggest, it is in the best interests of people from all ranks and racial/ethnic backgrounds to promote inclusive behaviors and policies. Fostering an open, supportive climate for all employees facilitates a focus on working toward a common good without diminishing differing individual experiences.

female and minority employees and increasing retention rates for minority managers with high potential. **Framing** requires leaders to positively and strategically present diversity to organization members as a learning opportunity, which may translate into learning new practices and markets that ultimately benefit the business. **Accountability**—the leader ensures that "human resource practices and decisions, such as those related to selection, promotion, and compensation, consider diversity goals and values" (p. 74); and **readiness**—"refers to leaders' understanding of the complexities of diversity in the organization and society . . . engag[ing] in self-exploration and, as a result, understand[ing] how privilege and ethnocentrism operate within their organizations and lives" (p. 75). In sum, leaders are expected to create an organizational culture and environment that is supportive of racial diversity and is an exemplar of workplace diversity.

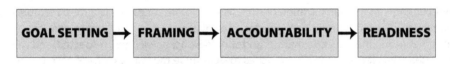

**Figure 9.1**   Diversity Management

Racial diversity can be achieved through proactive recruitment, which should be coupled with creating an inclusive working environment. Diversity and heterogeneity in recruitment ads is more attractive for female and minority job seekers than are homogeneous ads, whereas white males were indifferent toward both types of advertisements (K. Thomas & Davis, 2006). Another important factor in diversity management is diversity training and multicultural competence. Regardless of the impetus for diversity training (e.g., moral imperative, legal and social pressure, business necessity), the ultimate goal of racial and cultural sensitivity can be reached through training objectives that "provide knowledge, enhance self-awareness, change behavior, develop skills" (p. 77). In short, diversity training and workshops function as a form of intervention that ultimately prepares the organization and its members for change in the racial demographic. More pointedly, organizational members learn the skills and knowledge necessary for communicating competently and productively across racial lines, while achieving the goals of the organization.

Metaphors are frequently used in analyses of gender inequality in the workplace. The metaphor of a **glass ceiling** describes the barriers preventing women and people of color from advancing in the workplace, despite their qualifications or achievements. An article in 1992 used the metaphor of a **glass escalator** to describe the advantages for men in attaining leadership positions in professions predominantly populated by women (i.e., nursing, elementary school teaching, or social work). Two decades later, the author identified two major limitations of the concept—its failure to theorize race, sexuality, and

Box 9.8                                                          *Author Reflections*

## "Diversity Training" in the Workplace

In addition to my responsibilities as a university professor, I also am involved in various col-laborations with corporate, educational, health care, and community-based organizations. Most often, I work with these organizations to provide professional development opportu-nities related to diversity, inclusion, access, equity, and cultural competency for their mem-bers. Through this work, I attempt to utilize my expertise to enhance the ways in which people communicate in diverse settings. As you might expect, my focus is on having individ-uals understand the role that culture—race, ethnicity, age, gender, nationality, spirituality, ability, and sexual orientation—plays in communication. Working with organizations pro-vides a great opportunity to apply different theories and concepts to real-world contexts; it also allows me to stay current in terms of what's happening outside the walls of academia.

Working with various organizations on diversity-related issues, especially in the current sociopolitical climate, is important work. However, it is filled with a number of challenges. First, some organizations only engage in diversity training as a form of "window dressing." Sessions are typically not substantial (in terms of time, content, and quality); rather, they are frequently a means to an end (oftentimes to appease others). A second, related, challenge exists when the sessions are conducted without a visible commitment or strategic plan from organizational leadership. This results in a lack of incentive for participants to get involved and situates the issue as outside of the central mission of the organization (e.g., an add-on feature of less importance). Third, organizations want IDEA (Inclusion, Diversity, Equity, Access) engagement that provides easy answers to complex issues. In other words, they want a laundry list of "dos and don'ts"—something that facilitates cultural stereotypes and a false sense of security. A fourth challenge occurs when the organization only wants to focus on one aspect of diversity (e.g., race) without recognizing the need to address all aspects of diversity. This, as you will remember, goes against the idea of intersectionality explained in Chapter 5. Fifth, and finally, a challenge for providing effective diversity training exists when the focus is on eliminating personal biases. While this may be an important place to begin engaging participants, it does little to address institutional forms of oppres-sion that are oftentimes embedded within the organization itself (e.g., working toward an anti-racist organization).

Over the years, I have worked with some organizations whose efforts to provide profes-sional development opportunities to its organizational members were thwarted by some of the challenges identified here. Others have fearlessly confronted these issues and remain committed to addressing the tough issues related to race, ethnicity, and other salient aspects of identity. These are individuals who understand that the ability to communicate with diverse groups is vitally important to the future of the United States. Taking an entire course on interracial communication is a productive step to enhance your abilities. We hope, following graduation, you will join an organization that will provide additional oppor-tunities for professional development in this area.

—MPO

class (intersectionality) and outdated assumptions about traditional work organizations (C. Williams, 2013). The metaphor **concrete ceiling** (Davidson, 1997) underscores the intersectional bias that women of color face as they enter traditionally white and male organizational spaces. As Babers notes (2016), concrete has several qualities that make it even more problematic than glass as a barrier. Concrete is "practically impossible to break through by yourself," "impossible to see through," and has "no visible destination." A concrete ceiling signals a dead end; there is no visible path for escaping the current level. Although glass requires force and discomfort to break through, it can be shattered, and its transparency allows views of the next level. Women of color face unique barriers that prevent them from advancing. The advancement of nonwhite women is a perceived threat to those in power. Whether the motive is conscious or subconscious, barriers are erected to maintain the power imbalance in favor of whiteness that is a defining feature of much of U.S. and global society. This is also referred to as the **"black ceiling"** (Erskine et al., 2021) and defined as "attitudinal and organizational barriers that constrain Afro-Diasporic women from rising to senior leadership" (p. 39).

The ceiling metaphor has been applied to other groups as well, which is befitting of the pervasiveness of barriers to success amongst BIPOC in the workplace. The *bamboo ceiling* refers the disadvantages experienced by Asian individuals; the *stained-glass ceiling* is the barrier women confront in religious organizations, and the *celluloid ceiling* refers to the disadvantages of women in filmmaking (directing, writing, producing, editing, and cinematography). A metaphor linked to the effects of the various ceilings is *leaky pipeline*, which describes the decisions of employees to leave organizations because of structural barriers and lack of advancement opportunities.

Not surprisingly, most workplace cultures incorporate standards of professionalism defined by white, heterosexual men (Khosroshahi, 2021). Measures for performance reviews and for evaluating leadership qualities are centered on whiteness and masculinity. The first step in implementing an inclusive workplace is to recognize that how we hire and promote is often based on a certain prototype (M. Jackson & Rajai, 2021). The attributes sought for leaders— competitive, dominant, objective, self-confident, aggressive, ambitious—are overwhelmingly masculine. People of color do not match the measurements for leadership that were developed for white males. Women of color are at a double disadvantage; neither their race nor their gender match the prototype.

It is imperative that leaders must be aware of biases that result in glass or concrete ceilings. This is also true for Xerox, which has one of the most diverse workforces in the world. Its website claims diversity, inclusion, and belonging are essential parts of the company culture. It attributes innovative breakthroughs for its customers to the benefit of different ways of looking at their business because of the diversity of backgrounds and perspectives of its employees. Not only do customers benefit but also employees whose contributions result in feeling more engaged with their work. Since the 1960s, Xerox has encouraged independent caucus groups of employees. The groups incorporate self-advocacy and work with management to create an environment of inclusion and to achieve business objectives. In 2022, there were seven caucus groups established towards that end: African American, Latinx, Asian, women, African American women, LGBTQ+, and military veterans.

Thankfully, researchers identified three strategies companies and other institutions can use to adapt the organizational culture to its changing demographics (K. Thomas & Davis, 2006). The first strategy involves developing "communication structures [that allow] top leadership to hear underrepresented workers' voices" (p. 78), which might include formal coaching or mentoring of junior minority group members by senior members. For example, junior female engineers being mentored by senior executives in Xerox's Mentor Up Program received career advice and expanded networks while the executives learned about the conflicts women confront that can stifle their careers. Both mentor and protégé benefit from their interactions, and their experiences most likely will have a positive effect on the organization on a micro and macro level. The second strategy requires organization leaders to monitor all company materials and procedures to determine how racially sensitive and inclusive its efforts are in recruiting individuals from diverse racial and ethnic backgrounds. The third strategy involves the organization monitoring promotion policies and evaluating the process in terms of diversity outcomes. Employing these strategies requires a leadership team that is willing to make the investment to redefine itself and to allocate the necessary resources, time, and effort to create an authentically diverse and inclusive workplace. The strategies, strong leadership, and a high commitment level by organizational members can ultimately create an environment where BIPOC and all members feel supported by and connected to the company.

IBM has developed eight task forces (Asian, Black, Gay and Lesbian, Hispanic, Native American, People with Disabilities [PWD], white men, and women) composed of 15–20 executives representing each of IBM business segments. Task force members have in-depth, frank conversations about expectations of what is required of the company to make the group feel valued and welcome and to assist groups in maximizing their productivity, among other topics (D. Thomas & Kanji, 2017). IBM's efforts to diversify require buy-in from everyone and, more importantly, open and direct communication between employees and executives about how to create a truly inclusive work environment.

M. Jackson and Rajai (2021) have also contributed to this area of research by identifying three forms of cultural capital (knowledge, skills, abilities) of socially marginalized groups that can benefit organizations but are often unrecognized. *Resistance capital* consists of the skills people of color acquire through actively challenging inequality and oppressive systems. Employees with resistance capital can be valuable in changing the status quo and improving processes that may be hindering a company's growth. *Navigational capital* refers to the skills acquired because of the necessity to maneuver through social institutions that were not structured with communities of color in mind. POC who learn to navigate power structures can communicate those skills to others, increasing the retention of underrepresented talent. *Linguistic capital* is an accumulation of communication skills gained from interacting with individuals from other cultures and speaking multiple languages. Leaders and managers must be capable of establishing mutual understanding between different departments and employees. Linguistic capital facilitates communication between individuals who have different perspectives.

As we examine the salience of race within the workplace, we would be remiss not to discuss how European American males are dealing with racial/ethnic diversity. Do you assume that individuals who most benefit from existing systems are opposed to change? If you believe strongly in the idea that working hard will bring success, what happens when you see two equally qualified candidates for a job and a BIPOC applicant is hired instead of a European American applicant? Although you are in support of diversity, you are also concerned with how this is displacing others who are equally qualified for the same position.

Researchers conducted a national survey of 3,711 college-educated, heterosexual, professional, predominantly white men to examine both their attitudes toward and participation in their companies' diversity and inclusion (D&I) efforts (Kennedy & Jain-Link, 2020b). Only 10% thought D&I was not important; the researchers characterized this group as detractors. Persuadables, 48% of the sample, were those who said D&I was not very or was only somewhat important. Those who said D&I was very or extremely important were characterized as true believers—42% of the sample. The lead researcher commented that

> if corporate D&I professionals want to have more impact, [then] they should take a page from grassroots organizers by minimizing attention to the small percentage of men who are harsh critics, and instead nurture their base of support and the men who are persuadable. To do so, employers also need to reward and promote leaders who can build diverse, inclusive teams—showing this work is core to success at their organizations.

According to the findings, true believers have higher belonging scores than detractors, which are calculated by responses indicating feeling connected to, supported by, seen by, and proud to work at their organizations (Kennedy & Jain-Link, 2020a). The research suggests that higher belonging correlates with positive career outcomes such as engagement at work, willingness to recommend one's company as a good place to work, and feeling as though there are opportunities for advancement. Of men in top executive positions, 62% are true believers.

Given the support for D&I, why has there been little change? The research and anecdotal evidence tell us that there is a gap between belief and action. For example, fewer than half of true believers speak out when they see behavior demeaning to women, people of color, or LGBTQ individuals. Most have never attended an employee resource group for employees with a different background. Only 56% of true believers said they were involved with D&I efforts at their companies (Kennedy & Jain-Link, 2020a). The majority of men do not know how to support D&I. The reason most frequently cited for the lack of action was being too busy. That reason is shorthand for the belief that being active in DEI will not help in meeting business targets or in career advancement.

Kennedy and Jain-Link (2020a) suggest five ways to translate belief into action. First is to change reward structures so that inclusivity is a key factor in decisions about hiring, promotion, performance reviews, goal setting, and compensation. Second, senior leaders should build a more inclusive culture by prompting and engaging in conversations about sensitive topics like racism and sexism, modeling vulnerability, sharing their own experiences with bias, and encouraging true believers to communicate how incorporating different perspectives has helped advance their careers. Third, senior leads should create a culture of active allyship. Calling out microaggressions and intervening should be the norm rather than standing silent during discriminatory, intolerant incidents. Training to recognize the norms of white male culture that can exclude others helps develop an understanding of prejudice and privilege. Fourth, higher ups should encourage leaders to connect with individuals from underrepresented groups by, for example, serving as a sponsor for an employee resource group. Fifth, they should focus on the positive. Focus time and attention on individuals who accept D&I rather than on those who do not. Policies should ensure that detractors do not undermine underrepresented employees, but energies should be directed elsewhere. Shifting D&I from the periphery to the core of company operations "will take time, persistence, and learning new skills. But if inclusivity shifts from 'extracurricular' to 'core requirement' for leadership, we can meet the promises we've made to drive equity in our companies and in our world."

Our racial/ethnic identities are central to how we define ourselves, and that means we must be sensitive to how they influence our communicative experiences. The cultural context of communication is so extensive that people often are unaware of different subjective experiences of identity and communication patterns (Littlejohn et al., 2021). As such, for competent communication, we must be aware of different interests and perspectives. If we recognize and accept our differences—and are willing to adapt to difference—we will experience better understanding and better outcomes from interactions.

It is important to remember that the ability to communicate competently with others whose backgrounds and experiences may differ from ours builds relationships and supports mutual goal achievement. Recall the discussion of anxiety/uncertainty management in Chapter 6. Challenge yourself to leave your comfort zone. Chapter 6 also reviewed face-negotiation theory. Recall that the theory provides a framework for understanding how larger cultural dimensions impact communication choices. Individuals constantly negotiate their public image—how we want others to see us and how we treat others. Think about how you *really* interact with racially/ethnically different others. Do you understand their expectations? Remember, the other person may be thinking about you in the same way and may be unsure how to interact with you.

Effective communication refers to the exchange of messages that results in maximum understanding (Littlejohn et al., 2021). Mindfulness involves being aware of communication styles and strategies. Mindful individuals are aware of differences and adapt to the values, rules, and identities of others. They display a willingness to shift to new perspectives. All individuals seek security, inclusion, predictability, connection, and consistency. Skills in negotiating identities in interactions include careful observation, listening, empathy, politeness, reframing and collaboration. "Effective identity negotiation is present when both parties feel understood, respected, and valued" (p. 412). Identity shifting is a form of identity negotiation and involves changing language, behaviors, and perspectives to fit a particular organizational context. In other words, it can be a coping or a strategic strategy.

One aspect of managing diversity and inclusiveness is empowering/enabling employees (Itam & Bagali, 2018). Empowerment involves an individual or group having power, authority, or influence over events and outcomes important to them. Earlier, we mentioned the theory of corporate colonization in which the interests of the organization dominate the interests of the individual. Such an organization engages in legitimation, which privileges the management perspective. Habermas proposed a very different situation; in the ideal speech situation, the discourses of all members are legitimized in open dialogue (Littlejohn et al., 2021). Organizations that embrace D&I recognize that they need people who can interact competently with others. Encouraging and modeling strong communication skills is one means of empowering employees. This also requires leaders to assess their own communication to identify areas that need improvement. To empower employees, leaders should ask questions, communicate attention, discuss mistakes by providing positive feedback, and acknowledge success. Encouraging employees to develop strong communication skills will help them become better advocates for their ideas. The ability to capture attention increases the opportunities for employees to be heard. Through all of these efforts, employees who feel empowered will be more engaged with their organization.

As we can see, leaders/managers are responsible for assessing the effects of interactions between employees from diverse racial/ethnic groups and those in the majority and engaging organizational members in open communication about potential conflict as well as their roles in the organization. Because corporate America continually faces the urgency of racial/ethnic diversity, it is imperative that managers make a concerted effort to foster a positive social climate conducive to competent communication across racial borders. More importantly, the interpersonal communication skills and relationships developed between racially/ethnically different organizational members must become, and remain, a top priority.

## CONCLUSION

This chapter examined the significance of race within the workplace. Although efforts are being made to prepare corporate America, educational systems, and communities for racial diversity in traditionally European American contexts, people from all sides of the racial/ethnic divide have feelings of apprehension and discomfort. The good news, however, is that people are taking the initiative to improve race relations on both a micro- and macrolevel. In corporate America, we see that administrators and employees alike are struggling with this change in the environment. Although microcultural racial/ethnic group members face barriers to advancement, administrators are actively dealing with this glass ceiling and its effect on the overall well-being of its new organizational members. In our educational systems, students, faculty, and administrators are developing and creating programs and organizations that value the multiple identities of *all* students. Instead of making these students tokens, organizational members collectively celebrate racial/ethnic diversity through learning opportunities in and outside of the classroom.

Diversity-training programs are a method for increasing racial sensitivity and race consciousness. One challenge for diversity management is the promotion of more competent interracial communication. As the United States becomes increasingly diverse, both racially and ethnically, we must use our membership in different organizations to become social agents of change.

## KEY TERMS

| | |
|---|---|
| human relations theory | social context |
| REAL framework for action | chronological context |
| organizational culture | goal setting |
| politically responsive constructionist theory of communication (PRCT) | framing |
| | accountability |
| multiracial unity living experience program (MRULE) | readiness |
| | glass escalator |
| generalizing race | glass ceiling |
| localizing race | concrete ceiling |
| alluding to race | black ceiling |
| physical context | |

## RECOMMENDED CONTEMPORARY READINGS

Chancellor, R. L. (2019). Racial battle fatigue: The unspoken burden of Black women faculty in LIS. *Journal of Education for Library & Information Science, 60*(3), 182–189. https://doi.org/10.3138/jelis.2019-0007

Darling-Hammond, S., Lee, R. T., & Mendoza-Denton, R. (2020). Interracial contact at work: Does workplace diversity reduce bias? *Group Processes & Intergroup Relations, 24*(7), 1114–1131. https://doi.org/10.1177/1368430220932636

Dickens, D. D., Womack, V. Y., & Dimes, T. (2019). Managing hypervisibility: An exploration of theory and research on identity shifting strategies in the workplace among Black women. *Journal of Vocational Behavior, 113,* 153–163. https://doi.org/10.1016/j.jvb.2018.10.008

Everbach, T., Batsell, J., Champlin, S., & Nisbett, G. S. (2019). Does a more diverse newspaper staff reflect its community? A print and digital content analysis of the Dallas morning news. *Southwestern Mass Communication Journal, 34*(1), 1–18.

Kornbluh, M., Johnson, L., & Hart, M. (2021). Shards from the glass ceiling: Deconstructing marginalizing systems in relation to critical consciousness development. *American Journal of Community Psychology, 68*(1/2), 187–201.

Linares, C. E. (2018). Latinos first generation in the workplace: Perception of diversity and inclusion. *SAM Advanced Management Journal* (07497075), *83*(4), 54–60.

Paluck, E. L., Green, S. A., & Green, D. (2018). The contact hypothesis re-evaluated. *Behavioral Public Policy, 3*(2), 129–158. https://doi.org/10.1017/bpp.2018.25

Pitts, B. (2021). "Uneasy lies the head that wears a crown": A critical race analysis of the CROWN Act. *Journal of Black Studies, 52*(7), 716–735. https://doi.org/10.1177/00219347211021096

## OPPORTUNITIES FOR EXTENDED LEARNING

1. Visit the website of a company that provides products or services most people use and has a good reputation with consumers. What does the company identify as its core goals, values, and mission? Does it have a diversity management program in place? Search the website for diversity statements that may have been issued during summer 2020 and search the internet for any public responses. How committed to diversity does the company seem to be? What are the company's diversity goals? How realistic are they in creating an inclusive environment that goes beyond hiring diverse organizational members?

2. There has been a lot of debate about cancel culture being an extreme response to a company that has engaged in offensive or inappropriate behavior. The solution has been to "call out" the offender, expect a public apology, and vow economic consequences for the company. Do a search of companies that have been "cancelled." Focus on four, and (a) identify the questionable act, (b) identify the targeted audience, (c) explain the behavior's connection to racism, ethnocentrism, or prejudice, and (d) describe what the cancellation entailed. From your research, create an argument either for or against cancel culture and a solution(s) addressing company responsibility for addressing systemic racism.

3. In 1961, President John F. Kennedy issued Executive Order 10925, which decreed affirmative action as: The contractor will take affirmative action to ensure that applicants are employed, and that employees are treated during employment, without regard to their race, creed, color, or national origin. How does the definition compare to public perceptions? Compare and contrast how the definition creates dissonance for people who are either in support of or opposed to "leveling the playing field." Discuss as a class how affirmative action is still needed to provide BIPOC and physically challenged people equal access to opportunities traditionally denied to them.

4. Do an internet search for diversity resistance. After reading the articles you find, create two separate lists: one that includes 5 specific strategies that might cause resistance and 5 that could alleviate discomfort with workplace diversity. The list should involve strategies that create a climate that discourages hostile communication, fosters emotional and psychological support, and encourages interracial relationships between a variety of racial and ethnic groups in the workplace. As a class, create a Google doc so that you have a compilation of these strategies to consult for an in-class discussion on this topic. The discussion will include an assessment of how realistic, appropriate, and effective each strategy is. Be ready to provide suggestions for how the strategies can be modified to reach company goals.)

5. In communities of color, members sometimes clash with outgroup business owners operating within those communities. Search the internet for instances of such conflicts. Were there long-standing racial tensions? Did a specific event trigger open conflict? How have businesses responded? How are ethics and economics at odds with each other? How much should business owners and communities compromise to coexist? What effective strategies have been used and brought about healing? Having done the research, reflect on the effort and commitment that individuals must have if empathy, perspective-taking, and healing are to occur across racial lines.

6. Find a local business that seems to target certain racial/ethnic groups in the community or on your campus. Choose a business that you do not frequent or would have no personal need to visit. For example, if you are Latinx, then do not go the local mercado. Go to the business and make general observations of the people, products, and services provided as well as the overall setup. After leaving, immediately write down your field notes. Be sure to list the feelings you had about being in the minority in that situation and what that experience says about services targeting certain populations.

# 10

# Interracial Conflict

**CASE STUDY**   **Un-Fair Campaign on White Privilege Continues**

In January 2012, 15 community organizations partnered to launch the Un-Fair Campaign to address homogeneity in Duluth, Minnesota. Campaign members were very uncomfortable because people of color were not choosing to live in Duluth. The campaign drew attention to white privilege through the use of posters, billboards, speakers, and community events (Kraker, 2012). The goal of the campaign was to call attention to racial disparity in a city that was 90% white.

Members prioritized deep dialogue about white privilege and the causes of and solutions for racism. Organizers of the campaign noted that white people do not see privilege, and the first step is to make the problem visible. The Un-Fair Campaign is unique because it expects members to combat racism actively rather than passively identifying discrimination without taking action.

The Un-Fair Campaign regained nationwide attention in 2020 (Minneapolis Egotist, 2020). The campaign chose to take a very visible activist stance in protest of police brutality and the murders of George Floyd and Breonna Taylor. Images on billboards and posters (see https://tinyurl.com/3zawya7b) were of white faces with handwritten notes about white privilege scrawled across them. Some of the phrases on foreheads state, "It's hard to see racism when you're white," "Is white skin really fair skin?" and "I'm lucky to be white." Also written on the faces are explanations of whiteness and challenges to actively working against racism. The motto that weaves all of the images together is, "If you see racism, SPEAK up. Break the silence." The campaign continues to raise awareness of white privilege and encourage transformative activism by white people who can use their societal privilege to make a change.

How successful do you believe Un-Fair is in educating people about racism? How can initiatives like this prevent interracial conflict and promote interracial communication? How can people with societal power and privilege benefit from actively being involved in these efforts? What other similar organizations were formed because of the racial unrest of 2020?

In August 2016 then-San Francisco 49ers quarterback Colin Kaepernick and teammate Eric Reid knelt during the playing of the U.S. national anthem to bring attention to racial inequality and police brutality. They triggered a furor in the National Football League (NFL) and beyond. Reid (2017) said he was disturbed by "the incredible number of unarmed Black people being killed by the police." The killing of Alton Sterling in Reid's hometown of Baton Rouge, Louisiana, was even more personal because his family members still lived in the area. He became committed to doing something he believed was "respectful as possible." Although Kaepernick twice previously sat on the bench during the national anthem in protest over police brutality, neither Reid nor the news media noticed until the third game of the preseason. Backlash ensued. Reid and Kaepernick discussed how they could make a more powerful and positive impact. They spoke with Nate Boyer, a former NFL player and retired Green Beret, who suggested that kneeling was a respectful gesture. On September 1 before the final preseason game, Reid and Kaepernick knelt during the anthem. Reid compared kneeling to a flag being flown at half-mast to mark a tragedy. This landmark gesture catapulted race and race relations into the public sphere in very necessary yet complicated ways.

Reid (2017) expressed dismay that their protest was misconstrued as unpatriotic and disrespectful to the military, saying it was exactly the opposite. He and Kaepernick wanted to ensure that *all* people live in a fair and free society, which includes the right to protest. He remains heartbroken over the barrage of slurs against Kaepernick whom he considers courageous for seeking change on important issues. Remaining silent while unarmed Black persons are shot or when opinions are expressed that racism ended years ago and there is no white privilege was not an option for Kaepernick and Reid. Their protests focused attention on the racism that is in every part of our public and private lives, regardless of our race. Athletes in England (Axson, 2021), Tokyo, and New Zealand (R. Harris, 2021) have followed suit and are using their platforms to bring attention to racism by also "taking a knee."

Interracial conflict and tensions are nothing new in the United States, and neither is athlete activism against racism. At the 1968 Olympics in Mexico City, U.S. runners Tommie Smith and John Carlos "famously raised their fists in a Black Power salute" during the national anthem (Godin, 2020). The iconic picture capturing this courageous moment in history has come to represent the persistent racial divide in the United States. What is rarely discussed is that the medals Smith and Carlos earned were stripped away upon their return home. Conflict can result when an athlete holds views that differ from those of fans (Frisby, 2018). Since the August 2014 fatal shooting of unarmed, 18-year-old Michael Brown by a police officer in Ferguson, Missouri, athletes have been more active. Players for the St. Louis Rams walked on the field in the physical stance of "Hands up, don't shoot," which had become the protest chant after Brown's death. NBA players wore shirts saying "I can't breathe," the phrase uttered by Eric Garner before his death as the result of a police officer placing him in a choke hold for selling untaxed cigarettes on a New York sidewalk in July 2014. On May 25, 2020, George Floyd used the same words to plead with the Minneapolis police officer who planted a knee on his neck for 8 minutes and 46 seconds, ultimately killing him. Floyd unknowingly used a counterfeit $20 bill to buy cigarettes at a neighborhood convenience store in Minneapolis (Bogel-Burroughs & Wright, 2021). Despite the mounting tensions and threat of social isolation and death threats (Freeman, 2016), professional and high school athletes and their allies have chosen very visible and vocal ways to contribute to social justice and to foster interracial dialogue about this very pressing social issue.

Recognizing this communication phenomenon, communication researchers have conducted research on race in sports, with particular attention given to the language used by sportscasters to describe athletes and, more recently, the NFL's response to athlete activism. The findings reflect how we are socialized to think about and respond to racial differences. Denham et al. (2002) found that newscasters focused on the body size, natural athleticism, and strength of successful African Americans, and they focused on the intelligence, work ethic, and commitment to training of successful European Americans. These findings were consistent with the Foy and Ray (2019) study where they analyzed comments by announcers during NCAA basketball tournaments. Announcers were more likely to discuss the performance and mental abilities of lighter-skinned players and the physicality and athleticism of darker-skinned players.

Jason Lopez (2021) has broadened the scope of research on this issue by critiquing the NFL's "post-hoc" approach to its stance on athlete activism. As a multimedia brand, it was forced to respond to the opposing sides on the issue. Former President Trump's race-fueled reaction was to call all protesting athletes a "'son of a bitch' deserving to be fired." Nevertheless, athletes persisted in their commitment to standing up for what was right. The NFL's stance vacillated from supporting to condemning to co-opting the protests by players, thereby complicating the issue and impeding progress toward social justice. What are your thoughts on athlete activism? Are athletic events appropriate places for protests? If these platforms should not be used to address racism and other social issues, then what else can athletes do to reach large numbers of people?

Communication scholars have studied social conflicts for more than 30 years. This chapter draws from that research with a particular focus on interracial/interethnic conflict. Conflict is "the perceived and/or actual incompatibility of values, expectations, processes, or outcomes between two or more parties . . . over substantive and/or relational issues" (Ting-Toomey, 2000, p. 388). **Interracial conflict** is conflict between members of different races (i.e., African American/Asian American) and **interethnic conflict** is conflict between members of different ethnic groups (i.e., Cuban American/Puerto Rican American). The communication used in these interactions profoundly impacts conflict, in that it can either ease or create conflict. In either case, communication is the means for productive or destructive management of conflict (Hocker et al., 2022).

**Box 10.1**                                                    *Author Reflections*

### Racism Is Alive and Well

In October of 2001, I experienced a tense, horrific experience as a guest speaker for the Interfraternity Council (IFC). Around 1,000 male and female pledges were required to attend a monthly educational workshop, and I was asked to speak about interracial communication. I was totally unprepared for how the students responded to my message. Despite my conversational approach to such a sensitive topic, the students were hostile, which may have been due, in part, to their anger about the terrorist attacks one month earlier. Throughout my talk, students were mumbling inappropriate comments and demonstrating a great deal of resistance and anger towards me. The Q&A afterwards was incredibly uncomfortable.

At the conclusion of the event, the student who invited me hugged me and apologized profusely in my ear while we were on the stage. A few other IFC organization members apologized as well, including two female students who acted as "messengers" for friends characterized as too ashamed and humiliated to do so themselves. I graciously accepted their apologies. My students in attendance were livid that someone would speak to their professor that way and display such racist and prejudiced beliefs about African American, Arab American, and other racial/ethnic groups.

For my students and those willing to learn, the night's lessons were that racism is alive and well and racism needs to be actively addressed in the moment. Several of them, along with some IFC members, filed formal complaints with the Office of Greek Life. These students were willing to use their privilege and voices to hold IFC accountable for its behavior. All organizations were sanctioned by having a social taken away for the semester and being required to attend a series on racial awareness. I am not sure how effective either punishment was, but it was necessary to address the organization's behavior formally because it violated the university's Student Code of Conduct.

—TMH

Research on interracial and interethnic conflict is a rapidly growing area of study, and rightfully so. When racial and ethnic differences are present, they can complicate the conflict, although they do not have to. In this chapter, we provide background on the sources of conflict, different conflict styles, and barriers contributing to interracial conflict. We conclude by offering practical examples of how individuals and groups can create interracial unity and avoid interracial conflict.

## CONTEXTUAL SOURCES OF CONFLICT

Interracial/ethnic conflict is a dynamic process; any one episode is typically the result of multiple sources of conflict. In short, conflict simultaneously involves personal and cultural issues (Lawton et al., 2013). In order to

In interracial conflict, it is important to determine if the source of the conflict is a content issue or if it is directly related to racial or cultural differences.

understand how conflict often becomes racialized, we will first discuss various sources of interracial/ethnic conflict. We will also explore how anxiety, ingroup/outgroup tensions, relational conflict, interpersonal violence, perceptual differences, and stereotyping can fan the flames of contention between groups and make interracial communication difficult to manage.

## Contemporary Social Inequality

As discussed in Chapter 2, the United States is no stranger to ingroup/outgroup tensions. These tensions remain a part of our contemporary existence and continue to preserve present-day social inequality. History provides context for some interracial and interethnic conflict. In a capitalist society such as the United States, people find themselves competing for limited resources. Social inequalities—in terms of health, housing, employment, income, and education—exist and become a key source of frustration. Those tensions were heightened by the coronavirus pandemic that began in 2020. The world economy plummeted as global health was compromised. Competition increased for resources that became scarce, and businesses were shuttered. The pandemic also triggered racial discrimination against people of Asian descent (Addo, 2020). The Trump administration fueled the racism by calling the coronavirus the "Wuhan virus" or "China virus." Long-held negative perceptions of Asian Americans were unleashed, resulting in xenophobia, racism, and hate crimes targeted at Asian Americans and Pacific Islanders (AAPI) (Tessler et al., 2020).

The Stop AAPI Hate coalition began on March 19, 2020, in response to the escalation in xenophobia and bigotry during the COVID-19 pandemic. The organization tracks incidents of hate, violence, and harassment against Asian Americans and Pacific Islanders in the United States (Yellow Horse et al., 2021). From March 19, 2020, to December 31, 2021, the organization received reports of 10,905 hate incidents—63% for verbal harassment, 16.2% for physical assault, and 16.1% for deliberate avoidance (shunning). Chinese Americans reported the most hate incidents (42.8%) followed by Korean Americans (16.1%), Filipino Americans (8.9%), Japanese Americans (8.2%), and Vietnamese Americans (8%). Women reported 61.8% of the incidents.

Marginalized groups (most often people of color) in the United States remain victim to social beliefs denying the existence of social inequality. The United States remains divided in terms of the "haves" and the "have-nots," a division oftentimes occurring along racial lines. Inequities in employment, housing, health care, police protection, and the justice system are systemic and maintained by ideologies justifying them as being biological, which some call social Darwinism (Rudman & Saud, 2020). Crandall and Eshleman (2005) describe **social Darwinism** as an ideology in which hierarchies that prioritize the mistreatment of groups deemed "inferior" are necessary in order to "improv[e] the human race through natural selection. In this way, prejudice and discrimination are not only acceptable but inevitable, necessary, natural, and *moral*" (p. 250).

Intergroup competition already exists, and scarce resources escalate intergroup tensions. For example, research reveals a somewhat tenuous relationship between African Americans and Korean immigrants (Lang, 2020). In contexts with high tensions, groups view each other as a threat, placing strain on face-to-face interactions such as Korean immigrant retailers and African American customers. Social inequality shapes the context in which such interracial encounters occur. Other intergroup tensions involve Latinx employees of Korean-owned stores (NPR, 2020). Labor exploitation is the crux of the problem. Similar social inequalities have shaped the tensions between Blacks and Latinx people. The histories of the groups are linked "by parallel but not identical histories of labor exploitation, housing segregation, and cultural demonization. Yet while sharing the experiences of containment and confinement, Black and Brown people have also been continually pitted against one another" (G. Johnson, 2013, p. ix).

Both conflict and coalition have been present in relationships between the groups. Solidarity between Latinx and Blacks can occur (Terriquez & Milkman, 2021) when the groups work together toward managing conflicts. We live in a society that constantly mobilizes the resentment and anger of powerless people against each other, recruiting them into rounds of blaming and shaming that leave the real causes of their problems unaddressed. Racial groups have also been socialized to view other BIPOC as a threat to their own group's success, thus supporting the narrative that intergroup communication and peaceful coexistence is impossible. Not surprisingly, people pitted against each other will not magically unite simply because they are both oppressed (G. Johnson, 2013); rather, they must find a common cause that unites them and identify ways to address the issue that will benefit everyone. It is important to stress that all interracial interactions do not reach the level of violence and hostility witnessed on news outlets and social media, but they are a reminder of how important mutual understanding and cultural competence are in ingroup/outgroup interactions.

## Anxiety

Interpersonal interactions, in general, can be stress-inducing, and one's stress level may increase when interacting with an outgroup member. Stereotypes can make people anxious, whether they are being stereotyped or are stereotyping others. A common stereotype is that white people are prejudiced. In interracial interactions, white participants may experience anxiety that they will confirm the stereotype, while Black participants may be anxious about being the target of prejudice (Babbitt et al., 2018). Anxiety or a fear of being perceived as prejudiced or racist can influence communication in interactions. Interracial roommate pairs (whites and ethnic minorities) experience significantly more stress about appearing racist than do same-race roommate pairs (Shelton et al., 2010). Research has found that, as cues from one roommate feeling anxious increased over time, the other roommate was less likely to respond positively, which can also happen in other social contexts. Fear of being offensive may cause awkward interactions. A similar study found that white roommates who lived with an other-race roommate for four months had more diverse friends and believed diversity was more important than did white participants with a white roommate (Gaither & Sommers, 2013). Another study with similar findings informed intervention group participants that people tend to avoid interracial interactions because of anticipated anxiety but that engaging in interracial interactions could reduce future feelings of anxiety (Schultz et al., 2015). Participants in a control group received no guidance. Participants from both groups were asked to choose a Black or white interaction partner. Consistent with other research, intervention group participants were more likely to choose to interact with a Black partner, and they exhibited more positive nonverbal engagement during the interracial interaction.

Littleford et al. (2005) used a more applied approach by observing dyadic interracial and same-race interactions between whites, Blacks, and Asians and concluded that whites had more discomfort with ethnic minority partners than with white partners. As whites became less comfortable, they compensated by increasing the positive feelings they had toward Black partners and decreasing the positive feelings they had toward white partners. As their comfort decreased, they felt less positive when paired with white partners but did not change their feelings in interracial encounters with Black or Asian partners. When experiencing discomfort in interracial encounters, women increased their friendliness while men decreased theirs. For these participants, anxiety came from the stress of potential negative consequences, such as feeling embarrassed, being exploited by outgroup members, fear of rejection, or negative evaluations by others. This is also referred to as self-image threat (Harber et al., 2010). Another cause of anxiety is the teacher/student dynamic in interracial interactions (T. M. Harris, 2017). When discussing race-related topics, there may be an assumption that individuals who have suffered discrimination will assume the responsibility for teaching about their microculture and related experiences. As discussed in Chapter 8, the expectation that BIPOC will assume the role of educator is an emotional burden that should be avoided in interracial interactions and relationships.

Virtual reality (VR) is a new context for the exploration of interracial interactions, whether in virtual classrooms, online medical consultations, multiplayer games, or interracial romantic relationships (as discussed in chapter 7). While VR provides a digital space for practicing how to become a more competent communicator with outgroup members, individuals bring their prejudices with them into virtual spaces. These social interactions replicate real-world norms and behaviors (Taylor et al., 2020). Observations of participants in virtual spaces show that they experience discomfort and avoidance, engage in less eye contact, and maintain greater physical distance between themselves and outgroup members. The researchers argue that most VR study participants are white and have biases and discriminate against Black, dark-skinned, or ethnic-minority appearing avatars. These findings stress the need for greater intergroup contact by increasing racial/ethnic representation among VR developers and researchers. Other recommendations for evidence-based practices include: listening to and believing racial/ethnic minorities' reports of racial microaggressions; requirements that developers and users complete VR cultural competence, diversity, inclusion, and equity training; and the provision of opportunities for users to deliver anonymous feedback to those with societal power "without fear of repercussions" (p. 136).

## Hate Crimes

In some instances, interracial conflict can escalate to the point of physical violence. **Hate crime** is criminal behavior against an individual or property motivated by bias regarding ethnicity, gender, sexual orientation, disability, religion, or nationality. Hate crimes are extreme forms of interracial conflict. In one recent incident, a white woman purposely drove her SUV into a group of Black and Latinx children (P. Jones & Sahouri, 2021). There are numerous examples of behavior motivated by bias, and while some of the biased behavior will not escalate to the level of criminal behavior and hate crimes, the conflict is damaging nonetheless. Recent examples include high school basketball players throwing tortillas at rival Hispanic players (Mendoza, 2021); a Black a man, his son, and his Black realtor being handcuffed and guns drawn on them by police officers while house hunting (Yancey-Bragg, 2021); country singer Morgan Wallen yelling the n-word (Paulson, 2021); phone recordings of ESPN reporter Rachel Nichols berating Black reporter Maria Taylor (L. Reyes, 2021); and ESPN personality Stephen A. Smith's public criticism of Japanese baseball star Shohei Ohtani for not speaking English (Gardner, 2021).

Another aspect of hate crimes is grievances (whether real or perceived) that create explosive conditions leading to violence (United Nations, 2022). This is more evident due to social media, which is a significant driver of hate speech. Microculture members are increasingly targeted as "other" or as threats, and when there is intergroup communication online, it can be hostile and confrontational, thus predicting future offline violence (Gallacher, 2021). Conflicts are often fueled by misunderstanding and fear in physical areas undergoing change, such as gentrification or an influx of immigrants (Commission on Human Relations, n.d.), and can occur in schools or in the community. Conflicts can be addressed by prioritizing education and increasing channels of communication to help parties understand the other person's point of view are strategies to prevent violence. Competent interracial communication cannot completely solve these issues, but it is a starting point. If competently practiced early in life, then it can prevent interracial conflict from occurring and encourage people to work through their racial/ethnic differences.

## Intimate/Interpersonal Partner Violence (IPV)

As discussed in Chapter 7, stigmas associated with interracial romantic relationships cause conflict for the partners. People think the partners have low self-esteem, are rebelling against parents or society, or are exploring sexual myths. In short, these relationships have been stigmatized as "culturally suspect" due to racial differences (Brummett, 2017, p. 772). Further complicating matters is the conflicting research on **intimate/interpersonal violence** (IPV) in interracial and intraracial relationships. A longitudinal study involving a national U.S. sample of 10,110 participants found mutual IPV (i.e., both partners contribute) higher for interracial couples and monoracial Black couples than for white monoracial couples (B. Martin et al., 2013). Their findings suggest external stressors such as "negative responses from others and lack of acceptance from neighbors and the community" were catalysts for the IPV (p. 7). Another IPV study of 2,681 interracial couples from the United States and Canada found that interracial relationships had higher odds of IPV occurring compared to intraracial relationships (Brownridge et al., 2021). The risk factors were attributed to partner characteristics, such as young age, drug use, and jealous behavior, thus dispelling the myth of IPV being a natural or inevitable part of interracial relationships. As discussed in Box 8.3, Field et al. (2015) also used comparative data from the United States and Canada (1,174 university students) and found no differences between interracial and intraracial couples and reports of violence.

Collectively, the findings are contradictory yet consistent with past research on IPV. IPV happens in both interracial and intraracial relationships but should not be considered a natural part of relationships. In order to destigmatize IPV, researchers need to gather more information from interracial couples about motivations for and causes of such behavior. Findings might also speak to the negative impact family, friends, neighbors, and others have on either or both partners and the relationship.

## Ingroup/Outgroup Tensions

Perceptions and interpretations we have of others and who we believe them to be are affected by complex and nuanced cultural identities. As a result, interactions between individuals with different backgrounds and experiences have the potential for conflict. It is important to recognize that distinctive group identities, animosities, and category-based prejudices frame how we understand our differences (Glenn, 2019). While our interactions are not wholly negative or conflict-ridden, "[w]e need to develop greater awareness of the ways we deal with each other. We need skillful communication promoting mutual understanding, nonviolent conflict management, relationship enrichment, and tolerance for distinctive identity expression" (p. 54).

Much like conflict in our personal relationships, intergroup conflict is persistent, pervasive, and takes many forms—from the discrimination, prejudice, and stereotypes of daily life to the horrors of war and terrorism. However, intergroup conflict is very different because it is a multilevel phenomenon involving perceptions, emotions, individual behavior, and historical context.

> Whether actual or imagined, the perception that outgroup members constitute a threat to ingroup members' interests or survival creates a circumstance in which identification and interdependence with the ingroup are directly associated with fear and hostility toward the threatening outgroup. (Halevy & Cohen, 2019, p. 163)

---

**BOX 10.2**                                                            *CASE STUDY*

### Truth, Racial Healing, and Transformation

The W. K. Kellogg Foundation has collaborated with local communities and scholars throughout the country to design a program for racial healing on a national level. The program addresses interracial conflict on an interpersonal, communal, institutional, and judicial level. Plans for developing what became the Truth, Racial Healing, and Transformation (TRHT) process started in 2016 and involved the company partnering with leaders, scholars, community members, and organizations to develop the TRHT framework. The goal of the framework and process is to provide communities with the resources for facilitating healing and to create actionable change. This group also created an Implementation Guidebook and a series of discussions designed to educate communities about how racial hierarchies come into existence and what they can do to block them.

The program's areas of emphasis are narrative change, racial healing, relationship building, separation, the law, and economy. Narrative change examines "how to create and distribute new complex and complete narratives in entertainment, journalism, digital and social media, school curricula, museums, monuments and parks and in the way we communicate that can influence people's perspectives, perceptions and behaviors about and towards one another." Racial healing and relationship building involve healing past wounds and establishing mutual respect to "build trusting intergenerational and diverse community relationships that better reflect our common humanity."

Separation, law, and economy are systemic approaches to racism. They involve communities addressing difficult topics such as segregation, colonization and concentrated poverty in neighborhoods, identifying discriminatory laws and policies, and gaining knowledge about structured inequality and barriers leading to racial economic disparities. Ultimately, these efforts will lead to collaboration on solutions for equity in all areas of society.

Source: W. K. Kellogg Foundation. https://healourcommunities.org/

People opposing immigration argue undocumented immigrants are draining the economy, while supporters say they are integral to the economy. Opposers fear that jobs, as a limited resource, are being taken away from U.S. workers. Supporters believe undocumented immigrants accept jobs U.S. citizens are unwilling to do. Regardless of one's position, the sociopolitical climate continues to reveal deep-seated tensions between racial/ethnic groups that need to be both acknowledged and addressed. We provide a brief review of the history of these tensions in the United States to illustrate the range of situations in which conflict can occur.

Domination, slavery, colonization, and military conquests are a part of U.S. history. This systemic oppression created tensions that continue to impede positive relations between whites and different racial and ethnic groups. The long history of mistreatment, discrimination, and racism has fostered a general sense of mistrust and suspicion of whites among some communities of color (Babbitt et al., 2018). At times, individual knowledge of the history of mistreatment of one group at the hands of another increases the negativity between racial and ethnic groups, which can trigger conflict. In addition, conflict can result when community residents perceive an influx of new racial/ethnic groups as threats (Summers 2021). The majority group may feel their economic and social privileges are threatened, which has been the case for some whites and Blacks regarding the economic power of Asian Americans. The end result is increased ingroup/outgroup tension, which typically results in greater communication apprehension during interracial interactions.

As mentioned earlier, ingroup/outgroup tensions exist between some Korean Americans and African Americans in urban areas across the United States (Lang, 2020). The 1990 boycott of the Family Red Apple Grocery in New York City and the 1992 Los Angeles riots are exemplars of the long history of interracial/interethnic conflict between these two microcultural groups. Korean Americans moved into African American communities and established residences and businesses. African Americans subsequently accused Korean Americans of overcharging, rudeness, usurping business opportunities, and siphoning money out of the community (S. S.-H. Lee, 2018). Korean Americans responded by attributing the conflict to larger social issues, such as being villainized through the "Yellow Peril" (Yi & Hoston, 2021)

Another area of intergroup tensions is that between Latinx individuals and African Americans, which is affected by "many factors related to cultural differences, patterns of racial segregation, and endemic systems of white supremacy" (Corral, 2020). Latinx in the South perceive greater competition for resources (i.e., jobs, homes, food) with African Americans than with other outgroups. These tensions become compounded when we consider predictions of an influx of the Latinx population. If the population growth is due largely to immigration, then people arriving from other nations may have internalized the racial hierarchies/stereotypes of their home countries. The tensions also become further complicated when perceptions of competition result from media and political narratives emphasizing conflicting interests that actually may not exist. As such, it becomes very important to recognize group similarities regarding lack of power compared to European Americans, as it may overcome "a superficially fractious and tenuous relationship between Latinos and Blacks" (pp. 448–449).

Despite the negativity associated with interracial/interethnic conflict, efforts are being made to ease tensions, particularly in light of the racial unrest of 2020. Interracial coalitions are developing between AAPI, Blacks, whites, LGBTQIA+ members, and Latinx communities committed to addressing inequities creating these divisions. Moreover, they are willing to join the fight against hate crimes, racism, xenophobia, heteronormativity, and other forms of systemic oppression at the core of interracial conflict (I. Johnson & Pietri, 2020; Kantawala, 2021).

## Perceptual Differences

Racial/ethnic group members interpret their experiences through double-consciousness. They view life as a microcultural group member adapting, to some degree, to the macroculture. As a result, they define and perceive conflict differently. It is not always clear if the conflict is because of race, personality differences, racial bias, naiveté, miscommunication, or misperceptions. The conflict can intensify if European Americans seem oblivious to the degree of offense taken to unintentional, subtle forms of racially biased statements and questions. In addition to possessing different perceptions of what constitutes conflict, racial/ethnic groups also have different expectations of how conflict is to be resolved. Do the parties resolve it themselves or seek a mediator? What is considered most appropriate? Racial/ethnic groups may have different responses to this question, which makes recognizing "appropriate" behavior relative. Different vantage points can result in a polarized conflict situation where trust and respect are lacking, thereby perpetuating negative outgroup stereotypes.

One example of different communication styles creating conflict is verbal dueling. African Americans may engage in a rapid, artful exchange of nonserious insults (Lawton et al., 2013). This has been colloquially referred to as "playing the dozens" (Garner, 1983) and currently "joning" or "jonin'." Outgroup members may perceive this style as ingroup attacking behavior, which most likely is not the case. Because outgroup members have different values and communication behaviors, the likelihood of misinterpretation becomes greater. Compared to Asian American groups, the European American verbal style could be perceived as boastful (Ting-Toomey & Dorjee, 2019). In comparison to the African American verbal style, however, the European American style could be seen as understated. African Americans may perceive Asian American style as distant or evasive. These contrasting communication styles may unintentionally lead to conflict situations that individuals are actually trying to avoid. As Ting-Toomey and Dorjee explain,

> Interethnic frictions arise when a group uses its own verbal style yardstick to evaluate another group's verbal output. Even routine conversations can escalate into major conflicts because of our ignorance of each other's preferred verbal styles. More importantly, our ethnocentric evaluations can clutter our ability to listen clearly to ongoing communication from others. Recognizing and respecting verbal style differences requires mindfulness. (p. 227)

As with interpersonal communication, different perceptions exist between people, and in the case of interracial communication, they are due to ingroup communication traditions. While Black communication is frequently more expressive, white communication is often more reserved and feelings are contained. Intergroup conflict is further complicated because individuals are very likely to experience psychological distance in their interracial interactions due to differing interests, values, and norms, all of which inhibit the ability for different races to reach common goals (Orbe & Everett, 2006).

## Segregation

Recall from Chapter 8 that the contact hypothesis theorizes that increased intergroup contact will reduce intergroup bias. Obviously, when public spaces are racially segregated, opportunities for contact disappear. This becomes further complicated when there is residential preference of individuals to live in racially segregated areas. Researchers have conducted studies on this critical issue, with particular interest in whether residential preferences are motivated by quality of life indicators (such as quality of schools, property values, and safety) associated with race (the **racial proxy** hypothesis) or by explicit beliefs about race beyond its relation to social class and socioeconomic factors.

In their research on residential segregation, Swaroop and Krysan (2011) found that the racial proxy hypothesis applied more strongly to Blacks and

---

*Box 10.3*                                    *Student Reflections*

### The Move to a "Safer" Neighborhood

Growing up in what I would say were two different extremes really shaped my feelings and opinions on racial issues. Until I was 7 years old, I lived in a neighborhood where there were Mexicans, Puerto Ricans, African Americans, and Caucasians all in one block. Then, my father decided to move our family to a safer city, to get us out of the bad neighborhood we were living in. This is where my life, and views on race and issues surrounding it, changed drastically. I didn't understand why there were no kids that looked like me, or even more, why all the kids at my school were the same. I was no longer in a multicultural setting. Instead, I was getting asked why I talked the way I did, or what certain slang words that I used meant. As a child, I didn't understand.

As I got older I realized that the color of my skin, my last name, and even the way I talked, was going to impact the rest of my life. I would frequently have a racial slur thrown at me, even by those people who called themselves my friends. I have been called everything from the n-word to dirty Mexican, and the one that for some reason bothers me the most, white girl. Although I would like to think that most people don't look at you and automatically see the color of your skin, more and more, I feel that they do. But I am also glad that people recognize me as a Latina, because I am proud of my background and feel that it is a very important part of who I am.

Latinx, whose preferences for integrated neighborhoods were largely attributed to better socioeconomic conditions and fewer social problems than those in predominantly microculture communities. Whites reported less satisfaction in neighborhoods with more minority residents, which could be construed as feeling as though their social position is diminished by residing in proximity to microculture individuals. Blacks reported less satisfaction in neighborhoods with fewer Black residents; their preference for predominantly Black neighborhoods could result from fears of hostility and other forms of discriminatory treatment from whites. Latinx people, however, reported more satisfaction in neighborhoods with higher proportions of whites than in neighborhoods with predominantly Latinx residents. The majority of Latinx in the study were immigrants, which could have minimized concerns about discrimination. The researchers concluded that individuals balance both socioeconomic and race-related concerns.

Further evidence of intergroup conflict is white flight, which is the movement of whites away from previously all-white communities once African Americans establish residence there. Scholars continue to debate whether white flight is racially motivated or results from socioeconomic concerns. If race is a proxy

## Box 10.4

### Tackling Residential Segregation

Racial segregation is a type of interracial conflict born from racial tensions between residents in certain neighborhoods resisting integration. Jim Crow laws legalizing racial segregation were outlawed more than 100 years ago, but "white flight" kept segregation in place. White flight was the term used to describe the mass exodus of white families from metropolises to the suburbs during the Great Migration (1916–1970) (Waldek, 2020). The practice continues today and impacts race relations because people are avoiding racial integration.

White flight contributes to interracial conflict by preventing opportunities for racial groups to interact with each other. One possibility for counteracting white flight is for communities and policy makers to promote and work toward residential integration. The Century Foundation (2019) identified civic and social-emotional, educational, and economic benefits of integrated communities.

1. reduced racial bias to counter stereotypes
2. decreased anxiety about intergroup contact
3. increased likelihood of living in racially diverse neighborhoods after graduation from an integrated school
4. better treatment of outgroup members because of greater likelihood of establishing meaningful interracial relationships

The complete list does not include relational benefits; however, interracial friendships and marriages will organically emerge from integrated communities. Community members will also have reduced fear and anxiety about interracial interactions. They will also develop competent interracial communication skills and reduce the potential for interracial conflict.

for social and socioeconomic concerns, then white flight should be greater in poor neighborhoods. Kye and Halpern-Manners (2019) examined white flight in both poor and middle-class suburban neighborhoods. They found that white flight was more likely in middle-class neighborhoods with larger non-white presence than in poorer neighborhoods. When social spaces such as neighborhoods, worship centers, educational institutions, and social organizations are segregated, the lack of interracial contact increases the likelihood that stereotypes and false generalizations will make interracial/interethnic interactions potentially volatile. The authors further conclude that white flight "may actually be more common than recent neighborhood-level studies suggest" (p. 25).

## Stereotyping

As humans, we sort individuals into social categories and use those categories to interpret the behavior of others (Remedios & Sanchez, 2018). Those categories oftentimes evolve into stereotypes that involve overlapping and shifting social categories that can change as we learn new information. Most people tend to classify individuals primarily on the basis of who belongs to our group, distancing ourselves from outgroups (Chan & Jasso, 2021). That is especially the case when there are perceptions of interracial competition that results in hostile stereotypes of outgroup members (S. Park, 2021). The most effective means of combatting racial bias is through interracial dialogue, which can be very difficult to do since, all too often, such dialogues are avoided because of fears about anxiety and negative outcomes (Schultz et al., 2015).

Box 3.6 discussed the model minority stereotype. While widely accepted as normal and positive, it reinforces the existing racial hierarchy yet has been internalized by both micro- and macrocultural groups (Yi & Houston, 2020). It portrays Asian Americans as two-parent families, well-educated, hardworking, successful, prosperous, and seamlessly acclimating to the dominant culture. Not only does the model minority stereotype ignore the economic and cultural differences of Asian American groups but it also implies that other microcultural groups lack the values of the "American Dream." An accompanying stereotype is that some Asian Americans will become "honorary whites," and others will be classified as Black. Such thinking worsens racial tensions, pits groups against each other, and fuels the perception or myth of scarce resources for which microcultural groups must compete. It also causes triangulation, which is an example of overlapping stereotypes. While European Americans stereotype Asian Americans as superior to other groups, they also ostracize them as foreign (Huang, 2021).

Y. Y. Kim (1994) recognized stereotyping, and a lack of interest in communicating with other racial and ethnic groups, as a source for conflict. When different races are trying to uplift their own race while other races hold stereotypes against them, it can cause serious intergroup conflict. For example, Blacks and Latinx people both may view Asian Americans as difficult to get along with (S. S.-H. Lee, 2022). As such, the belief will likely influence interactions and limit the opportunity for communication to have positive outcomes.

The impact of racial group stereotypes varies depending on the status of the group (Corral, 2020). For example, negative valuations of the work ethic of African Americans are powerful predictors of white opinions about Black social justice movements. Those negative perceptions are extended to the social justice realm, which is likely an inaccurate and unfair assumption to make. Although Latinx hold similar negative racial stereotypes, the opinions are far less powerful in predicting Latinx's support for Black movements. Many Latinos simultaneously recognize the role of systemic racial discrimination in the Black-white divide and the need for racial justice for African Americans. This may be attributed to a recognition that Latinx as a group gain little from anti-Black beliefs in a U.S. racial hierarchy that oppresses both Latinx and African Americans.

Racial and cultural stereotypes often-times cloud our judgments during conflict, which makes it difficult to find solutions and perpetuates the belief that interracial relationships are not possible.

**Metastereotypes**—the perceptions that people have about the stereotypes that others have regarding them—also affect interactions. An individual may consciously communicate to challenge the negative stereotypes they *believe* an outgroup holds about them (Fowler & Gasiorek, 2020). As a result, perceptions of outgroup stereotypes can exacerbate tensions that are assumed but may not exist (Gaunt, 2011). There are also ramifications if a member of one's group acts in a manner that confirms a metastereotype. A consequence of witnessing stereotypically negative behavior by an ingroup member during an interracial interaction can result in heightened anxiety, motivation to disprove the stereotype, and/or a reduced desire for future interracial interactions with the member of the outgroup who witnessed the behavior (Taylor et al., 2021). While people may reasonably fear that they will also be viewed stereotypically, attention is focused on how an individual is perceived rather than on the interaction and the issue that needs attention.

Metastereotypes vary by gender, which highlights the value of considering the intersection of race and gender in interracial perceptions, expectations, and interactions (Babbitt et al., 2018). Both white and Black participants in studies perceive white men as more racially prejudiced than white women. White women were also seen as warmer than white men. Our expectations about gender differences in interracial contexts have implications for workplaces, schools, and other institutions, which further complicates interracial interactions in various social contexts. Black employees, for example, may expect to have—and may actually have—better experiences with white female colleagues.

Chapter 11 discusses the influence of the media on interracial interactions; therefore, we will offer only cursory comments here. Racial/ethnic groups are relegated to wholly negative stereotypes, while majority group members (e.g., whites) have considerably more representation and dominate most media outlets. These strikingly different images are problematic. "The media we consume isn't just entertainment. It seeps into our subconscious and shapes the way we think about the world—and the way we think about what's possible" (Metz, 2022). Shelley Lee (2022) explains that

> The reach of mass media—newspapers, television, and film—gave it enormous power to shape its consumers' innermost ideas and concepts about people and the world, and popular culture had an especially insidious history for Asian Americans. From the halting and menacing neighbor Mr. Yunioshi in *Breakfast at Tiffany's* to the alluring yet innocent prostitute in *The World of Suzie Wong*, Asian representation veered between buffoonish and degrading, if not completely erased. These realities, and the fact that well into the 1960s such characters were usually played by white actors in yellowface, spoke volumes about Asians' marginalization in the United States. (p. 125)

## CONFLICT STYLES

Intercultural communication research consistently shows culture as having a significant influence on conflict management. Culture is defined as a "learned system of traditions, symbolic patterns, and constructed and negotiated meanings that fosters a particular sense of shared, community-hood, identity-hood, and interaction habits among the aggregate members of a community" (Ting-Toomey, 2017, p. 124). As such, cultures shape our perceptions, judgments, and ideas about ourselves and others. Cultures orient us toward particular perspectives and away from others. What is normal for one group may seem strange or wrong to another. Whether people realize it or not, everyone belongs to multiple cultures; some are based on gender, age, class, sexual orientation, ability, religion, ethnicity, and nationality. As an extension of those cultures, we use different conflict styles depending on the situation and the participants. The influence of culture is often invisible, imperceptibly affecting conflict and attempts to resolve disagreements.

One major finding is that the greater the cultural distance between parties in a conflict, the greater the likelihood of mistrust or misunderstanding taking place. "The most inclusive and influential theory pertaining to culture and conflict may be the conflict face-negotiation theory (FNT), which provides a sound explanatory framework for explicating cultural, individual, and situational influences on facework behavior and conflict styles" (Q. Zhang et al., 2014). Stella Ting-Toomey began working on FNT in 1985 when conflict literature defined conflict avoidance style as low concern for self-interest and low concern for other interest. In her experience, shaped by her Chinese Confucius upbringing, the avoidance style was an artful way to defuse or deflate conflict issues (Ting-Toomey, 2019). The literature's definition of conflict compromising style as a quick closure, give-and-take concession also did not resonate with her. She regarded compromising as a long-term effort to build relationships and trust to accomplish goals. Her lived experience and observation in both Asian and U.S. cultures planted the seeds for FNT. Recognizing its continued relevance, the core assumptions of the theory were developed and refined from 1985 through 2015 (Ting-Toomey, 2017).

We presented FNT theory in Chapter 6. Recall that face refers to one's self-image in the presence of others, and facework consists of the verbal and nonverbal messages to address face—whether one's own, the other person's, mutual, or communal. Facework can maintain, defend, or save one's face and/ or uplift or undercut another's social image in an interaction (Ting-Toomey, 2017). Chapter 6 also highlighted the differences between individualistic cultures (emphasis on the needs of the individual) and collectivistic cultures (emphasis on the harmony of the collective). FNT addresses personal as well as cultural factors influencing our intercultural interactions. **Self-construal** refers to one's self-concept as independent or interdependent. Independent self-construals view the self as autonomous, and interdependent self-construals see the self as connected with others (Littlejohn et al., 2021). As such, if some individuals in intercultural interactions are seeking to achieve personal goals while other individuals are attempting to satisfy group goals, misunderstandings that can lead to conflict are inevitable. This underscores the importance of understanding the influence of culture on our communication.

To manage conflicts, one must be aware of individual, situational, and cultural factors contributing to the conflict and to how (or whether) it can be resolved. The more important the conflict issue, the more threat to face. This means that when face is threatened in conflict, people experience identity-based frustration, emotional vulnerability, anger, defensiveness, hurt, and feelings of vengeance—at either group or individual levels. "Cultural worldview perspectives, individual personality tendencies, relational parameters and situational pressures frame the underlying interpretations of what counts as a severe intercultural "face-threatening" interaction episode." (Ting-Toomey, 2017, p. 126). Thus, it is imperative that we use our critical thinking skills and practice cultural sensitivity when these situations arise.

## Individualistic and Collectivistic Styles

FNT provides a framework for understanding conflict styles. Members of individualistic cultures are more likely to use *competing* or *collaborating* conflict styles. Collectivistic culture members are more likely to use *compromising*, *accommodating*, or *avoiding* styles. A cross-cultural comparison of participants from China, Germany, Japan, and the United States regarding facework during interpersonal conflicts revealed the importance of culture (Oetzel & Ting-Toomey, 2003). Cultural individualism-collectivism directly and indirectly affected conflict styles. Independent self-construal was related to self-face, and interdependent self-construal correlated with other-face. Self-face was related to competing conflict styles, and other-face was related to the use of collaborating, compromising, accommodating, and avoiding styles.

Another cross-cultural study asked participants from the United States and from Ecuador to describe an interpersonal conflict (Neuliep & Johnson, 2016). The researchers found significant differences in facework and conflict styles. Ecuadorean participants were more likely to use avoiding, compromising, and accommodating conflict styles. The findings support the patterns identified by FNT. Thus, it should not be a surprise that collectivistic cultures such as Ecuador use conflict styles that show concern for protecting the face of others, while individualistic cultures such as the United States use conflict styles oriented to self-face.

In order to further increase our understanding of the influence of culture on message exchanges, anthropologist Edward Hall divided cultures into two categories to highlight differences in verbal and nonverbal communication. **High-context cultures** are marked by collective understanding. Communication focuses on more than the content of the message; rather, nonverbals (e.g., facial expressions, tone, body language) and the context in which the communication takes place are considered most important. These shared (collective) cultural values result in more indirect, subtle interactions. Conversely, **low-context cultures** focus on individual expression and directness. Information is communicated explicitly. High-context cultures are generally collectivistic and homogenous, emphasizing the group and relationships. Low-context cultures are more individualistic and diverse; communication is direct, explicit, and literal. As such, low-context communicators use direct verbal messages that could help prevent misunderstandings, but the explicit nature of the communication could be perceived as confrontational and could escalate a conflict. The indirect messages of high-context communicators might be intended as respectful but could be interpreted incorrectly because they lack specificity. Table 10.1 summarizes cultural influences on conflict.

As a culture, European Americans are individualistic/low context, while Latinx, Asian Americans, and African Americans are collectivistic/high context (Ting-Toomey et al., 2000). Asians tend to use higher degrees of obliging and avoiding conflict styles than European Americans (Ting-Toomey & Oetzel, 2001). In comparison, European Americans tend to use up-front, solution-oriented styles, such as competing and collaborating, in dealing with conflict problems. Mexican Americans utilize avoiding conflict styles to preserve relational harmony when conflict arises among close Mexican American friends (Garcia, 1996). Research on African Americans has concluded that they tend to use more emotionally expressive and involving modes of conflict (Ting-Toomey, 1986). Given these cultural differences, it is understandable that interracial (e.g., intercultural) conflicts will certainly arise when different groups interact.

**Table 10.1    Core Cultural Differences in Conflict**

| Individualistic/Low-Context Cultures | Collectivistic/High-Context Cultures |
|---|---|
| ***Issue orientation*** | ***Relational/face orientation*** |
| • Conflict is necessary to work out major differences and problems | • Conflict viewed as damaging to social status and relational harmony |
| • Conflict is functional when it provides a way to address problems | • Conflict reflects a lack of self-discipline and emotional immaturity |
| • Focus should be on specific issues; relational issues should be handled separately | • Topical issues and relational issues are intertwined and must be dealt with together |
| ***Goal orientation*** | ***Process orientation*** |
| • Focus is on achieving specific goals with an eye on the future | • Focus on the process and how it relates to the past, present, and future |
| • Conflict episodes must be isolated and addressed accordingly | • Conflict management has no clear beginning and end |
| • Conflict management should follow a preset schedule with clear agenda items | • Conflict management is a delicate, subtle process that has no predetermined schedule |
| ***Use of formal mediator*** | ***Use of informal mediator*** |
| • Preference for formally trained mediator | • Preference for informal mediator, usually a well-respected elder |
| • Mediator should be impartial and not know any parties involved | • Mediator should know all parties involved |
| • Mediator should only focus on the issue(s) at hand | • Mediator should attend to past events to help understand current conflict |
| ***Tangible power resources*** | ***Intangible power resources*** |
| • Power is reflected in the ability to reward and/or punish others | • Power is reflected in gains or losses in reputation, prestige, or status |
| • Struggles to gain more power happen both overtly and covertly | • Fewer struggles to gain more power exist; if they do, they happen covertly |
| • Power is asserted through threats, direct requests, and aggressive defense strategies | • Power is displayed subtly through indirect requests, tag questions, and inferences |
| ***Direct/competitive communication*** | ***Indirect/integrating communication*** |
| • Communicators have a responsibility to be open, direct, and clear | • Communicators have a responsibility to pick up on the hidden meaning and intentions of others |
| • Emphasis on verbal offense and defense to justify one's position | • Relies on ambiguous, indirect verbal and nonverbal messages |
| • Uses communication strategies that reflect a win/win competition between parties | • Uses communication strategies that reflect a win/win negotiation between parties |

---

**Box 10.5**                                                    *Research Highlight*

## Strategies for Reducing Racial and Ethnic Prejudice

Learning for Justice (n.d.) is a project of the Southern Poverty Law Center dedicated to fighting hate and bigotry and seeking justice for society's most vulnerable members. William Hawley and his colleagues developed principles and strategies for reducing racial and ethnic prejudice and promoting intergroup relations. Included here are the principles most appropriate for individual and group level work.

- Principle 1—address both institutional and individual sources of prejudice and discrimination.
- Principle 2—strive to influence the behavior of individuals, including their motivation and capability to influence others.
- Principle 3—attend to the dispositions and behavior of all racial and ethnic groups involved.
- Principle 4—include participants who reflect the racial, ethnic, and linguistic diversity of the context; structure strategies to ensure cooperative, equal-status roles for persons from different groups.
- Principle 5—ensure the support and participation of those with authority and power in any given setting.
- Principle 6—involve children at an early age; continually encourage new entrants to organizations and reinforce the importance of positive intergroup relations.
- Principle 7—incorporate ongoing opportunities to learn in educational institutions and in organizations; establish a continuing set of learning activities that are valued and pursued.
- Principle 8—examine similarities and differences across and within racial and ethnic groups, including differences related to social class, gender, and language.
- Principle 9—recognize the value of bicultural and multicultural identities of individuals and groups and the difficulties those who live in two or more cultures confront.
- Principle 10—expose the inaccuracies of myths that sustain stereotypes and prejudices.

A true commitment to reducing racism and prejudice requires everyone to do their part. Adopting several or all of these strategies is a great start. Individuals and organizations must challenge themselves to think more critically about communicating with others and making a conscious decision to adopt behaviors facilitating change and positive relationships.

## Racial/Ethnic Comparisons

From the outset of scholarship in the area of race, ethnicity, and conflict, researchers have compared the conflict styles of different groups (Donahue, 1985). In his foundational research on Black and white styles in conflict, Kochman (1981) found that the "Black mode of conflicts is high-keyed, animated, interpersonal and confrontational; the white mode of conflict is relatively low-keyed, dispassionate, impersonal, and non-challenging" (p. 18). Other researchers with similar interests explored realism and honesty among different groups. They found that Blacks viewed realism as telling it like it is whether you are being positive or negative (J. Martin et al., 1994). In comparison, whites' idea of realism was slightly different. Whites used the term honesty in the place of realism. Honesty may be unrealistic and can become problematic when disclosing positives and negatives. For example, if a Black person is too honest to a white person, the white person may get offended; similarly, if a white person is not "real" with a Black person, it can produce the same results. These differences can also create problems in the workplace. Research in the organizational context focused on the different perceptions of Black and white women regarding workplace conflict (Shuter & Turner, 1997). Each group perceived their own attempts to reduce conflict as most effective and enacted different strategies toward the same objective. Black women preferred getting the conflict out on the table to readily address and move past it and believed using a direct approach was most effective. In comparison, white women used more of an avoidance strategy and felt fear or anxiety when having to approach conflict directly.

Collier (1991) included three U.S. ethnic groups (Mexican, Blacks, and whites) in her study of conflict differences within friendships. Participants were asked to define friendship and conflict and share whether they felt that their friends handled conflict effectively or ineffectively. Collier found that each racial group defined conflict differently. White males defined conflict as a difference of opinion, an attack on a person's beliefs and opinions, an unresolved situation, and an inability to compromise; Black men saw conflict as a

---

**Box 10.6**                                          *Author Reflections*

### The Question That Kick-Started
### My Motivation to Research in the Field

People are always surprised when I tell them that my intentions for earning a PhD were so that I could teach communication classes, preferably at a community college that catered to first-generation college students. When I started my doctoral work, my goal was to do "just enough" research to complete the degree and secure a college teaching position. This made sense given that my goal was to focus on teaching; however, to be honest, I was also not interested in research because I did not feel as if I had anything to contribute. Up to that point, the research that I had read did not "speak" to me or my experiences.

Something happened during the first year of my doctoral program, however, that changed all that. I started reading research in communication and related fields on different racial and ethnic groups. While the topics—interracial dating, biracial identity development, racial stereotypes, African American nonverbal communication—were interesting, I found the research highly problematic. From my perspective, the social scientific research did not do anything more than promote cultural stereotypes of all racial and ethnic groups. In one graduate seminar on nonverbal communication, I vividly remember talking about this issue in class. As is usually the case, I shared my criticisms with a passion and forcefulness that was perceived by some as unproductive, defensive, and overly critical. My graduate professor, however, listened intently to my comments, validated my concerns, and then asked me: "So, what are you going to do about it? Keep reading research that you find problematic or make the commitment to advance the research?"

At that point in my doctoral program, I did not have the confidence or the expertise to think that I could make significant contributions to the field of communication. However, that one scenario planted a seed that would ultimately serve as the primary motivator for conducting research on various topics related to race, culture, and communication.

- What research have you read in this text that you find problematic?

- How might you use a class project, independent study, or graduate school to help advance different research?

—MPO.

disagreement, different views, and misunderstandings; and Mexican Americans described conflict in a more relational manner. The study also examined how each racial/ethnic group perceived competent communication during conflict episodes. Whites valued taking responsibility for behaviors, directness, equality, rational decision making, concern for others, and shared control. Blacks believed information should be given, opinions should be credible, criticism was inappropriate, and assertiveness was important. Mexican American answers were similar to those of whites in terms of concern about the other person but differed regarding confrontation. Unlike whites, Mexican Americans believed that, in some situations, confrontation was appropriate.

A study of acquaintance relationships (a relational context in which third-culture norms have not yet been established) compared Latinx, Black, Asian, and white conflict styles (Ting-Toomey et al., 2000). The researchers examined the relationship between ethnic identity salience (importance of ethnicity to an individual), larger U.S. cultural identity (importance of belonging to a larger national culture), and conflict management styles across the four groups. Strong identification with one's racial/ethnic group increased the likelihood of culturally oriented conflict behaviors. Blacks strongly identified with their own racial/ethnic group. Interestingly, Latinx and Asian Americans identified both with their racial/ethnic group and with U.S. culture. Whites identified primarily with the larger U.S. culture. Asian Americans used more avoiding strategies than did whites, and Latinx people used more third-party conflict styles than did Blacks.

---

**Box 10.7**                                            *Research Highlight*

### Conflict Styles When Negotiating a Child's Education Conflict

Conflict in interracial relationships and intraracial relationships is very similar; however, racial/ethnic differences are sometimes contributing factors. Lawton et al. (2013) explored conflict styles of married interracial couples and decisions related to their children's educa- tion and found couples experience challenges due to different cultural perspectives. The researchers asked couples to respond to a survey of conflict styles and used cultural con- tracts theory (see Chapter 6). The focus was on education due to noted racial/ethnic differ- ences regarding educational opportunities. They wanted to know if gender, age, and race were related to conflict styles and couple choices.

Wives, across all racial groups, reported having higher control or dominance in their edu- cation-related decisions. Asian and Latinx husbands were more likely to exercise control or resist conforming to their wives' cultural values. There were also issues of concern about reli- gious values in school (Latinx) and achievement and oversight (Asian). The researchers con- cluded that identities such as motherhood or race do influence conflict styles while dealing with educational choices; however, styles may change for interracial couples as the relation- ship matures or partners realize the advantages of their spouses' main concerns.

---

It is clear that conflict styles describe the overall pattern of a person's communication orientation during conflict. Style differences can escalate con- flicts. While people generally follow a predominant style based on their expe- riences, the context of the disagreement, and cultural influences, they can learn to alter their communication. As such, awareness about style differences is an initial step in recognizing patterns and adapting to situations to work toward better outcomes. Towards that end, the next section addresses various approaches to managing interracial conflicts competently.

## THINKING CRITICALLY ABOUT MANAGING INTERRACIAL CONFLICT

Since the racial unrest of 2020, there has been a growing interest in addressing racial inequities and racism, affecting everyone in varying degrees. Increased numbers of white people began searching for educational resources and opportunities to get involved in grassroot social justice move- ments. Many communication scholars became (re)committed to their race- related research and integrating it into their classrooms to encourage others in academe to recognize the value and practical nature of our work. Companies and universities seized the opportunity to address these issues in the work- place by hiring scholars and diversity experts for training sessions about becoming more inclusive and diverse. This was an excellent way to translate theory into practice in very material and practical ways. Scholars shared resources on social media and nurtured a renewed commitment to doing the difficult work society needs. There was a newfound appreciation for research centering on race and offering competent strategies for healthy interracial dialogue and understanding. In this section, we highlight how research makes important contributions to these efforts and consider the nuances making interracial conflict so difficult yet manageable.

---

### Box 10.8

## 10 Commandments for Dismantling Systemic Racism and Affirming the Rights and Dignity of Black, Brown, and Native People

The Sacramento Area Congregations Together (ACT) is made up of more than 56 schools, neighborhoods, and churches committed to transforming their community according to their shared faith values. The organization represents 60,000 families and is addressing issues that lead to justice and equity. Sacramento ACT (2020) prioritizes eradicating historical social inequities (i.e., racism, discrimination, disinvestment) adversely impacting communities of color. Its ultimate goal is to advance equity through public policy. Their approach is "congregation-based community organizing," and they created 10 commandments for achieving an inclusive and equitable community.

Commandment 1: Thou shall make no graven image of white supremacy, but thou shall dismantle all forms of systemic and structural racism.

Commandment 2: Thou shall honor all Black lives. in recognition of this, thou shall acknowledge Juneteenth and keep it holy.

Commandment 3: Thou shall not kill unarmed Black, Brown, and Native people but rather de-escalate, negotiate, and investigate.

Commandment 4: Thou shall not steal resources or rights from Black, Brown, and Native communities.

Commandment 5: Thou shall not bear false witness against peaceful protesters.

Commandment 6: Thou shall not hire nor harbor racist police officers.

Commandment 7: Thou shalt divest from the police state and invest in community.

Commandment 8: Thou shall establish accessible and affordable health care for Black, Brown, and Native people.

Commandment 9: Thou shall decarcerate noncriminal offenders unjustly sentenced.

Commandment 10: Thou shall enact reparations and restitution to Black people for the legacy of slavery in the state of California.

What are your initial thoughts about these commandments? How does each contribute to interracial unity? What are the connections between these commandments and other key concepts discussed in this book? How, if at all, might they be applied to other types of multiracial organizations beyond those focusing on spirituality or community service?

Examples of interracial conflict are plentiful and vary in levels of extremity, including hate crimes against AAPI (Yellow Horse et al., 2021); public figures using the n-word (Paulson, 2021); politicians calling COVID the "China virus" (Addo, 2020) and comparing face masks to the Holocaust (Fram, 2021); and gentrification that displaces people of color from their communities (Daniels, 2018; Lees, 2016). These real-life examples are evidence of the urgency of addressing interracial conflict, its systemic origins, and the need for everyone to join the efforts to eliminate interracial conflict. Conflict is inevitable due to competing goals and interests and should never be grounded in any oppressive ideologies (i.e., racism, ethnocentrism, etc.).

Harris and Abbott (2011) developed the **racial microaggression identification and confrontation model** as a skills-based exercise to help people think about the best approach to managing interracial conflict. The model was developed for instructional purposes and has been adapted for consulting work. Using the model to assess past behaviors can impact future behavior by determining what, if anything, one would do differently to resolve interracial conflict. It also helps determine if one is willing to take certain risks (such as losing a relationship) to directly confront racism, prejudice, or discrimination. The model is a four-step process requiring honest self-reflexivity about a past conflict situation.

- Step 1. *Identify the microaggression* involves contextualizing the encounter to ensure clarity about how the encounter evolved.

- Step 2. *Assess the contribution of three cues to the conflict.* The three cues are (a) relational, (b) contextual, and (c) emotional. **Relational cues** refer to considering the relationship between involved parties in the encounter. Confronting a stranger might have fewer risks than confronting a partner or relative. **Contextual cues** are the physical environment where the microaggression occurred (i.e., restaurant, home). A public setting could affect the communication. **Emotional cues** involve feelings triggered by the conflict, such as anger, frustration, or sadness. If the microaggression causes anger, then a person may prioritize emotional cues over relational and contextual ones.

- Step 3. *Determine reaction to racial microaggression.* How did I react? How comfortable am I with my response? How did the other person respond? How did I feel in that moment? What influenced my decision to respond in that way? There are no right or wrong answers; these questions are prompts to encourage honest behavior assessment in situations where different behavior might have made a difference.

- Step 4. *Reflect on the outcome*. A person evaluates how their reaction affected the relationship and what they would do differently if given another opportunity. This stage encourages the person to identify the lessons learned from an encounter that equips them for addressing future interracial conflicts.

As mentioned earlier, communication is the means for the productive or destructive management of conflict. Speaking to Gonzaga University students and faculty, Kecia Thomas, an expert on diversity, commented that race is a taboo topic for many and is difficult to discuss because we have not developed fluency around race (McKinstry, 2022). Society and individuals can work toward change by focusing on inclusion, challenging current mindsets, building community, and working through discomfort. The anxiety generated when interacting with people who are different from us can cause some discomfort. Once we acknowledge the discomfort, we can move on to seeing conflict as an opportunity to learn and grow.

It is reasonable to assume that the more power distance between groups, the greater the likelihood of conflict. Some researchers have used the metaphor of dance to describe how to manage social inequity and unequal power

**Table 10.2    Best Practices for Interracial Communication Management**

| Pre-Conversation: Prepare | During Conversation: Act | Post-Conversation: Implement and Move Forward |
|---|---|---|
| Choose to discuss the problem directly, one on one. | Make known your goals for the conversation. Discuss confidentiality. Use respectful communication so that each person will continue to participate and not leave, go silent, raise their voice or be defensive. Listen intently for the other's perspective. Active Listening skills are especially useful in conflict conversations. Be aware of and try to understand your own and the other person's feelings. Discuss perceptions and assumptions. Address the past as necessary. Focus on the problem, not the person. Address the problem instead of being defensive. Look for areas of agreement—your common ground—and build on those. Agree on what you both can do in the future and leave the rest. *Recognize that the conflict may be viewed from different racial perspectives/standpoints. *Be willing to discuss the race-related issues with openness and honesty. | Act with integrity to maintain your shared agreements. Recognize that change is difficult and sometimes we make mistakes as we change. Notice positive behaviors. Let go of past hard feelings and look for ways to work together productively, e.g., use common personal greetings, say thanks when appropriate, acknowledge and show appreciation for changed behavior, repeat common ideas and goals, etc. *Commit to perspective-taking to better understand your racially different partner. |
| Act sooner rather than later. Problems not acted on tend to fester, take up energy needed for work and family, and may affect personal well-being. Decide what you would like to achieve in the conversation, e.g. clarification, behavior change, mending of the relationship, etc. Invite the other person to participate in a conversation. Plan the logistics of a meeting, including when, where, who should participate, etc. *Consider the possibility that racial/ethnic/cultural differences might exist. | | |

*Strategies developed by Orbe and Harris
Source: University of Iowa, 2022

relations when tackling social challenges (Gallegos et al., 2020). Resistance to opposing points of view can be overcome by more frequent, respectful contact rather than avoiding interactions that might lead to conflict.

> Part of this requires more attention to the meaning and context of behavior and to the connotations and meanings of our words. Cultural humility teaches us that there are many competing and multiple perspectives on any issue, including our own. Engaging in more vibrant and productive conflict requires courage and authenticity. (p. 173)

To engage in productive conflict, we need to disrupt habitual patterns by questioning assumptions and developing a heightened awareness (Gallegos et al., 2020). Embrace conflict and engage in dialogue to identify shared concerns. Notice how members of groups interact across boundaries. We need to be attuned to recognizing unconscious bias and the prevalence of microaggressions in everyday interactions. For example, how do you react when someone expresses surprise that an African American is in an honors class? Consider the following observation:

> Small behaviors with potentially huge and unintended consequences demand our constant vigilance and willingness to change behavior that may have been normal or acceptable in the past. In particular, the systemic level of context needs more amplification. . . . Prejudice and oppression are systemic, which means that they do not require conscious individual behavior to continue perpetuating injustice. The personal/self and interpersonal are embedded in complex systems and cannot be considered in isolation. Using our dancing metaphor, context in social interactions is the music we dance to (even when we are not fully listening), therefore it behooves us to pay close attention to what we are hearing (and not hearing) and to what others hear (and do not hear), as well as to how the systems and structures in which we are embedded channel and affect our behavior and experiences and those of others. (p. 173)

---

### Box 10.9

## Increasing Anti-Racist Behavior on SNS

The rise in usage and popularity of social network sites (SNS) has prompted researchers to consider if the contact hypothesis holds up in digital spaces. Research has shown that SNS encourages greater intergroup contact, promotes intergroup harmony, and reduces prejudice and discrimination; however, there is no definitive answer about the specific variables that influence this process (Imperato et al., 2021). The anonymity available on the internet plus control over communication (such as ending uncomfortable dialogue with an outgroup member) facilitate reducing prejudice on SNS, making people feel safer, and reducing the anxiety related to self-disclosure, especially for those who are stigmatized and marginalized. The research offers hope that digital spaces can be used to establish intergroup connections and ultimately improve race relations.

In both direct and indirect forms of contact, cross-group friendship enhances positive intergroup attitudes by increasing empathy and perspective taking (Imperato et al., 2021). Feeling empathy toward an outgroup member with whom one interacts can be linked to a decrease in prejudice toward the other group and thus increase one's engagement in anti-racist behaviors. The role of digital empathy, however, remains controversial. Some research finds most online communication is emotive and people develop empathic online relationships. Other research points to the lack of nonverbal clues that are necessary for intimate interpersonal communication. However, online empathic feelings have been positively related with commitment to an online community and to antiracist behavior. Relational need is one of the reasons people use social networks and may be the engine that pushes people to build harmonious online relationships and to behave in a prosocial, anti-racist manner.

Spontaneous online intergroup contact can change how people categorize others, leading to more positive outgroup attitudes (Imperato et al., 2021). By increasing identity exploration, online intergroup contact increased the sensitivity of participants toward discrimination against sexual minorities on Facebook. In Facebook interactions of individuals with an outgroup member, ingroup members felt more committed to the online community, which increased sensitivity to the detection of online discrimination toward ethnic minorities. Interacting on a social network may have suppressed ingroup/outgroup dynamics with a shift from personal identity to a more inclusive group in the Facebook community.

# CONCLUSION

Interracial communication has gained increased attention due to the recent racial unrest in the United States that reverberated throughout the world. We were gripped by hundreds of accounts of interracial conflict on social media and the news detailing tensions between racial groups leading to unfortunate outcomes. While 2020 was very emotional, we should remain hopeful all interracial communication is not rife with conflict. Instead, it is an excellent site for bridging differences and fostering positive connections with people of other races. Kantawala (2021) asserts that creating "communities of practice" is a practical solution, which means people create a space "where information, insights, and advice are shared, thus extending conversations and developing networks of tacit and explicit knowledge" (p. 6) We can get there if we all commit to working together not only to have productive dialogue about these issues but also to recognize that interracial conflicts occur within marriages, families, friendships, and professional relationships. Resolving these conflicts requires normalizing the fact that conflict, or a clash of personal goals in relationships, is inevitable. The important point is that we can avoid allowing racial differences to define conflict.

Research on interracial conflict has shown that residential segregation, gentrification, anxiety, ingroup/outgroup tensions, relational conflict, violence, and perceptual differences are largely due to stereotyping. This means we must do the difficult yet necessary work of unlearning the racial stereotypes shaping how we perceive others and ourselves. Only then will healthy interracial communication occur. We hope this chapter provided you with a better understanding of interracial conflict. Unfortunately, 2020 showed us that the United States and the world have many unresolved issues around racism, which ultimately manifest in strife and contention between groups. It also showed us that we can stop the cycle of normalizing interracial conflict by working together and engaging in informed, competent communication.

## KEY TERMS

interracial conflict
interethnic conflict
hate crime
intimate/interpersonal violence
racial proxy
metastereotypes
self-construal
self-face

high-context cultures
low-context cultures
racial microaggression identification
  and confrontation model
relational cues
contextual cues
emotional cues
outcome

## RECOMMENDED CONTEMPORARY READINGS

Chen, S. G., & Hosam, C. (2022). Claire Jean Kim's racial triangulation at 20: Rethinking Black-Asian solidarity and political science. *Politics, Groups & Identities, 10*(3), 455–460. https://doi.org/10.1080/21565503.2022.2044870

Greenland, K., Augoustinos, M., Andreoli, E., & Taulke-Johnson, R. (2020). Cross-group friendships, the irony of harmony, and the social construction of "discrimination." *Ethnic and Racial Studies, 43*(7), 1169–1188.

MacNeil-Kelly, T. (2020). Exploring conflict within interracial dating dyads. In T. MacNeil-Kelly (Ed.), *The role of conflict on the individual and society* (pp. 53–70). Rowman & Littlefield.

Maxwell, K. E., & Chesler, M. (2021). Learning separately, learning together: White students' experiences in two different racial dialogues. *Journal of Diversity in Higher Education, 15*(3), 314–324. https://doi-org/10.1037/dhe0000303

Monaci, M. G. (2022). Interethnic workplace conflict: Reciprocal perception of Italian and immigrant blue-collar coworkers. *Europe's Journal of Psychology, 18*(2), 193–206. https://doi.org/10.5964/ejop.2395

Oliver, M. D., Datta, S., & Baldwin, D. R. (2019). Wellness among African-American and Caucasian students attending a predominantly white institution. *Journal of Health Psychology, 24*(12), 1637–1645.

Williams, J. C., & Wright, C. N. (2020). Developing implicit bias awareness in the communication classroom: From Project Implicit to Jane Elliott's *Brown eye blue eye*. *Communication Teacher, 34*(4), 320–326. https://doi-org.libezp.lib.lsu.edu/10.1080/17404622.2019.1706755

## OPPORTUNITIES FOR EXTENDED LEARNING

1. The 2022 invasion of Ukraine by Russia revealed ethnic tensions and interracial conflict on an international stage. It became even more racial when reports emerged of refugees being blocked from exiting the country for

safety reasons. Google "this is what a 50 km-long refugee crisis looks like." Make note of the actions engaged in by citizens and officials to deny the exit of Africans. What are some similarities and differences between Ukraine and the United States in their treatment of people from other countries? What immigration policies or laws have been created as a formal response to immigrants gaining citizenship in either or both countries? What language is used to express xenophobia, racial prejudice, racism, etc.? How have allies responded to these acts of aggression? What are some actions that can be taken to protect these law-abiding citizens?

2. Take an informal poll of your friends and ask them to identify conflict issues that create barriers to competent communication in interracial relationships. Use that list to explore some of the same or different issues that might occur in same-race relationships. What are the differences? Similarities? What are the best approaches to managing relational conflict? Why are conflicts in interracial relationships seen as more difficult to overcome than those in same-race relationships? What can partners do to overcome them? What can be done on a societal level?

3. Do a search for natural disasters or recent events in popular culture where racial/ethnic groups have experienced interracial conflict and BIPOC groups were treated differently because of their race. Try and locate online editorials, op-eds, blogs, or websites created in response to those events. How are the racial/ethnic standpoints of the authors of the posts/comments shaping their perception of the conflict? How are their viewpoints similar? Different? If they were all together in one room, how might they be able to have an effective conversation about this topic that would create mutual understanding and appreciation? Develop six strategies that can assist them in that goal.

4. The Association for Conflict Resolution is the largest national organization designed to promote peaceful, effective conflict resolution. Visit their homepage at http://www.acrnet.org/ and learn about some of the conflict resolution efforts across the world. Pay particular attention to how the site addresses issues of race and ethnicity. Is race invisible, marginalized, or central to how the organization engages in conflict resolution?

5. Review the "Best Practices" for effective conflict management by the University of Iowa in Table 10.2. After reviewing their suggested practices, which ones do you believe would be least or most effective in resolving interracial conflict? Are the strategies reasonable? Appropriate? How are they assessed to determine their effectiveness? In what other contexts can they be applied?

6. In a small group, discuss the different qualities or resources that an ideal romantic partner would need to possess. Review the different theories covered in Chapter 6. Which one of the theories do you think does the best job at explaining why some interracial interactions end in conflict and others do not? What particular concepts, models, and processes are included in the theories that specifically address the sources of conflict described in this chapter?

# 11

# Race/Ethnicity and the Mass Media

**CASE STUDY**　　　　**Double Standards in the Media's Depiction of the Royal Family**

The media have been accused of having a double standard when they report on Meghan Markle and Kate Middleton. Both women married members of Britain's royal family, with Kate marrying Prince William in 2011 and Meghan marrying Prince Harry in 2018. Specifically, the media are accused of purposely framing Meghan as someone "ignorant, uncouth, and unfit for the aristocracy."

Meghan is biracial and from the United States, while Kate is white and from Great Britain. The women have engaged in similar behaviors, but Meghan has come under much harsher scrutiny. When both women wore wedge shoes, Meghan was accused of breaking royal shoe protocol, and Kate was praised for wearing very versatile, stylish summer shoes. Kate was "glowing" while Meghan was "unbecoming" when pictured rubbing their pregnant bellies. Meghan was also accused by tabloids of seeking attention. There were many other behaviors for which Meghan was criticized, including crossing her legs and not wanting pictures taken of her.

The biased framing is not explicitly racist, but it can be inferred that the double standard is driven by racism and/or nationalism. Kate is presented as the default standard for being a royal, while Meghan is held to what some journalists label a "false royal protocol." (Meghan and Harry resigned from the royal family in April 2020.) The discriminatory treatment by the press contributed to Meghan suing *The Mail*. The years-long battle resulted in a $90 million settlement in her favor and the London High Court ordering the tabloid to run a front-page apology to her for breaching her privacy by publishing excerpts from a letter she wrote to her father. The case and verdict represent the lengths to which Meghan must go to protect herself from being attacked and misrepresented by the media.

How could this ruling affect future reports on Meghan or other people of color in the media? How can news outlets be held accountable for their biased reporting? Are more serious news sources guilty of the same patterns of behavior? What impact does this have on audiences? How can audiences be more critical consumers of the media?

Source: Friehl, M. (2019, November 7). Meghan Markle is being criticized for doing the same things that Kate Middleton is praised for. *Insider*.

In this chapter, we will challenge you to consider the different media representations of racial/ethnic groups. We will illustrate the important role of these images in shaping societal attitudes about race and how both macro- and microcultural group members are depicted in very problematic ways. We also address how certain representations have more negative outcomes for marginalized groups than for dominant groups and how racial divisions are maintained and perpetuated by stereotypes associated with certain groups. We provide an overview of the television shows and movies featuring, in alphabetical order, African Americans, Arab Americans, Asian Americans, European Americans, Latinx Americans, and Native Americans and discuss the images embedded within the media.

Sociologist Patricia Hill Collins (2022) uses the term *controlling images* to describe the stereotypes that objectify and dehumanize groups and provide the rationale for domination. Controlling images regulate opportunities, impose constraints, and channel emotions, while also organizing a person's experience and shaping expectations (Vasquez-Tokos & Norton-Smith, 2017). Social institutions circulate controlling images, which ultimately restricts microcultural groups' access to upward mobility and the power of self-definition. Unsurprisingly, the media are prime players in the circulation of these controlling images. Cydney Dupree (2022), who studies stereotyping and intergroup interactions, notes:

> From the first instant our eyes alight on a TV or phone screen, we are inundated with a curated set of images that (supposedly) depict the world around us. These images often show people of color through a stereotypical lens, and these stereotypes bleed into our everyday lives. . . . Stereotypes leak into conversations, even when we try to avoid them. (p. 33)

The media are oftentimes an important source of information for many (Murphy & Harris, 2017). When personal contact between racial groups is limited or nonexistent, there is a greater reliance on media stereotypes when formulating ideas about people outside one's race/ethnicity (Yuen, 2017). As a result, as studies show, the lack of direct interactions with particular racial groups leaves audiences to rely on stereotypes they see on screen. For example, Latinx stereotypes in the media can create associations of immigration with increased unemployment and crime.

Visual images and verbal messages in the media are very powerful and perform a disservice when messages are negative and highly stigmatized. The messages potentially serve as road maps for interracial interactions and may cause people to fear the unknown or perpetuate stereotypes (controlling images). The negative outcome is that interracial communication is perceived as too difficult or stressful to manage. Even when stereotypes seem positive or harmless, they create unrealistic (and often negative) expectations and assumptions that have a profound effect on individuals (Geena Davis Institute, 2021).

Our increasing dependence on social media and mass communication warrants better understanding of different racial/ethnic group members' use of (see Box 11.5) and experience with media and the impact media images have on interracial interactions. Mass media images serve three functions regarding race: (1) to *reflect* societal values and ideas about race/ethnicity; (2) to *reinforce* or *shape* widely shared ideals of "normal"; and (3) to serve as *gatekeepers* to information about race/ethnicity. We begin our exploration of the mass media and race/ethnicity with a brief overview of a few media theories designed to explain and understand media consumption. Our focus will then shift to racial/ethnic representations in the media.

## MEDIA THEORIES: AN INTRODUCTION

There are countless theories social scientists use to understand the motivations of media producers and consumers. In this section, we offer an overview of seven theories (presented in no particular order) that explore the connection between media and culture. We will then address how consumption of restrictive images of racial/ethnic groups has a negative impact on both micro- and macrocultural group members. We hope these theories will encourage you to increase your awareness of the effects of your media consumption.

### Cultivation Theory

Cultivation theory is among the most cited theories in communication research (Busselle & Van den Bulck, 2020), hence its inclusion. Television in the 1960s dominated leisure time and media use. By adulthood, most individuals spent more time watching TV than with any other socializing agent, including schools and parents. Scholar George Gerbner (1969) headed the Cultural Indicators Project at the Annenberg School for Communication at the University of Pennsylvania to study the messages television was sending and their effects on the audience. Cultivation theory proposes that, over time, heavy viewers of television develop views of the world similar to what they see on TV (Bryant & Finklea, 2023). Violent crime is a prime example of the distorted reality perpetuated in TV images—including the frequency of crime, the type of crime, and who commits the crime. The first major cultivation study found that heavier viewers were more likely to see the world as "mean"—filled with violence and crime (Gerbner & Gross, 1976). This was formerly known as the Mean World Syndrome.

Cultivation theory extends beyond violence in the media. TV messages draw a picture of a homogenized world, which Gerber referred to as mainstreaming. Television presents "an overarching message about good and bad, about what mattered in the world and what did not, and about who was powerful and who was not" (Busselle & Van den Bulck, 2020, p. 70). Content analyses of TV shows revealed "which groups in society were more likely to be presented as perpetrators of crime and violence, which groups were more likely to be powerless or victims, which groups were overrepresented, and which ones were underrepresented." More importantly, the presence or absence of groups signaled their place in society: "representation in the fictional world signifies social existence; absence means symbolic annihilation" (Gerbner & Gross, 1976, p. 182). Gerbner's research found that television often operates within the boundaries of commonly held beliefs, resulting in heavy TV viewers receiving reinforcement of the stereotypes and worldviews they already hold. This is possible because those images resonate with audiences. Resonance is the degree to which a mediated image is consistent with a person's lived experience.

Gerbner believed media narratives socialize us into roles of gender, age, class, vocation, and lifestyle. The media cultivate much of what we think, what we do, and how we conduct our affairs. While Gerbner focused on television, cultivation theory has been applied to multiple media channels.

> Just as citizens in previous decades were enveloped in the media environment of television, one must assume that, at least for important developmental periods of their lives, significant numbers of citizens today are enveloped in mediated environments that provide common messages on screens that vary in shape and size and are ubiquitous. Further, those messages, while distributed across thousands of different channels, may be relatively homogeneous with respect to important aspects of social reality. Citizens may communicate with a greater number of acquaintances and significant others than ever before through social networking systems. But similar to the powerful handful of television networks that existed at the inception of cultivation theory, a relatively small group of corporations control or influence a few powerful social media platforms. (Busselle & Van den Bulck, 2020, p. 77)

Unsurprisingly, media messages can lead to narrow perceptions of women, marriage and work, political views, and racial/ethnic microcultures. Heavy viewers ultimately fail to recognize racial, ethnic, and cultural diversity; thus, the social lines of difference (class, race, gender) are blurred, presenting a false perception that the world is homogenous. Heavy viewers also tend to accept the media representations of racially different others, leading to a belief in the accuracy of these stereotypical images. As such, heavy viewing is a barrier to positive race relations because of microcultural group underrepresentation and stereotype perpetuation on television.

## Cultural Studies

The most notable group of cultural scholars is associated with the Centre for Contemporary Cultural Studies at the University of Birmingham. British cultural scholars began writing in the 1950s and explored the gap between the intellectual upper class and their own working-class roots (Littlejohn et al., 2021). Stuart Hall became the director in 1969 and is credited with changing the focus to the media and for bringing issues of race and colonialism into cultural studies research. Cultural studies scholars investigate popular culture to determine the dominant norms and power structures in society and how members of social groups make sense of their everyday lives. A cultural critic might examine how a particular movie is positioned within social processes and how it relates to power structures. Cultural studies theorists are interested in any cultural practices in which negotiation over meaning takes place and in how power is embedded in media texts. This multidisciplinary approach is informed by Marxism, feminism, queer theory, and post-colonialism (Rai & Panna, 2015).

Cultural studies theorists explore the ways disparate elements—for example, economics, media, race, class, and property—are linked across similarities and differences (Littlejohn et al., 2021). These links are part of larger structures; therefore, scholars look at how ideologies coerce individuals into adopting a particular perspective. The television industry, for example, is a means of creating, reproducing, disputing, or changing culture. Cultural studies research looks at representation in media, the benefits and costs of mediated technology, and the different roles audiences play in relation to media. The media are part of the dominant order, but they have the potential to influence individuals' perceptions and opinions about issues of class, power, and domination. Multiple ideologies exist in society and compete for dominance, which Hall referred to as a *theatre of struggle*. Cultural studies scholars are particularly interested in dominant ideologies of capitalism, as they are the driving force behind most societies. They believe that helping people understand the ways ideologies of powerful groups are unwittingly perpetuated and developing ways to resist those ideologies will lead to positive social reform. The end goal of such scholarship is to encourage individuals to engage in social agency and resist dominant cultural agendas (Rai & Panna, 2015).

## Social Learning Theory

Social learning theory, later renamed social cognitive theory, emphasizes observational learning (Bryant & Finklea, 2023). An individual learns from observing other people's actions and the consequences of those actions. The observer can then reenact the learned behavior. There is also a vicarious capacity, which is the ability to learn without direct experience. So, for example, individuals can learn from behavior modeled in the media—whether depictions of prosocial or antisocial behavior. "A vast amount of information about human values, styles of thinking, and behavior patterns is gained from the extensive modeling in the symbolic environment of the mass media (Bandura, 2009, p. 98).

Four human capacities allow us to learn and acquire skills through watching behavior modeled by others: symbolization, self-regulation, self-reflection, and vicarious capability (Bandura, 2009). Simply put, a person stores and uses observed verbal and nonverbal behaviors as a guide for future behavior. This means that memories of events become symbolic representations for reenactment. By observing positive and negative consequences attached to certain actions, we can regulate and modify our behavior. People are influenced directly by experience and indirectly through observation and have the opportunity to reflect on their actions and how they align with values and goals.

To be clear, humans are not automatons merely imitating others; humans have agency (Krcmar, 2021). Four processes are required to reenact observed behavior: *attention, retention, motor reproduction,* and *motivation.* For example, an individual might pay attention to the behavior of a character in a movie, retain information about that behavior, and be physically capable of reproducing that behavior. However, without any desire (motivation) to repeat the action, there will be no imitation.

> Social cognitive theory argues that personal (e.g., personality factors, affective sensitivities), environmental (e.g., media exposure, family), and behavioral determinants interact with one another transactionally, ultimately meaning that the "causes" for human behavior—as well as learning, decision-making, and other related outcomes—are interrelated and cannot be isolated from one another. Each is in a transactional relationship with the other. (p. 101)

An important conclusion reached from content analyses of media is that racist or sexist behavior is modeled in media representations (Krcmar, 2021). If all four processes are present, social cognitive theory would predict that exposure to these depictions should yield effects consistent with the content. For example, a survey taken after participants watched teen movies that portrayed female characters as more socially aggressive than male characters found that viewing teen movies was associated with negative stereotypes about female gender roles. These findings support the primary arguments of the theory.

As you can see, social cognitive theory can contribute to understandings of interracial communication by exploring how racial representations or invisibility educate audiences about racial differences. If interracial interactions are either absent or framed as volatile, then audiences will believe this to be true in their daily lives. Similarly, casting underrepresented groups as terrorists or criminals increases the likelihood that these stereotypes will be accepted as truthful and accurate.

## Standpoint Theory

Standpoint theory was previously discussed in Chapter 1; however, we offer a brief discussion here to stress the influence our vantage points have on how we view the world (Buzzanell, 2015) and engage with media depictions. Feminist thought, Black feminist thought, Chicanx feminist thought, and multiracial feminism are all examples of standpoint theory. Each speaks to the multiple layers of oppression forcing women to the margins of society. Gender

Many assume that standpoints do not impact our experiences with television, film, or other forms of media. While common ground might exist, our standpoints will create different media experiences, which should be appreciated.

oppression is foundational to each school of thought and the corresponding social movements resisting said oppression. It also informs the theories and is an active form of consciousness (feminism) and social theory addressing systemic oppression (Kramarae, 1981; Tully, 2018).

Feminism is often conceptualized as a series of waves distinguished by different objectives (Foss et al., 2022). The first wave began in the mid-1800s and ended in 1920 with the ratification of the Nineteenth Amendment that gave women the right to vote. Legal and social equality for women was the focus of the second wave, which began in the 1960s. The third started in the early 1990s with a focus on individual activism; it emphasized differences among women's experiences. "Many feminists believe we are now in the fourth wave, which began sometime in the first two decades of this century and emphasizes intersectionality, individuality, and policing behavior" (p. 21). The wave metaphor has been criticized because of the tendency to see each wave as a separate entity and to assume that all feminists at a particular moment in time had the same concerns. There are many standpoints within the feminist movement, which is diverse, dynamic, and complex.

Tully (2018) references **millennial feminism**, which is led by millennials and focuses on "intersectionality, sex-positivity, media representation, voice, and the eradication of gender roles" (p. 197). Feminism in the fourth wave is marked by the prominence of mass media in advancing issues of equity and equality regarding gender and race. There are two ideological camps "one the individualist, pragmatic approach based on self-sufficiency, and the other the collective, idealistic approach which speaks to solidarity and community building" (Donegan, 2018). #MeToo's social feminism was heavily influenced by African American feminist scholars such as Kimberlé Crenshaw whose work centers Black women at the intersection of racism and sexism. Self-identified feminists have been successful using social media to bring attention to and galvanize social media movements such #MeToo, Time's Up, and Everyday Sexism, creating a "new collective face of feminism" (Haughton, 2019).

## Magic Bullet Theory, Two-Step Flow Theory, and Curated Information

Mass communication theories explain how the mass media influence attitudes and behaviors and how audiences are likely to react to mass media messages (Nwabueze & Okonkwo, 2018). Studies of propaganda by people such as Harold Lasswell after World War I created a belief that the mass media, particularly electronic media, had almost unlimited power to influence unsuspecting audiences and change attitudes and behavior (Bryant & Finklea, 2023). One of the earliest mass communication theories is the **magic bullet theory or hypodermic needle theory**. It asserts that mass media has a "direct, immediate and powerful effect on its audiences" (Nwabueze & Okonkwo, 2018, p. 1). The impact of media messages on audiences was compared to firing a bullet or injecting a drug, thus causing a desired change in the audience's behavior and psyche. This direct effects theory remained dominant until after the Great Depression.

Despite early claims about the media, empirical studies began to indicate less powerful mass media effects on audiences than originally assumed (Bryant & Finklea, 2023). Paul Lazarsfeld and his colleagues researched the effects of radio and found that interpersonal communication was an important moderating factor. In the 1940s, they examined the influences of mass media on public opinion during a presidential campaign. They introduced the **two-step flow theory**—an indirect effects theory—in which media messages influenced opinion leaders (often heavy users of mass media) who, in turn, influenced others in the community via interpersonal communication.

Thorson and Wells (2016) suggested a comprehensive approach—**curated information**—to explain message flow and media effects. The fragmentation and proliferation of media and technological changes such as multiplatform, multidevice digital networks have affected the messages people receive, create, and distribute. In the digital age, there are five sets of curating actors who produce, select, filter, and frame content: journalists, strategic communicators, individual media users, social contacts, and algorithmic filters. It stands to reason that the effects of messages depend on the curated information consumed.

We hope the theories discussed in this section have encouraged you to think about your own media consumption. As you can see, each of the theories can be used to explain how audiences engage with different forms of mass media and the impact on their behaviors and ways of thinking. This is particularly important for interracial communication since many people depend on the media to inform and educate them about outgroup members from a different racial/ethnic group.

# MASS MEDIA REPRESENTATIONS OF RACIALIZED OTHERS

The media's agenda may be to entertain or to educate, but multiple messages are communicated, thereby complicating the messages received. As a freethinking individual, pay attention to the images you view. Think critically, for example, about media representations of racial/ethnic groups across media. "Ample evidence shows how the manner of ethnic and racial representation in the media can result in either harm or benefit for different groups" (Hughey & González-Lesser, 2020, p. 2). For decades, scholars have investigated the influence of media exposure and its influence on our thinking and behavior. "We live in a media-saturated world, one in which we often do not recognize the extent of our immersion in media because of its banal normality" (p. 3).

As of June 2021, white audiences accounted for 66% of linear (i.e., scheduled) TV programming, while Black (13%) and Hispanic audiences (18%) accounted for markedly less (Nielsen, 2021). The disparities are partially due to whites being the largest racial demographic, with the percentages reflecting the demographics of the U.S. population. In the early days of streaming, content was aimed at a general population, but new platforms now target specific audiences. Latinx audiences spend less time with traditional TV than with streaming services. YouTube accounted for 21% of viewing minutes. Black audiences accounted for 39% of the minutes viewed on Tubi; Pluto also attracts a Black audience. Viewership is also greatly influenced by content and representation, with people of color choosing platforms and programs that reflect their unique experiences.

Despite increased options, mediated images remain problematic yet impactful in shaping how people view outgroup members. People of color have marginal representation in the media and, like other racial/ethnic groups, occupy both old and new stereotypes that make interracial interactions difficult (T. Harris & Scott, 2019). This is particularly true since the racial attitudes of people with limited interracial contact will be shaped by media images, thus profoundly impacting societal perceptions of difference (Washington & Harris, 2018). As you think critically about mass media and racial groups, we encourage you to pay attention to issues of (1) invisibility, (2) underrepresentation, (3) stereotypical depictions, and (4) misrepresentation.

---

### Box 11.1

### Racism in *Big Brother*: The Cookout Alliance

The reality competition show *Big Brother* made history when it crowned its first Black winner in the show's 23-year history. The season was historic because it had six Black houseguests *and* they secretly created an alliance (dubbed The Cookout) on the very first day that lasted through day 85. The other houseguests were unaware that the alliance was created with the "express intent of having the show see its first-ever Black winner" (Seemayer, 2021). The gaming strategy of creating private alliances is common for televised competition shows. The Cookout members also created interracial alliances with other houseguests, who all identified as white, but they remained dedicated to each other and their group mission.

*(continued)*

The Cookout was harshly criticized on social media and accused of "reverse racism." Members dismissed the allegations, stating reverse racism does not exist and stressing that their alliance formed and operated just like all the other alliances since the show's inception. Past winners and alliances have been primarily white houseguests competing and teaming together to eliminate other contestants and win the grand prize. Fan outrage was triggered because the alliance was all-Black and wanted a Black winner and no white male made it to the jury of eliminated players. Winner Xavier Prather said, "I came to this game wanting to do anything and everything I could to make sure that *Big Brother* season 23 would be remembered as crowning the first Black winner in US history." He stressed that this strategy was all about representation regardless which alliance member won.

Is there a double standard in how audiences watch this show? How are BIPOC affirmed by The Cookout's performance and strategy on this show? How does this relate to broader societal race issues? Why do people have a problem with The Cookout? What other shows or movies have experienced similar backlash? What is the best way for the media to address representation issues?

Chapter 3 presented an overview of the labels used to designate the main racial/ethnic groups in the United States. In this section, we present an overview of how each racial/ethnic group, listed in alphabetical order, is represented in the media and the media images typically associated with them. We discuss the roles reality television, film, social media, and other mass media outlets play in shaping societal perceptions of otherness. It is important to note that some groups have less information and examples due to the lack of actual representation and/or research about the groups. At the conclusion of this chapter, you should have a better understanding of the media's power to influence how we think about each other and our racial/ethnic affiliations.

## African Americans

African Americans have historically been plagued by racism, which remains a critical problem in society. Racially charged presentations date back to the late 1700s and caricatures of African slaves in theater presentations (R. Coleman, 2003). What is widely regarded as the first true Hollywood film was released in 1915 (Hunt & Ramón, 2022). *The Birth of a Nation* was blatantly racist, glorifying the Ku Klux Klan and featuring European American actors in blackface enacting potent Black stereotypes. The *Amos 'n' Andy* radio program began airing in 1925 and was an equally troubling representation of African Americans. The two main Black characters, again enacted by European Americans, were presented as lazy, uneducated imbeciles constantly involved in mishaps (Childs, 2021). Stereotypes were eventually integrated into television, which continued the use of European American performers in blackface using exaggerated behaviors. If African American actors were cast, then the roles were degrading, thus perpetuating controlling images that created a false impression of African American identity.

Early African American stereotypes have origins in slavery and include Jezebel, mammy, servant, matriarch, buffoon, minstrel, and slave (Jerald et al., 2017). Shows like *Amos 'n' Andy* (1951–1953), *Beulah*, (1950–1953), and *Jack Benny* (1950–1965) presented African Americans as unintelligent and content with a subservient, powerless social status. *Beulah* solidified the stereotypical domestic servant who happily and devotedly served her boss (Haggins, 2001, p. 250). It also centered the gender-neutral "pickaninny" stereotype of the dirty, bulging-eyed child with thick lips and unkempt hair eating a slice of watermelon and the "coon" stereotype of the foolish, idiotic, subservient, lazy, and "shiftless" nonthreatening African American, a role with which European American audiences were comfortable. The tragic mulatto (deceptive light-skinned African Americans "passing" for white) is another gender-neutral controlling image.

These controlling images are preserved and perpetuated by the media (T. Harris et al., 2018). African American men are stereotyped as Sambo (lazy, jolly, content with life), Uncle Tom (quiet, desires to please the white man), and Buck (strong, athletic, and sexually powerful). African American women are stereotyped as mammy (asexual, nurturing caregiver), Jezebel (sexually promiscuous), and Sapphire (sexually enticing). The video vixen is a 21st century adaptation of Jezebel borne out of the rap music industry (Fitts, 2008). The **Magical Negro** is a controlling image referring to a lead character spiritually gifted with the ability to aid their white lead counterparts (Glenn & Cunningham, 2009). Newer stereotypes include the **Black best friend**, whose purpose is to guide white characters through challenging circumstances (Nittle 2021b). **The thug** is a drug dealer, pimp, con artist, or other criminal stereotype of Black men being dangerous and involved in illicit activities. The **angry Black woman** is sassy, temperamental, difficult to work with, and has an attitude.

The 1970s to the 1980s marked an increase in shows featuring African Americans. Media critics argued that these shows—*Sanford and Son, Good Times, The Jeffersons, What's Happening!!, Diff'rent Strokes, 227,* and *Amen*—reinvented traditional stereotypes in a contemporary context (MacDonald, 1992). The tide turned with *The Cosby Show* (1984–1992), a seemingly positive portrayal of the African American family that has since been criticized for never dealing directly with race while subtly expressing Blackness through onset artifacts (e.g., statues, clothing displaying names of HBCU colleges, music, etc.). More recently, producer Kenya Burris created the sitcom *black-ish* (2015–2022) as a counternarrative to the long-standing stereotypes of African Americans, centering an upper-class Black family that explicitly addresses intersectionality through humor and seriousness.

Mass media representations of African Americans have overwhelmingly been through comedic roles (e.g., neominstrelsy) (Q. Lopez, 2018). Black writers and producers have been creating dramas, sitcoms, sci-fi mysteries to provide audiences with more relatable characters and story lines. This could have been in response to many early 21st century shows that lacked depth and reinscribed many of the previously discussed stereotypes. Black showrunner Shonda Rhimes, who has written multiple highly successful series, made history in 2012 with her political drama *Scandal*. Actress Kerry Washington starred as Olivia Pope—the first African American woman to lead a series since Diahann Carroll 44 years earlier. Despite the lead character being intelligent, powerful, and strong-willed, many criticized *Scandal* for objectifying and sexualizing Olivia as the president's mistress, thus perpetuating the Jezebel stereotype. Other shows have been launched on premium channels, streaming services, and linear television showing diversity through characters and across entertainment genres. *Black Panther*, a movie with an almost all-Black cast and a Black director, was a watershed moment for diversity and representation in 2018. It was the first Marvel movie with a Black superhero and shattered many of the stereotypes seen repeatedly in the media with its

---

**Box 11.2**                                              *Author Reflections*

## Absence of Diversity in Television

I really appreciate the entertainment and information I cull from mass media; however, I am frequently discomforted by and question the images embedded within them. There is considerable invisibility of microcultural group members in popular television programs and movies. After 18 years and 25 seasons, *The Bachelor* (ABC) franchise finally announced that a Black man, Matt James, would be the featured bachelor in 2021 (Bradley, 2020). *The Bachelorette* (ABC) in 2017 chose its first Black lead, Rachel Lindsay, for its 13th season. She threatened to cut ties with the franchise if it did not choose a Black bachelor. In addition to seeking more diverse leads and cast, she lobbied for more diverse people behind the cameras and decision makers. She eventually cut her affiliation after the February 2021 interview described below.

During Lindsay's season, *Bachelorette* contestant Lee Garrett was allowed to pick a fight with a Black contestant (an example of seeking formulaic controversy), and racist tweets he had written resurfaced. Lindsay was unaware of the contestant feud and Garrett's racist social media history, leaving her vulnerable had she selected him. Viewership dropped that season, making some wonder if it was tied to "Trumpish" ways of thinking (Bradley, 2020).

Rachel Kirkconnell was one of four final contestants chosen by Matt James when TikTok users accused her of "liking" racist posts, and photos of her from 2018 surfaced. She was dressed in antebellum attire at an Old South plantation-themed college party. Chris Harrison, host of *The Bachelor* since 2002, defended Kirkconnell on Lindsay's *Extra* show, saying we need compassion and making reference to "the woke police" (Rock, 2022). Shortly thereafter, Harrison stepped aside due to viewer and cast member backlash; he was replaced with former *Bachelorette* leads Tayshia Adams (Black) and Kaitlyn Bristowe (white). Lindsay received death threats and was accused of "cancelling" Harrison.

Was each situation handled fairly? Why or why not? Should the networks be held accountable for not diversifying their characters? Should the hosts? If not, then who can make these changes? What should networks do to address representation issues in this programming genre?

—TMH

depiction of African culture in the fictional nation of Wakanda (Bryant & Finklea, 2023). The film resonated so strongly with Black audiences that many dressed in African regalia at the theaters to celebrate this historic moment in media history.

## Arab Americans

Arab Americans have endured troubling images in all forms of media. Whether news or entertainment, media narratives can construct a reality that misrepresents a population. Machiavelli warned that mankind is often more influenced by things that *seem* rather than by things that *are* (Shaheen, 2009). For more than a century, Arab-as-villain stereotypes have conditioned viewers to dehumanize an entire group. Westerners have stereotyped Arabs as barbaric since the Crusades, which makes it no surprise that Hollywood largely portrays people from the Middle East as Muslims (Nittle, 2021a).

Historically, Arab Americans have been perceived as a homogenous ethnic group with a belief system different from that of people in the United States as a primarily Christian nation (T. Harris & DeTurk, 2012). Susan Fiske, a leading expert on prejudice, notes that people have negative reactions to others who are dramatically different (Resnik, 2017). This is particularly the case when primary exposure to those groups is through the media. This minimal, incomplete characterization activates an us-versus-them conflict. Her research finds that when people dehumanize others, the regions of their brains associated with disgust are activated, and the regions associated with empathy turn off.

One of the longest running stereotypes in Hollywood is the Arab terrorist (Raouf, 2020). After September 11th, Arab Americans were called Osama bin Laden, told to go back where they came from (even though many were born in the United States), and put on watch lists. Depictions on television became more negative and racist in such series as *24* (2001–2010), *24: Legacy* (2016–2017), and *JAG* (1995–2005). Repeated media exposure can cultivate a chronic accessibility to a stereotype—the automatic association of an individual with a stereotypical characterization because of repeated activation (Cohen et al., 2020). For example, viewers repeatedly exposed to the Muslim terrorist stereotype in the news may conclude that all Muslims are terrorists.

Three-quarters of U.S. Muslims believe there is a lot of discrimination against Muslims in the United States, 23% think racism is the most important problem faced, 13% identify ignorance/misconceptions of Islam, 10% say being viewed as terrorists, and 9% indicate negative media portrayals (Pew Research Center, 2017). This is important because nationality and religious identity for Arab Americans and Muslims remain conflated. Television shows perpetuate the apocalyptic and bigoted narrative through fictional terrorists armed with chemical, nuclear, or biological weapons on shows like *NCIS* (2003–present), *Homeland* (2011–2020), and *Quantico* (2015–2018), for example (Nittle, 2021a).

Other less violent yet problematic stereotypes associated with Arab Americans are gendered and common. Women are portrayed as belly dancers or as silent women shrouded in veils; all Arab Americans are depicted as perpetual foreigners, riding camels, and always in the desert (Nittle, 2021a). The characters in TV shows and movies are from unspecified Middle Eastern countries, thus misrepresenting a heterogenous racial/ethnic people. Arab Americans are from countries such as Lebanon, Syria, Iraq, Iran, Jordan, Saudi Arabia, Kuwait, Qatar, Bahrain, United Arab Emirates, Oman, and Yemen. Current shows and movies that positively represent Arab Americans and/or Muslim people are *Whispers* (2020–present*), The Bold Type* (2017–present), *Ramy* (2019–present), graphic novel *Persepolis* (reprint 2022), *Breaking Fast* (2020), *Caramel AKA Sukkar Banat* (2007), *Community* (2009–2015), and *Secret of the Nile* (2018) (Osman, 2021). The narratives center experiences and perspectives rarely seen in most forms of media. They also provide audiences with characters that are relatable for Arab Americans and break away from the controlling images that have dominated mass media.

When audiences identify with characters, they are more likely to be empathetic (Cohen et al., 2020). Thus, seeing the world through the eyes of a character can provide a better understanding of different perspectives and experiences. Identification, however, is not restricted to characters who are demographically similar. Studies have looked at how media characters can impact audience members. For example, one study found that Jewish students who identified with an Arab character had more positive attitudes about the conflict between Arabs and Israelis, greater willingness to interact with Arabs, and reduced stereotypes about Arabs (Tal-Or & Tsfati, 2016).

---

### *Box 11.3*

### Racial Profiling After September 11th

In the wake of 9/11, racial profiling of people appearing to be of Middle Eastern descent has evolved into a common practice among many people. Countless stories have been told about citizens reporting others as being potential terrorists. The media prime society to look for physical markers signifying someone's racial/ethnic group membership.

One example of a formal, systemic process is the U.S. Army's iWatch program. People are encouraged to "see something, say something" and report suspicious activity such as people drawing or measuring important buildings, asking questions about security forces or security procedures, leaving briefcases or suitcases behind, intruders in secure areas, or individuals wearing clothes that are too big or inappropriate for hot weather. While in theory heightened awareness was somewhat warranted, it has conditioned us to believe that "Arab racial background or Islamic faith [was/is] a factor or proxy for precursor terrorist activity" (T. Yin, 2010, p. 118).

Arab Americans are a diverse racial/ethnic group and should be presented as such. Counterimages based on the diversity of identities would create the multi-dimensionality essential to changes in societal attitudes towards this marginalized group. What are your thoughts about how Arab Americans are depicted in the media? Do you think the portrayals are unfair? Has what you have learned here prompted you to rethink racism in the media?

## Asian Americans and Pacific Islanders (AAPIs)

As discussed in Chapter 10 (as well as Chapter 12), hate crimes against AAPI people have increased since the pandemic. These violations of human rights underscore the need for investigations of cultural messages about microcultures to combat stereotypes that contribute to violence (Geena Davis Institute, 2021). One of the enduring stereotypes is the *perpetual foreigner*, which presents Asian Americans as foreigners with allegiance to their ancestral countries despite a U.S. nationality. Seeing individuals as foreign (i.e. outsiders) makes it more likely that they will be treated with hostility. This was evidenced when people of East Asian heritage were associated with images of **yellow peril**. Specifically, the character of Fu Manchu—a villain intent on world domination and a foe to democracy and Christianity—embodied this stereotype and was often portrayed by white actors in yellowface. It is no surprise that the stereotype can have profound consequences. Yellow peril was the manufactured fear that Asians were taking over and threatening U.S. society and culture. Repetition of the stereotype in the media resulted in paranoid xenophobia (J. Lee, 2018). As discussed in Chapter 3, 110,000 Japanese Americans were forcibly removed to internment camps during World War II, which was the result of an unfounded fear of the other.

Cultural stereotypes reflect assumptions that Asian Americans in general are (1) the model minority, (2) perpetual foreigners, (3) innately predatory (immigrants who never give back), (4) restricted to clichéd occupations (e.g., restaurant workers, laundry workers, martial artists, etc.), and (5) inherently comical or sinister (M. Park et al., 2021). We have previously discussed the negative aspects of the model minority stereotype (hardworking, well educated, talented in science and math) and its tendency to ignore diversity within the Asian community. The model minority myth makes Asian Americans invisible by assuming the positive stereotyping erases discrimination (Nunes, 2021). Cultural differences between East Asian heritage (Chinese, Korean, Japanese) and South Asian cultural traditions (Indians, Pakistani, Bangladeshi) explain why South Asians are more likely to achieve executive leadership despite generally facing more prejudice (attributable to darker complexions—colorism as discussed in Chapter 7). Scholars attribute the difference to communication patterns (Lu et al., 2020). Cultural traditions of East Asians encourage reserve, humility, and harmony, while South Asian culture encourages assertiveness in communication—a style that matches expectations for leadership communication in the United States. Regardless of one's ethnicity, all Asian Americans face hurdles in overcoming the stereotypes routinely seen in the media, but some cultural traditions help break the bamboo ceiling.

As with other racial/ethnic groups, the media reinforce Asian American stereotypes (Kao & Shinkoda, 2021). Images of people from macrocultures and microcultures exist in the same space, which means that, for example, stereotypes of one group as feminine elevates the masculinity of the other group. Romantic relationships on the screen generally involve a European American man and an Asian American woman. In the early days of film and television,

Asian American men were cast as effeminate laundry workers and cooks (Geena Davis Institute, 2021). More recently, they are typecast as nerdy, sidekicks, math geniuses, and unattractive to women—often speaking with heavy accents (which reinforce the perpetual foreigner stereotype). Newer and more negative gender-neutral stereotypes have emerged, such as technical robot, fresh off the boat, and Kung Fu warriors. The **technical robot** was introduced through *Top Chef* and *Project Runway* (G. Wang, 2010); in this stereotype, the unemotional (e.g., robot-like) Asian American is unassailable as a competitor but lacks creativity. Fresh off the boat is a derogatory term assuming a person is a new immigrant not yet adapted to a country's customs, language, and traditions (Abad-Santos, 2015). Kung Fu warriors invoke the stereotype of every Asian person as a martial artist (Guo & Harlow, 2014).

Controlling images of Asian Americans are also gendered and overwhelmingly negative—whether effeminate or unrelentingly cruel. Men are frequently asexual or associated with the emasculated stereotypes of eunuchs. Many were deferential to whites and nonthreatening. Charlie Chan was a detective who revealed his powers of deduction through fortune-cookie platitudes. In contrast, Fu Manchu was a diabolical representative of yellow peril (F. Wu, 2002). As for women, they are perceived as hypersexual, as evidenced by the **Lotus Blossom** stereotype (i.e., China Doll, Geisha Girl, Shy Polynesian Beauty) (Guo & Harlow, 2014). The stereotype presents a submissive, delicate character who is sexually available. Conversely, the **Dragon Lady** is cold, calculating, manipulative, and aggressive, while exuding exotic danger. The **Suzie Wong** stereotype suggests a woman with model minority, assimilation/dependency, and exoticism qualities (Balaji & Worawongs, 2010).

Pioneering East Asian actress Anna May Wong had a long career in Hollywood playing slave girls, prostitutes, temptresses, and doomed lovers (J. Lee, 2018). Early in the career of popular Asian American actor Lucy Liu, her characters in *Ally McBeal* and *Kill Bill* were cold and sexually manipulative. Later in her career, ethnicity did not play a part in her roles in *Charlie's Angels, Elementary,* and *Why Women Kill* (Sirikul, 2021). Recent shows and movies have been instrumental in helping destigmatize Asians. Television series and films, such as *The Half of It, Shadow and Bone,* and *Killing Eve,* are depicting Asian American characters with more nuance. The 2018 blockbuster hit *Crazy Rich Asians* was a Hollywood-backed film based on the first book in a trilogy written by Chinese-Singaporean author Kevin Kwan. The movie successfully centered Asian culture from an Asian American perspective. Despite its historic success, director Jon Chu was criticized for relegating Brown actors to subservient roles (Bose, 2021) and inaccurately depicting Singaporean diversity (Goh, 2018). Other Asian and Asian American films include *Parasite, The Farewell,* and *Minari* featuring well-rounded Asian American characters expressing the full spectrum of human emotions (Kao & Shinkoda, 2021). In 2020, *Parasite* made history by snagging the Oscar for best picture, becoming the first foreign language film to do so in Oscar's 92-year history. These efforts should inspire future film makers to be historically accurate so audiences can learn about Asian culture and avoid stereotypes related to culture, class, and nation.

## European Americans

European Americans are direct benefactors of racism and, as a result, are prevalent in the media and represented through diverse images. They have ethnic diversity (see Chapter 3) that is usually unacknowledged, unexplored, or unknown. European Americans are considered the default or norm for nearly every aspect of human life and are depicted as raceless, void of ethnicity, and from an array of professions, classes, and walks of life (Morris, 2016). A consequence of these depictions is that other races and ethnicities are viewed in a very negative light. European Americans in the media are typically Italians, Irish, and Jews, with each ethnic group being synonymous with white. Each ethnic group has had and continues to experience discrimination, racial prejudice, and xenophobia. While the groups benefit from their racial location, they are stigmatized in their portrayals in the media.

General portrayals include rich housewives, reality television stars, white-collar suburbanites, doctors, forensic scientists, lawyers, and love interests. There is some physical diversity, but the standard of beauty remains blonde hair, blue eyes, thin, and porcelain skin. In the shows *Real Housewives of New Jersey* (2009–present), *Sister Wives* (2010–present), *Dance Moms* (2011–2019), *Teen Mom* (2009–present), *Keeping Up With the Kardashians* (2007–2021), *Here Comes Honey Boo Boo* (2012–2017), *Gossip Girl* (2007–2012), *Jersey Shore* (2009–2012), and *Jersey Shore: Family Vacation* (2018–present), the European American characters possess negative qualities, such as intellectual inferiority, anger management issues, materialism, narcissism, immorality, and dysfunction (Gibson et al., 2018). Redneck humor is a genre that presents them as uneducated, "poor white trash," as seen in the reality television show *Duck Dynasty* (2012–2017) that showcases the multi-millionaire Robertson family. The brothers wore long beards, headbands, and overalls, spoke with strong Southern accents, and held strong conservative Christian values that fueled homophobic, racist, and xenophobic messages. The show was eventually canceled.

About 5.5% of the U.S. population identify as Italian Americans (Sawe, 2019). The predominant stereotypes are mobsters or thugs as seen in films such as *The Godfather*, *Goodfellas*, *Casino*, and *Donnie Brasco* and in television series including *The Sopranos*, *Growing Up Gotti*, and *Mob Wives* (Nittle, 2019). On the MTV reality series *Jersey Shore*, the characters were self-described as "Guido" and "Guidette," pejorative slang terms. The visual representations of the stereotypes depict Italian Americans as "lazy, promiscuous, narcissistic, violent, unthinking, vapid members of society whose main concern is the gym, tanning, and doing laundry" (Giannino, 2013, p. 3). The women are sexually promiscuous tramps, and men are uneducated, dishonest, and/or violent, sex-crazed womanizers.

Irish Americans are about 10.6% of the population (Sawe, 2019). They are stigmatized by the controlling (negative) images of the professional boxer, rebel, lazy and abusive drunk, hardworking blue-collar worker, and being hot-headed and belonging to a matriarch-led family (Dowd, 2016). The dominant stereotype portrays Irish Americans as "always willing to fight and die for causes domestic and foreign" (Fox, 2019, p. 46). Fairly recent TV shows containing these stereotypes are *The Mick* (2017–2018), *Blue Bloods* (2010–present), *Boardwalk Empire* (2009–2014), *Shameless* (2011–2021), and *Sons of Anarchy* (2008–2014).

Immigrants face xenophobia and stereotypes because they are a perceived threat to the status quo. When Jewish Americans immigrated to the United States in the 19th and 20th centuries, the country was undergoing a dramatic transformation with the rise of urbanization, industrialization, and the integration of women and microcultures into the workforce (Prell, 2021). Many stereotypes replicated those in Europe, and some were created by Jewish immigrants of different generations, genders, and socioeconomic statuses: the ineffective immigrant father, the noisy Eastern European Jewish woman, and the smothering Jewish mother. Other stereotypes surfaced: Jewish American Princess (i.e., materialistic, selfish, neurotic), nice Jewish boy (i.e., mensch, nerdy, physically week, neurotic), nice Jewish girl (i.e., old-fashioned, kind, domestic, nasally voice), and self-hating anti-Semitic Jew (Pickette, 2020).

The first Jewish female characters appeared on the TV shows *The Goldbergs* (1949–1957) and *The Gertrude Berg Show* (1961–1962). Jewish comedy through the first decade of the new millennium was marked by three phases (Ruggieri & Leebron, 2010). Phase 1 (1989–1992) marked a breakthrough of Jewish comedies with characters assimilated into mainstream society (read white) through the sitcom *Seinfeld*. Phase 2 (1992–1998) included shows influenced by *Seinfeld* featuring **crypto-Jews**, or seemingly Jewish characters who are racially/ethnically ambiguous, increasing their mainstream appeal. Phase 3 (1998–2010) sitcoms feature attractive, sexually confident female protagonists who use Yiddish expressions frequently. Recent shows centering Jewishness include *Crazy Ex-Girlfriend* (2015–2019), *The Goldbergs* (2013–present), *Unorthodox* (2020), *The Marvelous Mrs. Maisel* (2017–present), *Curb Your Enthusiasm* (2000–2020), and *Shtisel* (2013–2021). Much like *Crazy Ex-Girlfriend*, many of these shows embrace Jewish stereotypes while connecting Jewish femininity with psychosis (Pickette, 2020).

## Indigenous Americans

Indigenous Americans have been stereotyped to fit ideological needs (Fitzgerald, 2014). Many durable stereotypes surfaced during colonial times to justify conquest and dispossession. The term *Indian* was designated to frame them as a monolithic group—completely ignoring the diversity of many hundreds of tribes with different languages, traditions, and histories (Singer, n.d.). The stereotypes offered a polarized binary: either docile, childlike natives or aggressive, murderous heathens. Generations of viewers saw either rampaging, bloodthirsty savages or peaceful people willing to give up their sovereignty and assimilate into white culture. The "good" Indian helped the Europeans (thereby endorsing domination) and the "bad" Indian resisted Europeans who had arrived to civilize the wilderness (Hirschfelder & Molin,

2018). Out of these images grew the stereotypes of an evil, vicious, cruel, murderous enemy (the bloodthirsty savage) and the innocent, free-spirited child of nature (the noble savage). The representations invariably depicted the demise of "Indians"—portrayals that suggested they existed only in the past not in the present. The narrative structure featured Indigenous people—whether savage or noble—as a perpetual backdrop to a white person's story (Marubbio & Buffalohead, 2013). Whether positive or negative, the images deny both the lived reality and the survival efforts of Indigenous Americans.

These images perpetuate and instill the belief that being Indigenous American is a relic of the past. This invisibility suggests Indigenous Americans either do not exist or their numbers are too few to represent fairly. Very few shows had a prominent Indigenous American character: *The Lone Ranger* (1949–1957), *Dr. Quinn, Medicine Woman* (1993–1998), *Walker, Texas Ranger* (1993–2001), *Northern Exposure* (1990–1995), *MacGyver* (1985–1992), and *Quantum Leap* (1989–1993). From 1987 to 2009, Indigenous Americans were largely excluded from prime-time television; from 2017 to 2019, there were no lead characters of Indigenous heritage on scripted broadcast, cable, or digital shows (Bryant & Finklea, 2023). Native characters accounted for 0.5% or less on television. The few visible characters were portrayed on the Western frontier, limiting them to the western genre of movies and television. More recent depictions include alcoholism and untrustworthy Native casino owners (Dixon, 2020), and when Indigenous Americans appear in the news, the focus is generally on cultural festivals, reinforcing a stereotype of being mysterious and overly spiritual.

Film images prior to 1960 frequently presented Indigenous Americans wielding tomahawks, often intent on scalping settlers. There have been other outrageous *mis*representations. For example, the speech of Indigenous Americans is presented as substandard and *foreign*—not native. This is another example of stereotypes and ideology; it positions the language of Indigenous Americans as outside the national boundaries (Meek, 2006). Another significant threat to Indigenous representation is "playing Indian" (Hirschfelder & Molin, 2018). Children imitate the speech (or nonspeech) heard in media representations, buy toys and clothes based on the media images, and construct teepees. Organized sports teams have (or had) derogatory/stereotypical names (Braves, Chiefs, Indians, Savages, Redskins, and Warriors), "red-face" mascots, costumes, and fans who engage in demeaning war whooping and tomahawk chopping—all of which have become normalized. While some may argue that these depictions are harmless, research has shown otherwise. Studies have shown that media images of Native American mascots affect the moods of Indigenous American adolescents and young adults and lower their self-esteem (Yuen, 2017).

Wes Studi, an Indigenous American, has both experienced and countered the effects of deeply ingrained stereotypes. He grew up in Oklahoma and spoke only Cherokee until he was 5. After seeing Jay Silverheels on the TV series *The Lone Ranger*, he asked his father whether someone else could do what Jay Silverheels did. His father said that was unlikely because most actors were 6 feet tall with blue eyes and blond hair (Coyle, 2022). Hollywood was still casting white actors to play Indigenous people when Studi began pursuing an acting career in the 1990s. He received an honorary Oscar in 2019—the first Indigenous American to receive an Academy Award. He has played vengeful warriors and resistance leaders but has not been limited to what he calls "leather and feathers" characters. He is a recurring guest star in *Reservation Dogs* and appears in *Rutherford Falls*. He hopes the expanded roles will create a better understanding of Indigenous people and erase the stereotype that no one survived. At age 75, Studi was cast in a film where he plays the romantic lead. As the director of the film stated, the female and male lead actors in the film have appeared in more than a hundred films and never kissed anyone on screen—a revealing fact about who is allowed to fall in love in movies.

The shows *Rutherford Falls* (2021–present) and *Reservation Dogs* (2021–present) offer positive counterimages and narratives through Indigenous American characters, producers, and writers (Cimaglio & Hall, 2021); they are telling their own stories and celebrating Indigenous American culture in powerful and affirming ways. They challenge the stereotypes of what it means to be Indigenous while addressing the tragic history of colonization.

## Latinx

What images pop into your mind when you think of Latinx people? Are they positive or negative? Think about those images as we discuss how Latinx individuals are typically portrayed in the media.

In 2019, about 11% of news analysts, reporters, and journalists were Latinx, which included employees of Spanish-language networks (Galvan, 2021). The absence of Latinx in newsrooms and other media industries results in portrayals that affect how fellow Americans view this ethnicity. The most recurring stereotypes of Latinx Americans occur in the context of news (Dixon, 2020). The majority of news stories focus on illegal immigration and Latinx Americans as criminals, cultural threats, or competitors for jobs. Most news stories depict all undocumented immigrants as Latinx, which is a significant distortion of reality.

Latinx Americans comprise 18.5% of the U.S. population, but they were grossly underrepresented in scripted shows across broadcast (5.3%), cable (6.3%), and digital (5.7%) platforms during the 2018–2019 television season (Bryant & Finklea, 2023). This lack of representation results in stereotypical presentations rather than richer, more complete narratives. Of 1,200 popular films released between 2007 and 2018, 4.5% of more than 47,000 speaking roles went to Latinx actors (D. Kellner, 2020). Campaigns to increase diversity in Hollywood, such as #OscarsSoWhite, have resulted in actors of color landing more high-profile roles (S. Smith et al., 2019). However, Latinx trailed all ethnic groups in screen time. In an analysis of the top 200 movies from 2017 to 2018, the culture of Latinx characters was erased or minimized. Characters are not shown living with other family members, and there are no context cues such as flags, cuisine, clothing, or cultural artifacts related to their background. When Latinx teens view negative depictions of their culture, they have negative self-perceptions. Studies have found that exposure to films negatively affected school performance, social abilities, and self-esteem for Latinx teens.

In entertainment media, Latinx characters, particularly women, are stereotyped as hypersexualized and employed in low status jobs (Dixon, 2020). Latinx men with darker complexions are portrayed as aggressive and criminal, while those with lighter skin color are depicted as intelligent and articulate. Latinx characters are often depicted as living in poverty, attempting to cross the border, or as criminals. Latinx people in general are stereotyped as undocumented people, unintelligent, and hot-tempered (Erba, 2018). Latinx men are portrayed as drug dealers, gangbangers, dance kings, Latin lovers, and janitors (T. Anderson, 2017). Latinx women are portrayed as sexy sirens or housemaids; they are either manipulative temptresses or self-sacrificing with virginal qualities. Regardless of gender, hypersexual and criminal Latinx characters are associated with negative attitudes. The characters also usually speak Spanish only or very broken English. Through these depictions, audience attitudes are affected by both the quantity and quality of representation (Bryant & Finklea, 2023). Lack of representation results in stereotypical presentations rather than richer, more complete narratives. Studies have shown that one way to remedy this issue is to depict Latinx characters as professionals, leading to more favorable audience attitudes.

Notable television programs featuring a Latinx American characters include *I Love Lucy* (1951–1957), *Chico and the Man* (1974–1978), *Will & Grace* (1998–2006), *The West Wing* (1999–2006), *The Brothers Garcia* (2000–2003), *Dora the Explorer* (2000–2012), *George Lopez* (2002–2007), *Desperate Housewives* (2004–2012), *Ugly Betty* (2006–2010), *Modern Family* (2009–2020), *Glee* (2009–2015), *Ringer* (2011–2012), and *H8R* (2011). More recent shows are *Euphoria* (2020–present), *Lucifer* (2016–2021), *Pose* (2018–present), *Mr. Iglesias* (2019–2021), *Gentefied* (2020–present), *One Day at a Time* (2017–present), *Jane the Virgin* (2014–2019), and *Station 19* (2018–present). *Station 19* offers a counterimage of the Latinx community with Puerto Rican character Andrea "Andy" Herrera as the lieutenant and co-acting captain for fire station 19 in Seattle. Andy is a strong, multilayered female character who is very close with her father.

The Disney animated movie *Encanto* (2021) celebrates Columbian-Hispanic culture through the Madrigal family, a matrilineal family with supernatural power. The movie is groundbreaking because it showcases characters of all shades and hues within the Latinx community while also deviating from typical Disney movies that idealize marriage and have an antagonist (Sinha, 2022). *Encanto* "sheds light on personal struggles with vulnerability, self-acceptance, and embracing imperfections" while celebrating Latinx culture. *In the Heights*, originally a Lin-Manuel Miranda off-Broadway play that launched his career, became a movie in 2021. It is a vibrant portrayal of joys and struggles in a neighborhood (R. Reyes, 2021). One character is worried about college; her neighbors worry about gentrification; other characters run businesses. Miranda's tribute to his Washington Heights neighborhood depicts a diverse Latinx community of all ages and backgrounds (Puerto Rican, Dominican, Cuban) dealing with love, loss, and family issues.

More Latinx individuals as directors can certainly shift narratives away from stereotypes toward a nuanced picture of a vibrant and multifaceted community (Longoria & Smith, 2021). This will be difficult to achieve since Hollywood professes to be inclusive, but its practices do not match the rhetoric. The entertainment industry is fully capable of creating change, as evidenced by the following two examples. In the 1940s, films were produced to inspire soldiers and the nation during World War II. *Will & Grace* and *The Ellen Show* contributed funds to support marriage equality. Regarding Latinx people, similar efforts should be made in shifting the narrative in order to end decades of erasure, stereotyping, and marginalization through better representation.

---

**Box 11.4**                                            *Student Reflections*

### The Fight Against Mexican Stereotypes . . . on *Desperate Housewives*

This issue [of racial stereotypes in media] was addressed in an episode of *Desperate Housewives*. Gabrielle and her husband are attempting to adopt a baby because Gabrielle is unable to have children. They have searched for the right mother and finally came across a young woman who Gabrielle thought was a perfect mother for their future child. However, this young mother did not believe that Gabrielle and her husband should be able to adopt her daughter purely because of the fact that Gabrielle and her husband were Mexicans. This young Caucasian woman immediately judged Gabrielle and her husband once she found out that they were Mexican rather than Hispanic.

I think that this was an excellent topic for *Desperate Housewives* to address because Mexicans are constantly fighting against stereotypes. Some of the stereotypes that I have heard about the Mexican culture are that they are poor, dirty, and will do hard labor for a very small amount of money. I am sure if I thought harder I could come up with many more stereotypes. I believe that oftentimes people forget to discuss how this culture is constantly discriminated against in the United States, and I am thankful that *Desperate Housewives* has brought this issue to the forefront. Besides appearing in *Desperate Housewives*, the issue has grown in popularity because of the new government bills that attempt to send home illegal immigrants, with a focus on the immigrants from Mexico. There are so many different views about this issue, but personally I believe that they should be welcomed into this culture. While I know that I am not aware of all the issues surrounding the issue of illegal immigrants, I do believe that we have a right to attempt to allow anyone willing to work and find a better life into this country. Personally, I believe that this is why our country was founded in the first place, an attempt to find a better life away from the government and hardships of our motherland.

## MASS MEDIA VENUES AND CONSUMPTION

Various forms of media play a major role in the lives of most U.S. Americans. We will first discussion television because it is a media type to which most people have easy access.

### Television

Hollywood's racial and gender biases result in heroes portrayed by European Americans while members of microcultural groups are either erased or play subordinate roles as sidekicks, villains, or sexual objects (Yuen, 2017). One negative consequence of these disparities is their impact on microcultural groups. According to some research, prolonged television viewing predicts a decrease in self-esteem for all girls and African American boys but an increase

---

**Box 11.5**                                                **Author Reflections**

#### Interracial and Intraracial Conflict in Reality Television

I have a "nonscholarly" confession to make: I have always loved to watch television. While my viewing has fluctuated over time, I currently average at least 4 hours of television viewing a day. This may sound like a huge amount of time for a university professor actively involved in teaching, research, and community service. The good news is that a significant amount of my television viewing is tied to one of my research areas: representations of diversity within the media.

My recent research interests have focused on reality-based television. More specifically, I'm interested in those shows that feature different forms of interracial and intraracial conflict (something that seems to be a hallmark of many reality shows). For instance, I serve on a dissertation committee for a student who is studying audience perceptions of authenticity of the Kardashians' shows (focusing on the "big" wedding special). I am also interested in comparing and contrasting similar shows with a specific focus on representations of race/ethnicity. For instance, as someone who has seen both seasons of VH1's *Flavor of Love*, I am intrigued with how this show's depiction of female competition compares against other similar shows (e.g., *The Bachelor*), especially the ways in which "blackness" and "whiteness" intersect with representations of sexuality. My most recent focal point is on how whiteness is represented in terms of class and regionality—really fascinating stuff. Analyzing shows such as *Here Comes Honey Boo Boo, Buckwild*, and *Breaking Amish* provide interesting points of analysis.

- What types of media are you most interested in?
- What is your reality TV "guilty pleasure"?
- How concerned are you about the ways in which your racial/ethnic group is portrayed on reality TV?
- What can you learn from analyzing the ways in which race and ethnicity are represented in these shows?

—MPO

in self-esteem for European American boys. African Americans watch an average of 3.55 hours of live TV a day, while Asians watch 1.75 hours, and Hispanics watch 2.45 hours (Watson, 2019). Use of streaming services is similar across racial groups, with 51% of white adults, 50% of Latinx adults, and 50% of African American adults watching or streaming TV shows every day (Stoll, 2021). Respondents identifying as "other" consumed significantly less media at 14%. Data suggest that all racial groups are engaging with various media with different motivations.

Viacom/CBS (parent company of Paramount+, CBS, MTV, Nickelodeon and Comedy Central) surveyed more than 15,000 people in 15 countries to determine how consumers feel about how they are depicted in TV shows and movies (NickALive, 2021). The Global Insights project explored how television and entertainment teach people about themselves and others. Almost 8 in 10 people believed that it was important for television shows to offer representation of different groups and identities because portrayals on TV shows and movies influence perceptions in the real world. Almost 6 in 10 people believed that they did not see enough people like themselves on screen, and 52% believed they were not accurately represented. A consequence of poor representation it that it negatively impacts self-esteem, confidence, opportunities, and sense of belonging. People from microcultural communities often felt caricatured. Unfortunately, perpetuating harmful stereotypes remains highly damaging to audiences, While the first concern regarding representation was race/ethnicity in Australia, the Netherlands, Nigeria, Singapore, South Africa, the United Kingdom, and the United States, economic status ranked first in Argentina, Brazil, Chile, Germany, Italy, Malaysia, Mexico, and Poland.

## The Internet

Since its inception in the 1990s, the internet has become a primary source of communication for people. Smartphones, tablets, laptops, and desktop computers are used with such regularity that they are increasingly replacing tradi-

Social media and other forms of technology are an integral part of daily life for many, and research shows distinct patterns in their usages across racial/ethnic groups.

tional forms of interpersonal communication. This is potentially problematic for our relationships, and we must work to ensure that the art of human communication is not lost. The internet is different from other media because it allows users to become a part of a virtual community. Users transcend space and time and engage in on-screen conversations with people throughout the world.

| Box 11.6 | | | | |
|---|---|---|---|---|

### Table of Social Media Use

| Race | Use One Social Media Site | Facebook | Instagram | LinkedIn |
|---|---|---|---|---|
| Hispanic | 80% | 72% | 52% | 19% |
| Black | 77% | 74% | 49% | 29% |
| White | 69% | 64% | 35% | 27% |

Source: Pew Social Media Fact Sheet (2021)

While communication on the internet can certainly be positive, the sad reality is that racism exists there as well. Indeed, the internet facilitates wide circulation of racist views, which is a problem since social media platforms are widely used but unregulated. As such, extreme views and lies are available to a huge audience. (Suciu, 2021). The resurgence of white nationalism, rebranded as the Alt-Right, is largely due to virtual spaces and former President Donald Trump's active use of social media "to follow and repost comments by a number of online social media users with white supremacist ties" (Eschmann, 2020b, p. 419). Social media companies have provided targeting tools that aid in sowing division and distrust (Eisenstat, 2021). Algorithms determine what speech to amplify to keep users engaged, which can include connecting users to hate groups. There are no laws governing how social media companies should address hate speech, conspiracy theories, or incitement to violence.

While developing a formal approach in response to cyber racism may not be feasible for some people, behavioral change on the individual level is a great way to start. Users need to think critically about information on the internet to identify misinformation and unsupported assertions. Community activism, among other approaches, can be used to combat online aggression and intimidation. The Southern Poverty Law Center (SPLC) provides a list of 10 things we can do to fight hate: (1) act; (2) join forces; (3) support the victims; (4) speak up; (5) educate yourself; (6) create an alternative; (7) pressure leaders; (8) stay engaged; (9) teach acceptance; and (10) dig deeper (Via & Brooks, 2017).

## Implications and Consequences of Media Images

There is great concern about media images because of their profound effect on everyday life. Media is the dominant form of culture that socializes us (D. Kellner, 2020).

> Media culture divides the world into categories of "us" and "them" and tells us who are our friends and enemies, who we should love and hate, and who we are and should be. . . . Media spectacles demonstrate who has power and who is powerless, who is allowed to exercise force and violence, and who is not. They dramatize and legitimate the power of the powers that be and show the powerless that they must stay in their place. (p. 1)

Research continues to show a clear connection between racial/ethnic images in the media, societal stereotypes of others, and negative interracial/interethnic interactions (Lienemann & Stopp, 2013). Throughout this chapter, we see have seen how mass media images of underrepresented group members are especially powerful given the quality and quantity of portrayals. We also recognize the importance of having BIPOC behind the scenes creating the narratives we see in the media. One example is the recent work of Indian American actress/comedian/screenwriter/producer/director Mindy Kaling.

> This authentic scriptwriting can be attributed to Mindy Kaling's decision to hire young Indian American writers, which she has previously discussed in an interview with *The New York Times*. The positive effects of hiring actual South Asian writers is apparent in the show. The cultural "inside knowledge" is visible: the portrayal of the social phenomenon called "aunties," use of common South Asian nicknames, and popular Bollywood music (songs such as "Mehndi Laga Ke Rakhna" and "Nagada Sang Dhol") instead of the default instrumental Indian music we have heard countless times before. (Tariq, 2020)

Clearly, one effect mass media images have had on interracial communication is reinforcing existing racial/ethnic stereotypes. An equally important effect is related to how the mass media has presented examples of interracial communication. Most media texts create separate worlds for different racial/ethnic groups. For instance, the vast majority of television programs and films feature casts of one racial or ethnic group. Although some may include one or two token representations of outgroup members, their presence is marginal to the overall plot. When interracial communication does occur, it is done with little, or no, attention to any sort of racial/ethnic barriers. These depictions are too simplistic to model any concrete strategies for competent interracial communication for viewers. Some scholars, as explained in the next section, even see how these more positive images of race/ethnicity contribute to a new form of racism.

---

**Box 11.7**                                                    *Research Highlight*

## (Mis)representation and Invisibility in Mainstream Movies

Racial representation in entertainment media is an issue Hollywood directors/producers Spike Lee and Jordan Peel bring to society's conscience through their race-laden films such as *BlacKkKlansman* (2018), *Chi-Raq* (2015), *Da 5 Bloods* (2020), *Lovecraft Country* (2020), *Get Out* (2018), and *Us* (2019).

Brenda Cooper (1998) used relevancy as the framework in her research on the reactions of African Americans and non-African Americans to Lee's 1989 film, *Do the Right Thing*. Her analysis of the "white-black fault line" still holds true today. "While issues of racism appear irrelevant to the cultural subjectivities of the non-African American spectators, racism and its consequences are the major relevant issues in the viewing experiences of the African American spectators" (p. 205). Her primary argument is that African American audiences believe their experiences are mirrored by the characters and speak to "broader issues of societal discrimination and marginalization of people of their race" (p. 205). Non-African Americans do not make the same connection. By identifying with white characters, they discount (or justify) the racism in the film.

Lee has confronted fellow directors/producers Quentin Tarantino, Tyler Perry, and Clint Eastwood by questioning the authenticity, misrepresentation, and invisibility in the stories being told. For example, Lee accuses Tarantino of minimizing the historical significance of slavery in *Django Unchained* (2012), Perry of reifying minstrelsy in all of his films (specifically with character Madea), and Eastwood of invisibility by excluding African Americans from his war films. The tensions between the producers have been fairly volatile, with each taking a different stance on the issue of racial representation.

Cooper's research highlights the salience of audience racial differences and viewpoints in creating qualitatively different experiences with media. Her framework explains the producers' different stances on Lee's accusations about how they choose to (or not) represent African Americans in their movies.

Regardless of one's position, we must acknowledge that the movies' characters and stories individually and collectively impact understandings of "the other" for both ingroup and outgroup members. (Mis)representation and invisibility contribute to the perpetuation of controlling images that have existed for years and must be challenged by producers and viewers alike.

---

# FOSTERING AN ENLIGHTENED AND AVERSIVE RACISM

Adopting an attitude denying the existence or reality of racism is a very misinformed and naïve position to take toward race relations. Some may believe society is operating with a level playing field, but considerable evidence exists to the contrary. A truly informed understanding of under- and misrepresentation can only be gained through race narratives or stories, which we also hope leads to awareness and action. Enlightened racism and aversive racism are two ideologies about race that complicate this process and must be addressed. These two different forms of denial work against positive race relations and efforts to counter postracial ideology. Our discussion of media treatments of different racial/ethnic groups has revealed how imperative it is that everyone, regardless of their group membership, begin to think more critically about race in every social context.

**Enlightened racism** is the acknowledgement of the historical significance of racism in the United States but a failure to see its effect on historically oppressed groups. Jhally and Lewis (2003) introduced this concept in response to the overwhelming popularity of the *The Cosby Show* and the positive images of African Americans in prime-time television. Claire, a lawyer, and Cliff Huxtable, a doctor, were a successful professional New York City couple with four children. The family rarely, if ever, was seen dealing with issues of race, presenting viewers with a false representation of the African American family. Nothing in the series reflected the tremendous impact of institutionalized racism on life for African Americans in the United States. The series *Black-ish* (2014–2022) served as an antidote to this controlling image by introducing a similarly successful African American couple. André and Rainbow Johnson are an ad exec and anesthesiologist raising their five children in an upper-class Los Angeles, California, neighborhood. The family differs markedly from the *Cosby* family because they directly deal with race, racism, diversity, sexism, and other social issues, creating teachable moments for the audience by weaving facts and research into the storyline. The show did an excellent job of being real and not compromising the reality of racism but also not losing its audience by fixating on a single topic.

**Aversive racism** suggests that evaluations of racial/ethnic microcultures are characterized by a conflict between whites' "endorsement of egalitarian values and their unacknowledged negative attitudes toward racial/ethnic outgroups" (Mastro et al., 2008, p. 3). Individuals who adopt this attitude have an egalitarian disposition and "oppose racial discrimination on both legal and moral bases" (p. 3)—yet have antipathy towards race. They hold onto these beliefs because the cultures and ideologies of macro- and microcultural group members are naturally different, which gives rise to racial stereotyping (Rodenborg, & Boisen, 2013). Thus, our social identities serve as motivating factors for intergroup comparisons (Mastro et al., 2008). In the case of the media, a European American person might express a belief that all races are equal and should be treated fairly; however, when confronted with their personal racial biases, they do not recognize them as such and make other attributions (e.g., personality, preference).

Aversive racism is an inherent contradiction between one's denial of personal prejudice and underlying unconscious negative feelings and beliefs, which is rooted in normal, adaptive psychological processes (Dovidio, Gaertner, & Pearson, 2017). These processes involve people generally having an affinity for others who are similar to them. So, for example, an individual in contact with Arab Americans experiences anxiety and uneasiness rather than open hostility and fear, which would indicate racist tendencies. When watching television programs or movies with Arab American characters, that person will avoid discriminatory behaviors that appear racist and offer an alternate, more socially acceptable explanation. So, in this scenario, they might say they do not like that genre of media. Despite these efforts toward behavior management, racial prejudice still exists.

Both enlightened and aversive frameworks are problematic because they are racial ideologies that are significantly impacted by limited interracial interactions and negative media images of different racial/ethnic groups. This is evidenced by the fact that European Americans oftentimes engage in selective exposure when choosing movies (Weaver & Frampton, 2019). Many are apt to avoid movies with more than a few actors from other racial/ethnic groups, particularly when it is a romantic movie, which suggests an aversive racist attitude. One troubling trend was the interracial buddy film genre with the movie *Rush Hour* (J. Park et al., 2006). The lead characters are usually two males, one European American male and one either African American or Asian American. These movies have been very popular across all audience demographics, which may be due in part to conformity to comedic stereotypes.

Thornton (2011) uses the interracial buddy television show *Psych* to further illustrate this point. She argues the black/white pairing of the best friends Sean and Gus as a crime-stopping duo "adapts the assimilationist situation comedy to rhetorically intensify post-race ideology by encouraging a light-hearted, breezy attitude toward race and racism" (p. 424). Audiences are reassured of their enlightened racism "through three distinct modes of racial humor" that "mock 'PC,'" use comedy to frame blackness, and project "post-race fantasies of black-white sameness and interchangeability" (p. 424). Much like their on-screen counterparts, European Americans are attracted to these

## Box 11.8

### Blackfishing

A recent social media phenomenon is "blackfishing." Journalist Wanna Thompson popularized the term in 2019 and defines it as "when white public figures, influencers and the like do everything in their power to appear Black" (Karimi, 2021). Thompson further explains that this can be done by excessive tanning to gain racial ambiguity and wearing hairstyles and clothes "pioneered by Black women." Blackfishing allows white people to engage with black culture without having "the full experience of Blackness," particularly the systemic discrimination inherent with this reality. Public figures accused of this are hip hop star Iggy Azalea, singer Ariana Grande, and celebrity Kim Kardashian.

Blackfish is a combination of blackface and catfishing and involves a stranger creating a persona different from who they are normally. While some public figures say their appearance is normal and deny blackfishing, others apologize for any offense taken by or disrespect of Black people.

Who are some other public figures who are guilty of blackfishing? Why is this not a form of cultural appropriation? Is there any time when this is acceptable? Why or why not?

films because they represent the fantasy of interracial cooperation. The most appealing aspect is that these partnerships exist without challenging the status quo (Artz, 1998). For instance, two things exist in most interracial buddy films: (1) European American authorities are ultimately in charge, and (2) the lone African American hero is separated from his community. This is also seen in the one friend rule in interracial relationships in real life and the media, which Munn (2018) defines as a "social mechanism in which whites name a non-intimate, institutionally tied interracial friendship as 'close' to project a generalized value for diversity" (p. 474).

## BECOMING CRITICAL MEDIA CONSUMERS

The last few years have made it abundantly clear that issues of race are surfacing in all media—online newspaper, television, streaming services, social media, and the internet. This pervasiveness further stresses how important it is to address issues of racial/ethnic representation (invisibility, stereotyping, or strategic programming) because of the impact it has in shaping how people understand racial groups and race relations. The presence or absence of each media portrayal of underrepresented group members either advances or stunts the struggle toward interracial understanding. Because the media play such a central role in how persons come to understand self and others, we must rethink how we use and interpret messages communicated via mass communication channels. Additionally, we must think critically about the media's role in contributing to perceptions that hinder competent interracial communication from occurring.

Media outlets transmit standards of beauty, body image, fashion, and lifestyle, and the images therein set standards, influence beliefs, and create social hierarchies. The characters depicted in the media have an effect on how we view ourselves and others. When these images perpetuate negative stereotyping, there is a risk of diminishing the self-esteem of viewers. Such is the case when women and microcultures are underrepresented or unfairly portrayed. Viewers do not see themselves in the people presented as admirable by the media, which can lower self-confidence. This is also a problem for people with little or no direct contact with members of the groups portrayed; it can result in accepting media characterizations as reality (Yuen, 2017). Cydney Dupree (2022) cautions:

> Stereotypes force us into boxes, and we try to break free of them using the most primary tool available to us: our words. Yet until we enact large-scale cultural changes that challenge these stereotypes, we will all continue to be shackled by them. (p. 33)

In the 30th anniversary edition of her *Black Feminist Thought*, Patricia Hill Collins (2022) tells readers that much is riding on them regarding social change. She refers to a joint process of meaning-making—both her ideas and how readers interpret them. The meanings made emerge through conversations with the text and with others about the text. Her goal is to provide conceptual tools so readers think for themselves.

Cultural studies show how media culture constructs dominant views of the world and behavior. Some groups accept the standards and values of mainstream culture; other groups create oppositional identities. Cultural studies provide the tools to examine critically the representations of race, gender, and class. Douglas Kellner (2020) advises:

> The realities of twenty-first-century life, and the technological and information revolutions that characterize it, demand that all citizens become media literate. . . . Living in a media culture, it is the responsibility of everyone to become media literate and to learn to read, interpret, critique, contextualize, and even produce media culture. In today's media-and-technology-saturated world, everyone can contribute to discussion, critique, and media creation through social media and new technologies and platforms. Individuals can not only participate in critical discussions of their media culture, society, and politics, but increasingly can even create their own narratives, images, analyses and media artifacts as the tools of media production become part of the digital devices of everyday life. (pp. 2–3)

While the media presents narratives that influence individuals to conform to the established organization of society, they also provide the resources that can empower people to resist. Individuals can emulate, modify, or reject dominant meanings, values, and messages. They can invent their own meanings and identities through communication and social networking.

We can become activists by inserting ourselves in decision-making processes affecting mass media images of underrepresented group members (Dale & Overell, 2018). Audience activism is an effective strategy that can move us toward change. In light of developments in social media and its success in activating social movements such as Black Lives Matter, we suggest using online petition organizations such as Change.org and social media platforms such as Facebook and Twitter to draw attention to your cause. Global organization Plan International recommends (1) creating a hashtag (e.g., #MeToo) and recruiting a prominent user to amplify your movement, (2) using social media accounts to highlight problematic content, (3) engaging audiences in a challenge, and (4) securing media coverage,

Word of mouth and social media are tools for communicating about inclusive projects or for protesting problematic projects. Activist April Reign created the #OscarsSoWhite hashtag as a critique of the 2015 Oscars for not having a single acting nominee of color. Her efforts attracted sufficient support such that the Academy of Motion Pictures and Sciences revised its policies to be more inclusive. Social media protests can be paired with other protest measures, such as boycotts. Twitter is heavily monitored by studios and networks to learn reactions to a film or show; therefore, audiences are encouraged to use Twitter and other social media platforms to promote or protest what they see.

On a more personal level, we can use a number of approaches to think critically about mass media representations of race/ethnicity. For instance, we can examine the *types* (e.g., friendship, family, professional) and *quality* of interactions (e.g., affirming, hostile, devaluing) occurring between the persons in the media. Just as important is to maintain an increased awareness of the obvious—and not so obvious—ways that visibility, marginalization, and stereotyping occur within various mass media texts. As you read tweets, scan a magazine ad, watch television, or binge on a streaming series, ask yourself several questions. What is being communicated here—explicitly or implicitly—about race/ethnicity? Am I being entertained, informed, or both? How are these images consistent with, or different from, what mainstream media typically portrays? Is there anything here that I or others might find offensive? How accurate or inclusive are these media?

Be aware of your assumptions and biases, or blind spots (King, 2019). Think about the difference between bystanders and confronters. Rather than observing a wrong and thinking that things should be different, ask "what can I do differently" to confront bias (Rattan et al., 2019). By becoming more critical about our own use of the media, we can gain a better understanding of how influential the media are in shaping our attitudes, beliefs, and perceptions of self and others. If change does not start within ourselves, we will continue to be what we are: a society living in fear of difference and diversity.

The next time you sit down to watch television, read a newspaper, or watch Netflix or Hulu, there are a few things we would like you to consider as you absorb the images before you. In general, most people use the media in ways that are personally beneficial. In some cases, there is a desire to see oneself or one's racial group accurately and broadly represented. Unfortunately, certain images either perpetuate racial stereotypes or fail to represent some racial groups at all. Ponder the following points as you engage with media.

- Identify and recognize the myths and stereotypes perpetuated in the media about different racial/ethnic groups.
- Do research on how different racial communities have actively made the media more conscious of and responsible for their portrayals of racial/ethnic groups.
- Support television programs and networks (e.g., Black Entertainment Television [BET], Univision) that target different racial groups. Buy movie tickets for inclusive films, and stream inclusive video.
- Engage in open and honest dialogue with friends and peers from different racial/ethnic groups about racial/ethnic representation in the media.
- Engage in open and honest dialogue with your same-race friends about the way your own and other racial/ethnic groups are represented in the media.
- Be open to films, television programs, newspapers, magazines, music (and so on) targeted to racial/ethnic groups other than your own.
- Recognize that racial/ethnic stereotypes do exist and are often offensive to certain groups of people.
- Rethink the types of stereotypes you have about racial/ethnic groups.
- Rethink how you perceive racial/ethnic groups based on messages and images communicated in the media.

## CONCLUSION

In this chapter, we presented considerable information regarding the increasingly important role the mass media play in shaping our perceptions and understandings of race relations and racial groups in the United States and beyond. Particular attention was given to television, film, and social media because they are an integral part of our lives. We identified long-standing and new controlling images associated with different racial and ethnic groups and how they either positively or negatively impact our interracial interactions. This is especially important when people have limited exposure to racially different others or their exposure is solely from the media.

By examining specific areas of the media, we were able to demonstrate the power that lies in these images that have become normalized through various platforms. We also hope people will become more critical of and thoughtful about the many ways we are all exposed to messages that potentially taint our perceptions of others. As you journeyed through this chapter, we hope that you became more understanding of the media's impact on everyday life interactions and how these vary from person to person.

### KEY TERMS

| | | |
|---|---|---|
| cultivation theory | curated information | Lotus Blossom |
| cultural studies | Magical Negro | Dragon Lady |
| social learning theory | Black best friend | Suzie Wong |
| standpoint theory | angry Black woman | crypto-Jews |
| millennial feminism | the thug | enlightened racism |
| magic bullet theory | yellow peril | aversive racism |
| two-step flow theory | technical robot | |

### RECOMMENDED CONTEMPORARY READINGS

Black, J. E., & Harrison, V. R. (2018). A Native American "playing Indian": Internal colonization in professional wrestling rhetoric. *International Journal of Media & Cultural Politics, 14*(2), 173–185. https://doi-org.libezp.lib.lsu.edu/10.1386/macp.14.2.173_1

LeBlanc, A. K. (2018). "There's nothing I hate more than a racist:" (Re)centering whiteness in American Horror Story: Coven. *Critical Studies in Media Communication, 35*(3), 273–285. https://doi.org/10.1080/15295036.2017.1416418

Maheswara, A. M., & Fatwa, N. (2021). Representation of Middle Eastern Islamic locality in video games. *IBDA Jurnal Kajian Islam dan Budaya, 19*(1), 141–151. https://doi.org/10.24090/ibda.v19i1.4427

Matias, C. E. (2020). Do you SEE the words coming out of that text?: Seeing whiteness in digital text. *International Journal of Multicultural Education, 22*(2), 14–29.

Oh, D. C. (2020). "Opting out of that": White feminism's policing and disavowal of anti-racist critique in *The Unbreakable Kimmy Schmidt. Critical Studies in Media Communication, 37*(1), 58–70. https://doi.org/10.1080/15295036.2019.1690666

Sayfo, O. (2020). Hollywood (mis)representations of Arabs and the Middle East from a production perspective—The case of FX channel's *Tyrant. Series International Journal of TV Serial Narratives, 6*(1), 43–55. doi:10.6092/issn.2421-454X/10285

Strass, H. A., & Vogel, D. L. (2018). Do stereotypical media representations influence white individuals' perceptions of American Indians? *The Counseling Psychologist*, 46(5), 656–679. https://doi.org/10.1177/0011000018788532

Uzuegbunam, C. E. (2021). Oppositional gaze or revenge? A critical ideological analysis of foreignness and foreign identities in Nollywood feature films. *Catalan Journal of Communication & Cultural Studies*, 13(1), 121–139. https://doi.org/10.1386/cjcs_00042_1

## OPPORTUNITIES FOR EXTENDED LEARNING

1. Do an internet search for viewing trends or social media use among different racial ethnic groups. While reviewing the different websites, make note of (a) the sources of the information; (b) from where they gathered their data (i.e., Census Bureau, Pew Research Center); (c) viewing or usage trends by racial/ethnic group. What do current data say about who is using which type of media most or least? Are the sources reliable? How does this information help us understand the impact the media have on our perceptions of each other?

2. Watch a limited series or movie targeted to a cultural group different from your own. Compare and contrast how characters and story lines either perpetuate or challenge stereotypes. Generate a list of possible movements consumers can initiate to encourage the industry to dispel stereotypes.

3. Choose a company that makes one of your favorite products. Locate their website and Twitter and Instagram accounts and review them to determine how inclusive or exclusive they are in appealing to racially and ethnically diverse audiences. How long have they been inclusive? What strategies seem to be effective or ineffective? What statements have they issued in support of recent social movements? How committed to inclusivity do they appear? How have your findings influenced your decision to continue purchasing or not from this company?

4. Do an internet search of the college and national sports teams that use Indigenous tribal names. What is the current status of debate over continuing or discontinuing the name? How are the teams, sports officials, fans, and Native American tribes responding? How are these controlling images being challenged?

5. After reading the article by Vivian Dang (2021), "Cultural Appropriation of Food: Why It's So Personal" (https://tinyurl.com/2p8f5yr4), discuss the criteria that can be used to determine what qualifies as cultural appropriation. Is cultural appreciation a factor? What impact might this have on interracial communication?

# 12

# Moving from the Theoretical to the Practical

| CASE STUDY | Can a "Redemption Tour" Redeem Morgan Wallen? |

Country singer Morgan Wallen came under heavy criticism in early 2021 when tabloid TMZ released a video of him spewing the n-word and other profanities in front of his home with a group of friends while inebriated. The backlash was immediate. He was dropped from his recording label Republic Records, deemed ineligible for Academy of Country Music Awards nominations, and removed from major radio stations.

Wallen apologized on *Good Morning America* and explained that he did not use the slur in a derogatory manner and did not know the severity of his actions until he spoke with African American leaders after the incident. He was acting out of ignorance. During the same interview, Wallen stated he was donating $500,000 from his recently released album to Black musicians and groups such as the Black Music Action Coalition that support Black Lives Matter, He ultimately had meetings with prominent Black record executives and singers.

The incident did not significantly impact Wallen's reputation, as evidenced by his considerable record sales. Various media outlets reported that he did a lot of soul searching to understand his behavior, and even though there were some losses, he did not seem to be a typical victim of cancel culture. Wallen's case presents an opportunity to consider how to get through difficult racial incidents.

How can racial healing occur when a person's actions are very hurtful and bring up a painful history? How fair is it to judge the sincerity of someone's apology for racist behavior? Should we separate the art from the artist? Why or why not? How can we use these moments to have open dialogue about interracial communication?

Source: Curto, J. (2021, July 13). Morgan Wallen says he donated profits from album sales spike after racial-slur video. *Vulture*. https://tinyurl.com/y72w6wsa

A s the previous chapters have demonstrated, the issues of race, ethnicity, and communication have become incredibly complex. The myth of a post-racial era in the United States has assuredly been dispelled by the sociopolitical climate of the last several years and the racial unrest of 2020. Granted, race relations have improved in various capacities, but racism, prejudice, and stereotyping remain a staple in the diet of many U.S. Americans.

Earlier in the book we described theories that analyze the complexities associated with race, ethnicity, and communication. In this chapter, we present some practical approaches to competent interracial communication and an antiracist positionality. We hope that you will continue to apply concepts and knowledge gathered from previous chapters to the issues presented here and work towards being antiracist or actively fighting against racism. We begin by summarizing research describing what constitutes satisfying interracial communication from different perspectives. We discuss how this process must involve antiracist actions that confront racism in productive and substantive ways. Then we explain different race-related training models, levels of inter-

---

*Box 12.1*

### Standing in Solidarity with the AAPI Community

On March 8, 2021, The Professional Staff Organization of the University of Washington released a statement condemning the upsurge in racial violence committed against AAPI. The solidarity statement was made shortly after seven women were murdered in Atlanta, six of whom were of Asian descent. The tragic loss of life focused attention on the increasing anti-Asian violence since the beginning of the pandemic and demonstrated the PSO's antiracism position.

The PSO encourages others to take action against racism and racial violence and lists recommendations for doing so. Although specific to the Atlanta murders, the recommendations are also applicable to all other racially motivated acts of violence.

1. Learn the names and stories of those who have been lost.

2. Check in with family and friends in the AAPI community—listen to their stories, for as long they want to talk.

3. Contact your representatives and advocate for policies that thwart hate crimes and violence and support progress toward institutional antiracism and justice for all.

4. If you see racism, say something. Strong allyship behavior needs to be modeled over and over again.

5. Donate to stopaapihate.org. Historically, less than 1% of philanthropic resources go to AAPI communities.

6. Donate to napawf.org, the National Asian Pacific American Women's Forum, specifically their Atlanta chapter.

7. Get involved with groups like the Revolutionary Love Project who direct resources to victims' families and organizers.

racial attitudes, and how allies and advocate-mentors (individuals who act in the interest of social injustice) can promote the most productive attitudes in others. From there, we reengage the value of interracial dialogue. We conclude the chapter by highlighting intercultural dialectics as a practical guide to maximizing competent interracial interactions.

## SATISFYING INTERRACIAL COMMUNICATION

The work of Michael Hecht and colleagues was instrumental in providing models that identified satisfying communication from the perspectives of U.S. racial and ethnic microcultural group members. One line of research tapped into a Mexican American perspective regarding interracial communication (focusing on interactions with European Americans). Five themes emerged that affected how communication was experienced (Hecht & Ribeau, 1984; Hecht et al., 1990). These themes were not assumed to be complete but captured "how things operate"—what was important/unimportant, acceptable/unacceptable, and effective/ineffective in terms of satisfaction. The first theme, worldview, relates to sharing common experiences and interests, which is crucial to communication satisfaction. Acceptance was the second theme—a perception that one's ideas and culture were accepted, confirmed, and respected. The third theme, negative stereotyping, was a main source for dissatisfying communication. Being categorized solely in terms of one's ethnicity (as opposed to being seen as a unique person first) creates barriers between persons. Relational solidarity was the fourth theme, which relates to the positive value attributed to developing close interracial relationships. Finally, the researchers identified expressiveness as a theme. Interracial communication was satisfying when individuals could express themselves openly, honestly, and fully without fear of rejection, judgment, or retaliation. These themes remain valuable today when assessing relational expectations across races. In response to the racial unrest of 2020, communication scholars and society members are increasingly vocal about how partners having an antiracist ideology is integral to any interracial relationship (Desnoyers-Colas, 2021; Lapum et al., 2020). An antiracist ideology seems a reasonable sixth theme for all BIPOC's evaluation of competent communication across racial lines.

In parallel research investigating an African American perspective on interracial communication (again primarily with European Americans), similar themes were identified (Hecht et al., 1989; Ribeau et al., 1997). These included negative stereotyping, acceptance, emotional expressiveness, authenticity, understanding, goal attainment (achieving desired outcomes), and power dynamics (not feeling controlled or manipulated). Hecht and his colleagues used their data to identify a series of improvement strategies for enhancing competent interracial communication. Listed below are some of their practical guidelines for achieving satisfying interracial communication.

1. Engage in interracial communication with an open mind; do not dismiss others' points of view without sufficient consideration.

2. Identify a common threshold of language that is accessible to both parties (e.g., avoid cultural slang that might be unfamiliar to the other person).

3. Be genuine in how you present yourself and views of others.

4. Practice other orientation. In other words, attempt to involve the other person's perspective as you locate common ground. This will enhance understanding.

5. Do not be afraid to assert your point of view; discussing disagreements and confronting problematic issues can be beneficial to building long-term relationships.

6. Take advantage of teachable moments where learning about other cultures can occur naturally.

---

**Box 12.2**                                              *Research Highlights*

### Interracial Communication Barriers

Much of the interracial communication research conducted rarely focuses on white people and their experiences with interracial relationships. Castle Bell (2019) fills this void and explores how "fear, prejudice, and racism create communication barriers between Black and [w]hite individuals" (p. 243). Applying cultural contracts theory to 31 interviews with white people, Castle Bell found that they held ready-to-sign cultural contracts with Black community members, with no room for renegotiation. Interview narratives revealed an affinity for or against certain Black individuals. There was a preference for Black individuals wearing business attire and an aversion to Black people wearing baggy pants or hoodies. Other narratives revealed a fear of being in predominantly Black spaces, preferring not to be the sole white person in a room, believing Black people are responsible for the negative ascriptions white people have about them, and believing Black people hinder themselves. Although these experiences are limited to the few study participants, they provide insight into an under-researched phenomenon and speak to barriers to interracial communication that might be more common than we think. Racist, prejudiced, and stereotypical ways of thinking about Black people will either prevent interracial relationships from occurring at all or will have a negative impact on any relationships that develop.

---

## Race-Related Training Models

Researchers have found that race-related training models can be an appropriate means to foster more competent interracial interactions. They can be even more effective if they contain an antiracism component, which is "an active process of changing attitudes, beliefs, practices, and policies with the goal of dismantling systemic hierarchy and oppressive power" (Lapum et al., 2020, p. 51). An antiracist approach includes but is not limited to (1) "Identifying and challenging racism within institutions," (2) "Taking specific and directed action towards eliminating racism," and (3) "Recognizing self as an agent for change towards equity" (p. 49). While developed for nurses to learn an anti-racist approach to communication with their patients, these three elements should be adopted for all models of interracial communication to address systemic bias, power inequities, and white privilege.

Fredericks and Bargallie (2020) stress relationships in their case study on cross-cultural training in Australia related to racism against Aboriginal and Torres Strait Islander peoples. By centering otherness and a relational approach, trainings will ultimately lead to "curricula design and implementation" that prioritizes the centrality of "Indigenous people's voices, worldviews, knowledges and pedagogies" (p. 296). The researchers prioritize communication and relationships by underscoring the transformative potential of "open discussions on racism, privilege, discrimination and change" (p. 297).

This focus is akin to interracial relationships, where partners change and grow as a result of their connection to each other. Foeman (1997) was the first to suggest five interpersonal behavioral objectives of race relations training: (1) discuss race-related issues (demystification); (2) articulate; (3) examine; (4) find validity in the other groups' perspectives; and (5) utilize others' perspectives in order to work together effectively while striving toward common goals. These two research studies conducted 23 years apart demonstrate the significance of increasing sensitivity among people who were ignorant about the significance of race prior to a workshop. By sharing their experiences and perceptions of racism, participants/coworkers have a better understanding of how racial/ethnic identity locates them in society as well as in the organizational context.

A study of a comprehensive diversity training program for faculty by one of its participants offers another example of increased sensitivity through training (N. Hudson, 2020). Teaching Inclusion and Diversity Everywhere (TIDE) has been offered annually at California Polytechnic State University since 2016. The TIDE program increased awareness of the degree of discrimination present on campus and in society, revealed the negative impacts of discrimination on the well-being, health, and academic performance of microculture college students, and spurred rethinking of one's role as an educator. The training facilitators gathered quotations from students of color on campus. Examples included:

> I don't know how to explain how frustrating it is to tell people at your school, "I am experiencing racism every day," and their response is, "Then leave."

> Do you know what it's like to be a minority at (university)? It's being told that race is not an issue in our community. It's being told your anger is unjustified. . . . It's silence. It's discomfort. It's hell. (in N. Hudson, 2020, p. 4)

The training changed the frame through which N. Hudson (2020) viewed race relations. It prompted her to change her thinking, communication, and teaching so that microcultural students would not feel "othered" in her classroom. This study supports the argument that training programs for faculty in higher education are needed because "socialization in a covertly racist system perpetuates cultural stereotypes, implicit bias causes discrimination in the classroom, and discrimination in the classroom adversely affects academic performance" (p. 3). Higher education classrooms are diverse learning environments, providing opportunities for students to become aware of differences in social identity and appreciative of diversity and inclusion.

Recall our discussion about confronting racial microaggressions in chapter 10. The model by Harris and Abbot (2011) has recently been used in DEI organizational workshops to help organizational members confront and intervene in racial microaggressions (RM) in the workplace and in other interpersonal interactions. To review, the model contains four steps for analyzing past interracial encounters. **Step 1** *identifies* the context of the RM and how the

---

### Box 12.3

# 101 Tools for Tolerance v2

The Southern Poverty Law Center (http://www.dec17.org/101_tools.pdf) offers 101 tips people can use to combat racism on an individual level for themselves, family, school, workplace, and community. Collected below are a dozen personal strategies useful in making a difference.

1. Attend a play, listen to music, or go to a dance performance by artists whose race or ethnicity is different from your own.

2. Volunteer at a local social services organization.

3. Attend services at a variety of churches, synagogues, mosques, and temples to learn about different faiths.

4. Speak up when you hear slurs. Let people know that bias speech is always unacceptable.

5. Shop at ethnic grocery stores and specialty markets. Get to know the owners. Ask about their family histories.

6. Participate in a diversity program.

7. Start a monthly "diversity roundtable" to discuss critical issues facing your community; establish an equity forum.

8. Learn sign language.

9. Frequent businesses owned by members of microcultures and get to know the proprietors.

10. Examine the degree of diversity at all levels of your workplace. Are there barriers that make it harder for people of color and women to succeed? Suggest ways to overcome them.

11. Vary your lunch partners. Seek out coworkers of different backgrounds, from different departments, and at different levels in the company.

12. Fight against the "just like me" bias—the tendency to favor those who are similar to ourselves.

interaction evolved. **Step 2** *assesses* how one or more of three cues (relational, contextual, emotional) contributed to the chosen response. **Step 3** *determines the reaction* to an RM and what behaviors were involved. **Step 4** *reflects on the outcome* and requires the person to evaluate their response and the effect on the outcome. The end goal is to identify a communication strategy a person feels most comfortable using to confront a racial microaggression. Organizational members and people in general can use this model to improve race relations in the workplace and in other interpersonal spaces.

Three training models (didactic, experiential training, and groupwork) are useful in changing the behaviors of macrocultural and microcultural group members. The models vary in their approach to race relations, but all three have similar goals. Each provides information bases and social contexts designed to train participants, increase cross-racial dialogues, and encourage participants to apply this knowledge to their interracial interactions and larger social system.

The **didactic model** is one of the most common forms of race relations training. The teaching mechanism used in this model is lecture, in which the trainer presents facts and information to participants. This one-way approach confronts the macrocultural group members by making an information-based appeal. However, this style is very ineffective in bringing about change. First, the interpersonal goals of participants are not always met because they are not able to interact and exchange ideas and information. Second, macrocultural group members may perceive this approach as "defensive reeducation," which may indicate an inability to personalize and internalize information gained from the social experiences of the "others" (Foeman, 1997).

The **experiential training model** centers on the assumption that interaction among race relations training participants is necessary. Unlike the didactic model, the experiential training model depends heavily on the personal experiences of individuals from various racial/ethnic groups. All persons are expected to share their racialized realities with fellow participants in an effort to reduce prejudice through personal contact, which may in turn facilitate change. One primary drawback of this model is that people of color are perceived as spokespersons for all members of their respective racial/ethnic groups. Generalizing from one ethnic perspective to an entire microculture feeds into the vicious cycle of stereotyping. People of color participating in the training receive fewer benefits from the experience and have the additional stress of being perceived as representatives of all other racial/ethnic group members.

The **groupwork model** strikes a good medium between the didactic and experiential models in that trainers incorporate information and experience into the learning process. Doing so assists participants in discerning the social contexts in which interracial contact will occur, which ultimately expands each person's frame of reference and their understanding of and responses to cross-race issues (Foeman, 1997). Because they are dealing with a variety of people who have different learning styles, trainers use film, discussion, and role-play, among other strategies, to encourage learner participation. The most appealing aspect of this model is that it promotes dialogue (see next section) among and between participants, particularly microcultural group members. It is hoped that participants will act on the information they are provided.

> European Americans are not one-dimensional in their racial identities and there is an important psychological connection, conditioned by historic culture, between racial identity and where one stands on the racism to antiracism continuum. By better understanding their own historic backgrounds, EAs' growth in racial identity is possible along with progression from individual racism to individual antiracism. (Bowser & Hunt, 1996, p. 250)

Ideally, the use of any of these models will achieve the goal of sensitizing people to the realities of racism. Unfortunately, the possibility remains that not everyone will reach the same level of consciousness after completing a training session. For decades, Robin DiAngelo (2018) has conducted workplace racial equity training sessions. Her experiences resulted in identifying what she refers to as *white fragility*.

> Socialized into a deeply internalized sense of superiority that we either are unaware of or can never admit to ourselves, we become highly fragile in conversations about race. We consider a challenge to our racial worldviews as a challenge to our very identities as good, moral people. Thus, we perceive any attempt to connect us to the system of racism as an unsettling and unfair moral offense. The smallest amount of racial stress is intolerable—the mere suggestion that being white has meaning often triggers a range of defensive responses. These include emotions such as anger, fear, and guilt and behaviors such as argumentation, silence, and withdrawal from the stress-inducing situation. These responses work to reinstate white equilibrium as they repel the challenge, return our racial comfort, and maintain our dominance within the racial hierarchy. I conceptualize this process as white fragility. (p. 2)

Some individuals, however, work to overcome the discomfort associated with honest appraisals of privilege and attempt "to understand the racial realities of people of color through authentic interaction rather than through the media or through unequal relationships" (p. 148). It is clear that, for many of the aforementioned reasons, training can help to challenge socialization and misinformation if people are willing to work toward mutual understanding and cocreated meaning.

Bryan Stevenson is an NYU law professor, founder of the Equal Justice Initiative, and author of the book *Just Mercy* on which the 2020 movie of the same name was based. He is an ardent believer that we need to engage everyone in a meaningful conversation about what it would take to cleanse ourselves of the legacy of slavery (Klein, 2020). Many people either deny U.S. history or are silent or ignorant about it. Using Stevenson's metaphor, the smog created by our history of racial injustice corrupts our worldview. As such, moving forward requires talking honestly about who we are and how the current status came into existence. There is no way forward that does not involve some discomfort and some inconvenience, but we need to find the capacity to experience disquieting facts on the path to a more just society.

As we have reiterated throughout the text, interpersonal contact and communication are critical to race relations if racism is to become a part of our past. Therefore, it is reasonable that approaches created to change intergroup prejudices, stereotyping, and discriminatory behaviors would promote intergroup contact. We must acknowledge that intergroup contact is influenced by context, power dynamics, time, status, individuality, and acquaintance potential. By receiving information, education, sensitivity training, and problem-solving strategies in training workshops, all members of society can become more skilled in their approaches to interracial communication. Although personal relationships outside the workplace may not "naturally" develop in most contexts, the skills and knowledge gained from relationships with people from other racial groups are invaluable. The changing racial demographics of our country will undoubtedly affect all areas of life in society—schools, churches, parks, restaurants, corporate America, government, etc. Not only should we acknowledge the saliency of our racial/ethnic identities in a society consumed by race but we should also make a conscious effort to combat racism in the public and private areas of our lives.

| Box 12.4 | Student Reflections |
|---|---|

### My Reality Unveiled

The more I hang around my friends and actually listen to some of the things that come out of their mouths, the more I realize what a twisted world we live in. Before I began this class, I would venture to say that I felt as if I had a good understanding of what it means to be Black or white and everything else in between. I also have to admit that I was skeptical of the course and its content in general (being that some parts I felt I didn't agree with). So, now we are almost through with the semester, and I feel as if I have changed a bit in that my eyes have been opened a little more to some of the small, less obvious injustices that take place on a daily basis. This is not to say that I never noticed them before, but I guess after hearing and seeing them for so long and having grown accustomed to them, I was desensitized in a sense that blinded me or made me indifferent to them in my path to achieving my own goals.

In most situations I come in contact with, the person [who] is being offensive is no more knowledgeable about the problem than a dog drinking antifreeze. I feel as if most people are stuck in their ways and really use racism as an out or excuse for the things that bother them in life. A friend of mine and I were going through the bank drive-thru, and I was completely cut off by a burgundy Mitsubishi. His first remark was "damn n*****." I turned to him and said, "Now why would you say some sh*t like that?" In this case I chose to engage the conversation and we ended up going on for about an hour about why he couldn't just attribute the person's actions to just being inconsiderate and rude rather being Black. It almost makes me sick to even have to say that I had a conversation like that with someone I know. This is just one example of how it is more our responsibility to provoke this kind of awareness about these issues.

## Levels of Racial Attitudes

One of the objectives of many race relations training programs is to foster positive attitudes regarding interracial communication. This means reducing the level of negative attitudes for some participants and enhancing the positive attitudes of others. Depending on one's socialization, individuals develop attitudes about different racial and ethnic groups that influence their interracial communication (or lack thereof).

---

**Box 12.5**

### Hate Crimes

Statistics indicate that there was a 44% increase in hates crimes in 2020, and they were race-based. These heinous crimes, as well as many others, frequently go unreported. This may be attributed to feelings of powerlessness in confronting such crimes since the perpetrator(s) is usually a stranger. Berea College provides several guidelines for responding effectively to hate crimes (Department of Public Safety, 2022).

**Things you can do:**

• Counter hatred by advocating for hate crime prevention.

• Understand the motivation behind hate.

• Understand the difference between hate speech (which is not illegal) and hate crimes.

• Identify and assess the hate and violence behavior.

• Support victims of hate. This improves the overall climate of the community, helps ensure the health and well-being of community members, and can de-escalate tensions.

• Respond to all hate incidents. This can deter them from escalating into more violent hate crimes.

• Working with hate crime offenders is a significant prevention activity. Effective diversion programs and aftercare can reduce repeat offenses.

• By using tools from violence prevention and prejudice reduction programs, college students can become the most effective advocates for hate crime prevention on campus.

• Develop hate crime partnerships and coalitions to improve communication between campus groups.

---

Dorothy Riddle's (1994) Scale of Homophobia is a measure of attitude change and is a useful resource to understand different levels of attitudes. While it can be used to apply to different types of microcultural groups, we utilize it here for the specific purpose of understanding levels of *racial* attitudes (see Figure 12.1). We added the last level—celebration.

Repulsion is a negative attitude based in ethnocentrism, and a person sees anything different as wicked, crazy, immoral, or sinful. When Europeans first

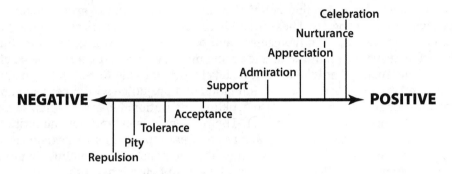

**Figure 12.1**  Attitudes Toward Differences

encountered the people of Africa and those indigenous to what is now known as the United States, they were repulsed by many of their customs, rituals, appearances, religious beliefs, etc. Today, some people maintain similar attitudes. Pity is another negative attitude where individuals have preferred norms and feel sorry for others who have perceived inferior lifestyles. The goal for those who are pitied is to have them become more like the people who pity them. The third attitude, tolerance, sounds positive but actually reflects a negative attitude. Tolerance means that someone is moderately respectful of other racial and ethnic groups, but the attitude is steeped in rejection and lack of acceptance. Tolerance "puts up with" people. A declaration such as "You have the right to your cultural beliefs, but I don't have to like them" captures an attitude of tolerance.

The next three attitudes about race are more positive, but they still have degrees of negativity associated with them. The fourth attitude is acceptance, which sounds positive. However, at the core of acceptance is an implied message that there is something to accept. "I don't see you as a member of a microculture; I see you as a person" sends an affirming message yet also fails to acknowledge the importance of one's race and ethnicity. Being colorblind may sound ideal for some, but it denies people the right to embrace important aspects of their identity. Support is a racial attitude that translates into efforts to safeguard the rights of all. People at this level typically do not recognize their own privilege but are aware of racial and ethnic oppression and want to do something to address it. The sixth attitude is admiration, a generally positive perspective whereby individuals acknowledge that racial and ethnic microcultures have great strength and perseverance to survive in an oppressive society. While individuals at this level typically are willing to examine their own privilege and biases, they sometimes can have greater admiration for different cultural aspects (e.g., art, food, religious beliefs) than for the people of the culture themselves.

The final three levels of racial attitudes bring the most productive perspectives into interracial interactions. The attitude of appreciation values diversity and demonstrates a genuine belief that all racial and ethnic group members are a valid part of society. These individuals are active learners as they work to combat discrimination in themselves and others. Nurturance goes a step further in its insistence that racial and ethnic microcultures are an indispensable part of our society. Individuals at this level work actively to cultivate the success of others by addressing discrimination and prejudice within personal and organizational contexts—and also tackling institutional barriers that sometimes are more difficult to confront. The final level is celebration, an attitude that honors everyone and everything as an integral part of human existence. A celebration attitude rejoices in settings that demonstrate a genuine commitment to embracing difference as natural, beautiful, and inherently valuable.

As you read through the descriptions of different levels of racial attitudes, what thoughts did you have about your own attitudes and those of others with whom you've interacted? Can you identify specific instances of your life when you unknowingly or knowingly changed levels? Can you understand how specific attitudes lead to particular communicative behaviors during interracial interactions? Figure 12.2 highlights the behaviors associated with different levels of racial attitudes.

Racial training programs work to change both attitudes and behaviors during interracial interactions. The next section highlights interesting communication research on the experiences of allies, individuals who use their social power and privilege to promote social justice for others. As you read through the section, think about the levels of attitudes from which allies operate. We hope this helps you understand how you can transform theoretical and conceptual resources into practice.

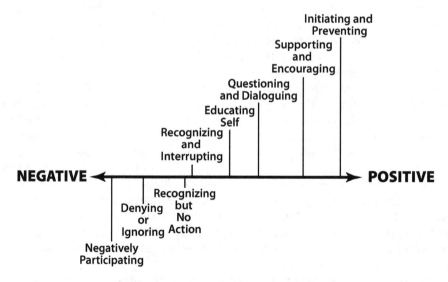

**Figure 12.2**  Communicative Behaviors Associated with Different Attitudes

## Working as Allies and Advocate-Mentors

An ally is frequently defined as an individual from an advantaged group who works to dismantle the privilege enjoyed by their group (Anderson & Accomando, 2019). For example, white people can work with Black Lives Matter, men can attend the Women's March, or cisgender individuals can work with LGBTQ movements. Because of the differential power relations between advantaged and disadvantaged group members, scholars and activists have long discussed the benefits and pitfalls of including allies in social movements (Selvanathan et al., 2020). While allies can use communicative interventions related to a number of social injustices (e.g., sexism, ableism, ageism, heterosexism, etc.), we will focus on European Americans who function as allies for people of color.

How do people become allies? There are multiple reasons why a person who is part of an advantaged group works actively to facilitate social justice for others. Research on allyship has found a number of motivations for taking action in support of microcultures. For example, Radke et al. (2020) identify four goals of activism: the desire to improve the status of a disadvantaged group, meeting personal needs, engaging in behavior that aligns with moral beliefs, and participation to maintain the status of one's own group. Among the reasons Selvanathan et al. (2020) offer include, while acknowledging there are undoubtedly other important motivations, feelings of anger over injustices, moral affirmation, and acceptance.

> To be effective proponents of social change, allies need to be responsive to identity-based needs of both advantaged and disadvantaged groups in society. We propose that allies' involvement in social change efforts has the potential to promote acceptance among members of the broader society who are advantaged and empowerment among members of the broader society who are disadvantaged. (p. 1352)

DeTurk (2011) outlines three primary reasons for allyship. First, allies may be motivated to action based on their identification with marginalization due to another salient identity marker. For instance, a European American woman or Jewish man may understand the consequences of sexism or anti-Semitism and have a desire to work against all types of oppression. Second, allies may have been socialized by family, friends, education, or travel to value differences. Typically, these individuals value and enjoy the benefits of racial diversity within their personal, social, and professional networks and work actively against barriers to racial inclusiveness. Third, allies may be influenced directly by role models, educators, or others who have inspired their social justice efforts. Most often, they have been inspired by individuals of different racial and ethnic backgrounds who have played an influential role in helping them confront their own prejudices.

DeTurk (2011) identified three different themes central to the lived experiences of allies working toward social justice. First, working as an ally reflects a person's enacted self, whereby individuals act on moral imperatives associated with social justice, diversity, and inclusion. Their goals are to

Political activism is one important strategy toward social justice advocacy, however other efforts can involve interpersonal, small group, and organizational initiatives.

affirm and support individuals who are marginalized because of their racial identities and to promote cultural change to eliminate racism.

> On the whole, people who identify as allies are passionate about social justice, enjoy learning and educating others, and seek a stronger sense of self through connection with culturally different others. Allies see their role as one of honoring differences, validating the identities of those outside the mainstream, and being visible and vocal advocates for the "underdog." (p. 575)

Second, allies draw from various forms of social and cultural capital to influence others. Recall from Chapter 7 that social capital refers to resources—knowledge, skills, experiences, associations with different groups—that give individuals advantages in society. Given their status as macroculture group members, allies use their social and cultural capital to advocate for and support people of color.

Third, allies experience tensions, such as self-interest versus moral commitments and support versus overprotectiveness. Striving to promote equality from a position of privilege in the system that confers it causes those tensions. Allies are motivated by both altruism and self-interest. White people sometimes engage in antiracism work in ways that reinforce their feelings of virtue rather than ways that lead to social justice; this is also referred to as performative activism. When privileged individuals advocate for less privileged people, there is a danger of reinforcing the oppression of the group whom one is supporting. Ally work

> is not easy. Although doing it is a choice that allies make—more so than responses to prejudice and discrimination faced directly by their targets—it can be both risky and exhausting, and those people who commit to doing it work hard to perform it effectively. They make tactical decisions about what forms of communication will be supportive to targets, persuasive to agents, and conducive to a just and respectful society while at the same time protecting their own safety and personal relationships. (DeTurk, 2011, p. 585)

Table 12.1 looks at issues in collective action for social change (Selvanathan et al., 2020). "Advantaged group allies and disadvantaged group members have divergent needs and motivations during efforts for social change" (p. 1347).

**Table 12.1    Allies in Social Justice**

| Issues | Advantaged Group Members | Disadvantaged Group Members |
|---|---|---|
| Group Identity | Emphasize common group identity with disadvantaged members | Emphasize microculture identities |
| Communication | Expresses empathy | Explicit challenges to inequality. |
| Help strategies | Help is sometimes dependency oriented | Autonomous help in which advantaged participate but remain out of spotlight |
| Needs | Acceptance; moral affirmation | Respect and empowerment |
| Outcomes of confronting inequality | Reinforcing ingroup morality motivates others to join. To be effective, need to frame inequality in terms of ingroup privilege | Challenges to inequality by allies promotes confidence and autonomy |
| Role models | Act as moral exemplars to promote ingroup pride | Observing outgroup change fosters hope |

The term "ally" has been criticized when it is claimed as an identity, which centers the privileged individual and shifts attention from a movement for social justice to an individual (Anderson & Accomando, 2019). In comparison, an advocate mentor speaks in support of or in defense of another person. An advocate is "one who pleads for or on behalf of a less powerful person. Their interest must be genuine, and they must be willing and committed to assertively addressing situations and people when the SOC [student of color] has unfairly been treated" (T. Harris & Lee, 2019, p. 107). As coined and defined by Harris and Lee, the advocate-mentor has societal privilege and "must verbally and nonverbally express a deep commitment to seeking social justice on behalf of [BIPOC]" (p. 107).

The advocate mentor also helps true supporters avoid the critical pitfall of performative allyship, which is a focus on being perceived as an ally—performing a role of someone who helps the disadvantaged. "Allyship remains contentious because of its performative (lip service) elements and the ways power, privilege, and oppression operate on and among marginalized communities at the expense of Black and Brown bodies" (A. Hall, 2021, p. 133). People with genuine concern must actively work towards meaningful antiracist action.

By identifying the tensions associated with working toward more positive, productive, and meaningful race relations, scholars provide great insight into the difficulty of such important work. In our next section, we highlight inter-cultural dialectics as a means of facilitating interracial interactions across diverse contexts.

## INTERCULTURAL DIALECTICS

A dialectic is a relationship between two opposing concepts that constantly push and pull one another (J. Martin & Nakayama, 2010). An example of opposing tensions or connected opposites is certainty←→uncertainty. Dialec-tics are a framework for addressing the tensions inherent in any relationship. As opposed to approaches that understand human existence through binary categories (e.g., good or bad, male or female, Black or white), a dialectical approach is based on the understanding that life is best understood as a "both/ and," not an "either/or" phenomenon. Table 12.2 illustrates three common dia-lectical tensions in relationships (Dumlao & Janke, 2012).

**Table 12.2   Dialectical Tensions in Interpersonal Relationships**

| Dialectical Tension | Issue | Considerations |
|---|---|---|
| Autonomy vs. Connection | Boundaries | What do we do together?<br>What do we do separately?<br>What proportion of independence and togeth-erness works for us? |
| Novelty vs. Predictability | Expectations | How comfortable are we with new experiences?<br>Does routine feel more comfortable?<br>What is the balance between the familiar and spontaneity? |
| Openness vs. Closedness | Managing Privacy | Does sharing information make us closer?<br>Does concealing information threaten the relationship?<br>What information do we need to keep private and what do we need to reveal? |

In this section, we apply intercultural dialectics to interracial communica-tion. In particular, we explain how a dialectical approach provides an excellent set of guidelines for high quality, and satisfying, interracial communication. Figure 12.3 illustrates six dialectics that characterize intercultural communi-cation (J. Martin, 2017). The dialectics, while neither exhaustive nor mutually exclusive, represent an ongoing exploration (J. Martin & Nakayama, 2010).

Cultural←→individual. Interracial communication scholars recognize that when individuals from different racial/ethnic backgrounds interact with one another, their behaviors reflect both individual and cultural influences. In other words, some of the behavior is unique to individual personalities, while other behavior is learned from one's culture(s). Competent interracial communicators recognize how a person's communication reflects both influences. Seeing a Chinese American woman as *both* an individual and as a member of a larger cultural group (and not one *or* the other) aids in successful negotiation of any tensions that arise.

Personal ←→ contextual. Some aspects of communication remain relatively constant while others change in different contexts. When communicating

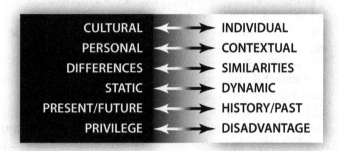

**Figure 12.3**
Intercultural Dialectics

### The Nameless Tailor

Something happened at dinner tonight with my family that made me feel uncomfortable and also made me question how sensitive my parents are to issues concerning race. While we were eating dinner, my mom told my dad that if he kept eating so much unhealthy food, he would gain back all the weight that he had lost in the previous six months. My dad's response to this was, "It's okay. I'll just take my pants back to China Lady and she can fix them for me." My dad has been going to the same tailor for the past 13 years and it astounded me that he did not know her name. Although I realize that my dad had had a few drinks, I still did not see this as an excuse for such an overtly racist remark.

Immediately I questioned my dad and asked him if he knew her name. After he told me that he did not know her name, it made me very upset and I launched into a tirade about how latent, subconscious prejudice and racism is more harmful than the blatant overt racism that most people think of when confronted with the topic of race. I told my family about the Crayola activity that we had completed the day before in class and how it had made me aware of a lot of subconscious racial tension and prejudices that I had carried all my life. Seeing as how I have never been a minority, the exercise forced me to analyze my own behavior and to see things from a minority's point of view. Although it is entirely possible that my reaction to my dad's comment had a lot to do with the fact that the Crayola activity was still very fresh in my mind, I would like to think that this would be my reaction in the face of any racist remarks for the remainder of my life.

within interracial contexts, we must recognize how verbal and nonverbal codes are simultaneously personalized and contextualized. A dialectical perspective helps us understand that seemingly inconsistent behaviors may be the result of a particular context rather than a person's individual inconsistency.

Differences ←→ similarities. In terms of interracial communication competence, this particular dialectic is crucial. In order to maximize your interactions, you must discern how you are similar to, and simultaneously different from, others. Historically, the tendency has been to overemphasize differences between different racial and ethnic groups. For instance, people thought about "whites" as the opposite of "Blacks" in many ways. More recently, efforts exist where people want to focus solely on similarities (e.g., insisting that there is only one human race). The most competent interracial communicators see others as both similar and different in multiple ways.

Static ←→ dynamic. This dialectic highlights the ever-changing nature of culture while simultaneously recognizing its consistency over time. Interracial communicators must be aware that cultural patterns change from generation to generation. Critics of post-racial discussions are quick to point out that racism still exists in the United States; however, they must also acknowledge how the U.S. culture is also changing in terms of race and racism.

Interracial worship is one example where communicators must negotiate the tension between the similarities of faith (i.e., relationship with the Creator) and differences of racial backgrounds (i.e., the cultural norms of worship).

Present/future ←→ history/past. Competent interracial communicators balance the recognition that history informs our present, and that our present is situated within our past. Too often European Americans want to ignore past racist transgressions and only understand current realities in isolation from any historical events. For example, from time to time, we will hear a white student say, "I never owned any slaves" and describe how their family's success is based on hard work and determination. In a similar vein, people of color will describe past racial atrocities without any mention of significant advances that have been made. Focusing solely on the past (without any recognition of how things have changed) or on the present (without any recognition that past influences inform current realities) fails to recognize the important role that both play in everyday interracial interactions.

Privilege ←→ disadvantage. In Chapter 3, we discussed the idea of societal privilege and focused on white privilege. In Chapter 5, we referred to other forms of privilege—male privilege, middle/upper-class privilege, heterosexual privilege, etc. This particular dialectic is based on the idea that every individual's social location includes areas of privilege as well as areas of disadvantage. For instance, men of color simultaneously function within male privilege and within the disadvantages of being a racial cocultural group member. Because we are all multicultural, no one's existence is completely privileged *or* disadvantaged. Instead, we have to realize we are all privileged in certain aspects of who we are *and* disadvantaged in others.

A dialectical perspective can expose hierarchies and power relations—the processes by which some people are included and others are not. A dialectical perspective helps in examining power hierarchies because it "foregrounds individual characteristics of competence with larger societal attitudes and laws" (J. Martin & Nakayama, 2015, p. 13). It may reveal a Eurocentric bias in assumptions about individual characteristics and skill sets. The intercultural dialectics explained in this section provide an excellent set of practical guidelines for individuals who are interested in working toward the most productive and satisfying communication with others. When engaged mindfully, tensions can lead to peak communicative experiences, like those highlighted next.

## THE REALITIES OF INTERRACIAL DIALOGUE

In Chapter 1, we explained the differences between talk, discussion, communication, and dialogue. To maximize interracial interactions, individuals must understand and work toward achieving communication where everyone is operating within shared meanings. Throughout the book, we have also highlighted different attempts, initiatives, and programs designed to facilitate interracial dialogue.

Dialogue is considerably more than conversation—much more than a turn-taking, sequential, or linear process (Heath & Isbell, 2017). It requires listening, inquiry out of curiosity rather than certainty, self-disclosure, open-mindedness, and exploration together. Sustained dialogue may be the ideal, but more often than not, people experience this form of peak communication as dialogic moments—times when fully engaged, diverse individuals synergistically transform in terms of how they see themselves, others, and society as a whole.

> We seek dialogic moments. We do not experience dialogue as uninterrupted; dialogic moments are not continuous. The etymological definition of dialogue defines "dia" not as two but as through, between, or across. Thus dialogic moments are not an individual experience but the sum of an experience between individuals. (p. 184)

Rather than reproducing understandings we already know, dialogue invents fuller, more complex meaning by integrating our own understanding with that of others.

In this section, we look at a research project that illustrates dialogue in a number of interracial interactions and explore how we can identify potential barriers to interracial communication.

---

| *Box 12.7* | *Research Highlights* |

## Interracial Dialogue Across Nations

The United States Institute of Peace (2015) is a federal institution created in 1984 to promote conflict resolution and prevention worldwide. Dialogue is one activity used regularly by experts at the institution to manage conflict nonviolently. The institution's website defines dialogue as a dynamic process of joint inquiry and listening to diverse views. To understand dialogue, the institution prepared a handout contrasting it with another form of communication—debate.

| Debate | Dialogue |
|---|---|
| oppositional: two sides oppose each other and attempt to prove each other wrong | collaborative: two or more sides work together to reach common understanding |
| winning is the goal | common ground is the goal |
| listens to the other to identify flaws and build counterargument | listens to the other to understand |
| defends assumptions and treats them as the truth | assumptions revealed for reevaluation |
| critiques the other position | analyzes own position |
| defends original proposal as the best solution and dismisses other solutions | open to achieving a better solution than any original proposal |
| closed-minded attitude; determined to be right | open-minded attitude; willing to change |
| search for differences | search for agreement |
| counter other position without regard for feelings or relationship; often belittles or deprecates | real concern for the other person; avoids alienating or offending |

Over a six-month period (June–December 2010), Orbe conducted a national study on public perceptions of President Obama's communication. This involved traveling to 12 different states and talking with 333 people who participated in 42 different focus groups. A key aspect of this research was exploring *diverse* perspectives. Accordingly, Orbe (2011) made sure that participants varied in terms of race/ethnicity, gender, age, education, socioeconomic status, and region. Some focus groups were homogeneous in terms of race and ethnicity (e.g., all African American or Latino groups in Virginia, Alabama, and California or all European American groups in Connecticut, North Carolina, Nebraska, and Ohio), while the majority of the groups involved a racially mixed group of participants. The decision to use focus group discussions to gather data (compared with one-on-one interviews) was based on the synergistic insight that could emerge from diverse group dynamics.

Generally, participants were relatively unfamiliar with one another. In each focus group, the session began with *talk* about the project but then quickly moved to a *discussion*. Most focus groups did not move beyond discussions (and in some cases, debates) about public perceptions of President Obama's communication. However, in a few instances when participants came into the focus group with a sense of familiarity with others, the group interaction moved from discussion to *communication* and/or *dialogue*. We share excerpts from two different sessions here to illustrate how dialogue can emerge within interactions about race.

The first excerpt comes from a focus group of 10 white students held on a college campus in rural southern Ohio. Participants discussed President Obama's comments about the incident in which Henry Louis Gates, an African American Harvard professor returning from a trip to China, was attempting to force open his own front door, which was jammed. A neighbor called the police about a possible burglary. Gates was arrested by a European American police officer for disorderly conduct. President Obama commented that the Cambridge police "acted stupidly in arresting somebody when there was already proof that they were in their own home" (Guskin et al., 2010). The sequence of events prompted what came to be known as the "Beer Summit" at the White House (Patterson, 2011).

As you read participants' opinions about the role that race played in this incident, take note of how this example of intraracial communication featured attempts to develop shared meaning amidst diverse perspectives. [WM#1 refers to a white male participant; WF#1 refers to a white female participant, etc.]

> WM#1: Going along with what she said, I believe that it is a *racial* thing but not necessarily a *racist* thing. [Emphasis added]
>
> WF#1: But President Obama is the person who brought it back to the race issue. I understand that he has a reason to be proud that he is the first African American to be president. But as the president, I feel that he shouldn't be dividing people into groups.
>
> WF#2: But it was a racial issue.
>
> WF#1: No, it wasn't! If any person who was breaking into a house at night . . .
>
> WM#1: It was during the day, wasn't it?

WF#1: Well, during the day, at night, whatever. If someone is breaking into a house, getting into a residence, it is going to look like someone is trying to rob it. Whether they are white, Black, purple, yellow, green—it is going to look like they are going to rob you. It is not a race issue . . .

WM#2: The fact is that [Gates] didn't get charged with breaking into his own house. He got charged with making trouble with the cop. So, he made it a race issue, but he would have gotten out of it with no trouble at all if he wouldn't have gotten all riled up and started trouble with the police officer. It is not a race thing. it is a . . . if someone is breaking into this house, the police are going to check it out. Then they find out, "Oh, this guy lives here, fine." But he decided to get excited and probably started yelling at the police officer and that's when he probably got arrested. He didn't get in trouble for breaking into his own house, he got in trouble for something that any white person, or Hispanic person, would get in trouble for if they were doing that.

WF#1: That's what I was saying . . . [Gates] automatically turned it into: "This cop is judging me because of my race." And then President Obama reacts to it with no information that was factual. He just jumps to a conclusion and says something that shouldn't have been said. . . . I think that he did it because other people expected him to. . . .

WF#3: The whole point is that none of us can know if it was racial or not. How can we say that it was racial or not? How would we know? And maybe that's the problem with what Obama said—how could he know? I don't know, maybe he had some obligation to defend the minority perspective.

WM#2: I don't know . . . as the first African American President, a lot of people might be quick to say that racism is over. And maybe he feels like it is important for him to highlight examples that demonstrate how that is not true. (Orbe, 2011, pp. 156–157)

In the excerpt above, participants struggled with trying to understand if the incident was personal (between two individuals who might have overreacted), racial (involving perceptions of race on both sides), and/or racist (a person in authority using power to act on a racial stereotype). This group of participants did not necessarily come to an agreement; however, they did work actively to develop shared meaning as they communicated about their individual perceptions.

Compare the intraracial interactions in the previous excerpts to the inter-racial interactions of another focus group. A dialogic moment occurred within a focus group of African American and European American students from a state university in Michigan. All of these students had just completed an 8-week summer session class together. The interaction began with a question about what their friends and family members thought about President Obama. Several African American participants were quick to describe how family members unconditionally supported the president—with little attention to his faults or shortcomings. However, another African American participant shared how his family members criticized President Obama for what they perceived as a lack of concerted efforts to address Black issues. A couple of the European American participants responded with surprise, stating their belief that all African Americans unconditionally supported President Obama. This

| Box 12.8 | Author Reflections |
| --- | --- |

### Hope for the Future: "Each One, Teach One"

At the turn of the 21st century, Hatch (2003) predicted that the current generation is tragically destined to pass on the problems of race to still another generation. I don't think that I am as pessimistic as Hatch; however, I am a realist and recognize that in all probability race will be an issue that my children's children will have to negotiate on some level. This has been confirmed by the problematic racialized realities experienced and witnessed in recent years.

The more I interact with my young adult children—aged 29, 28, and 25—and their friends, the more hopeful I am for the future. Clearly, each generation seems to be more and more open and less bogged down with negative racial baggage. As a parent of multiracial young adults, I believe that part of the job is to educate them about race and empower them with strategies to deal with everyday racism. Despite these attempts—including those found in various "teachable moments"—my children appear much more comfortable and confident when it comes to discussing race. I oftentimes sit in awe as I observe them interact with others; I can't help but think how much more at ease they are with their racial identities (and overall self-concepts) than I was at their ages. Lately, I've been able to see them take the lead in advocating for diversity, inclusion, access, and equity in their personal and professional lives. Ideally, their self-confidence will spread to future generations.

Part of my teaching philosophy is based on the "each one, teach one" principle. In this regard, I expect students to share what they've learned with others—to create an ongoing ripple effect. So, as you conclude this semester, the question is: What will you do with the information that you learned? How will it affect how you go about your everyday lives? How, if at all, will your experiences contribute to a more equitable, harmonious society?

—MPO

initial exchange led others in the group to share comments about their family's perceptions. For example, one white male participant revealed:

> My family is primarily conservative, I'm the only liberal in my family. So, they HATE everything that Obama does but only because he is a Democrat. I think that if it would be a Republican president doing the exact same stuff, they would be totally fine. But, just because he is a Democrat, they totally hate him. (quoted in Orbe, 2011, p. 144)

Other European Americans in the focus group shared similar accounts of their families; in particular, several described their parents' rejection of President Obama's candidacy, and subsequent politics, in terms of his political affiliation—not his race.

During these exchanges, a couple of the African American participants traded glances of suspicion with one another. This nonverbal communication occurred in several different focus groups across the United States. In the Michigan group, the comment of one young African American male participant reflected a moment of cross-racial transparency.

> This is all really interesting to me. . . . Your parents [referring to the white male quoted earlier] are so against Obama because he is [a] Democrat. And, in my mind, I was like, "Yeah, and probably because he is Black." I really hate that I think like that but I'm pretty sure that a lot of Black people feel that way. Especially for hard-core Republicans who are like, "Okay, he's a Democrat AND he's Black." Come on now! (quoted in Orbe, 2011, pp. 144–145)

Immediately, two other African American women verbalized their agreement, which led to the group dialogically disclosing how their own racial perceptions can hinder their ability to create and maintain meaningful interracial relationships. Several participants appeared moved by the openness and honesty of the exchange, including an African American man who concluded:

> And as Black people we have to get past that, but it is still heavy on our minds. Especially for people who are so against Obama, I always feel that it's because he's Black. We know that every white person who doesn't like Obama, it's not because he's Black. But I don't know what it is about our culture but we believe that. So earlier when you said that your parents don't like Obama because he is a Democrat, I even said to [an African American woman sitting next to him] "It's because he's Black." And she was like, "Yeah, I know." It is just so interesting that sometimes Black people—we—have a harder time getting over race than white people. (quoted in Orbe, 2011, p. 145)

Within this exchange, a diverse group of participants—in terms of race, gender, and political affiliations—developed a common understanding of a complex issue. Throughout the Michigan focus group, different participants disclosed information about themselves and their family members that allowed the group to recognize the vast diversity of opinion in seemingly homogenous groups and question their own racialized ingroup and outgroup perceptions. At one pivotal moment, an African American man shared his immediate [racialized] reaction to one of the European American participants. His honest self-disclosure, and subsequent critical self-reflection, led others to do the same. A productive communicative interaction moved toward one of personal transformation. The result was a dialogic moment where participants shared at a level that fostered a deeper understanding of the function that race plays—or does not play—in the perceptions of self and others.

So, what does it take for dialogue to occur in discussions about race? We must seek "I–You" encounters where both parties relate to each other as authentic beings (Arrington, 2020). People must be willing to resist the coercive influences of others, listen with empathy, and work to bring assumptions into clear view. The 2020 racial tensions spurred the American Association of Retired People (AARP), along with many organizations, practitioners, and scholars, to offer society a variety of resources to help understand the complexities of race and racism and how to have healthy and productive dialogue. AARP offered seven tips to approach conversations about race or other difficult topics that can make people uncomfortable (Spike, 2020).

1. *Check your own bias.* Every personal experience includes some prejudice. Think carefully about what biases you may have (due to age, gen-

der, race, etc.) before you begin a conversation. Be open to learning other perspectives.

2. *Set guidelines, boundaries and goals.* Uncertainty about how conversations will progress and people's reactions can be uncomfortable. Setting guidelines such as one person speaking at a time or specifying that conversations are confidential can ease uncertainty.

3. *Start on common ground.* To begin the conversation, investigate whether both parties have read a race-centered news article or book or seen a similarly themed movie. Another possibility was explored in Chapter 3. Visit Project Implicit, take the Race Implicit Bias Association test and discuss the results.

4. *Turn to facts.* The conversation can become emotional. Beginning with data can start the exchange on solid ground; disagreements may surface but they arise from facts rather than assumptions.

5. *Agree to disagree when necessary.* Not all dialogue will result in mutual understanding.

6. *Use FFF* statements. Expressing emotions by saying "I felt," "I found out," and "I feel" keeps the focus on feelings so that statements are less likely to provoke defensiveness.

7. *Actively listen.* Resist planning your response, which can mean that you do not hear what the other person is saying. Exchanging ideas requires full attention to the perspectives expressed.

Using any or all of these tips provide a solid foundation for continued dialogue. Only through practice and patience can one learn what works best for any given relationship.

---

**Box 12.9**                                                   *Author Reflections*

### Planting Seeds of Hope: A Journey Toward Positive Race Relations

Over the past 27 years, I have grown and learned quite a lot about race and positive race relations. My professional and personal lives have comingled, and I have become richer for it. I continue to approach each class I teach with a plan, a goal, a mission to make the lives of students the better for it. As I stand in the classroom, I feel as though I am serving a greater and higher purpose in the move towards positive race relations.

I could not imagine a life without the opportunity to speak, teach, and write about race. I get excited when students have a light bulb moment where they finally "get it." Whether it is realizing for the first time that white privilege is a part of their reality or that other microcultural groups also experience systemic oppression, I am honored and humbled by the fact that I am, in a very small way, a catalyst of sorts in their journey toward learning and understanding the very complex ways in which race really does matter.

*(continued)*

I would be remiss if I did not acknowledge that the many joys that come with my life are tempered by trials and tribulations because of my dual status—African American and female—in microcultures. I have been treated differently, poorly even, because I do not fit mainstream ideals of the standard of beauty or what is "typical." Thankfully, I have a wonderful network of family members, girlfriends, and colleagues who continually offer me the emotional and spiritual support necessary for withstanding the difficulties that come my way while continuing to do interracial communication research. These experiences eventually evolve into teachable moments that directly inform my scholarship, affirming my commitment to doing that which I am destined to do: teach, speak, and write about race whenever possible. My personal battles as an African American woman are certainly not in vain.

It is true that this journey toward positive race relations can be tiresome and exhausting; however, I am not on this journey alone. I become encouraged, excited, and honored when I meet others with a similar passion for and commitment to making this world in which we live a better place—where racial differences are appreciated, not tolerated. I am also affirmed by the knowledge that my purpose is to be on a lifelong journey of self-discovery while encountering opportunities to eradicate racism that culminate in a legacy of peace, love, and appreciation. I have no tangible legacy to leave to birth children, but I pray I have been successful in planting seeds of hope and trust in others. I believe that change is in fact a possibility—one relationship at a time.

—TMH

# CONCLUSION

It is our hope that this text has challenged you to think critically about interracial communication and your current levels of racial attitudes. Most people are either not challenged to think about or not invested in thinking about race (European Americans), while others are forced to think about it continually (microcultural racial/ethnic groups). To be clear, this does not mean European Americans are not sensitized to issues of race and racism in the United States. The lived realities for racial/ethnic microcultural groups, however, are markedly different because of dealing with racism, stereotyping, prejudice, and discrimination far too frequently.

The racial and ethnic landscape of the United States is continuing to shift, thus making it even more crucial that we give even greater priority to the important role that interracial communication plays in all areas of life. The racial tensions of 2020 had a devastating impact. Family members, friends, and society members were drawing lines in the sand as their opposing racial ideologies rose to the surface, pitting loved ones against each other. The same was partially true for strangers. Relationships were strained, redefined, or terminated, which made it impossible for healthy dialogue about race to occur. Thankfully, there are many who are interested in and committed to learning about and engaging with others regarding these very real issues.

In the first part of this book, we introduced the concept of interracial communication and provided a rationale for studying and applying different conceptual and theoretical principles to everyday lives. We also presented current scholarly research and information regarding race and ethnicity as sociopolitical constructions, the power of language and nonverbal cues, identity negotiation, and intersectionality. In the second part of the book, we applied a significant amount of this information to different contexts: colorism and global racial hierarchies, friendship and romantic relationships, organizations, conflict negotiation, and the mass media. This final chapter provides hope for change and highlights specific ways in which all of the information covered throughout the book can be translated into actions designed to dismantle racism. The concluding chapter speaks to the subtitle of the book: theory into practice.

The racial turmoil currently plaguing the United States further underscores the urgency of putting into action our ever-growing knowledge about race and humanity. There is no doubt that we *all* have some responsibility in engaging in high quality, productive interracial interactions. Systems of oppression can only remain intact if there are those who believe in and preserve them. Whether involvement is conscious or subconscious, overt or covert, or you are a direct benefactor or victim of racism, we are all impacted to varying degrees. It is our hope that each of us will feel compelled to address racism in whatever form we encounter it.

As noted in the confronting racial microaggressions model, we can all do our part by questioning someone's *intentionality* ("Did she or he mean to say that? Was their intention to harm?") when they make a covertly or overtly racist comment. We must also recognize that seemingly innocent comments can be just as harmful as the blatantly hurtful ones. It is our moral responsibility to question individuals when they say something disparaging to us, to someone we care about, or maybe even to a total stranger. No matter how difficult, we must challenge prejudice. Granted, some might hesitate to confront racism because of the potential damage to a relationship. Nevertheless, it is imperative that we become more proactive in eradicating racism on a micro-, interpersonal level if we are going to see the macrolevel change required to dismantle systemic racism.

Recent events are evidence that we are not living in a post-racial society. These numerous events include but are not limited to racialized police brutality, rampant voter suppression efforts against racial and ethnic groups, cultural genocide by oil pipelines in tribal lands, government seizure of tribal lands, anti-immigration policies targeting the Deferred Action for Childhood Arrivals (DACA) program, environmental racism (i.e., lead in tap water, toxic waste facilities in a community) in communities of color, the rise in hate crimes against AAPI people, and the All Lives Matter counterresponse to the BLM movement. The tensions and conflicts within each of these and many other issues center on racial and ethnic differences and threats to an imbalance of societal power benefiting the macroculture. Collectively, these events along with more subtle forms of racial microaggression offer undeniable evidence that the salience of race in every aspect of life cannot and should not be ignored. The less egregious recent historic moments playing out before us have revealed public displays of ignorance, inhumanity, and insensitivity. Yet, we remain encouraged and hopeful that these incidents will continue to inspire public and private dialogues on race matters. Structural and systemic racism is certainly difficult to dismantle, but we cannot give up. We must, at a minimum, commit to engaging in dialogue and communication in both public and private spaces with family, friends, and outgroup members to deconstruct the racist ideologies imbedded in Western culture.

## KEY TERMS

| | |
|---|---|
| didactic model | acceptance |
| experiential training model | support |
| groupwork model | admiration |
| repulsion | appreciation |
| pity | nurturance |
| tolerance | celebration |

## RECOMMENDED CONTEMPORARY READINGS

Ashby, K. M., Collins, D. L., Helms, J. E., & Manlove, J. (2018). Let's talk about race: Evaluating a college interracial discussion group on race. *Journal of Multicultural Counseling and Development, 46*(2), 97–114. https://doi.org/10.1002/jmcd.12095

Chebrolu, R. (2020). The racial lens of Dylann Roof: Racial anxiety and white nationalist rhetoric on new media. *Review of Communication, 20*(1), 47–68. https://doi.org/10.1080/15358593.2019.1708441

Davidson Mhonde, R., & Hingle, A. (2021). Resistance, reflexivity, and rest: Critical pedagogical rituals of "Ubuntu." *Communication Education, 70*(3), 336–338. https://doi.org/10.1080/03634523.2021.1912793

Ilchi, O. S., & Frank, J. (2021). Supporting the message, not the messenger: The correlates of attitudes towards Black Lives Matter. *American Journal of Criminal Justice, 46*(2), 377–398. https://doi.org/10.1007/s12103-020-09561-1

Jones, S. C. T., Anderson, R. E., & Stevenson, H. C. (2021). Not the same old song and dance: Viewing racial socialization through a family systems lens to resist racial trauma. *Adversity and Resilience Science, 2*(4), 225–233. DOI:10.1007/s42844-021-00044-8

Kelly, C. R. (2020). Donald J. Trump and the rhetoric of white ambivalence. *Rhetoric & Public Affairs, 23*(2), 195–223. https://doi.org/10.14321/rhetpublaffa.23.2.0195

McIntosh, D. M. D., & Eguchi, S. (2020). The troubled past, present disjuncture, and possible futures: Intercultural performance communication. *Journal of Intercultural Communication Research, 49*(5), 395–409. https://doi.org/10.1080/17475759.2020.1811996

Nuru, A. K., & Arendt, C. E. (2019). Not so safe a space: Women activists of color's responses to racial microaggressions by white women allies. *Southern Communication Journal, 84*(2), 85–98. https://doi.org/10.1080/1041794X.2018.1505940

Richardson, A. V. (2019). Dismantling respectability: The rise of new womanist communication models in the era of Black Lives Matter. *Journal of Communication, 69*(2), 193–213. https://doi.org/10.1093/joc/jqz005

Stokke, C. (2021). Unlearning racism through transformative interracial dialogue. *International Journal of Qualitative Studies in Education, 1*–17. https://doi.org/10.1080/09518398.2021.1930245

*OPPORTUNITIES FOR EXTENDED LEARNING*

1. Older research on interracial roommate conflicts found that white people attributed roommate behaviors to external/situational factors, whereas Black people attributed behaviors to internal causes and personality flaws of the roommates (Bresnahan et al., 2009). Brainstorm different roommate conflicts you have noticed. What do you believe would be the findings if the study were replicated today? What strategies should be in place to ensure positive race relationships?

2. The dramatic increase in hate crimes against AAPI individuals have undoubtedly broken the trust between AAPI and other racial groups. Download (https://tinyurl.com/ax34rhnb) and read the excerpt from *The Racial Healing Handbook* by Annalise Singh and Derald Sue. What do you think are the most productive activities for bringing about racial healing? How effective are these activities for different races and ethnicities? What are some other online resources that might be effective in addressing societal responses to hate crimes?

3. In 2017, PBS released the documentary *Accidental Courtesy* featuring musician Daryl Davis (https://www.pbs.org/independentlens/documentaries/accidental-courtesy/). The documentary chronicles Daryl's unusual hobby of meeting and befriending KKK members, many of whom are meeting a Black person for the first time. Daryl pursues an answer to the question, "How can you hate me when you don't even know me?" His journey questions and confronts racism one racist at a time. The documentary follows Daryl as he conducts interviews with current and former KKK leaders and with BLM activists who vehemently oppose his tactics. How effective is this method in facilitating racial reconciliation? Is there any hope that the contact hypothesis applies in these circumstances? What can be done to help these KKK leaders and members become *true* recovering racists?

4. In Chapter 3, the first opportunity for extended learning directed you to Project Implicit's website to take the Race IAT. A research study used the implicit association test to determine the effectiveness of online diversity education programs in reducing bias (Behm-Morawitz & Villamil, 2019). Students were tested at the beginning and end of the semester, and the findings show that the program was effective in decreasing bias against African Americans, increasing openness to diversity, and increasing internal motivations to control prejudice. Prior to learning these results, what were your opinions about online diversity education programs? Do you believe the Race IAT effectively measures changes in students? What do you think the results would be if the students were tested again the following semester, one year later, or two years later?

5. Communication scholar Michael Zirulnik was part of a team that in 2022 launched a website (speakingtruth.org) that invites descendants of slave owners to describe and reflect on their ancestors' roles in slavery. Designed as a pathway to national reconciliation regarding race, racism, and slavery, the website provides videos of individuals who are committed to critically examining their relatives' beliefs, understanding how their own lives have

benefitted from the past, and striving to create a concrete plan to make amends. Take some time to watch some of the videos on the Speaking Truth website, and then discuss with others the following questions: What are your initial reactions to learning these individual's stories? What role can these personal stories play toward racial reconciliation? How do the intentions and strategies of this website align with the ideas of this textbook generally and Chapter 12 more specifically?

6. Search the internet for articles and essays that examine racial conflict (keyword: *racial conflict* or *race relations + conflict*). What role does geography play in how the conflict originates and is resolved? Are certain racial/ethnic groups in conflict more than others? Is race a factor in the conflict, or is the conflict over a nonrace issue? Address whether race and/or racial/ethnic difference appears to contribute to the conflict. Apply strategies from this text that could resolve racial conflicts effectively.

7. Visit the section on ally theory on the Ally Group's website (https:// sites.google.com/view/theallygroup). As you read through the materials on this website, what connections can you make between how positive and negative attitudes toward various types of difference (e.g., race, sexual orientation, sex, abilities, gender, etc.) are similar and different?

8. Waymer (2021) recommends that white communication scholars become proactive in achieving racial justice in the field by addressing the lack of diversity in: graduate school enrollment, distinguished scholars recognized by the National Communication Association, and faculty throughout the discipline. What actions can scholars, professors, and students take to create racial justice in a field that is not very diverse? What can be done through curriculum? What are the benefits of diversifying journal articles, for example, for students and other scholars?

# Glossary

**abilities**  Physical, emotional, and mental capabilities.

**ability**  One of six interrelated factors in co-cultural theory that refers to a person's access to enact certain communicative practices.

**acceptance**  A generally positive racial attitude involving confirmation of and respect for one's ideas and culture; however there is an implied message of difference that needs to be accepted.

**accountability**  Taking responsibility for actions through self-assessment and analysis of situations. For example, a leader in an organization who values diversity must analyze company practices and decisions, such as those related to selection, promotion, and compensation.

**acculturation**  Learning and acquiring the elements of a new culture.

**admiration**  A generally positive racial attitude whereby individuals acknowledge that racial and ethnic microcultures have great strength and perseverance to survive in an oppressive society.

**African American**  A label used to describe people living in the United States whose ancestors can be traced to Africa; sometimes used interchangeably with **Black**.

**alluding to race**  Racializing dialogue by using language to convey a racial meaning indirectly rather than in an explicit statement.

**American Indian**  A label used to describe people living in the United States whose ancestors can be traced to the indigenous people of the land; sometimes used interchangeably with **Native American** and **First Nations People**.

**angry Black person**  A stereotype of a Black person or character as angry, hostile, and dangerous regardless of gender.

**antimiscegenation laws**  Laws that were enacted by 41 states that made intermixture between whites and non-whites through intermarriage illegal; born from fear that such unions would blur the lines of physiological differences (e.g., eye color, hair texture, facial features). between diverse ethnic and racial groups.

**anxiety**  An emotion triggered by uncertainty about a situation; according to anxiety/uncertainty management theory, anxiety is a basic cause of communication failure.

**appreciation**  A positive racial attitude (and the fourth stage of biracial identity development) that values diversity and demonstrates a genuine belief that all racial and ethnic group members are a valid part of society.

**Arab Americans**  A label used to describe people living in the United States who trace their ancestors to the Middle East.

**arbitrary nature of words**  The idea that words do not have inherent meaning;

meaning is in people, not the words that they use.

**artifacts**   A form of nonverbal communication that refers to physical and personal objects that are used personally (e.g., clothes, jewelry) or spatially (e.g., objects in one's personal or professional space).

**ascription**   The identity attributed to an individual or group by others. How others see us has a direct impact on how we see ourselves.

**Asian American**   A label used to describe people living in the United States whose ancestors can be traced to Asia.

**assimilation**   People adopting the dominant group's attitudes and beliefs while forsaking those of their primary racial/ethnic group.

**autonomy**   The final (sixth) stage of macrocultural identity development whereby individuals work to maintain a positive nonracist perspective.

**aversive racism**   Evaluations of racial/ethnic minorities that are characterized by a conflict between whites' endorsement of egalitarian values and their unacknowledged negative attitudes toward racial/ethnic out-groups.

**avowal**   The perceived identity that an individual enacts in a particular context.

**baby boomers**   Generation of individuals born 1946–1964.

**Banton's orders of interacial contact**   The first four orders (peripheral contact; institutionalized contact; pluralism, and assimilation) discourage an appreciation of racial/ethnic difference and two orders (acculturation and integration) encourage appreciation.

**biracial Americans**   A label used to describe people living in the United States who can trace their ancestors to two racial groups; sometimes used interchangeably with **multiracial Americans**.

**Black**   A label used to describe people across the world whose ancestors can be traced to Africa.

**Black best friend**   A stereotypical Black character who guides white characters out of challenging circumstances.

**Black ceiling**   Attitudinal and organizational barriers that constrain Afro-Diasporic women from rising to senior leadership.

**Brahmins**   A group under the caste system consisting of intellectuals and priests.

**branqueamento/blanqueamiento**   An ideology endorsing the belief of the superiority of whiteness and the desire to aspire to whiteness.

*Brown v. Board of Education*   The landmark U.S. Supreme Court case that desegregated all public educational institutions (e.g., elementary schools, high schools, and colleges and universities) throughout the nation.

**Buck**   Negative stereotype associated with African American males who are described as strong, athletic, and sexually powerful. It has its origins in slavery.

**caste system**   A caste system is a characterization system or structure used to rank people at birth due to class, race, or gender, for example. Caste systems place value on groups and influence opportunities one has in society.

**catfishing**   Purposeful act of deceiving others through the creation of a fake online identity.

**Caucasian**   A label used to describe people of European descent (originally a reference to people from the Caucasus Mountain region); Blumenbach differentiated five races stratified by perceived beauty with Caucasians at the top of the hierarchy.

**celebration**   The most positive racial attitude; individuals embrace an attitude that honors everyone and everything as integral to human existence.

**Charlie Chan**   A stereotype based on the detective character who possessed impressive powers of deduction but was deferential to whites.

**Chicana/o**   A label used to describe people in the United States who can trace their ancestors to Latin America; most often used by those who maintain a political consciousness regarding race and culture.

**choice of group categorization**   The second stage in multiracial identity development when individuals gain an increased awareness of their race/ethnic heritage and choose one particular identity.

**chosen people**   A belief that Europeans were the race chosen by God to reclaim the world in his name.

**chronological context**   The role of time in influencing workplace interactions (e.g., morning vs. afternoon meetings); one of Weick's three contexts that influence organizational communication.

**chronemics**   A form of nonverbal communication that focuses on how people use time to communicate their power, status, or level of interest in a person or activity.

**classism**   The top-down practice whereby middle- and upper-class persons perpetuate discriminatory behaviors toward those of lower-class standing.

**co-created cultural contracts**   These agreements are fully negotiable; the motivation is mutual satisfaction and respect that includes acknowledgement and validation of cultural differences.

**co-cultural group**   Groups that share an aspect of culture—based on gender, race, ethnicity, sexual orientation, abilities, etc.—that traditionally has been marginalized in society; sometimes used interchangeably with **minority** or **subcultural group**.

**coherence**   A concept, as articulated in complicity theory, that sees difference as complementary and constructs reality in a way that does not privilege one position at the expense of another.

**collectivism**   Cultural values that emphasize group identities, concerns, and needs over individual identities, concerns, and needs.

**colonialism**   A formal system of domination that removes the power of self-determination from one group and gives it to another.

**colorism**   A form of ingroup bias where members discriminate against each other because of skin color—the elevation of lighter skin tones over darker skin tones across all communities of color.

**commitment**   One of six core elements of community that refers to a strong willingness to coexist and work through any barriers that hinder a sense of community.

**communal frame**   A layer of identity that results from group associations of individuals bonded by a collective memory; one of four interconnected layers in identity theory.

**communicare**   Latin for "to make common"; serves as the root word for communication.

**communication**   A series of messages that ultimately result in creating shared meaning and mutual understanding.

**communication approach**   One of six interrelated factors in co-cultural theory that refers to the voice used by group members, such as nonassertive, assertive, or aggressive.

**community**   A group of individuals who practice inclusiveness, commitment, consensus, contemplation, vulnerability, and graceful fighting.

**complicity**   A concept, as articulated in complicity theory, that involves using language that highlights differences instead of commonalities and emphasizes division at the expense of unity.

**concrete ceiling**   The intersectional bias faced by women of color in traditional white male organizational spaces. Concrete is more impenetrable than glass and is not transparent; it signals a dead end with no visible path for advancing beyond the current level.

**conformity**   The second stage of microcultural identity development that includes an acceptance and internalization of macrocultural perspectives, values, and norms.

**consensus**   One of six core elements of community that refers to efforts seeking general agreement on key values, assumptions, and decisions.

**contact**   The first stage in macrocultural identity development that typically involves an unawareness of one's own racial identity.

**contact hypothesis**   A theory by Allport that increased interactions with racially different others will reduce prejudiced thoughts and beliefs in optimal conditions.

**contemplation**   One of six core elements of community that represents a reflective awareness of self, other, and the community itself.

**contextual cues**   In racial microaggressions, one of three cues to the conflict—the physical environment (i.e., restaurant, home, etc.) where the racial microaggression occurs can affect one's reaction.

**convergence**   A strategy, as described by communication accommodation theory, whereby individuals adapt their verbal and nonverbal communication to become more like the other person.

**coon**   Negative stereotype depicting African Americans as foolish and idiotic.

**coping**   Stage two of Foeman and Nance's interracial relational development model; in this stage, the couple move toward each other and away from others, solidifying their relationship.

**counterpublic**   A group that exists outside of state-sanctioned or mainstream spaces; counterpublics engage in social protests and other acts of civil disobedience to oppose the dominant sphere.

**cross-cultural adaptation**   The process of change that occurs over time when individuals whose primary socialization is in one culture come into continuous, prolonged contact with a new and unfamiliar culture.

**crypto-Jews**   Seemingly Jewish characters whose race/ethnicity is ambiguous, increasing the character's mainstream appeal.

**cultivation theory**   The theory proposes that significant exposure to television violence by heavy TV viewing (four or more hours a day) results in viewers being more likely to see the real world as similar to the distorted TV images—the Mean World Syndrome.

**cultural competency**   The ability to communicate in ways regarded as both effective and appropriate.

**cultural contracts theory**   Theory that argues people negotiate their identities through cultural contracts with others.

**cultural humility**   Remaining humble and respectful plus embracing a lifelong commitment to self-reflection, self-critique, and addressing one's biases.

**cultural racism**   Much like ethnocentrism, this involves people presenting their own racial/ethnic group's cultural preferences and values as superior to those of other groups; all aspects of one culture and heritage are deemed culturally acceptable, thus negating the value of all other racial/ethnic groups.

**cultural resources**   In romantic relationships, an emphasis on the importance of shared or similar cultural or racial/ethnic backgrounds, leading to similar values and opinions.

**cultural studies**   Area of study concerned with how ideologies are maintained by those with power.

**culture**   A set of learned and shared values, beliefs, and behaviors common to a particular group of people.

**curated information**   Developed by Thorson and Wells as a comprehensive approach to explain message flow and media effects; in the digital age, there are five curating actors who frame content: journalists, strategic communicators, individual media users, social contacts, and algorithmic filters.

**debate**   A competitive interaction in which the goal is to win an argument or convince someone, such as the other participant or third-party observers.

**decategorization**   Seeing someone as an individual rather than as a member of a group; an awareness of individual distinctiveness.

**dialogue**   Message exchange through which people who have different beliefs and perspectives develop mutual understanding that transforms how they see themselves and others.

**didactic training model**   A teaching mechanism that uses lecture to present facts and information to participants; this is a linear, or one-way, approach to race relations training.

**digital sexual racism**   Bias in online dating that reduces people to exotic caricatures through stereotyped thinking about race, masculinity, femininity, and class.

**discussion**   Involves multi-directional messages exchanged between two or more people—talking *with* rather than *at* others.

**disintegration**   The second stage of macro-cultural identity development that typically involves a growing awareness of one's own privilege.

**divergence**  A strategy, as described by communication accommodation theory, whereby individuals stress verbal and nonverbal differences in order to emphasize ingroup/outgroup status.

**Dragon Lady**  A stereotype of Asian women as cunning, manipulative, evil, aggressive—exuding exotic danger and determined to seduce and corrupt men.

**dyadic factors**  Similarities, reciprocity of liking, and self-disclosure are factors that impact friendships and interpersonal connections.

**emergence**  Stage three of Foeman and Nance's interracial relational development model; in this stage, the couple has solidified their relationship and present themselves as a couple to outsiders.

**emotional cues**  In microaggressions, one of three cues to the conflict—the feelings triggered by the interaction can include anger, frustration, or sadness.

**emotionality**  The negative emotions evoked by experiencing offensive behavior (whether first- or second-hand) are a barrier to interracial relationships if the feelings are not communicated and discussed.

**enacted frame**  A layer of identity where one's sense of self is performed to others; one of four interconnected layers in identity theory.

**enclave**  A public sphere produced when societal norms deny access or meaningful participation in dominant public spheres.

**endogamy**  Marriage that occurs when people marry within their group (e.g., race/ethnicity or religion).

**enlightened racism**  A perspective on racial relations that acknowledges the historical significance of racism in the United States but sees the 21st century as colorblind and a time when racial equality has increased opportunities to achieve the American Dream through hard work and determination.

**enmeshment/denial**  The third stage of biracial identity development characterized by emotional tension associated with

an identity that does not fully express all aspects of one's racial identity.

**environmental factors**  Opportunities to be together is a factor that impacts friendships and interpersonal connections.

**environmental nonverbal codes**  Natural and human-made features of different settings, such as temperature, lighting, furniture, colors, and materials that impact interactions in different spaces.

**essentialism**  The tendency to generalize cultural groups without recognition of ingroup differences.

**ethnic-racial socialization**  The process through which individuals learn from explicit and implicit messages what race and ethnicity mean to them.

**ethnicity**  A cultural marker that indicates shared traditions, heritage, and ancestral origins.

**ethnocentrism**  Belief in the normalcy or rightness of one's culture; consciously or unconsciously evaluating other cultures by using your own as a standard.

**eugenics**  The belief in improving the quality of the human species by encouraging the reproduction of persons believed to have desirable traits and discouraging the reproduction by those thought to have undesirable traits.

**European American**  A label used by people living in the United States who can trace their ancestors to Europe; oftentimes used interchangeably with Caucasian, white, or Anglo.

**experiential training model**  In race relations training, emphasizes the importance of interactions among participants who are expected to share their personal experiences to reduce prejudice through personal contact.

**expressiveness**  The ability to express oneself in open and honest ways without fear of rejection, judgment, or retaliation is a satisfying outcome in interracial communication.

**eyeball test**  A nonscientific, random measure of racial categorization used in everyday interactions by laypersons.

**face**   The desired identity we want others to see in us—one's self-image in the presence of others.

**facework**   The verbal and nonverbal messages to build and protect one's own face and to build or threaten the face of others. Facework can address self-face, other face, mutual face, or communal face.

**field of experience**   One of six interrelated factors in co-cultural theory that refers to the sum of lived experiences that influence one's communication behaviors.

**First Nations People**   A label used primarily in Canada to describe people living in North America whose ancestors can be traced to the indigenous people of the land; sometimes used interchangeably with **American Indian** and **Native American**.

**4-step framework for action**   The REAL framework steps developed by the Center for Creative Leadership (CLL) for inclusive leadership are: (1) revealing relevant opportunities, (2) elevating equity, (3) activating diversity, and (4) leading exclusively.

**framing**   A stage in the process of diversity management in organizations; the communication of leaders frames diversity as a strategic learning opportunity that can improve and expand the business.

**friendship**   A mutual involvement between two people that is characterized by affection, satisfaction, enjoyment, openness, respect, and a sense of feeling important to the other.

**Fu Manchu**   A stereotype portraying Asian men as cruel and cunning.

**gender**   A socialized and psychological aspect of identity that refers to levels of femininity and masculinity.

**generalized other**   A concept, central to symbolic interactionism, that refers to an individual's perception of how others see them.

**generalizing race**   Racializing dialogue that involves no explanatory properties associated with a specific racial category.

**Generation X**   Individuals born between 1965 and 1980.

**Generation Z**   Individuals born 1996–2010.

**glass ceiling**   The invisible barriers that prevent women and people of color from advancing in the workplace, despite their qualifications or achievements.

**glass escalator**   A new phenomenon in organizations referring to white men being promoted in the workplace at a much faster rate than women and minorities because of their status as a "new" minority group (e.g., being "marginalized" persons in a work environment where they are in the minority).

**goal setting**   A stage in the process of diversity management in organizations involving the establishment of diversity goals that can be measured by relationships with minority communities in and outside of the organization (such as the number of mentoring relationships and retention rates of high-potential minority managers).

**graceful fighting**   One of six core elements of community that involves a general acceptance that conflict should not be avoided but instead managed effectively to enhance the ultimate sense of community.

**group categorization**   The second stage of biracial identity development characterized by an increased awareness of race to the point of being pushed to choose an identity.

**group identification**   A desire to preserve the social history of one's racial/ethnic group, which directly influences efforts to prevent interracial marriages from occurring.

**group sanctions**   Institutions that impose sanctions to prevent marriage between people from different racial/ethnic backgrounds (i.e., antimiscegenation laws).

**groupwork model**   Training model incorporating elements from both the didactic and experiential; combining information and shared experiences promotes dialogue.

**haptics**   A form of nonverbal communication that focuses on how touch is used to communicate.

**hate crime**   Criminal behavior against an individual or property motivated by bias because of the victim's actual or perceived race, color, religion, disability, sexual orientation, or national origin.

**high context cultures**   Collectivistic cultures emphasize the group and relationships; communication is subtle and indirect—meaning depends on more than the content of the message and differences may exist between what is said and what is meant.

**Hispanic**   A label used to describe people who can trace their ancestors to Spanish-speaking countries; sometimes used interchangeably with **Latinx**.

**homogamy**   A person's preference for a mate who is close in social status and education.

**homophily**   A term that refers to the common experiences shared by two individuals.

**human relations theory**   The goal of the organization is to improve all interpersonal—including interracial—relationships among employees in the workplace; it takes into consideration the multiple identities of its organizational members.

**hypergamy**   An interest in or willingness to marry someone of a different status.

**hypervisibility**   Media representations so heavily stereotyped that they are accepted as accurate even when refuting information exists.

**hyper(in)visibility**   The use of pervasive stereotypes to justify causing harm to individuals; stereotyped media representations can promote interpersonal violence.

**hypodescent**   The "one-drop" rule; assigning a biracial or multiracial person to the racial group in their heritage that has the least social status.

**identity emergence**   Stage three of Foeman and Nance's interracial relational development model; in this stage, the couple makes their relationship official, presenting themselves to others as romantically involved.

**immersion/emersion**   The fifth stage of macrocultural identity development that is characterized by blaming microcultural groups for their own disadvantaged status.

**implicature**   A concept in complicity theory involving acceptance of the idea that we are all connected, interrelated, and interdependent—what affects one of us affects all of us.

**inclusiveness**   One of six core elements of community that refers to general acceptance and appreciation of differences.

**identity gaps**   The result of competing or contradicting frames of identity.

**individual factors**   Social skills, responsiveness, and physical attraction are factors that impact friendships and interpersonal connections.

**individualism**   A cultural value that emphasizes personal identity, rights, and needs over those of the larger group.

**integration**   The final (fourth) stage of microcultural identity development that focuses on achieving a public racial identity that is consistent with one's inner sense of self; the final stage of biracial identity development characterized by individuals' ability to recognize and value each aspect of their racial identity.

**intentionality**   The degree to which a certain behavior is viewed by an offended party as purposeful in causing hurt or harm.

**interracial relational development model**   A four-stage model developed by Foeman and Nance that describes the process of successfully managing IRRs (specifically African American/European American) in the face of external forces.

**interaction-based approach**   An approach to workplace communication that carries an expectation that community members will have constant interactions due to their roles.

**intercultural communication**   A broad term used to describe interactions between two individuals who are culturally different.

**interethnic communication**   Interactions between two individuals from two different ethnic groups.

**interethnic conflict**   Conflict between members of different ethnic groups.

**international communication**   Communication between nations, frequently through representatives of different countries.

**interpenetration**   In the communication theory of identity, the ways in which different frames of identity influence, confirm, and contradict one another.

**interpersonal communication**   Interactions between two individuals regardless of race; often used synonymously with intraracial communication.

**interpersonalizing cultural difference** Method to prepare students for living and working in a diverse society; four subprocesses require that partners (1) cultivate trust and establish a silent contract, (2) embrace similarity yet remember their differences, (3) explore other cultures, and (4) bridge difference to connect.

**interracial communication** Interactions between two individuals in a situational context where racial difference is salient issue.

**interracial conflict** Conflict between members of different races.

**intersectionality** An approach to understanding human communication through examinations of multiple aspects of cultural identity.

**intimate partner violence/interpersonal violence** Abuse or aggression that occurs in a romantic relationship.

**intraracial communication** Interactions between two individuals who identify with the same racial group.

**invisibility** Lack of media representation; certain groups are missing completely.

**"it's a preference"** The rationale offered for dating only within one's racial group—attributing the behavior to preference, not bias.

**Jezebel** Negative stereotype typically associated with African American women who are believed to be sexually promiscuous.

**Jim Crow** State and local laws across U.S. southern states that mandated racial segregation; Jim Crow era lasted from 1890s–1950s.

**kinesics** Nonverbal communication that encompasses all of the ways in which we use our hands, fingers arms, legs, and posture when communicating; also includes the various ways in which we use facial expressions and head movements.

**Kshatriyas** A group under the caste system consisting of rulers and warriors.

**Latinx American** A label used to describe people in the United States who can trace their ancestors to Latin America; most

often used by those concerned with preserving language and culture.

**linguistic profiling** Instances of racial discrimination when assumptions are made based on a person's vocalized patterns of speech (e.g., "sounding Black").

**localizing race** In racializing dialogue, limiting the use of race as an explanation for action to particular situations.

**Lotus Blossom** Stereotypical depiction of Asian women as a sexual-romantic object, utterly feminine and delicate that is a "welcome" respite from their often loud, independent American counterparts (e.g., China Doll, Geisha Girl, Shy Polynesian Beauty).

*Loving v. Virginia Supreme Court* Landmark court case that reversed the antimiscegenation laws in the United States.

**low context cultures** In individualistic cultures, communication is direct and explicit; the meaning of verbal messages is literal rather than embedded in the context or relational status of participants.

**Magical Negro** A negative stereotype associated with an African American male lead character who is spiritually gifted with the ability to aid their white lead counterparts.

**magic bullet theory** A mass communication theory that asserts mass media messages have a direct and powerful effect on audiences.

**maintenance** Stage four of Foeman and Nance's interracial relational development model; in this stage, the couple commits to preserving a long-term relationship; there is continual communication about how they present themselves and how others perceive them.

**Manifest Destiny** A concept related to chosen people; certain countries (e.g., European countries, the United States) had the right—granted by God—to extend their territorial dominion and power across continents in the interests of civilization.

**message orientation approach** A perspective of communication whereby both senders and receivers have some responsibility to create shared meaning.

**mestizaje** An ideology in which everyone is considered to have mixed heritage; it is one strategy to de-emphasizes privileges associated with phenotypically white characteristics.

**metastereotypes**  Perceptions that individual have of the stereotypes that other individuals have about them.

**microculture**  A group whose members are culturally different than those in the majority; used in place of less acceptable terms like minority or subgroup.

**millennial feminism**  Activism by millennials focused on intersectionality, sex-positivity, media representation, voice, and the eradication of gender roles.

**Millennials**  Generation of individuals born 1981–1995.

**mindfulness**  Constant awareness of one's actions and thoughts and what motivates them.

**minority**  See **microculture**.

**mistrust**  A lack of confidence in another person, suspicion and/or uncertainty about the truthfulness of communication.

**model minority**  A stereotype ascribed to all Asian Americans that they are industrious and successful; by extension, the stereotype attributes a lack of work ethic to other racial/ ethnic minorities, accounting for why they cannot achieve "the American Dream."

**money whitening effect**  Assigning color categories based on class; high-income people more likely to be classified as white.

**MRULE (multiracial unity living experience program)**  Michigan State University's multiracial residential student community to help students create genuine relationships and promote social justice.

**mulatto/a**  A term used historically in the United States to describe a person with one African American and one European American parent.

**multiracial Americans**  A label used to describe people living in the United States who can trace their ancestors to two or more racial groups; oftentimes used interchangeably with **biracial Americans**.

**nationality**  Reference to the nation in which one is born; used interchangeably with nation of origin.

**Native American**  A label used to describe people living in the United States whose ancestors can be traced to the indigenous people of the land; sometimes used interchangeably with **American Indian, First Nations People,** and **Indigenous Americans**.

**negative stereotyping**  Being categorized in terms of one's ethnicity rather than being seen as a unique individual creates barriers in interracial communication.

**neominstrelsy**  The 21st century representations of the blackface minstrel caricatures of African Americans that perpetuate media racism. These roles are usually found in sitcoms or provide comic relief for audiences.

**normalization**  Process of identifying and moving toward common ground on which to base transracial communication.

**nurturance**  A positive racial attitude that understands racial and ethnic microcultures as an indispensable part of our society.

**octoroon**  A term used historically in the United States to describe a person with one African American and seven European American parents.

**one-drop rule**  A social and/or legal guideline used in the United States that defines a person with *any* African ancestry as African American.

**organization**  A social collectivity (a group of people) where coordinated activities achieve both individual and collective goals; organizing is accomplished through communication.

**organizational culture**  A pattern of basic assumptions—invented, discovered, or developed by a given group as copes with problems of external adaptation and internal integration. The accumulated learning has worked well enough to be considered valid and is taught to new members as the correct way to perceive, think, feel, and behave.

**overaccommodation**  An aspect of convergence (adjusting one's communication to resemble that of another person) in which individuals fail to recognize that they are converging to a stereotype rather than actual communication behavior.

**perceived costs and rewards** One of six interrelated factors in co-cultural theory that refers to the ways in which individuals weigh the advantages and disadvantages of communicative choices.

**personal frame** A layer of identity that encompasses one's sense of self; one of four interconnected layers in identity theory.

**personal identity** The first stage of biracial identity development characterized by defining oneself by personality elements rather than by race.

**phenotypes** Observable characteristics of an individual (height, eye color, hair color, blood type and certain types of disease) that result from the interaction of genotypes with localized environments.

**physical context** In workplace communication, the physical environment where the communication takes place (e.g., boss's office, employee lounge); one of Weick's three contexts that influence organizational communication.

**pity** A negative racial attitude where individuals have preferred norms and feel sorry for others who have inferior lifestyles.

**pickaninny** Stereotype of the bulging-eyed child with thick lips and unkempt hair eating a slice of watermelon typically associated with African Americans.

**political correctness** A term popularized by the mass media to describe social movements to adopt a specific set of ideologies, concepts, and terms that reflect a sensitivity to issues of culture, power, and privilege.

**politically responsive constructionist theory of communication** Theory that recognizes the importance of political realities in sociohistorical context; communication in dialogic form constructs new possibilities rather than reproducing old experiences, challenging unexamined assumptions, facilitating voice, and developing an appreciation of otherness.

**preferred outcome** One of six interrelated factors in co-cultural theory that reflects the ultimate goal for a person's communi-

cation behavior (i.e., assimilation, accommodation, separation).

**proxemics** A form of nonverbal communication that focuses on how space is used to communicate.

**pseudo-independence** The fourth stage of macrocultural identity development that is characterized by European Americans who unconsciously believe that their culture is more advanced and civilized than others.

**public sphere** An area of social life where people come together and engage in sociopolitical issues; ideally, this engagement is a springboard to action.

**quadroon** A term used historically in the United States to describe a person with one African American and three European American parents.

**quasi-completed cultural contracts** Contracts that are partially pre-negotiated and partially open for negotiation; these contracts attempt to balance maintaining the status quo and asserting one's identity within existing structures.

**race** A sociopolitical construction that categorizes people into four primary groups.

**racial awareness** Stage one of Foeman and Nance's interracial relationship development model; involves partners becoming aware of a mutual attraction and the possibility for an intimate involvement.

**racial boundary-crossing** Lighter skinned individuals enjoy societal privileges and benefits associated with groups higher on the racial hierarchy than do darker skinned individuals from the same ethnic group.

**race checklist** Subjectively favorable beliefs about individuals based on stereotypes—a mental checklist of qualities or characteristics a person is expected to have as a member of a particular group.

**racial devaluation** Ascribing negative qualities based on racial categories and negative stereotypes.

**racial discrimination** Acting upon racial prejudice when communicating with others; all people can have racial bias—explicit or implicit.

**race fetishization** Sexual obsession with or unnatural preference for individuals solely because of their racial group membership.

**racial location**    People experience life from a particular vantage point; race, age, gender, class, sexual orientation, and spirituality contribute to how they see the world.

**racial microaggression identification and confrontation model**    Developed by Harris and Abbott (2011), this model contains four steps that guide people through how to reflect on past interracial encounters in order to address future racial microaggressions.

**racial motivation theory**    The theory that a person becomes involved in an interracial marriage (or relationship) *because* of racial difference.

**racial perspective**    A largely unconscious social location, informed by race and other cultural group membership, that influences one's perception of self, other, and society.

**racial preferences**    Described as a personal choice rather than discrimination, favoring or choosing one group or individual over another based on race—an illegal practice in education and employment but prevalent on social media apps.

**racial proxy**    Hypothesis that all neighborhood residents act on preferences to avoid neighborhoods with socioeconomic concerns (i.e., low incomes, poor schools and services, high levels of crime)—race is a stand-in for socioeconomic status rather than an indication of racial prejudice.

**racial reconciliation**    The process of healing the racial tensions and bridging the racial divide that exist between the races.

**racial standpoint**    An achieved viewpoint earned through critical reflections on power relations and taking a stance in opposition to dominant cultural systems.

**racism**    The systematic subordination of certain racial groups by racial groups in power.

**readiness**    A stage in the process of diversity management in organizations in which organizational leaders engage in self-exploration to understand how privilege and ethnocentrism operate within their lives and the complexities of diversity within the organization and society.

**ready-to-sign cultural contracts**    Pre-negotiated agreements designed to promote assimilation and maintain the status quo.

**reappropriating language**    Embracing a once-negative label and redefining it as a means of empowerment.

**regionality**    A specific area of a nation that has its own culture within the larger national culture.

**reintegration**    The third stage of macrocultural identity development that includes a sense of racial pride.

**relational cues**    In racial microaggressions, one of three cues to the conflict—the relationship (i.e., stranger, friend, relative, etc.) between the parties affects the encounter.

**relational frame**    A layer of identity that is negotiated through one's relationships with others; one of four interconnected layers in identity theory.

**relational solidarity**    Developing close interracial relationships contributes to satisfying interracial communication.

**religion**    A community of people who fellowship around common ways of worship.

**repulsion**    A negative racial attitude that is based in ethnocentrism and sees anything different as wicked, crazy, immoral, or sinful.

**resistance and separation**    The third stage of microcultural identity development that begins when individuals experience some tension trying to understand themselves in the context of ingroup/outgroup perceptions.

**salience**    The attention or importance individuals place on their intergroup differences.

**Sambo**    Negative stereotype of African Americans as lazy, jolly, and content with life.

**Sapir-Whorf hypothesis**    The idea that language shapes one's perception of reality; also known as the **Whorfian hypothesis**.

**Sapphire**    Negative stereotype typically associated with African American women believed to be sexually enticing.

**satellite**  A public sphere that allows for wider and more equitable public discourses than do dominant public spheres.

**self-construals**  One's self-perception as being either independent or interdependent of larger group influences.

**self-face**  Concern for one's own image.

**semantics of prejudice**  Language choice can intentionally or unintentionally reveal information about an individual's internal thoughts.

**sexual orientation**  An aspect of cultural identity that references the direction of an individual's sexuality: lesbian, gay, bisexual, transgender, queer (questioning), asexual, heterosexual.

**Shudras**  A group under the caste system consisting of servants and manual workers.

**significant others**  In symbolic interactionism, individuals who are significantly influential in identity development; these orientational others are, for most individuals, generally family members.

**Silent Generation**  Generation of individuals born 1925–1945.

**situational context**  One of six interrelated factors in co-cultural theory that recognizes the important role that the dynamics inherent in a particular setting play in communication behavior.

**situational factors**  Frequency of interaction and desire to interact with the other person are factors that impact friendships and interpersonal connections.

**skin whitening**  The use of a chemically-based product(s) to lighten one's skin tone.

**social capital**  Resources such as knowledge, skills, experiences, and associations with different groups that give individuals advantages in society; lighter skin tone is a form of social capital providing access to education, romantic partners, social networks, and jobs.

**social context**  In workplace communication, the relationships between communicators; one of Weick's three contexts that influence organizational communication.

**social Darwinism**  An ideology elevating hierarchies that prioritize the mistreatment of groups deemed "inferior" and are natural and necessary in order to improve the human race through natural selection.

**social learning theory**  Developed by psychologist Albert Bandura, the theory argues we learn by observing others through interpersonal relationships or vicariously through mass media.

**societal privilege**  An invisible package of unearned assets that majority members can rely on without much thought; a set of unearned entitlements only available to majority group members.

**socioeconomic status**  An aspect of cultural identity that refers to one's economic standing and the long-term values, norms, and behaviors that are associated with it.

**speech code**  A concept central to speech community theory that refers to a system of symbols, rules, and meanings related to communication behavior.

**speech community**  A concept central to speech community theory that describes when a group of people understand goals, norms, and styles of communication behavior in ways not shared by people outside the group.

**spirituality**  Reference to an individual's identification with, and belief in, a higher power or higher order of things.

**standpoint theory**  Developed by feminist sociology scholars, it acknowledges that our gender, race, class, and sexual orientation standpoints intersect and create a vantage point from which to view the world.

**stereotypes**  Overgeneralizations of group characteristics or behaviors that are applied universally to all individuals of that particular group.

**strangers**  Unfamiliar others from outside the primary cultural community.

**structural theory**  Explains the motivations for relational involvement; mutual attraction between relationally different partners is due to demographics (i.e., education, occupation, status).

**subaltern counterpublics**  A type of public sphere created and maintained by historically marginalized group members.

**support**  A positive racial attitude that translates into efforts to safeguard the rights of all; people are aware of racial and ethnic oppression and want to do something to address it.

**Suzie Wong**   A stereotype of Asian women suggesting assimilation/dependency and exoticism.

**talk**   Unidirectional messages sent with little attention to, or opportunity for, feedback; talk is one-way communication that often takes the form of a lecture.

**theory**   A way of seeing and thinking about the world; frameworks that provide insight into phenomena.

**technical robot**   Stereotype of Asian Americans as being unemotional (e.g., robot-like) technicians lacking creativity.

**three social forces**   Three difference variables that influence marriage patterns: (1) preferences for marriage candidates, (2) social group influence on mate selection process, and (3) constraints in the marriage market.

**thug**   A drug dealer, pimp, con-artist, or other criminal incorporated in the stereotype of Black men as dangerous and drawn to illicit activities.

**tolerance**   An unproductive racial attitude whereby someone is moderately respectful of other racial and ethnic groups, but the attitude is steeped in rejection and unacceptance.

**transnationalism**   A concept that captures how modern-day immigrants simultaneously live in two or more cultures and construct bicultural identities.

**transracial communication**   Interactions between individuals in a context where racial differences are transcended and commonalities are heightened.

**two-step flow theory**   This indirect effects theory tracks how media messages influence opinion leaders (i.e., politicians, friends) who, in turn, influence others in the community via interpersonal communication.

**uncertainty**   A cognition doubting one's ability to predict the outcome of interactions; according to anxiety/uncertainty management theory, a basic cause of communication failure.

**Uncle Tom**   Negative stereotype of African American males who are quiet and desire to please the white man.

**unconscious bias**   Sociocultural stereotypes about groups of people that individuals form outside their conscious awareness.

**unexamined identity**   The first stage of microcultural identity development that is characterized by an absence of any awareness of racial identity.

**Untouchables**   A group under the caste system consisting of workers who process animal and human waste.

**Vaishyas**   A group under the caste system consisting of merchants and traders.

**vocalics**   A form of nonverbal communication that includes any vocal-auditory behavior except for spoken words (e.g., pitch, volume, tone, pauses, laughter, and sarcasm); paralanguage.

**video vixen**   A 21st century adaptation of the Jezebel stereotype borne out of the rap music industry.

**visibility**   Representations in media that contribute to greater understanding of the human experience beyond mere stereotypes.

**vulnerability**   One of six core elements of community that includes discarding masks of composure and exposing one's inner self to others.

**white leader prototype**   A public relations theory that professional roles are racially constructed through ideological discourses that perpetuate white privilege.

**whiteness**   A social construction associated with privilege based on how European American identity is unmarked, neutral, and invisible.

**Whorfian hypothesis**   See **Sapir-Whorf hypothesis**.

**yellow peril**   Unfounded fear of Asian expansion by whites, which led to the societal oppression and stereotyping of Asian Americans as a racial group deemed inferior.

# References

Abad-Santos, A. (2015, January 15). What "fresh off the boat" means to Asian-Americans. *Vox.* https://www.vox.com/2014/5/15/5717046/what-fresh-off-the-boat-means-to-asian-americans

Acosta, I. (2021, September 24). Workplaces may be getting more inclusive, but Latino professionals still have challenges. *Fast Company.* https://www.fastcompany.com/90679785/workplaces-may-be-getting-more-inclusive-but-latino-professionals-still-have-challenges

Adams, C. (2020, June 18). Not all Black people are African American. Here's the difference. CBS News.

Adams, C. (2021, March 26). Evanston is the first U.S. city to issue slavery reparations. Experts say it's a noble start. NBC News.

Adams, E. A., Kurtz-Costes, B., Hoffman, A. J., Volpe, V. V., & Rowley, S. J. (2020). Longitudinal relations between skin tone and self-esteem in African American girls. *Developmental Psychology, 56*(12), 2322–2330.

Addo, I. Y. (2020). Double pandemic: Racial discrimination amid coronavirus disease 2019. *Social Sciences & Humanities Open, 2*(1), 100074.

Affram, A. A., Osei-Tutu, A., & Dzokoto, V. A. (2020). Conflict handling in Ghanaian in-law relationships: Implications for face concerns. *Journal of Family Communication, 20*(4), 285–297. https://doi.org/10.1080/15267431.2020.1822845

Aguilar, C. (2019). Undocumented critical theory. *Cultural Studies ↔ Critical Methodologies, 19*(3), 152–160. https://doi.org/10.1177/1532708618817911

Aguilar, C., & Juarez, D. (2023). Undocumented critical theory. In J. Austin, M. Orbe, & J. Sims (Eds.), *Communication theory: Racially and inclusive perspectives* (pp. 17–26). Cognella.

Alexander, B. K. (2021). Critical autoethnography as intersectional praxis: A performative pedagogical interplay on bleeding borders of identity. In R. Boylorn & M. Orbe (Eds.), *Critical autoethnography: Intersecting cultural identities in everyday life* (pp. 32–44). Routledge.

Alexander, B. K., Asaratnam, L., Avant-Mier, R., Durham, A., Flores, L., Leeds-Hurwitz, W., Mendoza, S., Oetzel, J., Osland, J., Tsuda, Y., Yin, J., & Halualani, R. (2014). Defining and communicating what "intercultural" and "intercultural communication" means to us. *Journal of International and Intercultural Communication, 7*(1), 14–37. https://doi.org/10.1080/17513057.2014.869524

Alexander, M. (2010). *The new Jim Crow: Mass incarceration in the age of colorblindness.* The New Press.

Alexander, S. (1994). Vietnamese Amerasians: Dilemmas of individual identity and family cohesion. In E. P. Salett & D. R. Koslow (Eds.), *Race, ethnicity and self: Identity in multicultural perspective* (pp. 198–216). MultiCultural Institute.

Alford, N. S. (2021, June 17). Why Rita Moreno's comment about *In the heights* was terribly wrong. CNN Opinion. https://www.cnn.com/2021/06/17/opinions/rita-moreno-in-the-heights-colorism-alford/index.html

Alharbi, A. (2018). Case study of three Arab American language identity: Bilingual, binational, or both. *Journal of Literature and Art Studies, 8*(8), 1235–1244.

Allen, B. J. (1998). Black womanhood and feminist standpoints. *Management Communication Quarterly, 11*, 575–586.

Allen, B. J. (2012). *Difference matters* (2nd ed.). Waveland Press.

Allen, B. J. (2016). Sapphire and Sappho: Allies in authenticity. In A. Gonzalez & Y.-W. Chen (Eds.), *Our voices: Essays in culture, ethnicity, and communication* (6th ed., pp. 217–221). Oxford University Press.

Allen, P. G. (1986). *The sacred hoop: Recovering the feminism in American Indian traditions.* Beacon Press.

Allport, G. W. (1958). *The nature of prejudice*. Doubleday.

Al-Ramahi, R., Ab Rashid, R., Al-Smadi, O., & Ismail, H. (2021). The discursive strategies used by Langston Hughes in the construction of whiteness and blackness. *Journal of Language and Linguistic Studies, 17*(1). http://jlls.org/index.php/jlls/article/view/2197

American Community Survey, (2020a). Disability characteristics. https://data.census.gov/cedsci/table?hidePreview=true&tid=ACSST5Y2020.S1810

American Community Survey (2020b). Selected characteristics of the foreign-born population by period of entry into the United States. Table S0502. https://data.census.gov/cedsci/table?y=2020&tid=ACSST5Y2020.S0502

Anderson, C., & Cromwell, R. L. (1977). "Black is beautiful" and the color preferences of Afro-American youth. *The Journal of Negro Education, 46*(1), 76–88.

Anderson, J. (2021, January 13). Capitol riot images showing Confederate flag a reminder of country's darkest past. *USA Today.* https://www.usatoday.com/story/news/2021/01/07/capitol-riot-images-confederate-flag-terror/6588104002/

Anderson, K. J., & Accomando, C. H. (2019). The pitfalls of ally performance: Why coalition work is more effective than ally theater. *Psychology Today.* https://www.psychologytoday.com/us/blog/benign-bigotry/201608/the-pitfalls-ally-performance

Anderson, K., Harwood, J., & Hummert, M. L. (2005). The grandparent–grandchild relationship: Implications for models of intergenerational communication. *Human Communication Research, 31*(2), 268–294.

Anderson, T. (2017, April 27). 4 Latino stereotypes in TV and film that need to go. *Los Angeles Times.*

Anguiano, C., Milstein, T., De Larkin, I., Chen, Y. W., & Sandoval, J. (2012). Connecting community voices: Using a Latino/a critical race theory lens on environmental justice advocacy. *Journal of International and Intercultural Communication, 6*(3), 403–421.

Antoine, D. M. (2011). Unethical acts: Treating Native men as lurking threat, leaving Native women without voice. *Journal of Mass Media Ethics, 26*(3), 243–265.

Arab American Institute. (2021). National Arab American demographics. https://www.aaiusa.org/demographics

Arrington, M. I. (2020). When teaching failed in the interracial communication course: On the need to teach dialogue and the need to teach dialogically. *Communication Education, 69*(4), 432–440. https://doi.org/10.1080/03634523.2020.1804068

Artz, B. L. (1998). Hegemony in Black and White: Interracial buddy films and the new racism. In Y. R. Kamalipour & T. Carilli (Eds.), *Cultural diversity in the U.S. media* (pp. 67–78). State University of New York Press.

Asante, M. K. (1988). *Afrocentricity*. Africa World Press.

Asante, M. K. (1998a). *The Afrocentric idea*. Temple University Press.

Asante, M. K. (1998b). Identifying racist language, linguistic acts, and signs. In M. L. Hecht (Ed.), *Communicating prejudice* (pp. 87–98). Sage.

Ashcraft, K. L., & Allen, B. J. (2003). The racial foundation of organizational communication. *Communication Theory, 13*(1), 5–38.

Austin, A. (2006). *Achieving blackness: Race, black nationalism, and Afrocentrism in the twentieth century.* New York University Press.

Austin, J. T., Orbe, M., & Sims, J. D. (Eds.). (2023). *Communication theory: Racially diverse and inclusive perspectives.* Cognella.

Awad, G. H., Hashem, H., & Nguyen, H. (2021). Identity and ethnic/racial self-labeling among Americans of Arab or Middle Eastern and North African descent. *Identity, 21*(2), 115–130. https://doi.org/10.1080/15283488.2021.1883277

Axson, S. (2021, July 15). Police arrest four people over racist abuse of England soccer players after Euro 2020 loss. *USA Today.* https://www.usatoday.com/story/sports/soccer/2021/07/15/euro-2020-four-people-arrested-over-racist-abuse-england-players/7975635002/

Babers, J. (2016, April 19). For women of color, the glass ceiling is actually made of concrete. *Aspen Institute.* https://www.aspeninstitute.org/blog-posts/for-women-of-color-the-glass-ceiling-is-actually-made-of-concrete/

Babbitt, L., Gaither, S., Toosi, N., & Sommers, S. (2018). The role of gender in racial meta-stereotypes and stereotypes. *Social Cognition, 36*(5), 589–601. https://doi.org/10.1521/soco.2018.36.5.589

Bahrainwala, L. (2021). Shithole rhetorics. *Journal of International and Intercultural Communication, 14*(3), 185–201. https://doi.org/10.1080/17513057.2020.1795224

Baia, L. R. (1999). Rethinking transnationalism: Reconstructing national identities among Peruvian Catholics in New Jersey. *Journal of Interamerican Studies and World Affairs, 41*(4), 93–109.

Bahk, C. M., & Jandt, F. E. (2004). Being White in America: Development of a scale. *Howard Journal of Communications, 15*, 57–68.

Balaji, M., & Worawongs, T. (2010). The new Suzie Wong: Normative assumptions of white male and Asian female relationships. *Communication, Culture & Critique, 3*(2), 224–241.

Baldwin, J. (1990). Quoted in introduction: A way of images. In J. L. Dates & W. Barlow (Eds.), *Split image* (pp. 1–21). Howard University Press.

Banaji, M. R., & Greenwald, A. G. (2013). *Blindspot: Hidden biases of good people.* Bantam Books.

Bandura, A. (2009). Social cognitive theory of mass communication. In J. Bryant & M. B. Oliver (Eds.), *Media effects: Advances in theory and research* (3rd ed., pp. 94–124). Routledge.

Banjo, O. (2011). What are you laughing at? Examining white identity and enjoyment of black entertainment. *Journal of Broadcasting and Electronic Media, 55*(2), 137–159.

Banks, J. A. (1976). The emerging stages of ethnicity: Implications for staff development. *Educational Leadership, 34*(3), 190–193.

Banks, T. (2000). Colorism: A darker shade of pale. *UCLA Law Review, 47*(6), 1705–1746.

Banton, M. (1967). *Race relations.* Tavistock.

Bardhan, N., & Orbe, M. (2012). Introduction: Identity research in intercultural communication. In N. Bardhan & M. Orbe (Eds.), *Identity research and communication: Intercultural reflections and future directions* (pp. xiii–xxv). Lexington Books.

Barker, V., & Giles, H. (2003). Integrating the communicative predicament and enhancement of aging models: The case of older Native Americans. *Health Communication, 15*(3), 255–275.

Barnett, L. (2004). The dimensions of colorism on race, class, and gender in the United States. *Conference Papers—American Sociological Association*, 1–23.

Batalova, J., Hanna, M., & Levesque, C. (2021, February 11). Frequently requested statistics on immigrants and immigration in the United States. Migration Policy Institute. https://www.migrationpolicy.org/article/frequently-requested-statistics-immigrants-and-immigration-united-states-2020

Baugh, J. (2000a). *Beyond Ebonics: Linguistic pride and racial prejudice*. Oxford University Press.

Baugh, J. (2000b). Racial identification by speech. *American Speech, 75*(4), 362–364.

Begley, S. (1995, February 13). Three is not enough. *Newsweek,* 67–69.

Behm-Morawitz, E., & Villamil, A. M. (2019). The roles of ingroup identification and implicit bias in assessing the effectiveness of an online diversity education program. *Journal of Applied Communication Research, 47*(5), 505–526.

Bell, K., Orbe, M., Drummond, D. K., & Camara, S. K. (2000). Accepting the challenge of centralizing without essentializing: Black feminist thought and African American women's communicative experiences. *Women's Studies in Communication, 23*(1), 41–62.

Bell, M. (2021). Invisible no more: White racialization and the localness of racial identity. *Sociology Compass, 15*(9). https://doi.org/10.1111/soc4.12917

Bell-Jordan, K. E. (2008). Black. White. And a survivor of the real world: Constructions of race on reality TV. *Critical Studies in Media Communication, 25*(4), 353–372.

Bennett-Alexander, D. D., & Harrison, L. F. (2016). My hair is not like yours: Workplace hair grooming policies for African American women as racial stereotyping in violation of Title VII. *Cardozo Journal of Law and Gender, 22,* 437–462.

Bergsieker, H. B., Shelton, J., & Richeson, J. A. (2010). To be liked versus respected: Divergent goals in interracial interactions. *Journal of Personality & Social Psychology, 99*(2), 248–264.

Bernstein, A. (2012, October 25). *Nightline takes a rare look inside the new KKK.* ABC News. http://abcnews.g.com/blogs/headlines/2012/10/nightline-takes-a-rare-look-inside-the-new-KKK/

Berry, S. (2019). Teaching to connect: Community-building strategies for the virtual classroom. *Online Learning, 23*(1), 164–183. https://doi.org/10.24059/olj.v23i1.1425

Bhandari, H., & Yasunobu, K. (2009). What is social capital? A comprehensive review of the concept. *Asian Journal of Social Sciences, 37*(3), 480–510.

Bhattacharya, K. (2021). Connecting with water spirits: An autoethnography of home and higher education. In R. Boylorn & M. Orbe (Eds.), *Critical autoethnography: Intersecting cultural identities in everyday life* (pp. 103–117). Routledge.

Bilge, N., Marino, M. I., & Webb, L. M. (2021). Definitions of ethnicity in communication scholarship: A new perspective. *Howard Journal of Communications, 32*(3), 213–234. https://doi.org/10.1080/10646175.2021.1871869

Blackstone, A. (2021, July 28). Meet the woman who founded an event series to address colorism in the Black community. Black Enterprise. https://www.blackenterprise.com/meet-the-woman-who-founded-an-event-series-to-address-colorism-in-the-black-community/

Blake, A. (2018, January 16). The Trump "shithole countries" flap takes an even more ridiculous turn. *The Washington Post.* https://www.washingtonpost.com/news/the-fix/wp/2018/01/16/the-trump-shithole-countries-flap-takes-an-even-more-ridiculous-turn/

Blake, J. (2021, August 15). Obama poses a question that we still can't answer. CNN Politics. https://www.cnn.com/2021/08/15/politics/obama-poses-a-question-that-we-still-cannot-answer/index.html

Blancero, D. M., Mouriño-Ruiz, E., & Padilla, A. M. (2018). Latino millennials? The new diverse workforce: Challenges and opportunities. *Hispanic Journal of Behavioral Sciences, 40*(1), 3–21.

Bloch-Eikon, Y. (2011). The polls—Trends: Public perceptions and the threat of international terrorism after 9/11. *Public Opinion Quarterly, 75*(2), 366–392.

Blubaugh, J. A., & Pennington, D. L. (1976). *Crossing difference . . . Interracial communication.* Charles E. Merrill.

Blumenbach, J. F. (1969). *On the natural varieties of mankind: De generis humani varietate nativa* (T. Bendyshe, Trans.). Bergman Publishers. [Original work published 1775]

Blumer, H. (1969). *Symbolic interactionism: Perspective and method*. Prentice-Hall.

Bogel-Burroughs, N., & Wright, W. (2021, April 19). Little has been said about the $20 bill that brought officers to the scene. *The New York Times*.

Bonilla-Rodriguez, D. M. (2016). Latinas in the workplace: Creating a path of success. In M. F. Karsten (Ed.), *Gender, race, and ethnicity in the workplace: Emerging issues and enduring challenges* (pp. 339–358). Praeger.

Bose, D. (2021, June 7). The director of *Crazy Rich Asians* says he regrets casting Brown actors in stereotypical roles in response to whitewashing criticism. *Insider*. https://www.insider.com/jon-chu-crazy-rich-asians-whitewashing-stereotypes-tropes-2021-6

Bowen, S. P. (2016). Jewish and/or woman: Identity and communicative style. In A. Gonzalez & Y.-W. Chen (Eds.), *Our voices: Essays in culture, ethnicity, and communication* (6th ed., pp. 47–52). Oxford University Press.

Bowman, N. A., & Park, J. J. (2015). Not all diversity interactions are created equal: Cross-racial interaction, close interracial friendship, and college student outcomes. *Research in Higher Education: Journal of the Association for Institutional Research, 56*(6), 601–621.

Bowser, B. P., & Hunt, R. G. (Eds.). (1996). *Impacts of racism on White Americans* (2nd ed.). Sage.

Boylorn, R. M. (2008). As seen on TV: An autoethnographic reflection on race and reality television. *Critical Studies in Media Communication, 25*(4), 413–433.

Boylorn, R. M., & Orbe, M. (Eds.). (2021). *Critical ethnography: Intersecting cultural identities in everyday life*. Routledge.

Bradley, L. (2020, June 12). *The Bachelor* can't right its racist history with one Black lead. *The Daily Beast*. https://www.thedailybeast.com/the-bachelor-cant-right-its-racist-history-with-black-lead-matt-james

Braithwaite, D. O., & Braithwaite, C. A. (2000). Understanding communication of persons with disabilities as cultural communication. In L. A. Samovar & R. E. Porter (Eds.), *Intercultural communication: A reader* (pp. 136–145). Wadsworth.

Braithwaite, D. O., & Thompson, T. L. (Eds.). (2000). *Handbook of communication and people with disabilities: Research and application*. Lawrence Erlbaum.

Brayboy, B. M. J. (2005). Toward a Tribal critical race theory in education. *The Urban Review, 37*(5), 425–446. https://doi.org/10.1007/s11256-005-0018-y

Bresnahan, M. J., Guan, X., Shearman, S. M., & Donohue, W. (2009). Roommate conflict: Does race matter? *Howard Journal of Communications, 20*, 394–412.

Brewer, S. (2006). *Borders and bridges: A history of U.S.–Latin American relations*. Praeger.

Brown, A. (2018, January 9). "Least desirable"? How racial discrimination plays out in online dating. Minnesota Public Radio: Web Edition Articles (MN).

Brown, M. K., & Chevrette, R. (2021). Teaching co-cultural theory, dis/ability, and normativity using *The Greatest Showman*. *Communication Teacher*. https://doi.org/10.1080/17404622.2021.1945640

Brownridge, D. A., Taillieu, T., Chan, K. L., & Piotrowski, C. (2021). Understanding the elevated prevalence of intimate partner violence in interracial relationships. *Journal of Interpersonal Violence, 36*(7–8), NP3844–NP3868.

Brummett, E. (2017). "Race doesn't matter": A dialogic analysis of interracial romantic partners stories about racial differences. *Journal of Social and Personal Relationships, 34*(5), 771–789.

Brummett, E. A., & Afifi, T. D. (2019). A grounded theory of interracial romantic partners' expectations for support and strain with family members, *Journal of Family Communication, 19*(3), 191–212.

Bryant, J., & Finklea, B. (2023). *Fundamentals of media effects* (3rd ed.). Waveland Press.

Budiman, A. (2020). Key findings about U.S. immigrants. Pew Research Center. https://www.pewresearch.org/fact-tank/2020/08/20/key-findings-about-u-s-immigrants/

Budiman, A., & Ruiz, N. (2021, April 29). Key facts about Asian Americans, a diverse and growing population. Pew Research Center. https://www.pewresearch.org/fact-tank/2021/04/29/key-facts-about-asian-americans/

Buggs, S. G. (2017a). Dating in the time of #BlackLivesMatter: Exploring mixed-race women's discourses of race and racism. *Sociology of Race and Ethnicity*, *3*(4), 538–551.

Buggs, S. G. (2017b). Does (mixed-) race matter? The role of race in interracial sex, dating, and marriage. *Sociology Compass*, *11*(11).

Burge, C. D., Wamble, J. J., & Cuomo, R. R. (2020). A certain type of descriptive representative? Understanding how the skin tone and gender of candidates influences black politics. *The Journal of Politics*, *82*(4), 1596–1601.

Burgoon, J. K., Manusov, V., & Guerrero, L. K. (2021). *Nonverbal communication* (2nd ed.). Routledge.

Burke, P. J., & Reitzes, D. C. (1981). The link between identity and role performance. *Social Psychology Quarterly*, *44*, 83–92.

Busselle, R., & Van den Bulck, J. (2020). Cultivation theory, media stories, processes, and reality. In M. B. Oliver, A. Raney, & J. Bryant (Eds.), *Media effects: Advances in theory and research* (4th ed., pp. 69–82). Routledge.

Buzzanell, P. M. (2015). Standpoint theory. In J. Bennett (Ed.), *The Sage encyclopedia of intercultural competence* (pp. 771–774). Sage.

Cabrera, N. L. (2019). Critical race theory v. deficit models. *Equity & Excellence in Education*, *52*(1), 47–54. https://doi.org/10.1080/10665684.2019.1630342

Calafell, B. M. (2010). Notes from an "angry woman of color": Academic policing and disciplining women of color in a post (fill in the blank) era. *Journal of Communication Inquiry*, *34*(3), 240–245.

Calvert, C. (1997). Hate speech and its harms: A communication theory perspective. *Journal of Communication*, *47*(1), 4–19.

Camara, S. K., & Orbe, M. (2010). Analyzing strategic responses to discriminatory acts: A co-cultural communicative investigation. *Journal of International*

*and Intercultural Communication*, *3*(2), 83–113.

Camara, S. K., & Orbe, M. (2011). Understanding interpersonal manifestations of reverse discrimination through phenomenological inquiry. *Journal of Intercultural Communication Research*, *40*(2), 111–134.

Campos-Vázquez, R., & Medina-Cortina, E. (2019). Skin color and social mobility: Evidence from Mexico. *Demography*, *56*(1), 321–343.

Canary, D., & Dindia, K. (Eds.). (1998). *Sex differences and similarities in communication: Critical essays and empirical investigations of sex and gender in interaction*. Lawrence Erlbaum.

Canotal, E. (2009, August 21). An overseas example of "lighter is better": The implications of colorism among male sex workers in Thailand. https://scholarworks.smith.edu/theses/1181/

Cantu, M. (2018, December 1). Colorism within the Latinx community. LJ Express. https://www.jackcentral.org/news/colorism-within-the-latinx-community/article_6095446a-1239-5b36-a47c-fc5b456f7d35.html

Carbado, D. W. (2013). Colorblind intersectionality. *Signs: Journal of Women in Culture and Society*, *38*(4), 811–845. https://doi.org/10.1086/669666

Carbaugh, D. (1999). "Just listen": "Listening" and landscape among the Blackfeet. *Western Journal of Communication*, *63*, 250–270.

Caring Across Generations. (2020). Conversation guide: Talking about race, racism, care, and caregiving. https://caringacross.org/blog/talking-about-race/

Carlo, G., McGinley, M., Hayes, R. C., & Martinez, M. M. (2012). Empathy as a mediator of the relations between parent and peer attachment and prosocial and physically aggressive behaviors in Mexican American college students. *Journal of Social and Personal Relationships*, *29*(3), 337–357.

Carlson, C. I., Wilson, K. D., & Hargrave, J. L. (2003). The effect of school racial composition on Hispanic intergroup relations. *Journal of Social and Personal Relationships, 20*(2), 203–220.

Carrillo Rowe, A. (2016). Women writing borders, borders writing women: Immigration, assimilation and the politics of speaking. In A. Gonzalez & Y.-W. Chen (Eds.), *Our voices: Essays in culture, ethnicity, and communication* (6th ed., pp. 308–321). Oxford University Press.

Carson, D. K., & Hand, C. (1999). Dilemmas surrounding elder abuse and neglect in Native American communities. In T. Toshio (Ed.), *Understanding the elder abuse in minority populations* (pp. 161–186). Brunner/Mazel.

Castle Bell, G. (2019). "There's a difference between Black people and n******": A cultural contracts exploration of interracial communication barriers. *Communication Quarterly, 67*(3), 243–270. https://doi.org/10.1080/01463373.2019.1573744

Castle Bell, G., & Hastings, S. O. (2011). Black and White interracial couples: Managing relational disapproval through facework. *Howard Journal of Communications, 22*(3), 240–259.

Cedillo, C. V. (2018). What does it mean to move? Race, disability, and critical embodiment pedagogy. *Composition Forum, 39.* https://files.eric.ed.gov/fulltext/EJ1188979.pdf

Cemone, C., Augoustinos, M., & Maass, A. (2020). The language of derogation and hate: Functions, consequences, and reappropriation. *Journal of Language and Social Psychology, 40*(1), 80–101. https://doi.org/10.1177/0261927X20967394

Century Foundation. (2019, April 29). The benefits of socioeconomically and racially integrated schools and classrooms. https://tcf.org/content/facts/the-benefits-of-socioeconomically-and-racially-integrated-schools-and-classrooms/?agreed=1

Chakravartty, P., Kuo, R., Grubb, V., & McIlwain, C. (2018). #CommunicationSoWhite. *Journal of Communication, 68,* 254–266.

Chan, N. K. M., & Jasso, F. (2021). From inter-racial solidarity to action: Minority linked fate and African American, Latina/o, and Asian American political participation. *Political Behavior.* https://doi.org/10.1007/s11109-021-09750-6

Chan, S. (1989). You're short, besides! In Asian Women United of California (Eds.), *Making waves: An anthology of writing by and about Asian American women* (pp. 265–272). Beacon Press.

Chan, S. (Ed.). (2003). *Remapping Asian American history.* AltaMira Press.

Charles, C. (2003). Skin bleaching, self-hate, and Black identity in Jamaica. *Journal of Black Studies, 33*(6), 711–728.

Charles, J. (2021). Colorism and the Afro-Latinx experience: A review of the literature. *Hispanic Journal of Behavioral Sciences, 43*(1/2), 8–31.

Chauhan, G., & Tiwari, A. (2019). Unfair promotion of whitening creams: Is beauty no more skin deep? *Media Watch, 10*(2), 365–373.

Chavez, K. R. (2012). Doing intersectionality: Power, privilege, and identities in political activist communities. In N. Bardhan & M. Orbe (Eds.), *Identity research and communication: Intercultural reflections and future directions* (pp. 21–32). Lexington Books.

Chavez, N., & Kaur, H. (2021, August 19). Why the jump in the Native American population may be one of the hardest to explain. CNN. https://www.cnn.com/2021/08/19/us/census-native-americans-rise-population/index.html

Chavez-Duenas, N. Y., & Adames, H. Y. (2014). Skin-color prejudice and within-group racial discrimination: Historical current impact on Latino/a populations. *Hispanic Journal of Behavioral Sciences, 36*(1), 3–26. https://doi.org/10.1177/0739986313511306

Chen, Y.-W. (2016). "What's in a name?" Shifting meanings, negotiating identities, and globalizing relationships. In A. Gonzalez & Y.-W. Chen (Eds.), *Our voices: Essays in culture, ethnicity, and communication* (6th ed., pp. 19–24). Oxford University Press.

Chen, Y.-W., & Collier, M. J. (2012). Intercultural identity positioning: Interview discourses from two-identity-based nonprofit organizations. *Journal of International and Intercultural Communication, 5*(1), 43–63.

Cheng, H. L. (2005). Constructing a transnational multilocal sense of belonging: An analysis of *Ming Pao* (West Canadian edition). *Journal of Communication Inquiry, 29*(2), 141–159.

Childs, D. (2021, February 8). Representations of African American characters on television and film. Democracy & Me. Cincinnati Public Radio.

Chuang, R., Wilkins, C., Tan, M., & Mead, C. (2021). Racial minorities' attitudes toward interracial couples: An intersection of race and gender. *Group Processes & Intergroup Relations, 24*(3), 453–467. https://doi.org/10.1177/1368430219899482

Cimaglio, Z., & Hall, E. (2021, November 21). Native Americans in entertainment: The "good" and the "bad." *State Hornet.* https://statehornet.com/2021/11/native-film-representation-good-bad/

Clark, K. D., & Diggs, R. C. (2002). Connected or separated? Toward a dialectical view of interethnic relationships. In T. McDonald, M. Orbe, & T. Ford-Ahmed (Eds.), *Building diverse communities: Applications of communication research* (pp. 3–26). Hampton Press.

Coates, T. (2012). Fear of a black president. *The Atlantic.* https://www.theatlantic.com/magazine/archive/2012/09/fear-of-a-black-president/309064/

Coates, T.-N. (2014, June). The case for reparations. *The Atlantic.* https://www.theatlantic.com/magazine/archive/2014/06/the-case-for-reparations/361631/

Cohen, J., Appel, M., & Slater, M. D. (2020). Media, identity, and the self. In M. B. Oliver, A. Raney, & J. Bryant (Eds.), *Media effects: Advances in theory and research* (4th ed., pp. 179–194). Routledge.

Cohen, M., & Avanzino, S. (2010). We are people first: Framing organizational assimilation experiences of the physically disabled using co-cultural theory. *Communication Studies, 61*(3), 272–303.

Cole, J. B. (1995). Commonalities and differences. In M. L. Andersen & P. H. Collins (Eds.), *Race, class, and gender: An anthology* (pp. 148–154). Wadsworth.

Coleman, L. M., & DePaulo, B. M. (1991). Uncovering the human spirit: Moving beyond disability and "missed" communications. In N. Coupland, H. Giles, & J. M. Wiemann (Eds.), *Miscommunication and problematic talk* (pp. 61–84). Sage.

Coleman, R. R. M. (2003). Black sitcom portrayals. In G. Dines & J. M. Humez (Eds.), *Gender, race, and class in media: A text-reader* (2nd ed., pp. 79–88). Sage.

Collier, M. J. (1991). Conflict competence within African, Mexican, and Anglo American friendships. In S. Ting-Toomey & F. Korzenny (Eds.), *Cross-cultural interpersonal communication* (pp. 132–154). Sage.

Collier, M. J. (2000). Cultural identity and intercultural communication. In L. A. Samovar & R. E. Porter (Eds.), *Intercultural communication: A reader* (pp. 16–33). Wadsworth.

Collier, M. J. (2002). Intercultural friendships as interpersonal alliances. In J. N. Martin, T. K. Nakayama, & L. A. Flores (Eds.), *Readings in cultural contexts* (pp. 301–309). Mayfield.

Collins, P. H. (1998). *Fighting words: Black women and the search for justice.* University of Minnesota Press.

Collins, P. H. (2016). Black feminist thought as oppositional knowledge. *Departures in Critical Qualitative Research, 5*(3), 133–144. https://doi.org/10.1525/dcqr.2016.5.3.133

Collins, P. H. (2019). *Intersectionality as critical social theory.* Duke University Press.

Collins, P. H. (2022). *Black feminist thought: Knowledge, consciousness, and the politics of empowerment* (30th anniversary ed.). Routledge.

Comeforo, K. (2021). My butch body: An autoethnography of gender and (dis)ease. In R. Boylorn & M. Orbe (Eds.), *Critical autoethnography: Intersecting cultural identities in everyday life* (pp. 71–81). Routledge.

Connell, R. W. (2005). *Masculinities.* Polity Press.

Cook, G. (2003, November 18). Study finds that racism can breed stupidity. *Kalamazoo (MI) Gazette,* p. A4.

Cooper, B. (1998). "The white-black fault line": Relevancy of race and racism in spectators' experiences of Spike Lee's *Do the Right Thing*. *Howard Journal of Communications, 9*(3), 205–228.

Cooper, B. C. (2018). *Eloquent rage: A Black feminist discovers her superpower.* St. Martin's Press.

Coopman, S. J. (2003). Communicating disability: Metaphors of oppression, metaphors of empowerment. *Communication Yearbook, 27,* 337–394.

Corbett, C. (2003). Introduction: When God became red. In R. A. Grounds, G. E. Tinker, & D. E. Wilkins (Eds.), *Native voices: American Indian identity and resistance* (pp. 189–193). University Press of Kansas.

Cornejo, M., & Kam, J. A. (2020). Exploring the ascribed and avowed identities of Deferred Action for Childhood Arrivals (DACA) recipients in early adulthood. *Cultural Diversity and Ethnic Minority Psychology.* Advance online publication. https://doi.org/10.1037/cdp0000378

Cornett-DeVito, M. M., & Worley, D. W. (2005). A front row seat: A phenomenological investigation of learning disabilities. *Communication Education, 54*(4), 312–333.

Corona, R., Velazquez, E., McDonald, S., Avila, M., Neff, M., Iglesias, A., & Halfond, R. (2017). Ethnic labels, pride, and challenges: A qualitative study of Latinx youth living in a new Latinx destination community. *Journal of Ethnic and Cultural Studies, 4*(1), 1–13.

Corral, Á. (2020). Allies, antagonists, or ambivalent? Exploring Latino attitudes about the Black Lives Matter movement. *Hispanic Journal of Behavioral Sciences, 42*(4), 431–454.

Covarrubias, P. O. (2008). Masked silence sequences: Hearing discrimination in the college classroom. *Communication, Culture, & Critique, 1,* 227–252.

Coyle, J. (2022, July 26). For once, Cherokee actor Wes Studi cast as romantic co-star. AP News. https://apnews.com/article/entertainment-movies-native-americans-wes-studi-8e9ce54075898da338c1c0bc83cd7690

Crandall, C. S., & Eshleman, A. (2005). The justification-suppression model of prej-udice: An approach to the history of prejudice research. In C. S. Crandall & M. Schaller (Eds.), *Social psychology of prejudice: Historical and contemporary issues,* pp. 237–267. Lewinian Press.

Crenshaw, K. W. (1995). Mapping the margins: Intersectionality, identity politics, and violence against women of color. In K. W. Crenshaw, N. Gotanda, C. Peller, & K. Thomas (Eds.), *Critical race theory: The key writings that formed the movement* (pp. 357–383). The New Press.

Crenshaw, K. W. (2012). From private violence to mass incarceration: Thinking intersectionally about women, race, and social control. *UCLA Law Review, 59,* 1419–1472.

Crenshaw, K. (2015, September 24). Why intersectionality can't wait. *The Washington Post.* Retrieved https://www.washingtonpost.com/news/in-theory/wp/2015/09/24/why-intersectionality-cant-wait/

Crenshaw, K., Gotanda, N., Peller, G., & Thomas, K. (Eds.). (1995). *Critical race theory: The key writings that formed that movement.* The New Press.

Cross, W. (2017). Ethnic racial identity models. Paper presented at the annual meeting of the National Cross-Cultural Counseling and Education Conference for Research, Action, and Change. https://digitalcommons.georgiasouthern.edu/ccec/2017/2017/17

Crutchfield, J., Fisher, A., & Webb, S. L. (2017). Colorism and police killings. *Western Journal of Black Studies, 41*(3/4), 81–91.

Cummings, M. S., & Roy, A. (2002). Manifestations in Afrocentricity in rap music. *Howard Journal of Communications, 13*(1), 59–76.

Cupach, W. R., & Imahori, T. T. (1993). Identity management theory: Communication competence in intercultural episodes and relationships. *International and Intercultural Communication Annual, 17,* 112–131.

Curington, C. V., Lundquist, J. H., & Lin, K.-H. (2021). *The dating divide: Race and desire in the era of online romance.* University of California Press.

Curtin, P. (2011). Discourses of American Indian racial identity in the public relations materials of the Fred Harvey Company: 1902–1936. *Journal of Public Relations Research, 23*(4), 368–396.

Dace, K. L., & McPhail, M. L. (2002). Crossing the color line: From empathy to implicature in intercultural communication. In J. N. Martin, T. K. Nakayama, & L. A. Flores (Eds.), *Readings in cultural contexts* (pp. 344–350). Mayfield.

Dale, C., & Overell, R. (2018). Introduction. In C. Dale & R. Overell (Eds.), *Orienting feminism: Media, activism, and cultural representation* (pp. 1–5). Palgrave Macmillan.

Dame-Griff, E. C. (2021). What do we mean when we say "Latinx"? Definitional power, the limits of inclusivity, and the (un/re)constitution of an identity category. *Journal of International and Intercultural Communication.* https://doi.org/10.1080/17513057.2021.1901957

Daniels, R. (2018). Displacing black people and culture, gentrification: The new "negro removal" program: A call for an emergency summit. *Journal of Pan African Studies, 12*(7), 7–11.

Davidson, J. R., & Schneider, L. J. (1992). Acceptance of Black-White interracial marriage. *Journal of Intergroup Relations, 24*(3), 47–52.

Davidson, M. J. (1997). *The Black and ethnic minority woman manager: Cracking the concrete ceiling.* Paul Chapman.

Davis, F. J. (1991). *Who is Black? One nation's definition.* Pennsylvania State University Press.

Davis, R. A. (1997). *The myth of Black ethnicity: Monophylety, diversity, and the dilemma of identity.* Ablex.

Davis, R. E., Alexander, G., Calvi, J., Wiese, C., Greene, S., Nowak, M., Cross, W. E., & Resnicow, K. (2010). A new audience segmentation tool for African Americans: The Black Identity Classification Scale. *Journal of Health Communication, 15*(5), 532–554.

Davis Tribble, B. L., Allen, S. H., Hart, J. R., Francois, T. S., & Smith-Bynum, M. A. (2019). "No [right] way to be a Black woman": Exploring gendered racial socialization among Black women. *Psychology of Women Quarterly, 43*(3), 381–397.

Dawson, M. (1995). A Black counterpublic? Economic earthquakes, racial agenda(s) and Black politics. In Black Public Sphere Collective (Eds.), *The Black public sphere* (pp. 199–227). University of Chicago Press.

Day, A. G. (1960). *Hawaii and its people.* Duell, Sloan & Pearce.

Deetz, S. (1992). *Democracy in an age of corporate colonialization: Developments in communication and the politics of everyday life.* State University of New York Press.

Deetz, S., & Simpson, J. (2004). Critical organizational dialogue: Open formation and the demand of "otherness." In R. Anderson, L. A. Baxter, & K. N. Cissna (Eds.), *Dialogue: Theorizing difference in communication studies* (pp. 141–158). Sage.

Degler, C. N. (1971). *Neither Black or White: Slavery and race relations in Brazil and the United States.* Macmillan.

Delgado, F. P. (1998). When the silenced speak: The textualization and complications of Latino/a identity. *Western Journal of Communication, 62,* 420–438.

Denham, B. E., Billings, A. C., & Halone, K. K. (2002). Differential accounts of race in broadcast commentary of the 2000 men's and women's final four basketball tournaments. *Sociology of Sport Journal, 19,* 315–332.

de Onís, C. M. (2017). What's in an "x": An exchange about the politics of "Latinx." *Chiricú Journal: Latina/o Literatures, Arts, and Cultures, 1*(2), 78–91. https://www.muse.jhu.edu/article/664597

Department of Public Safety (2022). A guide for responding to hate crimes/hate behaviors/hate acts. Berea College. https://www.berea.edu/public-safety/hate-guide/

Desnoyers-Colas, E. F. (2021). The proof is in the hovering: Disrupting racism in white spaces. *Women's Studies in Communication, 44*(2), 138–141.

DeTurk, S. (2011). Allies in action: The communicative experiences of people who challenge social injustice on behalf of others. *Communication Quarterly, 59*(5), 569–590.

Diamond, J. (1994, November). Race without color. *Discover,* 83–89.

DiAngelo, R. (2018). *White fragility. Why it's so hard for white people to talk about racism.* Beacon Press.

Dias, E. (2021, September 11). Muslim Americans' "seismic change." *The New York Times.* https://www.nytimes.com/2021/09/08/us/9-11-american-muslims.html

Dixon, A. R., & Telles, E. E. (2017). Skin color and colorism: Global research, concepts, and measurement. *Annual Review of Sociology, 43,* 405–424.

Dixon, J., Durrheim, K., Tredoux, C., Tropp, L., Clack, B., & Eaton, L. (2010). A paradox of integration? Interracial contact, prejudice reduction, and perceptions of racial discrimination. *Journal of Social Issues, 66*(2), 401–416.

Dixon, T. L. (2020). Media stereotypes: Content, effects, and theory. In M. B. Oliver, A. Raney, & J. Bryant (Eds.), *Media effects: Advances in theory and research* (4th ed., pp. 243–257).

Dixon, T. L., Schell, T. L., Giles, H., & Grogos, K. L. (2008). The influence of race in police-civilian interactions: A context analysis of videotaped interactions taken during Cincinnati police traffic stops. *Journal of Communication, 58*(3), 530–549.

Dixson, A. D., & Rousseau, C. K. (2005). And we are still not saved: Critical race theory in education 10 years later. *Race, Ethnicity, and Education, 8*(1), 7–27.

Docan-Morgan, S. (2011). "They don't know what it's like to be in my shoes": Topic avoidance about race in transracially adoptive families. *Journal of Social and Personal Relationships, 28*(3), 336–355.

Dodd, C. H., & Baldwin, J. R. (1998). The role of family and macrocultures in intercultural relationships. In J. N. Martin, T. K. Nakayama, & L. A. Flores (Eds.), *Readings in cultural contexts* (pp. 335–344). Mayfield.

Domke, D., McCoy, K., & Torres, M. (2003). News media, immigration, and priming of racial perceptions. In D. I. Rios & A. N. Mohamed (Eds.), *Brown and black communication: Latino and African American conflict and convergence in mass media* (pp. 123–142). Praeger.

Donahue, W. A. (1985). Ethnicity and mediation. In W. B. Gudykunst, L. P. Stewart, & S. Ting-Toomey (Eds.), *Communication, culture, and organizational processes* (pp. 134–154). Sage.

Donegan, M. (2018, May 11). How #MeToo revealed the central rift within feminism today. *The Guardian.* https://www.theguardian.com/news/2018/may/11/how-metoo-revealed-the-central-rift-within-feminism-social-individualist

Don-Yehiya, E. (2012). Orthodox and other American Jews and their attitude to the State of Israel. *Israel Studies, 17*(2), 120–128.

Dovidio, J. F., Gaertner, S. L., & Pearson, A. R. (2017). Aversive racism and contemporary bias. In C. G. Sibley & F. K. Barlow (Eds.), *The Cambridge handbook of the psychology of prejudice* (pp. 267–294). Cambridge University Press.

Dovidio, J. F., Love, A., Schellhaas, F., & Hewstone, M. (2017). Reducing intergroup bias through intergroup contact: Twenty years of progress and future directions. *Group Processes & Intergroup Relations, 20*(5), 606–620.

Dowd, C. (2016). The Irish-American identities of Robert E. Howard and Conan the Barbarian. *New Hibernia Review, 20*(2), 15–34.

Drew, E. M. (2011). Pretending to be "postracial": The spectacularization of race in reality TV's *Survivor. Television and New Media, 12*(4), 326–346.

Drummond, D. K., & Orbe, M. P. (2009). "Who are you trying to be?" Identity gaps within intraracial encounters. *Qualitative Research Reports in Communication, 10*(1), 81–87.

Drummond, D. K., & Orbe, M. P. (2010). Cultural contracts: Negotiating a ubiquitous U.S. dominant worldview on race and ethnicity. *Communication Studies, 61*(4), 373–390.

Du Bois, W. E. B. (2012). *The souls of Black folks.* Signet Classics. [Original work published 1903]

Dumlao, R., & Janke, E. (2012). Using relational dialectics to address differences in community-campus partnerships. *Journal of Higher Education Outreach and Engagement, 16*(2), 79–103.

Dupree, C. H. (2022, July 4/July 11). How stereotypes shape our words. *Time, 200*(1–2), 33.

Durham, A. (2021). Wounded: Diagnosis (for a) Black woman. In R. Boylorn & M. Orbe (Eds.), *Critical autoethnography: Intersecting cultural identities in everyday life* (pp. 21–31). Routledge.

Edgar, A. N., & Johnson, A. E. (2018). *The struggle over Black Lives Matter and All Lives Matter.* Lexington Books.

Edgerly, L. (2011). Difference and political legitimacy: Speakers' construction of "citizen" and "refugee" personae in talk about Hurricane Katrina. *Western Journal of Communication, 75*(3), 304–322.

Ehrenhalt, J. (2018, November 5). Mix it up at lunch: Not just for kids! *Learning for Justice Magazine.*

Ehrenreich, B. (1990). Are you middle class? In M. L. Andersen & P. H. Collins (Eds.), *Race, class, and gender: An anthology* (pp. 100–109). Wadsworth.

Eisenstat, Y. (2021, January 11). How to hold social media accountable for undermining democracy. *Harvard Business Review.*

Eleftheriadou, Z. (2010). *Psychotherapy and culture: Weaving inner and outer worlds.* Routledge.

Eligon, J. (2020, June 26). A debate over identity and race asks, are African Americans "Black" or "black"? *The New York Times.* https://www.nytimes.com/2020/06/26/us/black-african-american-style-debate.html

Ellison, S. (2020, October 13). How the 1619 Project took over 2020. *The Washington Post.* https://www.washingtonpost.com/lifestyle/style/1619-project-took-over-2020-inside-story/2020/10/13/af537092-00df-11eb-897d-3a6201d6643f_story.html

Ellithorpe, C. (2016, March 3). Are interracial daters truly undesirable or insecure, compared to same-race dates? Examining the personal attributes of interracial daters. *The Social Relations Collaborative.* http://www.socialrelationslab.com/relating-results---a-blog/are-interracial-daters-truly-undesirable-or-insecure-compared-to-same-race-daters-examining-the-personal-attributes-of-interracial-daters

El Nasser, H. (2003, February 17). Black America's new diversity. *USA Today,* p. 3A.

Endale, L. (2018). The multidimensional model of Black identity and Nigrescence theory: A philosophical comparison. *Journal of Pan African Studies, 12*(4), 509–525.

Engen, D. (2016). Invisible identities: Notes on class and race. In A. Gonzalez & Y.-W. Chen (Eds.), *Our voices: Essays in culture, ethnicity, and communication* (6th ed., pp. 253–259). Oxford University Press.

Erba, J. (2018). Media representations of Latina/os and Latino students' stereotype threat behavior. *The Howard Journal of Communications, 29*(1), 83–102.

Erikson, E. H. (1963). *Childhood and society* (2nd ed.). Norton.

Erskine, S. E., Archibold, E. E., & Bilimoria, D. (2021). Afro-Diasporic women navigating the black ceiling: Individual, relational, and organizational strategies. *Business Horizons, 64*(1), 37–50. https://doi.org/10.1016/j.bushor.2020.10.004

Eschmann, R. (2020a). Digital resistance: How online communication facilitates responses to racial microaggressions. *Sociology of Race and Ethnicity, 7*(2), 264–277. https://doi.org/10.1177/2332649220933307

Eschmann, R. (2020b). Unmasking racism: Students of color and expressions of racism in online spaces. *Social Problems, 67*(3), 418–436.

Evia, C., & Patriarca, A. (2012). Beyond compliance: Participatory translation of safety communication for Latino construction workers. *Journal of Business and Technical Communication, 26*(2), 340–367.

Ezekiel, R. S. (1997). *The racist mind: Portraits of American neo-Nazis and Klansmen.* Penguin.

Faulkner, S. L. (2006). Reconstruction: Being LGBTQ and Jewish. In M. Orbe,

B. J. Allen, & L. A. Flores (Eds.), *The same and different: Acknowledging the diversity within and between cultural groups* (pp. 95–120). National Communication Association.

Faulkner, S. L., & Hecht, M. L. (2011). The negotiation of closetable identities: A narrative analysis of lesbian, gay, bisexual, transgendered, queer Jewish identity. *Journal of Social and Personal Relationships, 28*(6), 829–847.

Feliciano, C. (2015). Shades of race: How phenotype and observer characteristics shape racial characterization. *American Behavioral Scientist, 60*(4), 390–419. https://doi.org/10.1177/0002764215613401

Fernando, C., & Nasir, N. (2021, January 14). Years of white supremacy threats culminated in Capitol riots. *Associated Press News.* https://apnews.com/article/white-supremacy-threats-capitol-riots-2d4ba4d1a3d55197489d773b3e0b0f32

Field, C., Kimuna, S., & Lang, M. (2015). The relation of interracial relationships to intimate partner violence by college students. *Journal of Black Studies, 46*(4), 384–403.

Field, D., & Travisano, R. (1984). Social history and American preoccupation with identity. *Free Inquiry in Creative Sociology, 12,* 51–56.

Fine, M. (1991). New voices in the workplace: Research directions in multicultural communication. *The Journal of Business Communication, 28,* 259–275.

Fine, M., & Johnson, F. (2016). Creating a family across race and gender borders. In A. Gonzalez & Y.-W. Chen (Eds.), *Our voices: Essays in culture, ethnicity, and communication* (6th ed., pp. 222–229). Oxford University Press.

Fitts, M. (2008). "Drop it like it's hot": Culture industry laborers and their perspectives on rap music video production. *Meridians: Feminism, Race, Transnationalism, 8*(1), 211–235.

Fitzgerald, M. R. (2014). *Native Americans on network TV.* Rowman & Littlefield.

Flores, R., & Telles, E. (2012). Social stratification in Mexico: Disentangling color, ethnicity, and class. *American Sociological Review, 77*(3), 486–494.

Floyd, N. E. (2010). Identity and achievement: A depth psychology approach to student development. *Small Group Research, 41*(1), 71–84.

Flynn, J. (2022, April 5). 31 alarming employment discrimination statistics: The state of employment discrimination in the U.S. Zippia.

Foeman, A. K. (1997, July). Managing multiracial institutions: Goals and approaches for race-relations training. *Communication Education, 40*(3), 255–265.

Foeman, A. K., & Nance, T. (1999). From miscegenation to multiculturalism: Perceptions and stages of interracial relationship development. *Journal of Black Studies, 29*(4), 540–557.

Foeman, A. K., & Nance, T. (2002). Building new cultures, reframing old images: Success strategies of interracial couples. *The Howard Journal of Communications, 13,* 237–249.

Folb, E. A. (1997). Who's got room at the top? Issues of dominance and nondominance in intracultural communication. In L. A. Samovar & R. E. Porter (Eds.), *Intercultural communication: A reader* (8th ed., pp. 138–146). Wadsworth.

Fong, M. (2000). The crossroads of language and culture. In L. A. Samovar & R. E. Porter (Eds.), *Intercultural communication: A reader* (9th ed., pp. 211–216). Wadsworth.

Fonseca, F. (2021, May 19). Navajo nation surpasses Cherokee to become largest US tribe. *U.S. News.*

Forbes, D. A. (2009). Commodification and co-modification: Explicating black female sexuality in organizations. *Management Communication Quarterly, 22*(4), 577–613.

Ford-Ahmed, T., & Orbe, M. (1992, November). *African American graduate students, their majority host institution and ethnic prejudice: A bright side?* [Paper presentation]. Speech Communication Association 77th Annual Convention, Chicago.

Foss-Snowden, M. S. (2011). The mid-education of race: Communication, coding, and the illogic of the current approach. In D. A. Brunson, L. L. Lampl, & F. F.

Jordan-Jackson (Eds.), *Interracial communication: Contexts, communities, and choices* (pp. 36–45). Kendall Hunt.

Fowler, C., & Gasiorek, J. (2020). Implications of metastereotypes for attitudes toward intergenerational contact. *Group Processes & Intergroup Relations, 23*(1), 48–70.

Fox, B. (2019). Sots, songs, and stereotypes: 1916, the Fighting Irish, and Irish-American nationalism in *Finnegans Wake. James Joyce Quarterly, 56*(1), 45–61.

Foy, S. L., & Ray, R. (2019). Skin in the game: Colorism and the subtle operation of stereotypes in men's college basketball. *American Journal of Sociology, 125*(3), 730–785. https://doi.org/10.1086/707243

Fram, A. (2021, July 20). Marjorie Taylor Greene apologizes for comparing Covid face masks, Holocaust. *USA Today.* https://www.usatoday.com/story/news/politics/2021/06/15/marjorie-taylor-greene-apologizes-equating-face-masks-holocaust/7697785002/

Frankenberg, R. (1993). *White women, race matters: The social construction of whiteness.* University of Minnesota Press.

Fraser, N. (1992). Rethinking the public sphere: A contribution to the critique of actually existing democracy. In C. Calhoun (Ed.), *Habermas and the public sphere* (pp. 109–142). MIT Press.

Fredericks, B., & Bargallie, D. (2020). Situating race in cultural competency training: A site of self-revelation. *M/C Journal, 23*(4), 295–308.

Freeman, K. (2016, September 16). First home game for Brunswick High School since player said he received racial threats. FOX. https://fox8.com/news/first-home-game-for-brunswick-high-school-since-player-said-he-received-racial-threats/

Freire, P. (2000). *Pedagogy of the oppressed* (30th anniversary ed.). Continuum. [Original work published 1970]

Frey, W. H. (2021, June 23). All recent US population growth comes from people of color, new census estimates show. Brookings. https://www.brookings.edu/research/all-recent-us-population-growth-comes-from-people-of-color-new-census-estimates-show/

Frisby, C. (2018). "Oh, see what we say": A content analysis of partisan media's framing of the "take a knee" silent protest by the NFL. *American International Journal of Humanities and Social Science, 4*(3), 6–18.

Fry, R. (2020, April 28). Millennials overtake Baby Boomers as America's largest generation. Pew Research Center.

Fry, R., Kennedy, B., & Funk, C. (2021, April 1). STEM jobs see uneven progress in increasing gender, racial and ethnic diversity. Pew Research Center.

Fujioka, Y., Ryan, E., Agle, M., Legaspi, M., & Toohey, R. (2009). The role of racial identity in responses to thin media ideals: Differences between white and black college women. *Communication Research, 36*(4), 251–274.

Funderburg, L. (1993). *Black, White, other: Biracial Americans talk about race and identity.* Morrow.

Gaither, S. E., & Sommers, S. R. (2013). Living with another-race roommate shapes Whites' behavior in subsequent diverse settings. *Journal of Experimental Social Psychology, 49,* 272–276.

Gajanan, M. (2020, June 26). Unilever will drop the word "fair" from its skin-lightening creams. *Time.* Time.com/5860313/unilever-fair-and-lovely-name-change-colorism/

Gallacher, J. D. (2021). *Online intergroup conflict: How the dynamics of online communication drive extremism and violence between groups* [Doctoral dissertation, University of Oxford]. file:///C:/Users/csr/Downloads/Gallacher_Thesis_ORA_Online_Intergroup_Conflict.pdf

Gallegos, P. V., Wasserman, I. C., & Ferdman, B. M. (2020). The dance of inclusion: New ways of moving with resistance. In K. Thomas (Ed.), *Diversity resistance in organizations* (2nd, pp. 165–177). Routledge.

Gallois, C., Ogay, T., & Giles, H. (2005). Communication accommodation theory. In W. B. Gudykunst (Ed.), *Theorizing about intercultural communication* (pp. 121–148). Sage.

Galupo, M. P. (2007). Friendship patterns of sexual minority individuals in adulthood. *Journal of Social and Personal Relationships, 24*(1), 139–151.

Gangotena, M. (2016). The rhetoric of la familia among Mexican Americans. In A. Gonzalez & Y.-W. Chen (Eds.), *Our voices: Essays in culture, ethnicity, and communication* (6th ed., pp. 65–76). Oxford University Press.

Garcia, W. R. (1996). Respeto: A Mexican base for interpersonal relationships. In W. Gudykunst, S. Ting-Toomey, & T. Nishida (Eds.), *Communication in personal relationships across cultures* (pp. 55–76). Sage.

Gardner, S. (2021, July 12). ESPN's Stephen A. Smith apologizes for comments about Shohei Ohtani. *USA Today.* https://www.usatoday.com/story/sports/media/2021/07/12/espn-stephen-a-smith-apologizes-comments-shohei-ohtani/7945619002/

Garner, T. (1983). Playing the dozens: Folklore as strategies for living. *Quarterly Journal of Speech, 69*(1), 47–57. https://doi.org/10.1080/00335638309383634

Gaunt, R. (2011). Effects of intergroup conflict and social contact on prejudice: The mediating role of stereotypes and evaluations. *Journal of Applied Social Psychology, 41*(6), 1340–1355.

Geena Davis Institute. (2021, Summer). I am not a fetish or model minority: Redefining what it means to be API in the entertainment industry. seejane.org/wp-content/uploads/api-study-2021-8.pdf.

Geertz, C. (1976). From the native's point of view: On the nature of anthropological understanding. In P. Rabinow & W. M. Sullivan (Eds.), *Interpretive social science* (pp. 225–241). University of California Press.

Genç, E., & Su, Y. (2021). Black and White couples: Exploring the role of religiosity on perceived racial discrimination and relationship satisfaction. *American Journal of Family Therapy*, 1–21.

Gerbner, G. (1969). Toward "cultural indicators": The analysis of mass mediated public message systems. *AV Communication Review, 17*, 137–148. https://doi.org/10.1007/BF02769102

Gerbner, G., & Gross, L. (1976). Living with television: The violence profile. *Journal of Communication, 26*(2), 173–199.

Giannino, S. (2013). Guidos and guidettes: Exploring editorial news media frames of Italian Americans on *Jersey Shore*. *Review of Journalism and Mass Communication, 1*(1), 1–13.

Gibson, B., Hawkins, I., Redker, C., & Bushman, B. J. (2018). Narcissism on the *Jersey Shore*: Exposure to narcissistic reality TV characters can increase narcissism levels in viewers. *Psychology of Popular Media Culture, 7*(4), 399–412.

Giles, H. (1973). Accent mobility: A model and some data. *Anthropological Linguistics, 15*, 87–109.

Giles, H., Linz, D., Bonilla, D., & Gomez, M. L. (2012). Police stops of and interactions with Latino and white (non-Latino) drivers: Extensive policing and communication accommodation. *Communication Monographs, 79*(4), 407–427.

Giles, H., Taylor, D. M., & Bourhis, R. Y. (1973). Towards a theory of interpersonal accommodation through language: Some Canadian data. *Language in Society, 2*, 177–192.

GilkesBorr, T. (2019). The strategic pursuit of black homophily on a predominantly white campus. *Journal of Higher Education, 90*(2), 322–346.

Gittens, R. A. (2021). Atlanta's pink trap house: Reimagining the Black public sphere as an aesthetic community. *Theory & Event, 24*(2), 434–455. https://doi.org/10.1353/tae.2021.0021

Gladwell, M. (1996, April/May). Black like them. *The New Yorker*, 74–80.

Glenn, C. L., & Cunningham, L. J. (2009). The power of black magic: The magical negro and white salvation in film. *Journal of Black Studies, 40*(2),135–152.

Glenn, P. (2019). Core intercultural conflict communication practices: Insights from diverse fields. *Journal of Promotional Communications, 7*(1), 53–62.

Godin, M. (2020, January 14). Athletes will be banned from protesting at the 2020 Tokyo Olympics. But the games have a long history of political demonstrations. *Time.*

Goffman, E. (1959). *The presentation of self in everyday life*. Anchor/Doubleday.

Goh, L. S. (2018, September 26). Imperial fantasies: On the costs of misrepresentation. *Bitch Media*. https://www.bitchmedia.org/article/crazy-rich-asians-representation

Gong, G. (2016). When Mississippi Chinese talk. In A. Gonzalez & Y.-W. Chen (Eds.), *Our voices: Essays in culture, ethnicity, and communication* (6th ed., pp. 77–84). Oxford University Press.

Gonzalez, M. C. (2002). Painting the white face red: Intercultural contact presented through poetic ethnography. In J. N. Martin, T. K. Nakayama, & L. A. Flores (Eds.), *Readings in intercultural communication: Experiences and contexts* (pp. 386–397). McGraw-Hill.

Good, B. (2021, December 1). American Library Association documents 155 attempts at banning books about POC or LGBTQ issues in the last 6 months. *Diversity Inc*. https://www.diversityinc.com/american-library-association-documents-155-attempts-at-banning-books-about-poc-or-lgbtq-issues-in-the-last-6-months/

Goodnight, G. T. (1997). Opening up "the spaces of public dissension." *Communication Monographs, 64*, 270–275.

Gordils, J., Elliot, A., & Jamieson, J. (2021). The effect of perceived interracial competition on psychological outcomes. *PLoS ONE, 16*(1), e0245671.

Gordon, M. M. (1964). *Assimilation in American life*, Oxford University Press.

Gosset, T. F. (1963). *Race: The history of an idea in America*. Schocke.

Gould, S. J. (1994, November). The geometer of race. *Discover*, 65–69.

Graves, J. L. (2004). *The race myth: Why we pretend race exists in America*. Dutton.

Gravois, J. (2005, April 8). Teach impediment: When the student can't understand the instructor, who is to blame? *The Chronicle of Higher Education*, pp. A10–A12.

Griffin, E., Ledbetter, A., & Sparks, G. (2019). *A first look at communication theory*. McGraw-Hill.

Griffin, R. A. (2010). Critical race theory as a means to deconstruct, recover and

evolve in communication studies. *Communication Law Review, 10*(1), 1–9.

Groscurth, C. R. (2003). Dialectically speaking: A critique of intergroup differences in African American language research. *Journal of Intergroup Relations, 30*(2), 47–64.

Gudykunst, W. B. (1988). Uncertainty and anxiety. In Y. Y. Kim & W. B. Gudykunst (Eds.), *Theories in intercultural communication* (pp. 125–128). Sage.

Gudykunst, W. B. (1993). Toward a theory of effective interpersonal and intergroup communication: An anxiety/uncertainty management (AUM) perspective. In R. L. Wiseman & J. Koester (Eds.), *Intercultural communication competence* (pp. 33–71). Sage.

Gudykunst, W. B. (1995). Anxiety/uncertainty management (AUM) theory: Current status. In R. L. Wiseman (Ed.), *Intercultural communication theory* (pp. 8–58). Sage.

Gudykunst, W. B. (2005). An anxiety/uncertainty management (AUM) theory of effective communication: Making the mesh of the net finer. In W. B. Gudykunst (Ed.), *Theorizing about intercultural communication* (pp. 281–322). Sage.

Gudykunst, W. B., & Hammer, M. (1988). The influence of social identity and intimacy of interethnic relationships on uncertainty reduction processes. *Human Communication Research, 14*, 569–601.

Guo, L., & Harlow, S. (2014). User-generated racism: An analysis of stereotypes of African Americans, Latinos, and Asians in YouTube videos. *The Howard Journal of Communications, 25*(3), 281–302.

Gupta, J. (2020). About Jyoti. Jyotigupta.squarespace.com/about; video channel youtube.com/user/colorsofbrown/videos

Gurung, R. A. R., & Duong, T. (1999). Mixing and matching: Assessing the concomitants of mixed-ethnic relationships. *Journal of Social and Personal Relationships, 16*(5), 639–657.

Guskin, E., Khan, M. S., & Mitchell, A. (2010, July 26). The arrest of Henry Louis

Gates, Jr. Pew Research Center. https://www.pewresearch.org/journalism/2010/07/26/arrest-henry-louis-gates-jr/

Habermas, J. (1989). *The structural transformation of the public sphere: An inquiry into a category of bourgeois society* (T. Burger, Trans.). MIT Press.

Haggins, B. L. (2001). Why "Beulah" and "Andy" still play today: Minstrelsy in the new millennium. *Emergences: Journal for the Study of Media and Composite Cultures, 11*(2), 249–267.

Hajek, C., & Giles, H. (2002). The old man out: An intergroup analysis of international communication among gay men. *Journal of Communication, 52*(4), 698–714.

Hajek, D., Martinez, A., & Dickens, K. (2021, October 10). A Black family got their beach back—And inspired others to fight against land theft. National Public Radio.

Halevy, N., & Cohen, T. (2019). Intergroup conflict 2020. *Negotiation and Conflict Management Research, 12*(2), 161–173.

Hall, A. R. (2021). "Check yo' stuff" allies: A forum on the personal/political challenges of coalition-building in precarious times, *Women's Studies in Communication, 44*(2), 131–137. https://doi.org/10.1080/07491409.2021.1923328

Hall, E. T. (1959). *The silent language*. Doubleday.

Hall, E. T. (1983). *The dance of life: The other dimension of time*. Doubleday.

Hall, J. N. (2020). The other side of inequality: Using standpoint theories to examine the privilege of the evaluation profession and individual evaluators. *American Journal of Evaluation, 41*(1), 20–33. https://doi.org/10.1177/1098214019828485

Hall, M. L. (2012). (Re)thinking conceptualizations of Caribbean immigrant identity performances: Implications for intercultural communication research. In N. Bardhan & M. Orbe (Eds.), *Identity research and communication: Intercultural reflections and future directions* (pp. 191–204). Lexington Books.

Hall, R. E. (Ed.). (2013). *The melanin millennium: Skin color as 21st century international discourse*. Springer Netherlands.

Halualani, R. T. (1998). Seeing through the screen: "A struggle of culture." In J. N.

Martin, T. K. Nakayama, & L. A. Flores (Eds.), *Readings in cultural contexts* (pp. 264–274). Mayfield.

Hamlet, J. D. (2016). The reason why we sing: Understanding traditional African American worship. In A. Gonzalez & Y.-W. Chen (Eds.), *Our voices: Essays in culture, ethnicity, and communication* (6th ed., pp. 85–89). Oxford University Press.

Hamri, S. (Director), & Turner, K. (Writer). (2006). *Something new* [Film]. Gramercy Pictures & Homegrown Pictures.

Hao, R. N. (2011). "America has a dominant language—Learn it!": An analysis of whiteness in the construction of international teaching assistant identity in the *Daily Egyptian*. In D. A. Brunson, L. L. Lampl, & F. F. Jordan-Jackson (Eds.), *Interracial communication: Contexts, communities, and choices* (pp. 286–306). Kendall Hunt

Hao, R. N. (2021). Performing fortune cookie: An autoethnographic performance on diasporic hybridity. In R. Boylorn & M. Orbe (Eds.), *Critical autoethnography: Intersecting cultural identities in everyday life* (pp. 45–56). Routledge.

Harber, K. D., Stafford, R., & Kennedy, A. A. (2010). The positive feedback bias as a response to self-image threat. *British Journal of Social Psychology, 49*, 207–218.

Hardiman, R. (1994). White racial identity development in the United States. In E. P. Salett & D. R. Koslow (Eds.), *Race, ethnicity, and self: Identity in multicultural perspective* (pp. 117–142). National Multicultural Institute.

Harding, S. (Ed.). (2004). *The feminist standpoint theory reader: Intellectual and political controversies*. Routledge.

Harlow, S., & Benbrook, A. (2019). How #Blacklivesmatter: Exploring the role of hip hop celebrities in constructing racial identity on Black Twitter. *Information, Communication & Society, 22*(3), 352–368.

Harris, A. P. (2008). From color line to color chart? Racism and colorism in the new century. *Berkeley Journal of African-American Law & Policy, 10*, 52–69.

Harris, D. R., & Sim, J. J. (2001). *An empirical look at the social construction of* race: *The case of multiracial adolescents* (Research Report No. 00–452). University of Michigan, Population Studies Center.

Harris, R. (2021, July 21). Soccer players kneel to start new era of Olympic activism. *Associated Press News.* https://apnews.com/article/2020-tokyo-olympics-sports-race-and-ethnicity-racial-injustice-soccer-18c738309b73ef7c2237e948f1870ca7

Harris, T. M. (2016). "I know it was the blood": Defining the biracial self in a Euro-American society. In A. Gonzalez & Y.-W. Chen (Eds.), *Our voices: Essays in culture, ethnicity, and communication* (6th ed., article 31). Oxford University Press.

Harris, T. M. (2017). Performing otherness as an instructor in an interracial communication classroom: An autoethnographic approach. In A. Atay & S. T. Toyosaki (Eds.), *Critical intercultural communication pedagogy* (pp. 131–152). Routledge.

Harris, T. M., & Abbott, B. (2011). Reframing the rhetoric of race through classroom discourse. In D. A. Brunson, L. L. Lampl, & F. F. Jordan-Jackson (Eds.), *Interracial communication: Contexts, communities, and choices* (pp. 286–306). Kendall Hunt.

Harris, T. M., & DeTurk, S. (2012). Promoting interracial communication within religious organizations. In S. M. Croucher & T. M. Harris (Eds.), *Religion & communication: An anthology of extensions in theory, research, & method* (pp. 81–102). Peter Lang.

Harris, T. M., & Hill, P. S. (1998). "Waiting to exhale" or "breath(ing) again": A search for identity, empowerment, and love in the 1990s. *Women & Language, 11*(2), 9–20.

Harris, T. M., Janovec, A., Murray, S., Gubbala, S., & Robinson, A. (2018). Communicating racism: A study of racial microaggressions in a southern university and the local community. *Southern Communication Journal, 84*(2), 72–84.

Harris, T. M., & Lee, C. (2019). Advocate-mentoring: A communicative response

to diversity in higher education. *Communication Education, 68*(1), 103–113. https://doi.org/10.1080/03634523.2018.1536272

Harris, T. M., & Sanders, M. (in press). *Bridgerton*: A case study in critical cultural approaches to racial representations in popular culture. In T. Nakayama & R. Halualani (Eds.), *Handbook of critical intercultural communication* (2nd ed.). Wiley-Blackwell.

Harris, T. M., & Scott, K. (2019). Girlfriends—There, through thick and thin! African American female sisterhood and the quest for happiness. In S. B. White & K Harris (Eds.), *Representations of Black womanhood on television: Being Mara Brock Akil* (pp. 13–32). Lexington Books.

Harris, T. M., & Trego, A. (2008). Something old, something new: A cinematic representation of interracial romance in the 21st century. *International & Intercultural Communication Annual, 31*, 227–253.

Harter, L. M., Scott, J. A., Novak, D. R., Leeman, M., & Morris, J. F. (2006). Freedom through flight: Performing a counter-narrative of disability. *Journal of Applied Communication, 34*(1), 3–29.

Harwood, J., Soliz, J., & Lin, M.-C. (2006). Communication accommodation theory: An intergroup approach to family relationships. In D. O. Braithwaite & L. A. Baxter (Eds.), *Engaging theories in family communication: Multiple perspectives* (pp. 19–34). Sage.

Haslam-Ormerod, S. (2019, January 11). "Snowflake millennial" label is inaccurate and reverses progress to destigmatize mental health. *The Conversation.* https://theconversation.com/snowflake-millennial-label-is-inaccurate-and-reverses-progress-to-destigmatise-mental-health-109667

Hassan, A., & Carlsen, A. (2018, August 17). How "crazy rich" Asians have led to the largest income gap in the U.S. *The New York Times.*

Hatch, J. B. (2003). Reconciliation: Building a bridge from complicity to coherence in the rhetoric of race relations. *Rhetoric & Public Affairs, 6*(4), 737–764.

Haughton, P. (2019, March 3). Fourth-wave feminism and how social media shapes our protests. Activism Has blog. https://wpmu.mah.se/nmict191group4/2019/03/03/fourth-wave-feminism-and-how-social-media-shapes-our-protests/

Heath, R. G., & Borda, J. L. (2021). Reclaiming civility: Towards discursive opening in dialogue and deliberation. *Journal of Deliberative Democracy, 17*(1), 9–18.

Heath, R. G., & Isbell, M. G. (2017). *Interorganizational collaboration: Complexity, ethics, and communication.* Waveland Press.

Hecht, M. L., Faulkner, S. L., Meyer, C. R., Niles, T. A., Golden, D., & Cutler, M. (2002). Looking through *Northern Exposure* at Jewish American identity and the communication theory of identity. *Journal of Communication, 52,* 852–870.

Hecht, M. L., Jackson, R. L., II, & Ribeau, S. (2003). *African American communication: Exploring identity and culture* (2nd ed.). Lawrence Erlbaum.

Hecht, M. L., & Ribeau, S. A. (1984). Ethnic communication: A comparative analysis of satisfying communication. *International Journal of Intercultural Relations, 8,* 135–151.

Hecht, M. L., Ribeau, S. A., & Alberts, J. K. (1989). An Afro-American perspective on interethnic communication. *Communication Monographs, 56,* 385–410.

Hecht, M. L., Ribeau, S. A., & Sedano, M. V. (1990). A Mexican American perspective on interethnic communication. *International Journal of Intercultural Relations, 14,* 31–55.

Hecht, M. L., Warren, J. R., Jung, E., & Krieger, J. L. (2005). The communication theory of identity: Development, theoretical perspective, and future directions. In W. B. Gudykunst (Ed.), *Theorizing about intercultural communication* (pp. 257–278). Sage.

Hegde, R. S. (1998). Swinging the trapeze: The negotiation of identity among Asian Indian immigrant women in the United States. In D. V. Tanno & A. Gonzalez (Eds.), *Communication and identity across cultures* (pp. 34–55). Sage.

Hellman, R. (2020, July 13). Expert prescribes identification, empathy for better interracial communication. KU News Service. https://today.ku.edu/2020/07/09/expert-prescribes-identification-empathy-better-interracial-communication

Helms, J. E. (1990). *Black and White racial identity: Theory, research, and practice.* Greenwood Press.

Helms, J. E. (1994). *A race is a nice thing to have: A guide to being a White person or understanding the White persons in your life.* Content Communications.

Hendrix, K. G. (2016). Home as respite for the working-class academic. In A. Gonzalez & Y.-W. Chen (Eds.), *Our voices: Essays in culture, ethnicity, and communication* (6th ed., pp. 260–266). Oxford University Press.

Herek, G. M. (2000). Sexual prejudice and gender: Do heterosexuals' attitudes toward lesbians and gay men differ? *Journal of Social Issues, 56,* 251–266.

Hernandez, J. (2021, October 5). Tesla must pay $137 million to a Black employee who sued for racial discrimination. National Public Radio. https://www.npr.org/2021/10/05/1043336212/tesla-racial-discrimination-lawsuit

Herring, R. D. (1994). Native American Indian identity: A people of many peoples. In E. P. Salett & D. R. Koslow (Eds.), *Race, ethnicity, and self: Identity in multicultural perspective* (pp. 170–197). MultiCultural Institute.

Hewlett, S. A., Allwood, N., & Sherbin, L. (2016, October 11). U.S. Latinos feel they can't be themselves at work. *Harvard Business Review.*

Heyward, G. (2021, September 25). Reparations for Black residents are becoming a local issue as well as a national one. *The New York Times.* https://www.nytimes.com/2021/09/25/us/reparations-legislation.html

Hirschfelder, A., & Molin, P. F. (2018, February 22). I is for ignoble: Stereotyping Native Americans. Jim Crow Museum, Ferris State University. https://www.ferris.edu/HTMLS/news/jimcrow/native/homepage.htm

Hocker, J., Berry, K., & Wilmot, W. (2022). *Interpersonal conflict* (11th ed.). McGraw-Hill.

Hodge, J. L. (1989). Domination and the will in Western thought and culture. In C. E. Jackson & E. J. Tolbert (Eds.), *Race and culture in America: Readings in racial and ethnic relations* (pp. 27–48). Burgess.

Hohmann-Marriott, B. E., & Amato, P. (2008). Relationship quality in interethnic marriages and cohabitations. *Social Forces* 87(2), 825–855.

Hoijer, H. (1994). The Sapir-Whorf hypothesis. In L. A. Samovar & R. E. Porter (Eds.), *Intercultural communication: A reader* (7th ed., pp. 194–200). Wadsworth.

Holder, A. (2012, April 24). The issue of colorism: Dark-skinned girls, light-skinned girls. *Trinidad Express* Newspapers. https://trinidadexpress.com/news/local/the-issue-of-colorism/article_da5e1b4e-d84e-565e-81ab-8298dfe24a70.html

Holloway, J. E. (Ed.). (1990). *Africanisms in American culture.* Indiana University Press.

Holt, B. (2021, February 8). Racism thrives in the online dating world. Mashable. https://mashable.com/article/racism-online-dating

Homsey, D. M., & Sandel, T. (2012). The code of food and tradition: Exploring a Lebanese (American) speech code in practice in Flatland. *Journal of Intercultural Communication Research, 41*(1), 59–80.

hooks, b. (1992). *Black looks: Race and representation.* South End Press.

Hopkins, P., Botterill, K., Sanghera, G., & Arshad, R. (2017). Encountering misrecognition: Being mistaken for being Muslim. *Annals of the American Association of Geographers, 107*(4), 934–948. https://doi.org/10.1080/24694452.2016.1270192

House, C. A. (2018). Crying for justice: The #BLACKLIVESMATTER religious rhetoric of Bishop T. D. Jakes. *Southern Communication Journal, 83*(1), 13–27. https://doi.org/10.1080/1041794X.2017.1387600

Houston, L., Grandey, A. A., & Sawyer, K. (2018). Who cares if "service with a smile" is authentic? An expectancy-based model of customer race and differential service reactions. *Organizational Behavior and Human Decision Processes, 144,* 85–96. https://doi.org/10.1016/j.obhdp.2017.10.001

Houston, M. (1997). When Black women talk with White women: Why dialogues are difficult. In A. Gonzalez, M. Houston, & V. Chen (Eds.), *Our voices: Essays in culture, ethnicity, and communication* (2nd ed., pp. 187–194). Roxbury.

Houston, M. (2002). Seeking difference: African Americans in interpersonal communication research, 1975–2000. *Howard Journal of Communications, 13,* 25–41.

Houston, M., & Wood, J. T. (1996). Difficult dialogues, expanded horizons: Communicating across race and class. In J. T. Wood (Ed.), *Gendered relationships* (pp. 39–56). Mayfield.

Howard, A. (1980). Hawaiians. In S. Thernstorm (Ed.), *Harvard encyclopedia of American ethnic groups* (pp. 449–452). Harvard University Press.

Howell, W. S. (1982). *The empathic communicator.* Wadsworth.

Hu, J., Leonardelli, G. J., & Toh, S. M. (2016). The White leader prototype in China? A test of cultural exposure and White dominance. *Academy of Management Annual Meeting Proceedings, 2016*(1), 1.

Huang, H.-Y., & Chen, H.-L. (2019). Constructing collective memory for (de)colonisation: Taiwanese images in history textbooks, 1950–1987. *Paedagogica Historica, 55*(1), 101–120.

Huang, T. J. (2021). Perceived discrimination and intergroup commonality among Asian Americans. *The Russell Sage Foundation Journal of the Social Sciences* 7(2), 180–200.

Hudson, N. J. (2020). An in-depth look at a comprehensive diversity training program for faculty. *International Journal for the Scholarship of Teaching and Learning, 14*(1). https://doi.org/10.20429/ijsotl.2020.140103

Hudson, T. D. (2022). Interpersonalizing cultural difference: A grounded theory of the process of interracial friendship development and sustainment among college students. *Journal of Diversity in Higher Education, 15*(3), 267–287.

Hughes, D., Rodriguez, J., Smith, E. P., Johnson, D. J., Stevenson, H. C., & Spicer, P. (2006). Parents' ethnic-racial socialization practices: A review of research and directions for future study. *Developmental Psychology, 42*(5), 747–770. https://doi.org/10.1037/0012-1649.42.5.747

Hughey, M., & González-Lesser, E. (2020). Introduction. In M. Hughey & E. González-Lesser (Eds.), *Racialized media: The design, delivery, and decoding of race and ethnicity* (pp. 1–18). New York University Press.

Huling, N., Murray, C., & Houston, M. (2016). Sister-friends: Reflections on Black women's communication in intra- and intercultural friendships. In A. Gonzalez & Y.-W. Chen (Eds.), *Our voices: Essays in culture, ethnicity, and communication* (6th ed., pp. 57–64). Oxford University Press.

Hunt, D., & Ramón, A. (2022). Hollywood diversity report 2022. The Division of Social Sciences at UCLA.

Hunter, M. (2002). "If you're light you're alright": Light skin color as social capital for women of color. *Gender and Society, 16*(2), 1751–1793.

Hunter, M. (2007). The persistent problem of colorism: Skin tone, status, and inequality. *Sociology Compass, 1*(1), 237–254.

Huntington, S. P. (2005). Hispanic immigration threatens to divide America. In J. D. Toor (Ed.), *Race relations: Opposing viewpoints* (pp. 62–79). Greenhaven Press.

Hymes, D. (1974). *Foundations in sociolinguistics: An ethnographic approach.* University of Pennsylvania Press.

Imperato, C., Keum, B. T., & Mancini, T. (2021). Does intercultural contact increase anti-racist behavior on social network sites? *Social Sciences, 10,* 207.

Indian Country Today. (2021, August 13). 2020 census: Native population increased by 86.5 percent. https://indiancountrytoday.com/news/2020-census-native-population-increased-by-86-5-percent

Isaksen, J. (2011). Obama's rhetorical shift: Insight for communication studies. *Communication Studies, 52*(4), 456–471.

Itam, U., & Bagali, M. (2018). Diversity and inclusion management: A focus on employee engagement. In N. Sharma, V. Singh, & S. Pathak (Eds.), *Management techniques for a diverse and cross-cultural workforce* (pp.149–171). IGI Global.

Jackson, B. W., & Hardiman, R. (1983). Racial identity development. *The NTL Managers' Handbook, 13*(2), 107–119.

Jackson, C. E., & Tolbert, E. J. (Eds.). (1989). *Race and culture in America: Readings in racial and ethnic relations.* Burgess.

Jackson, M., & Rajai, P. (2021, January 20). Does your definition of leadership exclude women of color? *Harvard Business Review.*

Jackson, R. L. (1999). *The negotiation of cultural identity.* Praeger.

Jackson, R. L. (2000). So real illusions of black intellectualism: Exploring race, roles, and gender in the academy. *Communication Theory, 10,* 48–63.

Jackson, R. L. (2002a). Cultural contracts theory: Toward an understanding of identity negotiation. *Communication Quarterly, 50,* 359–367.

Jackson, R. L. (2002b). Exploring African American negotiation in the academy: Toward a transformative vision of African American communication scholarship. *Howard Journal of Communications, 13,* 43–57.

Jackson, R. L. (2006). *Scripting the black masculine body: Identity, discourse, and racial politics in popular media.* State University of New York Press.

Jackson, R. L., & Castle Bell, G. (2023). Cultural contracts theory. In J. Austin, M. Orbe, & J. Sims (Eds.), *Communication theory: Racially and inclusive perspectives* (pp. 37–46). Cognella.

Jackson, R. L., & Crawley, R. L. (2003). White student confessions about a black male professor: A cultural contracts theory approach to intimate conversations about race and worldview. *Journal of Men's Studies, 12*(1), 25–41.

Jackson, R. L., & Hopson, M. C. (Eds.). (2011). *Masculinity in the black imagination: Politics of communicating race and manhood.* Peter Lang.

Jackson, R. L., Johnson, A. L., Hecht, M. L., & Ribeau, S. A. (2020). *African Ameri-*

can communication: *Examining the complexities of lived experience* (3rd ed.). Routledge. https://doi.org/10.4324/9781351103244

Jackson, S. J., & Welles, B. F. (2015). Hijacking #myNYPD: Social media dissent and networked counterpublics. *Journal of Communication, 65*, 932–952. https://doi.org/10.1111/jcom.12185

Jacobs, J. H. (1992). Identity development in biracial children. In M. P. P. Root (Ed.), *Racially mixed people in America* (pp. 190–206). Sage.

James, A. D., & Tucker, M. B. (2003). Racial ambiguity and relationship formation in the United States: Theoretical and practical considerations. *Journal of Social and Personal Relationships, 20*(2), 153–169.

James, N. C. (2016). When Miss America was always white. In A. Gonzalez & Y.-W. Chen (Eds.), *Our voices: Essays in culture, ethnicity, and communication* (6th ed., pp. 137–141). Oxford University Press.

Jayson, S. (2010, November 18). Tired of the baby boomers. *USA Today*, pp. 1D, 2D.

Jerald, M. C., Ward, L. M., Moss, L., Thomas, K., & Fletcher, K. D. (2017). Subordinates, sex objects, or sapphires? Investigating contributions of media use to Black students' femininity ideologies and stereotypes about Black women. *Journal of Black Psychology, 43*(6), 608–635.

Jha, M. (2016). *The global beauty industry: Colorism, racism, and the national body*. Routledge.

Jha, S., & Adelman, M. (May 01, 2009). Looking for love in all the white places: A study of skin color preferences on Indian matrimonial and mate-seeking websites. *Studies in South Asian Film & Media, 1*(1), 65–83

Jhally, S., & Lewis, J. (2003). Enlightened racism: *The Cosby Show*, audiences and the myth of the American dream. In W. Brooker & D. Jermyn (Eds.), *The audience studies reader* (pp. 279–286). Routledge.

Jimenez, N. (2017, August 19). Charlottesville violence shows we haven't come that far on racism. *USA Today*. https://www.usatoday.com/story/news/columnists/nick-jimenez/2017/08/19/jimenez-charlottesville-violence-shows-we-havent-come-far-racism/578030001/

Johannesen, R. L. (1971). The emerging concept of communication as dialogue. *Quarterly Journal of Speech, 57*, 373–382.

Johnson, A. (2017). From academe, to the theatre, to the streets: My autocritography of canonical exception and aesthetic cleansing in the wake of Ferguson. *Qualitative Inquiry, 1*–13. https://doi.org/10.1177/1077800416684869

Johnson, A. (2018). Straight outta erasure: Black girl magic claps back to the hyper(in)visibility of Black women in *Straight outta Compton. National Political Science Review, 19*(2), 34–49.

Johnson, A. (2021). Negotiating more, (mis)labelling the body: A tale of intersectionality. In R. Boylorn & M. Orbe (Eds.), *Critical autoethnography: Intersecting cultural identities in everyday life* (pp. 57–70). Routledge.

Johnson, A., & Petermon, J. (2023). Theory of hyper(in)visibility. In J. Austin, M. Orbe, & J. Sims (Eds.), *Communication theory: Racially and inclusive perspectives* (pp. 261–270). Cognella.

Johnson, G. T. (2013). *Spaces of conflict, sounds of solidarity: Music, race, and spatial entitlement in Los Angeles*. University of California Press.

Johnson, I. R., & Pietri, E. S. (2020). An ally you say? Endorsing White women as allies to encourage perceptions of allyship and organizational identity-safety among Black women. *Group Processes & Intergroup Relations, 1*–21.

Jones, N., Marks, R., Ramirez, R., & Rios-Vargas, M. (2021). 2020 census illuminates racial and ethnic composition of the country. United States Census Bureau. https://www.census.gov/library/stories/2021/08/improved-race-ethnicity-measures-reveal-united-states-population-much-more-multiracial.html#:~:text=The%20White%20and%20Black%20or,people%2C%20a%20230%25%20change

Jones, P., & Sahouri, A. M. (2021, August 20). Woman who intentionally drove SUV into Black, Latina children sentenced on federal hate crime charges. *USA Today*. https://www.usatoday.com/story/news/nation/2021/08/20/des-moines-woman-intentionally-hit-children-sentenced-federal-hate-crime/8217297002/?utm_source=feedblitz&utm_medium=FeedBlitzRss&utm_campaign=usatodaycomnation-topstories

Joseph, R. L. (2011). Imagining Obama: Reading overtly and inferentially racist images of our 44th president, 2007–2008. *Communication Studies, 62*(4), 389–405.

Juang, L. P., Yoo, H. C., & Atkin, A. (2017). A critical race perspective on an empirical review of Asian American parental racial-ethnic socialization. In Y. Choi & H. Hahm (Eds.), *Asian American parenting: Family process and intervention* (pp. 11–36). Springer. https://doi.org/10.1007/978-3-319-63136-3_2

Jun, J. (2012). Why are Asian Americans silent? Asian Americans' negotiation strategies for communicative discriminations. *Journal of International and Intercultural Communication, 5*(4), 329–348.

Jun, J., Woo, B., Kim, J. K., Kim, P. D., & Zhang, N. (2021). Asian Americans' communicative responses to COVID-19 discrimination in application of co-cultural theory. *Howard Journal of Communications, 32*(3), 209–327. https://doi.org/10.1080/10646175.2021.1922103

Jung, E., & Hecht, M. L. (2004). Elaborating the communication theory of identity: Identity gaps and communication outcomes. *Communication Quarterly, 52*, 265–283.

Jung, E., & Hecht, M. L. (2008). Identity gaps and level of depression among Korean immigrants. *Health Communication, 23*(4), 313–325.

Kalmijn, M. (1998). Intermarriage and homogamy: Causes, patterns, trends. *Annual Review of Sociology, 24*, 395–421.

Kantawala, A. (2021). Bending the arc of justice: Communities of practice. *Journal of the National Art Education Foundation*. https://doi.org/10.1080/00043125.2021.1919483

Kao, G., Joyner, K., & Balistreri, K. S. (2019). *The company we keep: Interracial friendships and romantic relationships from adolescence to adulthood*. Russell Sage Foundation.

Kao, G., & Shinkoda, P. (2021, April 12). Media bears responsibility for reinforcing Asian American stereotypes. *Variety*.

Karanja, T. N. (2019). The tales of interracial relationships—How interracial couples in Sweden experience being treated in everyday life. (Dissertation, Malmö universitet/Hälsaochsamhälle). http://urn.kb.se/resolve?urn=urn:nbn:se:mau:diva-25302

Karimi, F. (2021, July 8). What's blackfishing? CNN. https://www.cnn.com/2021/07/08/entertainment/blackfishing-explainer-trnd/index.html

Kay, P., & Kempton, W. (1984). What is the Sapir-Whorf hypothesis? *American Anthropologist, 86*, 65–73.

Kellner, D. (2020). *Media culture: Cultural studies, identity, and politics in the contemporary moment* (2nd ed., 25th anniversary ed.). Routledge.

Kellner, G. (1994). *Hispanics and United States film: An overview and handbook*. Bilingual Review/Press.

Kellogg, A. H., & Liddell, D. L. (2012). "Not half but double": Exploring critical incidents in the racial identity of multiracial college students. *Journal of College Student Development, 53*(4), 524–541.

Kendi, I. X. (2019). *How to be an antiracist*. One World.

Keneally, M. (2018, August 8). What to know about the violent Charlottesville protests and anniversary rallies. ABC News. https://abcnews.go.com/US/happen-charlottesville-protest-anniversary-weekend/story?id=57107500

Kennedy, J. T., & Jain-Link, P. (2020a, October 5). Getting involved in diversity and inclusion is optional: That's a problem. *Fortune*. https://fortune.com/2020/10/05/corporate-diversity-inclusion-programs-training/

Kennedy, J. T., & Jain-Link, P. (2020b). *What majority men really think about diversity and inclusion (and how to engage them in it)*. Coqual. https://coqual.org/

wp-content/uploads/2021/04/Belonging-Majority-Men-2-Press-Release-Updated.pdf

Kent, A. H., & Ricketts, L. (2020, December 2). Has wealth inequality in America changed over time? Here are key statistics. Federal Reserve Bank of St. Louis.

Kezar, A., Fries-Britt, S., & Espinosa, L. (2020, June 15). Are campus leaders prepared for the impact of the racial crisis? *Inside Higher Ed.* https://www.insidehighered.com/views/2020/06/15/many-colleges-must-work-harder-engage-racial-healing-opinion

Khakimova, L., Zhang, Y. B., & Hall, J. A. (2012). Conflict management styles: The role of ethnic identity and self-construal among young male Arabs and Americans. *Journal of Intercultural Communication Research, 41*(1), 37–57.

Khan, R. (2011, January 22). Stop using the word "caucasian" to mean white. *Discover Magazine.* https://www.discovermagazine.com/mind/stop-using-the-word-caucasian-to-mean-white

Khosroshahi, H. (2021, May 10). The concrete ceiling. *Stanford Social Innovation Review.*

Kich, G. K. (1992). The developmental process of asserting a biracial, bicultural identity. In M. P. P. Root (Ed.), *Racially mixed people in America* (pp. 304–317). Sage.

Kilvington, D. (2021). The virtual stages of hate: Using Goffman's work to conceptualise the motivations for online hate. *Media, Culture & Society, 43*(2), 256–272. https://doi.org/10.1177/0163443720972318

Kim, Y. Y. (1994). Interethnic communication: The context and the behavior. *Communication Yearbook, 17,* 511–538.

Kim, Y. Y. (2007). Ideology, identity, and intercultural communication: An analysis of differing academic conceptions of cultural identity. *Journal of Intercultural Communication Research, 36*(3), 237–253.

King, M. (2019, June 21). Three ways to tackle a lack of diversity in media. *Forbes.*

Klein, E. (2020, July 20). Bryan Stevenson on how America can heal: A conversation about truth and reconciliation in the US. https://www.vox.com/21327742/bryan-stevenson-the-ezra-klein-show-america-slavery-healing-racism-george-floyd-protests

Kochman, T. (1981). *Black and White styles in conflict.* University of Chicago Press.

Kouri, K. M., & Lasswell, M. (1993). Black-White marriages: Social change and intergenerational mobility. *Marriage and Family Review, 19*(3–4), 241–255.

Kraker, D. (2012, January 24). Edgy posters, billboards come out against racism in Duluth. MPR News.

Kramarae, C. (1981). *Women and men speaking.* Newbury.

Krcmar, M. (2021). Social cognitive theory. In M. B. Oliver, A. Raney, & J. Bryant (Eds.), *Media effects: Advances in theory and research* (4th ed., pp. 100–114). Routledge.

Kroskrity, P. V. (2018). On recognizing persistence in the Indigenous language ideologies of multilingualism in two Native American communities. *Language & Communication, 62,* 133–144. https://doi.org/10.1016/j.langcom.2018.04.012

Krysan, M., Couper, M. P., Farley, R., & Forman T. A. (2009). Does race matter in neighborhood preferences? Results from a video experiment. *AJS, 115*(2), 527–59.

Kuhn, M. H., & McPartland, T. S. (1954). An empirical investigation of self-attitudes. *American Sociological Review, 19,* 68–76.

Kunst, J. R., Onyeador, I. N., & Dovidio, J. F. (2021). Knowledge about individuals' interracial friendships is systematically associated with mental representations of race, traits, and group solidarity. *Personality and Social Psychology Bulletin.*

Kurt, D. (2022, February 28). Corporate leadership by race. Investopedia.

Kye, S. H., & Halpern-Manners, A. (2019). Detecting "white flight" in the contemporary United States: A multicomponent approach. *Sociological Methods & Research, 51*(1), 3–33.

Labov, W. (1972). *Sociolinguistics patterns.* University of Pennsylvania Press.

Lambert, A. A., & Orbe, M. (2019). #Black-LivesMatter political discourse: A Burkeian analysis of controversial comments at Aretha Franklin's funeral. *Journal of Contemporary Rhetoric, 9*(3/4), 126–138. http://contemporaryrhetoric.com/wp-content/uploads/2019/12/Lambert_Orbe_9_3_4_3.pdf

Landor, A. M., & Smith, S. M. (2019). Skin-tone trauma: Historical and contemporary influences on the health and interpersonal outcomes of African Americans. *Perspectives on Psychological Science, 14*(5), 797–815.

Lang, C. (2020). The Asian American response to Black Lives Matter is part of a long, complicated history. *Time.* https://time.com

Langston, D. (2020). Tired of playing monopoly? In M. L. Andersen & P. H. Collins (Eds.), *Race, class, and gender: Intersections and inequalities* (10th ed., pp. 119–128). Cengage.

Lapum, J., St-Amant, O., Hughes, M., & Garmaise-Yee, J. (Eds.). (2020). *Introduction to communication in nursing.* Ryerson University. Open Access.

Larson, K. R., & McHendry, G. F., Jr., (2019). Parasitic publics. *Rhetoric Society Quarterly, 49*(5), 517–541. https://doi.org/10.1080/02773945.2019.1671986

Lasker, G. W., & Tyzzer, R. N. (1982). *Physical anthropology.* Holt.

Lawless, B. (2016). More than white: Locating an invisible class identity. In A. Gonzalez & Y.-W. Chen (Eds.), *Our voices: Essays in culture, ethnicity, and communication* (6th ed., pp. 267–272). Oxford University Press.

Lawton, B., Foeman, A., & Braz, M. (2013). Interracial couples' conflict styles on educational issues. *Journal of Intercultural Communication Research, 42*(1), 35–53.

Lazarsfeld, P. F., & Merton, R. K. (1954). Friendship as a social process: A substantive and methodological analysis. In M. Berger (Ed.), *Freedom and control in modern society* (pp. 18–66). Van Nostrand.

Le, C. N. (2022). The model minority image. Asian Nation. http://www.asian-nation.org/model-minority.shtml#sthash.ZmiOX7xz.dpbs

Leading Effectively Staff. (2022). 5 powerful ways to take REAL action on DEI (diversity, equity, & inclusion). Center for Creative Leadership. https://www.ccl.org/articles/leading-effectively-articles/5-powerful-ways-to-take-real-action-on-dei-diversity-equity-inclusion/

Learning for Justice (n.d.). Strategies for reducing racial and ethnic prejudice: Essential principles. https://www.learningforjustice.org/professional-development/strategies-for-reducing-racial-and-ethnic-prejudice-essential-principles

Lechuga, M. (2020). Mapping migrant vernacular discourses: Mestiza consciousness, nomad thought, and Latina/o/x migrant movement politics in the United States. *Journal of International and Intercultural Communication, 13*(3), 257–273. https://doi.org/10.1080/17513057.2019.1617332

LeCroy, C. (1988). Parent–adolescent intimacy: Impact on adolescent functioning. *Adolescence, 23*(89), 137–147.

Lee, J. (2018). East Asian "China Doll" or "Dragon Lady"? *Bridges: An Undergraduate Journal of Contemporary Connections, 3*(1).

Lee, S. (Writer/Director). (1991). *Jungle fever* [Film]. Universal Pictures.

Lee, S. (2017). Yes, even online dating has white privilege. *Huffington Post.* https://www.huffpost.com/entry/yes-even-online-dating-has-white-privilege_b_9066266

Lee, S. S.-H. (2018). From unwatchable life to consumable spectacle: On history and the Black-Korean conflict. *Asian Diasporic Visual Cultures & the Americas, 4*(3), 280–296.

Lee, S. S.-H. (2022). *Koreatown, Los Angeles: Immigration, race, and the "American dream."* Stanford University Press.

Lees, L. (2016). Gentrification, race, and ethnicity: Towards a global research agenda? *City & Community, 15*(3), 208–214.

Leudar, I., & Nekvapil, J. (2011). Practical historians and adversaries: 9/11 revisited. *Discourse and Society, 22*(1), 66–85.

Leung, A. (2021, July 21). Biden administration exploring policy changes to make US census more accurate and inclusive of race and ethnicity. *Diversity Inc.* https://www.diversityinc.com/biden-administration-exploring-policy-changes-to-make-us-census-more-accurate-and-inclusive-of-race-and-ethnicity/

Lewis, K. (2016). Preferences in the early stages of mate choice. *Social Forces, 95*(1), 283–320.

Lienemann, B. A., & Stopp, H. T. (2013). The association between media exposure of interracial relationships and attitudes toward interracial relationships. *Journal of Applied Social Psychology, 43,* E398–E415.

Littleford, L. N., Wright, M. O., & Sayoc-Parial, M. (2005). White students' intergroup anxiety during same-race and interracial interactions: A multimethod approach. *Basic and Applied Social Psychology, 27*(1), 85–94.

Littlejohn, S. W., Foss, K. A., & Oetzel, J. G. (2021). *Theories of human communication* (12th ed.). Waveland Press.

Livingston, G., & Brown, A. (2017, May 18). Intermarriage in the U.S. 50 years after *Loving v. Virginia.* Pew Research Center.

Logan, N. (2011). The white leader prototype: A critical analysis of race in public relations. *Journal of Public Relations Research, 23*(4), 442–457. https://doi.org/10.1080/1062726X.2011.605974.

Logan, N. (2021). Breaking down barriers of the past and moving toward authentic DEI adoption. In. D. Pompper (Ed.), *Public relations for social responsibility: Affirming DEI commitment with action* (pp. 3–18). Emerald Publishing.

Longoria, E., & Smith, S. L. (2021, August 27). Hollywood has the power to combat damaging stereotypes about Latinos. *Time.*

Lopez, J. K. (2021). Rewriting activism: The NFL takes a knee. *Critical Studies in Media Communication, 38*(2), 183–196.

Lopez, Q. (2018). Minstrelsy speaking: Metaparodic representations of blackface and linguistic minstrelsy in Hollywood films. *Discourse, Context & Media, 23,* 16–24.

Lorde, A. (1984). *Sister outsider.* Crossing Press.

Louis, P.-A. (2021, July 17). Overlooked no more: "Skipped History" explores forgotten events. *The New York Times.* https://www.nytimes.com/2021/07/17/us/overlooked-no-more-skipped-history-explores-forgotten-events.html

Lu, J. G., Nisbett, R. E., & Morris, M. W. (2020). Why East Asians but not South Asians are underrepresented in leadership positions in the United States. *PNAS Proceedings of the National Academy of Sciences of the United States of America, 117*(9), 4590–4600.

Lui, M., Robles, B. J., Leondar-Wright, B., Brewer, R. M., & Adamson, R. (2006). *The color of wealth: The story behind the U.S. racial wealth divide.* The New Press.

Luna, A. (1989). Gay racism. In M. S. Kimmel & M. A. Messner (Eds.), *Men's lives* (pp. 440–447). Macmillan.

Lundquist, J. H., & Lin, K.-H. (2015). Is love (color) blind? The economy of race among gay and straight daters. *Social Forces, 93*(4), 1423–1449.

MacDonald, J. F. (1992). *Black and white TV: Afro-Americans in television since 1948.* Nelson-Hall.

MacLeod, J. (2009). *Ain't no makin' it: Aspirations & attainment in a low-income neighborhood* (3rd. ed.). Westview Press.

Mahalingam, R. (2006). Cultural psychology of immigrants: An introduction. In R. Mahalingam (Ed.), *Cultural psychology of immigrants* (pp. 1–12). Lawrence Erlbaum.

Mallinson, C., & Brewster, Z. W. (2005). "Blacks and bubbas": Stereotypes, ideology, and categorization processes in restaurant servers' discourse. *Discourse & Society, 16*(6), 787–807.

Mandelbaum, D. G. (Ed.). (1949). *Selected writings of Edward Sapir.* University of California Press.

Marcelo, A. K., & Yates, T. M. (2019). Young children's ethnic–racial identity moderates the impact of early discrimination experiences on child behavior problems. *Cultural Diversity and Ethnic Minority Psychology, 25*(2), 253–265. https://doi.org/10.1037/cdp0000220

Maree, J. G. (2021). The psychosocial development theory of Erik Erikson: Critical overview. *Early Child Development and Care, 191*(7/8), 1107–1121. https://doi.org/10.1080/03004430.2020.1845163

Marine, B. (2021, January 5). Are you really sure you love *Bridgerton? W Magazine.* https://www.wmagazine.com/story/bridgerton-netflix-criticism

Marsiglia, F. F., & Hecht, M. L. (1999). The story of Sara: Raising a Jewish child around the Christmas tree. In D. O. Braithwaite & J. T. Woods (Eds.), *Case studies in interpersonal communication processes and problems* (pp. 44–51). Thomson Learning.

Marta, R., Merry, M., Kurniawan, F., Seftira, H., & Amanda, M. (2021). Tidayu ethnic harmonization in semiotic review of face negotiations conflict styles. *Edulite: Journal of English Education, Literature and Culture, 6*(2), 369–382.

Martin, B. A., Cui, M., Ueno, K., & Fincham, F. D. (2013). Intimate partner violence in interracial and monoracial couples. *Family Relations, 61*(1), 202–211.

Martin, J. N. (2017). Dialectics of culture and communication. In Y. Y. Kim (Ed.), *The international encyclopedia of intercultural communication.* Wiley-Blackwell. https://doi.org/10.1002/9781118783665.ieicc0215

Martin, J. N., Hecht, M. L., & Larkey, L. K. (1994). Conversational improvement strategies for interethnic communication: African American and European American perspectives. *Communication Monographs, 61,* 236–255.

Martin, J. N., Krizek, R. L., Nakayama, T. K., & Brodford, L. (1996). Exploring Whiteness: A study of self-labels for White Americans. *Communication Quarterly, 44,* 125–144.

Martin, J., & Nakayama, T. (2010). Intercultural communication and dialectics revisited. In T. K. Nakayama & R. T. Halualani (Eds.), *The handbook of critical intercultural communication* (pp. 59–83). Blackwell.

Martin, J. N., & Nakayama. T. K. (2015). Reconsidering intercultural communication competence in the workplace: A dialectical approach. *Language and Intercultural Communication, 1,* 13–28.

Martin, J. N., & Nakayama, T. K. (2018). *Intercultural communication in contexts* (7th ed.). McGraw-Hill.

Martinez, D. E., & Gonzalez, K. E. (2020). "Latino" or "Hispanic"? The sociodemographic correlates of panethnic label preferences among U.S. Latinos/Hispanics. *Sociological Perspectives, 64*(3), 365–386.

Marubbio, M. E., & Buffalohead, E. L. (2013). *Native Americans on film: Conversations, teaching, and theory.* University Press of Kentucky.

Mastro, D. E., Behm-Morawitz, E., & Kopacz, M. A. (2008). Exposure to television portrayals of Latinos: The implications of aversive racism and social identity theory. *Human Communication Research, 34*(1), 1–27.

Mathews, T. J., & Johnson, G. S. (2015). Skin complexion in the twenty-first century: The impact of colorism on African American women. *Race, Gender & Class, 22*(1–2), 248–274.

Matsuda, M. J., Lawrence, C. R., Delgado, R., & Crenshaw, K. W. (Eds.). (1993). *Words that wound: Critical race theory, assaultive speech, and the First Amendment.* Westview Press.

McAllister, G., & Irvine, J. (2000). Cross-cultural competency and multicultural communication. *Review of Educational Research, 70,* 3–24.

McCann, R. M., & Giles, H. (2002). Ageism and the workplace: A communication perspective. In T. D. Nelson (Ed.), *Ageism* (pp. 163–199). MIT Press.

McCann, R. M., Kellerman, K., Giles, H., Gallois, C., & Viladot, M. A. (2004). Cultural and gender influences on age identification. *Communication Studies, 55*(1), 88–106.

McClintock, E. A., & Murry, V. M. (2010). When does race matter? Race, sex, and dating at an elite university. *Journal of Marriage and Family, 72*(1), 45–72. https://doi.org/10.1111/j.1741-3737.2009.00683.x

McIntosh, D. M. D., Moon, D. G., & Nakayama, T. K. (Eds.). (2018). *Interro-*

*gating the communicative power of whiteness.* Routledge.

McIntosh, P. (1988). White privilege and male privilege: A personal account of coming to see correspondences through work in women's studies. Working Paper 189, Wellesley Centers for Women. https://www.wcwonline.org/Fact-Sheets-Briefs/white-privilege-and-male-privilege-a-personal-account-of-coming-to-see-correspondences-through-work-in-women-s-studies-2

McIntosh, P. (1992). White privilege and male privilege. In A. L. Andersen & P. H. Collins (Eds.), *Race, class, and gender: An anthology* (pp. 65–69). Wadsworth.

McIntosh, P. (2009). White privilege: Unpacking the invisible backpack. In E. Disch (Ed.), *Reconstructing gender: A multicultural anthology* (5th ed., pp. 78–83). McGraw-Hill.

McKay, V. C. (2000). Understanding the co-culture of the elderly. In L. A. Samovar & R. E. Porter (Eds.), *Intercultural communication: A reader* (pp. 180–188). Wadsworth.

McKinney, J. P., McKinney, K. G., Franiuk, R., & Schweitzer, J. (2006). The college classroom as a community: Impact on student attitudes and learning. *College Teaching, 54*(3), 281–284. https://doi.org/10.3200/CTCH.54.3.281-284

McKinstry, S. (2022, February 24). Dr. Kecia M. Thomas: Navigating the workplace as pets or threats. *Gonzaga Bulletin.*

McLuhan, M., & Fiore, Q. (2005). *The medium is the massage.* Gingko Press.

McPhail, M. L. (1991). Complicity: The theory of negative difference. *Howard Journal of Communications, 3*(1&2), 1–13.

McPhail, M. L. (1994a). The politics of complicity: Second thoughts about social construction of racial equality. *Quarterly Journal of Speech, 80*(3), 343–357.

McPhail, M. L. (1994b). *The rhetoric of racism.* University Press of America.

McPhail, M. L. (1996a). Race and sex in black and white: Essence and ideology in the Spike Lee discourse. *Howard Journal of Communications, 7*(2), 127–138.

McPhail, M. L. (1996b). *Zen in the art of rhetoric: An inquiry into coherence.* State University of New York Press.

McPhail, M. L. (1998a). From complicity to coherence: Rereading the rhetoric of Afrocentricity. *Western Journal of Communication, 62*, 114–140.

McPhail, M. L. (1998b). Passionate intensity: Louis Farrakhan and the fallacies of racial reasoning. *Quarterly Journal of Speech, 84*(4), 416–429.

McPhail, M. L. (2002). *The rhetoric of racism revisited: Reparations of separation?* University Press of America.

McPhail, M. L. (2009). The politics of complicity revisited: Race, rhetoric, and the (im)possibility of reconciliation. *Rhetoric & Public Affairs, 12*(1), 107–123. https://doi.org/10.1353/rap.0.0078

McPhail, M. (2023). Complicity theory. In J. Austin, M. Orbe, & J. Sims (Eds.), *Communication theory: Racially and inclusive perspectives* (pp. 187–196). Cognella.

Mead, G. H. (1934). *Mind, self, and society.* University of Chicago Press.

Meek, B. A. (2006). And the Injun goes "how!" Representations of American Indian English in white public space. *Language in Society, 35*, 93–128.

Meltzer, B. N., & Petras, J. W. (1970). The Chicago and Iowa Schools of symbolic interactionism. In T. Shibutani (Ed.), *Human nature and collective behavior* (pp. 74–92). Prentice-Hall.

Melville, M. B. (1988). Hispanics: Race, class, or ethnicity? *Journal of Ethnic Studies, 16*(1), 67–84.

Mendoza, J. (2021, June 22). California school district apologizes for "racism, classism" after tortilla-throwing incident. *USA Today.* https://www.usatoday.com/story/news/education/2021/06/21/tortillas-thrown-latino-team-california-basketball-game/5296806001/

Menjivar, J. (2021, April 1). Confront colorism guide. DoSomething.org. https://www.dosomething.org/us/articles/confront-colorism-guide

Merino, M.-E., & Tileaga, C. (2011). The construction of ethnic minority identity: A discursive psychological approach to ethnic self-definition in action. *Discourse and Society, 22*(1), 86–101.

Merrill, H. (2006). *An alliance of women: Immigration and the politics of race.* University of Minnesota Press.

Merskin, D. (2004). The construction of Arabs as enemies: Post–September 11 discourse of George W. Bush. *Mass Communication & Society, 7*(2), 157–175.

Metz, N. (2022, July 8). How can we come together with our world in tatters? *Chicago Tribune,* sec. 2, p. 8.

Millen, K., Dorn, B., & Luckner, J. L. (2019). Friendships and self-determination among students who are deaf or hard of hearing. *American Annals of the Deaf, 163*(5), 576–595.

Miller, A. N., & Harris, T. M. (2005). Communicating to develop white racial identity in an interracial communication class. *Communication Education, 54*(3), 223–242.

Miller, B., Catalina, S., Rocks, S., & Tillman, K. (2021). It is your decision to date interracially: The influence of family approval on the likelihood of interracial/interethnic dating. *Journal of Family Issues,* 1.

Miller, N. (2002). Personalization and the promise of contact theory. *Journal of Social Issues, 58*(2), 387–410.

Miller, R., Liu, K., & Ball, A. F. (2020). Critical counter-narrative as transformative methodology for educational equity. *Review of Research in Education, 44*(1), 269–300. https://doi.org/10.3102/0091732X20908501

Miller, R. L., & Rotheram-Borus, M. J. (1994). Growing up biracial in the United States. In E. P. Salett & D. R. Koslow (Eds.), *Race, ethnicity and self: Identity in multicultural perspective* (pp. 143–169). Multicultural Institute.

Mills, M. A. (2021). *The colors of love: Multiracial people in interracial relationships.* New York University Press.

Min, P. G. (Ed.). (2006). *Asian Americans: Contemporary trends and issues.* Pine Forge Press.

The Minneapolis Egotist. (2020, August 18). Unfair campaign receives national attention again, eight years after its inception. https://www.themplsegotist.com/news/unfair-campaign-receives-national-attention-again-eight-years-after-its-inception/

Minniear, M., & Soliz, J. (2019). Family communication and messages about race and identity in Black families in the United States. *Journal of Family Communication, 19*(4), 329–347. https://doi.org/10.1080/15267431.2019.1593170

Mitchell Dove, L. (2021). The influence of colorism on the hair experiences of African American female adolescents. *Genealogy, 5*(1), 5.

Mizuno, T. (2003). Government suppression of the Japanese language in World War II assembly camps. *Journalism and Mass Communication Quarterly, 80*(4), 849–865.

Moffit, K. R. (2020). "Light-skinned people always win": An autoethnography of colorism in a mother–daughter relationship. *Women, Gender, and Families of Color, 8*(1), 65–86. https://doi.org/10.5406/womgenfamcol.8.1.0065

Moffitt, U., & Syed, M. (2020). Ethnic-racial identity in action: Structure and content of friends' conversations about ethnicity and race. *Identity: An International Journal of Theory and Research, 21*(1), 67–88. https://doi.org/10.1080/15283488.2020.1838804

Monk, E. P., Jr., (2021a). Colorism and physical health: Evidence from a national survey. *Journal of Health & Social Behavior, 62*(1), 37–52.

Monk, E. P., Jr., (2021b). The unceasing significance of colorism: Skin tone stratification in the United States. *Daedalus, 150*(2), 76–90.

Montagu, A. (1964). *The concept of race.* Free Press of Glencoe.

Montagu, A. (1978). *Touching: The human significance of the skin* (2nd ed.). Harper & Row.

Montagu, A. (1997). *Man's most dangerous myth: The fallacy of race* (6th ed.). AltaMira Press.

Moon, D. G., & Rolison, G. L. (1998). Communication of classism. In M. L. Hecht (Ed.), *Communicating prejudice* (pp. 122–135). Sage.

Moore, C., Barbour, K. J., & Lee, K. (2017). Five dimensions of online persona. *Persona Studies, 3*(1), 1–12. https://doi.org/10.21153/ps2017vol3no1art658

Moreman, S. T. (2011). Qualitative interviews of racial fluctuations: The "how" of Latina/o-White hybrid identity. *Communication Theory, 21*(2), 197–216.

Morrison, K. R., & Chung, A. H. (2011). "White" or "European American"? Self-identifying labels influence majority group members' interethnic attitudes. *Journal of Experimental Social Psychology, 47*(1), 165–170. https://doi.org/10.1016/j.jesp.2010.07.019

Moss, K. (2003). *The color of class: Poor whites and the paradox of privilege.* University of Pennsylvania Press.

Moss, K., & Faux, W. V., II (2006). The enactment of cultural identity in student conversations on intercultural topics. *Howard Journal of Communications, 17*, 21–37.

Mudambi, A. (2019). South Asian American discourses: Engaging the yellow peril-model minority dialectic. *Howard Journal of Communications, 30*(3), 284–298.

Mujahid, A. M. (2003, July). In a virtual internment camp: Muslim Americans since 9/11. *SoundVision.* https://www.soundvision.com/article/in-a-virtual-internment-camp-muslim-americans-since-911

Munn, C. W. (2018). The one friend rule: Race and social capital in an interracial network. *Social Problems, 65*, 473–490. https://doi.org/10.1093/socpro/spx020

Muraco, A. (2005). Heterosexual evaluations of hypothetical friendship behavior based on sex and sexual orientation. *Journal of Social and Personal Relationships, 22*(5), 587–605.

Murphy, M., & Harris, T. M. (2017). White innocence and Black subservience: The rhetoric of White heroism in *The Help. The Howard Journal of Communications, 29*(1), 325–334. 10.1080/10646175.2017.1327378.

Murthy, D. (2020). From hashtag activism to inclusion and diversity in a discipline. *Communication, Culture, and Critique, 13*(2), 259–264.

Muthuswamy, N., Levine, T., & Gazel, J. (2006). Interaction-based diversity initiative outcomes: An evaluation of an initiative aimed at bridging the racial divide on a college campus. *Communication Education, 55*(1), 105–121.

Mutua, E. M. (2016). Deconstructing the refugee body: Toward an intercultural understanding of refugee and host communities. In A. Gonzalez & Y.-W. Chen (Eds.), *Our voices: Essays in culture, ethnicity, and communication* (6th ed., pp. 283–289). Oxford University Press.

Nakamura, D. ((2021, August 30). U.S. hate crimes rose in 2020 to the highest level since 2008, propelled by increasing assaults on Black and Asian victims, FBI reports. *The Washington Post.* https://www.washingtonpost.com/national-security/hate-crimes-fbi-2020-asian-black/2021/08/30/28bede00-09a7-11ec-9781-07796ffb56fe_story.html

Nakashima, C. (1992). Blood quantum: Native American mixed bloods. In M. P. P. Root (Ed.), *Racially mixed people in America* (pp. 162–180). Sage.

Nakayama, T. (2017). What's next for whiteness and the internet? *Critical Studies in Media Communication, 34*(1), 68–72. https://doi.org/10.1080/15295036.2016.1266684

Nakayama, T. K., & Halualani, R. T. (Eds.). (2011). *The handbook of critical intercultural communication.* Wiley-Blackwell.

Nance T. A., & Foeman, A. K. (2002). On being biracial in the United States. In J. N. Martin, T. K. Nakayama, & L. A. Flores (Eds.), *Readings in intercultural communication: Experiences and contexts* (pp. 35–43). McGraw-Hill.

National Public Radio (NPR). (2020). Latinos and Asians grapple with racism, allyship amid ongoing protests. *Weekend Edition Sunday.*

National Research Council. (2004). *Measuring racial discrimination.* National Academies Press.

Nazione, S., & Silk, K. (2011). Employees' views of discrimination in a community health department. *Howard Journal of Communications, 22*(2), 200–221.

Neergaard, L. (2006, September 12). Where you live a significant factor in how long you live, new study finds. *Kalamazoo (MI) Gazette*, p. A8.

Nelson, S. C., Syed, M., Tran, A. G. T. T., Hu, A. W., & Lee, R. M. (2018). Pathways to ethnic-racial identity development and psychological adjustment: The differential associations of cultural socialization by parents and peers. *Developmental Psychology, 54*(11), 2166–2180. https://doi.org/10.1037/dev0000597

Nero, C. I. (2016). Black queer identity, imaginative rationality, and the language of home. In A. Gonzalez & Y.-W. Chen (Eds.), *Our voices: Essay in culture, ethnicity, and communication* (6th ed., pp. 142–147). Oxford University Press.

Neuliep, J. W., & Johnson, M. (2016). A cross-cultural comparison of Ecuadorian and United States face, facework, and conflict styles during interpersonal conflict: An application of face-negotiation theory. *Journal of International and Intercultural Communication, 9,* 1–19.

Ng, E., White, K. C., & Saha, A. (2020). #CommunicationSoWhite: Race and power in the academy and beyond. *Communication, Culture, and Critique, 13*(2), 143–151. https://doi.org/10.1093/ccc/tcaa011

Ng, M. T. (2004). Searching for home: Voices of gay Asian American youth in West Hollywood. In J. Lee & M. Zhou (Eds.), *Asian American youth: Culture, identity, and ethnicity* (pp. 269–284). Routledge.

NickALive! (2021, October 28). ViacomCBS releases the findings of its newest Global Insights project, Reflecting Me: Global representation on screen. Nickalive.net/2021/10/viacomcbs-releases-findings-of-its.html

Nielsen. (2021, August). Tailored content strategies are driving viewership growth among streaming platforms. https://www.nielsen.com/insights/2021/tailored-content-strategies-are-driving-viewership-growth-among-streaming-platforms/

Nishime, L. (2012). The case for Cablinasian: Multiracial naming from Plessy to Tiger Woods. *Communication Theory, 22*(1), 92–111.

Nittle, N. K. (2019, July 28). Stereotypes of Italian Americans in film and television. ThoughtCo. https://www.thoughtco.com/stereotypes-of-italian-americans-fil-television-2834703

Nittle, N. K. (2021a, March 17). Common Arab stereotypes in TV and film. ThoughtCo.

Nittle, N. K. (2021b, September 8). 5 common Black stereotypes in TV and film. ThoughtCo. https://www.thoughtco.com/common-black-stereotypes-in-tv-film-2834653

Norwood, K. (2015). "If you is white, you's alright. . . ." Stories about colorism in America. *Washington University Global Studies Law Review, 14,*(4), 585–607.

Notopoulos, K. (2018, February 27). Tinder says it is really into interracial love. *Buzzfeed News.* https://www.buzzfeednews.com

Nunes, L. (2021, June 28). Lessons from the bamboo ceiling. Association for Psychological Science. https://www.psychologicalscience.org/observer/bamboo-ceiling

Nwabueze, C., & Okonkwo, E. (2018). Rethinking the bullet theory in the digital age. *International Journal of Media, Journalism and Mass Communications, 4*(2), 1–10.

O'Brien Hallstein, D. L. (2000). Where standpoint stands now: An introduction and commentary. *Women's Studies in Communication, 23*(1), 1–15.

Oetzel, J. G., & Ting-Toomey, S. (2003). Face concerns in interpersonal conflict: A cross-cultural empirical test of the face-negotiation theory. *Communication Research, 30*(6), 599–624. https://doi.org/10.1177/0093650203257841

Olivier, J., Clair, M., & Denis, J. S. (2019). Racism in the era of Trump. *The Blackwell Encyclopedia of Sociology,* 1–10. https://doi.org/10.1002/9781405165518.wbeos1238

Olsen, K. (2006, Fall). We were still the enemy. *Teaching Tolerance,* 36–41.

Ono, K. A. (2010). Postracism: A theory of the "post"—As political strategy. *Journal of Communication Inquiry, 34*(3), 227–233.

Orbe, M. (1998). *Constructing co-cultural theory: An explication of culture, power, and communication.* Sage.

Orbe, M. (1999). Communicating about "race" in interracial families. In T. Socha & R. Diggs (Eds.), *Communication, race, and family: Exploring communication in black, white, and biracial families* (pp. 167–180). Lawrence Erlbaum.

Orbe, M. (2003). African American first-generation college student communicative experiences. *Electronic Journal of Communication, 13*(2–3).

Orbe, M. (2005). "The more things change. . .": Civil rights health assessment in a "majority–minority" U.S. community. *Howard Journal of Communications, 16*(3), 177–200.

Orbe, M. (2011). *Communication realities in a "post-racial" society: What the U.S. public really thinks about Barack Obama*. Lexington Books.

Orbe, M. (2012). Researching biracial/multiracial identity negotiation: Lessons from diverse contemporary U.S. public perceptions. In N. Bardan & M. Orbe (Eds.), *Identity research and communication: Intercultural reflections and future directions* (pp. 165–178). Lexington Books.

Orbe, M. (2015). #AllLivesMatter as post-racial rhetorical strategy. *Journal of Contemporary Rhetoric, 5*, 90–98.

Orbe, M. (2016). Diverse understandings of a "post-racial" society. In K. Sorrells & S. Sekimoto (Eds.), *Globalizing intercultural communication: A reader* (pp. 23–42). Sage.

Orbe, M. (2018). Pedagogy of the taboo: Theorizing transformative teaching-learning experiences that speak truth(s) to power. In A. Atay & S. Toyosaki (Eds.), *Theorizing critical intercultural communication pedagogy* (pp. 93–107). Lexington Books.

Orbe, M. (2019). Cultural communication competency as a two-way street: My journey from medical avoidance to patient self-advocacy. In P. M. Kellett (Ed.), *Narrating patienthood: Engaging diverse voices on health, communication, and the patient experience* (pp. 35–46). Lexington Books.

Orbe, M. (2021a). The normative nature of racial microaggressions in the legal field: Exploring the communicative experiences of U.S. attorneys of colour. *Journal of Intercultural Communication Research, 50*(3), 207–244. https://doi.org/10.1080/17475759.2020.1866644

Orbe, M. (2021b). Socioeconomic (im)mobility: Resisting classifications within a "post-projects" identity. In R. Boylorn & M. Orbe (Eds.), *Critical autoethnography: Intersecting cultural identities in everyday life* (pp. 203–215). Routledge.

Orbe, M., & Albrehi, F. (2023). Co-cultural theory. In J. Austin, M. Orbe, & J. Sims (Eds.), *Communication theory: Racially and inclusive perspectives* (pp. 65–78). Cognella.

Orbe, M., Allen, B. J., & Flores, L. A. (Eds.). (2006). *The same and different: Acknowledging the diversity within and between cultural groups* [Paper presentation]. National Communication Association 92nd Annual Convention, Washington, DC.

Orbe, M., & Drummond, D. K. (2009). Negotiations of the complicitous nature of US racial/ethnic categorization: Exploring rhetorical strategies. *Western Journal of Communication, 73*(4), 437–455.

Orbe, M., & Drummond, D. K. (2011). Competing U.S. cultural worldviews: A phenomenological examination of the essential core elements of transnationalism and transculturalism. *The Qualitative Report, 16*(6). www.nova.edu/ssss/QR/QR16-6/orbe.pdf

Orbe, M., Drummond, D. K., & Camara, S. K. (2002). Phenomenology and black feminist thought: Exploring African American women's everyday encounters as points of contention. In M. Houston & O. I. Davis (Eds.), *Centering ourselves: African American feminist and womanist studies of discourse* (pp. 123–144). Hampton Press.

Orbe, M., & Elliott, R. R. (2012). Race, religion, and contemporary U.S. culture: A semiotic analysis of mass mediated signifiers. In S. M. Croucher & T. M. Harris (Eds.), *Religion & communication: An anthology of extensions in theory, research, & method* (pp. 159–174). Peter Lang.

Orbe, M., & Everett, M. A. (2006). Interracial and interethnic conflict and communication in the United States. In J. Oetzel & S. Ting-Toomey (Eds.), *The Sage handbook of conflict communication* (pp. 575–594). Sage.

Orbe, M., & Kinefuchi, E. (2008). Crash under investigation: Engaging complications of complicity, coherence, and implicature through critical analysis. *Critical Studies in Media Communication, 25*(2), 135–156.

Orbe, M., & Roberts, T. L. (2012). Co-cultural theorizing: Foundations, applications, and extensions. *Howard Journal of Communications, 23*, 293–311.

Osman, S. M., (2021, September 29). 12 movies & TV shows with accurate Arabic characters, not offensive stereotypes. SheKnows. https://www.sheknows.com/entertainment/slideshow/2490779/movies-tv-shows-arabic-characters/

Padden, C., & Humphries, T. (1988). *Deaf in America: Voices from a culture*. Harvard University Press.

Page, C. (1994, January 5). Uneasy journey to political correctness. *Louisville (KY) Courier-Journal*, p. A19.

Palmer, P. J. (1993). *To know as we are known: Education as a spiritual journey*. Harper.

Papamarko, S. (2017, March 21). Why black women and Asian men are at a disadvantage when it comes to online dating. *Toronto Star*. https://www.thestar.com/life/2017/03/21/racism-and-matchmaking.html

Parameswaran, R., & Cardoza, K. (2009). Melanin on the margins: Advertising and the cultural politics of fair/light/white beauty in India. *Journalism & Communication Monographs, 11*(3), 213–274.

Park, J. H., Gabbadon, N. G., & Chernin, A. R. (2006). Naturalizing racial differences through comedy: Asian, black, and white views on racial stereotypes in *Rush Hour 2*. *Journal of Communication, 56*, 157–177.

Park, M., Choi, Y., Yoo, H. C., Yasui, M., & Takeuchi, D. (2021). Racial stereotypes and Asian American youth paradox. *Journal of Youth and Adolescence: A Multidisciplinary Research Publication, 50*(12), 2374–2393.

Park, S. (2021). Asian Americans' perception of intergroup commonality with Blacks and Latinos: The roles of group consciousness, ethnic identity, and intergroup contact. *Social Sciences 10*, 441.

Parlsoe, S. M., & Campbell, R. C. (2021). "Folks don't understand what it's like to be a native woman": Framing trauma via #MMIW. *Howard Journal of Communications, 32*(3), 197–212. https://doi.org/10.1080/10646175.2021.1871867

Parrillo, V. N. (1996). *Diversity in America*. Pine Forge Press.

Parrish-Sprowl, J. (2016). I am hearing impaired: Negotiating identity in a hearing world. In A. Gonzalez & Y.-W. Chen (Eds.), *Our voices: Essays in culture, ethnicity, and communication* (6th ed., pp. 51–56). Oxford University Press.

Patel, S. (2019). "Brown girls can't be gay": Racism experienced by queer South Asian women in the Toronto LGBTQ community. *Journal of Lesbian Studies, 23*(3), 410–423. https://doi.org/10.1080/10894160.2019.1585174

Patterson, R. E. (2011). The "Beer Summit" and what's brewing: Narratives, networks, and metaphors as rhetorical confinement in the age of Obama. *Communication Studies, 62*(4), 439–455.

Pattisapu, K., & Calafell, B. M. (2012). (Academic) families of choice: Queer relationality, mentoring, and critical communication pedagogy. In N. Bardhan & M. Orbe (Eds.), *Identity research and communication: Intercultural reflections and future directions* (pp. 51–68). Lexington Books.

Patton, T. O. (2004). In the guise of civility: The complicitous maintenance of inferential forms of sexism and racism in higher education. *Women's Studies in Communication, 27*(1), 60–87.

Paul, S., Rafal, M., & Houtenville, A. (2021). Annual disability statistics compendium: 2021. University of New Hampshire, Institute on Disability. https://disabilitycompendium.org/sites/default/files/user-uploads/Events/2022ReleaseYear/2021_Annual_Disability_Statistics_Compendium_WEB.pdf

Paulin, D. R. (1997). De-essentializing interracial representations: Black and white border-crossings in Spike Lee's *Jungle Fever* and Octavia Butler's *Kindred*. *Cultural Critique, 36*, 165–193.

Paulson, D. (2021, July 23). Morgan Wallen says "I was just ignorant" about use of slur, reveals rehab stint. *The Tennessean*. https://www.tennessean.com/story/entertainment/music/2021/07/23/morgan-wallen-interview-i-just-ignorant-use-racial-slur-singer-says/8067143002/

Paychex. (2019, August 1). Employment and discrimination: Exploring the climate of workplace discrimination from 1997 to 2018. Paychex Workx. https://www.paychex.com/articles/human-resources/eeoc-workplace-discrimination-enforcement-and-litigation

Peck, M. S. (1987). *The different drum: Community making and peace*. Simon & Schuster.

Pedraza, S. (2006). Assimilation or transnationalism? Conceptual models of the immigrant experience in America. In R. Mahalingam (Ed.), *Cultural psychology of immigrants* (pp. 33–54). Lawrence Erlbaum.

Pennington, D. L. (1979). Black-white communication: An assessment of research. In M. K. Asante, E. Newark, & C. A. Blake (Eds.), *Handbook of intercultural communication* (pp. 383–402). Sage.

Perry, A. (2005, November 28). Letter from Bombay: Could you please make me a shade lighter? *Time*. http://content.time.com/time/subscriber/article/0,33009,1134744-2,00.html

Petermon, J., D. (2014). *Hyper (in)visibility: Reading race and representation in the neoliberal era* [Doctoral dissertation, University of Santa Barbara]. Open Access Dissertations, Alexandria. https://www.alexandria.ucsb.edu/lib/ark:/48907/f3cc0xvc

Petermon, J. D. (2018). Race (lost and found) in Shondaland: The rise of multiculturalism in prime-time network television. In R. Griffin & M. Meyer (Eds.), *Adventures in Shondaland: Identity politics and the power of representation* (pp. 101–119). Rutgers University Press.

Peters, M. A., & Besley, T. (2021). Models of dialogue. *Educational Philosophy and Theory, 53*(7), 669–676. https://doi.org/10.1080/00131857.2019.1684801

Pettigrew, T. F., Fredrickson, G. M., Knoble, D. T., Glazer, N., & Ueda, R. (1982). *Prejudice: Dimensions of ethnicity*. Belknap Press of Harvard University Press.

Pettigrew, T. F., Tropp, L. R., Wagner, U., & Christ, O. (2011). Recent advances in intergroup contact theory. *International Journal of Intercultural Relations, 35*(3), 271–280.

Pew Research Center. (2017, July 26). U.S. Muslims concerned about their place in society but continue to believe in the American dream.

Pew Research Center. (2020, February 6). What census calls us.

Pew Research Center. (2021, April 7). Social media fact sheet. https://www.pewresearch.org/internet/fact-sheet/social-media/?menuItem=2fc5fff9-9899-4317-b786-9e0b60934bcf#who-uses-social-media

Philipsen, G. (1975). Speaking "like a man" in Teamsterville: Culture patterns of role enactment in an urban neighborhood. *Quarterly Journal of Speech, 61*, 13–22.

Philipsen, G. (1976). Places for speaking in Teamsterville. *Quarterly Journal of Speech, 62*, 15–25.

Philipsen, G. (1997). A theory of speech codes. In G. Philipsen & T. L. Albrecht (Eds.), *Developing communication theories* (pp. 119–156). State University of New York Press.

Phinney, J. S. (1993). A three-stage model of ethnic identity development in adolescence. In M. E. Bernal & G. P. Knight (Eds.), *Ethnic identity: Formation and transmission among Hispanics and other immigrants* (pp. 61–79). State University of New York Press.

Pickette, S. (2020). Suffering, stereotypes, and psychosis: The representation of Jewish femininity in *Crazy ex-girlfriend*. *Journal of Modern Jewish Studies, 19*(1), 51–70.

Pimentel, C., & Balzhiser, D. (2012). The double occupancy of Hispanics: Counting race and ethnicity in the U.S. census. *Journal of Business and Technical Communication, 26*(3), 311–339.

Pindar, L., & Jones, K. O. (2012). Understanding the roles of religion, faith, and communication in managing disability: Lessons learned, opportunities and needs for further research. In S. M. Croucher & T. M. Harris (Eds.), *Religion & communication: An anthology of extensions in theory, research, & method* (pp. 13–22). Peter Lang.

Pinsker, J. (2021, March 29). Trump's presidency is over. So are many relationships. *The Atlantic.* https://www.theatlantic.com/family/archive/2021/03/trump-friend-family-relationships/618457/

Plaut, V. C., Thomas, K. M., Hurd, K., & Romano, C. A. (2018). Do color blindness and multiculturalism remedy or foster discrimination and racism? *Current Directions in Psychological Science, 27*(3), 200–206.

Pluralism Project. (2020a). Many local traditions. Harvard University.

Pluralism Project. (2020b). Myth of the "vanishing Indian." Harvard University.

Pluralism Project. (2020c). Struggle and survival: Native ways of life today. Harvard University.

Ponterotto, J. G., & Pedersen, P. B. (1993). *Preventing prejudice: A guide for counselors and educators.* Sage.

Poston, W. S. C. (1990). The biracial identity development model: A needed addition. *Journal of Counseling and Development, 69,* 152–155.

Prell, R.-E. (2021, June 23). Jewish gender stereotypes in the United States. *Jewish Women's Archive.* https://jwa.org/encyclopedia/article/stereotypes-in-united-states

Presbitero, A., & Attar, H. (2018). Intercultural communication effectiveness, cultural intelligence and knowledge sharing: Extending anxiety–uncertainty management theory. *International Journal of Intercultural Relations, 67,* 35–43.

Professional Staff Organization. (2021, March 18). Statement of solidarity with AAPI community. University of Washington. https://www.washington.edu/pso/2021/03/18/aapi-solidarity/

Purdie-Vaughns, V., & Eibach, R. P. (2008). Intersectional invisibility: The distinctive advantages and disadvantages of multiple subordinate-group identities. *Sex Roles, 59*(5/6), 377–391.

Putman, A., & Kvam, D. S. (2021). "I'm generally just a white European mutt": Communication strategies for interpreting and sharing DNA-based ancestry test results. *Journal of International and Intercultural Communication.* https://doi.org/10.1080/17513057.2021.1942144

Putman, A., & Thompson, S. (2006). Paving the way: First-generation Mexican American community college students in a border community. In M. Orbe, B. J. Allen, & L. A. Flores (Eds.), *The same and different: Acknowledging the diversity within and between cultural groups* (pp. 121–142). National Communication Association.

Qian, Z. (1998). Changes in assortative mating: The impact of age and education. 1970–1990. *Demography, 35*(3), 279–292.

Radke, H., Kutlaca, M., Siem, B., Wright, S., & Becker, J. (2020). Beyond allyship: Motivations for advantaged group members to engage in action for disadvantaged groups. *Personality and Social Psychology Review, 24*(4), 291–315. https://doi.org/10.1177/1088868320918698

Rafalow, M. H., Feliciano, C., & Robnett, B. (2017). Racialized femininity and masculinity in the preferences of online same-sex daters. *Social Currents, 4*(4), 306–321. https://doi.org/10.1177/2329496516686621

Rai, R., & Panna, K. (2015). *Introduction to culture studies* (4th ed.). Himalaya Publishing House.

Raible, J. W. (2009). Checklist for allies against racism. https://johnraible.wordpress.com/checklist-for-allies-against-racism/

Ramirez-Sanchez, R. (2008). Marginalization from within: Expanding co-cultural theory through the experience of the *Afro punk. Howard Journal of Communications, 19,* 89–104.

Rangel, I. (2020, March 4). "Snowflake," "entitled": Here's what you get wrong about millennials. *Florida Today.* https://www.floridatoday.com/story/opinion/2020/03/04/millennials-arent-all-snowflakes/4938220002/

Ranzini, G., & Rosenbaum, J. E. (2020). It's a match (?): Tinder usage and attitudes toward interracial dating. *Communication Research Reports, 37*(1/2), 44–54.

Rao, P. (2019, April 9). Paying a high price for skin bleaching. *Africa Renewal.* https://www.un.org/africarenewal/magazine/april-2019-july-2019/paying-high-price-skin-bleaching

Raouf, T. (2020, September 22). The ongoing problem with Middle Eastern representation on TV. *Nerdist.*

Rathbun, L. (2001). The debate over annexing Texas and the emergence of Manifest Destiny. *Rhetoric and Public Affairs, 4*(3), 459–493.

Rattan, A., Chilazi, S., Georgeac, O., & Bohnet, I. (2019, June 6). Tackling the underrepresentation of women in media. *Harvard Business Review.*

Ray, G. B. (2009). *Language and interracial communication in the United States: Speaking in black and white.* Peter Lang.

Razack, S., & Joseph, J. (2021). Misogynoir in women's sport media: Race, nation, and diaspora in the representation of Naomi Osaka. *Media, Culture & Society, 43*(2), 291–308. https://doi.org/10.1177/0163443720960919

Razzante, R. J., Boylorn, R. M., & Orbe, M. (2021). Embracing intersectionality in co-cultural and dominant group theorizing: Implications for theory, research, and pedagogy. *Communication Theory, 31*(2), 228–249. https://doi.org/10.1093/ct/qtab002

Razzante, R. J., & Orbe, M. (2018). Two sides of the same coin: Conceptualizing dominant group theory in the context of co-cultural theory. *Communication Theory, 28*(3), 354–375. https://doi.org/10.1093/ct/qtx008

Reid, E. (2017, September 25). Eric Reid: Why Colin Kaepernick and I decided to take a knee. *The New York Times.* https://www.nytimes.com/2017/09/25/opinion/colin-kaepernick-football-protests.html

Reilly, K. (2016, August 21). Here are all the times Donald Trump insulted Mexico. *Time.* https://time.com/4473972/donald-trump-mexico-meeting-insult/

Reimers, D. M. (2005). *Other immigrants: The global origins of the American people.* New York University Press.

Reiter, L. (1989). Sexual orientation, sexual identity, and the question of choice. *Clinical Social Work Journal, 17*, 138–150.

Remedios, J. D., & Sanchez, D. T. (2018). Intersectional and dynamic social categories in social cognition. *Social Cognition, 36*(5), 453–460.

Rengifo, A. F., & Slocum, L. A. (2020). The identity prism: How racial identification frames perceptions of police contact, legitimacy, and effectiveness. *Law & Social Inquiry, 45*(3), 590–617. https://doi.org/10.1017/lsi.2019.72

Resnik, B. (2017, March 7). The dark psychology of dehumanization, explained. Vox.

Reyes, L. (2021, August 26). Report: ESPN removes Rachel Nichols from all NBA programming in fallout over Maria Taylor spat. *USA Today.* https://www.usatoday.com/story/sports/nba/2021/08/25/espn-removes-rachel-nichols-nba-programming-per-report/5592458001/

Reyes, R. A. (2021, June 10). *In the heights* defies stereotypes, portrays Latinos in 3 dimensions. *USA Today.*

Ribeau, S. A. (2004). How I came to know in self-realization there is truth. In A. Gonzalez, M. Houston, & V. Chen (Eds.), *Our voices: Essays in culture, ethnicity, and communication* (4th ed., pp. 32–37). Roxbury.

Ribeau, S. A., Baldwin, J. R., & Hecht, M. L. (1997). An African American communication perspective. In L. A. Samovar & R. E. Porter (Eds.), *Intercultural communications: A reader* (pp. 147–154). Wadsworth.

Rich, A. L. (1974). *Interracial communication.* Harper & Row.

Rich, A. L., & Ogawa, D. M. (1972). Intercultural and interracial communication: An analytical approach. In L. A. Samovar & R. E. Porter (Eds.), *Intercultural communication: A reader* (pp. 22–29). Wadsworth.

Richeson, J. A., Baird, A. A., Gordon, H. L., Heatherton, T. F., Wyland, C. L., Trawalter, S., & Shelton, J. N. (2003). An fMRI investigation of the impact of interracial contact on executive function. *Nature Neuroscience, 6,* 1323–1328.

Rickford, J. R., & Rickford, R. J. (2000). *Spoken soul: The story of Black English.* John Wiley & Sons.

Riddle, D. (1994). The Riddle scale. Alone no more: Developing a school support system for gay, lesbian and bisexual youth. St Paul: Minnesota State Department.

Rinderle, S. (2006). Quienes son/quienes somos: A critical analysis of the changing names for people of Mexican descent across history. In M. Orbe, B. J. Allen, & L. A. Flores (Eds.), *The same and different: Acknowledging the diversity within and between cultural groups* (pp. 143–165). National Communication Association.

Ritter, Z. S. (2015). Taboo or tabula rasa: Cross-racial/cultural dating preferences amongst Chinese, Japanese, and Korean international students in an American university. *Journal of International Students, 5*(4), 405–419.

Roberts, D. (2015). *Loving v. Virginia* as a civil rights decision. *New York Law School Law Review, 59*(1), 175–209.

Robnett, B., & Feliciano, C. (2011). Patterns of racial-ethnic exclusion by internet daters. *Social Forces 89*(3), 807–828.

Rock, A. (2022, April 20). Chris Harrison & Rachel Lindsay: What happened between the *Bachelor* nation stars. Hollywood Life.

Rockquemore, K. A., & Brunsma, D. L. (2002). *Beyond black: Biracial identity in America.* Sage.

Rockquemore, K. A., & Laszloffy, T. (2005). *Raising biracial children.* AltaMira Press.

Rodenborg, N. A, & Boisen, L. A. (2013). Aversive racism and intergroup contact theories: Cultural competence in a segregated world. *Journal of Social Work Education, 49*(4), 564–579.

Rodrigues, P. (2016). "I am not Jamal": Asian Indians, simplistic perceptions, and the model minority myth. In A. Gonzalez & Y.-W. Chen (Eds.), *Our voices: Essays in culture, ethnicity, and communication* (6th ed., pp. 97–106). Oxford University Press.

Rodriguez, A. (2002). Culture to culturing: Re-imaging our understanding of intercultural relations. *Journal of Intercultural Communication, 5.* https://www.immi.se/intercultural/nr5/rodriguez.pdf

Root, M. P. P. (1992). Within, between, and beyond race. In M. P. P. Root (Ed.), *Racially mixed people in America* (pp. 3–11). Sage.

Root, M. P. P. (Ed.). (1996). *The multiracial experience: Racial borders as the new frontier.* Sage.

Roper, L. (2019). The power of dialogue and conversation in higher education. *New Directions for Student Leadership, 163,* 15–28. https://doi.org/10.1002/yed.20344

Rose, S. F., & Firmin, M. W. (2016). Racism in interracial dating: A case study in southern culture and fundamentalism. *Christian Higher Education, 15*(3), 140–152.

Rosenthal, L., & Starks, T. J. (2015). Relationship stigma and relationship outcomes in interracial and same-sex relationships: Examination of sources and buffers. *Journal of Family Psychology, 29*(6), 818–830.

Rosner, H. (2021, October 8). The long American history of "missing white woman syndrome." *The New Yorker.* https://www.newyorker.com/news/q-and-a/the-long-american-history-of-missing-white-woman-syndrome

Ross, C. L., & Woodley, X. M. (2020). Black-White identity development: Understanding the impact of personal and collective racial identity factors on interracial marriages. *Journal of Couple & Relationship Therapy, 19*(1), 26–50.

Roth, W. D. (2018, July 8). Genetic ancestry tests don't change your identity, but you might. PBS News Hour, Science. https://www.pbs.org/newshour/science/genetic-ancestry-tests-dont-change-your-identity-but-you-might

Rothstein, R. (2014, April 17). *Brown v. Board* at 60. Economic Policy Institute.

Rothstein, R. (2017). *The color of law: A forgotten history of how our government segregated America.* Liveright Publishing.

Rowe, A. C., & Malhotra, S. (2006). (Un)hinging whiteness. In M. Orbe, B.

J. Allen, & L. A. Flores (Eds.), *The same and different: Acknowledging the diversity within and between cultural groups* (pp. 166–192). National Communication Association.

Roy, R. N., James, A., Brown, T. L., Craft, A., & Mitchell, Y. (2020). Relationship satisfaction across the transition to parenthood among interracial couples: An integrative model. *Journal of Family Theory & Review, 12*(1), 41–53.

Royer, D. W. (2014, September). *Race, religion, and multiracial congregations in America* [Conference session]. 33rd Annual Research-to-Practice Conference in Adult and Higher Education, Muncie, Indiana.

Rubin, D. I. (2021). *The Jewish struggle in the 21st century: Conflict, positionality, and multiculturalism.* Brill.

Rudman, L. A., & Saud, L. H. (2020). Justifying social inequalities: The role of social Darwinism. *Personality & Social Psychology Bulletin, 46*(7), 1139–1155.

Ruggieri, D. G., & Leebron, E. J. (2010). Situation comedies imitate life: Jewish and Italian American women on prime time. *The Journal of Popular Culture, 43*(6), 1266–1281.

Sacramento ACT. (2020, September 2). 10 commandments for dismantling systemic racism and affirming the rights and dignity of Black, Brown and Native people. https://www.sacact.org/news/2020/9/25/10-commandments-for-dismantling-systemic-racism-and-affirming-the-rights-and-dignity-of-black-brown-and-native-people

Sahay, S., & Piran, N. (1997). Skin-color preferences and body satisfaction among south Asian-Canadian and European-Canadian female university students. *Journal of Social Psychology, 137*(2), 161–171.

Salazar, L. R., Garcia, N., Diego-Medrano, E., & Castillo, Y. (2021). Workplace cyberbullying and cross-cultural differences: Examining the application of intercultural communication theoretical perspectives. In L. R. Salazar (Ed.), *Handbook of research on cyberbullying and online harassment in the workplace* (pp. 284–309). IGI Global.

Sanders, J. M. (2020). Seeking acceptance: LGBTQ and membership in Alcoholics Anonymous (AA). *Alcoholism Treatment Quarterly, 38*(4), 430–445. https://doi.org/10.1080/07347324.2020.1738295

Sanders, M. S., & Ramasubramanian, S. (2012). An examination of African Americans' stereotyped perceptions of fictional media characters. *Howard Journal of Communications, 23*(1), 17–39.

Sanders, S., & Orbe, M. (2016). TIPs to maximize meaningful professional development programs and initiatives: A case study in theoretically-grounded diversity education. In C. Scott & J. Sims (Eds.), *Developing workforce diversity programs, curriculum, and degrees in higher education* (pp. 235–257). IGI Global Publishing.

Saraswati, L. A. (2021). Beauty and cosmopolitan whiteness. Inside Indonesia. insideindonesia.org/beauty-and-cosmopolitan-whiteness

Sarup, M. (1996). *Identity, culture, and the postmodern world.* University of Georgia Press.

Satran J. (2016, January 4). Eva Longoria reveals she was "an ugly duckling" as a child. *Huffington Post.*

Saulny, S. (2011, January 29). Black? White? Asian? More young Americans choose all of the above. *The New York Times.* https://www.nytimes.com/2011/01/30/us/30mixed.html

Sawe, B. (2019, July 18). Largest ethnic groups and nationalities in the United States. World Atlas. https://www.worldatlas.com/articles/largest-ethnic-groups-and-nationalities-in-the-united-states.html

Schein, E. H. (2017). *Organizational culture and leadership* (5th ed.). Jossey-Bass.

Schieferdecker, D., & Wessler, H. (2017). Bridging segregation via media exposure? Ingroup identification, outgroup distance, and low direct contact reduce outgroup appearance in media repertoires. *Journal of Communication, 67*(6), 993–1014. https://doi.org/10.1111/jcom.12338

Schultz, J. R., Gaither, S. E., Urry, H. L., & Maddox, K. B. (2015). Reframing anxiety to encourage interracial interactions. *Translational Issues in Psychological Science, 1*(4), 392–400.

Schwartzman, L. F. (2007). Does money whiten? Intergenerational changes in racial classification in Brazil. *American Sociological Review, 72*(6), 940–963.

Scott, K. D. (1996, June). *Style switching as ideological position in Black women's talk* [Paper presentation]. Annual meeting of the Speech Communication Association's Black Caucus/African American Communication and Culture Division Summer Conference, Frankfort, KY.

Scott, K. D. (2016). Broadening the view of Black language use: Toward a better understanding of words and worlds. In A. Gonzalez & Y.-W. Chen (Eds.), *Our voices: Essays in culture, ethnicity, and communication* (6th ed., pp. 201–207). Oxford University Press.

Sebring, D. L. (1985). Considerations in counseling interracial children. *The Personnel and Guidance Journal, 13*, 3–9.

Seemayer, Z. (2021, September 30). *Big brother*: The Cookout Alliance on making history and those claims of "reverse racism." ET. https://www.etonline.com/big-brother-the-cookout-alliance-on-making-history-and-those-claims-of-reverse-racism-173092

Seidman, S., Meeks, C., & Traschen, F. (1999). Beyond the closet: The changing social meaning of homosexuality in the United States. *Sexualities, 2*(1), 9–34.

Selvanathan, H. P., Lickel, B., & Dasgupta, N. (2020). An integrative framework on the impact of allies: How identity-based needs influence intergroup solidarity and social movements. *European Journal of Social Psychology, 50*(6), 1344–1361. https://doi.org/10.1002/ejsp.2697

Sengupta, A. (2018, May 9). Is fashion's newfound "inclusivity" only skin deep? Refinery29. https://www.refinery29.com/en-us/multiracial-women-fetishized-in-fashion-industry-controversy

Serwer, A. (2019, December 23). The fight over the 1619 Project is not about the facts. *The Atlantic.* https://www.theatlantic.com/ideas/archive/2019/12/historians-clash-1619-project/604093/

Shaheen, J. G. (2009). *Reel bad Arabs: How Hollywood vilifies a people.* Olive Branch Press.

Shakirova, R., Safina, A., & Akhunzianova, R. (2018). Communicative failures and their causes as a result of unsuccessful communication. *International Journal of Engineering and Technology, 7*, 469–473. https://doi.org/10.14419/ijet.v7i4.38.24606.

Shand-Baptiste, K. (2020, April 8). No, Karen is not the equivalent of the n-word for white women—This isn't a debate worth having. *Independent.* https://www.independent.co.uk/voices/karen-n-word-racism-white-women-julie-bindel-coronavirus-a9453201.html

Shapiro, A. R. (2020, August 21). The racist roots of the dog whistle. *The Washington Post.* https://www.washingtonpost.com/outlook/2020/08/21/racist-roots-dog-whistle/

Shelton, J., Trail, T. E., West, T. V., & Bergsieker, H. B. (2010). From strangers to friends: The interpersonal process model of intimacy in developing interracial friendships. *Journal of Social & Personal Relationships, 27*(1), 71–90.

Shepard, C. A., Giles, H., & Le Poire, B. A. (2001). Communication accommodation theory. In W. P. Robinson & H. Giles (Eds.), *The new handbook of language and social psychology* (pp. 33–56). John Wiley.

Shih, K. Y., Chang, T.-F., & Chen, S.-Y. (2019). Impacts of the model minority myth on Asian American individuals and families: Social justice and critical race feminist perspectives. *Journal of Family Theory & Review, 11*(3), 412–428. https://doi.org/10.1111/jftr.12342

Shin, Y., & Hecht, M. L. (2017). Communication theory of identity. *The international encyclopedia of intercultural communication.* Wiley Online Library. https://doi.org/10.1002/9781118783665.ieicc0008

Shively, M. G., Jones, C., & DeCecco, J. P. (1984). Research on sexual orientation: Definitions and methods. *Journal of Homosexuality, 9*, 127–137.

Shome, R. (2011). "Global motherhood": The transnational intimacies of white femininity. *Critical Studies in Media Communication, 28*(5), 388–406.

Shrikant, N. (2018). "There's no such thing as Asian": A membership categorization analysis of cross-cultural adaptation in an Asian American business community. *Journal of International and Intercultural Communication, 11*(4), 286–303. https://doi.org/10.1080/17513057.2018.1478986

Shuter, R., & Turner, L. H. (1997). African American and European American women in the workplace: Perceptions of conflict communication. *Management Communication Quarterly, 11*(1), 74–96.

Sigelman, L., Bledsoe, T., Welch, S., & Combs, M. (1996). Making contact? Black–white social interaction in an urban setting. *American Journal of Sociology, 101*(5), 1306–1332.

Sigelman, L., Tuch, S. A., & Martin, J. K. (2005). What's in a name? Preference for "black" versus "African American" among Americans of African descent. *Public Opinion Quarterly, 69*(3), 429–439.

Silverman, R. E. (2021). Tikkun olam from a queer Jewess perspective. In R. Boylorn & M. Orbe (Eds.), *Critical autoethnography: Intersecting cultural identities in everyday life* (pp. 175–187). Routledge

Silverstein, J. (2021). The 1619 Project and the long battle over U.S. history. *The New York Times*. https://www.nytimes.com/2021/11/09/magazine/1619-project-us-history.html

Simpson, J. L. (2008). The color-blind double bind: Whiteness and the (im)possibility of dialogue. *Communication Theory, 18*(1), 139–159.

Simpson, J. S., Causey, A., & Williams, L. (2007). "I would want you to understand it": Students' perspectives on addressing race in the classroom. *Journal of Intercultural Communication Research, 36*(1), 33–50.

Sing, B. (1989). *Asian Pacific Americans: A handbook on how to cover and portray our nation's fastest growing minority group*. National Conference of Christians and Jews.

Singer, B. (n.d.). Native Americans in movies. Film reference. https://www.encyclopedia.com/arts/encyclopedias-almanacs-transcripts-and-maps/native-americans-and-cinema

Sinha, A. (2022, January 2). *Encanto summary & review—A magical movie that breaks all stereotypes*. Digital Mafia Talkies. https://dmtalkies.com/encanto-summary-review-2021-disney-animated-film/

Sirikul, L. (2021, July 22). The evolution of the Asian heroine in Hollywood. *Nerdist*. https://nerdist.com/article/asian-heroines-hollywood-depiction/

Small, A. (2010, January 9). Land acknowledgements accomplish little. *Inside Higher Ed*. https://www.insidehighered.com/views/2020/01/09/why-land-acknowledgments-arent-worth-much-opinion

Smith, A. (1973). *Transracial communication*. Prentice-Hall.

Smith, D. E. (1987). *The everyday world as problematic: A feminist sociology of knowledge*. Northeastern University Press.

Smith, H. L. (2019). Has nigga been reappropriated as a term of endearment? A qualitative and quantitative analysis. *American Speech, 94*(4), 420–477. https://doi.org/10.1215/00031283-7706537

Smith, S. L., Choueiti, M., Case, A., Pieper, K., Clark, H., Hernandez, K., Martinez, J., Lopez, B., & Mota, M. (2019, August). Latinos in film: Erasure on screen & behind the camera across 1,200 popular movies. USC Annenberg Inclusion Initiative.

Snowden, F. (1970). *Blacks in antiquity: Ethiopians in Greco–Roman experience*. Belknap Press of Harvard University Press.

Sodowsky, R. G., Kwan, K. L. K., & Pannu, R. (1995). Ethnic identity of Asians in the United States. In J. Ponterotto, J. M. Casas, L. A. Suzuki, & C. M. Alexander (Eds.), *Handbook of multicultural counseling* (pp. 123–154). Sage.

Soto-Vasquez, A. D. (2018). The rhetorical construction of U.S. Latinos by American presidents. *Howard Journal of Communications, 29*(4), 353–367. https://doi.org/10.1080/10646175.2017.1407718

Souleymanov, R., Brennan, D. J., George, C., Utama, R., & Ceranto, A. (2020). Experiences of racism, sexual objectification and alcohol use among gay and bisexual men of color. *Ethnicity & Health, 25*(4), 525–541. https://doi.org/10.1080/13557858.2018.1439895

Spaights, E., & Dixon, H. (1984). Socio-psychological dynamics in pathological Black–White romantic alliances. *Journal of Instructional Psychology, 11*(3), 133–138.

Speer, S., & Potter, J. (2000). The management of heterosexist talk: Conversational resources and prejudiced claims. *Discourse & Society, 11*, 543–572.

Spellers, R. E. (2002). Happy to be nappy! Embracing an Afrocentric aesthetic for beauty. In J. N. Martin, T. Nakayama, & L. A. Flores (Eds.), *Readings in intercultural communication: Experiences and contexts* (pp. 52–59). McGraw-Hill.

Spickard, P. R. (1989). *Mixed blood: Intermarriage and ethnic identity in twentieth-century America.* University of Wisconsin Press.

Spickard, P. R. (1992). The illogic of American racial categories. In M. P. P. Root (Ed.), *Racially mixed people in America* (pp. 12–23). Sage.

Spieldenner, A. R., & Castro, C. F. (2010). Education and fear: Black and gay in the public sphere of HIV prevention. *Communication Education, 59*(3), 274–281.

Spike, C. (2020, September 22). How to have a respectful conversation about racial justice. AARP. https://www.aarp.org/home-family/friends-family/info-2020/having-racial-justice-conversations.html

Squires, C. R. (2002). Rethinking the Black public sphere: An alternative vocabulary for multiple public spheres. *Communication Theory, 12*(4), 446–468. https://doi.org/10.1111/j.1468-2885.2002.tb00278.x

Squires, C., & Orbe, M. (2023). (Counter)public sphere theory. In J. Austin, M. Orbe, & J. Sims (Eds.), *Communication theory: Racially and inclusive perspectives* (pp. 239–250). Cognella.

Stackman, V. A., Reviere, R., & Medley, B. C. (2016). Attitudes toward marriage, partner availability, and interracial dating among Black college students from historically Black and predominantly White institutions. *Journal of Black Studies, 47*(2), 169–192.

Stanton, M. (1971). A remnant Indian community: The Houma of southern Louisiana. In J. K. Moorland (Ed.), *The not so solid South: Anthropological studies in a regional subculture* (pp. 82–92). University of Georgia Press.

Steele, C. K. (2016). Pride and prejudice: Pervasiveness of colorism and the animated series *Proud family. Howard Journal of Communications, 27*(1), 53–67.

Stewart, C. O., Pitts, M. J., & Osborne, H. (2011). Mediated intergroup conflict: The discursive construction of "illegal immigrants" in a regional U.S. newspaper. *Journal of Language and Social Psychology, 30*(1), 8–27.

Stewart, D.-L. (2017, March 30). Language of appeasement. *Inside Higher Ed.* https://www.insidehighered.com/views/2017/03/30/colleges-need-language-shift-not-one-you-think-essay

Stewart, F. (2020). Exploring Afrocentricity: An analysis of the discourse of Oprah Winfrey. *Journal of Black Studies.* https://doi.org/10.1177/0021934720947654

Stokel-Walker, C. (2018, September 29). Why is it OK for online daters to block whole ethnic groups? *The Guardian.*

Stokke, C. (2021). Unlearning racism through transformative interracial dialogue. *International Journal of Qualitative Studies in Education.* https://doi.org/10.1080/09518398.2021.1930245

Stoll, K. (2021). Frequency of watching or streaming TV shows among adults in the United States as of February 2020, by ethnicity. Statista. https://www.statista.com/statistics/1118986/frequency-of-watching-or-streaming-tv-shows-by-ethnicity/

Stotlzfus-Brown, L. (2021). Deep south Mennonite, transgender Amish: A critical autoethnography of white cisheteronormativity. In R. Boylorn & M. Orbe (Eds,), *Critical autoethnography: Intersecting cultural identities in everyday life* (pp. 130–142). Routledge.

Stout, C., & LeMee, G. (2021, July 22). Efforts to restrict teaching about racism and bias have multiplied across the U.S. *Chalkbeat*. https://www.chalkbeat.org/22525983/map-critical-race-theory-legislation-teaching-racism

Stow, S. (2017). American skin: Bruce Springsteen, Danielle Allen, and the politics of interracial friendship. *American Political Thought, 6*(2), 294–316.

Stromberg, E. (Ed.). (2006). *American Indian rhetorics of survivance: Word medicine, word magic*. University of Pittsburgh Press.

Suarez-Orozco, M. (2000). Everything you ever wanted to know about assimilation but were afraid to ask. *Daedalus, 129*, 1–30.

Sue, D. W. (2016). *Race talk and the conspiracy of silence: Understanding and facilitating difficult dialogues on race*. Wiley.

Sugino, C. M. (2020). Multicultural incorporation in Donald Trump's political rhetoric. *Southern Journal of Communication, 85*(3), 191–202. https://doi.org/10.1080/1041794X.2020.1780301

Summers, B. T. (2021). Reclaiming the chocolate city: Soundscapes of gentrification and resistance in Washington, DC. *Environment and Planning D: Society and Space, 39*(1), 30–46.

Swahn, M. H., Mahendra, R. R., Paulozzi, L. J., Winston, R. L., Shelley, G. A., Taliano, J., Frazier, L., & Saul, J. R. (2003). Violent attacks on Middle Easterners in the United States during the month following the September 11, 2001 terrorist attacks. *Injury Prevention, 9*, 187–189.

Swaroop, S., & Krysan, M. (2011). The determinants of neighborhood satisfaction: Racial proxy revisited. *Demography, 48*(3), 1203–1229.

Swencionis, J. K., Dupree, C. H., & Fiske, S. T. (2017). Warmth-competence trade-offs in impression management across race and social-class divides. *Journal of Social Issues, 743*(1), 175–191. https://doi.org/10.1111/josi.12210

Syed, M., & Fish, J. (2018). Revisiting Erik Erikson's legacy on culture, race, and ethnicity. *Identity: An International Journal of Theory and Research, 18*(4), 274–283. https://doi.org/10.1080/15283488.2018.1523729

Tajfel, H. (1978). Social categorization, social identity, and social comparison. In H. Tajfel (Ed.), *Differentiation between social groups* (pp. 61–76). Academic Press.

Tal-Or, N., & Tsfati, Y. (2016). When Arabs and Jews watch TV together: The joint effect of the content and context of communication on reducing prejudice. *Journal of Communication, 66*, 646–668.

Tanno, D. V. (1998, May). *A characterization of dialogue* [Paper presentation]. National Communication Association Ethics Conference Biannual Meeting, Gull Lake, MI.

Tanno, D. V., & Gonzalez, A. (1998). Sites of identity in communication and culture. In D. V. Tanno & A. Gonzalez (Eds.), *Communication and identity across cultures* (pp. 3–10). Sage.

Tariq, M. (2020). "Never have I ever": Authentic Indian representation results in show's massive success. *Hollywood Insider*. https://www.hollywoodinsider.com/never-have-i-ever-review-indian/

Tatum, B. D. (2017). *Why are all the Black kids sitting together in the cafeteria? And other conversations about race*. Basic Books.

Tavernise, S., Mzezewa, T., & Heyward, G. (2021, August 14). Many theories behind rise in multiracial Americans. *The New York Times*. https://www.nytimes.com/2021/08/13/us/census-multiracial-identity.html

Taylor, C. (1992). *Multiculturalism and the politics of recognition*. Princeton University Press.

Taylor, J., & Richardson, B. (2006). Powerlessness, resistance, and the understood "they": Sexual harassment at the intersection of race and gender. In M. Orbe, B. J. Allen, & L. A. Flores (Eds.), *The same and different: Acknowledging the diversity within and between cultural groups* (pp. 68–94). National Communication Association.

Taylor, V. J., Valladares, J. J., Siepser, C., & Yantis, C. (2020). Interracial contact in virtual reality: Best practices. *Policy Insights from the Behavioral and Brain Sciences, 7*(2), 132–140.

Taylor, V. J., Yantis, C., Bonam, C., & Hart, A. (2021). What to do? Predicting coping strategies following ingroup members' stereotypical behaviors in interracial interactions. *Personality and Social Psychology Bulletin, 47*(7), 1084–1100.

Tedeschi, J. T., & Norman, N. (1985). Social power, self-presentation, and the self. In B. R. Schlenker (Ed.), *The self and social life* (pp. 293–322). McGraw-Hill.

Telles, E., & Garcia, D. (2013). Mestizaje and public opinion in Latin America. *Latin American Research Review, 48*(3), 130–152.

Telzer, E. H., & Vazquez Garcia, H. A. (2009). Skin color and self-perceptions of immigrant and U.S.-born Latinas: The moderating role of racial socialization and ethnic identity. *Hispanic Journal of Behavioral Sciences, 31*(3), 357–374.

Terriquez, V., & Milkman, R. (2021). Immigrant and refugee youth organizing in solidarity with the movement for Black lives. *Gender & Society, 35*(4), 577–587.

Tessler, H., Choi, M., & Kao, G. (2020). The anxiety of being Asian American: Hate crimes and negative biases during the COVID-19 pandemic. *American Journal of Criminal Justice, 45*(4), 636–646.

Thomas, D. A., & Kanji, A. (2017). IBM'S diversity strategy (a case study analysis). https://www.slideshare.net/ajzam99/ibms-diversity-strategy-a-case-study-analysis

Thomas, K. M., & Davis, J. L. (2006). Best practices in diversity management. In M. Karsten (Ed.), *Gender, race, & ethnicity in the workplace: Issues and challenges for today's organizations* (Vol. 3, pp. 69–84). Praeger/Greenwood.

Thompson, M. S., & Keith, V. M. (2001). The blacker the berry: Gender, skin tone, self-esteem, and self-efficacy. *Gender and Society, 15*(3), 336–357.

Thornton, D. (2011). *Psych's* comedic tale of Black-White friendship and the lighthearted affect of "post-race" America. *Critical Studies in Media Communication, 28*(5), 424–449.

Thorson, K., & Wells, C. (2016). Curated flows: A framework for mapping media exposure in the digital age. *Communication Theory, 26*(3), 309–328.

Ting-Toomey, S. (1986). Conflict communication styles in Black and White subjective cultures. In Y. Y. Kim (Ed.), *Interethnic communication: Current research* (pp. 75–88). Sage.

Ting-Toomey, S. (1988). Intercultural conflict styles: A face negotiation theory. In Y. Y. Kim & W. B. Gudykunst (Eds.), *Theories in intercultural communication* (pp. 213–235). Sage.

Ting-Toomey, S. (1993). Communicative resourcefulness: An identity negotiation perspective. In R. Wiseman & J. Koester (Eds.), *Intercultural communication competence* (pp. 17–39). Sage.

Ting-Toomey, S. (2000). Managing intercultural conflicts effectively. In L. A. Samovar & R. E. Porter (Eds.), *Intercultural communication: A reader* (pp. 388–400). Wadsworth.

Ting-Toomey, S. (2017). Conflict face-negotiation theory: Tracking its evolutionary journey. In X. Dai & G.-M. Chen (Eds.), *Conflict management and intercultural communication* (pp. 123–143). Routledge.

Ting-Toomey, S. (2019). Playing with facework: The meandering theorizing journey. Society for Intercultural Education Training and Research. https://www.sietarusa.org/blog/7341756

Ting-Toomey, S. (2023). Conflict face-negotiation theory in intercultural-interpersonal contexts. In J. Austin, M. Orbe, & J. Sims (Eds.), *Communication theory: Racially and inclusive perspectives* (pp. 53–64). Cognella.

Ting-Toomey, S., & Dorjee, T. (2019). *Communicating across cultures* (2nd ed.). The Guilford Press.

Ting-Toomey, S., & Oetzel, J. G. (2001). *Managing intercultural conflict effectively.* Sage.

Ting-Toomey, S., Yee-Jung, K. K., Shapiro, R. B., Garcia, W., Wright, T. J., & Oetzel, J. G. (2000). Ethnic/cultural identity salience and conflict styles in four U.S. ethnic groups. *International Journal of Intercultural Relations, 24*, 47–81.

Tolbert, E. J. (1989). General introduction. In C. E. Jackson & E. J. Tolbert (Eds.), *Race and culture in America: Readings in racial and ethnic relations* (pp. 1–21). Burgess.

Torchinsky, R. (2022, April 14). Judge cuts the payout in a Black former Tesla contractor's racial discrimination suit. National Public Radio.

Touré. (2011). *Who's afraid of post-blackness? What it means to be black now.* Free Press.

Troy, A. B., Lewis-Smith, J., & Laurenceau, J.-P. (2006). Interracial and intraracial romantic relationships: The search for differences in satisfaction, conflict, and attachment style. *Journal of Social and Personal Relationships, 23*(1), 65–80.

Trump, D. J. (2020, September 17). *Our heroes will never be forgotten* [Speech transcription]. *The American Mind.* https://americanmind.org/features/reclaiming-american-history/remarks-by-president-trump-at-the-white-house-conference-on-american-history/

Tsunokai, G. T., Kposowa, A. J., & Adams, M. A. (2009). Racial preferences in internet dating: A comparison of four birth cohorts. *Western Journal of Black Studies, 33*(1), 1–15.

Tukachinsky, R., Mastro, D., & Yarchi, M. (2017). The effect of prime time television ethnic/racial stereotypes on Latino and Black Americans: A longitudinal national level study. *Journal of Broadcasting & Electronic Media, 61*(3), 538–556. https://doi.org/10.1080/08838151.2017.1344669

Tully, M. (2018). Constructing a feminist icon through erotic friend fiction: Millennial feminism on *Bob's burgers. Critical Studies in Media Communication, 35*(2), 194–207.

Turner, J. C. (1987). *Rediscovering the social group.* Basil Blackwell.

Tyler, I. (2018). Resituating Erving Goffman: From stigma power to Black power. *The Sociological Review, 66*(4), 744–765. https://doi.org/10.1177/0038026118777450

Tyree, T. C. M., Byerly, C. M., & Hamilton, K.-A. (2012). Representations of (new) black masculinity: A news-making case study. *Journalism, 13*(4), 467–482.

Umaña-Taylor, A. J., & Hill, N. E. (2020). Ethnic-racial socialization in the family: A decade's advance on precursors and outcomes. *Journal of Marriage and Family, 82*(1), 244–271. https://doi.org/10.1111/jomf.12622

United Nations. (2022, April 22). Minorities and their rights matter to prevent conflict, says expert. https://www.ohchr.org/en/stories/2022/04/minorities-and-their-rights-matter-prevent-conflict-says-expert

University of Iowa. (2022). Best practices for effective conflict management. https://conflictmanagement.org.uiowa.edu/best-practices

Uotinen, V. (1998). Age identification: A comparison between Finnish and North American cultures. *International Journal of Aging and Human Development, 46*, 109–124.

Urban, E. L., & Orbe, M. (2010). Identity gaps of contemporary U.S. immigrants: Acknowledging divergent communicative experiences. *Communication Studies, 61*(3), 304–320.

Urban, E. L., Orbe, M., Tavares, N., & Alvarez, W. (2010). Exploration of Dominican international student experiences. *Journal of Student Affairs Research and Practice, 47*(2), 233–250.

U.S. Institute of Peace. (2015). Comparison of dialogue and debate. https://www.usip.org/sites/default/files/2017-01/Dialogue%2Bvs%2BDebate%2B%2BUSIP%2BGlobal%2BCampus.pdf

Valentine, G. (1995, Spring). Shades of gray: The conundrum of color categories. *Teaching Tolerance, 47.*

Valentino, N. A., & Brader, T. (2011). The sword's other edge: Perceptions of discrimination and racial policy opinion after Obama. *Public Opinion Quarterly, 75*(2), 201–226.

Vasquez-Tokos, J., & Norton-Smith, K. (2017). Talking back to controlling images: Latinos' changing responses to racism over the life course. *Ethnic and Racial Studies, 40*(6), 912–930.

Vavrus, M. D. (2010). Unhitching from the "post" (of postfeminism). *Journal of Communication Inquiry, 34*(3), 222–227.

Verkuyten, M., & Yogeeswaran, K. (2020). Cultural diversity and its implications for intergroup relations. *Current Opinion in Psychology, 32*, 1–5. https://doi.org/10.1016/j.copsyc.2019.06.010

Verma, S. B. (2010). Obsession with light skin—Shedding some light on use of skin lightening products in India. *International Journal of Dermatology, 49*(4), 464–465.

Vertovec, S. (2001). Transnationalism and identity. *Journal of Ethnic and Migration Studies, 27*(4), 573–582.

Via, W., & Brooks, L. (2017). *Ten ways to fight hate: A community response guide* (5th ed.). Southern Poverty Law Center. https://www.splcenter.org/20170814/ten-ways-fight-hate-community-response-guide

Vidali, A. (2009). Rhetorical hiccups: Disability disclosure in letters of recommendation. *Rhetoric Review, 28*(2), 185–204.

Villarreal, A. (2021, May 19). Only 17% in US say race relations better one year after Floyd's murder, poll finds. *The Guardian.* https://www.theguardian.com/us-news/2021/may/19/us-race-relations-poll

Vore, A. (2021, October 1). "Elderly"—A label journalists should avoid. *San Diego Union-Tribune.*

Waisanen, D. (2012). Bordering populism in immigration activism: Outlaw-civic discourse in a (counter)public. *Communication Monographs, 79*(2), 232–255.

Waldek, S. (2020). What is White flight? *House Beautiful.* https://www.housebeautiful.com/lifestyle/a34319800/what-is-white-flight/

Waldrop, J., & Stern, S. (2003). *Disability status 2000: Census 2000 brief.* U.S. Department of Commerce/Economics and Statistics Administration.

Wander, P. C., Martin, J. N., & Nakayama, T. (1999). Whiteness and beyond: Sociohistorical foundations of Whiteness and contemporary challenges. In T. K. Nakaywna & J. N. Martin (Eds.), *Whiteness: The communication of social identity* (pp. 13–26). Sage.

Wang, F. K.-H. (2016, January 11). 50 years later, challenging the "model minority myth" through #ReModelMinority. NBC News.

Wang, G. (2010). A shot at half-exposure: Asian Americans in reality TV shows. *Television & New Media, 11*(5), 404–427.

Wang, M.-T., Henry, D. A., Smith, L. V., Huguley, J. P., & Guo, J. (2020). Parental ethnic-racial socialization practices and children of color's psychosocial and behavioral adjustment: A systematic review and meta-analysis. *American Psychologist, 75*(1), 1–22. https://doi.org/10.1037/amp0000464

Wang, M.-T., Smith, L. V., Miller-Cotto, D., & Huguley, J. P. (2020). Parental ethnic-racial socialization and children of color's academic success: A meta-analytic review. *Child Development, 91*(3). https://doi.org/10.1111/cdev.13254

Warren, J. T., & Hytten, K. (2004). The faces of whiteness: Pitfalls and the critical democrat. *Communication Education, 53*(4), 321–339.

Washington, M. (2012). Interracial intimacy: Hegemonic construction of Asian American and Black relationships on TV medical dramas. *Howard Journal of Communications, 23*(3), 253–271.

Washington, M., & Harris, T. M. (2018). The interracial gaze and Shonda Rhimes' post-racial promised land. In R Griffin & M. D. E. Meyer (Eds.), *Identity politics and the power of representation: Adventures in Shondaland* (pp. 156–175). Duke University Press.

Waters, M. (1999). *Black identities: West Indian dreams and American realities.* Harvard University Press.

Watson, A. (2019). Media consumption among ethnic groups in the U.S.—Statistics & facts. Statista. https://www.statista.com/topics/5108/ethnic-groups-in-the-us-media-consumption/#topicHeader__wrapper

Watts, E. K. (2016). Confessions of a thirty-something hip-hop (old) head. In A. Gonzalez & Y.-W. Chen, (Eds.), *Our voices: Essays in culture, ethnicity, and communication* (6th ed., pp. 208–213). Oxford University Press.

Weaver, A. J., & Frampton, J. R. (2019). Crossing the color line: An examination of mediators and a social media intervention for racial bias in selective exposure to movies. *Communication Monographs, 86*(4), 399–415.

Weber, D. E. (2016). Constructing U.S. American Jewish male identity. In A. Gonzalez & Y.-W. Chen (Eds.), *Our voices: Essays in culture, ethnicity, and communication* (6th ed., pp. 156–161). Oxford University Press.

Weick, K. (1979). *The social psychology of organizing*. Random House.

Weiss, E. L. (2015). Building community in a diverse college classroom. In J. E. Coll & E. L. Weiss (Eds.), *Supporting veterans in higher education: A primer for administrators, faculty, and academic advisors* (pp. 104–129). Lyceum Books.

Welner, K. G. (2006). K–12 race-conscious student assignment policies: Law, social science, and diversity. *Review of Educational Research, 76*(3), 349–382.

West, C. (1982). *Prophecy deliverance: An Afro-American revolutionary Christianity*. Westminster Press.

West, C. (1993). *Race matters*. Beacon Press.

Whitehead, K. A. (2009). "Categorizing the categorizer": The management of racial commonsense in interaction. *Social Psychology Quarterly, 72*(4), 325–342.

Whitehead, K. A., & Lerner, G. H. (2009). When are persons "white"? On some practical asymmetries of racial reference in talk-in-interaction. *Discourse and Society, 5*, 613–641.

Whitesides, J. (2017, February 7). From disputes to a breakup: Wounds still raw after U. S. election. *Reuters.* https://www.reuters.com/article/us-usa-trump-relationships-insight/from-disputes-to-a-breakup-wounds-still-raw-after-u-s-election-idUSKBN15M13L

Wiggins-Romesburg, C. A., & Githens, R. P. (2018). The psychology of diversity resistance and integration. *Human Resource Development Review, 17*(2), 179–198.

Wilder, J. (2015). *Color stories: Black women and colorism in the 21st century*. Praeger.

Wilder, J., & Cain, C. (2011). Teaching and learning color consciousness in Black families: Exploring family processes and women's experiences with colorism. *Journal of Family Issues, 32*(5), 577–604.

Wilkie, S. (2021, February 6). Opinion: Land acknowledgements fall short in honoring Indigenous people. *Cherokee Phoenix.* https://www.cherokeephoenix.org/opinion/opinion-land-acknowledgments-fall-short-in-honoring-indigenous-people/article_cdf8233f-f107-5cb6-a9c5-e89823a10e2d.html

Williams, A. (2020). Black memes matter: #LivingWhileBlack with Becky and Karen. *Social Media & Society, 6*(4), 1–14. https://doi.org/10.1177/2056305120981047

Williams, C. (2013). The glass escalator, revisited: Gender inequality in neoliberal times. *Gender & Society, 27*(5), 609–629. https://doi.org/10.1177/0891243213490232

Williams, S. A. S., Hanssen, D. V., Rinke, C. R., & Kinlaw, R. (2020). Promoting race pedagogy in higher education: Creating an inclusive community. *Journal of Educational and Psychological Consultation, 30*(3), 369–393. https://doi.org/10.1080/10474412.2019.1669451

Willis, G. (2003). *"Negro president": Jefferson and the slave power*. Houghton Mifflin.

Willis, H. A., & Neblett, E. W. (2020). Racial identity and changes in psychological distress using the multidimensional model of racial identity. *Cultural Diversity and Ethnic Minority Psychology, 26*(4), 509–519. https://doi.org/10.1037/cdp0000314

Wilmot, W. W. (1995). *Relational communication*. McGraw-Hill.

Wilson, J. D. (2021). *Becoming disabled: Forging a disability view of the world*. Lexington Books.

Winker, K. J. (1994, May 11). The significance of race. *The Chronicle of Higher Education*, pp. A10–A11.

Winn, P. (1995). *Americas: The changing face of Latin America and the Caribbean*. Pantheon.

Witteborn, S. (2004). Of being an Arab woman before and after September 11: The enactment of communal identities in talk. *Howard Journal of Communications, 15*, 83–98.

Wong (Lau), K. (2002). Migration across generations: Whose identity is authentic? In J. N. Martin, T. K. Nakayama, & L. A. Flores (Eds.), *Reading in cultural contexts* (pp. 95–100). Mayfield.

Wong (Lau), K. (2016). Working through identity: Understanding class in the context of race, ethnicity, and gender. In A. Gonzalez & Y.-W. Chen (Eds.), *Our voices: Essays in culture, ethnicity, and communication* (6th ed., pp. 273–280). Oxford University Press.

Wong, P., Manvi, M., & Wong, T. H. (1995). Asiacentrism and Asian American studies. *Amerasia Journal, 12*, 137–147.

Wood, J. T. (Ed.). (1996). *Gendered relationships*. Mayfield.

Wood, J. T. (1997). *Communication theories in action: An introduction*. Wadsworth.

Wood, J. T. (2005). Feminist standpoint theory and muted group theory: Commonalities and divergences. *Women and Language, 28*(2), 61–64.

Wood, J. T., & Dindia, K. (1998). What's the difference? A dialogue about differences and similarities between women and men. In D. J. Canary & K. Dindia (Eds.), *Sex differences and similarities in communication: Critical essays and empirical investigations of sex and gender in interaction* (pp. 19–40). Lawrence Erlbaum.

Woods, F. A., & Ruscher, J. B. (2021). "Calling-out" vs. "calling-in" prejudice: Confrontation style affects inferred motive and expected outcomes. *British Journal of Social Psychology, 60*, 50–73.

Wright, L. (1994, July 25). One drop of blood. *The New Yorker*, 46–55.

Wu, F. H. (2002). *Yellow: Race in America beyond black and white*. Basic Books.

Wu, M.-H. (2021). A critical examination of Asian students' interracial and interethnic friendships at a multiracial urban school. *Urban Education, 56*(3), 424–450.

Wynne, G. (2020, July 20). Racial fetishization is a big problem online. Here's what dating apps & users can do. *Bustle*. https://www.bustle.com/wellness/racial-fetishization-big-problem-online-what-dating-apps-users-can-do

Xia, R. (2020, August 2). Manhattan Beach was once home to Black beachgoers, but the city ran them out. Now it faces a reckoning. *Los Angeles Times*. https://www.latimes.com/california/story/2020-08-02/bruces-beach-manhattan-beach

Yancey, G. (2003). A preliminary examination of differential sexual attitudes among individuals involved in interracial relationships: Testing "jungle fever." *The Social Science Journal, 40*, 153–157.

Yancey-Bragg, N. (2021, August 10). "Sheer terror": Black real estate agent, clients handcuffed by Michigan police during home tour. *USA Today*. https://www.usatoday.com/story/news/nation/2021/08/09/michigan-police-handcuff-black-real-estate-agent-clients-home-tour/5535620001/

Yellow Horse, A. J., Jeung, R., & Matriano, R. (2022, March 4). Stop AAPI Hate national report, 3/19/2020–12/31/2021. https://stopaapihate.org/wp-content/uploads/2022/03/22-SAH-NationalReport-3.1.22-v9.pdf

Yen, H. (2009, June 29). Generation gap widest since 1969, survey finds. *Kalamazoo (MI) Gazette*, p. A5.

Yep, G. A. (2002). Navigating the multicultural identity landscape. In J. N. Martin, T. K. Nakayama, & L. A. Flores (Eds.), *Readings in cultural contexts* (pp. 60–66). Mayfield.

Yep, G. A. (2013). Privilege and culture. In A. Kurylo (Ed.), *Inter/cultural communication* (pp. 163–184). Sage.

Yep, G. A. (2016). Toward thick(er) intersectionalities: Theorizing, researching, and activating the complexities of communication and identities. In K. Sorrells & S. Sekimoto (Eds.), *Globalizing intercultural communication: A reader* (pp. 86–94). Sage.

Yep, G. A. (2019). A thick intersectional approach to microaggressions. *Southern Communication Journal, 84*(2), 113–126. https://doi.org/10.1080/1041794X.2018.1511749

Yi, S.-H., & Hoston, W. T. (2020). Demystifying Americanness: The model minority myth and the Black-Korean Relationship. *Journal of Ethnic and Cultural Studies, 7*(2), 68–89

Yin, J. (2018). Beyond postmodernism: A non-western perspective on identity.

*Journal of Multicultural Discourses,* *13*(3), 193–219. https://doi.org/10.1080/ 17447143.2018.1497640

Yin, T. (2010). Through a screen darkly: Hollywood as a measure of discrimination against Arabs and Muslims. *Duke Forum for Law & Social Change, 2,* 103–123.

Yomtoob, D. (2013). Caught in code: Arab American identity, image, and lived reality. In R. Boylorn & M. Orbe (Eds.), *Critical autoethnography: Intersecting cultural identities in everyday life* (pp. 144–158). Left Coast Press.

Young, S. L. (2015). It's not just Black and white: Exploring a pedagogy of racial visibility and the biracial Korean/white self. *Departures in Critical Qualitative Research, 4*(4), 8–32. https://doi.org/ 10.I525/dcqr.2015.4.4.8

Youngblood, J. D., & Winn, J. E. (2004). Shout glory: Competing communication codes experienced by the members of the African American Pentecostal Genuine Deliverance Holiness Church. *Journal of Communication, 54*(2), 355–370.

Yuen, N. W. (2017). *Reel inequality: Hollywood actors and racism.* Rutgers University Press.

Zamudio-Suarez, F. (2021, February 2). Race on campus. *The Chronicle of Higher Education.* https://www.chronicle.com/ newsletter/race-on-campus/2021-02-02

Zhang, Q., Ting-Toomey, S., & Oetzel, J. (2014). Linking emotion to the conflict face-negotiation theory: A U.S.–China investigation of the mediating effects of anger, compassion, and guilt in interpersonal conflict. *Human Communication Research, 40*(3), 373–395.

Zhang, Y. B., & Giles, H. (2018). Communication accommodation theory. In Y. Y. Kim (Ed.), *The international encyclopedia of intercultural communication* (pp. 95–108). Wiley. https://doi.org/10.1002/ 9781118783665.ieicc0156

Zuberi, T. (2000). Deracializing social statistics: Problems in the quantification of race. *Annals of the American Academy of Political and Social Science, 568,* 172–175.

# Index

hooks, b., 108
Houston, M., 27, 77, 202, 215
Huling, N., 126
Hurricane Katrina, 63, 80
Hypergamy, 211, 212
Hyperinvisibility, 162–163
Hypervisibility, 162–163
Hypodescent, 43, 176

IBM, 249
Identity. *See* Cultural iden-
    tity
Ideology
    biological foundations of
        race and, 36–38
    challenging existing,
        38–39
    chosen people, 32–34
    colonialism, 36, 171, 172,
        177, 178, 189, 293
    colorism and, 171–173,
        182, 185–188, 190
    Manifest Destiny, 32–34,
        37, 133
    Marxism, 158, 293
    mestizaje, 113, 175
    "post-racial," 4–5, 39,
        47–48, 52, 107, 324,
        340, 349
    racism, 34–35, 202, 306,
        307, 317
    social Darwinism, 262
    theatre of struggle, 294
    white leader prototype,
        240
Ifill, G., 125
Image management, 98, 99
Imahori, T. T., 86
Immigration/immigrants
    Arab, 67–68
    Asian, 68–70
    Black, 66–67
    Central American, 49, 50
    colorism and, 173, 183
    countries of origin, 50
    illegal, 63, 308, 310
    Jewish, 71–72
    Korean, 262
    Mexican, 49, 50

migration tensions and,
    49–51
myths about U.S., 55
patterns of, 49
population growth from,
    9, 267
as source of conflict, 267
transnationalism and,
    128
Implicature, 161
Impression management
    theory, 98, 99
Inclusiveness, 21, 252, 335
India
    caste system in, 177–178
    colorism and, 177
    skin color and, 186,
        187–188
Indigenous Peoples. *See*
    Native Americans
Indigenous Peoples' Day, 29
Individualism, 148–149
Inequalities
    of African Americans, 46
    contemporary social,
        261–262
    mass media and, 292
    as sources of conflict, 262
Institute of Peace, 342
Institutions
    colorism and, 181
    dominant societal,
        104–106
    as sources of conflict,
        271
Integration, 46, 66, 93, 94,
    96, 147, 183, 209, 232,
    270, 306
Intentionality, 81, 82,
    215–216, 349
Intercultural dialectics, 16,
    325, 338–341
Inter-Fraternity Council
    (IFC), 260
International Teaching
    Assistant (ITA), 60
Internet
    African Americans and,
        298–299
    colorism and, 176

immigrants and, 128
mass media and, 313
as a mass media venue,
    312–313
online dating and, 204
self/others and, 320
Internment camps, Japa-
    nese Americans in, 303
Interpenetration, 101
Interpretive theories,
    150–157
Interracial communication
    models, 142–144
Interracial friendships
    (IRFs)
    Banton's six orders of
        interracial contact,
        209
    challenges to, 214–216
    contact hypothesis and,
        210–211, 213
    critical thinking about
        racial stereotypes
        and, 210–211
    definition, 199
    factors affecting, 199–200
    mental models of inter-
        racial relationships
        and, 208
    politics and, 200
    relationship inventory,
        212
Interracial Relational
    Development Model
    (IRDM), 219
Interracial relationships
    coping strategies for, 223
    current mental models
        of, 208–214
    self-esteem and, 220
    social forces and, 216–219
    socioeconomic status
        and, 216, 217
    virtual dating, 204–208
Interracial romantic rela-
    tionships (IRRs)
    attitudes about intermar-
        riage, 201–202, 220
    myths/misconceptions
        about, 221–222